'For nearly two decades Professor Mulheron has been living, teaching, writing about, providing expert opinions on and helping to draft legislation in respect of class actions on a global scale. Now she has produced this excellent and eminently accessible text offering invaluable and practical insights and advice for anyone who wishes to understand how class actions are meant to work, how they do work in practice, and what considerations legislators and lawmakers should take into account when introducing or amending class action legislation in their jurisdictions. Her analysis of the government's dual role as legislator and potential class action party makes this work unique.'

John P. Brown, Litigation Partner, McCarthy
Tétrault LLP, Canada

'This excellent and stimulating new book from the leading academic commentator on class and group actions will be required reading for all those interested in the field, exploring and analysing from a comparative perspective the symbiotic relationship that exists between class actions and the government.'

Duncan Fairgrieve, Senior Fellow in Comparative Law, British
Institute of International and Comparative Law,
and Professor of Comparative Law,
Université Paris Dauphine PSL

'This is a first-class book – clear and comprehensive. As usual, Rachael Mulheron has researched her subject thoroughly and produced an authoritative work which will assist both practitioners and scholars.'

Sir Rupert Jackson QC, 4 New Square, London

'The leading comparative scholar of class action law has done it again. Here, Professor Mulheron reviews the often-overlooked relationship between the class action and government in the UK, United States, Canada, and Australia; the government as system engineer, as operator, and as a party or beneficiary. A work that is comprehensive and erudite, with abundant utility for practitioners and judges as well as for teachers and students.'

Craig E. Jones QC, Professor,
Thompson Rivers University Faculty of Law

'Mulheron weaves together a stunning kaleidoscope to view class actions through the lens of government. Her imaginative analytical framework and choice of targeted examples deliver fascinating insights into the class action regimes in their cultural and political context, but with a rigour that Mulheron unfailingly delivers. A must for the novice and the specialist.'

Peta Spender, Professor of Law,
Australian National University

CLASS ACTIONS AND GOVERNMENT

The relationship between class actions and government makes for a nuanced and fascinating study. Government sets the scene by implementing and designing the regime, by choosing whether to act as a seed-funder for the regime, and by deciding to what extent it should regulate the regime against worldwide classes being litigated on its doorstep. It can then become a key player in the litigation itself. Government may be a representative claimant bringing the action, or a class member, or a potential financial beneficiary. Most commonly of all, it may be a defendant, being sued under the very regime which it enacted into law. With numerous opt-out class action regimes around the common law world in place, and others on the horizon, the book takes a comparative perspective throughout, and concludes with a series of recommendations, drawn from that comparative analysis of government's intricate interplay with class actions.

RACHAEL MULHERON is Professor of Tort Law and Civil Justice at Queen Mary University of London. She is widely published in the class actions field and is also the author of the textbook, *Principles of Tort Law* (Cambridge University Press, 2016, 2nd edn 2020). Professor Mulheron was academic member of the Civil Justice Council of England and Wales between 2009 and 2018 and, in that capacity, chaired various working parties, provided an empirical study on class actions, and served as principal author of various other reports and publications for the government. She also served as a member of the relevant rules-drafting committee in 2015 which prepared rules of court for the United Kingdom's first opt-out class action.

CLASS ACTIONS AND GOVERNMENT

RACHAEL MULHERON

Queen Mary University of London

CAMBRIDGE
UNIVERSITY PRESS

CAMBRIDGE
UNIVERSITY PRESS

University Printing House, Cambridge CB2 8BS, United Kingdom

One Liberty Plaza, 20th Floor, New York, NY 10006, USA

477 Williamstown Road, Port Melbourne, VIC 3207, Australia

314–321, 3rd Floor, Plot 3, Splendor Forum, Jasola District Centre, New Delhi – 110025, India

79 Anson Road, #06–04/06, Singapore 079906

Cambridge University Press is part of the University of Cambridge.

It furthers the University's mission by disseminating knowledge in the pursuit of education, learning, and research at the highest international levels of excellence.

www.cambridge.org
Information on this title: www.cambridge.org/9781107043978
DOI: 10.1017/9781107358317

First published 2020

Printed in the United Kingdom by TJ International Ltd, Padstow Cornwall

A catalogue record for this publication is available from the British Library.

Library of Congress Cataloging-in-Publication Data
Names: Mulheron, Rachael P, author.
Title: Class actions and government / Rachael Mulheron, Queen Mary University of London.
Description: Cambridge, United Kingdom ; New York, NY, USA : Cambridge University Press, 2020. | Includes bibliographical references and index.
Identifiers: LCCN 2019033432 (print) | LCCN 2019033433 (ebook) | ISBN 9781107043978 (hardback) | ISBN 9781107358317 (epub)
Subjects: LCSH: Class actions (Civil procedure) – Political aspects – English-speaking countries.
Classification: LCC K2243 .M85 2020 (print) | LCC K2243 (ebook) | DDC 347/.053–dc23
LC record available at https://lccn.loc.gov/2019033432
LC ebook record available at https://lccn.loc.gov/2019033433

ISBN 978-1-107-04397-8 Hardback

To Brenda, in gratitude for unstinting friendship and support
over the years

and

With sincere thanks to the British Academy for the provision
of generous and valuable financial support for this project

SUMMARY OF CONTENTS

CONTENTS

FIGURES AND TABLES

Figures

Tables

PREFACE

The relationship between class actions and government is a little like that of bees and flowers: one simply cannot survive and flourish without the other; they are mutually reliant. Yet, the interplay between the class action and government (in all of its guises) has not been much written upon in class actions scholarship to date. It is the purpose of this book to seek to fill that niche by adopting a comparative perspective towards the topic.

This book arose out of a confluence of my teaching, research, and law reform work in the class actions area. For example, I was intrigued by the willingness of North American and Australian law reformers to advocate, and implement, an opt-out class action device several decades ago when it may not have been as apparent that many suits against governments would eventuate under those regimes. That reality has been certainly readily apparent since, and it is hypothesised that this has had something of a 'chilling effect' upon procedural reform in some other jurisdictions.

Moreover, the battle (and it is, make no mistake, a battle) to achieve law reform in this area is highly dependent upon the way in which the political wind is blowing. The very willingness to enact legislation at all is oft-said to depend upon 'evidence of need', to which any law reformer will grimly smile at the notion of 'proving a negative', and will bite back the riposte (and draw the metaphor noted by various scholars and commentators in this context) that the voice in the cornfield who told Kevin Costner's character in *Field of Dreams* (1989), '[i]f you build it, they will come', was one worth listening to. Yet, there are now numerous opt-out class actions around the common law world in place, and others are possibly on the horizon or have been mooted.

Once enacted, government becomes a 'key player' in the litigation ('the match', as Part II's heading notes). It may fulfil the roles of representative claimant; of class member; of defendant (as mentioned); and of beneficiary. The study of governmental interplay in class actions jurisprudence makes for a fascinating study. It is a field in which there are various drafting options, and these are considered from a comparative perspective throughout the book.

As always, the production of this book has been a concerted team effort. The support, encouragement, wise counsel, and good humour provided by my parents, friends, and colleagues at Queen Mary University of London throughout the undertaking of this work are gratefully appreciated.

Moreover, grateful thanks are due to the British Academy which, by virtue of the award of a Mid-Career Fellowship, enabled me to undertake this work for a period which was free of teaching and administrative responsibilities. I will be forever grateful for this support and generosity that enabled me to enjoy such a reflective and quiet interlude in which to research and to write the manuscript.

Grateful thanks are also due to the editors, typesetters, and proofreaders at Cambridge University Press. The book has benefited tremendously from the proofreading undertaken by my parents; but, as ever, all remaining errors are solely my responsibility.

The law is stated, from the materials that were available to me, as at 30 April 2019.

Rachael Mulheron
London
June 2019

TABLE OF CASES

TABLE OF LEGISLATION

Australia

European Union

The Netherlands

Scotland

United States

ABBREVIATIONS

General

[6]	paragraph 6
56	page 56
§ or s 21	section 21
r 12.3	rule 12.3
aff'd	affirmed
A-G or AG	Attorney-General
ALI	American Law Institute
ALRC	Australian Law Reform Commission
Alta	Alberta
Am	American
Ann	Annual
Ass	Assurance
Assn	Association
Aust or Aus	Australian
BC	Borough Council
BC	British Columbia
BIS	Department for Business, Innovation and Skills
Bull	Bulletin
c	chapter
CC	County Council
ch	chapter
CJ	Chief Justice
CJC	Civil Justice Council of England and Wales
cl, cll	clause/s
Co	Company or Corporation
Comm	Commission or Committee
Comp	Comparative
Comp	Competition
Commr	Commissioner
Corp	Corporation

CP	Consultation Paper
CPR	Civil Procedure Rules
Cth	Commonwealth
DC	District Council
Dept	Department
Dist	District
Div	Division
DP	Discussion Paper
ed	editor
edn	edition
Euro	European
EWLC	England and Wales Law Commission
fn	footnote
GLO	Group Litigation Order
Govt	Government
Hosp	Hospital
Ins	Insurance
Intl	International
J	Journal
J, JJ	Judge or Justice, Judges or Justices
LBC	London Borough Council
Litig	Litigation
LJ	Lord Justice
LRC	Law Reform Commission
M	Million
MBC	Metropolitan Borough Council
MOJ	Ministry of Justice
MR	Master of the Rolls
NSW	New South Wales
NZ	New Zealand
OFT	Office of Fair Trading
OLRC	Ontario Law Reform Commission
P	President
Pt	Part
PD	Practice Direction
pp	pinpoint
Prod/s	Product/s
Q	Quarterly
QC	Queen's Counsel
Qld	Queensland
reg/s	regulation/s
ref'd	refused

Rep	Report
Rev	Review
rev'd	reversed
s, ss	section/s
SC	Shire Council
SME	small and medium-sized enterprises
Soc	Society
Sys	System
U or Uni	University
UK	United Kingdom
US	United States
Vic	Victoria
WP	Working Paper

Courts

CA	Court of Appeal (of the jurisdiction referred to by the reporter series)
CAT	Competition Appeal Tribunal
Ch	Chancery Division of the High Court of England and Wales
DC	District Court (of the jurisdiction referred to by the reporter series)
Div Ct	Superior Court of Justice (Divisional Court of Ontario)
EWCA	Court of Appeal of England and Wales
EWHC	High Court of England and Wales
FCA	Federal Court of Australia
Full FCA	Full Bench of the Federal Court of Australia
Gen Div	Ontario Court of Justice (General Division)
HC	High Court (of the jurisdiction referred to by the reporter series)
HCA	High Court of Australia
HL	House of Lords
QB	Queen's Bench Division
SC	Supreme Court (of the relevant jurisdiction)
SCC	Supreme Court of Canada
SCJ	Superior Court of Justice (Ontario)
SDNY	United States District Court, Southern District of New York (sample jurisdiction)
2d Cir	United States Court of Appeals for the Second Circuit

Legislation

CA 1998	Competition Act 1998 (UK)
CPA (Ont)	Class Proceedings Act, SO 1992, c 6

CPA (BC)	Class Proceedings Act, RSBC 1996, c 50
FCA 1976	Federal Court of Australia Act 1976
FRCP	Federal Rules of Civil Procedure (US)

Law Reports

AC	Law Reports, Appeal Cases (Third Series) (1891–)
ACWS (3d)	All Canada Weekly Summaries, Third Series
All ER	All England Law Reports
ALR	Australian Law Reports
Alta LR (3d)	Alberta Law Reports, Third Series
App Cas	Appeal Cases (1875–90)
BCJ	British Columbia Judgments
BCLR (3d)	British Columbia Law Reports, Third Series
Cal 2d	California Reports, Second Series
CCLT (3d)	Canadian Cases on the Law of Torts, Third Series
Ch	Law Reports, Chancery Division (Third Series) (1891–)
Ch D	Law Reports, Chancery Division (Second Series) (1875–90)
CLR	Commonwealth Law Reports
CPC (3d)	Carswell Practice Cases, Third Series
DLR (4th)	Dominion Law Reports, Fourth Series
ER	English Reports
F 2d	Federal Reporter, Second Series
F 3d	Federal Reporter, Third Series
FCR	Federal Court Reports (Australia)
FLR	Federal Law Reports (Australia)
FRD	Federal Rules Decisions
F Supp	Federal Supplement
F Supp (2d)	Federal Supplement, Second Series
IR	Irish Reports
KB	Law Reports, King's Bench
Lloyd's Rep	Lloyd's Law Reports
NSWLR	New South Wales Law Reports
OAC	Ontario Appeal Cases
OJ	Ontario Judgments
OR (2d)	Ontario Reports, Second Series
OR (3d)	Ontario Reports, Third Series
QB	Law Reports, Queen's Bench (1891–)
QBD	Queen's Bench Division (1876–90)
SA	South African Law Reports
SASR	South Australian State Reports
SC	Session Cases (Scotland)

SCR	Supreme Court Reports, Canada
SLT	Scots Law Times
Sol Jo	Solicitors' Journal
US	United States Supreme Court Reports
VLR	Victorian Law Reports
VR	Victorian Reports
WLR	Weekly Law Reports (UK)
WWR	Western Weekly Reports

NOTES ON MODE OF CITATION

Throughout this book, the following protocols are adopted:

1 In the footnotes, the order of preference of case law citations is as follows:

    (a) where the case has been designated a neutral citation by the adjudicating court, the neutral citation is used;

    (b) where the case has been reported in an authorised series of reports, the authorised citation is used in addition to the neutral citation;

    (c) in the absence of (b), where the case has been reported in an unauthorised series of reports, the unauthorised citation is used in addition to the neutral citation;

    (d) in the absence of (a)–(c), the case is cited in the following manner: (court, date of decision).

2 Paragraph numbers are used in preference to page numbers, where pinpoints from primary or secondary sources are required.
Occasionally, where a primary or secondary source was accessed online and could not be located in hard copy feasibly or at all, so as to locate a pinpoint for a quotation, the following is noted: (accessed online, no pp available).

3 For each case, the court is referred to in parentheses in all instances where it is not obvious from the report series or citation which court made the decision.

4 The scholarship and opinion of many entities and persons are referenced throughout this book, and have been cited and pinpointed in accordance with British citation conventions. All reasonable efforts have been made to pinpoint as accurately and fulsomely as possible.

5 Wherever quotations appear from primary or secondary sources, in the interests of brevity, footnotes within those quotations have not be

reproduced unless otherwise shown; and the conventional usage of 'footnotes omitted' should be assumed throughout.

6 In the text and footnotes, references to the masculine gender should be taken to import the feminine gender, unless expressly indicated otherwise.

Introduction

A   About This Book

The relationship between government and class actions is a challenging one – combining leaps of faith, conflicts, tensions, and truly complex jurisprudence. Government may be the 'pursuer' in one class action, and the 'pursued' in another. It may (indirectly) fund one class action, and (indirectly) receive funding from another. It may draft one kind of class action regime, but actually implement a different type altogether. It may quite like the idea of its courts being at the hub of global class actions litigation, but hesitate (and actually legislate against) making that a reality for its own class action. These (and other) dichotomies and tensions make for an absorbing study. This book examines that relationship in detail, and in particular, analyses the following, and often controversial, roles of government: as class action enabler, as designer, as funder, as gatekeeper, as representative claimant, as class member, as defendant, and finally, as beneficiary.

At the outset, it is important to explain what is meant by 'government' and by 'class action' in this book, given its title and its subject matter.

1   The Meaning of 'Government'

The word 'government' is a Middle English word[1] which was originally derived from Old French,[2] from Latin,[3] and from Greek,[4] meaning 'to steer'

---

[1] See: *Oxford Dictionary of English* (2nd edn, revised, Oxford University Press, 2005) 749.
[2] ibid, from Old French *'governer'*.
[3] ibid, from Latin *'gubernare'*.
[4] ibid, from Greek *'kubernan'*.

or 'to rule'. It may not be susceptible to more than one pronunciation[5] – but, as a concept, it certainly gives rise to more than one meaning,[6] depending upon the context in which it is used. That reality is evident throughout this book. Depending upon the chapter and the context, 'government' may take on one or more of **four** possible meanings.

(a)   Depending upon the Context

First, the term, 'government', it is used in the sense of *the Ministers of the Crown for the time being, and of their government departments*, both of which are the organs of central government and which are responsible for various spheres of public administration, including legislative policy.[7] The relevant minister/s who head the departments are politically responsible for those policy decisions, as to what legislation will go forth for consideration in the Parliamentary chamber; whilst much of the 'finer detail' of drafting, consulting upon, and implementing law reform proposals is undertaken by the permanent civil servants who staff them.[8] Where the role of government as enabler, designer, funder, and gatekeeper is considered later in this book,[9] these organs of government are vital to that process. If class actions reform is sectoral[10] rather than generic,[11] then any one of a number of departments (and their relevant ministers) may 'carry the ball forth into the ruck' for their particular sector (and for none others). Indeed, the very unpredictability of the government organ from which class actions reform may emanate is one of the challenges of law reform in this area. For example, in the United Kingdom, whilst much attention was focused upon the prospect of promulgating a generic class action via the Ministry of Justice in

---

[5] Note the amusing anecdote by R Burchfield (ed), *New Fowler's Modern English Usage* (3rd edn, revised, 1998) 339: '[w]hile preparing my booklet *The Spoken Word* (1981) for the BBC, I found that this belonged to a small group of words that gave maximum offence to listeners if pronounced in a garbled manner, with the first *n* silent, i.e., as gavement, or even gavment'.

[6] See at least four different meanings attributed to the word in: *Oxford Dictionary of English* (n 1) 749.

[7] E Martin and J Law (eds), *Oxford Dictionary of Law* (6th edn, 2006) 243, 342; and J Penner, *The Law Student's Dictionary* (13th edn, 2008) 131.

[8] *Oxford Dictionary of Law*, ibid, 243.

[9] All of which are considered in Part I of the book.

[10] i.e., a class action regime which applies to one particular sector of the economy or society, to the exclusion of others which are not specified in the governing legislation.

[11] i.e., a class action which is capable of applying to all, or almost all, causes of action which arise across multiple sectors of economic or social activity and which apply to all or most affected parties, whether individual or corporate.

2010–11,[12] HM Treasury, quietly and without herald, published a consultation paper which proposed an opt-out class action solely for financial services claims,[13] and duly promulgated a bill by which to implement the reform.[14]

Secondly, the term 'government' is used in the sense of *Parliament*, i.e., 'the supreme legislative power in a State',[15] or 'the highest legislature'.[16] The Parliament of any country is constituted according to its customs. For example, in the United Kingdom, Parliament consists of Her Majesty the Queen, the House of Commons, and the House of Lords;[17] whilst in Australia, federal Parliament practically consists of Her Majesty the Queen's representative, the Senate, and the House of Representatives.[18] The functions of any Parliament are, simply put, to enact legislation, to sanction taxation and public expenditure, and to scrutinise critically government policy and administration. In this guise, the role of Parliament is relevant in any chapter of this book in which regard is had to the detailed content of class actions legislation. Parliamentary debates, and the Hansard record of cross-party standing committees which may examine a bill during the course of its passage through Parliament, often reveal the extent of disagreement about either key drafting points or of wider policy, and occasionally signal that a particular provision in a draft bill was revised, or even deleted, in light of the scrutiny to which it was subjected. The principal exception to this is where class actions laws are delegated to rule-making bodies or committees. Such entities tend to have the power to make 'rules of court relating to practice or procedure'.[19] Hence, as a general rule, rule-making bodies cannot enact, alter or revoke substantive law, and any attempt

---

[12] Following from the law reform recommendation for a generic class action which was proposed by the Civil Justice Council, *Improving Access to Justice through Collective Actions: Final Report (A Series of Recommendations to the Lord Chancellor)* (November 2008). The Ministry of Justice formally responded: *The Government's Response to the Civil Justice Council's Report: 'Improving Access to Justice through Collective Actions'* (July 2009); and see too: the Rt Hon Bridget Prentice, *Justice: Collective Actions* (Written Ministerial Statement, 20 July 2009).

[13] HM Treasury, *Reforming Financial Markets* (Cm 7667, 2009).

[14] Financial Services Bill (Bill 51 09–10), introduced to Parliament on 9 November 2009. The chequered history of this Bill, which was ultimately enacted as the Financial Services Act 2010, c 28, but not with the class action sections included, is discussed in detail by the author in: 'Recent Milestones in Class Actions: A Critique and a Proposal' (2011) 127 *Law Quarterly Review* 288.

[15] *Law Student's Dictionary* (n 7) 131.

[16] *Oxford Dictionary of English* (n 1) 1280.

[17] *Oxford Dictionary of Law* (n 7) 381.

[18] *Butterworths Concise Australian Legal Dictionary* (1997) 74.

[19] See, e.g.: Civil Procedure Act 1997 (UK), s 1(1).

to do so will be *ultra vires* their rule-making powers which are delegated to those bodies by Parliament. The extent to which such delegation has occurred throughout various common law jurisdictions to date, either permissibly or impermissibly, has been discussed by the author elsewhere,[20] and will not be revisited herein.

Thirdly, 'government' may be used in the sense of **the Crown**, as that body which is capable of suing or of being sued, to the extent that Parliament has permitted that course.[21] The Crown, albeit 'legally ill-defined',[22] does not mean 'the monarchy'[23] for the purposes of this book. Rather, it is taken to mean (and where appropriate from the context) that corporation sole[24] which represents 'the entire administrative edifice of the executive government';[25] or alternatively, 'the state in all its aspects ... such as Crown dependencies, provinces or states'.[26] As evident from the Table of Cases,[27] and depending upon the jurisdiction, the Crown may be denoted, in litigation, by terms such as 'the state', 'the State of [jurisdiction]', 'the Crown', 'the Crown in Right of [jurisdiction]', 'Her Majesty the Queen in Right of [jurisdiction]', or just by the relevant jurisdiction's name (e.g., 'Victoria'). The division between the Crown on the one hand, and the monarch (i.e., the sovereign who is filling the office of Crown or of the corporation sole at any given time) on the other, is necessary, precisely because it is not possible to sue the sovereign personally.[28] In that sense, it is said that 'the Crown never dies',[29] whereas the monarch inevitably will. As will be discussed in this book, the Crown may certainly constitute a class action claimant or defendant.

Finally, the term 'government' may, depending upon the context, refer to **government agencies**, consisting of 'executive agencies'[30] or 'Crown corporations'.[31] These are typically statutory bodies corporate which are

---

[20] *The Class Action in Common Law Legal Systems: A Comparative Perspective* (Hart Publishing, 2004) 38–42.

[21] Per, e.g.: Crown Proceedings Act 1947 (UK), ss 1, 2.

[22] As noted in the definition of 'the Crown' (*Wikipedia*, accessed 12 March 2019).

[23] As it is often defined, see, e.g.; *Oxford Dictionary of English* (n 1) 415.

[24] i.e., a corporation consisting of one person only, where that person constitutes an artificial legal person which has the capacity to sue or to be sued, and in which title to property may be vested: *Oxford Dictionary of Law* (n 7) 131.

[25] *Butterworths Legal Dictionary* (n 18) 99.

[26] Per definition of 'the Crown' (*Wikipedia*, accessed 12 March 2019).

[27] See pp xxi–xxxix.

[28] See, e.g., the discussion in: *Oxford Dictionary of Law* (n 7) 142.

[29] *Law Student's Dictionary* (n 7) 78.

[30] *Oxford Dictionary of Law* (n 7) 210.

[31] See: *Butterworths Legal Dictionary* (n 18) 99.

created by the Crown or which carry on duties on behalf of the Crown or the 'parent' government, but which do not have policymaking powers. They generally operate under delegated statutory powers in order to deliver public services (e.g., a Prisons Service, an industry regulator, or an Immigration Agency).[32] In particular, these bodies may also sue or be sued in class actions litigation, as later chapters discuss.

(b) What Does Not 'Count'

Although frequent references are made, throughout this book, to the recommendations of law reform commissions and to decisions issued by the judiciary, these entities are not considered to comprise part of 'government'. Whilst law reform commissions are frequently statutory corporations which are established by a legislative enactment, and fulfil the role of 'advisory public bodies' to keep the law of a jurisdiction under review and to recommend reform where required,[33] they are not an organ of 'government'. As one source explains, they are 'usually independent from governmental control, providing intellectual independence to accurately reflect and report on how the law should progress'.[34]

The judiciary is, likewise, that arm of authority, appointed by the Crown or by the state (depending upon the jurisdiction), which interprets laws and which adjudicates upon disputes of fact and/or law. To the extent that curial or extra-curial commentary by judges has been important in encouraging the implementation of class actions legislation – as an 'independent voice' from those of the policymaking and the legislative arms of government – that is duly noted in chapter discussion where relevant.[35] However, neither of these entities is part of 'government' for the purposes of the scholarly examination undertaken in this book.

2   The Meaning of 'Class Action'

Whilst the term, 'class action', may generically cover a wide array of group litigation mechanisms, the focus of this book is upon the *opt-out*

---

[32] *Oxford Dictionary of Law* (n 7) 210.

[33] See, e.g., the discussion of the Law Commission of England and Wales: '[t]he Law Commission is a statutory independent body that keeps the law under review and recommends reform where it is needed. ... [it] is an advisory non-departmental public body, sponsored by the Ministry of Justice': 'Law Commission', available at: www.gov.uk/government/organisations/law-commission.

[34] Discussion of 'law reform' (*Wikipedia*, accessed 11 March 2019).

[35] See, in particular, Chapter 2 of this volume, 'Government as Class Actions Enabler'.

class action. The phrase of 'class action' will be used throughout this book in place of synonymous terms such as 'collective action', 'collective proceedings', or 'group actions' (unless those terms are specified within original quotations or legislative wording). The opt-out species of the class action is defined as follows:[36]

> A class action is a legal procedure which enables the claims (or part of the claims) of a number of persons against the same defendant to be determined in the one suit. In a class action, one or more persons ('representative claimant') may sue on his or her own behalf and on behalf of a number of other persons ('the class') who have a claim to a remedy for the same or a similar alleged wrong to that pursued by the representative claimant, and who have claims that share questions of law or fact in common with those of the representative claimant ('common issues'). Only the representative claimant is a party to the action. The class members are not usually identified as individual parties but are merely described. Should they not wish to participate, class members are permitted to opt-out of the class action in the time and manner prescribed. Unless they opt-out, class members are bound by the outcome of the litigation on the common issues, whether favourable or adverse to the class, although they do not, for the most part, take any active part in that litigation.

There are many other forms of class action other than that defined above, and indeed, many other collective redress mechanisms altogether, on the 'statute books' throughout the common law world, which facilitate, to a greater or lesser degree, the recovery of compensation.[37] These are summarised in Table 1.1 overpage.[38] Except to the extent that discussion of these

---

[36] Reproduced from: Mulheron, *The Class Action* (n 20) 3, drawing from a number of law reform commission reports, including those from: Australia, South Africa, Alberta, and Ontario.

[37] The vast array of collective redress mechanisms is evident from scholarly works such as: P Karlsgodt (ed), *World Class Action: A Guide to Group and Representative Actions around the Globe* (Oxford University Press, 2012); C Hodges, *Multi-Party Actions* (Oxford University Press, 2001), especially Pt II, and the case studies in Pt V; E Lein et al (eds), *Collective Redress in Europe: Why and How?* (BIICL, 2015); Ontario LRC, *Report on Class Action* (1982), chs 2 and 3; *Class and Group Actions 2019* (11th edn, Global Legal Group, 2018); A Zuckerman, *Zuckerman on Civil Procedure: Principles of Practice* (3rd edn, Thomson Sweet and Maxwell, 2013), ch 12.

[38] The author has discussed these options in detail in the following sources, from which the summary in the Table is drawn: 'From Representative Rule to Class Action: Steps Rather than Leaps' (2005) 24 *Civil Justice Quarterly* 424; 'Some Difficulties with Group Litigation Orders – and Why a Class Action is Superior' (2005) 24 *Civil Justice Quarterly* 40; *Reform of Collective Redress in England and Wales: A Perspective of Need* (Research Paper for the CJC, 2008), Pt II; and 'Opting In, Opting Out, and Closing the Class: Some Dilemmas for England's Class Action Lawmakers' (2010) 50 *Canadian Business Law Journal* 376, Section II.

Table 1.1 *Collective redress: the other options*

	The regime	A brief description
1.	an opt-in class action	all putative class members must take some prescribed step within a prescribed period in order to join the action, to be bound by any judgment or settlement on the common issues, and to receive compensation in the event of success. The class members are identified by name, rather than merely described by characteristics or event. However, the class members do not need to file individual proceedings; an entry of their names onto a group register, whether maintained by the representative claimant, the court, or other, is sufficient to signify membership of the class.
2.	group litigation	this is similar to an opt-in class action, except that each class member must file individual proceedings, whereupon the claims are then grouped, and case-managed, in the one action.
3.	a compulsory class action	all persons falling within the class description are bound by the class action, with no opportunity for the class members to exclude themselves from the action (also called a 'mandatory class'). Under some variations of the compulsory class action: either class members can opt out of the class action but only with judicial permission, or an otherwise opt-out class action can be rendered compulsory per judicial discretion in appropriate circumstances.
4.	a mixed-model class action	a number of variations on the opt-out class action exist, e.g.: a class action which can be formed on either opt-in or opt-out principles, depending upon judicial election, having regard to the circumstances; or an opt-in class is the primary legislatively-dictated model, unless the court deems an opt-out class to be better suited to the circumstances; or an opt-out regime is legislatively specified for the principal class, with an opt-in class also being legislatively specified for a particular sub-class or in particular circumstances.
5.	the representative rule	the longstanding rule (originating in equity and then embraced in court rules applying to common law courts too) which permits a proceeding by the

Table 1.1 (*cont.*)

	The regime	A brief description
		representative claimant on behalf of a class, where numerous class members (or 'two or more' class members) share the 'same interest' with the representative claimant. This is probably a compulsory class, although theoretically at least, exclusions from the class may be permissible.
6.	joinder	joinder typically describes a procedure in which two or more parties may be named in the one set of proceedings, on the basis that their claims may conveniently be disposed of in that one set of proceedings.[39] Each of the parties is a named party in those initiating proceedings.
7.	consolidation	this typically describes a procedure in which the court may combine two or more already-commenced proceedings, as part of its case-management powers, for the sake of efficiency and to avoid inconsistent outcomes, where those cases share sufficient commonality of fact or of law.[40] The parties are named parties in the separately issued proceedings.
8.	a test action	a proceeding which is instituted to establish the outcome on a point of law or fact, in order to establish a precedent for those similarly situated parties who have either instituted proceedings, or who have registered their name on a group register, or who are yet to institute proceedings. The outcome of the test action has precedential value for other similar cases, but it is not binding *res judicata* upon those other cases who are not parties to the test action.
9.	a lead action	a case which is chosen from a number of cases already instituted by similarly situated parties, with those other actions stayed, pending the outcome of the lead

---

[39] See, e.g.: CPR 7.3 (in general); CPR 19.2(2)(b) ('there is an issue involving the new party and an existing party which is connected to the matters in dispute in the proceedings, and it is desirable to add the new party so that the court can resolve that issue'); and CPR 19.3 (where two or more persons are jointly entitled to a remedy).

[40] See, e.g., CPR 3.1(2)(g).

Table 1.1 (*cont.*)

	The regime	A brief description
		action. This term is often used interchangeably with the term, 'test case'.[41]
10.	a settlement-only class action	under this more limited model, the parties to a proposed collective settlement may jointly request the court to declare that settlement binding on all members of the class unless a member elects to opt out. The settlement will not be binding upon the class members until the court assesses the reasonableness and fairness of the proposal.[42]

devices is necessary to expound the background to, or the theory or practice of, opt-out class actions,[43] they will **not** comprise any focus of this book.

For three reasons, however, this book focuses upon *opt-out class actions*, and their interplay with government.

First, of all the aforementioned collective redress devices mentioned, it is the opt-out class action which is most evolving and considered by law reformers around the common law world. At the time of writing, there

---

[41] e.g., in the English Civil Procedure Rules, references to 'test case' encompass scenarios where a number of individual actions have been commenced, and one is selected from that cadre for litigation: CPR 19.13(b) and CPR 19.15.

[42] As implemented by the Collective Settlement of Mass Damage (Wet Collectieve Afwikkeling Massaschade) (WCAM), which entered into force in The Netherlands in July 2005, and which is contained in the Dutch Civil Code, arts 7:907–7:910. Under that regime, the settlement proceedings consist of four separate phases (as detailed, e.g., in: A Knigge and I Wijnberg, *Class/collective Actions in The Netherlands: Overview* (Class Actions Global Guide, Practical Law, updated as at 1 July 2018); and J Fleming and J Kuster, 'The Netherlands', in Karlsgodt (ed), *World Class Action* (n 37), ch 14. On 19 March 2019, the Dutch Senate passed legislation to facilitate an opt-out class action for either judgments or settlements, and which is not restricted to representative organisations. See further: H Schrama and M Sinnighe Damste, 'Class Action for Damages in the Netherlands' (*Loyens Loeff Newsletter*, 20 March 2019); C Van Rest and B Keizers, 'A Collective Action for Damages in the Netherlands is a Fact!' (*Hogan Lovells*, 2 April 2019). At the time of writing, the statute has not been proclaimed into force. An unauthorised copy of A Bill on Redress of Mass Damages in a Collective Action (Wet affwikkeling Massaschade in Collectieve Actie) is available at: www.houthoff.com/doc/ English_translationbill_on_Redress_of_Mass_Damages_in_a_collective_action.pdf.

[43] See, e.g., discussion in Chapter 2.B, as to the perceived or actual problems and deficiencies with some of these devices as a 'prompter' for class actions reform.

are several law reform reports – e.g., in Hong Kong,[44] Western Australia,[45] the United Kingdom,[46] and South Africa[47] – whose recommendations for the implementation of opt-out class actions reform have gone unheeded by their respective governments. There are even jurisdictions which have ignored the much more modest recommendations for *opt-in* class actions reform.[48] In Scotland, and following two reviews of civil process which recommended an opt-in or opt-out (generic) regime,[49] depending upon judicial choice, the Scottish Parliament has finally enacted relevant legislation to that effect,[50] with relevant rules of

---

[44] LRC of Hong Kong, *Class Actions* (2012) [3.72], and Recommendation 2(1), p 106; and on an opt-out basis: Recommendation 3, p 122.

[45] LRC of Western Australia, *Representative Proceedings: Final Report* (Project 103, 2015), and Recommendations 1 and 2 (that 'Western Australia enact legislation to create a scheme in relation to the conduct of representative actions, and that the legislative scheme be based on Part IVA of the Federal Court of Australia Act 1976 (Cth)').

[46] CJC, *Improving Access to Justice: Final Report* (2008) (n 12), recommending that 'collective claims may be brought on an opt-in or opt-out basis, subject to court certification': Recommendation 3, p 5.

[47] South African Law Comm, *The Recognition of Class Actions and Public Interest Actions in South African Law* (Project 88, 1998), recommending the introduction of an opt-out class action, and drafting appropriate legislation (in ch 6) to give effect to that recommendation. In the absence of legislation, South African courts have judicially fashioned a class action on the basis of: the Constitution of the Republic of South Africa, 108 of 1996, ch 2, and s 38(c). See too: *Nkala v Harmony Gold Mining Co Ltd* [2016] ZAGPJHC 97, [238] ('South Africa does not have legislation governing class action claims. The rules governing class actions have been developed by the courts. In the absence of legislative regulation in South Africa, the courts are duty bound to continue the development of class action proceedings').

[48] LRC of Ireland, *Multi-Party Litigation* (Rep 76, 2005), with a recommendation that the class action 'would operate on the opt-in principle' (at [2.26]); of which it has been said that, '[t]his recommendation has yet to be implemented and does not form part of the government's current legislative programme': *The Class Actions Law Review: Ireland* (2nd edn, *The Law Reviews*, May 2018). See too: Scottish Law Comm, *Multi-Party Actions* (1996), with a recommendation that 'persons . . . who wish to be group members should be required . . . to elect to be members of the group' (at [4.55]).

[49] *Report of the Scottish Civil Courts Review* (2009), viii ('[w]e have identified further gaps of which the most important is the absence of an efficient procedure for multi-party actions . . . subject to suitable safeguards, multi-party litigations have a valuable role to play in modern civil justice'), and Recommendation 163, which recommended the introduction of a multi-party procedure, initially for the Court of Session only, and where it would be for the court to decide whether, in the particular circumstances of a case, an 'opt in' or 'opt out' model would be desirable. This recommendation was approved subsequently by Sheriff Taylor in: *Review of Expenses and Funding of Civil Litigation in Scotland* (2013), ch 12, [11]–[19].

[50] Civil Litigation (Expenses and Group Proceedings) (Scotland) Act 2018, s 20, permitting 'grouped proceedings' in the Court of Session: s 20(1), which may be brought as opt-in, opt-out, or either opt-in or opt-out proceedings: s 20(7).

court presently being drafted.[51] Elsewhere, a review of whether opt-out class actions should be introduced into domestic law is actively underway;[52] as is a review of how a long-established opt-out class action could be revised and improved in light of a quarter of a century of jurisprudence.[53] Reviews of long-established class actions have also been undertaken over the years.[54] All of this demonstrates the developing, and at times problematical, jurisprudence which accompanies this important civil procedural regime. With that in mind, it is anticipated that an examination of the interplay between government and opt-out class actions will assist policymakers and lawmakers in several jurisdictions to consider the complex issues that may arise, both in drafting the actual content of class actions legislation, and in studying the merits or demerits of setting up accoutrements such as a dedicated class actions fund.

Secondly, it is apparent that, across those jurisdictions in which opt-out class actions have achieved a firm hold, the government has featured heavily as a 'player' in class actions litigation. Governments are frequently sued as class actions defendants;[55] the basis upon which a government can sue as representative claimant is far from straightforward;[56] how a government is to be treated as class member varies widely;[57] and whether financial windfalls to governments (from unclaimed residual damages funds) should ever be countenanced (and, if so, the criteria governing those distributions) has been most controversial.[58] A dedicated study of these conundrums is warranted, in order to learn lessons and to recommend 'best practice' arising out of the varying judicial decisions and legislative drafting precedents.

---

[51] The relevant court rules are being developed by the Scottish Civil Justice Council, according to that body's *Annual Report 2017/18 and Annual Programme 2018/19*, p 13.

[52] e.g., New Zealand Law Comm, *Review of Class Actions and Litigation Funding* (May 2018), with the reference discussed at: www.lawcom.govt.nz/news/review-class-actions-and-litigation-funding. For an interesting and topical analysis of the New Zealand class action litigation procedure, and why reform is required, see: N Chamberlain, 'Contracting-Out of Class Action Litigation: Lessons from the United States' [2018] *New Zealand Law Review* 371; and by the same author: 'Class Actions in New Zealand: An Empirical Study' [2018] *New Zealand Business Law Quarterly* 132.

[53] Law Reform Commission of Ontario, *Class Actions: Objectives, Experiences and Reforms* (CP, March 2018).

[54] Australian LRC, *Integrity, Fairness and Efficiency – An Inquiry into Class Action Proceedings and Third-Party Litigation Funders* (Rep 134, December 2018); Victorian LRC, *Access to Justice: Litigation Funding and Group Proceedings* (2018).

[55] See Chapter 8, 'Government as Class Actions Defendant'.

[56] See Chapter 6, 'Government as Representative Claimant'.

[57] See Chapter 7, 'Government as Class Member'.

[58] See Chapter 9, 'Government as Class Actions Beneficiary'.

Thirdly, the wide-reaching effects of lawsuits conducted under opt-out class action regimes – whatever their outcome – has been judicially acknowledged, frequently and globally. The scale of that reach matters to government, in each of the four guises considered in this book. For example:

- in Canadian jurisprudence, it has been stated that –

  > there is an element of social engineering in class proceedings, with the exposure to liability encouraging proper conduct and discouraging misbehaviour.[59]

- whilst, in the United Kingdom, the Competition Appeal Tribunal has noted that –

  > The introduction of collective proceedings on an opt-out basis for violations of competition law amounts to legislation in the field of social or economic policy. . . . The [legislation] covers in particular the victims of that violation, whose rights the regime helps to vindicate, as well as the broader interest of society of establishing an effective redress mechanism for violations of competition law.[60]

- whilst, in Australia, in an early class actions case, Kirby J stated that –

  > it is clear that the Parliament intended to arm the Federal Court with a wide and flexible armoury of powers, capable of being adapted to the particular needs and novel circumstances of representative proceedings . . . Representative proceedings are not traditional litigation; nor should they be subjected to all of the requirements of such litigation. . . . it is inappropriate to impose upon such grants of power strictures derived from earlier times and traditional powers in litigation between individual parties.[61]

- whilst the US Supreme Court has remarked that –

  > The aggregation of individual claims in the context of classwide suit is an evolutionary response to the existence of injuries unremedied by the regulatory action of government. Where it is not economically feasible to obtain relief within the traditional framework of a multiplicity of small individual suits for damages, aggrieved persons may be without any effective redress unless they may employ the class action device.[62]

---

[59] *Farkas v Sunnybrook & Women's College Health Sciences Centre* (Ont SCJ, 25 August 2009) [52] (Perell J).

[60] *Gibson v Pride Mobility Products Ltd (Application for a Collective Proceedings Order)* [2017] CAT 9, [44].

[61] *Graham Barclay Oysters Pty Ltd v Ryan* [2002] HCA 54, (2002) 211 CLR 540, [267].

[62] *Deposit Guaranty Nat Bank, Jackson, Miss v Roper*, 445 US 326, 339, 100 S Ct 116, 63 L Ed 2d 427 (1980).

Hence, the fact that government activities affect the social, economic, and cultural fabric of national, state, local, and/or indigenous communities means that the interplay of government with the class action device which facilitates compensatory redress creates a 'perfect storm' of **impact** upon individuals and businesses, and sometimes, even upon government itself. That interplay is thoroughly deserving of close study.

B A Comparative Study

As the aforementioned judicial statements make plain, how policy-makers and lawmakers should respond to alleged grievances on a widespread scale – by consumers and others – is a problem that has been, and is being, confronted in many jurisdictions. A plethora of discussion and consultation papers and reform reports emanating from the European Commission, Canada, Australasia, Asia, Africa, Ireland, the United States, and the United Kingdom,[63] dealing solely or principally with collective redress, bear testament to the conundrum of how to achieve efficiency of process and accessibility of redress via multi-party litigation, at reasonable transaction costs, and with a tight control over both frivolous litigation and abusive scenarios. It is precisely for commonly occurring conundrums such as this that comparative studies are particularly apposite (as the author has discussed elsewhere[64]).

However, the comparative study undertaken in this book has a twist. Not every role of government which is examined in this book warrants a comparative treatment from around the common law world. Rather, specific experiments, or parallels and differences, may be sufficient – and indeed preferable – as a more focused study. For example, a government decision to establish a dedicated class actions fund has been implemented in Ontario, and that conveys considerable lessons for other jurisdictions which may have considered, but not yet implemented, that step.[65] Escheat distributions to government are more common in the United States than in any other common law jurisdiction, hence giving rise to more judicial observations upon their merits and disadvantages than anywhere else.[66]

---

[63] These are all collected in the Bibliography, under 'Reports, Discussion Papers and Published Research Papers'.

[64] *The Class Action* (n 20) 15–20.

[65] See Chapter 4, 'Government as Class Actions Funder'.

[66] See Chapter 9, 'Government as Class Actions Beneficiary'.

Moreover, the surprising parallels of reform processes between Australia and the United Kingdom, twenty-five years apart, may lend interest to other jurisdictions which are mulling over class actions reform.[67] These examples are typical of why the topics covered in this book frequently warrant a focused, rather than a generalised, comparative study.

The principal jurisdictions that will comprise the focus of study in this book (the Comparator Jurisdictions) are those of Australia, Canada, the United Kingdom, and the United States. All are now established opt-out class actions jurisdictions, albeit with very differing degrees of experience. A brief description of their *legislative footing*, from longest standing to most recently enacted, follows.

1   United States

The modern-day opt-out class action took effect in the United States on 1 July 1966, when an amended version of rule 23 of the Federal Rules of Civil Procedure (FRCP 23) was enacted. As the oldest of the regimes considered in this book, it represents, as one commentator accurately put it, 'a model for both what to do and what not to do, as policymakers consider reforms in other countries'.[68]

The process of promulgating any new or amended rule of civil procedure occurs pursuant to the enactment of the Rules Enabling Act of 1934.[69] This is an Act of Congress which empowers the US Supreme Court 'to prescribe general rules of practice and procedure and rules of evidence for cases in the United States district courts (including proceedings before magistrate judges thereof) and courts of appeals'[70] – provided always that '[s]uch rules shall not abridge, enlarge or modify any substantive right'.[71] The Judicial Conference is the main policymaking and rule-making body of the US courts, and it is this body which is authorised by

---

[67] See Chapter 2, 'Government as Class Actions Enabler'.

[68] Karlsgodt (ed), *World Class Action* (n 37) 'Introduction', xxxvii.

[69] Pub L 73–415, 48 Stat 1064, enacted 19 June 1934, 28 USC. Its long title is: 'An act to give the Supreme Court of the United States authority to make and publish rules in actions at law'. It was enacted by the 73rd US Congress.

[70] Per § 2072(a).

[71] Per § 2072(b).

Congress to promulgate rules of civil procedure which have the effect of law.[72]

The FRCP were amended in 1966, following considerable disquiet about the then-existing FRCP 23.[73] The US Supreme Court's Rules Advisory Committee prepared a draft of a revised rule in March 1964,[74] which was forwarded to the Judicial Conference's Standing Committee on Rules of Practice and Procedure. A consultation period followed. That resulted in some amendments being made at the suggestion of both judiciary and legal practitioners; the draft rules were presented again to the Standing Committee in June 1965; and they were recommended (with a few additional changes) to the Judicial Conference in September 1965. Then, on 28 February 1966,[75] and acting pursuant to the rule-making powers that were delegated to them under the Act of 1934, the Judicial Conference's Standing Committee approved and adopted the draft FRCP 23 which had been presented to them some five months earlier. That draft was then duly transmitted to Congress;[76] and on 1 July 1966, the amended FRCP 23 took effect, thus commencing the era of the modern opt-out class action.

There was, however, a dissenter on the Judicial Conference's Standing Committee, viz, Justice Black.[77] More than fifty years later – and during

---

[72] See: *How the Rulemaking Process Works* (US Courts Newsletter, available at: www .uscourts.gov/rules-policies/about-rulemaking-process/how-rulemaking-process-works). A convenient summary of the history and tasks of the Judicial Conference of the United States is contained at: https://en.wikipedia.org/wiki/Judicial_Conference_of_the_United_States.

[73] As described in, e.g.: *Notes Accompanying Federal Rules of Civil Procedure*, Title IV, Parties, Rule 23, Class Actions, 'Notes of Advisory Committee on Rules – 1966 Amendment' (Legal Information Institute, Cornell Law School, available at: www .law.cornell.edu/rules/frcp/rule_23); and B Kaplan, 'Continuing Work of the Civil Committee: 1966 Amendments of the Federal Rules of Civil Procedure' (1967) 81 *Harvard Law Review* 356, 357–58. Some particular difficulties with the former US FRCP 23, in particular, the so-called spurious class action, are described in Chapter 2.

[74] Contained in: *Report of the Committee on Rules of Practice and Procedure of the Judicial Conference of the United States*, Standing Committee on Rules of Practice and Procedure, 'Preliminary Draft of Proposed Amendments to Rules of Civil Procedure for the United States District Courts' (1964) 34 *Federal Rules Decisions* 325, 385–87.

[75] Kaplan, 'Continuing Work' (n 73); and see, for further detail: A Conte and H Newberg, *Newberg on Class Actions* (4th edn, West Group, 2002), vol 1, § 1.10, 'Major innovations of 1966 amendments to Rule 23'.

[76] See: *Report of the Judicial Conference of the United States*, 39 *Federal Rules Decisions* 69, 'Amendments to Rules of Civil Procedure; Supplemental Rules for Certain Admiralty and Maritime Claims; Rules of Criminal Procedure'. Rule 23 constituted only a small portion of the Judicial Conference's report, but arguably had the biggest impact of any amendment contained in that volume of the FRD.

[77] The dissenting opinion is contained in 39 FRD 69, 272–75. Justice Douglas also dissented in part (at 276–79), but not on the subject of the class actions amendment.

which time the US federal class action has been termed many things: 'a Frankenstein monster posing as a class action';[78] 'one of the most important procedural mechanisms for handling disputes arising from large scale, small claim phenomena';[79] the 'single most significant procedural event in civil litigation today';[80] and that '[m]issing from public view are the cases in which attorneys have risked bankruptcy to proceed with suits that will alter the lives of large groups of people'[81] – it is interesting to revisit the misgivings which Justice Black expressed, at the time, about the class actions rule. In particular:[82]

> Despite my continuing objection to the old rules, it seems to me that since they have at least gained some degree of certainty, it would be wiser to 'bear those ills we have than fly to others we know not of,' unless, of course, we are reasonably sure that the proposed reforms of the old rules are badly needed. But I am not. The new proposals, at least some of them, have ... objectionable possibilities that cause me to believe our judicial system could get along much better without them.[83]

and:

> I particularly think that every member of the Court should examine with great care the amendments relating to class suits. ... they place too much power in the hands of the trial judges and the rules might almost as well simply provide that 'class suits can be maintained either for or against

[78] *Eisen v Carlisle and Jacquelin*, 391 F 2d 555, 572 (2d Cir, 1968) (Lumbard CJ dissenting) (specifically because of the complexity and length of the litigation). This sparked a refutation by one noted class actions scholar: A Miller, 'Of Frankenstein Monsters and Shining Knights: Myth, Reality, and the "Class Action Problem"' (1979) 92 *Harvard Law Review* 664, especially 679–82.

[79] A Miller, '*McIntyre* in Context: A Very Personal Perspective' (2012) 63 *South Carolina Law Review* 465, 471.

[80] S Partridge and K Miller, 'Some Practical Considerations for Defending and Settling Products Liability and Consumer Class Actions' (2000) 74 *Tulane Law Review* 2125, fn 10 (referring specifically to class certification).

[81] *Newberg on Class Actions* (n 75), vol 1, § 1.1, p 2.

[82] Justice Black also had a more general concern, that 'the provisions of 28 USC § 2072 (1964), under which these rules are transmitted ... which provide for giving transmitted rules the effect of law as though they had been properly enacted by Congress, are unconstitutional': 39 FRD 69, 272. In an obituary published following his death on 25 September 1971, and following his thirty-four years of service on the US Supreme Court, the author wrote: 'To Justice Black, who many observers believe influenced American life more than any of his colleagues in modern time, the Constitution was his bible. A well-thumbed copy was always in his pocket. When challenged about the effect of unpopular decisions, he would say simply: "The Court didn't do it. The Constitution did it"': 'Justice Black Dies at 85; Served on Court 34 Years' *NY Times* (New York, 25 September 1971).

[83] 39 FRD 69, 273.

particular groups whenever in the discretion of a judge he thinks it is wise.'
The power given to the judge to dismiss such suits or to divide them up
into groups at will subjects members of classes to dangers that could not
follow from carefully prescribed legal standards enacted to control class
suits.[84]

As discussed later in this book,[85] the very complexity of class actions
legislative design and judicial interpretation since has principally been
aimed at defining, and redefining, those 'legal standards to control class
suits' that Justice Black presciently forecast in 1966.

After the federal class action rule was amended in 1966, that version
became the most widely adopted model for US state class action rules.[86]
However, some states retained the earlier version of FRCP 23 (that which
covered so-called spurious class actions);[87] a very small number still
disallow state class actions altogether;[88] whilst others have subsequently
amended the federal class actions rule.[89] This book will focus upon the
federal class action rule, given that it is the best known and most oft-cited
US class action rule from a comparative perspective.

---

[84] ibid, 274, quoting from a memorandum which Justice Black previously submitted to the
Judicial Conference whilst the rules were in draft form only.

[85] See Chapter 3, 'Government as Class Actions Designer'.

[86] *Newberg on Class Actions* (n 75), vol 4, § 13.1, 399.

[87] ibid, § 13.3. See too: Karlsgodt (ed), *World Class Actions* (n 37) 27–28.

[88] e.g., Virginia does not have a state class action regime ('[w]hile virtually every other
jurisdiction in the country has a statutory scheme for class actions, usually based upon
Federal Rule 23, it is widely accepted that Virginia is the anomalous, class-free zone':
D Munro, 'Class Actions in Virginia state courts? Or is it just *Bull?*' (2012) 23 *Journal of
the Virginia Trial Lawyers Association* 26, 26); and nor does Mississippi (on 17 May 2018,
'the state supreme court rejected a petition to add a class mechanism to the state civil
procedure rules': P Cooper, 'Mississippi Won't Add Class Action Rule' *Bloomberg News*,
(18 May 2018)); although claimants can still file class actions in federal courts in both
states.

[89] *Newberg on Class Actions* (n 75), § 13.13. See additionally, e.g., *The Law of Class Action:
Fifty-state Survey 2015–16* (American Bar Assn, 2016); K Lambert, 'Class Actions
Settlements in Louisiana' (2000) 61 *Louisiana Law Review* 89, 91 ('[t]he recent adoption
in Louisiana of a new procedural scheme for class actions, based upon FRCP 23, presents
a unique opportunity to take a fresh look at this crucial facet of class action practice within
the state'); P Schenkkan, 'State Class Action Reform: Lessons from Texas' (2005) 12
Andrews Class Action Litigation Reports 15, outlining a number of variations between the
Texas and federal class actions rules. Indeed, Texas remains an anomaly, in that 'the Texas
Supreme Court has narrowly interpreted the state's class action requirements under
Texas Rule of Civil Procedure 42 such that it is extremely difficult to have a class action
certified by a Texas state court. That trend does not appear to be reversing anytime soon':
K Kliebard *et al.*, *Class/collective Actions in the United States: Overview* (Class Actions
Global Guide, Practical Law, updated as at 1 September 2018).

Five decades after its enactment, attempts are still being made to revise the text of the US federal class action rule,[90] evidencing that, even in the jurisdiction in which opt-out class actions has been most heavily litigated, rebalancing and clarification are still the subject of divided reform attention.

2 Canada

The first jurisdiction in Canada to implement an opt-out class action was Québec,[91] a civil law jurisdiction. However, it is the common law jurisdictions within Canada which implemented opt-out class actions which are the focus of this book. The first common law jurisdiction to enact such legislation was Ontario,[92] followed by British Columbia,[93] Saskatchewan,[94] Newfoundland and Labrador,[95] Manitoba,[96] Alberta,[97] New Brunswick,[98] and Nova Scotia.[99] The federal jurisdiction of Canada also enables opt-out class proceedings.[100]

At this stage, only Prince Edward Island and the three territories[101] have not enacted class actions legislation.[102] However, and in the context of a class suit *against the provincial government of Prince Edward Island*, the Supreme Court of that jurisdiction has recently taken the

---

[90] By virtue of the Fairness in Class Action Litigation Act of 2017 (HR 985), introduced to the House of Representatives on 9 February 2017 by Representative Bob Goodlatte, Republican of Virginia. The legislation was passed in March 2017, but 'remains under review by the Senate. The proposed changes are considered controversial by some, and there is no indication as to when the Senate will move forward on the issue': Kliebard, ibid. For further detail, see, e.g.: H Erichson, 'Searching for Salvageable Ideas in Ficala' (2018) 87 *Fordham Law Review* 19; R Marcus, 'Revolution v Evolution in Class Action Reform' (2018) 96 *North Carolina Law Review* 903.

[91] An Act Respecting the Class Action, SQ 1978, c 8, in force, 19 January 1979; and CCP (Que), arts 999–1030.

[92] Class Proceedings Act, SO 1992, c 6, which commenced operation on 1 January 1993.

[93] Class Proceedings Act, RSBC 1996, c 50, in force 1 August 1995, and first enacted as SBC 1995, c 21.

[94] Class Actions Act, SS 2001, c C-12.01, in force 1 January 2002.

[95] Class Actions Act, SNL 2001, c C-18.1, in force 1 April 2002.

[96] Class Proceedings Act, CCSM c C130, in force 1 January 2003.

[97] Class Proceedings Act, SA 2003, c C-16.5, in force 1 April 2004.

[98] Class Proceedings Act, SNB 2006, c C-5.15, in force 30 June 2007.

[99] Class Proceedings Act, SNS 2007, c 28, in force 3 June 2008.

[100] Federal Courts Rules, SOR/98-106, Pt 5.1.

[101] Yukon, Northwest, and Nunavut.

[102] Although representative proceedings are available in those jurisdictions, as discussed in: Y Martineau and A Lang, 'Canada', in Karlsgodt (ed), *World Class Actions* (n 37) 56–58.

extraordinary step of seeking to judicially implement a class actions regime which bears great similarity with other Canadian statutory regimes (and of permitting the class action to proceed).[103] In doing so, the Supreme Court stated that, '[t]o be clear, legislation is by far the best way to provide for class proceedings from the point of view of certainty to parties and the availability to legislators of public consultation. In this context, judge-made rules are a "second best" alternative. In the absence of legislation, this decision is at least a start.'[104]

Ontario's Class Proceedings Act started its passage in the Ontario Parliament as Bill 28, An Act respecting Class Proceedings.[105] Together with a companion bill by which to arrange funding of the regime,[106] these were introduced by the Liberal Government in June 1990.[107] However, with the calling of the Ontario general election in 1990, both Bills were 'washed up' in accordance with the usual procedure which occurs during Parliamentary purdah.[108] The Liberal Government was unexpectedly defeated at the general election, and a new government was formed by the New Democratic Party in September 1990.[109] What happened next in

[103] See: *King & Dawson v Government of PEI* [2019] PESC 27 (class of residents of Prince Edward Island with mental disabilities alleged that, in breach of the Canadian Charter of Rights and Freedoms, the government excluded people with disabilities caused by mental illness from qualification for benefits through the provincial Disability Supports Program; the 'class action', devised by the court, was certified to proceed in class action form: at [108]).

[104] ibid, [16].

[105] For a detailed scholarly account of the background to the Ontario class actions legislation, see: S Chiodo, 'The Class Actions Controversy: The Origins and Development of the Ontario Class Proceedings Act' (2018–19) 14 *Canadian Class Action Review*, and in particular, 'The Report of the Attorney General's Advisory Committee on Class Action Reform (1985–1993)', ch 4 of the journal issue, 89–170.

[106] There was a companion bill, Bill 29, An Act to amend the Law Society Act to provide for Funding to Parties to Class Proceedings.

[107] *Hansard* (Legislative Assembly of Ontario, 34th Parliament, 2nd Session, 12 June 1990, Attorney-General, Mr Ian Scott, member of the Liberal Party representing St George-St David, at 1530), available at: www.ola.org/en/legislative-business/house-documents/parliament-34/session-2/1990-06-12/hansard.

[108] 'Purdah' means the pre-election period between the time an election is announced and the date the election is held, during which time political communications, Parliamentary business, and civil servants' conduct, are highly regulated. See, e.g.: www.parliament.uk/site-information/glossary/purdah/.

[109] In a fascinating political vignette, it is reported that: '[t]he governing Ontario Liberal Party led by Premier David Peterson was unexpectedly defeated. Although the Peterson government, and Peterson himself, were very popular, he was accused of opportunism in calling an election just three years into his mandate. In a shocking upset, the New Democratic Party, led by Bob Rae, won a majority government. This marked the first time the NDP had won government east of Manitoba, and to date the only time the NDP formed the government in

Ontario is ironic, for as discussed later,[110] the first opt-out class action Bill in the United Kingdom's history was also 'washed up' upon the calling of the 2010 UK general election, and the outcome was very different. That Bill never came back to the UK Parliament, after the proposing government was voted out of power following the 2010 general election.[111] However, the same fate did **not** befall the two Ontario Bills. They were introduced again to the Legislative Assembly of Ontario by the new Attorney-General, receiving their First Reading on 17 December 1990.[112] The main Bill was introduced in positive terms:

> The Class Proceedings Act, 1990, will make available a comprehensive procedure for claims on behalf of numerous persons who have suffered the same loss or injury. The procedure is designed to provide a more efficient and streamlined method for the court to deal with complex litigation affecting the interests of hundreds or even thousands of persons.[113]

However, Bill 28 did not receive its Second Reading until almost a year later, on 18 November 1991.[114] One Canadian scholar notes that, '[t]here is little to explain this delay, although the Rae government may well have been distracted by the severe difficulties which it faced in its first year and thereafter, as well as the deepening recession in Ontario'.[115] During the course of its Third Reading, on 27 April 1992, when the Bill was again moved by the Attorney General, the following exchange is of interest, with a suggestion of some reluctance on the part of Parliament to follow through with the enactment:[116]

Ontario. Not even the NDP expected to come close to winning power; indeed, Rae had already made plans to retire from politics after the election' ('1990 Ontario general election', *Wikipedia*, accessed 21 March 2019).

[110] See Section B(4).

[111] After thirteen years in power, the Labour Government (led by Prime Minister, the Rt Hon Gordon Brown) was replaced by a coalition of the Conservative Party (led by the Rt Hon David Cameron, who became Prime Minister) and the Liberal Democrat Party (led by the Rt Hon Nick Clegg, who became Deputy Prime Minister), no party achieving an outright majority at that election.

[112] *Hansard* (Legislative Assembly, 35th Parliament, 1st Session, 17 December 1990, moved by Mr Howard Hampton, at 1510), available at: www.ola.org/en/legislative-business /house-documents/parliament-35/session-1/1990-12-17/hansard.

[113] ibid.

[114] *Hansard* (Legislative Assembly, 35th Parliament, 1st Session, 18 November 1991, moved by Mr Winninger, on behalf of Mr Hampton, at 1630), available at: www.ola.org/en/ legislative-business/house-documents/parliament-35/session-1/1991-11-18/hansard.

[115] Chiodo, 'The Report of the Attorney General's Advisory Committee' (n 105) 156 (footnote omitted).

[116] *Hansard* (Legislative Assembly, 35th Parliament, 2nd Session, 27 April 1992, moved by Attorney-General, Mr Hampton, Member of New Democratic Party (Rainy River)),

The Hon Mr Hampton (Attorney General): A number of steps must be taken before Bill 28 can be proclaimed. . . . The first step is to design the class proceedings fund. . . . Second, we will need to . . . give considerable attention to the Québec experience with its class actions assistance fund. As you know, Québec has had class actions for some time and it has considerable experience with some of these things. Next . . . [c]onsideration will need to be given to whether it is necessary to amend any of the rules to accommodate class proceedings or whether forms of notice for class proceedings should be added to the rules. After that, . . . we will have to consult with the Law Society of Upper Canada. Class proceedings raise certain ethical issues, such as the potential conflict of interest between the lawyer's duty to the representative plaintiff and to other members of the class. Finally, one of the issues which will be germane here will be judicial education. Class proceedings will mean a major change for the judiciary. . . .

Mr Ian G Scott (and previous Attorney General): I am fascinated to hear the way the minister introduced the bill, because he described in detail, more elaborate than I would have thought necessary, the work that has to be done ahead of us, all this education and so on. I drew from that the inevitable conclusion that the minister has no early intention of proclaiming this bill if it's passed. . . .

Mr Hampton: . . . we anticipate . . . that we will need at least six months to implement the legislation. Following passage by the House and royal assent, we will have to work through all the steps I have indicated . . .

Mr Robert Chiarelli: [117] . . . I will be less delicate than the former Attorney General . . . What we have just seen from the Attorney General is a very transparent attempt to further delay this legislation. . . . In November 1991, at second reading, the opposition parties both spoke to this legislation and both wanted it to proceed as quickly as possible. We finished the debate in about 15 or 20 minutes. The government had no further matters to bring forward . . . The matter was referred to committee. In committee, both opposition parties had no amendments to bring forward, the government had no amendments to bring forward, and yet despite the request of the opposition parties, the government refused to bring the legislation back in December and have it voted on for third reading and royal assent before the Christmas break. That was in December 1991. . . . The minister knew he had the full support of this Legislature, the full support of the legal profession, the full support of the public and he

available at: www.ola.org/en/legislative-business/house-documents/parliament-35/session-2/1992-04-27/hansard). The quotes of Mr Hampton and Mr Scott are to be found at 1520–30.

[117] *Hansard* (Legislative Assembly, 35th Parliament, 2nd Session, 27 April 1992, moved by Mr Chiarelli, Member of the Liberal Party (Ottawa West), at 1530).

sat idly by. I believe the reason and the rationale are that this government is not now committed to this legislation for some unstated and unknown reason which we can only speculate on …

Mr Gilles Bisson: [118] … I just want to remind the member from the opposition that it was the recommendation of the former Attorney General, within the Liberal government, that this particular bill go back for consultation in order to really cover the bases that needed to be done to put this bill forward. If there was a delay, it was because of that.

Mr Chiarelli: [119] … It's this type of legislation that would enable people who have been injured by the Dalkon Shield, for example, to take a class action and get some remedy for the wrongs that've been done to them. In Ottawa-Carleton there was an environmental spill a number of years ago that destroyed the water system of a number of people in Manotick. This type of legislation would enable them to take some kind of action as a class. Because this legislation was delayed, those people cannot have the benefit of the protection of the law. Justice delayed is justice denied.

Such skirmishings have been reflected in each of the other Comparator Jurisdictions, and demonstrate that the passage of such important legislation is never smooth-sailing! In any event, the Ontario opt-out class action duly achieved its Third Reading, received Royal Assent on 25 June 1992,[120] and came into force on 1 January 2003.

3   Australia

Australia's federal opt-out class action, contained in Part IVA of the Federal Court of Australia Act 1976,[121] took effect on 4 March 1992.[122] The regime, which applies to representative claimants whose causes of

---

[118] *Hansard* (Legislative Assembly, 35th Parliament, 2nd Session, 27 April 1992, moved by Mr Bisson, Member of the New Democratic Party (Cochrane South), at 1640), available at: www.ola.org/en/legislative-business/house-documents/parliament-35/session-2/1992-04-27/hansard).

[119] *Hansard* (Legislative Assembly, 35th Parliament, 2nd Session, 27 April 1992, at 1650).

[120] *Hansard* (Legislative Assembly, 35th Parliament, 2nd Session, 25 June 1992, moved by the Speaker, the Hon David Warner, at 2320), available at: www.ola.org/en/legislative-business/house-documents/parliament-35/session-2/1992-06-25/hansard-1.

[121] Sections 33A–33ZJ.

[122] It was inserted into the principal Act by s 3 of the Federal Court of Australia Amendment Act 1991.

action arise under federal jurisdiction,[123] is also regulated by court rules[124] and by practice direction.[125]

The relevant Bill which proposed the federal class action in 1991 was promulgated by the Labor Government of the time.[126] Characteristically of this area of reform, considerably divided opinion abounded prior to the implementation of Pt IVA, in Australian Parliamentary debates of twenty-five years ago.[127] Emotive language and rhetoric were used on both sides. The proponents of the regime argued that: the new regime would promote access to justice,[128] and would serve to enforce the substantive law;[129] a number of 'checks and balances' would preclude any 'US-style' excesses;[130] and 'ethical businesses' had nothing to fear from the regime.[131] The primary purposes of the regime were put in these terms by the then-Attorney-General:

---

[123] The federal court principally deals with claims under federal legislation under its original jurisdiction, although this is expanded somewhat by an accrued jurisdiction (i.e., 'the litigious or justiciable controversy between the parties of which the federal claim or cause of action forms part': *Re Wakim, ex p McNally* [1999] HCA 27, 198 CLR 511, 583–84, citing: *Stack v Coast Securities (No 9) Pty Ltd* (1983) 154 CLR 261 (HCA) 290). Recently, however, the High Court of Australia has admonished the use of the 'imprecise' term, 'accrued jurisdiction', preferring the notion that what is required is 'one matter', even where that combines federal and non-federal law: *Rizeq v Western Australia* [2017] HCA 23, (2017) 344 ALR 421, [55].

[124] See: Division 9.3 of the Federal Court Rules 2011 (Cth).

[125] Per: Class Actions Practice Note (GPN-CA) relating to representative proceedings commenced under Pt IVA.

[126] Pursuant to an enactment of the Keating Government, the federal executive government led by Prime Minister Paul Keating of the Australian Labor Party.

[127] The relevant extracts of the Parliamentary debates are conveniently located in App 3–5, and 7, of D Grave and K Adams, *Class Actions in Australia* (Lawbook Co, 2005).

[128] 'the public interest demands that access to the courts be made easier and less costly for those with limited means. Grouped proceedings are a step in that direction': *Hansard* (Senate, 13 November 1991, Senator Spindler, at 3022). This Senator also noted that, 'the greatest credit must go to the ALRC, whose report on this matter is of outstanding quality' (at 3023).

[129] 'The only likely costs to business of the reforms in the Bill will be through people being able to enforce existing substantive rights which claimants could not previously afford to enforce, even though the liabilities existed': *Hansard* (House of Representatives, 14 November 1991, Mr Duffy MP and A-G, at 3175).

[130] 'I not believe that this particular proposal will lead Australia to go down the United States road . . . and to become an overly litigious society . . . we have set our face firmly against some features of the American legal system, such as contingency fees': *Hansard* (Senate, 13 November 1991, Senator Tate, at 3025).

[131] '[The proposed reform] is to the benefit of ethical businesses which honour their legal obligations without having to be forced to do so by legal action': *Hansard* (House of Representatives, 14 November 1991, Mr Duffy MP and A-G, at 3175).

Such a procedure is needed for two purposes. The first is to provide a real remedy where, although many people are affected and the total amount at issue is significant, each person's loss is small and not economically viable to recover in individual actions. It will thus give access to the courts to those in the community who have been effectively denied justice because of the high cost of taking action. The second purpose of the bill is to deal efficiently with the situation where the damages sought by each claim are large enough to justify individual actions and a large number of persons wish to sue the respondent. The new procedure will mean that groups of persons, whether they be shareholders or investors, or people pursuing consumer claims, will be able to obtain redress and do so more cheaply and efficiently than would be the case with individual actions.[132]

Predictably, there was vociferous and strident criticism of the Bill by the opposition. In the Senate (the Australian Government's Upper House), Senator Durack called it 'a rather loony proposal', and a Bill that would 'involve major, some would even say revolutionary, changes'.[133] He further emphasised the uncertainty which would accompany the new law;[134] the lengthy delay that preceded the legislative enactment;[135] the fear of 'US-style litigation';[136] and a preference for amending the 'representative action' to make it more fit for purpose, rather than introducing an entirely new procedure.[137] The most detailed criticism of the Bill came from the Rt Hon Peter Costello, then a member of the main opposition party, the Liberal Party, and later to become Treasurer of Australia:[138]

---

[132] Second Reading Speech, *Hansard* (House of Representatives, 14 November 1991, Mr Duffy MP and A-G, at 3174).

[133] *Hansard* (Senate, 13 November 1991, Senator Durack, at 3018 and 3019). As one Australian class actions scholar has wryly noted, not only is the Pt IVA regime 'still in operation unaltered, but it has also been emulated' by state class legislatures since: V Morabito, 'Empirical Perspectives on 25 Years of Class Actions', in D Grave and H Mould (eds), *25 Years of Class Actions in Australia* (Ross Parsons, 2017), ch 4, 43.

[134] e.g., 'this legislation ... will introduce new and uncertain burdens on our court system. ... it is a revolutionary proposal. ... it will be a bonanza for lawyers': *Hansard* (Senate, 13 November 1991, at 3021).

[135] e.g., 'this legislation ... has had a long gestation. Many had hoped that it would have been stillborn and would not have been brought into the Senate. ... the speech by Senator Tate on this Bill is remarkably bland. It is almost as if he is trying to hide this creature to which the ALRC gave birth': ibid, 3019.

[136] e.g., '[i]t is a question of whether we are having a class action along the lines of the American system ... we are starting to become a community nearly as legally driven as is the United States community. I do not think we ought to be encouraging this system any further': ibid, 3020–21.

[137] '[we should] seek to improve the existing representative action that has long standing and experience in our legal system': ibid, 3020.

[138] House of Representatives (Higgins). Mr Costello served as Federal Treasurer from 1996–2007, under the Howard Liberal Government.

[The Bill] is bad legislation. ... Firstly, under the proposals in this Bill, individual rights will be exercised on behalf of individuals thrown into classes at the choice of people who decide to initiate class actions. The Bill is flawed because it is an attack on the way legal rights are traditionally exercised in this country. Secondly, this Bill is a step on the way to making Australia a more litigious society ... and that is not in the interests of the public in the long term. Thirdly, the Bill is flawed because it will change the nature of legal practice. Hitherto, lawyers have provided services to those wanting to exercise their legal rights, who consult them and ask those lawyers to act on their behalf. ... Lawyers will have an incentive to spruik for actions on behalf of people who did not know the action is being brought, who have not consulted the lawyer to bring the action, and who may not even want the action to be brought on their behalf. Fourthly, this is flawed legislation because no grounds have been shown which will justify the changes introduced by this Bill. If the object is to reduce the costs of litigation, the proposals in this Bill are a wholly unnecessary overreaction. ... It is like having open-heart surgery to treat a headache.[139]

However, despite such criticism, the political winds blew sufficiently in favour of the reform. The Bill was ultimately passed in the Australian House of Representatives by a majority of 12;[140] and by a majority of 6 in the Senate.[141] In fact, prior to the Third Reading, Mr Costello moved further amendments to the Bill,[142] but those were unsuccessful, with the response of the Government indicative of the acerbity which accompanied the passage of this Bill:

[the debate] has been going on for years and years, and the Opposition knows it. The basic fact of the matter is that Opposition members are terrified of any legislation that will protect the consumer in a way that does not protect the people who are out there making mistakes. No matter how much the Opposition blustered around with its innuendo or whatever it likes, there is no reason for the Government to accept these amendments. This is a Bill that is respected and wanted by the people of Australia and will accordingly be passed by this Parliament.[143]

[139] Second Reading, *Hansard* (House of Representatives, Mr Peter Costello, 26 November 1991, at 3284).
[140] By a majority of 66 ayes to 54 noes: *Hansard* (House of Representatives, 26 November 1991, vote, at 3297).
[141] By a majority of 34 ayes to 28 noes: *Hansard* (Senate, 13 November 1991, vote, at 3028).
[142] Including, significantly, to convert the regime to an opt-in regime only – see the proposed amendment to s 33E of the Bill: *Hansard* (House of Representatives, 26 November 1991, Mr Costello, at 3289).
[143] The amendments were hence negatived: *Hansard* (House of Representatives, 26 November 1991, Mr Peter Staples, Lab, Jagajaga, Minister for Aged, Family and Health Services, at 3297).

The amending Act received Royal Assent on 4 December 1991,[144] and took effect three months later, on 4 March.

There are only three opt-out state class actions operative in Australia at the time of writing: in Queensland (via legislation[145] and practice direction[146]); in New South Wales (via legislation[147] and practice note[148]); and in Victoria (via legislation[149] and practice note[150]). The state regimes are 'substantially modelled' on the federal regime,[151] although with some minor differences.[152] As further evidence of the expanding reach of opt-out class actions, the potential introduction of such a regime is also under Parliamentary consideration in the state of Tasmania at the time of writing.[153] That regime is being 'largely modelled' on the New South Wales provisions.[154]

As discussed in detail later in the book,[155] the Australian regimes differ from their Comparator Jurisdiction counterparts, in that a formal

---

[144] Federal Court of Australia Amendment Act 1991, No 181 of 1991. The amending Act was itself repealed on 10 March 2016, by virtue of the Amending Acts 1990 to 1999 Repeal Act 2016, which in no way affects the continued operation of Pt IVA.

[145] Civil Proceedings Act 2011, Pt 13A, inserted by the Limitation of Actions (Institutional Child Sexual Abuse) and Other Legislation Amendment Act 2016 (Qld). The regime, the most recent state regime, took effect on 1 March 2017.

[146] Per: Supreme Court Practice Direction 2 of 2017 (27 February 2017), published by: The Hon Chief Justice Catherine Holmes, Chief Justice of the Supreme Court of Queensland.

[147] Per: Civil Procedure Act 2005 (NSW), Pt 10. This regime took effect on 4 March 2011. Part 10 was inserted by Sch 6 of the Courts and Crimes Legislation Further Amendment Act 2010 (NSW).

[148] Practice Note No SC GEN 17 – Supreme Court Representative Proceedings (31 July 2017), published by: The Hon Chief Justice Tom Bathurst, Chief Justice of the Supreme Court of New South Wales.

[149] Per: Supreme Court Act 1986 (Vic), Pt 4A. The regime commenced operation on 1 January 2000.

[150] Practice Note SC GEN 10 Conduct of Group Proceedings (Class Actions) (30 January 2017), published by: V Macgillivray, Executive Associate to the Chief Justice.

[151] See, e.g., *Hansard* (New South Wales Legislative Assembly, 24 January 2010, Mr John Hatzistergos A-G). Indeed, as The Hon Bernard Murphy notes, '[i]t is said that imitation is the most sincere form of flattery, and a good indication that the federal regime is operating well is the fact that several state governments have adopted the same procedures': 'The Operation of the Australian class action regime' (Bar Assn of Queensland, Gold Coast, 9 March 2013) [5.3].

[152] For a brief discussion of these, see: B Newbold *et al.*, *Class/collective actions in Australia: Overview* (Class Actions Global Guide, Practical Law, updated as at 1 August 2018).

[153] Contained in the Supreme Court Civil Procedure Amendment Bill 2018, Pt VII. If enacted, the class action will be inserted into the Supreme Court Civil Procedure Act 1932 (Tas). The Bill has been moved for its Second Reading at the time of writing.

[154] According to the Second Reading Speech by the Hon Elise Archer MP, reproduced at: www.parliament.tas.gov.au/bills/Bills2018/pdf/notes/52_of_2018-SRS.pdf, at 2.

[155] See Chapter 3, Section C(2).

certification regime is not included in any of the federal or state regimes. However, in the alternative, a defendant to a class action may seek interlocutory relief on the grounds that the representative claimant has not satisfied the required threshold criteria.[156]

The area of class actions remains under regular review in Australia, with the law reform commissions of Western Australia, Victoria, and Australia all considering class actions reform within the last five years.[157]

4 United Kingdom

After a significant false start,[158] the United Kingdom's first opt-out class action was implemented on 1 October 2015, via a mixture of overarching primary legislation[159] and underpinning court rules.[160]

The regime contains a 'twist' upon the types of opt-out class actions featured elsewhere in the Comparator Jurisdictions, because it adopts an opt-in or opt-out approach to the formation of the entire class, depending upon judicial determination on a case-by-case basis.[161] Thus (and unusually), there are a number of options open to the representative claimant. The regime explicitly permits representative claimants to institute their claim on either an opt-in or an opt-out approach, and leave it to the adjudicating tribunal (the Competition Appeal Tribunal, or 'CAT'[162]) to decide the basis upon which the claim should proceed;[163] or the claim can be brought on an opt-in basis

---

[156] Pursuant to Pt IVA, ss 33L–33N.

[157] See Bibliography, 'Official Reports and Discussion Papers'.

[158] Most notably, via the proposed enactment of an opt-out regime contained in the Financial Services Bill 2009–10, as noted in Chapter 2, and described in detail by the author in: 'Recent Milestones' (n 14).

[159] The regime is principally contained in the Competition Act 1998 ('CA 1998'), ss 47A–49E, and with various consequential amendments contained in the Enterprise Act 2002.

[160] Supporting court rules are contained in the Competition Appeal Tribunal Rules 2015 (SI 1648/2015) ('CAT Rules'), rr 73–98. These rules were the subject of a formal consultation, as part of the *Competition Appeal Tribunal Rules of Procedure: Review by the Rt Hon Sir John Mummery* (closing 3 April 2015).

[161] CA 1998, s 47B(7)(c); and CAT Rules, r 79(3).

[162] Exclusive jurisdiction is vested in this tribunal: CA 1998, s 47A(1). The regime deals with claims for damages, for 'a sum of money' or for injunctive relief in England, Wales and Northern Ireland, and for any of these except for injunctive relief in Scotland: CA 1998, s 47A(3).

[163] As in: *UK Trucks Claim Ltd v Fiat Chrysler Automobiles NV* (Case 1282/7/7/18, published 29 June 2018).

only;[164] or the claim can be instituted on a solely opt-out basis;[165] or even should the representative claimant frame the claim as an opt-out class action, it is conceivable that the CAT could specify that the proceedings should be opt-in proceedings only (although, to date, that is the only eventuality which has not occurred under the limited case law).

Introduced by the Consumer Rights Act 2015,[166] the regime (hereafter, 'the UK Competition Law Class Action') is aimed solely at facilitating private actions for anti-competitive conduct. Any grievance of the class must arise either from an 'infringement decision' (i.e., such that the class action is a follow-on action[167]), or from 'an alleged infringement' (i.e., that the class action is a 'stand-alone action'[168]) of prohibitions on anti-competitive behaviour stipulated in either the Competition Act 1998 or the EU Treaty.[169] Of the six actions filed to date, four have been follow-

---

[164] As in: *Road Haulage Assn Ltd v Man SE* (Case 1289/7/7/18, published 27 July 2018).

[165] As in: *Gibson v Pride Mobility Products Ltd* [2017] CAT 16 (President Roth J, and members Glynn and Stuart, dated 31 March 2017); and *Merricks v Mastercard Inc* [2017] CAT 16 (President Roth J, and members Mayer and Potter, dated 21 July 2017), successfully appealed and the rejection of certification set aside: *Merricks v Mastercard Inc* [2019] EWCA Civ 674 (Patten, Hamblen and Coulson LJJ, 16 April 2019), with leave to appeal to the SC being sought at the time of writing; and the two most recent cases filed: *Gutmann v First MTR South Western Trains Ltd* (Case 1304/7/7/19) and *Gutmann v London and South Eastern Rwy Ltd* (Case 1304/7/7/19), both published 11 March 2019.

[166] As a result of its genesis (in a section entitled, 'Private Actions in Competition Law'), the regime is sometimes called the 'Consumer Rights Act regime', although it is firmly ensconced in the Competition Act 1998.

[167] As the Competition Markets Authority ('CMA') explains, '[w]here the CMA, a sector regulator or the European Commission has made a final decision that competition law has been infringed, that decision will be binding on both the ordinary courts and the CAT. A claimant can therefore use the decision as proof that competition law has been broken and may rely on certain findings of fact in it, so that in most cases they will need to prove only that they have suffered loss from the infringement': *Competition Law Redress: A Guide to Taking Action for Breaches of Competition Law* (CMA 55, May 2016) [3.6].

[168] i.e., '[a] standalone action is a claim brought where the claimant seeks itself to prove that competition law has been broken without relying on an infringement decision made by the European Commission, the CMA or another competition authority (or a judgment of an appeal court confirming such a decision)': ibid, [3.4].

[169] Per: CA 1998, s 47A(2). The key provisions of both EU and UK competition law prohibit two types of behaviour: anti-competitive agreements between businesses; and abuses of a dominant market position by businesses. The prohibitions in Chapters 1 and 2 of the CA 1998 apply where there is an effect on UK trade; the prohibitions in Arts 101 and 102 of the Treaty on the Functioning of the European Union (TFEU) apply where the effect is on trade between EU Member States.

on,[170] whereas two have been stand-alone actions.[171] By comparison with the regimes enacted in the other Comparator Jurisdictions, the UK's regime is, most decidedly, **not** generic[172] in nature. For several years prior to its implementation, there was a detailed debate surrounding the generic-versus-sectoral type of class action amongst UK law reformers and lawmakers, as detailed later in the book,[173] but ultimately, the legislation encompassed sectoral reform only.

It remains solely for conjecture as to when any generic opt-out class action regime may be legislatively implemented in the UK. In the author's view (which is stated in a personal capacity only, and undoubtedly may be subject to a contrary view!), such a law reform development is at least five to ten years away. This view is based upon various factors. First, it is undoubtedly the case that tangible pressures have been visited upon the Ministry of Justice and other government departments, given various Brexit-related ramifications upon the policy and legislative capacities of the government to consider, consult upon, and enact non-Brexit-related legislation. As the Chair of the Civil Contingencies Secretariat of the Cabinet Office recently stated:[174]

> The National Audit Office's report on contingency preparations for no-deal Brexit underlines the scale of the challenge Government faces, including preparing to respond to issues at the border, with the transport system and with food and health supplies. Most of these would be major projects in their own right, yet Government departments have been work-ing on these plans alongside plans for an exit with a deal – a costly and time-consuming duplication of effort.

Secondly, the England and Wales Law Commission has not sought to engage with the topic by means of law reform study at any stage over the past fifteen years, and nor is there any sign of its doing so in the future. This inactivity – by contrast to many other common law

---

[170] i.e., *Gibson, Merricks*, and the two trucks cartel cases (nn 163–64).

[171] i.e., the two train tickets cases, alleging abuse of dominant position (n 165).

[172] i.e., it is not capable of dealing with any cause of action arising, whether under common law or statute.

[173] See Chapter 2, pp 97–99. See too, Mulheron, 'The United Kingdom's New Opt-Out Class Action' (2017) 37 *Oxford Journal of Legal Studies* 814, 816–21.

[174] The Rt Hon Meg Hillier MP (*Commons Select Committee Parliament News*, 12 March 2019), quoted at: www.parliament.uk/business/committees/committees-a-z/commons-select/public-accounts-committee/news-parliament-2017/chairs-comments-nao-report-17-191/, and citing: Comptroller and Auditor General, *Contingency Preparations for Exiting the EU with No Deal* (HC 2056, 12 March 2019).

jurisdictions[175] – has deprived the issue of both law reform momentum and visibility.[176] Thirdly, the competition law class action is
destined to serve as something of a 'test case' for class actions,[177] and
yet, by their very nature, sectoral regimes do not produce as much
litigation as do generic regimes, particularly in their early stages. They
tend to be 'slow-burners'. Competition law class actions are also prone
to throw up issues that do not usually manifest in cases which are
based upon other causes of action – for example, whether a follow-on
class action must relate solely to the initial infringement decision or
could be based upon a market-wide 'policy' of infringement by
a cartellist;[178] and the standard of accuracy and the type of methodology which econometric expert evidence about the class's aggregated
losses must achieve at certification,[179] are not issues that arise in most
class actions.[180] These three factors, whether alone or in combination,
do not serve to foster and encourage further generic opt-out class
action reform in the United Kingdom for the foreseeable future.

The UK Competition Law Class Action was introduced to the UK
Parliament on 23 January 2014,[181] and received Royal Assent on 26 March

[175] See the extensive list of reports in the Bibliography, 'Reports, Discussion Papers and
Published Research Papers'.
[176] The author corresponded with the EWLC in 2004, requesting that the topic of class
actions be included in the then-Ninth Programme of Law Reform, but that request was
declined.
[177] In this respect, the UK Government partly adopted the recommendation of the CJC,
Improving Access to Justice: Final Report (2008) (n 12), that 'there is merit in
introducing for a short period of time a discrete, rather than generic, collective
action within the civil courts ahead of the scheduled introduction of the generic
action. An obvious example of how this could be achieved would be through the
introduction of a discrete, stand-alone collective action for claims arising out of
competition law breaches which have caused harm to individual consumers': at 139,
and see too, Recommendation 1, p 5.
[178] This was the issue in *Gibson* [2017] CAT 9.
[179] This was the issue in *Merricks v Mastercard Inc* [2017] CAT 16, leave to appeal granted:
Merricks v Mastercard Inc [2018] EWCA Civ 2527; with decision of the CAT reversed:
Merricks v Mastercard Inc [2019] EWCA Civ 674. Leave to appeal to the Supreme Court
has been filed.
[180] There are, indeed, numerous other unique issues arising out of competition law
class actions, including limitation periods, the pass-through issue, and the class
definition, which is why they attract their own chapter or section in several noted
works, e.g.,: J Brown et al., *Defending Class Actions in Canada* (3rd edn, CCH
Canadian Ltd, 2011); *Newberg on Class Actions* (n 75), ch 18; Ontario LRC, *Report
on Class Actions* (1982), ch 5.3(c).
[181] Introduced to the Commons by the Conservative and Liberal Democrat Coalition
Government, promulgated by the Business, Innovations and Skills Dept (BIS), under
the Secretary of State, the Rt Hon Dr Vince Cable MP.

2015. Between those two dates, there were various stages at which the regime appeared to be, if not scuppered, then under serious threat. For example, there was an attempt to convert the Bill to an opt-in regime only[182] (which amendments were not moved[183]); and the wide-ranging Bill became so bogged down in debates about 'ticket touting'[184] (of all things) that Parliament was forced to obtain a grant for an extension of the debate on the Bill or else, it would have lapsed.[185] Notwithstanding these hiccups, the UK Competition Law Class Action survived, and came into effect on 1 October 2015.

Hence, it is fully apparent from these brief synopses of the legislative background to the enactments in the Comparator Jurisdictions that none of their passages was smooth nor unanimous. The opponents' voices tended to raise common themes, which manifest to this day, where opt-out class action reform is contemplated. However, the fact that these enactments made it into law have enabled huge numbers of class members in these jurisdictions to achieve some measure of redress which otherwise likely would not have been feasible.

C   The Coverage of the Book

The book is divided into two Parts. To adopt a sporting analogy, Part I (which contains Chapters 2–5) considers the role of government in preparing the way for a class action to be implemented, i.e., the steps that are involved when a government is 'preparing a path to the stadium'. Part II, on the other hand, considers (in Chapters 6–9) what role the government plays in class litigation itself, i.e., once 'the matches are underway in the stadium'.

1   Part I of the Book

In Chapter 2, the role of government as the 'enabler' of a class actions regime is considered. Experience around the Comparator Jurisdictions

---

[182] Per Amendments 67 and 68 of the Fifth Marshalled List of Amendments to be moved in Grand Committee, dated 29 October 2014, proposed by Lord Hodgson of Astley Abbotts, prior to the House of Lords Grand Committee debate. See 'Bill Documents', at: https://publications.parliament.uk/pa/bills/lbill/2014-2015/0029/amend/ml029-V.htm.

[183] As evident in: *Hansard* (HL Deb, 3 November 2014, col GC584).

[184] See, e.g., the Marshalled List of Motions to be moved on consideration of Commons Reason, dated 24 February 2015, at: https://publications.parliament.uk/pa/bills/lbill/2014-2015/0081/amend/ml081-i.1-7.html.

[185] Consumer Rights Bill (Carry-Over Extension), *Hansard* (HC, 21 January 2015, vol 590, col 677). The Bill was extended by sixty-seven days, until 30 March 2015.

has shown that there is a common set of 'typical triggers' (eight are identified) which typically prompt a government to consider that it is appropriate and desirable to implement a legislative class actions procedural device. Essentially, any law reform is predicated upon an evidence of the need for a change to the status quo – and in the case of the opt-out class action, that 'need' must inevitably be constructed by means of the litigation that is not being brought in the domestic jurisdiction at all. Proving that need must (in the author's view[186]) entail both an 'inward-looking' and an 'outward-looking' analysis. Overlaying all of this is the direction of the political wind. Even with what may appear to law reformers to be a convincing case, class actions reform may languish, unenacted and politically unpalatable, for some years, or entirely. This reluctance may, arguably, be attributed to an inherent conflict of interest, whereby a government may be unwilling to legislate for a procedural regime under which it may itself be sued by a class of persons with an alleged grievance against the government.

The role of government as the 'designer' of a class actions regime is considered in Chapter 3. Across the spectrum – from the commencement of the action, throughout its conduct, and via its funding and costs regimes – the class action involves up to **100** different design choices. Some of these will be made by the legislature, whilst in other instances, silence (or opaqueness) on the face of the legislative drafting will require the courts to make those design decisions, thereby building up a body of precedential law. Whichever authority makes the decisions, it is, by any measure, an extraordinarily complex procedural mechanism. In addition to articulating those design features, this chapter emphasises that no class actions regime is drafted in isolation. There is a veritable wealth of comparative jurisprudence to investigate and to learn from, and in that respect, a case study of how the UK Government learnt from the lessons of the Australian federal class actions regime, enacted a quarter of a century earlier, is of great scholarly interest.

Chapter 4 examines the concept of the government as 'funder' of a class action. Parliament may choose to permit any one or more funding avenues to underpin a class actions regime. These may include: third party funding via a litigation funding agreement entered into by either the representative claimant or the class members with a commercial funder; legal aid funding; contingency fees (whether multiplier- or percentage-based) which are charged by the class lawyers; before-the-event insurance funding via

---

[186] As evidenced in her empirical study: *Reform of Collective Redress* (n 38), Pts III and IV.

insurance policies held by the class members; after-the-event insurance funding secured (usually) by the representative claimant; and specialist avenues such as union funding or *pro bono* litigation. Whilst these are, themselves, of interest,[187] the focus of this chapter falls upon, instead, a legislative decision to establish a specialist class actions fund. This type of dedicated fund, seeded by public or statutorily designated monies, is intended to be self-funding and self-replenishing. It has been oft-considered by law reform opinion, but not often implemented. This chapter examines a quarter of century of jurisprudence which has accompanied the Ontario Class Proceedings Fund – its problems, issues, advantages, and evolution. It was truly an experiment of class actions funding, and many lessons may be learnt by other lawmakers and policymakers from that jurisprudence.

The reality is that, in a world in which the supply of goods and services on a global basis is a reality for many defendant manufacturers and entities, class members who maintain a grievance against that defendant may reside in a variety of countries. For any domestic class action, one of the key design issues is to what extent non-resident class members may comprise part of the class of litigants. If their inclusion is permitted by which to create a cross-jurisdictional class action, such that the 'gates of the stadium are open to them', then another key issue is to ascertain upon what basis the domestic court may validly assert personal jurisdiction over them. Parliament may elect to stipulate that all non-resident class members must opt in to the class action, in what is otherwise an opt-out class action for domestic class members. In other cases, the legislature may leave this issue unaddressed on the face of the regime, meaning that the basis for jurisdiction is solely for the courts to adjudicate and to reason. Chapter 5 considers how this 'gate-keeper' role is acquitted by Parliament in class action regimes, where cross-jurisdictional class actions are concerned.

2 Part II of the Book

The class action device is particularly impactful for government, because of the various roles that government, in different guises, may fulfil in the class action.

---

[187] The author has considered these other options elsewhere: *Costs and Funding of Collective Actions: Realities and Possibilities* (A Research Paper for the European Consumers' Organisation (BEUC), February 2011).

Whilst a government has no choice as to whether it is sued in a class action, any decision to sue on behalf of a class, as representative claimant, must be consciously and deliberately taken. Whether or not that step is open to the government depends upon how the class action regime is designed. As Chapter 6 analyses, there are three different scenarios that may confront a governmental representative claimant. The first is where the government shares exactly the same cause of action and type of damage as do the class members (e.g., where all of those parties were the victims of a price-fixing cartel concerning widgets, which both government and class members purchased). The second scenario is where the government has a cause of action in its own right, which it does not share with the class member, but which raises common issue/s of fact or law with the class members – a difficult scenario to adjudicate. The third scenario is where the government lacks any claim against the defendant whatsoever, but where it is permitted to bring the class action as an 'ideological claimant'. For the purposes of this chapter, the government, as representative claimant for the class, is taken to include the following: (1) any level of government, from federal to state/provincial to local council/authority to indigenous councils/bands; and (2) any governmental entity or instrumentality (e.g., a department, statutory authority, or regulator) which is established as a creature of statute and which receives some public funding from Consolidated Revenue.

More rarely, the government may be a mere class member, possessing a grievance against a defendant, whilst leaving the pursuit of the class action to another as representative claimant. One of the design issues confronting Parliament is whether a government (or government officer) must opt out of the action to exclude itself or that individual from the action; or whether the different status of a government (or government officer) requires that, by contrast to other class members, it or he/she must opt in to the action in order to be bound by the outcome of it. A second conundrum is who, precisely, should be considered a 'government officer' for this purpose. These controversial issues are examined in Chapter 7.

The prospect of government as class actions defendant looms very large under class action regimes enacted throughout the Comparator Jurisdictions. Indeed, as Chapter 8 demonstrates, the panoply of scenarios in which government has been sued by classes of its citizens (whether individuals, businesses, or both) under generic class action regimes (not always successfully, it must be said) is extraordinary – from those with gambling addictions, to those who claim that educational, social or housing services are inadequate, and many other grievances in between. Whether they succeed or fail, such suits may have various implications – legal, reputational, and political – for that governmental defendant. The consequences of a sectoral regime for a government are entirely different (and diminished); indeed, a governmental defendant may be unthinkable (or very unlikely) under the type of sectoral regime enacted. Where a government is sued as class action defendant, the Crown is the appropriate defendant in most cases. Additionally, as the chapter discusses, government entities may also be the subject of a class action suit. The analysis in this chapter concludes with the types of common law causes of action that frequently feature in class action suits against governments.

Rather than being sued under a class action, government may actually *benefit* from a class action – in the form of, say, an escheat distribution to the government's Consolidated Revenue Fund. This sum of money is typically derived from undistributed damages awards, whether from judgment or settlement. What should happen with such residues is a controversial design issue, and it is fair to say that escheat distributions have not featured positively in many law reform or judicial opinions on the subject! Indeed, they generally rank either alongside, or below, the option of reverting any unclaimed residue to the defendant. To that end, the judicially imposed factors that demonstrate that an escheat distribution either is, or is not, permissible, are of great interest. A 'benefit' may also accrue to a government if it is designated, judicially, to be a *cy-près* beneficiary; or if it is designated, statutorily, to be a recipient of residual funds. More indirectly, the enforcement of those substantive laws which have been enacted by Parliament, by means of the class actions device, is worth noting (albeit that a lack of empirical evidence on this point has been noted). Across these various issues, some very interesting jurisprudence has emerged on the topic of how, precisely, governments may benefit from class action suits, and this is examined in Chapter 9.

The book is intended to have relevance and utility for policymakers and lawmakers in those jurisdictions in which opt-out class actions have already been enacted, and where they are actively, or potentially, under consideration. With that in mind, each chapter concludes with a list of drafting and/or operational recommendations, which are collected and reproduced in Chapter 10, preceded by some closing thoughts upon the fascinating interplay between class actions and government.

PART I

Preparing a Path to the Stadium

2

Government as Class Actions Enabler

A   Introduction

The processes of law reform that led to the enactment of opt-out class action regimes around the Comparator Jurisdictions have often been both long (an 'elephantine gestation period', as one Canadian scholar aptly put it[1]) and tortuous. Rarely has the eventual outcome quite matched that which a preceding reform agency's report recommended or suggested. Significant and vehement opinions opposing such reform have frequently hallmarked the reformist and political discussions; and following enactment, the regimes have often been 'slow-burners' whilst litigants, lawyers, courts and funders adjust to the new law.

All of this is traceable to the fact that opt-out class actions change the procedural, legal, and cultural fabric of society in a way that has few equivalents in civil procedure. As the authors of the leading treatise on US class actions state:

> Because class suits can have far-reaching effects to bring about institutional or governmental change, to internalize substantial environmental costs that the public would otherwise pay, or to disgorge significant profits arising from unlawful or tortious conduct, class actions are controversial.[2]

---

[1] G Watson, 'Is the Price Still Right?' (Administration of Justice Conference, Toronto, 15 October 1997) 3, cited in: V Morabito, 'Ideological Plaintiffs and Class Actions: An Australian Perspective' (2001) 34 *University of British Columbia Law Review* 459, fn 19, referring to the introduction of Ontario's Class Proceedings Act, SO 1992, c 6, which took effect on 1 January 1993, some eleven years after the law reform report which had recommended the implementation of opt-out class actions for that jurisdiction: Ontario LRC, *Report on Class Actions* (1982).

[2] A Conte and H Newberg, *Newberg on Class Actions* (4th edn, Thomson West Group, 2002), §1.1, 3.

The Rand Institute also properly called attention to the political ramifications of any such reform, remarking that:

> class actions [for damages] pose a dilemma for public policy because of their capacity to do both good and ill for society. . . . Those who believe that the social costs of damage class actions outweigh their social benefits think that the best course of action would be to . . . rely . . . on administrative agencies and public attorneys-general to enforce regulations, and on individual litigation to secure financial compensation for individuals' financial losses. Those who believe that the social benefits of damage class action outweigh their costs say that prohibiting private collective litigation . . . would be unacceptable. They have less faith in the capacity of regulatory agencies and public attorneys to enforce regulations . . . [and] argue that . . . consumer protection statutes were enacted with the understanding that claims brought under [them] would be so small that the only practical way for individuals to assert the rights granted by the statutes would be through collective litigation. Because the controversy over class action litigation springs from sharp differences in political and social values, it is difficult to resolve.[3]

With these controversies in mind, it is only natural that governments should take a cautious and pragmatic attitude towards such reform, and that it should be predicated upon 'evidence of need' before the class action device is introduced.[4] This has been a challenge with which law reform commissions have regularly grappled in this field.[5]

No single factor necessarily establishes that 'need'. Rather, the history of class actions law reform demonstrates that several triggers have often

---

[3] D Hensler *et al.*, *Class Actions Dilemmas: Pursuing Public Goals for Private Gain: Executive Summary* (RAND Institute for Civil Justice, 1999) 25.

[4] See, e.g.: *Hansard* (HL 20 July 2009, vol 496 col 103WS), per the Hon Bridget Prentice, Parliamentary Under-Secy of State for Justice ('the Government do not think it would make sense to impose a one size fits all policy [of class actions reform] across the whole economy. Each sector will be responsible for deciding whether to introduce a right of action and for developing the required legislation, where there is evidence of need, and following an assessment of economic and other impacts').

[5] e.g.: Alberta Law Reform Institute, *Class Actions* (Rep 85, 2000), ch 3, 'Need for Reform'; Attorney-General's Law Reform Advisory Council, *Class Actions in Victoria: Time for a New Approach* (1997), ch 3, finding the then-existing legislation to 'lack guidance on a number of important issues' (at [3.33]); Australian LRC, *Grouped Proceedings in the Federal Court* (Rep 46, 1988), ch 2, 'Are new procedures needed to deal with multiple wrongs?'; Manitoba LRC, *Class Proceedings* (Rep 100, 1999), ch 3, 'The need for reform'; Ontario LRC, *Report on Class Actions* (1982), chs 3 and 4; Federal Court of Canada, The Rules Committee, *Class Proceedings in the Federal Court of Canada* (DP, 2000), ch 3, 'Need for reform'; and the author's empirical study, *Reform of Collective Redress in England and Wales: A Perspective of Need* (Research Paper for the Civil Justice Council of England and Wales, 2008) which comprised part of the CJC's reform study: *Improving Access to Justice through Collective Actions: Final Report* (November 2008), Pt 7.

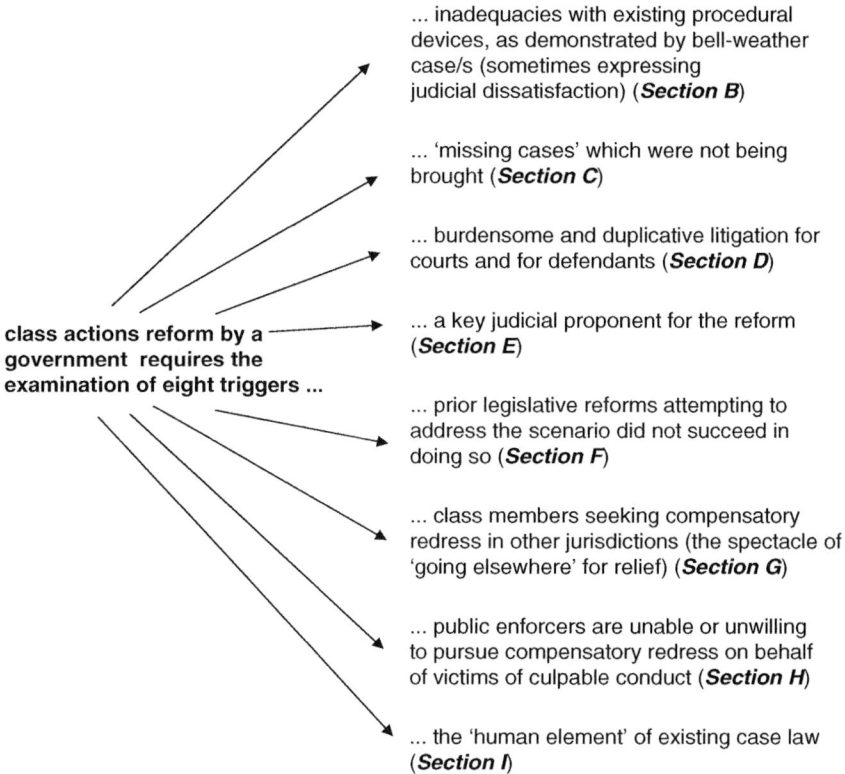

class actions reform by a government requires the examination of eight triggers ...

... inadequacies with existing procedural devices, as demonstrated by bell-weather case/s (sometimes expressing judicial dissatisfaction) (**Section B**)

... 'missing cases' which were not being brought (**Section C**)

... burdensome and duplicative litigation for courts and for defendants (**Section D**)

... a key judicial proponent for the reform (**Section E**)

... prior legislative reforms attempting to address the scenario did not succeed in doing so (**Section F**)

... class members seeking compensatory redress in other jurisdictions (the spectacle of 'going elsewhere' for relief) (**Section G**)

... public enforcers are unable or unwilling to pursue compensatory redress on behalf of victims of culpable conduct (**Section H**)

... the 'human element' of existing case law (**Section I**)

Figure 2.1   Government as 'enabler' of class actions reform.

converged fairly contemporaneously to warrant that political step being taken. In the author's view (and building upon previous analysis[6]), there are **eight** triggers which are typically to be found to manifest in a jurisdiction prior to opt-out class actions reform. These are shown in Figure 2.1 above.

Each of these triggers is examined by reference to the experience of the Comparator Jurisdictions in the order in which they appear in Figure 2.1.

As already discussed,[7] several jurisdictions (including that of the United Kingdom) have opt-out class actions law reform recommendations languishing and unenacted. An examination of the triggers discussed in the

---

[6] This chapter draws upon, develops, and updates the author's previous analysis: 'Class Actions and Law Reform: Insights from Australia and England, a Quarter of a Century Apart', in D Grave and H Mould (eds), *25 Years of Class Actions in Australia* (Ross Parsons, 2017), ch 14; and *Reform of Collective Redress*, ibid.

[7] See Chapter 1, pp 9–11.

following section – in the context of their own jurisdictional landscapes – may assist policymakers and lawmakers in those jurisdictions to consider whether, absent reform, a realistic opportunity for claimants to test their grievances, and for courts to achieve economies and efficiencies, are at continuing risk of being compromised.

B   The Inadequacies of Existing Procedural Regimes

Any law reform initiative is assisted by pointing to bell-weather or oft-cited cases which signify or symbolise what is wrong with the existing collective redress devices (whether as enacted or as judicially interpreted). Judicial pronouncements which reflect frustration with the status quo, and/or a hope for something better, also often underpin why these cases are so significant. Several collective redress mechanisms have drawn adverse comment, prior to the enactment of opt-out class actions reform.

1   The Representative Rule

The traditional representative rule originated in the early English Chancery courts.[8] It was a legal device which was transposed to many common law jurisdictions thereafter.[9]

The rule's requirement[10] that the representative claimant show that it shared the 'same interest' with other aggrieved persons who alleged that they had suffered loss and damage by reason of D's conduct has been so stringently and narrowly interpreted as to almost render the rule

---

[8] Originally enacted in the Rules of Procedure scheduled to the Supreme Court of Judicature Act 1873 (Eng) (36 and 37 Vict c 66) r 10; then reproduced almost in the same terms in RSC 1883, Ord 16, r 9; and then by RSC 1965, Ord 15, r 12; and, since 2000, see: CPR 19.6(1). For a fascinating history of how aggregated litigation developed in English medieval society, see the following, by S Yeazell: *From Medieval Group Litigation to the Modern Class Action* (Yale University Press, 1987); 'Group Litigation and Social Context: Toward a History of the Class Action' (1977) 77 *Columbia Law Review* 866; 'From Group Litigation to Class Action Part I: The Industrialization of Group Litigation' (1980) 27 *UCLA Law Review* 514; and 'From Group Litigation to Class Action Part II: Interest, Class, and Representation' (1980) 27 *UCLA Law Review* 1067; and additionally: R Marcin, 'Searching for the Origin of the Class Action' (1974) 23 *Catholic U Law Review* 515.

[9] As discussed in: Mulheron, *The Class Action in Common Law Legal Systems: A Comparative Perspective* (Hart Publishing, 2004), ch 4, 77–94, and the case law and secondary sources referenced therein.

[10] The English rule currently contained in CPR 19.6(1) states: '(1) Where more than one person has the same interest in a claim – (a) the claim may be begun; or (b) the court may order that the claim be continued, by or against one or more of the persons who have the same interest as representatives of any other persons who have that interest.'

nugatory. Whilst there were hopes that the rule could offer a flexible and useful regime which could cater for the resolution of mass grievances,[11] and whilst some judges have earnestly sought to bestow upon the rule precisely that effect,[12] the rule remains beset with a considerable degree of 'judicial baggage', which has tended to stultify the application of the rule (a reality revisited recently in England in a high-profile claim instituted against Google[13]). Those various problems of judicial interpretation, as they have applied in English litigation, have been discussed by numerous scholars[14] (and by the author[15]) elsewhere, and will not be revisited here.

The significant point, for present purposes, is that the inadequacies of the rule were often displayed in key cases in several of the jurisdictions, the legislatures of which then went on to enact opt-out class actions. For example:

- in **Alberta**, in *Western Canadian Shopping Centres Inc v Dutton*[16] – which concerned an allegation that interest was not paid upon debentures held by putative Canadian immigrants and which were managed by the defendants – the Alberta Court of Appeal was required to consider Alberta's then-representative action,[17] and allowed the claim

---

[11] As discussed, e.g., in: *Esanda Finance Corp Ltd v Carnie* (1992) 29 NSWLR 382 (CA) 395 (Kirby P); and see too, Ontario LRC, *Report on Class Actions* (1982) ('[w]hen this Rule first came before the courts in England, they adopted a very liberal attitude toward it', citing, e.g. *Duke of Bedford v Ellis* [1901] AC 1 (HL), and *Taff Vale Rwy Co v Amalgamated Socy of Rwy Servants* [1901] AC 426 (HL).

[12] Notably, in *Prudential Ass Co Ltd v Newman Industries Ltd* [1981] 1 Ch 229 (Vinelott J).

[13] *Lloyd v Google LLC* [2018] EWHC 2599 (QB) (the claim failed for a lack of the requisite 'same interest'). Also unsuccessful in: *Rendlesham Estates plc v Barr Ltd* [2014] EWHC 3968 (TCC), [2015] 1 WLR 3663.

[14] See, e.g.: J Sorabji, 'The Hidden Class Action in English Civil Procedure' (2009) 28 *Civil Justice Quarterly* 498, 510–11 ('[i]t might be said that as an English class action, the representative rule remains hidebound by restrictive authorities and remains a well-hidden part of English civil procedure. This need not remain the case'); C Hodges, *Multi-Party Actions* (Oxford University Press, 2001) [9.03]–[9.08]; Ontario LRC, *Report on Class Actions* (1982) 10–16; J Seymour, 'Representative Proceedings and the Future of Multi-Party Actions' (1999) 62 *Modern Law Review* 565; and by the same author: '*Independiente Ltd v Music Trading On-Line (HK) Ltd*: A little knowledge is a dangerous thing?' (2005) 24 *Civil Justice Quarterly* 16.

[15] See, e.g.: 'From Representative Rule to Class Action: Steps rather than Leaps' (2005) 24 *Civil Justice Quarterly* 424; '*Emerald Supplies Ltd v British Airways plc*: A Century Later, the Ghost of *Markt* Lives On' (2009) 8 *Competition Law Journal* 159; and 'A Missed Gem of an Opportunity for the Representative Rule' [2012] *European Business Law Review* 49.

[16] [1998] ABCA 392, 73 Alta LR (3d) 227.

[17] Alberta Rules of Court, Alta Reg 390/68, r 42 (requiring that 'numerous persons have a common interest in the subject of an intended action').

to proceed in that form. However, it remarked that, '[w]e find it necessary to comment on the inadequacy of Rule 42. The problems encountered in dealing with this application indicate the inadequacy of Rule 42 for dealing with representative actions. . . . this area of the law is clearly in want of legislative reform to provide a more uniform and efficient way to deal with class action law suits.'[18] On further appeal, the Canadian Supreme Court also permitted the action to proceed, whilst noting that, '[i]n the absence of comprehensive class-action legislation, courts must address procedural complexities on a case-by-case basis. Courts should approach these issues as they do the question of whether a class action should be allowed: in a flexible and liberal manner, seeking a balance between efficiency and fairness.'[19] The Court of Appeal's reservations were cited by the jurisdiction's law reformers as evidence of 'shortcomings of existing procedures',[20] and an opt-out class action was subsequently enacted in 2004;[21]

- in **Ontario**, in *Naken v General Motors of Canada Ltd* – which concerned a claim that General Motors had misrepresented the quality of its 1971 and 1972 Firenza vehicles and that they were not reasonably fit for use – the Supreme Court of Canada disallowed the representative action, scathingly remarking of the representative rule that, 'consisting as it does of one sentence of some thirty words, [it] is totally inadequate for employment as the base from which to launch an action of the complexity and uncertainty of this one'.[22] The case was cited by the Ontario Law Reform Commission as a leading example of how an expanded class actions procedure could be effective and efficient;[23] and 11 years later, that became a reality;[24]

- in **Manitoba**, in *Ranjoy Sales & Leasing Ltd v Deloitte, Haskins & Sells Ltd* – which concerned a claim brought by the creditors of two bankrupt

---

[18] [1998] ABCA 392, 73 Alta LR (3d) 227, [20].

[19] [2001] 2 SCR 534, 201 DLR (4th) 385, 94 Alta LR (3d) 1, [51].

[20] Alberta Law Reform Institute, *Class Actions* (Rep 85, 2000), xxi.

[21] Class Proceedings Act, SA 2003, c C-16.5, in force 1 April 2004.

[22] [1983] 1 SCR 72, 105, 144 DLR (3d) 385.

[23] See OLRC, *Report on Class Actions* (1982) 99–100, 'The Faulty Firenzas'. The report was handed down after the Ontario Court of Appeal had permitted the representative action to proceed, but as the OLRC itself foreshadowed (at 100), that decision was overruled by the Supreme Court. For an excellent detailed analysis of the important role which *Naken*, in particular, came to represent in Canadian class action reform, see, by S Chiodo: 'Class Actions in England, North America and Australia' (2018–19) 14 *Canadian Class Action Review* 15, 26–32; and 'The Early Campaign for Reform and the OLRC Report' (2018–19) 14 *Canadian Class Action Review* 47, 81–88.

[24] Class Proceedings Act, SO 1992, c 6, in force 1 January 2003.

companies – Monnin CJM declared that Manitoba's representative rule[25] 'must not be rendered useless', whilst the province 'wait[ed] for legislation on the matter ... or for specific practice rules which have not yet evolved'.[26] Subsequently, the Manitoba Law Reform Commission could only cite three cases in which the rule had been successfully invoked (and noted that *Ranjoy* itself settled without a trial), contributing to the conclusion by the same Commission that a new class action procedure was required.[27] Manitoba enacted an opt-out class action in 2003;[28]

- in the **United Kingdom**, in *Emerald Supplies Ltd v British Airways plc*[29] – in which a flower importer attempted to claim for the economic losses caused by an international air cargo cartel – the Court of Appeal called the case 'fatally flawed',[30] and the Vice-Chancellor of the Chancery Court had not found the rule to be satisfied at first instance either.[31] As the author has commented elsewhere, the failure by English claimants to litigate this cartel occurred exactly a century after the leading (and doomed) representative rule case of *Markt & Co Ltd v Knight Steamship Co Ltd*[32] – and '[b]oth decisions demonstrate a judicial shackling of the rule, to the point where it lacks any degree of reasonable utility at all, except in the most limited of cases.'[33] The UK Government agreed that the *Emerald* decision exemplified 'the difficulties with using the procedures under the Civil Procedure Rules in the ordinary courts',[34] and it recommended 'a limited opt-out collective actions regime, with safeguards, for competition law'.[35] This became a reality on 1 October 2015;[36]

- in **Australia**, in *Dillon v Charter Travel Co Ltd*[37] – in which a group of passengers claimed for damages arising from their involvement in the

---

[25] Contained in Queen's Bench Rules, Man Reg 553/88, r 12.01.

[26] (1984), 16 DLR (4th) 218, 31 Man R (2d) 87, [9].

[27] *Class Proceedings* (Rep 100, 1999) 7–8.

[28] Class Proceedings Act, CCSM c C130, in force 1 January 2003.

[29] [2010] EWCA Civ 1284, [2011] 2 WLR 203 (Mummery, Toulson and Rimer LJJ concurring).

[30] ibid, [62].

[31] *Emerald Supplies Ltd v British Airways plc* [2009] EWHC 741 (Ch) (Chancellor Morritt).

[32] [1910] 2 KB 1021 (CA).

[33] See: Mulheron, 'A Century Later, the Ghost of *Markt* Lives On' (n 15) 159.

[34] BIS, *Private Actions in Competition Law: Government Response* (2013) [3.6].

[35] ibid, [5.14].

[36] The Consumer Rights Act 2015, Sch 8, which inserted relevant provisions into the Competition Act 1998 and the Enterprise Act 2002, and with supporting court rules contained in the Competition Appeal Tribunal Rules 2015 (SI 1648/2015), rr 73–98.

[37] (1988) ATPR 40–872.

sinking of a cruise vessel which struck a shoal off the southern tip of New Zealand and then sank – a representative action was denied, a fact which the Australian Law Reform Commission cited as an example of the limitations of the representative rule.[38] Following the publication of that report, the 'tortuous' case of *Esanda Finance Corp v Carnie*,[39] which concerned the New South Wales version of the representative rule,[40] displayed all the usual controversies. However, the High Court of Australia deliberately interpreted the rule's 'same interest' widely, as requiring 'a community of interest in the determination of any substantial question of law or fact that arises in the proceedings',[41] whilst noting that '[m]uch as one might prefer to have a detailed legislative prescription by statute or rule of court regulating the incidents of representative action',[42] that did not then exist. A decade later, Australia's federal opt-out class action was enacted.[43]

2 Opt-In Regimes

Opt-in regimes undoubtedly have their place in civil procedure.[44] For example, since the opt-in Group Litigation Order (GLO) was enacted in the **United Kingdom** in 2000,[45] 105 actions have been certified, across a range of subject matter.[46]

However, they do have a number of procedural problems which have been judicially acknowledged, *viz*: the task of 'book-building',[47] and of

---

[38] *Grouped Proceedings in the Federal Court* (Rep 46, 1988) [42], fn 47; and [64], fn 83.

[39] (1995) 182 CLR 398 (HCA), and described as such by Toohey and Gaudron JJ (at 405). Earlier, the case had been struck out by the NSWCA, by majority: Gleeson CJ and Meagher JA, Kirby P dissenting.

[40] Supreme Court Rules 1970 (NSW), Pt 8, r 13(1).

[41] (1995) 182 CLR 398 (HCA), point 4 of Brennan J's judgment.

[42] ibid, point 6 of the judgment of Mason CJ, Deane and Dawson JJ.

[43] Federal Court of Australia Act 1976 ('FCA 1976'), Pt IVA, which took effect on 3 March 1992.

[44] For definition, see Table 1.1; and further discussed, by reference to relevant authorities, in: Mulheron, 'Some Difficulties with Group Litigation Orders – and Why a Class Action is Superior' (2005) 24 *Civil Justice Quarterly* 40.

[45] Contained in CPR 19.III, rr 19.10–19.15.

[46] See the register of GLOs maintained by HM's Courts and Tribunals Service at: www .gov.uk/guidance/group-litigation-orders accessed 28 April 2019. For a recent scholarly, practical and detailed study of the commencement and conduct of group litigation orders, see: D Grave, M McIntosh and G Rowan (eds), *Class Actions in England and Wales* (Sweet & Maxwell, 2018).

[47] A costly task that may fall to a third party funder, if involved, as discussed, e.g., in: M Power, 'Roundtable: Litigation Funding' (*Law Society Gazette*, 13 March 2017); and

maintaining (and updating) the group register of named claimants and/ or filing individual and particularised claim forms; the 'frontloading' of the claims, to particularise each claimant's grievance; being required to advertise the action, which can prompt judicial disapproval; a poor cost–benefit analysis, particularly where the size of the opt-in class (and the damages per class member) are forecast to be modest; sometimes low participation rates; the operation of limitation periods for those who have not opted in; whether a court may order claimants to join an opt-in class rather than to institute separate proceedings; and managing and allocating the costs of the action, given that group members are not generally immunised against costs for either the generic or the individual issues.[48]

The BIS Department made the point, when recommending an opt-out class action for competition law grievances, that 'opt-out collective actions are novel, which is why the actions are limited to competition cases – where many claims, particularly those brought on behalf of consumers, cannot be effectively brought in any other way'.[49] Although not mentioned in that document, it is notable that the GLO opt-in regime had not witnessed a single competition law claim since its inception (and, at the time of writing, still has not).

Furthermore, the opt-in regime enacted in the United Kingdom in 2002, the s 47B regime under the Competition Act 1998[50] (but only technically available from 2005, when the sole representative claimant under the regime was designated[51]) was not particularly effective either. The regime was dedicated entirely to 'consumer claims'[52] (i.e. excluding businesses which had suffered detriment) which were follow-on actions from an anti-competitive infringement.[53] It was abolished as part of the 2015 reforms, and in that time, there was a solitary action brought under it – *Consumers' Association (Which?) v JJB Sports plc*,[54] where the class

---

J Geisker and J Tallis, 'Australia', in *Third Party Litigation Funding Law Rev* (2nd edn, 16 November 2018).

[48] Itemised by the author, by reference to specific case law, in: *Reform of Collective Redress* (n 5), ch 6, 25–31. Earlier: 'Some Difficulties with Group Litigation Orders' (n 44); and *The Class Action* (n 9) 94–110.

[49] *Private Actions in Competition Law: Government Response* (2013) [5.52].

[50] Inserted by the Enterprise Act 2002 (UK), s 19.

[51] Per the Specified Body (Consumer Claims) Order 2005, SI 2005/2365. The designation of the English Consumers' Association, Which?, occurred on 1 October 2005.

[52] Competition Act 1998 (UK) (CA 1998), s 47B(7).

[53] CA 1998, s 47B(5) and (6).

[54] UK CAT Case No 1078/7/9/07. The author has described the details, and ramifications, of this case, elsewhere, e.g. ' A Channel Apart: Why the United Kingdom has Departed from

members sued in respect of price-fixing arrangements among the manufacturers and distributors of either replica Manchester United football
shirts or replica England shirts. Only 144 claimants were noted on the
original claim form (the average uplift per replica shirt was £15), and the
claim eventually settled on confidential terms. The English Consumers'
Association, as the sole representative designated under the regime,
categorically expressed its reluctance to commit precious resources
(both time and money) to pursue these actions.[55] Ultimately, the futility
of this s 47B regime was a key prompt for the UK Government's decision
to enact the 2015 Consumer Rights Act regime. The Government
remarked upon 'the inadequacy of the current opt-in collective action
in competition law', and that it was 'difficult to bring cases'.[56]

It is also noteworthy that some recent high-profile cases have shone
a light upon the complexities of conducting opt-in group litigation in the
United Kingdom. For example, a recent action instituted by over 600
sub-postmasters against the entity that operates the network of over
11,000 Post Office branches throughout the United Kingdom (*Bates
v Post Office Ltd*), has encountered a number of procedural issues.[57] In
Harcus Sinclair LLP v Harcus Sinclair UK Lte, Chancellor Vos noted that,
in respect of the intention to apply for a GLO in relation to the
Volkswagen diesel emissions scandal, the case would be complex, antici-
pating 'different firms of solicitors acting for different groups of claimants', and that 'such litigation inevitably involves numerous separate
Claim Forms being brought together by a Group Litigation Order'.[58] And
in the case of *Winstone v MGB Ltd*[59] – arising out of the routine use by

the European Commission's Recommendations on Class Actions' (2015) 17 *Cambridge
Yearbook of European Legal Studies* 36, 47–49; and *Reform of Collective Redress* (n 5), ch 8.

[55] As expressly stated by Which? in-house lawyers, quoted in the research report: ibid, at
39–41. For discussion by experienced litigators of its many problems, see: M Raja and
P Lomas, 'A Lawyer's Perspective', in E Lein *et al.* (eds), *Collective Redress in Europe: Why
and How?* (BIICL, 2015) 67–72; and see too: J Sorabji, 'Collective Actions Reform in
England and Wales', in D Fairgrieve and E Lein (eds), *Extraterritoriality and Collective
Redress* (Oxford University Press, 2012), ch 3, 51 ('[t]he great step forward, it turned out,
was anything but that').

[56] BIS, *Private Actions in Competition Law: Government Response* (2013) [3.6].

[57] See the separate judgments in: [2019] EWHC 871 (QB); [2018] EWHC 2698 (QB); and
[2017] EWHC 2844 (QB), re GLO #97.

[58] [2019] EWCA Civ 335, [64]. A separate GLO in relation to the VW emissions infringement has already been ordered (GLO #105), with six common 'defining issues' specified:
see the GLO summary at: www.gov.uk/guidance/group-litigation-orders#VW-NOx-
emissions-group-litigation.

[59] [2019] EWHC 265 (Ch).

the defendant of 'phone-hacking' as a journalistic tool, and which led to a large number of claims from those who claimed that their private information was accessed by means of voicemail interception and their right to privacy thereby infringed – Mr Justice Norris made the point that this case was not being conducted under the GLO umbrella at all. Rather, the claims 'are gathered together in "waves" (recorded in "group registers"). Each claimant in a wave will have his or her own solicitor, but there is a "lead solicitor" who deals with common issues relating to that wave';[60] and furthermore, 'it is important for the case management of multiple cases that each case is conducted substantially according to the same ground rules'.[61]

This *ad hoc* case management of complex and difficult litigation represents the status quo, given the absence of any *generic* opt-out class action in UK law which had been recommended for implementation by the Civil Justice Council of England and Wales in 2008,[62] to cope with this type of array of grievances across different subject matters. Of course, it cannot be predicted whether these cases could have been conducted more economically, efficiently, and with a greater accessibility for claimants to seek to achieve redress, under an opt-out class action. However, without that option on the statute books, there is no choice for such claimants but to persevere with the status quo. The only substantive change in the landscape since the CJC's 2008 recommendation is that an opt-out class action for competition law grievances has been introduced;[63] for everything else, the Council's 'key findings' remain as true now as they were then: '[e]xisting procedure does not provide sufficient or effective access to justice for a wide range of citizens, particularly but not exclusively consumers, small businesses, and employees wishing to bring collective or multi-party claims';[64] and '[t]here are meritorious claims that could fairly be brought with greater efficiency and effectiveness on a collective rather than unitary basis.'[65]

Half a world away, in **Victoria**, opt-in procedures have also figured largely in reform initiatives. The Victorian legislature had made

---

[60] ibid, [10].

[61] ibid, [38].

[62] *Improving Access to Justice: Final Report* (n 5) Recommendation 1 ('[a] generic collective action should be introduced'), at p 21; and 'key finding #3' ('[t]here is overwhelming evidence that meritorious claims, which could be brought are currently not being pursued'), at p 17.

[63] Described in: Chapter 1, Section B(4).

[64] ibid, 'key finding #1', at p 17.

[65] ibid, 'key finding #4'.

a conscious decision to overcome the deficiencies of the traditional representative rule[66] by enacting a new opt-in regime, contained in ss 34 and 35 of the Supreme Court Act. This regime was an opt-in regime, in the sense that all persons being represented in the proceeding had to consent in writing to being represented,[67] and had to be named in the originating process.[68] It was intended to be able to be used, even if different contracts were being relied upon by the class members, and even if their damages were different and would require individual assessment[69] (both being anathema to the representative rule's jurisprudence[70]). However, in *Zentahope Pty Ltd* v. *Bellotti*,[71] the Supreme Court of Victoria described ss 34 and 35 as being 'overly brief and enigmatic provisions' from which 'the Court strives by successive decisions to divine meaning', and most critical of all, that 'the legislature should give careful and early consideration to the repeal of ss 34 and 35'. Subsequent judicial comment rather understatedly remarked that, '[t]he new sections did not work very well'.[72] The regime was also described by law reformers as being 'silen[t] on a number of important issues', and with all the attendant problems that opt-in regimes typically entailed.[73] Following upon those reformers' recommendation, an opt-out class action was ultimately enacted in Victoria in 2000.[74]

3   Other Procedural Mechanisms

The devices of consolidation and joinder (also called 'permissive joinder'[75]) also had their critics amongst law reform bodies, preceding

---

[66] Then contained in: Supreme Court Act 1984, s 62(1C), and discussed in: *Marion v Esanda Ltd* [1986] VR 735.

[67] Per Supreme Court Act 1986, s 35(2)(a).

[68] Per ibid, s 35(2)(b). Those written consents by the class members had to be filed in the court at the same time that the originating process was commenced: s 35(3).

[69] Explicitly noted in: *Hansard* (Legislative Council, 5 December 1986, col 1659, Mr J Kennan A-G), as cited in: Attorney-General's Law Reform Advisory Council, *Class Actions in Victoria – Time for a New Approach* (1997) [3.1].

[70] As discussed in Section B(1).

[71] (VSC Appeal Div, 2 March 1992), all quotes at 24 (Fullagar J).

[72] *P Dawson Nominees Pty Ltd v Multiplex Ltd* [2007] FCA 1061, [45], although Finkelstein J disputed that ss 34 and 35 created an 'opt-in procedure in the strict meaning of that expression', an observation which this author finds somewhat puzzling.

[73] *Class Actions in Victoria* (n 69), especially [3.4] and [3.9]–[3.16].

[74] Supreme Court Act 1986, Pt 4A.

[75] Manitoba LRC, *Class Proceedings* (Rep 100, 1999) 64.

opt-out class actions reform. For example, the **Australian**,[76] **Manitoba**,[77] **Alberta**,[78] and **Ontario**[79] Law Reform Commissions all expressly cited the drawbacks of trying to use the joinder or consolidation procedures, by reference to specific cases.

In some cases, a voluntary informal grouping has been necessary, only because other procedural options have failed. For example, in **Alberta**, the Law Reform Institute referred to the case of *Holtslag v Alberta*,[80] in which a group of aggrieved homeowners alleged that the government of Alberta authorised and endorsed the use of pine shakes as a roofing material when it knew or should have known that it was unsuitable. The group's attempt to use the representative rule failed;[81] the Queen's Bench of Alberta wryly noted that, '[t]his application is a good example of why some governments have enacted legislation permitting class representative actions and prescribing rules which permit and govern such actions. Unfortunately, the Province of Alberta has, to date, chosen not to do so';[82] and following that unfortunate episode, the Alberta Law Reform Institute noted that the case had to proceed by the claimants forming 'a voluntary association in order to work together in pursuing their claims'.[83] This Institute's report also contains a fascinating vignette of how over 200 wrongful sterilisation claims commenced against the Alberta Government were the subject of strict and active case management, and where the case management judge permitted 'that a plaintiff committee be formed so that defence counsel would not have to deal with 60–70 individual lawyers', albeit that '[t]he case management required about a year of the judge's time',[84] and was 'uneven, being re-created case by case'.[85]

In the **United States**, the inadequacies of the 'spurious class action' which was contained in the original Federal Rules of Civil Procedure 23,

---

[76] *Grouped Proceedings in the Federal Court* (1988) [46], fn 53, citing: *Payne v Young* (1980) 145 CLR 609 (HCA) 618, and Mason J's description of the limitation of joinder; and [50].

[77] *Class Proceedings* (Rep 100, 1999) 9, citing: *Lytton v Barrett* [1996] AJ No 895 (QB). Also: '[r]ules on joinder and adding parties are useful, but cannot replace class proceedings because they can result in cumbersome and expensive proceedings': at 12.

[78] *Class Actions* (Rep 85, 2000) [43], citing: *Athabasca Realty Co v Humeniuk* (1978), 14 AR 79 (TD) 83; *Hagman v Omar Holdings Ltd* (1984), 55 AR 44, 45.

[79] *Report on Class Actions* (1982) 82–86.

[80] [2006] ABCA 51, 265 DLR (4th) 518, leave to appeal *ref'd*: (SCC, 14 September 2006).

[81] *Holtslag v Alberta* [2000] ABQB 351.

[82] ibid, [4]–[5].

[83] *Class Actions* (Rep 85, 2000) [41].

[84] ibid, [46], fn 58. The litigation was settled in 1999.

[85] ibid, [56].

was also considered to be 'little more than a permissive joinder device, which would be binding only on the original parties to the suit and those who might subsequently intervene'.[86] That rule applied where 'there [was] a common question of law or fact, affecting the several rights and a common relief [was] sought'.[87] It was judicially held that any judgment in a spurious class action did not bind members of the class who had not become parties.[88] Some courts sought to provide the spurious action with utility and liberality, i.e., that in spurious class actions, interventions 'should be liberally allowed' in order to increase their utility;[89] that the action could cope with class members who had claims for varying amounts of damages;[90] and that the court can determine the spurious class action even where 'there is joined a large number of parties who have only one question of law or fact in common'.[91] However, the reality remained that the device was of limited utility where similarly situated parties neglected or refused to join or to intervene. Any judgment rendered in the spurious class action could not bind them. There was also a minimum individual monetary threshold of $3,000 (which could not be aggregated to exceed that threshold) before the claim could be prosecuted in a federal court, which some spurious class actions could not meet.[92] Academic commentary has not been kind to the rule. For example, Rabiej has noted that class actions law decided under the spurious class action was

> becoming hopelessly inconsistent, ... failed to distinguish clearly which claims were suitable for class treatment, ... left the courts wrestling with ways to adapt the spurious class action to fit individual actions, creating a patchwork of *ad hoc* jurisprudence, ... [and] the extent of notice

---

[86] *Newberg on Class Actions* (n 2) §1.10, 33, citing: *Oppenheimer v FJ Young & Co*, 144 F 2d 387 (2nd Cir, 1944). See too, e.g.: *Hunter v Southern Indemnity Underwriters*, 247 F Supp 242, 244 (Ed Ky, 1942); and *Eisen v Carlisle and Jacquelin*, 391 F 2d 555, 560 (2nd Cir, 1968).

[87] FRCP 23(a)(3) (1938).

[88] *Fox v Glickman Corp*, 355 F 2d 161, 163, 164 (2nd Cir, 1965) ('in a spurious class action the judgment binds only participating parties, [any] subsequent assertion that a judgment would bind members of a class with similar interests, made in deciding on the propriety of a spurious class action in that case, was presumably intended to refer only to those members who initiated or intervened in the suit'); *Kainz v Anheuser-Busch Inc*, 194 F 2d 737, 742 (7th Cir, 1952) ('plaintiffs may ... maintain the suit as a spurious class suit under Rule 23(a)(3), though the judgments are several and no one is bound unless he is present').

[89] *Rosen v Bergman*, 640 FRD 19, 22 (SDNY, 1966).

[90] *Rath v Armour & Co*, 136 NW 2d 142, 145 (ND, 1965).

[91] *Hess v Anderson, Clayton & Co*, 20 FRD 466, 482 (SD Cal, 1957).

[92] e.g., *Wagner v Kemper*, 213 FRD 128 (WD Miss, 1952); *Knowles v War Damage Corp*, 171 F 2d 15 (DDC, 1949).

provided to class members varied from case to case depending on the discretion of the individual trial judge.[93]

As the authors of *Newberg on Class Actions* concluded, '[u]nder heavy criticism, original Rule 23 was completely rewritten, and sweeping innovations were introduced with the 1966 amendments'.[94]

In addition, the various attendant difficulties associated with the existing test/lead action device[95] were referred to by the **Ontario**,[96] **Manitoba**,[97] **Alberta**,[98] and **Australian**[99] Law Reform Commissions as further evidence as to why an expanded class actions procedure was required for those jurisdictions.

C 'Missing Cases'

One of the key foundational aspects of class actions reform is to establish that there is a 'gap' – an unmet need for access to a legal procedure by which to test a grievance commonly held. Of course, some multiparty litigation will fail on the merits – the high-profile litigation centred on bank charges both in the United Kingdom[100] and in Australia[101] being examples of that truism. However, the inability to bring actions at all must be

---

[93] K Rabiej, 'The Making of Class Action Rule 23: What Were We Thinking?' (2005) 24 *Mississippi College Law Review* 323, 333. For earlier comment about the difficulties of the previous FRCP 23, see, e.g.: Note, 'Aggregation of Claims in Class Actions' (1968) 68 *Columbia Law Review* 1554; Note, 'Class Actions and Interpleader: California Procedure and the Federal Rules' (1953) 6 *Stanford Law Review* 120; Note, 'Federal Class Actions: A Suggested Revision of Rule 23' (1946) 46 *Columbia Law Review* 818, 823.

[94] *Newberg on Class Actions* (n 2), §1.10, 33.

[95] Discussed by the author in: *The Class Action* (n 9) 102–05, by reference to secondary sources and case law.

[96] *Report on Class Actions* (1982) 86–88.

[97] *Class Proceedings* (Rep 100, 1999) 11, citing: *Muir v Alberta* (1996), 132 DLR (4th) 695 (Alta QB).

[98] *Class Actions* (Rep 85, 2000) [38]–[49].

[99] *Grouped Proceedings* (1988) [54]–[56], citing: *Kaur v Minister for Immigration, Local Govt and Ethnic Affairs* (case withdrawn); and the English case of *Davies v Eli Lilly & Co Ltd* [1987] 3 All ER 94 (CA); and see too, [63], citing: *Anderson v HFC Financial Services Ltd* [1988] VR 251; and *Green v Daniels* (1977) 13 ALR 1 (HCA).

[100] *Office of Fair Trading v Abbey National plc* [2009] UKSC 6, [2010] 1 AC 696. The case was brought by the OFT in the Commercial Court against seven banks, to test whether the provisions of the 1999 Regulations applied to unauthorised overdraft charges. The Supreme Court found in the banks' favour.

[101] *Paciocco v Australia and New Zealand Banking Group Ltd* [2016] HCA 28, (2016) 333 ALR 569. The action was pursued under Part IVA and alleged that the provisions for the various bank fees were unenforceable as penalties, or that their inclusion contravened various statutory provisions relating to unconscionable conduct. These claims failed.

a concern to any law reformer – and, notwithstanding the considerable challenge of 'proving the negative', there were numerous examples identified by reformers which preceded opt-out class actions reform being enacted across the Comparator Jurisdictions. An analysis of these studies (together with the author's own[102]) suggests that, considered in combination, these 'missing cases' tend to be identified via one of **three** avenues.

1   Known Disasters or Grievances

First, it may be possible to point to actual real-life events which feasibly gave rise to loss or damage on the part of several individuals and/or businesses, but from which no effective collective redress litigation had commenced at the time of the reformists' studies.

In **Ontario**, the OLRC correctly noted the challenge for law reformers in this context, that '[t]he exact effect of the procedural deficiencies ... cannot be stated or measured in the abstract with any degree of precision'.[103] However, by way of example, the Commission referred[104] to several instances of widespread grievances[105] which, at the time of that report, were bogged down in negotiations, out-of-court processes, or unitary litigation only.

In **Australia**, the ALRC noted that whether the need for a new procedure had been established must depend upon whether there were 'situations where effective grouping procedures [were] necessary to ensure access to legal remedies' or '[were] necessary to promote efficiency and consistency in dealing with multiple claims'.[106] In response to the challenge that 'actual instances of cases should be shown', where a court-based remedy was denied because costs or other factors deterred the claimants from proceeding, the ALRC nominated several examples of real-life scenarios[107] which would

---

[102] *Reform of Collective Redress* (n 5), especially Pt IV.

[103] *Report on Class Actions* (1982) 90.

[104] ibid, 90–98.

[105] Citing: the Mississauga train derailment in November 1979; health hazards caused by urea formaldehyde insulation in homes in 1976–77; and the collapse of a businessman's financial empire, giving rise to substantial investor losses.

[106] *Grouped Proceedings* (1988) [62].

[107] Citing, e.g., film for a camera going out of production, rendering the instant camera useless; serious programme errors in a software product; misrepresentations to lease-holders in a large shopping centre that a major department store and food retailer would be taking up leases, but when it opened, there was no major retailer on site; franchisees entering into franchise agreements on the basis of representations about the profitability of food outlets and levels of advertising: *Grouped Proceedings* (1988) [65].

have benefited from a grouping procedure in Australian courts, but where no litigation was identified by the Commission.

2 Litigation Elsewhere, with No Domestic Equivalent

Secondly, it may be possible to point to a specific service or product which has been distributed on a global, transnational or national basis, where: a defect or some culpable conduct has been alleged in relation to that service or product; and litigation arising from that allegation has been instituted elsewhere; but there is absolutely no equivalent litigation in the domestic jurisdiction.

In **Manitoba**, the relevant Commission considered a number of tort, contract, and commercial cases instituted in those Canadian jurisdictions (*viz*, Québec, Ontario, and British Columbia) which had implemented class actions as at the date of that report, but which had no litigious equivalent in Manitoba.[108] It stated that, '[i]t is sobering to realize that Manitobans could not, from a practical perspective, assert many of the tortious, contractual, commercial or other claims described earlier',[109] particularly given that they were the sort of claims that could feasibly arise in any jurisdiction.

In the **United Kingdom**, the failed representative rule arising from a cartel involving numerous airlines concerning fuel surcharges in *Emerald Supplies* has already been mentioned.[110] As the author has commented elsewhere,[111] *Emerald* occurred exactly a century after the leading (and doomed) representative rule case of *Markt & Co Ltd v Knight Steamship Co Ltd*[112] – and yet the failure by English claimants to litigate this cartel was in stark contrast to the opt-out class litigation in Australia,[113] Canada,[114] and the United States[115] arising from that same cartel. The lack of domestic redress in the United Kingdom concerning

---

[108] *Class Proceedings* (Rep 100, 1999) 17–21.
[109] ibid, 23.
[110] See p 45.
[111] Mulheron, 'A Century Later, the Ghost of *Markt* Lives On' (n 15) 159.
[112] [1910] 2 KB 1021 (CA).
[113] Settled on 6 June 2014 for $38M (see the website of Maurice Blackburn, 'Air Cargo Class Action', available at www.mauriceblackburn.com.au/past-class-actions/air-cargo-class-action/).
[114] See e.g., formerly *Nutech Brands Inc v Air Canada* [2009] CanLII 7095 (Ont SCJ) and then litigated under the title *Airia Brands Inc v Air Canada* [2011] ONSC 6286, which ultimately went to the CA: *Airia Brands Inc v Air Canada* [2017] ONCA 792, 11 CPC (8th) 35, special leave ref'd: [2018] CanLII 99652 (SCC).
[115] *In re Air Cargo Shipping Services Antitrust Litig*, 2009 US Dist LEXIS 97365 (EDNY, August 21, 2009); affirming 2008 US Dist LEXIS 107882 (EDNY, September 26, 2008).

this cartel was also mentioned by the Government in its law reform consultation response.[116] Further, in the legal and empirical study that preceded the recommendation that a generic class action be introduced to UK civil procedure,[117] it was plain that numerous rather common grievances pursued under the opt-out regimes in Canada and Australia had no equivalent in England and Wales; and actions brought in other jurisdictions re global products or services (e.g., particularly pharmaceutical products or medical devices) had not been pursued in this jurisdiction either. This was notwithstanding that product liability cases may be pursued under both negligence and via a more-favourable-to-the-consumer strict liability regime in English law[118] (they operate as side-by-side regimes[119]), suggesting that the substantive law was not a key problem, but the procedural framework by which to enforce that substantive law may have been. Again, this evidence was cited in the CJC's final report, and was used to support the recommendation that an opt-out class action be introduced[120] (although, to reiterate, that recommendation has not yet been acted upon by the UK Government).

3   Regulatory Fines with No Ancillary Civil Redress

Thirdly, it may be possible to point to examples of cases in which a regulator has identified the existence of culpable conduct, and where some injunctive or penalty order may have been awarded against the defendant, but where no compensatory redress in relation to that conduct has followed. That is treated as a separate trigger later in the chapter.[121]

4   Anecdotal Evidence

Responses to questionnaires and the conduct of interviews with either lawyers or third-party funders, where feasible, is undoubtedly one way of gaining insights as to cases that are not being brought.

---

[116] BIS, *Private Actions in Competition Law: Government Response* (2013) [3.6] and fn 7.

[117] Mulheron, *Reform of Collective Redress* (n 5).

[118] Per the Consumer Protection Act 1987; and note *A v National Blood Authy* [2001] EWHC 446 (QB) [13] (the Act's purpose was to 'increase consumer protection . . . [and] to render compensation of the injured consumer easier, by removing the concept of negligence as an element of liability': Burton J).

[119] Discussed in detail by the author in: *Principles of Tort Law* (Cambridge University Press, 2016) ch DP, 'Defective Products'.

[120] CJC, *Improving Access to Justice: Final Report* (n 5) 98–99.

[121] See Section H.

Any paucity of case law may be attributed to difficulties with the substantive law or with procedural hurdles. Indeed, lawyers who were interviewed[122] prior to the CJC's reform recommendations attributed the bereft competition law private enforcement landscape in the **United Kingdom** to both. On the other hand, in the case of a copper cartel which related to the supply of copper tubing,[123] one respondent noted that UK consumers were likely to be met with the plea of a passing-on defence; and additionally, the supply chain was of such length and complexity that any consumer who fitted copper tubing into his or her central heating system would find the proof of causation of damage very difficult to prove.[124] On the other hand, another respondent to the questionnaire remarked that he had investigated a price-fixing allegation in relation to a particular brand of motor vehicle, where the amount per claimant customer was estimated to be only £4,000–£5,000, and there approximately 10,000–15,000 claimants were affected. From a procedural point of view, that respondent concluded that the cost–benefit ratio of bringing this stand-alone action did not warrant private action; and that the task of identifying the asset owners at the outset would have been very difficult, absent an order directed to the defendant to disclose sales records.[125]

An opt-out class action does not erase all procedural difficulties by any means; and, except to the extent that legislation countenances, is not a device that can amend the substantive law. However, the cost–benefit ratio, and the ability to fund such actions, may look more positive when viewed on a collective basis. Notably, in an era in which one English Court of Appeal has acknowledged[126] that third-party funders are, quite properly, as much driven by commercial gain as by the purpose of facilitating access to justice; and another differently constituted Court of Appeal has stated[127] that the UK Competition Law Class Action 'was

---

[122] Mulheron, *Reform of Collective Redress* (n 5), especially Sections 9 and 10.

[123] Resulting from an EC infringement decision dated 16 December 2003, resulting in a fine of 78,730,000 Euros against five companies.

[124] *Reform of Collective Redress* (n 5) 59 (quoting Mr David Greene, Litigation Partner, Edwin Coe LLP).

[125] ibid, 65 (quoting an anonymous respondent).

[126] *Excalibur Ventures LLC v Texas Keystone Inc* [2016] EWCA Civ 1144, [28] ('I do not myself think that commercial funders are greatly motivated by the need to promote access to justice, and nor do I suggest that they should be. They are ... making an investment and are motivated by largely commercial considerations. Those whose money they invest would no doubt be aggrieved if it were otherwise': Tomlinson LJ).

[127] *Merricks v Mastercard Inc* [2019] EWCA Civ 674, [60].

obviously intended to facilitate a means of redress which could attract and be facilitated by litigation funding', it is unsurprising that all six actions filed under the UK Competition Law Class Action to date are being third-party funded.[128]

D   Burdensome and Duplicative Litigation

Another scenario which tends to trigger the prospect of opt-out class actions reform is where there are *too many* cases on foot arising from an event, causing judicial inefficiencies, duplicative litigious costs, and the prospect of inconsistent judgments.

In **Australia**, the ALRC referred to a number of real-life cases in which numerous claims were filed, but where (it was suggested) a singular class action may have dealt with the scenario much better: 300 claims for work-related asbestos exposure; 'hundreds of people' affected by bush-fires; and 'a number' of students alleging misrepresentations regarding a college's facilities.[129] Subsequent to the ALRC's report, the high-profile 1991 blood contamination case of *E v Australian Red Cross Socy*[130] had a significant impact. Wilcox J, who decided the case, was a Commissioner of the ALRC, from 1985 until the class actions report was completed,[131] and hence, had a great familiarity and affinity with its proposals. Claimant E claimed that he had received, at the Royal Prince Alfred Hospital in Sydney, a transfusion of frozen blood plasma which was HIV-infected. E sued the Australian Red Cross Society, the NSW Division of that Society, and the Central Sydney Area Health Service, alleging negligence. He claimed that the procedures adopted by the NSW Division by which those persons within the known AIDS high-risk categories were excluded from the blood donor pool were inadequate; that the Red Cross failed to provide face-to-face questioning and counselling of donors or to

---

[128]   *Gibson v Pride Mobility Products Ltd* [2017] CAT 9 (funded by Burford Capital (UK) Ltd); *Merricks v Mastercard Inc*, ibid (originally funded by Gerchen Keller Capital LLC, later acquired by Burford Capital (UK) Ltd; and with the appeal to the Court of Appeal funded by Innsworth Litigation Funding); and two cases arising from the EC's 'trucks cartel' infringement decision: *Road Haulage Assn Ltd v Man SE* (Case 1289/7/7/18) (funded by Therium Capital); and *UK Trucks Claim Ltd v Fiat Chrysler Automobiles NV* (Case 1282/7/7/18) (funded by Affiniti Finance Ltd); and *Gutmann v First MTR South Western Trains Ltd* (Case 1304/7/7/19) and *Gutmann v London and South Eastern Rwy Ltd* (Case 1304/7/7/19) (both funded by Woodsford Litigation Funding).
[129]   *Grouped Proceedings in the Federal Court* (1988) [64].
[130]   [1991] FCA 20, 27 FCR 310.
[131]   Noted in *Grouped Proceedings* (n 129), 'Participants', at xvii.

have any system permitting an embarrassed donor anonymously to request that his or her donation be discarded; and given that no specific test for HIV infection was then available, the Red Cross should have implemented a surrogate test for hepatitis B core antibodies, which would have identified many of the high-risk donors. One difficulty was that there were 42 other similar cases, where the factual circumstances by which those claimants contracted either HIV or hepatitis B were quite different; and some claims required expediting because of the claimants' shortened life expectancy. In an important passage, Wilcox J lamented that:

> [i]f there were in force in this Court provisions relating to grouped proceedings, such as those recommended by [the ALRC], it would have been possible for the Court to determine all common questions of fact or law at a single hearing in such a manner as to make the result binding on all applicants and all respondents. . . . The result would have been to avoid the repetition in each of the later cases of most of the evidence in this case, with consequential savings in costs and the earlier finalisation of the whole litigation. But that recommendation has not become law. So it will be necessary to deal with each of the cases separately.[132]

The case was undoubtedly a primer for the implementation of the 1992 federal class action reforms.[133]

Various law reform commissions whose reports preceded the enactment of opt-out class actions in their jurisdictions have particularly emphasised the need to avoid inconsistent outcomes arising from unitary litigation *en masse* – **Manitoba**,[134] **Alberta**,[135] and **Ontario**[136] being examples. In **Australia**, the ALRC also referred to Victorian[137] and West Australian[138] decisions in which their respective courts had differed as to liability in asbestos litigation, thereby causing inconsistency and uncertainty for the litigants concerned.[139]

---

[132] [1991] FCA 20, [7], (1991) 27 FCR 310, 314.

[133] The significance of this case to the federal reforms has also been made by other Australian scholars, e.g.: D Grave, K Adams and J Betts, *Class Actions in Australia* (2nd edn, Lawbook Co, 2012) 49–50; V Morabito, 'Class Action Against Multiple Respondents' (2002) 30 *Federal Law Review* 295, 299.

[134] *Class Proceedings* (Rep 100, 1999) 4, 17, 25, 31.

[135] *Class Actions* (Rep 85, 2000) [114].

[136] *Report on Class Actions* (1982) 81, 86.

[137] *CSR v Rabenalt* (Vic SC, 18 December 1987).

[138] *Joosten v Midalco Pty Ltd* [1979] WASC 206.

[139] *Grouped Proceedings in the Federal Court* (1988) [66].

The **United States** reforms were also responsive to a burdensome difficulty, *viz*, the difficulty for courts in determining *which type* of class action
should apply under the previous FRCP 23(a), i.e., whether the claim was a
'true' class action (involving 'joint, common, or secondary rights');[140] a
'hybrid' category (involving 'several' rights related to 'specific property');[141]
and the 'spurious' class action identified previously.[142] As academic scholars
attest:

> [t]he classification turned on an analysis of the abstract nature of the
> rights involved that often verged on the metaphysical. For this and other
> reasons, class actions did not play a major role in federal litigation from
> 1938, when the original Federal Rules of Civil Procedure became effective,
> until 1966.[143]
>
> [s]erious problems with the three categories emerged during FRCP
> 23(a)'s twenty-eight year existence. The categories engendered confusion
> and provided ingenious lawyers and judges considerable leeway to con-
> strue the rule liberally, expanding its reach. Placing a particular action
> within one of the three categories often proved to be contentious.[144]

and:

> For the members of the Advisory Committee, Rule 23 was a risible proce-
> dural contraption. Legal realism had exploded the sort of formalism embo-
> died in [the classification], and the rule-makers were unsympathetic and
> unconcerned with the 'jural relations' rationale underlying the classifica-
> tion. More damning, the rule-makers uniformly believed that categorizing
> class actions by the nature of pre-established rights worked terribly.[145]

The old rule was also very inefficient. The potential for class members to
delay their opting-in to the spurious class action until judgment in the
class's favour had been levied was also decried by both judges[146] and

---

[140] FRCP 23(a)(1) (1938).

[141] FRCP 23(a)(2) (1938).

[142] FRCP 23(a)(3).

[143] S Burbank and S Farhang, 'Class Actions and the Counter-revolution against Federal
Litigation' (2017) 165 *University of Pennsylvania Law Review* 1495, 1499 (internal
citations omitted).

[144] J Rabiej, 'The Making of Class Action Rule 23 – What Were We Thinking?' (2005) 24
Mississippi College Law Journal 323, 331.

[145] R Murphy, 'Competing Ideologies at the Formation of the Federal Class Action Rule:
Legal Process versus Legal Liberalism' (2018) 10 *Drexel Law Review* 389, 400.

[146] *American Pipe & Construction Co v Utah*, 414 US 538, 547 (1974) ('[a] recurrent source
of abuse under the former Rule lay in the potential that members of the claimed class
could in some situations await developments in the trial or even final judgment on the
merits in order to determine whether participation would be favorable to their
interests').

academic commentary[147] as causing abuses within the US civil procedural system. The fact that spurious class actions were not accorded
a binding effect on absent class members who did not opt in also made
the possibility of settlement unattractive to defendants,[148] rendering
common grievances more burdensome to the courts where the class
members' claims were individually recoverable. All of this was a key
motivator for the enactment of the revised rule in 1966.

One of the most startling examples of duplicative and burdensome
litigation in the **United Kingdom** arose in the previously mentioned
bank charges litigation[149] – and although this did not lead to the generic
opt-out class action recommended by the Civil Justice Council, the
episode did generate some extraordinary figures, peaking at approximately 7,000–8,000 claims per month filed in the county courts at the
height of the litigation during March–May 2007. These were in addition
to the recourse which many bank customers had to the Financial
Ombudsman Service, and to claims management services.[150] The courts
had to deal with battles by the banks to stay blocks of these cases, with
about 30 per cent of those applications being resisted; with stock defences
being filed by the banks, and settlements ensuing, in many cases, either
a few days before the hearing or on the morning of the hearing itself; with
the risk of inconsistent judgments being delivered. The banks themselves
suffered, in rare but highly publicised cases, the ignominy of missing
a judgment by default and enduring a bailiff visiting the bank to tag
computers and other items.[151] The case was surely an exemplar of what
an opt-out class could have achieved[152] – although, to reiterate, this

---

[147] S Cohn, 'The New Federal Rules of Civil Procedure' (1966) 54 *Georgia Law Journal* 1204,
    1225 ('[t]he new rule eliminates the unfairness of what the Advisory Committee terms
    one-way intervention by a spurious class member, who, under the old rule, could remain
    uncommitted until the termination of the litigation'); M Carroll, 'Class Action Myopia'
    (2016) 65 *Duke Law Journal* 843, fn 50.

[148] J Underwood, 'Rationality, Multiplicity & Legitimacy: Federalization of the Interstate
    Class Action' (2004) 46 *South Texas Law Review* 391, fn 101, citing: E Sherman,
    'American Civil Justice in a Global Context' (2002) 52 *De Paul Law Review* 401, 404.

[149] Culminating in the test case: *OFT v Abbey National plc* [2009] UKSC 6, [2010] 1 AC 696.

[150] Indeed, the Ministry of Justice had to take the unusual step of issuing guidance, in
    recognition of the substantial role that claims management businesses were undertaking:
    *Claims Management Services Regulation: Claims in Respect of Bank Charges: Guidance
    Note* (27 July 2007).

[151] See, for further details of this extraordinary episode in English litigation: Mulheron, *The
    Reform of Collective Redress* (n 5), Section 17, 121–31.

[152] As argued by the author elsewhere: 'The Case for an Opt-out Class Action for European
    Member States: A Legal and Empirical Analysis' (2009) 15 *Columbia Journal of European
    Law* 409, 448–50; and 'Disgruntled Customers and Bank Charges: Class Action (Reform)

episode did not relate to the field of that anti-competitive conduct which ultimately became the subject of opt-out class action reform.

E   A Key Judicial Proponent for Reform

Ultimately, law reform is – or should be – a democratic, albeit political, process, involving, by necessity, members of the executive, law reformers, and informed 'interested citizens' on the one hand, and the government of the day on the other. Another 'actor' in the process, who can often assume a significant role, is that of senior judiciary who are prepared to support the reform initiative. Not only do such office-bearers frequently witness the shortcomings of the existing panoply of the law firsthand in the courtroom, but they also command the respect of government.

The **United Kingdom's** implementation of an opt-out regime for competition law grievances was notable for the extra-curial comments made by Sir Gerald Barling, the then-president of the Competition Appeal Tribunal, in 2011.[153] As well as noting that the decision in *Emerald* 'would appear to render the [representative] rule of doubtful assistance in a case where damages are an element of the cause of action', his Lordship added that 'there are a number of benefits that may flow from introducing an opt-out regime, at least in the UK', and that its 'main gain would be the removal of the often significant hurdle of enticing a sufficient number of consumers to sign up to a claim where its financial value to each claimant is relatively small, but where the collective loss is enormous'.[154] The president also noted that, in his view, defendants in competition law cases would be able to 'achieve closure more completely [under an opt-out regime] than at present'.[155] The importance of such comments, by a senior member of the judiciary in the United Kingdom, cannot be overstated.

The important contribution and impact of Wilcox J to the class actions reform process in **Australia** (via his membership of the ALRC during the 'grouped proceedings' project, and via his judgment in *E v*

Activity', in S Grundmann *et al.* (eds), *Financial Services, Financial Crisis and General European Contract Law: Failure and the Challenges of Contracting* (Wolters Kluwer, 2011), ch 11, 279–98.

[153] The Hon Mr Justice Barling, 'Collective Redress for Breach of Competition Law: A Case for Reform?' (2011) 10 *Competition Law Journal* 5.

[154] ibid, quotes at 11, 19–20, respectively.

[155] ibid, 19.

Australian Red Cross Socy)[156] has already been mentioned.[157] Reflecting a quarter of a century later, Wilcox J remarked that, as the Australian regime did not provide for a class action public fund, and as the government of the day announced that it did not intend to establish such a fund, 'I wondered whether anyone would ever use the new legislation'.[158] Additionally, Kirby J was an important supporter of class actions reform in Australia. A former president of the ALRC, he was involved in the class actions reference to the ALRC.[159] His Honour's strong dissenting opinion in the NSW Court of Appeal in *Carnie v Esanda Finance Corp Ltd*[160] was ultimately upheld on further appeal to the High Court, his reasoning paving the way for the representative action to proceed in that case. Displaying a purposive approach towards the wording of the representative rule, Kirby J remarked that:

> [o]nce these are excised, what remains is a proper case for a representative order. The class of person affected is clear, defined and now closed. The primary relief sought is a declaration as to the meaning of an Act of Parliament as it affects the members of that class in respect of which all of them will have a common interest and a common legal grievance. So far as the orders are concerned ... they seek relief which is wholly beneficial to all the persons represented.[161]

However, independently of that desire to make the *existing* procedural rules work for the collective good of aggrieved persons, Kirby J was a strong advocate of *additional* procedural tools, including the class action. Writing extra-curially in 1983, Kirby J contrasted the extensive federal causes of action in the United States with the more limited options in Australia at that time: '[i]n Australia, the same panoply of Federal causes of action susceptible to collection in federal class action procedures do not exist', and noted that, as of 1979, the ALRC had recommended the introduction of class actions into Australia, 'on

---

[156] (1991) 27 FCR 310.

[157] See Section D.

[158] The Hon Murray Wilcox, 'Class actions in Australia: Recollections of the Early Days', in Grave and Mould (eds), *25 Years of Class Actions* (n 6) ch 2, 7. The controversial subject of a public fund is explored in Chapter 4 herein, 'Government as Class Actions Funder'.

[159] Noted in ALRC, *Grouped Proceedings in the Federal Court* (Rep 46, 1988), 'Participants', at xvii.

[160] (1992) 29 NSWLR 382 (Gleeson CJ and Meagher JA in the majority).

[161] ibid, 403 (dissenting).

a tentative basis and subject to strict controls'.[162] His presidency of the ALRC[163] has been described as being 'a period characterised by remarkable vigour and innovation. He believed that all Australians should be able to participate in the law reform process.'[164] That ethos undoubtedly helped with the advancement of class actions reform in the jurisdiction, especially where political opposition to the enactment at the time was quite vociferous ('a rather loony proposal', and a bill that would 'involve major, some would even say revolutionary, changes', as one Senator said at the time).[165]

The reform which occurred in the **United States** in 1966, which amended FRCP 23 from the form of the 'spurious class action', was not, perhaps, identifiable to any particular judicial member, but there is no doubt that appellate courts rued the lack of utility provided by the spurious class action, which added to the momentum for reform. Take one such example, from the United States Court of Appeals for the Second Circuit:

> there still seems considerable confusion as to the meaning and effect of the third group of class actions authorized by FRCP 23(a)(3), a confusion not lessened by the load it bears in its popular legal cognomen of 'spurious class action.' There is perhaps something anomalous in apparent legal participation in a lawsuit by persons unnamed and unidentified as individuals who, unless they show themselves by intervening, remain legally unaffected by any action taken in the case. The legal rationale lags behind the practical utilities found in the device and its 'psychological value' on courts and potential litigants. It stands as an invitation to others affected to join in the battle and an admonition to the court to proceed with proper circumspection in creating a precedent which may actually affect non-parties, even if not legally *res judicata* as to them. . . . [but] it cannot make the case of the claimed representatives stronger, or give them rights they would not have of their own strength, or affect legally the rights or obligations of those who do not intervene.[166]

---

[162] M Kirby, *Reform the Law: Essays on the Renewal of the Australian Legal System* (Oxford University Press, 1983), 164, 168.

[163] During the period 1975–84.

[164] ALRC, *Annual Report* (Rep 90, 2000).

[165] *Hansard* (Commonwealth Senate, 13 November 1991, Senator Durack, at 3018–19). Others were, however, far more supportive, with Senator Spindler noting that, 'the greatest credit must go to the ALRC, whose report on this matter is of outstanding quality' (at 3023). For a description of the political backdrop, see V Morabito, 'Ideological Plaintiffs and Class Actions' (n 1) [6]. The relevant extracts of *Hansard* are conveniently located in App 4–7 of D Grave and K Adams, *Class Actions in Australia* (Lawbook Co, 2005).

[166] *All American Airways v Elderd*, 209 F 2d 247, 248 (2nd Cir, 1954).

Furthermore, Judge Frankel, an eminent and respected US jurist,[167] was (amongst other areas[168]) a key proponent of the FRCP 23 reforms, arguing that the amended rule would provide class members with small claims with an avenue by which to seek redress for alleged large-scale competition law infringements;[169] and that any fears that the rule was invalid and unconstitutional should be baseless, 'having in mind the weighty presumption of validity with which the Supreme Court's imprimatur invests the rule'.[170] Ultimately, that view was affirmed by the US Supreme Court.[171]

F   Previously Existing Reforms Were Ineffective

The enactment of legislation, a short time previously, which had proven to be less-than-useful, was undoubtedly an implicit 'motivator' to the achievement of class actions reform in several jurisdictions. After all, lawmakers do not enjoy enacting legislation for no reason or utility. Efforts to draft, consult upon, and then enact, legislation (whether primary or secondary) are disappointing, when they are futile. That has been a precursor to more substantive reform.

---

[167] Formerly Columbia Law School Dean, and variously described in academic scholarship as: 'a noted jurist prominent in public debates over judicial administration and the legal function': J Stempel, 'Erie under Advisement' (2011) 44 *Akron Law Review* 907, fn 175; a 'prominent jurist' of class actions law: M Black, 'Class Actions Pursuant to Tennessee Rule of Civil Procedure 23' (1979) 46 *Tennessee Law Review* 556, 571; and see too, the moving tribute to this legal scholar, judge, lawyer and reformer in: G Lynch, 'Marvin Frankel: A Reformer Reassessed' (2009) 21 *Federal Sentencing Reports* 235 ('Frankel was what used to be called a "lion of the bar" – a lawyer with a distinguished and varied career, much of it devoted to the lucrative private practice of law combined with leadership in establishment law reform activities'). The 'joke' related in the article (at fn 3) is always a sobering lesson worth remembering: 'Legal fame is transient. As the old joke . . . has it, a successful legal career has four stages: (1) Who's Frankel? (2) I want Frankel. (3) Get me someone like Frankel, only younger and cheaper. (4) Who's Frankel?'.

[168] Judge Frankel's work helped to establish sentencing guidelines for the US federal courts: https://en.wikipedia.org/wiki/Marvin_E._Frankel#Legacy; and see too, his groundbreaking book, *Law Without Order* (Hill & Wang, New York, 1973).

[169] M Frankel 'Amended Rule 23 From a Judge's Point of View', Paper presented at the symposium on Amended Rule 23, and published in: (1966) 32 *ABA Antitrust Law Journal* 251. Judge Frankel's thoughtful and erudite contributions to the interpretation of the rule were academically noted at the time, e.g.: B Kaplan, 'Continuing Work of the Civil Committee: 1966 Amendments of the Federal Rules of Civil Procedure' (1967) 81 *Harvard Law Review* 356, fn 155; C Wright, 'Class Actions' (1970) 47 *Federal Rules Decisions* 169; G Wright, 'The Cost-Internalization Case for Class Actions' (1969) 21 *Stanford Law Review* 383; and since, e.g.: *Newberg on Class Actions* (n 2), §1.10, 36–37.

[170] 'Some Preliminary Observations Concerning Civil Rule 23' (1967) 43 *Federal Rules Decisions* 39, 45.

[171] *Phillips Petroleum Co v Shutts*, 472 US 797, 105 S Ct 2965 (1985).

In **Victoria**, the preceding law reform report[172] only cited two cases[173] brought under the Victorian opt-in class action contained in the now-repealed ss 34 and 35 of the Supreme Court Act 1986, and concluded that the regime contained 'a number of legal barriers, which prevent reliance on the ss 34 and 35 procedure in circumstances where a class action is appropriate'.[174]

In the **United Kingdom**, that reality was also borne out by the now-repealed s 47B opt-in regime, noted previously.[175] Whilst one respondent to the Government's consultation suggested that a single litigated case[176] 'should not automatically lead to a conclusion that the current regime is failing',[177] the Government disagreed. Rather, it considered that the one case demonstrably proved that the regime was 'inadequate'.[178] Indeed, it was surely hard to conclude anything else, when Which? itself was on record as stating that it would not litigate another case whilst the regime remained an opt-in one.[179]

Moreover, having regard to the **Australian** federal regime, the ALRC[180] had regard to amendments to the South Australian Supreme Court Rules, by which to introduce a new representative action, enacted on 1 January 1987.[181] It was a development on the traditional representative action, in that it required 'common questions of fact or law requiring adjudication', and that it would not be a bar to the action if 'the relief claimed includes claims for damages that would require individual assessment'.[182] As the ALRC noted, the rule most definitely 'abandoned the "same interest" test',[183] and was 'wider in scope'[184] – but it also failed to provide much guidance as to what would be needed to advance such an action. Significantly, as at the date of the

---

[172] *Class Actions in Victoria* (n 69) (authored by V Morabito and J Epstein).
[173] *Zentahope Pty Ltd v Bellotti* (VSC App Div, 2 March 1992); and *Dagi v BHP Minerals Pty Ltd* (VSC, 8 November 1994).
[174] *Class Actions in Victoria* (n 69) [3.33].
[175] See Section B(2) above.
[176] *Consumers' Assn (Which?) v JJB Sports plc.*
[177] *Private Actions in Competition Law: Government Response* (2013) [5.2], citing: Herbert Smith submission.
[178] ibid, [3.6].
[179] Quoted in: *Reform of Collective Redress* (n 5) 40–41.
[180] *Grouped Proceedings in the Federal Court* (Rep 46, 1988) [44].
[181] Supreme Court Rules 1987 (SA), r 34.01, and reproduced in *Grouped Proceedings*, ibid, App C, 'Other Models for Class Actions'. That rule has since been repealed and replaced by the following representative proceeding: Supreme Court Civil Rules 2006 (SA), Div 3, rr 80–84.
[182] ibid, rr 34.01(1) and 34.03(a), respectively.
[183] *Grouped Proceedings* (1988) 198.
[184] ibid, [45].

ALRC's 1988 report on class actions, the rule had not been used once.[185] The ALRC was clearly committed to producing a new regime which provided more fulsome guidance and utility for resolving collective disputes than the South Australian model had supplied.

G   The Spectacle of 'Going Elsewhere'

The potential prospect of domestic class members having to look to another 'legal backyard' in order to have their disputes resolved heralds the embarrassing and frustrating spectacle of domestic litigants having another jurisdiction's courts determining their rights, in the absence of 'anything better back home'.

A recent example of that unwelcome scenario occurred in the state of **Queensland**. The Brisbane floods litigation arose from the inundation of land downstream of Wivenhoe Dam by floodwater from the Brisbane River and tributary streams in January 2011. In the absence of any opt-out class action then-enacted in Queensland, litigation was commenced in the neighbouring state of New South Wales,[186] which *did* have an opt-out class action available for use.[187] The New South Wales Supreme Court has jurisdiction over the subject matter of the dispute, and over the Queensland individuals and businesses who are claiming compensation for the loss and damages suffered.[188] The merits of the claim are yet to be decided at the time of writing.[189] However, the fact that the floods litigation ended up being adjudicated in a competitive neighbouring state jurisdiction attracted both media[190]

---

[185]   Noted ibid, [44].

[186]   *Rodriguez & Sons Pty Ltd v Queensland Bulk Water Supply Authy* [2015] NSWSC 838 and [2015] NSWSC 1352; and *Lynch v Queensland Bulk Water Authy trading as Seqwater*, which commenced on 23 December 2016.

[187]   Civil Procedure Act 2005, Pt 10, in force 4 March 2011.

[188]   Pursuant to the Jurisdiction of Courts (Cross-Vesting) Act 1987 (Qld) and equivalent legislation in all Australian States, including that of New South Wales, s 4 provides that: '[t]he Supreme Court of another State or of a Territory has and may exercise original and appellate jurisdiction with respect to State matters'. These statutes were enacted as part of a national scheme to create a national legal system.

[189]   The trial is part-heard; with interlocutory skirmishings relating to expert evidence, e.g.: *Rodriguez & Sons Pty Ltd v Queensland Bulk Water Supply Authy t/as Seqwater (No 18)* [2018] NSWSC 1828; and, separately, *(No 19)* [2019] NSWSC 262; hearings recommenced in March 2019; and judgment on the claims of negligence, trespass and nuisance is awaited at the time of writing.

[190]   See, e.g.: 'Queensland floods class action to begin in NSW Supreme Court' *Weekend Australian* (Sydney, 8 July 2014); '2011 Queensland Floods: Class action begins in NSW Supreme Court' *Courier-Mail* (Brisbane, 3 December 2017); 'New flood class

and Parliamentary[191] comment, and was undoubtedly a key trigger for the enactment of the Queensland opt-out class action in 2015.[192]

In **Manitoba**, the preceding law reform commission report[193] made the point that, in the breast implant litigation which was settled in an Alabama court,[194] that settlement excluded Ontario and Québec residents because those Canadian jurisdictions had their own opt-out class actions. However, other Canadian provincial residents were included in that US class action as non-residents, but:

> on the much less favourable terms for non-Americans. In short, any resident of Manitoba may be included in class proceedings regimes which have an extra-Manitoba aspect even if such a proceeding could not be commenced in this jurisdiction. Accordingly, any discussion of whether Manitoba ought to adopt a class proceedings regime must consider whether Manitobans should be content to leave proceedings respecting mass claims to Ontario, British Columbia, Québec, and American federal and state courts, plaintiffs, and lawyers.[195]

In **Alberta** too, the relevant Institute remarked that, because of the restrictions associated with Alberta's representative rule, in particular,

---

action seeks compensation for what might have been' *Brisbane Times* (Brisbane, 23 March 2017).

[191] See: *Hansard* (Legislative Assembly, 55th Parliament, 1st Session, 8 November 2016, Mr Ryan, col 4285, at 4.12pm) ('[f]or many, many years the majority of those groups in Queensland who would like to bring a class action have either had to go interstate or into the federal jurisdiction to bring those causes of action because it was just too difficult to bring a class action in the Queensland regime. It was nearly impossible . . . the changes to the Civil Proceedings Act will . . . ensure that those people who do have a class action do not have to go interstate and incur the additional stress and cost associated with going interstate or into the federal jurisdiction to bring those class actions. That will be very welcome.'). See too: *Hansard* (Legislative Assembly, 55th Parliament, 1st Session, 8 November 2016, Ms Howard, col 4287, at 4.27pm); and *Hansard* (Legislative Assembly, 55th Parliament, 1st Session, 8 November 2016, Mr Dick, col 4311, at 5.09pm) ('[w]e live in a competitive federation and our courts in Queensland, particularly our Supreme Court, needs the opportunity to supervise class actions initiated in this jurisdiction. Again, that is not just about the state court system, particularly the Supreme Court, being competitive; it is about providing justice to Queenslanders through the class action mechanism that has required them in the past to seek redress through jurisdictions outside of Queensland. That is a very important reform.').

[192] Civil Proceedings Act 2011, Pt 13A, inserted by the Limitation of Actions (Child Sexual Abuse) and Other Legislation Amendment Act 2016 (Qld). The regime took effect on 1 March 2017.

[193] *Class Proceedings* (Rep 100, 1999).

[194] *In re Silicone Gel Breast Implant Product Liab Litig*, (1994) US Dist LEXIS 12521 (ND Ala, 1 September 1994).

[195] *Class Proceedings* (1999) 15 (internal citations omitted).

'Alberta citizens have sometimes been obliged to pursue their claims in other jurisdictions.'[196]

The incorporation of non-residents in a domestic class action has developed into a complex and divergent issue in opt-out class actions jurisprudence in the Comparator Jurisdictions, as discussed later.[197] For present purposes, the unequal treatment of domestic and non-resident class members has undoubtedly been a trigger for class actions reform.

That scenario emerged in **Australia** too. In his fascinating discussion of many product liability and other claims involving Australian residents which were litigated in the USA, Cashman remarks that, '[i]n order to make a fully informed decision [as to whether Australian claimants should bring legal claims in foreign jurisdictions], it is necessary to consider a number of legal, logistical, evidentiary, procedural and pecuniary considerations'.[198] The author proceeds to make the point that, '[t]he historical unavailability of class action procedures in Australia was a significant consideration weighing in favour of seeking to bring proceedings in the United States, before the introduction of class actions in Australia'.[199] Several of the cases cited by that author,[200] in which Australian claimants commenced claims in the United States and/ or participated in judicially approved class settlement agreements in that jurisdiction, were notably from that pre-1992 period. Moreover, the *Dalkon Shield* litigation,[201] which was commenced in the NSW Supreme Court as a series of lead claims representing approximately 1,500 women – but which was adjourned, pending the outcome of proceedings in the USA – was cited by the ALRC, in its 1988 report, as

---

[196] *Class Actions* (Rep 85, 2000) [99].

[197] See Chapter 5, 'Government as "Gate-keeper": Cross-Border Class Actions'.

[198] P Cashman, *Class Action Law and Practice* (Federation Press, 2007) 673, and see the further detailed discussion of several relevant cases in ch 10, 673–710.

[199] ibid, 674.

[200] e.g., *Corrigan v Bjork-Shiley Corp*, 182 Cal App 3d 166 (9 June 1986) (heart valve); *In re Silicone Gel Breast Implant Prods Liab Litig (MDL 926) Lindsey v Dow Corning Corp (Settlement Approval)* (ND Alabama, 1 September 1994); and re an unsuccessful attempt to join the English litigation regarding the Myodil contrast medium; and re the discontinuance of the English Benzodiazepine drug litigation because of withdrawal of legal aid. The latter tops the list of legal aid funding (£30M) allocated to group litigation in England for the period 1995–2005: Mulheron, *Reform of Collective Redress* (n 5) Table 11, at 76.

[201] This concerned an intrauterine contraceptive device. Claims against AH Robins (whether in Australia or the USA) variously related to alleged: loss of fertility; pelvic inflammatory disease; sepsis; miscarriages; and death, arising from the use of the device. Also discussed in Cashman (n 198) 686–87.

an example illustrating how '[a] grouping procedure would enable pro-ceedings to be commenced on behalf of all affected'.[202]

In the **United Kingdom** too, the spectacle of price-fixed victims having to join a US class action in order to participate in a judicially sanctioned settlement drew attention to just how lacking the landscape of private enforcement of competition law was in the United Kingdom. In the *British Airways/Virgin Fuel Surcharge Cartel Settlement*, approved by the Northern District of California,[203] the claim concerned price-fixed fuel surcharges paid by passengers (individuals and businesses) of BA and Virgin, on long-haul passenger fares between August 2004 and March 2006. Those class members domiciled in the United Kingdom were certified for the purposes of settlement as two sub-classes: BA's UK Settlement Class, and Virgin's UK Settlement Class.[204] Separate class representatives were appointed for those UK Settlement Classes.[205] The US District Court asserted jurisdiction over 'each of the parties to the Settlement Agreements, and the members of the proposed Settlement Classes'.[206] The settlement was rightly praised as a legal milestone, as being the first time that a domestic US class and an English class had been treated entirely equivalently in respect of the compensation awarded in a US class action.[207] However, the fact that the UK class members had to resort to the US settlement at all followed directly from the fact that the representative rule – of the type litigated in *Emerald Supplies* – was so patently ineffective.[208]

In the Civil Justice Council's analysis of collective redress in 2008, the point was also made that, in several identified actions across a range of subject matters (including blood contamination[209] and securities

---

[202] *Grouped Proceedings* (Rep 46, 1988) [63], citing *Burford v AH Robins Pty Ltd* (NSWSC, 12530/1986).

[203] *In re Intl Air Transport Surcharge Antitrust Litig*, 2008 US Dist LEXIS 500415 (ND Cal, 25 April 2008, Judge Breyer), referring to settlement agreements dated 15 February 2008 approved pursuant to FRCP 23(e).

[204] Long Form Notice, order 3, p 3–4.

[205] ibid, order 4, pp 5–6.

[206] ibid, order 1, p 3.

[207] e.g., C Ruckin, 'Cohen Milstein Lands $200M BA–Virgin Settlement' (*Legal Week*, 15 February 2008).

[208] Discussed further by the author in: 'The Case for an Opt-out Class Action for European Member States' (n 152) 441–48; and 'The Recognition and *Res Judicata* Effect of a United States Class Actions Judgment in England: A Rebuttal of *Vivendi*' (2012) 75 *Modern Law Review* 180, 186–90.

[209] *Factor VIII or IX Concentrate Blood Prods Liab Litig*, 408 F Supp 2d 569, 576–82 (ND Ill 2006), aff'd: 484 F 3d 951 (7th Cir, 2007).

litigation[210]), English claimants 'sought to be joined to a US opt-out action, in the absence of any opt-out regime in England under which the action could have been commenced. This has not always ended happily for English claimants, as both judicial decisions under FRCP 23, and the practical experience of UK law firms, attest.'[211] It was certainly one of the factors which prompted the CJC's recommendation that a generic class action ought to be introduced into the civil procedure of the jurisdiction[212] (as yet unenacted).

H   Public Regulators Are Unable or Unwilling to Pursue Redress

Governmental agencies and statutorily created regulators may act in particular sectors of society (e.g., in respect of financial services, data protection, competition law, health, and the securities market) in order to recover compensation on behalf of aggrieved citizens and businesses. The facts that: 'the *locus* of information about the identity of injurers' can be difficult for victims to ascertain, such that 'society may need to rely instead on public investigation and prosecution';[213] and regulators have the ability to render three types of intervention (fines, behavioural remedies, and structural remedies) so as to create a deterrent effect,[214] are just two rationales that support the use of public enforcement where appropriate. The role of 'public enforcement', and its comparative rationales, costs, and outcomes with those of 'private enforcement', whilst lying outside the scope of this book, have been discussed in detail elsewhere.[215]

---

[210] *In re Parmalat Securities Litig,* 497 F Supp 2d 526, 538–40 (SDNY, 2007); *In re SCOR Holding (Switzerland) AG Litig,* 537 F Supp 2d 556, 569 (SDNY, 2008).

[211] CJC, *Improving Access to Justice: Final Report* (n 5) Pt 7, 99.

[212] ibid, Recommendation 3, p 5, and discussed further at 145–50.

[213] M Polinsky and S Shavell, *Public Enforcement of Law* (Stanford Institute for Economic Policy Research, May 2006) 2, available at: https://siepr.stanford.edu/sites/default/files/publications/05–16_0.pdf.

[214] K Huschelrath and S Peyer, *Public and Private Enforcement of Competition Law: A Differentiated Approach* (CCP Working Paper 13–5, April 2013) 3–4.

[215] For discussion of regulatory redress, consumer ombudsmen, and statutory compensation schemes, see, e.g.: K Huschelrath and H Schweitzer (eds), *Public and Private Enforcement of Competition Law in Europe: Legal and Economic Perspectives* (Springer-Verlag, ZEW Economic Studies Series Title, 2014); *Ombudsman Schemes: Guidance for Departments* (Cabinet Office, April 2010); *An Introduction to Collective Redress Schemes* (Pinsent Masons, April 2016); I Kim, 'Public Enforcement', in A Marciano and G Ramello (eds), *Encyclopaedia of Law and Economics* (Springer, 2016); C Hodges and S Voet, *Delivering Collective Redress: New Technologies* (Hart Publishing, 2018); H Jackson and J Zhang, 'Private and Public Enforcement of Securities Regulations', in

Undoubtedly, if public enforcers had the resources and willingness both to prosecute culpable defendants, and to pursue compensatory redress on behalf of victims of that behaviour, then the need for private enforcement via civil litigation would be reduced, if not obviated. However, the inability or unwillingness of public regulators to fulfil that role has been a key trigger in prompting opt-out class actions reform.

In **Alberta**, the Law Institute agreed with the view that class members could not afford 'to leave the enforcement of standards to government'.[216] In **Ontario** too, the Law Commission considered[217] various alternatives to an expanded class actions procedure, including 'a revamped system of administrative agencies or small claims courts, or a new network of bodies dispensing arbitration or mediation services', but concluded that it would require intense resourcing which may not be forthcoming, and would develop ad hoc solutions to grievances which did not necessarily have precedential effect.

In **Australia**, the ALRC noted that, '[i]n some cases of multiple wrong-doing, action can be taken by a public agency either to seek individual remedies on behalf of the persons affected, to obtain a general remedy or, in some cases, to inquire into the circumstances and thereby assist individuals in pursuing their own remedies'.[218] However, the limitations of this arm of enforcement were candidly admitted. The ALRC noted that the essential focus of public enforcement agencies 'is regulatory'; that the pursuit of redress in the case of multiple wrongdoing, 'is incidental' to that purpose in many cases; and that 'the effective operation of the provisions depends upon the policy or resources of the relevant agency, rather than on the needs of a particular individual.'[219] The ALRC concluded that '[a]ction by public authorities cannot be regarded as an effective substitute for private action'.[220] Subsequent to that report, the two principal corporate regulators in Australia[221] were noted as being keen to extol the virtues that private enforcement had provided to the Australian landscape, and had 'expressed support for the role that class

---

J Gordon and W Ringe (eds), *The Oxford Handbook of Corporate Law and Governance* (Oxford University Press, 2018).

[216] Alberta Law Reform Institute, *Class Actions* (Rep 85, 2000) [91].

[217] *Report on Class Actions* (1982) 207–11.

[218] *Grouped Proceedings* (1988) [33].

[219] ibid, [36], referring to the then Trade Practices Commission and National Companies and Securities Commission.

[220] ibid, [38].

[221] The Australian Securities and Investments Commission and the Australian Competition and Consumer Commission.

actions play in providing access to justice and assisting the regulation of corporate misconduct'.[222]

In the **United Kingdom**, the Government was even more reluctant to give much credence to the effectiveness of public enforcement, at least in the field of UK competition law. It stated that:

> [t]here are many cases where it would be inappropriate for the Office of Fair Trading, the sectoral regulators or the European Commission to take action. In prioritising its work, the OFT considers a range of factors, including impact, strategic significance, risks and resources. This prioritisation allows the OFT to focus on cases which cause the most significant detriment to the UK economy as a whole or involve the most important deterrent effect (or both). However, it leaves a number of cases where it would be an inefficient use of public resource to bring the full force of an investigation to bear. Furthermore, even in cases where the OFT does find a breach of competition law, although a fine is imposed, there is no specific provision to make redress to those who have suffered loss.[223]

The relevant Secretary of State put it baldly, that:

> While the public competition authorities are at the heart of the regime, they have finite resources and cannot do everything. What is needed from Government is to create the legal framework that will empower individual consumers and businesses to represent their own interests.[224]

This view was borne out by the fact that the lack of private enforcement in anti-competitive conduct, following on from infringement findings, was stark, with the number of follow-on actions being brought in UK courts being limited to a handful only.[225]

I   The 'Human Element'

It is significant that the reform push which led to the introduction of class actions reform in several of the Comparator Jurisdictions had regard to

---

[222] The Hon Justice Bernard Murphy and V Morabito, 'The First 25 Years: Has the Class Action Regime Hit the Mark on Access to Justice?', in Grave and Mould (eds), *25 Years of Class Actions* (n 6) [3.2.5], citing a number of statements and sources to that effect.

[223] BIS, *Private Actions in Competition Law: A Consultation on Options for Reform* (2012) [3.15] (footnotes omitted).

[224] Rt Hon Dr Vince Cable MP, Secretary of State for Business, Innovation and Skills, writing the preface of: *Private Actions for Competition Law: Government Response* (January 2013) 3.

[225] Discussed in: Mulheron, *Reform of Collective Redress* (n 5) Pt III, Section 9, referring to infringement findings made by the Office of Fair Trading and the European Commission 2001–7.

the 'non-cost barriers' which litigants confront, in seeking redress for alleged grievances. This 'human element' – having regard to the often intangible aspects of what causes ordinary people, and SMEs, to hesitate to sue – was important. It provided a further impetus for reform.

In Canadian class actions reform, the Law Commissions of **Manitoba,**[226] **Ontario,**[227] and **Alberta,**[228] all referred to the social or psychological reasons as to why people fail to pursue legal remedies to which they are actually or potentially entitled.

In **Australia**, the ALRC referred to three points in its final report: the ignorance which litigants may have of the law; language barriers; and a possible fearfulness of the steps needed to enforce their rights against defendants.[229] Earlier in the Discussion Paper, the ALRC mentioned several further barriers that may hinder access to justice, *viz*: the practicalities and inconvenience of attending court to resolve the dispute; fear, or cynicism, of the legal system; the consequences which may flow for the litigant from the litigation; and 'a feeling of helplessness', the 'David-versus-Goliath' element of litigation against Government or big business, particularly where costs-shifting applies.[230] The illness of the claimants may also feature. Recall, for example, the dire life expectancies which several of the litigants were confronting, following HIV infection from blood donations, in New South Wales – this was explicitly referred to by Wilcox J in *E v Australian Red Cross Society*, as a reason as to why collective evidence on some of the common issues of fact or of law would have probably led to 'the earlier finalisation of the whole litigation'.[231] In **Victoria** too, the reluctance about suing – 'attributable to a number of reasons other than lack of interest in the class suit' – was explored.[232]

In the **United Kingdom**, the author's empirical study[233] in 2008 revealed no fewer than almost 20 factors (noted in Table 2.1 overpage) which could deter would-be claimants from suing individually, or from opting in to group litigation. They are simply reflections of human nature in all of its guises.

---

[226] *Class Proceedings* (Rep 100, 1999) 2.
[227] *Report on Class Actions* (1982) 127–29.
[228] *Class Actions* (Rep 85, 2000) [101], [114], [119].
[229] *Grouped Proceedings in the Federal Court* (Rep 46, 1988) [15].
[230] ALRC, *Access to the Courts II: Class Actions* (DP 11, 1979) [17].
[231] [1991] FCA 20, (1991) 27 FCR 310, 314–15.
[232] *Class Actions in Victoria* (n 69) [3.17]–[3.24], quote at [3.18].
[233] Mulheron, *Reform of Collective Redress* (n 5), Table 5, 33–34.

Table 2.1 *Why litigants may not wish to opt in*

The litigants . . .

Social or psychological reasons:
(1)   do not feel engaged with the legal process, or have a very limited understanding of the legal system;
(2)   do not consider that the system will deliver cheaply and efficiently (i.e. a cynicism);
(3)   have language or cultural differences which puts them off the litigious process;
(4)   feel antagonistic towards other class members;
(5)   believe that litigation is never useful or worthwhile;
(6)   fear shame or stigmatisation because of the claim that they would otherwise make;
(7)   do not wish to revisit a painful or traumatic episode in their past;

Reasons to do with the defendant:
(8)   fear recriminations or reprisals from the defendants, if they sue individually;
(9)   could be 'bought off' by goodwill gestures from defendants;
(10) retain loyalty and goodwill towards the defendant, thereby deterring litigation;

Procedural reasons:
(11) are beyond the reach of knowing of the existence of a cause of action on their part;
(12) mistakenly perceive that they are already part of a claim, and that they will receive a beneficial outcome from someone else's litigation;
(13) believe that some other avenue will deliver compensation to them (e.g., public enforcement, or a criminal compensation fund);
(14) prefer to 'piggy back' on someone else's litigious effort, rather than to pursue the action themselves;
(15) believe that their claims are statute-barred, and not worth pursuing;
(16) believe that they lack sufficient documentary evidence to pursue their claim, and have not checked whether some other avenue (e.g., sworn statements) may be sufficient;

Economic reasons:
(17) are put off by the costs implications of suing (particularly if they lose);
(18) think that the litigation is 'not worth the candle', given their own very small individual claim;
(19) prefer to 'go it alone', because they think that they will recover more compensation that way.

These factors were cited in the CJC's report,[234] as another reason for its recommendation that a better procedural tool, *viz*, an opt-out class action, was warranted. Potential ignorance of the law in this field – or the sheer difficulty of proving covert cartels, or of the situation which would have prevailed in the absence of the alleged anti-competitive conduct – were also referred to in the Government Response to the Consultation on *Private Actions in Competition Law*.[235]

Finally, it is worth noting that one of the key drivers for the enactment of the amended FRCP 23 in the **United States** was the desire to facilitate lawsuits for civil rights plaintiffs. In the 1960s, these rights had 'come to the fore', and '[e]quipping these rights-holders was at the heart of the revisions of Rule 23, drafted in the 1960s'.[236] Although it was the declaratory, rather than the damages, class action that was the focus of civil rights claims,[237] the US federal class action for damages, contained in FRCP 23(b)(3), has also been used for that purpose.[238] However, and notably, an oft-cited US empirical study of class actions which was undertaken by the Rand Institute remarked that 'the world of class actions in 1995–96 was primarily a world of Rule 23(b)(3) damage class actions, not the world of civil rights and other social policy reform litigation that John Frank tells us the 1966 rule drafters had in mind'.[239]

---

[234] *Improving Access to Justice: Final Report* (n 5) 100.

[235] ibid, [3.12].

[236] See the discussion in, e.g.: J Resnik, '"Vital" State Interests: From Representative Actions for Fair Labor Standards to Pooled Trusts, Class Actions, and MDLs in the Federal Courts' (2017) 165 *University of Pennsylvania Law Review* 1765, 1780, 1788, 1797; D Marcus, 'The History of the Modern Class Action, Part I' (2013) 90 *Washington University Law Review* 587, 608.

[237] See *US Advisory Committee's Note to FRCP 23* (1966) ('[i]llustrative [of (b)(2) actions] are various actions in the civil-rights field where a party is charged with discriminating unlawfully against a class, usually one whose members are incapable of specific enumeration'); and Kaplan, 'Continuing Work of the Civil Committee' (n 169) 389 ('[n]ew subdivision (b)(2) builds on experience mainly, but not exclusively, in the civil rights field').

[238] See, e.g., the case law discussed in: *Newberg on Class Actions* (n 2) §4.14.

[239] D Hensler *et al*, *Class Action Dilemmas: Pursuing Public Goals for Private Gain* (RAND Institute for Civil Justice, 2000) 53. See too (at 12): '[t]he race relations echo of [the 1960s] was always in the committee room. If there was [a] single, undoubted goal of the committee, the energizing force which motivated the whole rule, it was the firm determination to create a class action system which could deal with civil rights and, explicitly, segregation. The one part of the rule which was never doubted was (b)(2) and without its high utility, in the spirit of the times, we might well have had no rule at all.'

J Conclusion

For jurisdictions such as South Africa, the United Kingdom, Western Australia, and Hong Kong, where opt-out class actions recommendations remain unenacted, then pointing to an ongoing 'evidence of need' will be essential to achieving the desired outcome. After all, law reform is a 'long end game'. The 'elephantine gestation period' is fairly common across the jurisdictions.

For those jurisdictions which are presently considering opt-out reform, or which have recommended opt-in law reform in the past, the various 'lessons' from class actions reform which have arisen in the Comparator Jurisdictions and which share considerable commonality, may be of utility. Evidence of the need for reform – by reference to, say, a leading problematical case, or missing cases, or judicial efficiencies being witnessed under the existing regimes – is essential. A high-profile judicial supporter of the reform proposals is undoubtedly helpful, standing apart from the policy and executive functions. Any recent legislative enactments which failed to quite 'fit the bill' may assist greatly to emphasise the need for further change. Attempts by domestic litigants to seek redress in other jurisdictions (whether successfully, or with disappointing outcomes) may demonstrate how the domestic legal landscape is deficient. Empirical evidence of how ordinary litigants find the existing legal landscape, and the limitations of public enforcement being able to deliver redress to those litigants, may also supplement the 'evidence-of-need' evidentiary basis in any law reform project.

As a final concluding point: whether a government should wish to enact a class action, because of a desire to deter unlawful conduct and modify the behaviour of a particular defendant, or category of defendant, is rather a moot point, and for this reason, this factor has **not** been included in the motivators discussed in this chapter. Undoubtedly, some law reform opinion from the Comparator Jurisdictions (*viz*, Canada[240] and the United Kingdom[241]) has regarded behaviour modification as one of the true objectives of the class action device. US

---

[240] Manitoba LRC, *Class Proceedings* (1999) 28, 30,35; Alberta Law Reform Institute, *Class Actions* (2000) [115]; Ontario LRC, *Report on Class Actions* (1982) 140–46; Rules Committee of the Federal Court of Canada, *Class Proceedings in the Federal Court of Canada* (DP, 2000) 13.

[241] BIS, *Private Actions in Competition Law: Government Response* (2013) 6 (the implementation of an opt-out class action would 'act as a further deterrent to anyone thinking of breaking the law'), and [7.17].

courts[242] have long maintained that the enforcement of laws and the deterrence of violations is an important consequence of achieving class certification, whilst Canadian cases have reiterated that class actions 'generat[e] "a sharper sense of obligation to the public by those whose actions affect large numbers of people".'[243] It enhances accountability – '[c]lass actions thus deter repeated breaches because defendants recognize they will continue to be held accountable to the public.'[244] But not all law reform opinion has agreed, regarding any deterrent effect of class actions reform as a mere by-product of what is a compensatory regime.[245] Furthermore, the Law Commission of Ontario has recently stated that, '[n]otwithstanding the importance of behaviour modification to class action theory, little is known about the extent to which defendants are either specifically or generally deterred from wrongdoing as a result of class actions. . . . interviewees offered some specific examples: in employee over-time cases, employers changed policies as a result of litigation; payday loans litigation contributed to legislative changes in the industry; . . . while few interviewees could prove that class actions encourage behaviour modifica-tion, almost all interviewees interviewed believed it to be true.'[246] The Commission will be undertaking the valuable exercise of testing empirical and anecdotal evidence regarding the behaviour modification objective. For

---

[242] e.g.: *US Parole Comm v Geraghy*, 445 US 388, 403, 100 S Ct 1202 (1980); *Deposit Guaranty National Bank, Jackson, Missouri v Roper*, 445 US 326, 339, 100 S Ct 1166 (1980).

[243] Noted in, e.g.: *Williams v Canon Canada Inc* [2011] ONSC 6571, [124]; *78115 Ontario Inc v Sears Canada Inc* [2010] ONSC 4571, [30]; *Norman v Thunder Bay Regional Health Sciences Centre* [2015] ONSC 3252, [34]; *Hollick v Toronto (City)* [2001] SCC 68, [2001] 3 SCR 158, [15]; *Western Canadian Shopping Centres Inc v Dutton* [2001] SCC 46, [2001] 2 SCR 534, [27]; *Penney v Bell Canada* [2010] ONSC 2801, [45], all citing: Ontario Attorney-General's Advisory Committee, *Report on Class Action Reform* (1990) 17. Earlier Canadian case law is discussed in: Mulheron, *The Class Action* (n 9) 63–66.

[244] *Elliot v Joseph Brant Hosp* [2013] ONSC 124, [41], discussing how infection control practices in hospitals changed in light of the events that gave rise to this class action, where it was alleged that the defendant was negligent in its operation of Brant Hospital, which caused 223 persons to be infected with C difficile from 2006–7, of which 91 died.

[245] See, e.g., the Scottish and Australian LRCs, that the 'sole proper object [of a class action] is to obtain compensation', and that any 'greater enforcement of legal liabilities [was] incidental' to the primary goal of providing access to the remedy that the law prescribes: respectively in *Multi-Party Actions* (1996) [2.23]; and *Grouped Proceedings in the Federal Court* (Rep 46, 1988) [67], [323]. For this reason, the author discusses deterrence as a 'non-common objective' of class actions reform: *The Class Action* (n 9) 63.

[246] *Class Actions: Objectives, Experiences and Reforms* (CP, March 2018) 25–26. See earlier, the comment by a principal researcher on that project: J Kalajdizic, 'Consumer (In)Justice: Reflections on Canadian Consumer Class Actions' (2011) 50 *Canadian Business Law Journal* 356, n 49 ('[w]hether corporate and governmental defendants actually modify future conduct as a direct consequence of settlement payments is simply unknown').

present purposes, however, the author does not treat a government's wish to modify defendant behaviour as a motivator of class actions reform. Compensatory redress is, and always has been, the primary motivator of such regimes.

RECOMMENDATIONS: GOVERNMENT AS CLASS ACTIONS ENABLER

§ 2.1 Upon a review of a civil procedural landscape, class actions reform may tend to be indicated, where a number of the following circumstances are present – where:

(1) the existing procedural regimes are struggling, or unable, to cope with group actions, because the requirements contained within those regimes cannot be met, whether because of legislative drafting or judicial interpretation;

(2) a number of 'missing cases' are recognised, i.e., where mass disasters, regulatory fines, equivalent litigation elsewhere, yield no compensatory redress in the domestic landscape, or where anecdotal evidence from claimant lawyers points to 'deserving' cases not instituted;

(3) multiple claims arising out of the same dispute or event create burdensome or duplicative litigation;

(4) a senior and respected judicial figure emphasises the need for class actions reform, either curially or extra-curially;

(5) legislative regimes which were enacted in order to diversify and expand the collective redress regimes available have been under-utilised or otherwise unsuccessful;

(6) attempts have been made to create 'add-on' classes of domestic class members to class actions instituted in other jurisdictions, and another 'backyard';

(7) public regulators either state on the record, or exhibit from their litigious (non)activity, that they are unable or unwilling to devote the resources necessary to institute civil actions for compensatory redress, over and above their public enforcement function; and

(8) empirical and/or anecdotal evidence suggests that groups of people or businesses have been unwilling to litigate grievances or disputes, for economic, social, psychological, or personal reasons.

§ 2.2 The potential for class actions regimes to modify defendant behaviour and to create a deterrent effect upon potential defendants or across an industry or sector of enterprise/society may be a by-product of litigation, but should not be regarded as a motivator or objective of class actions reform. Compensatory redress (e.g., damages, restitutionary relief, and other permissible damages awards) is the objective.

3

Government as Class Actions Designer

A Introduction

The introduction of any opt-out class action regime merits a close analysis of the strengths and weaknesses with opt-out models which have manifested elsewhere. With well over 150 years of combined opt-out regime experience in the Comparator Jurisdictions to draw upon, it is evident that there have been many significant design issues for lawmakers – be they the judiciary, rule-makers or legislators – when deciding how to frame the regime.

This chapter posits that the design of a class action regime is necessarily underpinned by **two** significant features, as Figure 3.1 overpage shows:

Of course, design is not set in stone. For example, the US federal class actions rule was amended on 1 December 2018.[1] The purpose of those 'meaningful, but not breathtaking'[2] amendments was 'to take account of issues that have emerged since the rule was last amended in 2003';[3] to 'modernize' class actions procedure in relation to the giving of class

---

[1] The amendments resulted from the evaluative work undertaken by a subcommittee of the US Advisory Committee on Civil Rules which commenced in 2014. The Supreme Court approved the amendments on 26 April 2018 (see letter from Roberts J to the Speaker of the House of Representatives of the same date, available at: www.supremecourt.gov/orders/courtorders/frcv18_5924.pdf). The changes were communicated to Congress, and by their taking no action, the changes took effect on 1 December 2018. A current version of FRCP 23 is conveniently available at: www.federalrulesofcivilprocedure.org/frcp/title-iv-parties/rule-23-class-actions/.

[2] As noted, and usefully described, in: J Barkett, *The 2018 Amendments to the Federal Class Actions Rule* (American Bar Assn, 2018), available at: www.americanbar.org/content/dam/aba/administrative/litigation/materials/2017–2018/2018-sac/written-materials/miami-class-actions-amendments-to-the-federal-class.pdf). See too: *A Practitioner's Guide to the December 2018 Federal Rule Amendments* (Practical Law, 1 December 2018).

[3] *US Advisory Committee Note to Rule 23* (2018), 1.

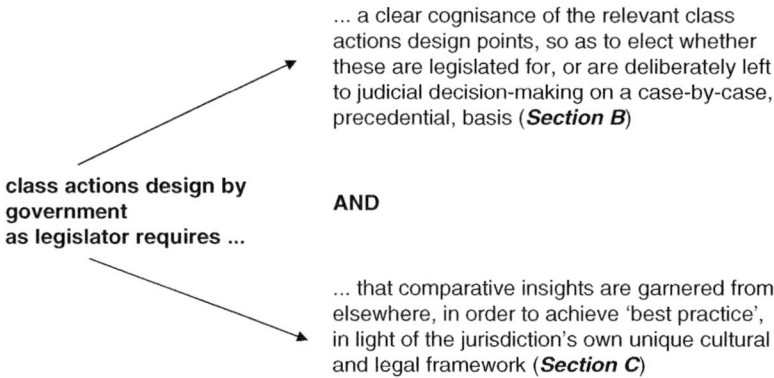

Figure 3.1 Government as 'designer' of the class action.

actions notice;[4] whilst also formalising and unifying practices relating to class actions settlement which many federal courts had already been putting into effect.[5] Moreover, the British Columbia class actions statute was amended in 2018 to create multijurisdictional opt-out class actions,[6] significantly converting their regime from the former requirement that non-residents had to opt in to a British Columbia domestic class action.[7] As discussed later,[8] that amendment likely had political momentum, in that it rendered British Columbia a more attractive jurisdiction in which to file national and global class actions (with all the attendant jurisdictional ramifications that those actions entail). Further, at the time of writing, the Law Commission of

---

[4] For example, the new FRCP 23(c)(2)(B) permits notice of class certification via 'electronic means, or other appropriate means'. This terminology will permit notice by email, text, and social media postings, thus expediting and modernising class action notice. Hence, '[t]he amendment should streamline and simplify the current process, which generally provides notice through first-class mail or publication': M Crandley, 'Federal Rule Changes Coming in December' (*National Law Review*, 26 September 2018).

[5] The desire to achieve uniformity across court process was a key motivation for the amendments, as discussed, e.g., in: J Morrison, 'Proposed Rule 23 Amendment for Class Action Settlement: Sea Change or Codification of the Status Quo?' (*Class Action Lawsuit Defense*, 11 May 2018); and see too: *US Advisory Committee Note to Rule 23* (2018), 3 ('[t]he central concern in reviewing a proposed class-action settlement is that it be fair, reasonable, and adequate. Courts have generated lists of factors to shed light on this concern. Overall, these factors focus on comparable considerations, but each circuit has developed its own vocabulary for expressing these concerns').

[6] By virtue of the Class Proceedings Act, RSBC 1996, c 50, s 4. This provision was inserted by Class Proceedings Amendment Act, 2018, s 5.

[7] Per Class Proceedings Act, RSBC 1996, c 50, s 16(2).

[8] Chapter 5 of this volume, 'Government as "Gate-Keeper": Cross-Border Class Actions'.

Ontario[9] is considering whether or not to suggest amendments to its jurisdiction's class action regime, whilst the Australian Law Reform Commission has recently studied the Australian landscape in detail.[10]

No one pretends that class actions are perfect, or that their design is immutable. But a detailed awareness of design issues, and of comparative jurisprudence, will enhance the desired outcome that the regime achieves procedural fairness for both claimant classes and for defendants, whilst fitting within the wider cultural and legal requirements of the jurisdiction's civil procedure.

Section B posits **100** separate design points to do with class actions commencement, conduct, and costs and funding, whilst Section C undertakes a case study setting out several aspects in which UK lawmakers learnt from the experiences amassed over a quarter of a century of Australian class actions jurisprudence. For those jurisdictions which have developed a sophisticated body of class actions jurisprudence, the debate has shifted from 'whether' to 'how' – and those lessons are crucial for any other legislature which has concluded that the triggers for class actions reform are met,[11] and that such a regime should duly be implemented.

B   100 Points of Class Action Design

This part of the chapter[12] sets out the 'design framework' of a modern opt-out class action regime[13] – from its beginning through to its end;

---

[9] *Class Actions: Objectives, Experiences and Reforms* (CP, March 2018). Consultation concluded on 31 May 2018, and at the time of writing, the final report is awaited, which 'may make recommendations for law reform where appropriate to do so': see announcement at: www.lco-cdo.org/en/our-current-projects/class-actions/.

[10] *Integrity, Fairness and Efficiency: An Inquiry into Class Action Proceedings and Third-Party Litigation Funders* (Rep 134, December 2018), published 25 January 2019; and earlier: *Inquiry into Class Action Proceedings and Third-Party Litigation Funders* (DP 85, May 2018).

[11] As explored in Chapter 2, 'Government as Class Actions Enabler'.

[12] Most of these issues are discussed by the author in much closer detail, in the light of a comparative analysis of the Australian federal, Canadian provincial and United States' federal regimes, in: *The Class Action in Common Law Legal Systems: A Comparative Perspective* (Hart Publishing, 2004); *The Modern Cy-près Doctrine: Applications and Implications* (Routledge Cavendish, 2006); and in various articles, such as: 'Justice Enhanced: Framing an Opt-Out Class Action for England' (2007) 70 *Modern Law Review* 550; and in 'Cy-près Damages Distributions in England: A New Era for Consumer Redress' (2009) 20 *European Business Law Review* 307; 'A Spotlight on the Settlement Criteria under the United Kingdom's New Competition Class Action' (2016) 35 *Civil Justice Quarterly* 1; and 'Third Party Funding and Class Actions Reform' (2015) 131 *Law Quarterly Review* 291.

[13] Sixty points of this 'design framework' were originally presented by the author at the Civil Justice Council (CJC) conference, *Consumer Redress Stakeholder Consultation Pt III*,

and costs and funding, as an integral part of the regime, are also addressed.

Procedural aspects 'at the beginning' dominate the framework, for this is the 'engine room' which fires up or extinguishes the class action at the very outset. It is a moot point whether the 'beginning procedures' are overly stated/prescriptive, but at least in the UK and Commonwealth jurisdictions, it seems to reflect an attitude of the law reform commissioners and legislatures to ensure, and demonstrably so, that their collective frameworks were not merely transplants of the US opt-out class action regime.

It must be emphasised that not all of these 'design issues' would necessarily require legislative articulation. Some would be dealt with sufficiently by establishing judicial precedent; by protocol or practice direction; or even by negotiation between the parties during the course of the litigation. All, however, have arisen as contentious points in class actions jurisprudence, and for many of them, *different* solutions are possible. It would always be up to the lawmakers as to how many of these 'design points' they were prepared to legislate for, thereby providing certainty but perhaps at the expense of flexibility (if the legislation was fairly prescriptive). If one envisages the relatively light-handed US federal class action as a 'first generation' opt-out regime,[14] and the subsequent more detailed enactments of Australia's federal regime and Canada's provincial regimes as 'second generation' statutes,[15] then England's version is a 'third generation' statute.[16] Each successive regime has profited from the opportunity to learn from the experiences of those earlier regimes. Some of those lessons are explored later in Section C.

Meanwhile, dividing the 100 'design points' into their four relevant sections:

26–27 March 2008, and was subsequently published in: 'Building Blocks and Design Points for an Opt-out Class Action' [2008] *Journal of Personal Injury Law* 308, 316–23. That publication intentionally excluded issues to do with costs and funding, but those matters **are** duly considered in this chapter.

[14] FRCP 23 only consists of subsections (a)–(h).

[15] Australia's federal regime in Pt IVA of the Federal Court of Australia Act 1976 consists of thirty-four detailed sections, while Ontario's Class Proceedings Act, SO 1992, c 6, consists of thirty-seven sections.

[16] The regime was contained in the Consumer Rights Act 2015, Sch 8, which inserted replacement and amending provisions into the Competition Act 1998 ('CA 1998') and the Enterprise Act 2002. Schedule 8 consists of twenty pages of legislative text. A supporting set of court rules was inserted in the Competition Appeal Tribunal Rules 2015 (SI 1648/2015), Pt 5 ('CAT Rules'), rr 73–98. See: Chapter 1 of this volume, Section B(4).

1   At the Beginning

(a)   Pleadings Matters

1. In accordance with usual pleadings requirements, *no frivolous, vexatious or abusive claims* should be permitted; and /or there must be *reasonable grounds* for bringing the claim.
2. Will the regime permit claimant, as well as defendant, classes? If so, any requirements specific to *defendant classes* must be considered.
3. The class's claim should also comply with any *specific pleadings requirements* for the class action, *viz*, that the pleadings (a) specify the common issues of fact or law, (b) describe the class and sub-classes (if any), and (c) specify the causes of action and the remedies sought for each class (and for each sub-class, if any).
4. Where the representative claimant is filing the class's claim under a *sectoral class actions regime* (rather than under a generic class action), the claim must fit within the scope of that sectoral regime.
5. In respect of any *'follow-on' class action*, the scope of the claim being prosecuted on behalf of the class must relate sufficiently to the infringement that was the subject of the original regulatory decision.

(b)   The Procedural Peculiarities of the Class Action

6. As a further brake/moderation on the ability to start a class action, should the claimant class be required to satisfy legislatively prescribed *preliminary merits test/s*? If so, which precise preliminary merits tests should be required – the claim's prospects of success; a cost–benefit analysis in the class's favour; a minimum financial threshold of individual and/or class claims; or other?
7. Would a *pre-certification 'class action protocol'* be desirable, requiring certain 'up-front disclosures', e.g., information about the size of class; the alleged common and individual issues; or the facts that go to prove why a class action would be superior to other means of resolving the dispute?
8. Should *a certification hearing* be mandated, as a 'gateway' through which all opt-out class actions must pass before they have judicial permission to proceed?
9. The class action should be the *superior avenue* for resolving the class members' disputes. If another procedural regime available to claimants is more efficient and less burdensome – say, a test or lead case, an existing opt-in regime, a representative rule, a sectoral regime, some regulatory complaints procedure, or the use of consolidation or joinder – then the class action should not proceed.
10. The class action should be *manageable* from the court's point of view (of which the court must be satisfied at the outset – subject to where the class action is certified for settlement purposes only, where there will be no trial).

11. Should any *type of legal issue be excluded* from the scope of the class action regime, i.e., should some disputes or causes of action be 'carved out' from the coverage of the class action regime?

12. Should the ability to commence a class action be precluded by some *other form of dispute resolution*? For example, can the parties deliberately 'trump' a class action by means of an arbitration clause inserted in their contract?

13. In what circumstances may a class action be *certified for the purposes of creating a settlement class* by consent – and which certification criteria can be 'overlooked' for that purpose, in the safe and certain knowledge that no trial court will ever have to hear and decide the merits of the action?

(c)   A Spotlight on the Class

14. A sufficient *minimum number* of class members must exist to form a class – and how this minimum threshold is defined will need to be legislatively articulated.

15. The class members' claims must be *sufficiently common*. The concept of 'commonality' requires a consideration of whether: (a) there must be some common 'cause of action' in play, (b) a common issue of fact or law is sufficient, or (c) some sort of 'predominance' of common issues is necessary or unnecessary.

16. There must be no insoluble *conflict of interests* arising as between representative claimant and absent class members.

17. It should be possible for a class member to *know whether or not he/she is a member of the class*, by perusing the class definition; subject to any defence that may be successfully pleaded and proved against that member (e.g., whether or not the class member suffered damage by reason of the defendant's breach, or whether the class member successfully passed the loss on).

18. The class must be defined in a way that is fair to both claimants and defendant – *not overly broad*, so that the common issues do not bear any relationship to some of the class members, but *not so narrow* that the defendant is facing the prospect of repetitive litigation arising out of the same grievance.

19. Is it permissible to *'tie' class membership to an external party* (rather than to the series of events out of which the dispute arose)? For example, should it be acceptable to tie class membership to those members whom a law firm or a third-party funder represents, or does that contravene the 'spirit', or even 'the letter', of the opt-out regime?

20. The formation of *sub-classes*, for issues that are common to that sub-class only but which are not common across the class as a whole, should be permitted.

21. What is the status of *absent class members* – e.g., relating to their right to give evidence at certification or at trial, the disclosure (if any) that should be

permitted against them, and the scope of the legal duty of care owed to them by the law firm which acts on behalf of the representative claimant?

22. How (if at all) should **non-resident class members** be encompassed by the domestic class action? Worldwide classes purportedly provide the defendant with 'global peace', but can conflict with the domestic jurisdiction's principles of private international law. For example, should non-resident class members be required to opt in to the class action, in order to signify formally their submission to the jurisdiction of the domestic court?

23. Whether any type of entity/person (e.g., government entities and officials) should be **excluded from being a class member** – or only be permitted to be a class member upon certain prerequisites being satisfied, such as opting in to an otherwise opt-out class action – should be considered.

24. For non-resident class members, if they do not have to opt in (legislatively), then upon what legal basis can the domestic court **assert personal jurisdiction over those non-resident class members**?

(d)   A Spotlight on the Defendant/s Being Sued

25. Proper **standing requirements** should apply, where multiple defendants are being sued in the class action. In the absence of any pleadable conspiracy or aiding and abetting allegation amongst defendants, whether it is required that every representative claimant has a pleadable cause of action against every defendant named in the action, or whether it is sufficient that, as against each defendant, there is *a* representative claimant who can plead a cause of action, should be legislatively prescribed, for the avoidance of doubt.

26. A class action must be **fair to the defendant**. For example, this will require consideration of the certification requirements which must be met by the class, the rights of disclosure and appeal to which the defendant is entitled under the regime, and the *res judicata* principles that apply.

27. Whether any particular types of defendants (e.g., Ministers of the Crown) should be **excluded** from the scope of the class action regime – or whether those particular types of defendant should only be prosecuted with the leave of the court – should be legislatively clarified.

(e)   A Spotlight on the Representative Claimant

28. The representative claimant must be **adequate to represent the absent class members**. What criteria will apply, by which to assess that adequacy?

29. The circumstances in which **substitution of the representative claimant** may validly occur, during the conduct of the action, should be legislatively stated.

30. If costs-shifting is preserved under the class action regime, then the representative claimant must have, or be able to put in place, the *financial means and capacity* to conduct the class action, to fund any adverse costs award, and to meet any security for costs order made against it. Should that be legislatively prescribed, or left to judicial criteria-setting?

31. The *legal representation must be adequate* to represent the representative claimant and the absent class members. Should criteria for that adequacy be legislatively prescribed?

32. The *status of 'ideological claimants'*, *viz*, trade or consumer associations – and the criteria permitting their appointment as representative claimant, and whether they should act as sole/preferred, or supplementary/optional, representative claimants – should be legislatively prescribed.

(f)   Potential Abuse of Process Issues

33. The extent (if any) to which the defendant may *contact absent class members* directly before the class action is certified (with a view, e.g., to individually settling with those absent class members) will need to be (probably judicially, rather than legislatively) considered, in order to set the parameters of acceptable litigious conduct, and to prevent claims of inappropriate or abusive process.

34. To what extent does the *Henderson rule* apply to class actions? Is the representative claimant permitted to frame the action around certain common issues, hiving off other common issues relevant to another line of argument for a 'rainy day' (i.e., for the day that the first class action loses on the common issues)? The operation of the *Henderson* rule has an impact upon the degree of finality which a class action may achieve for both class and defendant.

35. How should *parallel litigation* against the defendant, arising out of the same subject-matter, be handled? What criteria governing carriage motions, and the criteria for selecting one or more claims in preference to the other claims, should apply?

36. How should other *'multiple litigation' against the defendant* be handled? That is, where more than one class member institutes individual actions against the defendant (whether actions were instituted prior to certification of the class action, or by opt-out class members after certification), what criteria for stay, compulsory joinder, or other avenue, should apply?

37. Where class actions have been instituted in more than one jurisdiction, should a legislative list of criteria, similar to *a forum non conveniens analysis*, be stipulated, by which to choose the appropriate forum?

38. How should *overlapping classes* be dealt with, where some class members are involved in more than one class action, with the inevitable risk of their double-recovery?

2   *During the Action*

(a)   The Opting-Out Process

39. The class members must be **adequately informed** about their opt-out rights under the class action, giving them a realistic opportunity to opt out. What manner of giving notice is to be permitted? For example, when and how often should notice be given, is each notice to be mandatory or discretionary, can either group or individual notice be permitted, and what appropriate use can be made of the internet and websites for disseminating opt-out notice?
40. **Who pays** for the opt-out notice, both upfront, and ultimately, if a costs-shifting regime is preserved for the class action?
41. The **content** of the opt-out notice, the appropriate length of the opt-out period (e.g., whether any minimum or maximum opt-out periods should be set), and **how** to opt out, need to be considered.
42. Should those who opt out of the class action be permitted **an opportunity to opt back into that action**, whether on the same or on less favourable terms, in order to share in either a judgment award or a settlement fund?

(b)   Court Control

43. The extent to which close **judicial case-management** of the class action will be permitted, or even mandatory, requires consideration.
44. The court should have the legislative capacity to **exercise broad powers** (e.g., to enable it to narrow/widen the common issues, to amend the class definition, to direct amendments to the pleadings, etc.) in order to permit the class action to dispose of the dispute as expeditiously and as proportionately as possible.

(c)   Conducting the Class Action

45. When, and how, is **the class to be closed**, membership-wise? At some point (and with very limited exception), the class must convert from opt-out to opt-in. In most scenarios, the class members, hitherto described, will have to 'put their feet on the sticky paper', thereby giving rise to the 'take-up rate' of the action.
46. In what circumstances can **communications** be made by the representative claimant (or by its lawyers) **to absent class members** throughout the conduct of the action, either as formal notice which requires court approval, or as general correspondence which does not?
47. To what extent (if any) may **the defendant contact absent class members directly**, *after* the class action is certified (with a view to individually settling

with those absent class members)? This will depend upon the parameters of acceptable litigious conduct and of inappropriate or abusive process.

48. Against which person/s (e.g., the representative claimant, absent class members, third parties) may **disclosure** be sought, with or without leave?

49. In what circumstances and upon what criteria may the class action be **de-certified**, following certification?

(d)   Limitation Periods

50. The limitation period **may stop running (i.e., be tolled)** for both representative claimant and absent class members, either when the representative claimant files the class action, or when (or if) the action is certified. The precise circumstances at which the limitation period is tolled must be legislatively prescribed.

51. The limitation period will **start running again** upon certain events happening; these triggers should be legislatively prescribed.

(e)   The Substantive Law

52. Whether any **amendment of the substantive law** for any particular cause of action, or for any element of a cause of action, is desirable, in order to ensure that class actions litigation is not used so as to distort the law and punish a particular category of defendant in a manner that was not envisaged pre-class actions reform, may require consideration.

3   At the End

(a)   Settlement of the Class Action

53. Settlement agreements must be subject to **a fairness hearing**. This is, essentially, to preserve fairness for absent class members and for the defendant, but also serves to protect the interests of the representative claimant and the lawyers (e.g., where judicial approval is sought for remuneration to the representative claimant and for legal fees, respectively).

54. **Adequate notice** of a forthcoming fairness hearing, and about any verdict reached at that hearing, should be provided for. Should the timing and content of those notices require judicial approval?

55. What **'fairness criteria'** should apply to a settlement agreement? Should these be left to judicial development or legislatively prescribed? Is evidence from

representative claimants, absent class members, the defendant, the lawyers acting on each side, and experts, permissible at the fairness hearing?

56. Are *'bar orders'* permissible, whereby a settling defendant obtains an order that it is not to be exposed to any claims for indemnity and contribution from a non-settling defendant, in the event that the non-settling defendant loses at trial?

57. What procedures by which absent class members may (a) *object to a settlement*, or (b) opt out of a settlement (if a second opt-out stage is permitted at all), should be judicially or legislatively prescribed?

58. The procedure (if any) by which absent class members may *opt back into a class* for the purposes of settlement need to be considered.

(b)   Awarding Damages

59. Damages assessment may be individually assessed, or based upon a *class-wide aggregate assessment*, depending upon the circumstances. What prerequisites for an award of aggregate assessment, and what level of accuracy required for such an assessment, should apply? Should these be judicially or legislative prescribed?

60. Are any *types of damages precluded* from being awarded in the class actions context – e.g., punitive, exemplary, aggravated, nominal, restitutionary, or other?

61. Whether class members must – or merely may – have *an opportunity to come forward* to claim damages, prior to any distribution of the damages award (or settlement fund), should be considered, either judicially or legislatively.

62. Should a *civil penalty* be permitted to be awarded against the defendant in a class action, as an alternative to damages?

(c)   Treating Undistributed Residues

63. How should *distribution of undistributed residues* be handled, and at what point should it be declared that an undistributed residue does indeed arise?

64. Should a direct distribution to class members be permitted, not by an individual assessment of each class member's entitlement, but on the basis of *an average or pro rata assessment* for those class members who have come forward to claim?

65. Should *cy-près distributions* be permitted? If so, what are the prerequisites governing such distributions? Should a *cy-près* order on either a price-rollback or distribution-to-organisation basis be permitted, or barred? Should a *cy-près* distribution be made on a 'next best' or a 'as near as' basis?

66. Should *coupon recovery* ever be permitted (i.e., compensation 'in like', rather than in monetary terms), or should that be banned outright by either the legislature or the judiciary?

67. Should a **reversionary distribution to the defendant** be countenanced? If so, what level of priority should a reversion be given amongst the menu of options by which to treat undistributed residues?
68. Should an undistributed residue be permitted to **escheat to the government**, as part of its general Consolidated Revenue Fund, or more specifically to nominated government entities as an earmarked escheat, whether under the relevant class action legislation or under general escheat provisions?

(d)   Handling Class Members' Individual Issues

69. The means of **determining the individual issues** (if any) which remain after the determination of the common issues (whether by judgment or pursuant to a settlement agreement) must be clear and explicit, and yet be imbued with the utmost flexibility.
70. Should **class members have the right to insist upon** individual assessment and direct distribution? Or, in the interests of proportionality, may the managing judge approve an average distribution or a *cy-près* distribution, regardless of individual class members' indications to the contrary?

(e)   Rights of Appeal

71. **Appeals from certification orders** (e.g., who has the right to appeal, whether an appeal is 'as of right' or only with leave) needs to be considered.
72. **Appeal rights regarding the judgment of the common issues** (who, when, and with or without leave), and appeal rights regarding judgment on individual issues (who, when, thresholds, and with or without leave), as well as appeal rights arising from any judicially-approved settlement agreement, need to be considered.
73. Does any **right of appeal** lie from a question of law only, from a mixed question of law and fact, or from a particular specified point?

4   Costs and Funding

(a)   A Spotlight on the Defendant

74. Which **costs rules** will apply to the class action regime – costs-shifting, one-way costs-shifting, or no-way costs-shifting?
75. In what circumstances, if any, may a **costs-shifting rule be departed from**, thus depriving a successful defendant of its costs?

76. In what circumstances, if any, may a *no-way costs-shifting rule be departed from*, thus exposing a losing representative claimant or a losing defendant to an award of costs (e.g., in the case of vexatious, improper or abusive proceedings)?

77. Should *different costs scales, fixed costs, or costs-capping*, apply to class actions litigation?

(b)   A Spotlight on the Class

78. Is the *representative claimant permitted to receive any compensation* for the time and effort expended by that party on behalf of the class? If so, what criteria should apply, and must any such amount be capped under the regime?

79. The extent, if any, to which the costs, expenses and disbursements incurred on behalf of the class in achieving a successful outcome (which are not recovered from the unsuccessful defendant may be claimed from the damages award or settlement fund – ancillary to the *'common fund' doctrine* – should be considered, whether legislatively or judicially.

80. Should any claim of costs, expenses and disbursements incurred on behalf of the class be authorised for payment *prior to the distribution of the proceeds of the claim to individual class members*? Or should such payments only be possible after direct distributions have been made to those class members coming forward to claim?

81. What, precisely, is *included within the types of costs, expenses and disbursements* (e.g., does it include, e.g., a third-party funder's success fee; and an after-the-event insurance premium)?

82. The *notification to the class members* of any actual or potential costs liability to which they may be subject, by virtue of payment of the costs, expenses, and disbursements from the damages award or settlement fund, should be legislatively or judicially stipulated, given the burdens upon class members which these payments entail.

83. *An express immunity from costs* incurred by the representative claimant on the class's behalf, where the class action is unsuccessful on the common issues, whilst typical of class actions regimes, requires legislative authorisation.

84. May *class members be solicited for contributions* towards the representative claimant's costs, expenses and disbursements? If so, what sanctions (if any) may apply if the request for solicitations is ignored by any class member?

(c)   A Spotlight on the Class Lawyers

85. Should it be permissible for the *class lawyers to fund the action on a contingency basis* – via no-win-no-fee arrangements of any sort – by

agreement between the representative claimant and the class lawyers, or whether such funding should be barred?

86. If permitted, **what type of contingency fee** – a flat-rate basis, a multiplier basis, an uplift basis, a percentage-of-recovery basis, or a hybrid basis that combines the aforementioned or combines some of these and an hourly rate – should be permitted?

87. Should there be **caps applied to the contingency fees** capable of being charged to the representative claimant by class lawyers – either generally, or differing according to the different causes of action/types of class members?

88. Whether, when, and against what criteria a litigation funding agreement between the representative claimant and the class lawyers should be **judicially scrutinised and approved** must be considered.

89. In what circumstances may a **non-party costs order** (including a security for costs order) be made against the class lawyers who are funding the class action?

90. Whether class lawyers are lawfully permitted to enter into contingency funding agreements with individual class members at the outset of the action, thereby **defining (and 'tying') the class** by reference to both the underlying cause of action and the funding agreement – or whether that arrangement contravenes the 'spirit' or the 'letter' of an opt-out regime – should be judicially or legislatively stipulated.

91. Any **hybrid arrangements as between class lawyers and third-party funders**, permitting both to fund different aspects of the class action, require clarification, whether by the legislature, the judiciary, or the regulatory authority which regulates the conduct of the said lawyers.

(d)   A Spotlight on External Funding Sources

92. Should a **special class actions fund** be established by the government from which to fund class actions? If so, what costs awards (if any) may be awarded against that fund?

93. Should some **contingency aid fund** be permitted to fund class actions (amongst other litigation)? If so, how should that fund derive its funds?

94. Should **third-party funders** be permitted to fund class actions litigation? If so, in what circumstances may a litigation funding agreement be tainted with champerty and maintenance?

95. Whether, when, and against what criteria, a third-party funder's litigation funding agreement with the representative claimant should be **judicially scrutinised and approved**, and whether this should be legislatively or judicially stipulated.

96. Whether, and if so in what circumstances, the fact that the representative claimant is using an external source of funding, and the identity of that funder, should be **disclosed to the defendant**, requires consideration.

97. Should **caps apply to the success fees** capable of being charged to the representative claimant by a third-party funder?

98. In what circumstances may a **non-party costs order** (including a security for costs order) be made against a third-party funder which is funding the class action, whether stipulated in the class actions regime or in general legislation?

99. Whether third-party funders are lawfully permitted to enter into litigation funding agreements with individual class members at the outset of the action, thereby **defining (and 'tying') the class** by reference to both the underlying cause of action and the funding agreement – or whether that arrangement contravenes the 'spirit' or the 'letter' of an opt-out regime – must be judicially or legislatively stipulated.

100. Whether third-party funding requires the **oversight of formal regulation** – whether in the context of class actions litigation, or more generally – requires consideration, given the potential vulnerability to which class members are subject by virtue of the funder's position.

C   Some Comparative Design Lessons

The second strand of government as 'designer' is to take on board the experiences learnt from elsewhere. The legislature and rule-making bodies which seek to design a class action regime face a conundrum which is not unique to their own jurisdiction. Elsewhere, similar problems are being confronted in a search for an efficient resolution of grievances on a large scale. It is a problem of civil procedure which, as one comparative scholar aptly puts it, 'legitimately encourage[s] a search for help in the reasoning ... of other countries'.[17]

This section of the chapter discusses how the drafting of some features of the UK Competition Law Class Action was influenced by the statutory wording contained in the Australian federal class action which was enacted some twenty-five years earlier.[18] In several aspects, the UK legislature studied, and departed from, the legislative choices made by the Australian drafters. Whether these choices are correct remains to be seen, as the UK regime develops.

1   The Two Jurisdictions under Scrutiny

The year 2017 marked the twenty-fifth anniversary of Australia's federal opt-out class action. Contained in Pt IVA of the Federal Court of

---

[17] B Markesinis, *Foreign Law and Comparative Methodology* (Hart Publishing, 1997) 204.

[18] For details of this regime, see Chapter 1, Section B(3).

Australia Act 1976, the regime represented a watershed in Australian jurisprudence. There have been state replicas (of sorts) since,[19] but the federal action was a vanguard and a milestone in several respects. Not only did it signify a deliberate legislative departure from the often-awkward representative rule derived from English law, but it ushered in a newly independent era of Australian law. After 4 March 1992, it became feasible for thousands of Australian class members to be joined in the one action for compensatory redress, for a grievance which had been experienced on a global scale – without having to seek to join actions in the United States or United Kingdom to do so.[20]

The legislators in Australia undoubtedly learnt many lessons from some of the misgivings about the US federal regime,[21] just as the UK reformers did of the Australian federal regime during the course of the UK reform.[22] The timeline in Table 3.1 overpage outlines the key events of these three regimes.

Although the Australian regime was undoubtedly influential when it came to drafting the UK class action for competition law claims a quarter of a century later,[23] they do, in one respect, differ markedly. The Australian Pt IVA regime is, and was always intended to be, generic. It can cater for any cause of action which arises under the federal jurisdiction.[24] The ALRC envisaged that it would have that scope of

---

[19] In Victoria: Supreme Court Act 1986, Pt 4A; in New South Wales: Civil Procedure Act 2005, Pt 10; and in Queensland: Civil Proceedings Act 2011, Pt 13A. For a convenient summary of the two former state regimes, see, e.g.: M Legg and R McInnes, *Annotated Class Actions Legislation* (LexisNexis, 2014).

[20] As discussed in Chapter 1, Section B(3); and see also: P Cashman, *Class Action Law and Practice* (Federation Press, 2007) 601 ('Australian claimants are occasionally involved in group or class action litigation before English and US courts. Mass tort and product liability proceedings before US courts often encompass foreign claimants, including from Australia').

[21] e.g., the ALRC made extensive reference to the FRCP 23 regime in *Grouped Proceedings in the Federal Court* (Rep 46, 1988), ch 9, and App C, 'Other Models for Class Actions', noting the 'significant differences between the United States class action procedure and the grouped procedure recommended in this Report': at 191.

[22] e.g., Australian jurisprudence was referred to by the Civil Justice Council, when formulating its recommendation for the introduction of opt-out class actions: *Improving Access to Justice through Collective Actions: Final Report* (November 2008) 44–45, 98; by BIS, *Private Actions in Competition Law: Government Response* (2013) [5.13]; and in the author's research report submitted to BIS's predecessor, Dept for Business, Enterprise and Regulatory Reform: *Competition Law Cases under the Opt-out Regimes of Australia, Canada and Portugal* (October 2008).

[23] For example, written memos about aspects of the Australian regime (amongst others) were provided by the author to BIS, and to the CAT Rules Working Party, during the course of 2014–15.

[24] Per FCA 1976, Pt IVA, ss 33B and 33G.

Table 3.1 *Timeline: The class actions regimes of Australia, the United States, and the United Kingdom*

---

1 July 1966: FRCP 23 was adopted by US Supreme Court order, acting pursuant to the Rules Enabling Act (Justice Black dissenting), following a draft prepared by the Advisory Committee in 1964

February 1977: Referral by A-G to the ALRC, 'to review the laws . . . relating to . . . class actions . . . ; and to report upon (a) the adequacy thereof; (b) any desirable changes to the existing law in relation thereto . . . ; and (c) any related matter'

13 December 1988: ALRC, *Grouped Proceedings in the Federal Court* tabled

11 December 1989: Federal Court (Grouped Proceedings) Bill 1989 (a private member's Bill) introduced by Senator Haines which ultimately lapsed (but was a 'prod' for reform)

12 September 1991: Federal Court of Australia Amendment Bill 1991 introduced by Senator Tate, Minister for Justice and Consumer Affairs, for its First Reading

5 March 1992: Pt IVA of the FCA 1976 took effect, inserted by s 3 of the Federal Court of Australia Amendment Act 1991

1 December 2003: amendments to FRPC 23, in respect of the appointment of class counsel and the awards of lawyers' fees, together with settlement processes, including a second opportunity to opt out

November 2008: the Civil Justice Council recommended a generic opt-out class action for England and Wales: *Improving Access to Justice through Collective Actions: Final Report*; but rejected in July 2009 in favour of sectoral reform: *Government Response*

January 2013: the Dept for Innovation, Business and Skills (UK) recommended the introduction of a sectoral opt-out class action for competition law grievances: *Private Actions in Competition Law: Government Response*

26 March 2015: the Consumer Rights Act 2015 (UK) was enacted, just prior to the rise of Parliament for the 2015 general election

1 October 2015: Sch 8 of the Consumer Rights Act 2015 took effect, facilitating a follow-on or stand-alone class action for competition law grievances

1 December 2018: amendments to FRCP 23, in respect of class actions notice and settlement processes

---

operation,[25] and the Federal Parliament carried that vision forth in its generic action, and 'a significant part of the Government's equity and

---

[25] *Grouped Proceedings in the Federal Court* (1988) [324], 'Evaluation of the proposal'. As to the range of claims that potentially could be covered, the ALRC itemised these very widely: 'transport disasters, employment, public utilities and services, accidents, wrongful application of social security or taxation laws, breaches of trade practices law, and production of goods and services': at [325].

access policies embodied in its social justice program'.[26] The breadth of the types of claims since has reflected that widely construed objective[27] (albeit that the current actions on foot tend to predominate in certain areas[28]). On the other hand, the UK's regime pertains **only** to competition law grievances, whether stand-alone or follow-on (the latter where some infringement has been found by either the Office of Fair Trading or the European Commission).[29] It is ironical that this particular sector was chosen by the UK Government, at a time when competition law class actions are on the distinct wane under Australia's federal regime. In

---

[26] *Hansard* (House of Representatives, 14 November 1991, Mr Duffy MP and A-G, at 3175).

[27] The vast range of grievances litigated under the Australian regimes have included (but not been limited to) claims arising from: misleading and deceptive practices relating to products and services; defective pharmaceutical and medical devices; rating agencies in the fallout of the global financial crisis; real estate transactions, insurance and insurance products, agricultural products, medical services, and the employment relationship; environmental contamination and flooding; food consumption; overcharges in financial transactions with banks and credit card companies; franchise disputes; Indigenous rights; anti-competitive conduct; taxation disputes; misconduct or mismanagement of the company or of its affairs, or for other investment losses; employment discrimination; and defamation arising from credit references. See, especially, the discussion in, e.g.: V Morabito, *An Empirical Study of Australia's Class Action Regimes: Class Action Facts and Figures (First Report)* (December 2009), especially the Tables at pp 24–26, and as updated in: *Class Action Facts and Figures – Five Years On (Third Report)* (November 2014), Pt VI, Tables at 10–12. The range has also been evaluated in, e.g.: ALRC, *Integrity, Fairness and Efficiency: An Inquiry into Class Action Proceedings and Third-Party Litigation Funders* (Rep 134, December 2018), App F, 'ALRC Snapshot: Class Action Proceedings Finalised in the Federal Court of Australia (1997–October 2018)'; The Hon Justice Bernard Murphy and Prof V Morabito, 'The First 25 Years: Has the Class Action Regime Hit the Mark on Access to Justice?', in D Grave and H Mould (eds), *25 Years of Class Actions in Australia* (Ross Parsons, 2017) 22–28; D Grave, K Adams and J Betts, *Class Actions in Australia* (2nd edn, Lawbook Co, 2012) 37–38; Chief Justice Allsop, 'Class Actions' (Keynote address to the Law Council of Australia Forum, 13 October 2016); The Hon Justice Murphy, 'The Operation of the Australian Class Action Regime' (speech to the Bar Assn of Queensland, 9 March 2013), section 5.7, available at: www.fedcourt.gov.au/digital-law-library/judges-speeches/justice-murphy /murphy-j-20130309; S Stuart-Clark *et al.*, 'Australia', in P Karlsgodt (ed), *World Class Actions: A Guide to Group and Representative Actions around the Globe* (Oxford University Press, 2012), ch 22, 417–24; Mulheron, *Reform of Collective Redress in England and Wales: A Perspective of Need* (Research Paper for the CJC, 2008), Table 12.

[28] The latest statistics from the Federal Court of Australia illustrate that the ninety-four class actions presently on foot nationally in the federal registries are concentrated in the areas of corporate insolvency, and in corporate regulation and consumer protection: see Federal Court of Australia Law and Practice, *Class Actions Statistics* (2018), available at: www.fedcourt.gov.au/law-and-practice/class-actions/class-actions#statistics.

[29] i.e., the regime caters for class actions arising from an 'infringement decision' or 'an alleged infringement' in either the CA 1998 or the Treaty on the Functioning of the EU, per CA 1998, s 47A(2).

August 2016, Morabito published the fourth report in his series of groundbreaking empirical studies of Australian class actions, and remarked that, '[t]he total lack of cartel class actions over the last nine years highlights, on its own, the fact that formidable barriers are faced by those wishing to act on behalf of groups of victims of cartels'.[30]

Be that as it may, the UK decision to pursue sectoral reform was settled much earlier in the reform process, in 2009, when the Ministry of Justice (MOJ) stated that 'the Government considers that the only practical way forward is on a sector by sector basis . . . (where a sector is a discrete area of economic or social activity, within which particular issues, including specific types of legal claim, may arise)'.[31] It based this view on two grounds: there were 'structural differences' among the different sectors, which may necessitate different legislative frameworks; and 'it will be necessary to undertake a full [economic] assessment of the likely economic and other impacts before implementing any reform. However, a meaningful global impact assessment would be virtually impossible to achieve.'[32] This political position was entirely at odds with the earlier 2008 recommendation of the Civil Justice Council of England and Wales,[33] and of the even earlier recommendations of the Lord Chancellor's Department in 2001,[34] and of Lord Woolf,[35] both of whom had advocated that a generic 'multi-party action' be considered for England and Wales. The sectoral approach to class actions reform was, in this author's opinion, deeply flawed for several reasons.[36] Notably, the only reform of compensatory collective redress which has occurred since then has been strictly opt-in, in respect of certain infringements of the General Data Protection Regulations,[37] and only where 'data

---

[30]   *An Empirical Study of Australia's Class Action Regimes: Facts and Figures on Twenty-four Years of Class Actions in Australia (Fourth Report)* (August 2016) 18. Professor Caron Beaton-Wells makes the same point in: 'Private Enforcement of Competition Law in Australia – Inching Forwards?' (2016) 39 *Melbourne University Law Review* 681, and outlines a variety of reasons, including difficult limitation periods, for that scenario.

[31]   See the Government's Response to the CJC's Report: MOJ, *Improving Access to Justice through Collective Actions* (2009) [12].

[32]   Respectively: ibid, [12] and [13].

[33]   *Improving Access to Justice: Final Report* (n 22), Recommendation 1, and pp137–40.

[34]   *Representative Claims: Proposed New Procedures* (2001) [13]. As the CJC Report states, this proposal 'would, if implemented, have introduced a generic representative action procedure for all civil claims': *Improving Access to Justice*, ibid, 52, [12].

[35]   Lord Woolf MR, *Access to Justice: Final Report to the Lord Chancellor on the Civil Justice System in England and Wales* (1996), ch 17, conclusions (1)–(18).

[36]   'Recent Milestones in Class Actions Reform in England: A Critique and a Proposal' (2011) 127 *Law Quarterly Review* 288, 299–313.

[37]   Data Protection Act 2018, s 168.

subjects have given their authorisation to the representative body'[38] (albeit with the possibility of opt-out representative actions in this field in the future, depending upon the outcome of a further governmental review[39]). It is truly a very fragmented landscape in the United Kingdom.

It is relevant to now consider briefly **four** specific areas, regarding certification, **plus** a funding issue, in which the UK drafters departed from the Australian legislative drafting and/or policy, by way of example. The lessons of the Australian experience were well-learnt. This represents a tangible example of using comparative law to gain from the experience of another jurisdiction, whilst duly acknowledging the significant steps that were taken by the Australian legislature and judiciary in developing and finessing a complex process of civil procedure. In the task undertaken in this section of the chapter, it is important, and appropriate, that due tribute be made to the several judges of the Australian Federal Court who, in the early years of Pt IVA's operation, had to interpret Parliament's intention, and to seek to ensure that the regime *actually worked*, to deliver justice to representative claimant, defendant, and absent class members. This required that minute attention be given to the meaning of individual words and phrases. These early decisions are now part of the fabric of Australian class actions jurisprudence. We now take them for granted. Yet, for example, it is easy to forget that the word, 'substantial', in section s 33C(1)(c), required an appeal to the High Court of Australia as to what that one word actually meant.[40] The various judges were charged with the task of interpreting an entirely new legislative regime – and their important pronouncements did not go unnoticed by the UK law reformers and drafters.

2 *To Certify or Not to Certify?*

Whether or not to insist upon a formal authorisation procedure was an important issue for UK reformers, conscious of the Australian

---

[38] Per ibid, s 188. Various lobby groups pressed for such reforms on an opt-out basis, but these were unsuccessful, as discussed in, e.g.: B Hurst, 'The "Tidal Wave" of Data Protection-related Class Actions: Why We're not Drowning Just Yet . . . ' (*Bird & Bird Information Bulletin*, November 2018); and 'Watch Out for GDPR-related Claims: It's Not all about Fines . . . ' (*Walker Morris Update*, 25 July 2018).

[39] The Data Protection Act 2018, ss 189(2)(c) and s 190(1)(b) impose a duty on the Secretary of State to carry out a review of the opt-in representative arrangement and to consider the merits of permitting opt-out representative actions, and to report to Parliament on these matters, within thirty months of 25 May 2018.

[40] *Wong v Silkfield Pty Ltd* (1999) 199 CLR 255 (HCA).

legislature's decision to eschew certification under Pt IVA. Under the latter's de facto certification,[41] the representative claimant commences a proceeding that must accord with the requirements of section s 33C; and then the defendant may apply for an order that the proceeding no longer continue as a class action (hereafter, a 'discontinuance order'),[42] or on the basis that the requirements of section s 33C have not been met.

This lack of formal certification was a deliberate decision of the Australian drafters. The ALRC certainly recommended against it, arguing that there was 'no value in imposing an additional costly procedure, with a strong risk of appeals involving delay and expense, which will not achieve the aims of protecting parties or ensuring efficiency'.[43] It was one of several respects in which the US-style class action was consciously departed from. As Wilcox J recalls (he was a member of the ALRC at the relevant time), the drafters were anxious that, '[i]n the interests of saving unnecessary work, and therefore expense, it seemed obvious that ... we should dispense with the American certification process, in favor of allowing a respondent, who wished to challenge the applicability of the class action procedure, to move for a dismissal or stay of the proceedings.'[44]

However, the absence of any formal class action procedure has led to some allegations by commentators over the years that the Australian regime is too liberal, too claimant-friendly – that Australia is 'now regarded as the place, outside of the United States, where a corporation will most likely find itself defending a class action';[45] that the Australian regime effectively reverses the burden of proof, requiring that the defendant 'disprove that the case should proceed as a class action';[46] and that '[t]here is a real value in having a structured and formal occasion on

---

[41] Described as such, earlier in the regime's life, by legal commentators, e.g.: J Spender, 'Securities Class Actions: A View from the Land of the Great White Shareholder' (2002) 31 *Common Law World Review* 123, 139; V Morabito, 'Class Actions Against Multiple Respondents' (2002) 30 *Federal Law Review* 295, 297–98; S Stuart-Clark and C Harris, 'Multi-Plaintiff Litigation in Australia: A Comparative Perspective' (2001) 11 *Duke Journal of Comparative and International Law* 289, 295–96, 317.

[42] Per FCA 1976, ss 33L, 33M or (the most-frequently employed) 33N.

[43] *Grouped Proceedings in the Federal Court* (Rep 46, 1988) [146]–[147] (quote in [147]), and cited in, e.g.: *Dorajay Pty Ltd v Aristocrat Leisure Ltd* [2005] FCA 1483, [102]; *Perera v GetSwift Ltd* [2018] FCAFC 202, [55].

[44] The Hon Murray Wilcox, 'Class Actions in Australia: Recollections of the Early Days', in Grave and Mould (eds), *25 Years of Class Actions* (n 27), ch 2, 6.

[45] Piper Alderman, 'Class Actions in Australia: A Plaintiff's Paradise?' (*Lexology*, 19 February 2010) 2.

[46] Stuart-Clark *et al.* (n 27) 411; and Stuart-Clark and Harris (n 41) 295–96.

which the class action is subject to scrutiny, such as is provided by the US certification system'.[47] On the other hand, some scholars have strongly supported the absence of certification in Australia. Their reasons have included that: up to 80 per cent of those cases for which the defendant sought discontinuance continued as class actions; and that where the defendant lost that 'de-certification' battle, class-wide settlements were not the invariable result.[48]

Undoubtedly, as some Australian federal courts have recognised, there is a different ethos, and legal consequences, where there is no certification procedure in place. For example, in *Perera v GetSwift Ltd*, the Full Federal Court recently noted (in the context of a carriage motion) that, 'distinctions are important', and that, under Pt IVA, a class action 'can be issued as of right and continue', provided that no discontinuance order is made, and that Australian federal class actions are 'presumptively entitled to go forward, absent vexation, oppression or an abuse of power'; whereas '[i]n the Canadian provinces, there is no presumptive entitlement to go forward until certification'.[49] With a somewhat more critical tone, Finkelstein J remarked that, whilst Pt IVA does not require certification, '[i]n most jurisdictions, there is a certification procedure', and that '[e]xperience of class actions suggests that the absence of a certification process is itself the cause of numerous interlocutory applications with resultant expense and delay'.[50] The design of the Australian regime has also placed inordinate importance upon the discontinuance order – particularly that of section 33N(1)[51] – and upon what is relevant (and irrelevant) to that assessment, and of its legal consequences for the representative claimant and for the class members. Judicial clarification of these issues has been required from time to time.[52]

Despite such reservations, there has been no amendment to Pt IVA in order to introduce a formal certification procedure. Indeed, quite the

---

[47] 'Ripe for Reform: Improving the Australian Class Action Regime' (US Chamber Institute for Legal Reform, March 2014) 5.

[48] V Morabito and J Caruana, 'Can Class Action Regimes Operate Satisfactorily Without a Certification Device? Empirical Insights from the Federal Court of Australia' (2013) 61 *American Journal of Comparative Law* 579, and see too: V Morabito, 'Empirical Perspectives on 25 Years of Class Actions', in Grave and Mould (eds), *25 Years of Class Actions* (n 27), ch 4, 54.

[49] [2018] FCAFC 202, [196].

[50] *P Dawson Nominees Pty Ltd v Multiplex Ltd* [2007] FCA 1061, [18].

[51] i.e., that the proceeding no longer continue as a representative proceeding.

[52] See, e.g., the careful articulation in: *Bywater v Appco Group Australia Pty Ltd* [2018] FCA 707, [14]–[19], by reference to earlier case law.

contrary. In developments since the UK Competition Law Class Action came into effect in 2015, the Victorian,[53] Western Australian,[54] and Australian[55] Law Reform Commissions have re-endorsed the view that certification is not necessary for the Australian landscape. The Victorian Commission cited concerns such as the importance of keeping class actions regimes harmonised throughout the Australian landscape, thus rendering it difficult to introduce certification in Victoria alone; that no reviews of the Australian civil justice system had actively called for a certification procedure to be introduced; that there was no evidence of widespread systematic abuse in Victorian class actions, absent a certification procedure; and that there was a risk that the introduction of a certification requirement would cause 'significant complexity, cost and delay in the conduct of litigation'.[56] The Western Australian Commission conceded that there were 'competing views about the merits of a certification regime', but was not prepared to recommend that, when it would be 'fundamentally inconsistent' with the other enacted regimes in Australia.[57] The Australian Law Reform Commission noted that, despite several submissions which 'urged' that a statutory certification procedure be implemented in Pt IVA, the Commission 'remains unpersuaded that the introduction of a certification procedure would enhance the practice and procedure of the class action regime in Australia. In particular, the ALRC notes that Canada is currently considering whether its certification procedure should be abandoned, given the additional costs and delay that it imposes on parties and that, in Australia, class action litigation is subject to rigours [sic] pre-trial case management by the Courts'.[58]

---

[53] Victorian LRC, *Litigation Funding and Group Proceedings* (March 2018); and earlier: *Civil Justice Review Report* (Rep 14, 2008). The latter Commission (chaired by Professor Peter Cashman) was asked, in March 2018, whether there should be further regulation of group proceedings, including certification requirements, but it did not so recommend.

[54] *Representative Proceedings* (Rep 103, 2015) [5.92]. This report preceded the UK's regime by four months.

[55] *Integrity, Fairness and Efficiency: Final Report* (2018) (n 27); and earlier: (DP 85, May 2018) [6.20], noting that there were 'a number of protections and safeguards' in the regime.

[56] *Litigation Funding and Group Proceedings* (March 2018) [4.30]–[4.59], Recommendation 9, quote at [4.51].

[57] *Representative Proceedings* (Rep 103, 2015) [5.89]–[5.92].

[58] *Integrity, Fairness and Efficiency: Final Report* (2018) (n 27) [4.48]. Whether certification should be abandoned is currently being considered by the LRC of Ontario, as part of its study: *Class Actions: Objectives, Experiences and Reforms* (CP, March 2018). One question being posed is 'whether Ontario should abandon the requirement for certification, or

Predictably, the most recently enacted Australian state regimes, in Queensland[59] and New South Wales,[60] do not embrace a certification process either. In fact, there is only one regime in any Australian state representative proceeding which does entail certification,[61] but it is not a regime which replicates Pt IV A.

A quarter of a century of Australian experience did not convince the UK law reformers. The 'no certification' approach was not one which they wished to emulate. Both the Civil Justice Council, and later the government department which was responsible for promulgating the UK Competition Law Class Action, strongly recommended that some authorisation procedure be compulsory. The CJC, having made specific reference to the Australian regime, noted that '[t]he possibility of such large scale procedural skirmishing must be avoided in any reformed process', and that certification was 'an absolutely mandatory element of any collective action introduced in England'.[62] The justifications for rejecting the Australian approach were numerous. In a jurisdiction such as England's which strove for case-management, the court should act as 'a diligent gatekeeper' of any such action (rather than rely upon the defendant to apply to bring the action to a halt); and certification allowed the court to assess all forms of redress, including ADR, ombudsman schemes, and regulatory redress, to 'ensur[e] that the use of civil process is, in and of itself, the most appropriate, the superior, means of prosecuting any claim'.[63] That latter requirement meant that the public interest was served by ensuring that limited judicial resources were used fairly

---

preliminary hearings altogether?' (at 7, and Consultation Question 5). The Commission stated: '[t]here were many comments, from both plaintiff and defense counsel, that the statutory criteria in s 5 of the CPA were basically sound and should remain unchanged. . . . [but they] also often criticized how these criteria were applied in practice, such as the amount of evidence allowed by judges on certification motions [which] . . . indirectly turned the courts' focus to the merits . . . some defense counsel advocated that s 5 be explicitly changed to allow assessment of cases on the merits. Several counsel noted the volume of evidence produced and disclosed by parties [for] was a significant and growing issue, especially for cases involving historical evidence': at 12. See too: S Chiodo, 'Class Actions Twenty-five Years On' (2018–19) 14 Canadian Class Actions Review 189, 202–06 (noting that certification motions in Canada 'remain protracted, time-consuming and expensive': at 205).

[59] Civil Proceedings Act 2011, Pt 13, and see the commencement provisions in s 103B.
[60] Civil Procedure Act 2005, Pt 10, and see the commencement provisions in s 157.
[61] Supreme Court Civil Rules 2006 (South Australia), Div 3, rr 80–84. An application for a certification hearing is to occur within twenty-eight days of the defendant filing its defence: r 81(3).
[62] Improving Access to Justice: Final Report (n 22), Recommendation 4, and 153.
[63] ibid, 151–54.

and efficiently, in accordance with the Civil Procedure Rule's overriding objective which governs all litigation,[64] and which is duly repeated for the Competition Appeal Tribunal.[65] The government's response to the proposed UK competition law class action also noted that 'strong safeguards would be needed as part of an opt-out regime', one of which **must** be certification.[66] Specifically, 'there should be a strong process of judicial certification, including a preliminary merits test, an assessment of the adequacy of the representative, and a requirement that a collective action must be the best way of bringing the case'.[67]

All of this stamped the new regime with the ethos that certification was part and parcel of the case management to which **all** cases are subject in English litigation. To revert to the terminology of *Perera*,[68] there should be no presumptive entitlement for the representative claimant to go forward until the CAT decreed that outcome. The reality was that the UK Competition Law Class Action was never going to be enacted without the tight judicial control upfront which certification entails. It accords with the 'overriding objective' that permeates all UK civil litigation, and without it, the government was rightly concerned that the sub-parts of that objective would be seriously undermined.

In any event, the first certification decision handed down under the UK Competition Law Class Action, in *Gibson v Pride Mobility Products Ltd*,[69] bears testament to the efficiency with which class claims can be structured by the court, early in the proceedings, to either suit the regime or be disposed of altogether. In many respects, the case was a useful 'advertisement' for the benefits of certification. Not only did it clarify a point of law which will benefit other cases going forward, but it helped to focus the present case's concentration on that particular point, eventually leading to its withdrawal. The CAT required that the class's claim should demonstrate loss flowing from the *precise infringements* by the defendant which had been earlier found by the regulator, for the purposes of this follow-on action. As initially couched, the class's follow-on

---

[64] Per CPR 1.1(1).

[65] See CAT Rules, r 4, 'Governing Principles', which is in similar terms to the CPR's provisions noted ibid.

[66] *Private Actions in Competition Law: Government Response* (January 2013) [5.13], [5.16], [5.35]–[5.37].

[67] ibid, [5.55].

[68] See n 49 above.

[69] [2017] CAT 9. The decision is critiqued by the author in: 'The United Kingdom's New Opt-out Class Action' (2017) 37 *Oxford Journal of Legal Studies* 814.

claim was far too wide, and was 'misconceived as a matter of law'.[70] It was not proper (said the CAT) to claim losses incurred by those class members who purchased all thirty-two models of mobility scooters supplied by the defendant, Mobility Products, as part of some wider policy of resale price maintenance. The class action had to focus upon the *seven* specific models in the Pride range of mobility scooters which were affected, and upon those *eight* retailers with whom the regulator found that the defendant entered into agreements or concerted practices which had an anti-competitive object or effect. This decision meant that the class required narrowing, and the aggregate damages across that narrower class required recalculating, in order to rematch the original infringements. The representative claimant was provided with an opportunity to recast its economic evidence,[71] across a smaller band of purchasers than the entire market for Pride's mobility scooters.[72] The CAT made the point that it was not its role, at certification, 'to choose between the approaches of the two expert economists'[73] – but it was vital that the class definition, and the common issues, be correctly identified. Ultimately, the action was discontinued by the representative claimant, and the class action ended on 11 May 2017.[74] Hence, this first case prosecuted under the UK competition law class action aptly demonstrates the benefits of the certification process. Without it, the case would have required interlocutory applications by the defendant to seek to narrow the scope of the class, so as to align the follow-on action with the infringements found; with the inevitable delay and costs entailed. It was restructured by the CAT early in its life – and the representative claimant was duly given the opportunity to meet the challenge of reformulating her claim on behalf of the class and producing new economic evidence, which, ultimately, was not feasible. The end result was the saving of time and costs for all parties of prosecuting a flawed follow-on class claim.

The second filed action, that of *Merricks v Mastercard Inc*, was more complex (unsurprisingly, given that it is the largest-ever damages action filed in the United Kingdom[75]). The certification requirements were

---

[70] ibid, [112].

[71] Damages may be awarded 'without undertaking an assessment of the amount of damages recoverable in respect of the claim of each represented person': per CA 1998, s 47C(2).

[72] [2017] CAT 9, [114].

[73] ibid, [106].

[74] *Gibson v Pride Mobility Products Ltd* (Order of the President, Roth J, 25 May 2017).

[75] M Walters, 'Appeal Court Revives Mammoth £14bn Mastercard Group Action' (*Law Society Gazette*, 16 April 2019) ('[t]he £14bn damages claim was the largest sum claimed in English legal history').

again cited and applied by the CAT to foreclose the action,[76] but that decision has been the subject of a successful appeal,[77] and with a further permission to appeal to the Supreme Court under consideration at the time of writing.[78] The case concerns two key legal issues: the evidential threshold test required to be met when assessing aggregate damages; and the legal and practical mode of distributing those damages to the class members,[79] both by reference to the statutory wording used in the UK Competition Law Class Action. Again, in the author's view, a certification hearing was the best avenue by which to decide such important and precedential legal issues for the regime as a whole, especially so early in its life.

3   The Representative Claimant

In three respects, the UK lawmakers departed from the Australian class actions regime, when dealing with the representative claimant.

First, who can act in that capacity? There are **three** potential design choices: (1) the widest option, whereby the representative claimant may be **either** any class member with a direct cause of action against the defendant/s, **or** the so-called ideological claimant which may represent the interests of the class members but which does not have any direct cause of action; (2) mid-spectrum, any (and **only** a) directly-affected class member could have standing; or (3) at the narrowest, **only** the ideological claimant could sue.

The problem arising under the Australian regime concerned section 33C(1)(a), that '7 or more persons have claims against the same person';

---

[76] [2017] CAT 16, [22] ('[c]ertification in turn involves two aspects: (i) that the claims raise 'common issues'; and (ii) that the claims are suitable for collective proceedings: s 47B(6)').

[77] The CAT itself refused permission to appeal: *Merricks v Mastercard Inc* [2017] CAT 21; but application for leave was made directly to the CA: *Merricks v Mastercard Inc* [2018] EWCA Civ 2527 (Patten, Hamblen and Coulson LJJ) (leave to appeal permitted); and with the appeal allowed, and a re-hearing of certification by the CAT ordered: *Merricks v Mastercard Inc* [2019] EWCA Civ 674 (same court).

[78] The Court of Appeal denied the defendant permission to appeal, ibid (per oral judgment on 16 April 2019), but a direct application to appeal to the Supreme Court has been filed at the time of writing.

[79] Further analysis of this important decision has been undertaken by the author elsewhere: 'The Mere Mirage of a Class Action? A Challenge to *Merricks v Mastercard Inc*' (2018) 37 *CJQ* 216 (co-authored with D Edlin, re the first instance decision); and 'Revisiting the Class Action Certification Matrix in *Merricks v Mastercard Inc*' [2019] *King's Law Journal* (https://doi.org/10.1080/09615768.2019.1656392, in press) (re the Court of Appeal decision).

when read with section 33D(1), that a person 'who has a sufficient interest to commence a proceeding on his or her own behalf against another person has a sufficient interest to commence a representative proceeding against [the defendant] on behalf of other persons referred to in [s 33C(1)(a)]'. On the face of these provisions, option (2) seemed to apply – and some early Australian judgments certainly thought so.[80] However, the standing issue under Pt IVA turned out to be much more complex than that. Both a union[81] and the national consumer watchdog at the time (the ACCC[82]) were able to sue as representative claimants, on the basis that they did have a claim against the defendant under a statutory entitlement to sue for relief for themselves and others, conferred by statutes other than by Pt IVA (and, hence, they had a different cause of action from those of the class members).[83] In *Giraffe World*, Lindgren J later doubted that the ACCC was an appropriate representative claimant, 'where its only "claim" is its statutory standing to seek relief in the public interest' under a different statute'[84] (a topic to which attention will return in a later chapter[85]). It was all rather unsatisfactory and opaque.[86] The UK regime sought to remove any such uncertainty, by specifically permitting option (1), the widest possible form of standing:[87]

---

[80] *ACCC v Giraffe World Aust Pty Ltd* [1998] FCA 819, (1998) 84 FCR 512, 516 ('the representative party is necessarily one of the group of seven or more persons "on whose behalf a representative proceeding is commenced"'); *Symington v Hoechst Schering Agrevo Pty Ltd* [1997] FCA 969, (1997) 78 FCR 164, 167 ('the ... representative party ... must himself or herself have standing to sue the particular respondent').

[81] *Finance Sector Union of Australia v Commonwealth Bank of Australia Ltd* (1999) 94 FCR 179 (Full FCA). For an examination of the very extensive role that unions have played in Pt IVA class actions – whether as representative claimant, as a claimant who did not represent the class, as legal representative, or as funder – see: V Morabito and J Caruana, 'Australian Unions: The Unknown Class Action Protagonists' (2011) 30 *Civil Justice Quarterly* 382. These authors note that, despite the result in *Finance Sector*, unions rarely adopted the role of class representative thereafter (at 392).

[82] *Australian Competition and Consumer Commission (ACCC) v Chats House Investments Pty Ltd* (1996) 71 FCR 250, 254 (Branson J); and *ACCC v Golden Sphere Intl Inc* (1998) 83 FCR 424, 445 (O'Loughlin J).

[83] In the union's case, the Workplace Relations Act 1996, s 178(5)(d); and in the ACCC's case, the Trade Practices Act 1974, s 80(1).

[84] (1998) 84 FCR 512, 516.

[85] See Chapter 6, 'Government as Representative Claimant'.

[86] For academic critique, see: V Morabito, 'Ideological Plaintiffs and Class Actions: An Australian Perspective' (2001) 34 *University of British Columbia Law Review* 459, [44]; and Mulheron, *The Class Action* (n 12) 305–09.

[87] CA 1998, s 47B(8). The same approach is taken under the new Scottish generic regime: Civil Litigation (Expenses and Group Proceedings) (Scotland) Act 2018, s 20(3).

> The Tribunal may authorise a person to act as the representative in collective proceedings –
>
> (a) whether or not that person is a person falling within the class of persons described in the collective proceedings order for those proceedings (a 'class member'), but
>
> (b) only if the Tribunal considers that it is just and reasonable for that person to act as a representative in those proceedings.

This drafting choice was recommended by the Civil Justice Council,[88] and by the Department which promulgated the statute.[89] It was also the preferred choice in the financial services regime which ultimately 'washed up' in 2010.[90] As the author has discussed elsewhere, the UK lawmakers were never going to embrace option (3), given unsatisfactory experience with that previously,[91] but were prepared to incorporate ideological claimants as part of a very broad standing base. As it turned out, the very first class action filed under the UK Competition Law Class Action entailed just such a claimant.[92] Dorothy Gibson, General Secretary of the National Pensioners' Convention, had not purchased a mobility scooter, and hence, had no direct cause of action herself.[93] The CAT approved of her representation of the class at certification.[94]

The second divergence between the UK Competition Law Class Action and the Australian Pt IVA class action regime concerns an absence of conflicts of interest as between the representative claimant and the class members. There is no express reference in the Australian statute to this issue, but the requirement of adequate representation[95] was judicially interpreted, in *ACCC v Golden Sphere International Inc*,[96] to mean precisely that. This was always going to be a sensitive issue for UK drafters, given that potential conflicts of interest featured in both the

---

[88] *Improving Access to Justice: Final Report* (n 22), Recommendation 2, p 141–43.

[89] BIS, *Private Actions in Competition Law: Government Response* (January 2013) [5.30], [5.32].

[90] Per cl 18(5) of the Financial Services Bill 2009 ('A person may be authorised . . . to bring proceedings even if the person would not otherwise be regarded as having any interest, or any sufficient interest, in the proceedings').

[91] 'The United Kingdom's New Opt-out Class Action' (n 69) 827–33, citing the experience under the now-repealed s 47B of the CA 1998.

[92] *Gibson v Pride Mobility Products Ltd* [2017] CAT 9.

[93] ibid, [128].

[94] ibid, [139], [145].

[95] Per FCA 1976, s 33T(1).

[96] (1998) 83 FCR 424, 446.

Chancellor's[97] and the Court of Appeal's[98] decisions to deny the representative proceeding in *Emerald Supplies Ltd v British Airways plc*. The class members and the representative lacked the requisite 'same interest'. The case was such an important prompter for the new regime that any of its significant points were undoubtedly taken much heed of.[99] Hence, UK lawmakers preferred that an absence of any conflict of interest should be an express mandatory legislative criterion, when determining whether it is 'just and reasonable' for that party to so act.[100]

Thirdly, nowhere in the Australian regime is it stated that the financial resources of the representative claimant are relevant to the question of adequate representation. Security for costs applications against that representative are explicitly preserved in the Australian legislation[101] (as they are under the UK regime[102]) – but the UK legislature went further – much further. It is a mandatory certification requirement that the representative 'will be able to pay the defendant's recoverable costs if ordered to do so',[103] and will be able to satisfy any undertaking as to damages required by the CAT, where an interim injunction is sought.[104] The CAT is also entitled to order the representative claimant to provide 'an estimate of and details of arrangements as to costs, fees or disbursements'.[105] The provision has been put to good effect. For example, in the first certification decision of *Gibson v Pride Mobility Products Ltd*, the details of Ms Gibson's use of third-party funding, and an ATE policy taken out to cover adverse costs, together with detailed costs budgets, were scrutinised closely by the CAT, and considered to be adequate.[106]

---

[97] [2009] EWHC 741 (Ch) [36]–[37] ('the conflict between different members of the class is not a consequence of any esoteric defence of "passing on" but is inherent in damage being a necessary ingredient in the cause of action').

[98] [2010] EWCA Civ 1284, [69] (Mummery LJ, with Toulson and Rimer LJJ agreeing) ('[t]he potential conflicts arising from the defences that could be raised by BA to different claimants . . . reinforce the fact that they do not have the same interest and that the proceedings are not equally beneficial to all those to be represented').

[99] Discussed further by the author in: 'The Impetus for Class Actions Reform in England arising from the Competition Law Sector', in S Wrbka *et al.* (eds), *Collective Actions: Enhancing Access to Justice and Reconciling Multilayer Interests?* (Cambridge University Press, 2012), ch 15.

[100] See CAT Rules, r 78(2)(b).

[101] Per a combined reading of FCA 1976, ss 33ZG(c)(v) and 56.

[102] Per CAT Rules, r 98(1).

[103] CAT Rules, r 78(2)(d).

[104] CAT Rules, r 78(2)(e).

[105] CAT Rules, r 78(3)(c)(iii).

[106] [2017] CAT 9, [140]–[145].

Each of these three divergences implemented by the UK lawmakers built upon the lessons learnt via Australia's twenty-five years of experience of seeking to ensure that the party representing the class was adequate to do so.

4   The 'Multiple Defendant' Conundrum

Price-fixing litigation is one scenario which, of its very nature, raises the problem of what standing is necessary in the event of numerous defendants, because a number of alleged cartellists may be the subject of an alleged or proven infringement.

There are **three** design options by which to handle standing against multiple defendants:

(i) at the strict end of the spectrum, it is necessary that each and every representative claimant (and class member) has standing against each defendant;

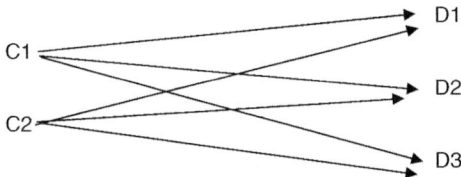

(ii) mid-spectrum, it is necessary that at least one representative claimant has a claim against each defendant (even if other representatives and class members do not); or

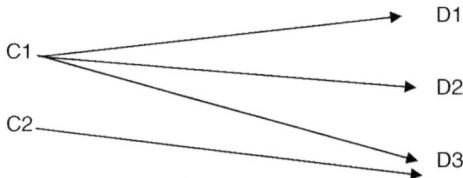

(iii) at the most liberal end, it is necessary that each defendant has a claim brought against it by *a* representative claimant, but not necessarily by the same representative claimant.

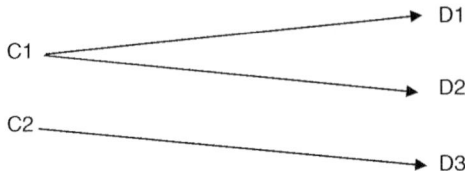

It is an issue which was statutorily silent under Australia's federal opt-out regime, and which the Australian federal court judiciary had to resolve. The judicial treatment of this issue had not been entirely straightforward (as the author[107] and others[108] have explained elsewhere). Early in the life of Pt IVA, Wilcox J declared[109] that option (1) was necessary, a view that was upheld at appellate level in the tobacco litigation of *Philip Morris (Australia) Ltd v Nixon*,[110] where the class action against six tobacco companies was disallowed, due to a failure to comply with the requisite standing requirements. Of most interest to UK law reformers was that the issue was re-ventilated in the competition law context in *Bray v Hoffman-La Roche Ltd*,[111] a vitamin price-fixing case involving eleven cartellists. Some representative claimants (and class members) did not consume any defendants' vitamins at all. The majority of the Full Federal Court[112] again preferred the view that each representative claimant must have a claim against each defendant named in the proceedings; but that strict view was softened by three caveats. First, not all *class members* had to have a claim against each and every defendant. Secondly, each of the representative claimants and class members had a claim for injunctive relief against the cartellists, which relaxed the requirement substantially from what it would have been, had the court insisted upon each representative claimant suffering loss by the acts or omissions of each defendant. Third, where either collective conduct or conspiracy is alleged (as in this case), it is easier to establish a class action against multiple defendants.[113]

---

[107] This section summarises the author's treatment of this issue in: *The Class Action* (n 12) 144–57; and *Competition Law Cases* (n 22) 42–44.

[108] e.g., V Morabito, 'Class Actions Against Multiple Respondents' (2002) 30 *Federal Law Review* 295, and by the same author: 'Standing to Sue and Multiple Defendant Class Actions in Australia, Canada and the United States' (2003) 41 *Alberta Law Review* 295; Victorian LRC, *Civil Justice Review Report* (2008) 528–31; Grave et al., *Class Actions in Australia* (n 27) 140–54.

[109] *Ryan v Great Lakes Council* (1997) 78 FCR 309. See too: *Symington v Hoechst Schering Agrevo Pty Ltd* (1997) 78 FCR 164 ('the applicant, or each one of several applicants, and each group member must have a claim against each respondent; it is not sufficient for one applicant to make a claim against one respondent and another applicant or a group member to make a claim against some other respondent').

[110] (2000) 170 ALR 487 (Full FCA) [126]–[127].

[111] [2003] FCAFC 153. An application for special leave to the High Court was argued, but ultimately discontinued: *BASF Australia Ltd v Bray* [2004] HCA Trans 206.

[112] Carr and Finkelstein JJ, with Branson J dissenting.

[113] ibid, [122]–[130] (Carr J) [243] (Finkelstein J). Cf Branson J [199].

Controversy persisted, however. In 2014, the Full Federal Court was again confronted with the issue in *Cash Converters Intl Ltd v Gray*.[114] It was common ground that, in light of *Philip Morris* and *Bray*, the *representative claimant* must have a claim against each defendant,[115] but did each *class member* need to have a claim against each defendant? After noting that there was conflicting authority at the level of the Full Federal Court and at first instance, and after yet another exercise in construing the legislative wording, the Full Federal Court concluded that it was **not** necessary that each class member have a claim against each defendant.[116]

The difficulties surrounding the issue in Australia are illustrated further by the fact that the New South Wales state class action regime was worded differently from the federal and other state regimes. In a provision unique to that regime, it is provided that:[117]

> **s 158(2)** The person may commence representative proceedings on behalf of other persons against more than one defendant irrespective of whether or not the person and each of those persons have a claim against every defendant in the proceedings.

That provision has recently been interpreted in *Fernandez v New South Wales*,[118] a class action arising out of the payment for medical care granted to non-Australian permanent residents. There were sixteen defendants (the state government, and fifteen local health districts). The representative claimants, Mr Fernandez and Ms Fotu, only had dealings with two of those local health districts, and a dispute arose as to whether they had standing to sue the other thirteen on behalf of the class. Garling J concluded (tentatively, in rejecting a summary judgment application by the defendant) that the aforementioned provision was a 'critical provision',[119] and that its 'preferable construction ... do[es] not require the plaintiff in representative proceedings or the group members, to have a claim against every defendant ..., providing that either a plaintiff or a group member has such a claim'.[120] By reflecting option (3), this evidences a more liberal attitude on the part of the both

---

[114] [2014] FCAFC 111 (Jacobson, Middleton, and Gordon JJ).
[115] ibid, [13].
[116] ibid.
[117] Civil Procedure Act 2005 (NSW), s 158(2), which took effect on 4 March 2011.
[118] [2019] NSWSC 255.
[119] ibid, [47].
[120] ibid, [65], and hence, choosing not to adopt the *Bray* interpretation, which was discussed in [50].

legislators and judiciary regarding standing against multiple defendants. Indeed, some commentators have suggested that New South Wales will be favoured for forum-shopping purposes for that reason.[121]

The UK's class action drafters were fully aware of the multiple defendant problem arising under Australia's federal regime – and, ultimately, their choice was to enact option (iii) for the UK Competition Law Class Action:[122]

> The following points apply in relation to claims in collective proceedings –
>
> (a) it is not a requirement that all of the claims should be against all of the defendants to the proceedings.

It is to be expected that this provision would be judicially interpreted in the same manner in which the relevant New South Wales standing provision has been interpreted in *Fernandez*, i.e., in a claimant's favour. In any event, this is a tangible example of how the convolutions of Australian judicial reasoning have been explicitly avoided by the UK drafters – and will be especially important for relevant multi-defendant stand-alone or follow-on cartel cases commenced under the UK regime in the future.

5   The Three Thresholds

At its essence, any sort of class action requires the twin pillars of commonality of grievance, together with a sufficient number of persons who share those grievances. In both respects, the UK reformers considered that the Australian drafters may have set the bar a little too high, and that 'brakes' upon the class action proceeding were better implemented by tougher requirements for the representative claimant and various other criteria (all of which are reproduced in Table 3.2, later in this chapter[123]). However, in respect of how meritorious the claim must be, in order for it to be instituted as a class action at all, the UK law reformers considered that the Australian requirements were not quite strong enough, and

---

[121] J Emmerig *et al.*, 'Supreme Court of New South Wales Relaxes Requirements for Class Actions' (Jones Day Publications, April 2019), available at: www.jonesday.com /Supreme-Court-of-New-South-Wales-Relaxes-Requirements-for-Class-Actions-04–08-2019/#.

[122] Per CA 1998, s 47B(3)(a).

[123] See pp 126–127.

introduced several additional preliminary merits criteria. These various issues are discussed below.

(a)   Commonality

Re-commonality, an identical formula as is used in Pt IVA[124] – 'the same, similar or related issues of fact or law' – is used in the UK Competition Law Class Action,[125] but in a different way. Although Wilcox J stated (extra-curially[126]) that the 'related' requirement imposed a burden that was 'difficult to state', different courts concluded that it is a very low threshold to surmount. Variously, it must mean 'a connection wider than identity or similarity',[127] that it represented a 'reasonably liberal approach' to certification,[128] that it contemplates 'a broad and indirect connection between two subject matters',[129] and that it does not require that the class members share the same 'claims' against the defendant.[130] However, so far as the author can identify, it is still not possible to identify any case in which the representative claimant has proven the also-required criterion of a 'substantial common issue of law or fact',[131] and yet has failed to prove the separate criterion of a 'same, similar or related issue' (or vice versa). Hence, it is difficult to know what the 'related' criterion adds to the commencement matrix in Australia (and some scholars have noted that the requirement is 'relatively easy for applicants to establish in practice'[132]).

The UK drafters approached the drafting differently (and, it is suggested, more elegantly), by stating that the class members must have claims that 'raise common issues',[133] where 'common issues' means 'the

---

[124] FCA 1976, s 33C(1)(b).

[125] CA 1998, s 47B(6); and CAT Rules, r 73(2).

[126] 'Representative Proceedings in the Federal Court: A Progress Report' (1997) 15 *Australian Bar Review* 91, 92.

[127] *Zhang de Yong v Minister for Immigration, Local Govt and Ethnic Affairs* (1993) 45 FCR 384, 404–05.

[128] *AS v Minister for Immigration and Border Protection* [2014] VSC 593, [54]. The same wording is repeated in the Victorian state regime.

[129] *Rickhuss v Cosmetic Institute Pty Ltd* [2018] NSWSC 1848, [60], referring to the identical provision in the New South Wales regime.

[130] Most recently affirmed in: *Gill v Ethicon Sàrl (No 3)* [2019] FCA 587, [6].

[131] Per FCA 1976, s 33C(1)(c).

[132] e.g., Grave *et al.*, *Class Actions in Australia* (n 27) 159. Also: Stuart-Clark *et al.* (n 27) 408 ('[t]hese requirements . . . continue to be applied liberally'); Morabito, 'Class Actions Against Multiple Respondents' (n 108) 295, 323–24 ('[t]he inclusion of the word "related" . . . tends to suggest that this provision was not intended to place, in the path of potential representative parties, a significant barrier').

[133] CAT Rules, r 79(1)(b).

same, similar or related issues of fact or law'.[134] In that respect, the criterion is not *additional* under the UK regime – it is *definitional*. Nothing has turned on that phrase in any contentious way to date.

The UK drafters also entirely avoided any 'threshold requirement'[135] of a 'substantial' common issue, as appears in section 33C(1)(c). That one word entailed a great deal of controversy in the early days of Pt IVA jurisprudence.[136] It was eventually interpreted, in *Wong v Silkfield Pty Ltd*,[137] to mean an issue which was not 'ephemeral or nominal'; one which was 'real or of substance';[138] but not one 'of special significance'.[139] Nor did it mean that the common issues had predominance over the individual issues on a numerical basis;[140] or that a common issue could resolve the claims of the class members once and for all, or that the common issue would have a 'major impact on the litigation';[141] or that the common issue would advance the determination of liability across multiple causes of action[142] – all of which had been upheld in earlier proceedings at federal court level. As one court recently explained, the word 'substantial' is one which is 'protean', and that, in *Wong*, '[t]he court's reasoning permitted context to determine where on the continuum the intended meaning was to be found'.[143]

However, given the judicial uncertainty as to how the term should be interpreted – and then, how 'watered down' that requirement of substantiality ultimately became – it is not surprising that the UK drafters did not adopt it.

(b)   Preliminary Merits

As with all litigation, the claimant must show that a viable cause of action is being pleaded against the defendant. The Australian federal regime requires that the representative claimant has 'a claim',[144] and provides

---

[134] CA 1998, s 47B(6); and CAT Rules, r 73(2).
[135] Per *Wong v Silkfield Pty Ltd* (1999) 199 CLR 255, [28].
[136] As discussed, e.g., in: Grave *et al.*, *Class Actions in Australia* (n 27) 165–67; Mulheron, *The Class Action* (n 12) 190–210; Stuart-Clark and Harris (n 41) 319, and by the same authors: 'Class Actions in Australia: (Still) a Work in Progress' (2008) 31 *Australian Bar Review* 63, 75–76; Morabito, 'Class Actions Against Multiple Respondents' (n 108) 328.
[137] (1999) 199 CLR 255, [27].
[138] ibid, [28].
[139] ibid.
[140] Per *Connell v Nevada Financial Group Pty Ltd* (1996) 139 ALR 723 (FCA).
[141] Per the majority in *Wong v Silkfield Pty Ltd* (1998) 90 FCR 152 (Full FCA).
[142] Per *Milfull v Terranora Lakes Country Club Ltd* (FCA, 16 June 1998).
[143] *Stojanovski v Australian Dream Homes* [2015] VSC 404, [45], [47], and cited in: *Dimitropoulos v Capital Constructions Pty Ltd* [2018] NSWCATAP 100, [74].
[144] Per FCA 1976, Pt IVA, s 33C(1)(a).

that nothing affects the court's powers 'in relation to a proceeding in which no reasonable cause of action is disclosed or that is oppressive, vexatious, frivolous or an abuse of the process of the court'.[145] (The Canadian regimes also typically provide that the claim must 'disclose a cause of action'.[146]) This relatively undemanding threshold is repeated in the UK Competition Law Class Action. Any suit must meet the threshold of showing a 'reasonable cause of action',[147] to prevent its being a frivolous suit; and default judgment[148] and summary judgment[149] remain options for all defendants if the substantive causes of action being pleaded against them look unarguable, weak or vexatious.

UK reformers were aware that the Australian federal regime contained a merits criterion which, if met, could provide the court with a ground for staying or for discontinuing a class action:

> s 33M Where ... the cost to the respondent of identifying the group members and distributing to them the amounts ordered to be paid to them would be excessive, having regard to the likely total of those amounts

The provision has not proven to be straightforward to apply in the very limited case law which has turned upon its wording.[150] Academic[151] and law reform[152] opinion has not been particularly kind to the provision either.

However, it was plain that the ethos demonstrated by the Australian legislators – that some higher threshold was required – was preferable to UK policymakers and lawmakers, rather than the type of explicit statement by the Canadian legislatures that a certification order 'is not a determination of

---

[145] Per s 33ZG(b).

[146] e.g., Ontario's Class Proceedings Act, SO 1992, s 5(1)(a); Newfoundland and Labrador's Class Actions Act, SNL 2001, c C-18.1, s 5(1)(a), albeit that Canadian courts accept that an assessment of merits 'could indirectly become relevant' during parts of the certification analysis (especially, commonality, superiority and class definition): see, e.g., *Warner v Smith & Nephew Inc* [2016] ABCA 223, [82]–[90].

[147] CAT Rules, r 41.

[148] CAT Rules, r 42.

[149] CAT Rules, r 43.

[150] e.g., it was not successful in: *Bray v F Hoffman-La Roche Ltd* [2002] FCA 1405, [61].

[151] Grave *et al.*, *Class Actions in Australia* (n 27) 512–13; V Morabito, 'The Federal Court of Australia's Power to Terminate Properly Instituted Class Actions' (2004) 42 *Osgoode Hall Law Journal* 473, 490; Mulheron, 'Justice Enhanced' (n 12) 568–71.

[152] Victorian LRC, *Civil Justice Review* (Rep 14, 2008) 539–40, arguing that the provision acts as an impediment to *cy-près* relief under the regime.

the merits of the proceedings'.[153] The UK Government considered that an analysis of 'the strength of the claims'[154] (which makes no appearance in the Australian regime) was 'particularly important for opt-out proceedings, as cases can be brought without class members' knowledge or consent, as they do not need to actively participate in the claim'.[155] Moreover, the preceding consultation report had also stressed that a preliminary merits assessment[156] (falling short of a 'full merits test'[157]) was an important part of upfront judicial scrutiny.

As a result, a cost–benefit test[158] and a financial threshold test[159] (the meanings of which are not entirely clear,[160] and which have yet to be judicially scrutinised[161]) were implemented by the UK lawmakers. The representative claimant must also 'believe that the claims … have a real prospect of success',[162] and 'the estimated amount of damages that individual class members may recover' also potentially matters.[163] By enacting these requirements, the UK lawmakers considered, but eschewed, other options for preliminary merits which had been recommended elsewhere.[164]

---

[153] e.g., Ontario's Class Proceedings Act, SO 1992, c 6, s 5(5); Newfoundland and Labrador's Class Actions Act, SNL 2001, c C-18.1, s 6(2); Saskatchewan's Class Actions Act, SS 2001, c C-12.01, s 7(2); Manitoba's Class Proceedings Act, CCSM c C130, s 5(2); British Columbia's Class Proceedings Act, RSBC 1996, c 50, s 5(7); Nova Scotia's Class Proceedings Act, SNS 2007, c 28, s 8(2); New Brunswick's Class Proceedings Act, RSNB 2011, c 125, s 7(2); Alberta's Class Proceedings Act, SA 2003, c C-16.5, s 6(2).

[154] CAT Rules, r 79(3)(a). This criterion applies when the CAT must choose between opt-in and opt-out.

[155] BIS, *Competition Appeal Tribunal (CAT) Rules of Procedure: Government Response* (September 2015) [3.16].

[156] BIS, *Private Actions in Competition Law: Government Response* (January 2013) [5.55].

[157] BIS (n 155) [3.16].

[158] CAT Rules, r 79(2)(b).

[159] CAT Rules, r 79(3)(b).

[160] See critique of the preliminary merits criteria by the author in: 'The United Kingdom's New Opt-out Class Action' (n 69) 837–42.

[161] An opportunity to do so may arise in any re-hearing of certification in *Merricks v Mastercard Inc*, as ordered by the Court of Appeal: [2019] EWCA Civ 674, and as speculated upon by the author in: 'Revisiting the Class Action Certification Matrix in *Merricks v Mastercard Inc*' (2019) 30 *King's Law Journal* 396.

[162] CAT Rules, r 75(2)(h). Whilst there has been no judicial pronouncement as yet, it is likely that the representative claimant's belief must be based on reasonable grounds, i.e., an objective test: as argued in: A Higgins, 'Driving with the Handbrake On: Competition Class Actions under the Consumer Rights Act 2015' (2016) 79 *Modern Law Review* 442, 451; Mulheron, 'The United Kingdom's New Opt-Out Class Action' (n 69) 834.

[163] CAT Rules, r 79(3)(b).

[164] *US Advisory Committee on Rules of Civil Procedure* (1996), cl 23(c)(F) (the court must consider 'whether the probable relief to individual class members justifies the costs and burdens of the litigation'); Ontario LRC, *Report on Class Actions* (1982), 862, Draft Bill, cl

Undoubtedly, those criteria which **were** implemented will (it is suggested) provide some considerable challenges for a representative claimant under the UK Competition Law Class Action, and some significant scope for argument. Ultimately, though, these 'brakes'[165] were preferred by the UK drafters, over and above the option of requiring a 'substantial common issue', as demonstrated shortly in Table 3.2.

(c)   Numerosity

The numerosity of the class has also been approached quite differently under the UK and Australian regimes. The latter requires a minimum of seven in the class (per section 33C(1)(a)). Rarely has this been an issue under the Australian federal regime in competition law (or, indeed, any) cases – although, surprisingly, it was contentious in the very early competition law class action of *Gold Coast City Council v Pioneer Concrete (Qld) Pty Ltd.*[166] That case arose out of price-fixing (and collusive tendering) of pre-mixed concrete over a five-year period. Drummond J remarked that:

> it might be thought that, in an area as large as the City of the Gold Coast, there would be, at the very least, seven persons who would fall within the class defined by the applicant. But the Gold Coast City Council, despite the attack made on the representative proceedings in this respect, has not produced any evidence confirming the existence of any person or organisation within the definition of group membership interested in recovering losses suffered as a result of the defendant's conduct by means of the representative action.[167]

The UK drafters elected to opt for the requirement of 'two or more claims' for the UK Competition Law Class action.[168] This option

---

3(3)(a) (the court must be satisfied that 'the action is brought in good faith and there is a reasonable possibility that material questions of fact and law common to the class will be resolved at trial in favour of the class'); OLRC, ibid, cl 6(1) (the court must consider whether 'the adverse effects of the proceedings upon the class, the courts or the public, would outweigh the benefits to the class, the courts or the public that might be secured if the action were certified'); Law Reform Committee of South Australia, *Relating to Class Actions* (Rep 36, 1977) 12, cl 3(3)(a) (the action must be 'brought in good faith and appears to have merit'); South African Law Comm, *The Recognition of Class Actions and Public Interest Actions in South African Law* (1998) 87, Draft Public Interest and Class Actions Act, cl 6(2)(b) (the court must 'take into account the existence of a prima facie cause of action', although the term, 'prima facie' was to 'probably mean that he or she only needs to aver fact that, if true, would establish a cause of action': 42–43).

[165] Reproduced at pp 126–127.

[166] (FCA, 9 July 1997).

[167] ibid, accessed via LexisNexis, no pinpoint available.

[168] CA 1998, s 47B(1). The same minimum threshold of two persons is provided for in the Scottish generic regime: Civil Litigation (Expenses and Group Proceedings) (Scotland) Act 2018, s 20(2).

particularly avoids the Australian conundrum of having to prove a minimum of seven members, whilst reconciling that with section 33H(2)'s statement that '[i]n describing or otherwise identifying group members . . .., it is not necessary to name, or specify the number of, the group members' (a provision thankfully not reproduced in the UK Competition Law Class Action). In other words, under the Australian federal regime, the class representative must prove the existence of seven class members, but does not need to name or to identify them. The tension between these two provisions was one which Wilcox J valiantly attempted to resolve in *Tropical Shine Holdings Pty Ltd v Lake Gesture Pty Ltd*,[169] but (in the author's view[170]) unconvincingly.

The fact that Australian federal courts have long been unwilling to declare that a class action was invalidly commenced because there were fewer than seven class members[171] only reinforces the point that the UK drafters were correct to set a 'bare threshold' as the prescribed minimum number. Certainly, the 'two or more' criterion may be criticised as 'all but remov[ing] a numerosity requirement'.[172] However, it presents a workable solution, when viewed within the context of the UK Competition Law Class Action regime as a whole. After all, there are numerous other criteria that will screen out unsuitable claims.[173]

6 A Funder's Success Fee

The usual accoutrements of costs and funding, as occur under Australia's federal regime, were implemented within the UK competition class action. Costs-shifting applies.[174] Security for costs orders may be made against the representative claimant.[175] Class members are 'immunised' from costs,[176] although the represented person will bear costs associated with the determination of individual issues.[177]

---

[169] (1993) 45 FCR 457.

[170] *The Class Action* (n 12) 118–19.

[171] See the discussion in, e.g.: Grave *et al.*, *Class Actions in Australia* (n 27) 136–39; Mulheron, ibid, 117–21.

[172] As described by the Manitoba LRC, *Class Proceedings* (Rep 100, 1999) 49, although that Commission ultimately endorsed the criterion, without detailed discussion.

[173] The view expressed in: *The Class Action* (n 12) 129. Those 'other criteria' contained in the UK Competition Law Class Action are collected in Table 3.2, later in this chapter.

[174] FCA 1976, s 33ZG(c)(v); CAT Rules, r 98(1).

[175] FCA 1976, s 33ZG(c)(v); CAT Rules, r 59(1).

[176] FCA 1976, s 43(1A); CAT Rules, r 98(1).

[177] CAT Rules, r 98(1)(b), r 98(2).

However (and in common with the Australian landscape), third-party funding is **not** prohibited under the UK Competition Law Class Action. Whilst the UK Government was clearly concerned about 'incentivising lawyers to bring cases',[178] thereby expressly prohibiting percentage contingency fees in the context of opt-out class proceedings;[179] and whilst it specifically recommended against any third party funder from being the representative claimant,[180] there was no ban on third-party funders from acting on a contingency basis. Indeed, the use of third-party funding for collective redress has been endorsed at a very senior judicial level in both the United Kingdom[181] and in Australia.[182] However, the UK reformers were very conscious of the conundrum: how does the litigation funder recover its 'success fee' from the class members, in an opt-out class action? There are **four** options for doing so:[183]

 (i) via a contractual entitlement as between the funder and the class members, by virtue of 'tied' or 'closed classes' – albeit that the UK lawmakers were aware, at the time of their own reforms, of the

---

[178] BIS, *Private Actions in Competition Law: A Consultation on Options for Reform* (April 2012) 5, and Box 6; and: *Government Response* (January 2013) [5.43]–[5.45]; [5.62]–[5.63].

[179] CA 1998, s 47C(8). Conditional fees are, however, still permitted.

[180] *Private Actions in Competition Law: Government Response* (2013) [5.32].

[181] See, e.g.: *Giles v Thompson* [1994] 1 AC 142 (HL); *R (Factortame) Ltd v Sec of State for Transport (No 8)* [2002] EWCA Civ 932; *Arkin v Borchard Lines Ltd* [2005] EWCA Civ 655, and the various other appellate authorities traced and analysed in: R Mulheron and P Cashman, 'Third Party Funding of Litigation: A Changing Landscape' (2008) 27 *Civil Justice Quarterly* 312; and since then, see, e.g.: Sir Rupert Jackson, *Review of Civil Litigation Costs: Final Report* (December 2009), ch 33, [4.3]; and also, by the same author: *Sixth Lecture in the Civil Litigation Costs Review Implementation Programme* (RCJ, 23 November 2011) [4.3]; and *Excalibur Ventures LLC v Texas Keystone Inc* [2016] EWCA Civ 1144.

[182] As just a sample: *Campbells Cash and Carry Pty Ltd v Fostif Pty Ltd* [2006] HCA 41 (Gleeson CJ, Gummow, Hayne, Crenna, Kirby JJ; with Callinan and Heydon JJ dissenting on this point); *Project 28 Pty Ltd (formerly Narui Gold Coast Pty Ltd) v Barr* [2005] NSWCA 240; *Clairs Keeley (a firm) v Treacy* [2004] WASCA 277; and the several other authorities cited in: Australian LRC, *Integrity, Fairness and Efficiency: Final Report* (2018) (n 27), especially ch 2.

[183] This section condenses the analysis of Canadian, US, and Australian law, in: Mulheron, 'Third Party Funding and Class Actions Reform' (n 12) Pt III. Various of the options are also discussed in, e.g.: Higgins, 'Driving with the Handbrake On' (n 162) 458–67; D Grave and J Betts, 'The Commission Recommendation on Common Principles for Collective Redress: Some Reflections from Australia', in E Lein *et al.* (eds), *Collective Redress in Europe: Why and How?* (BIICL, 2015) 227–9; R Gamble, 'Jostling for a Piece of the (Class) Action: Third Party Funders and Entrepreneurial Lawyers Stake their Claims' (2017) 46 *Common Law World Review* 3.

strong division of judicial opinion in Australia in favour of,[184] or opposing,[185] that avenue of assuring remuneration of the funder;[186] of the resulting propensity for competing 'closed' class actions against the same defendant and relating to the same grievance;[187] and of the fact that the New South Wales state regime had explicitly permitted such closed classes on the face of its statute;[188]

(ii) via the equitable 'common fund' doctrine: i.e., where there is 'the creation, preservation or increase of a fund in which others have an interest'[189] – and which received judicial approval under the Australian federal class action regime, just after the UK Competition Law Class Action came into force, in *Money Max Int Pty Ltd v QBE Ins Group Ltd*;[190]

---

[184] i.e., *P Dawson Nominees Pty Ltd v Multiplex Ltd* [2007] FCA 1061, (2008) 25 ACLC 1192 (Finkelstein J); and on appeal: *Multiplex Funds Management Ltd v P Dawson Nominees Pty Ltd* [2007] FCAFC 200, (2007) 244 ALR 600 (Jacobson J, with Lindgren and French JJ concurring).

[185] e.g.: *Dorajay Pty Ltd v Aristocrat Leisure Ltd* (2005) 147 FCR 394 (Stone J); *Rod Investments (Vic) Pty Ltd v Clark* [2005] VSC 449 (Hansen J); *Jameson v Professional Investment Services Pty Ltd* [2007] NSWSC 1437, [107] (Young CJ).

[186] Described in: ALRC, *Inquiry into Class Action Proceedings and Third-Party Litigation Funders* (DP 85, June 2018) [1.79]–[1.80], [6.11]–[6.14], and in the *Final Report* (2018) (n 27) [2.72]–[2.73].

[187] Discussed, e.g., in: B Phi, 'Arming the Courts in Collective Redress: A Move to "Australian-Style" Class Actions in the UK?' (2017) 36 *Civil Justice Quarterly* 197, 209–10; V Morabito, *An Empirical Study of Australia's Class Action Regimes (Second Report)* (September 2010), ch 2 (although Professor Morabito concluded that the judicial permission of tied classes 'has not increased the frequency with which this problem has been dealt with by the Federal Court', given that the phenomenon had *already* occurred prior to that: at 28); by the same author: 'Empirical Perspectives', in Grave and Mould (eds), *25 Years of Class Actions* (n 27), ch 4, 59–61; R Overington, 'Resolving Multiple Claims: How Efficient is the Class Action Regime?', in Grave and Mould (eds), ibid, ch 7.

[188] Civil Procedure Act 2005 (NSW), Pt 10, s 166(2). This was one of the most significant differences between this state regime and the earlier federal regime, as noted in: Beech-Jones (The Hon Justice Robert), 'Representative Actions in NSW Courts' (23 March 2017) 2.

[189] *Alyeska Pipeline Service Co v Wilderness Socy*, 421 US 240, 257 (1975); and discussed in further detail, by reference to US case law, in: Mulheron, 'Third Party Funding and Class Actions Reform' (n 12) 296–98.

[190] [2016] FCAFC 148 (26 October 2016), the impact of which was considered subsequently in: *Blairgowrie Trading Ltd v Allco Finance Group Ltd (R&M appointed) (in liq) (No 3)* [2017] FCA 330 (31 March 2017). See, for recent critical analysis: ALRC, *Inquiry into Class Action Proceedings and Third-Party Litigation Funders* (DP 85, June 2018) [6.15]–[6.19]; J Betts *et al.*, 'Litigation Funding for Class Actions', and S Khouri *et al.*, 'Litigation Funding and Class Actions: Idealism, Pragmatism and a New Paradigm', both contained in Grave and Mould (eds), *25 Years of Class Actions* (n 27), chs 10 and 11 respectively.

(iii) by judicial reliance upon some sort of general judicial supervisory power, vested by virtue of the governing legislation – i.e., under Pt IVA, 'to make any order the Court thinks appropriate or necessary to ensure that justice is done in the proceeding';[191] and

(iv) finally, via an express statutory provision which creates a form of statutory charge in favour of the funder – somewhat analogous to the charge which may be ordered to attach to the recovered damages under Pt IVA, for the amount by which solicitor-and-own-client costs exceeds recoverable costs.[192]

For UK purposes, two cautionary statements by Australian federal judges turned out to be prescient for the sectoral reforms which occurred in 2015. First, in *Blairgowrie Trading Ltd v Allco Finance Group Ltd (R&M Appointed)*, Wigney J stated:

> There is something to be said for the proposition that some form of common fund approach, similar to the common fund doctrine in the United States, should be adopted in Australia to deal with the reality of commercial litigation funding in representative proceedings. It would, however, perhaps be preferable for that to occur as a result of legislative reform, rather than by way of the piecemeal utilisation by judges of general discretionary powers such as ss 23 and 33ZF.[193]

However, given that it took the Australian judiciary almost twenty-five years to adopt a form of 'common fund' order (probably against all expectations of the drafters of Pt IVA[194]) – and given that there is no history of such a fund in English law in **any** context – then it was unlikely that such a doctrine (whether based in equity or on restitutionary principles[195]) was likely to be invoked under the UK Competition Law Class Action, in a funder's favour. The 'legislative reform' suggested by Wigney J was always going to be a more practicable solution. The second significant statement was that of Stone J, much earlier, in *Dorajay*:[196]

---

[191] Per FCA 1976, s 33ZF(1). For an excellent analysis of this provision, see: M Legg and J Metzger, 'Section 33ZF: Class Actions Problem Solver?' in Grave and Mould (eds), (n 27), ch 16. A somewhat similar provision exists in the CAT Rules, r 88(1) ('[t]he Tribunal may, at any time, give any directions it thinks appropriate for the case management of the collective proceedings').

[192] Per FCA 1976, s 33ZJ(2).

[193] [2015] FCA 811, [227].

[194] Murphy and Morabito, 'The First 25 Years', in Grave and Mould (eds), *25 Years of Class Actions* (n 27) 39.

[195] The US jurisprudence is split on this point: Mulheron, 'Third Party Funding' (n 12) 296–98.

[196] (2005) 147 FCR 394, [111] and [117].

Parliament has made a clear choice [in Pt IVA], and it is not for the courts to hold otherwise. Therefore it is necessary to address whether [a tied class] has the effect of implementing an opt-in procedure or otherwise subverting the process that the legislature has adopted . . . [t]he legislature made a clear choice [to adopt an opt-out regime] that was consistent with the recommendation of the Australian Law Reform Commission on this issue. Whatever advantages, real or apparent, may flow from the ability to identify each member of the class at the outset, a decision to apply an opt-in procedure can only be made by the legislature.

The UK Competition Law Class Action regime explicitly requires that the CAT certify the proceedings as either opt-out or opt-in.[197] The criteria for deciding how the class is to be formed do **not** encompass any criterion such as: how is the class action to be funded?[198] If the action is certified as an opt-out proceeding, then for the funder and class members to enter into a tied class thereafter would raise the very concerns expressed by Stone J – and doubly so, as it would be in *direct contravention* of the CAT's order.

In light of the various options for resolving this conundrum, the UK drafters chose option (iv). An amendment was inserted into the Consumer Rights Bill 2015, during its passage through Parliament.[199] The eventual provision became s 47C(6) of the Competition Act 1998 (with emphasis added):

> In a case within subsection (5) [where the CAT makes an award of damages in opt-out collective proceedings], the Tribunal may order that all or part of any damages not claimed by the represented persons within a specified period is instead to be paid to the representative in respect of all or part of *the costs or expenses incurred by the representative in connection with the proceedings*.

The UK Government was very concerned to ensure that the compensatory principle was given effect to, by ensuring that the class members would have first right to claim the damages recovered. In that regard, s 47C(6) is notably different from the 'common fund' doctrine, in that the claiming class members obtain their **full** compensation under s 47C(6); it is not necessary that they each pay a proportion of their damages to the funder. The italicised part of the provision constitutes a type of 'second charge', and covers expenses incurred by the representative claimant

---

[197] CA 1998, s 47B(7)(c).
[198] Per CAT Rules, r 79(3).
[199] See *Hansard*, HL, vol 756, 3 November 2014, GC585–GC588.

such as legal fees; the cost of an ATE premium taken out to cover the
risk of losing and having to pay adverse costs; and a funder's success fee.
This was confirmed in the second action filed under the CRA regime –
that of *Merricks v Mastercard Inc*.[200] Mastercard submitted that the
funder's fee was not a 'cost or expense', and thus, was uncovered by
s 47C(6)'s operation,[201] but that point was decided against it.[202] This
was an important precedent, for had the defendant's argument succeeded, then short of s 47C(6) being redrafted, funders may have been
unwilling to fund actions under UK Competition Law Class Action,
given the difficulties (or impossibility) of the other three options canvassed earlier in this section. As it is, the ethos of s 47C(6) has drawn
criticism from legal practitioners[203] and scholars,[204] because of the fact
that there is no guarantee that any of the damages award will remain
after distribution to the class members, by which to pay those 'costs and
expenses'. However, in this author's view, 100 per cent take-up rates are
unlikely to occur under the UK Competition Law Class Action (especially in cases of widespread but individually low losses); and the
solution reached by virtue of s 47C(6) was a necessary compromise
solution to what had become a point of real controversy in Australian
jurisprudence.

In summary, both this issue, and particular words and phrases used in
Australia's de facto certification framework, have conveyed some very
important lessons for the UK's competition law class action. Undoubtedly
there will be conundrums arising about some of the choices made by the
UK drafters, but there has been a genuine attempt to learn from the
Australian experiences of certification.

D   Conclusion

The twenty-fifth anniversary of the Australian federal class action, in
2017, precisely coincided with the first class action certification decision

---

[200] [2017] CAT 16.

[201] See, in particular, the second day of the certification application transcript, in which the
point was contested, and the author's 'Third Party Funding' article (n 12) was discussed
in opposing submissions, available at: www.catribunal.org.uk/files/1266_Walter_hugh_
Transcript__Hearing_2_190117.pdf.

[202] [2017] CAT 16, [109]–[117]. The issue was not dealt with on further appeal.

[203] This was a cited concern by panel and audience members, e.g., at the conference: 'Rapid
Response Seminar: *Merricks v Mastercard Inc*' (BIICL, London, 16 May 2019).

[204] A Higgins and A Zuckerman, 'Class Actions Come to England (Editorial)' (2016) 35
Civil Justice Quarterly 1, 12–13.

under the UK Competition Law Class Action.[205] A quarter of a century and half a world apart, the same conundrum – of how to deliver access to justice to large classes, or to defendants who successfully defend such a claim, with full *res judicata* effect – is being tackled by jurists and legislators, in somewhat different ways.

There have been numerous problems of application, and conundrums of statutory interpretation, to resolve over the twenty-five years of Australian jurisprudence – and, where the legislature has remained deliberately or inadvertently silent, the federal courts (and more recently, state courts), both at first instance and on appeal, have been prepared to judicially craft solutions to make the regimes work. It has been a successful example of pragmatism, vision and compromise. Lessons have been learnt from that experience by UK lawmakers, regarding the legal treatment of: the requirement of certification; the certification criteria; the type of representative claimant permitted; standing against multiple defendants; and the threshold requirements of commonality and numerosity. However, there is unease in some Australian quarters, as to the role of third-party funding, and the preoccupation of funders with shareholder class actions that rely upon infringements of the continuing disclosure requirements prescribed by the Corporations Law. Chief Justice Allsop offers an important reflection on the current status of the federal action:

> The variety of subject matters and the number of cases are not such as to indicate an abuse of the class action vehicle into socially useless litigation. Nevertheless, it is critical to ensure that how these cases come forward and how they are being run satisfies the requirement of social utility. This is most particularly so in an environment in which commercially driven litigation funders (domestic and international) now provide significant financial support to the propounding of claims. (Something in the order of 50% of class action claims are funded in this way.)[206]

The Australian Law Reform Commission fully shares these concerns, and has recommended a review of the continuing disclosure obligations and their interplay with federal class actions.[207] It noted that the reality that

---

[205] *Gibson v Pride Mobility Products Ltd* received its certification decision (which declined certification, but which provided a further opportunity for repleading) on 31 March 2017: [2017] CAT 9, ironically twenty-five years to the month after the Australian federal regime took effect.

[206] Chief Justice Allsop, 'Class Actions' (Keynote address to the Law Council of Australia Forum, 13 October 2016).

[207] *Integrity, Fairness and Efficiency: Final Report* (2018) (n 27), ch 9, 'A Review of the Substantive Law that Underpins Shareholder Class Action Proceedings?'.

Table 3.2 *The certification criteria under the UK's Competition Law Class Action*

1	**Minimum numerosity** —
	• there must be 'two or more claims' – s 47B(1)
2	**Commonality** —
	• class members must have claims that 'raise common issues' – r 79(1)(b), where 'common issues' means 'the same, similar or related issues of fact or law' – r 73(2); and CA 1998, s 47B(6)
3	**An adequate class definition** —
	• the claims must be 'brought on behalf of an identifiable class of persons' – r 79(1)(a)
	• the CAT must consider 'whether it is possible to determine for any person whether he is or is not a member of the class' – r 79(2)(e)
4	**Superiority** —
	• the class action must be 'an appropriate means for the fair and efficient resolution of the common issues' – r 79(2)(a)
	• the CAT must consider 'the availability of ADR and any other means of resolving the dispute' – r 79(2)(g)
5	**Preliminary merits** —
	• the representative claimant 'believes that the claims . . . have a real prospect of success' – r 75(2)(h)
	• when selecting opt-in or opt-out, the CAT shall consider 'the strength of the claims' – r 79(3)(a)
6	**Cost–benefit analysis** —
	• the CAT will consider 'the costs and the benefits of continuing the collective proceedings' – r 79(2)(b)
	• when selecting opt-in or opt-out, the CAT shall consider 'the estimated amount of damages that individual class members may recover' – r 79(3)(b)
7	**Need** —
	• the CAT must consider 'whether any separate proceedings making claims of the same or a similar nature have already been commenced by members of the class' – r 79(2)(c)
8	**General suitability** —
	• class members' claims must be 'suitable to be brought in collective proceedings' – r 79(1)(c), and CA 1998, s 47B(6)
	• the CAT must consider 'whether the claims are suitable for an aggregate award of damages' – r 79(2)(f)
	• the CAT must consider 'the size and the nature of the class' – r 79(2)(d)

Table 3.2 (*cont.*)

9	***Representative claimant —***

- it must be 'just and reasonable' that the person acts as a representative – r 78(1)(b), and CA 1998, s 47B(8)(b)
- the representative must be 'able to pay the defendant's recoverable costs if ordered' – r 79(2)(d), or satisfy any undertaking as to damages re injunctive relief – r 78(2)(e)
- no conflicts of 'material interests' between the representative and the class members – r 79(2)(b)
- if the representative is a class member, his 'suitability to manage the proceedings' – r 78(3)(a)
- if the representative is not a class member, then 'whether it is a pre-existing body and the nature and functions of that body' – r 78(3)(b)
- there must be a plan for the class action which is satisfactory – r 78(3)(c)

'representative proceedings on behalf of shareholders are more frequently supported by litigation funders than representative proceedings on behalf of poor and disadvantaged groups',[208] and that a 'thorough understanding' of the substantive law of the interaction with the relevant corporations law and of the earlier-enacted Pt IVA regime was essential.[209] From the vantage point of the UK jurisdiction in which opt-out class actions reform is in its infancy, it is remarkable how the current emphasis under the Australian federal regime has moved onto the law and practicalities of how class actions *are funded*; the judicial interpretations of key words and phraseology having been substantially resolved over the course of twenty-five years.

More widely, a quarter of a century of comparative class actions jurisprudence has given rise to 100 design points of great comparative importance for UK policymakers and drafters, and for those lawmakers who may be considering class actions reform elsewhere. The UK Competition Law Class Action is at the beginning of its journey. Being a 'third generation' class actions statute, it may yield some lessons for other jurisdictions' lawyers, jurists and commentators, as the body of jurisprudence slowly builds up. In this modern era of the class action, an ongoing cross-fertilisation of ideas across jurisdictions, by which to solve collective redress conundrums, is more important than ever.

---

[208] ibid, [9.89].
[209] ibid, [9.90].

RECOMMENDATIONS: GOVERNMENT AS CLASS ACTIONS DESIGNER

§ 3.1 Across the ambit of class actions commencement, conduct, costs, and funding, there are at least 100 design issues which arise. Not all of these will be dealt with via either legislative enactment or court rules; judicial precedent, practice directions, and practices developed in the legal marketplace may govern some of these design issues.

§ 3.2 No legal regime is entirely transplantable to another jurisdiction. Cultural, historical, and legal factors will dictate the extent to which the design of a class action in one jurisdiction may be successfully transposed to another, by reference to the lessons learnt from the former's experiences.

4

Government as Class Actions Funder

A   Introduction

The costs rules and funding of class actions is perhaps the most crucial aspect of the regime. Without effective procedural law, substantive law cannot be enforced; and without fair costs rules and effective avenues for funding, procedural law cannot facilitate claims. Hence, costs and funding are at the root of all civil procedure – and especially so, given the 'forest fire' of resource-intensive, expensive, expert-reliant and lengthy litigation that most class actions invoke.[1]

Difficult decisions abound, when designing a costs and funding framework. On the subject of costs, legislative choices must be made across a range of matters, *viz*: the type of costs rule (i.e., costs-shifting/loser pays, no-costs-shifting, or one-way costs-shifting) that will govern the class actions litigation (and those circumstances in which any exceptions to the stipulated costs rule will apply);[2] whether costs-capping, a fixed costs regime, or some different costs scale should apply to either all or part of class actions litigation;[3] the extent to which non-party costs orders may

---

[1] To adopt an analogy espoused by Perell J in *Heller v Ubertechnologies Inc* [2018] ONSC 1690, [1].

[2] The ordinary costs-shifting rule applies to the UK Competition Law Class Action: CAT Rules, r 98(1). In fact, all three costs rules have been implemented or recommended variously throughout the Comparator Jurisdictions, as discussed by the author in: *The Class Action in Common Law Legal Systems: A Comparative Perspective* (Hart Publishing, 2004), ch 12, Section C; and 'Costs-Shifting, Security for Costs, and Class Actions: Lessons from Elsewhere', in D Dwyer (ed), *The Tenth Anniversary of the Civil Procedure Rules* (Oxford University Press, 2010), ch 10, 183. It is not only the primary costs rule which matters, but also, the prescribed legislative circumstances (if any), or the general discretion vested in the court, in which the primary costs rule may be departed from in any given case.

[3] Discussed, by reference to the Comparator Jurisdictions, in: *The Class Action*, (n 2) ch 12 (C)(1)(b).

be made against funders or lawyers;[4] the methods (if any) by which the class lawyers for the successful representative claimant may be paid for their costs and disbursements, over and above the recoverable costs that may be payable by the unsuccessful defendant;[5] and the circumstances in which an order for security for costs may be made against the representative claimant (or against non-parties to the litigation[6]).

On the funding side, if anything, there are even more difficult legislative choices to be made, e.g., whether or not third party funding is permitted (and the extent, if any, to which that type of funding is regulated);[7] whether or not lawyers may charge contingency fees, and if so, of what type;[8] the availability (if any) of legal aid for class litigation (and to which parties the means test is applied);[9] the extent (if any) to which class members may be liable (or requested) to fund the action via solicitations;[10] the extent to which insurers are willing and able to fund

[4] This will be permissible under the UK Competition Law Class Action, pursuant to the Senior Courts Act 1981, s 51, and CPR 46.2.

[5] A feature of Australian class actions design, per FCA 1976, s 33ZJ(2), but not widely replicated, see: *The Class Action* (n 2) 461–64.

[6] Permitted under the UK Competition Law Class Action: CAT Rules, r 45(5)(h).

[7] See Chapter 3, 'Government as Class Actions Designer', Section C(6). A comparative analysis of third party funding in Australia, England and Canada, and of the self-regulation avenue adopted by UK policymakers, is undertaken by the author elsewhere: 'Third Party Funding and Class Actions Reform' (2015) 131 *Law Quarterly Review* 291; and 'England's Unique Approach to the Self-Regulation of Third Party Funding: A Critical Analysis of Recent Developments' (2014) 73 *Cambridge Law Journal* 570.

[8] The types of contingency fees – whether multiplier or percentage-based – have been a point of controversy in class actions jurisprudence: *The Class Action* (n 2) 468–79, and continue to be so. See, e.g., the law reform consideration in: Victorian LRC, *Access to Justice – Litigation Funding and Group Proceedings* (March 2018); ALRC, *Integrity, Fairness and Efficiency – An Inquiry into Class Action Proceedings and Third-Party Litigation Funders: Final Report* (Rep 134, December 2018); and LRC of Ontario, *Class Actions: Objectives, Experiences and Reforms* (CP, March 2018), especially consultation question 4, at 24. Percentage, but not multiplier, contingency fees are barred under the UK Competition Law Class Action: CA 1998, s 47C(8). The promulgating Dept was concerned about 'incentivising lawyers to bring cases': BIS, *Private Actions in Competition Law A Consultation on Options for Reform* (April 2012) 5, and Box 6; and *Government Response* (January 2013) [5.43]–[5.45]; [5.62]–[5.63].

[9] e.g., whether it is applied to the means of all those represented, or just to the representative claimant. As the ALRC noted, '[i]t would be rare for all members of the group to satisfy the means test': *Grouped Proceedings in the Federal Court* (1988) [304]. See too, the Scottish Law Commission's view that, '[i]f civil legal aid were to be available to the representative plaintiff in a class action it was likely that the financial conditions would have to be disapplied': *Multi-Party Actions* (1996) [8.46].

[10] There is no express permission for this under the UK Competition Law Class Action, although it has been permitted elsewhere in the Comparator Jurisdictions: *The Class Action* (n 2) ch 12, 464–66.

the representative claimant's own-side disbursements and/or the opponent's adverse costs of the class action (whether before-the-event (BTE) insurers with whom individual class members had already taken out a policy prior to the commencement of the class action, or after-the-event (ATE) insurers who contract with the representative claimant only);[11] whether a statutory charge should be imposed upon the entire damages or a portion of the damages (such as the unclaimed part) in order to fund the costs incurred by the representative claimant in prosecuting the action;[12] and whether (in the absence of any such statutory charge), a 'common fund' should be judicially created (whether on restitutionary or equitable principles).[13]

The aforementioned issues (constituting several of the 'design issues' referenced in an earlier chapter[14]) represent a very complex landscape for the drafters of any class actions regime. However, the significant issue for consideration in this chapter is the extent to which the government of the day chooses to assist with the financing of class actions litigation by establishing a dedicated class actions fund, as an alternative funding avenue to 'everything else' (as Figure 4.1 overpage shows).

Where a specialist class actions fund is established by virtue of statute, which is seeded by statutorily designated monies, and which is intended

[11] BTE insurance may be difficult, however, whether because class actions are excluded from coverage of the policy, or because combining class members' individual coverage is practically difficult, as discussed in: CJC, *The Law and Practicalities of Before-the-Event (BTE) Insurance: An Information Study* (November 2017) 59–61. The author was principal author of the report.

[12] Permitted under the UK Competition Law Class Action: CA 47C(6). For judicial consideration of the provision, see: *Merricks v Mastercard Inc* [2017] CAT 16, [109]–[117]. The background and effect of that provision is discussed by the author in: 'Third Party Funding and Class Actions Reform' (n 7) 307–10.

[13] The doctrine has been judicially recognised in US jurisprudence, as discussed in Mulheron, 'Third Party Funding and Class Actions Reform' (n 7) 296–98; A Higgins, 'Driving with the Handbrake On: Competition Class Actions under the Consumer Rights Act 2015' (2016) 79 *Modern Law Review* 442, 459–60. It was judicially approved in Australia in: *Money Max Int Pty Ltd v QBE Ins Group Ltd* [2016] FCAFC 148 (26 October 2016), the impact of which was considered subsequently in, e.g.: *Blairgowrie Trading Ltd v Allco Finance Group Ltd (R&M appointed) (in liq) (No 3)* [2017] FCA 330; *Westpac Banking Corp v Lenthall* [2019] FCAFC 34; and *Brewster v BMW Aust Ltd* [2019] NSWCA 35. See, for detailed discussion in the Australian context, ALRC, *Inquiry into Class Action Proceedings and Third-Party Litigation Funders* (DP 85, June 2018) [6.15]–[6.19], and the *Final Report* (2018) (n 8) 96–99; and J Betts *et al.*, 'Litigation Funding for Class Actions', and S Khouri *et al.*, 'Litigation Funding and Class Actions: Idealism, Pragmatism and a New Paradigm', both in D Grave and H Mould (eds), *25 Years of Class Actions in Australia* (Ross Parsons, 2017), chs 10 and 11 respectively.

[14] See Chapter 3, Section (B)(4).

... the government's establishment of a dedicated class actions fund, seeded by public or statutorily designated monies, which is intended to be self-funding and self-replenishing (**Sections B–E**)

class actions funding may depend upon ...

OR

... external sources of funding which do not depend upon public monies (e.g., third party funding; contingency fee funding by class lawyers; the resources of the representative claimant or of the class members themselves; union funders; before-the-event insurance; or after-the-event insurance)

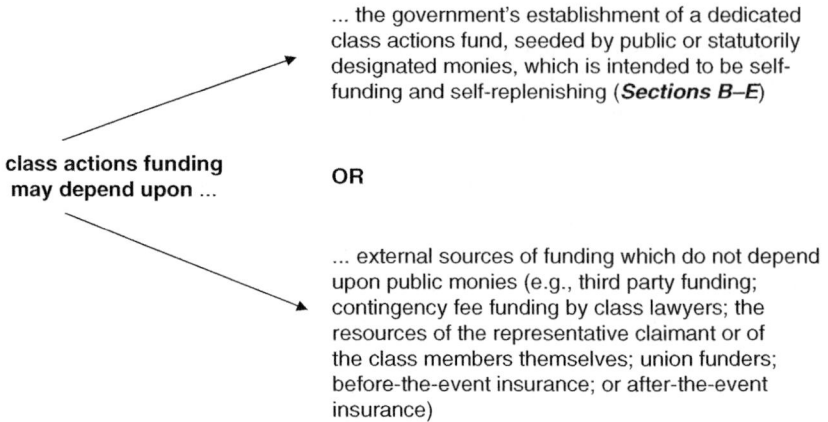

Figure 4.1   Funding a class actions regime

to be self-funding, then the government of the day is a class actions funder – for absent that legislative framework, the relevant actions which are reliant upon that funding would not otherwise have been litigated. In general terms, a class actions fund is self-replenished by levies on damages achieved (either by judgment, settlement, or both) in successful class actions. The fund typically finances either some or all of the legal expenses incurred by the representative claimant; and it may also indemnify that funded representative claimant against adverse costs awards, should he lose the class action.[15] A fund of this type has been supported by law reform opinion on the basis that it 'would be an acknowledgment that there is a public purpose to be served by enhancing access to remedies ... especially where many people have been affected'.[16] Notably, though, some law commissions have strongly

---

[15] Discussed further in: Mulheron, *Costs and Funding of Collective Actions: Realities and Possibilities* (Research Paper for the European Consumers' Organisation (BEUC), February 2011) 96.

[16] ALRC, *Grouped Proceedings in the Federal Court* (1988) [308]. The idea was also strongly supported by the Federal Court of Canada Rules Committee on the basis that it was 'the most attractive method of supporting class proceedings': *Class Proceedings in the Federal Court of Canada* (DP 2000) 102. The Hong Kong LRC, *Class Actions* (2012) [8.69], [8.127]–[8.129]; the Victorian LRC, *Civil Justice Review* (Rep 14, 2008), ch 10; South Australian LRC, *Report Relating to Class Actions* (Rep 36, 1977) 10; the Victorian Attorney-General's Law Reform Advisory Council, *Class Actions in Victoria: Time for a New Approach?* (1997) [7.34], recommendation 16, and the Civil Justice Council of England and Wales, *The Future Funding of Litigation: Funding Options and Proportionate Costs: Alternative Funding Structures* (June 2007), ch B, all recommended such a fund. None of these recommendations has been acted upon.

recommended *against* the option,[17] or have considered that it was politically unrealistic.[18]

In one of the many ironies of class action implementation across the Comparator Jurisdictions, the Ontario Law Reform Commission vehemently criticised the suggestion that a special fund be created,[19] whilst the Australian Law Reform Commission strongly recommended 'a public funding solution . . . to assist a principal applicant to meet the respondent's costs if the case is unsuccessful'.[20] Ultimately, though, the situations reversed! The Ontario class action regime implemented a class actions fund[21] (contemporaneously with the commencement of its class actions statute[22]), and the Australian regime did not (to some judicial[23] and law reform[24] chagrin). The Ontario Attorney-General's Advisory Committee which considered class actions for Ontario again in 1990[25] was concerned about the potentially chilling effect which an

---

[17] Note, e.g., the change of view of the South African Law Commission from its Working Paper (where it supported the idea of a class actions fund) to its Final Report (where it recommended against it): *The Recognition of Class Actions and Public Interest Actions in South African Law* (Project 88, 1998) [5.19.9], [5.19.13].

[18] Scottish Law Commission, *Multi-Party Actions* (1996)[5.21]–[5.31], [5.48], [5.50] ('[i]n the absence of any indication that public funding would be available to establish a class action fund . . . we do not recommend the establishment of such a fund'). The same doubts were held by the Alberta Law Reform Institute, *Class Actions* (Rep 85, 2000) [391], and the Manitoba LRC, *Class Proceedings* (Rep 100, 1999) 86.

[19] *Report on Class Actions* (1982) 713. This is partly because the OLRC recommended (at 706) that there should be a no-costs regime for class proceedings (hence, there was no need for the creation of any special fund to cover adverse costs), but the Ontario legislature also rejected that recommendation, in favour of costs-shifting.

[20] *Grouped Proceedings in the Federal Court* (1988) [301], [309] (the recommendation), and [311]–[314].

[21] By virtue of: the Law Society Amendment Act (Class Proceedings Funding), SO 1992, c 7, and the Ontario Regulation 771/92: Class Proceedings, enacted pursuant to the Law Society Act, RSO 1990, c L.8.

[22] Class Proceedings Act, SO 1992, c 6.

[23] e.g., *Woodlands and Ballard v Permanent Trustee Co Ltd* (1995) 58 FCR 139, [21]–[22] ('if such a fund had been established, it would have been a means of resolving the present problem. However, the Government did not adopt this recommendation. No fund was established.').

[24] ALRC, *Integrity, Fairness and Efficiency: Final Report* (2018) (n 8) [2.8] ('neither the Part IVA, nor any other relevant legislation, dealt with the issue of an appropriate costs regime— leaving unanswered the difficult question of how to relieve a principal applicant from the brunt of an adverse costs order should the proceeding fail. A recommendation to establish a public fund to protect principal applicants in the face of such an eventuality was not adopted by the government of the day').

[25] *Report of the Attorney General's Advisory Committee on Class Action Reform* (Ministry of the Attorney General, 1990).

adherence to a costs-shifting rule would have upon any new regime. That Committee considered that such a fund was really necessary, so that the objective of increasing access was not undermined.[26]

The resulting Ontario's Class Proceedings Fund has been an interesting class actions experiment. It is 'unique',[27] and remains the only one of the Comparator Jurisdictions to have implemented that experiment.[28] The Class Proceedings Fund – a true 'statutory funder'[29] – is administered by the Law Foundation of Ontario[30] via the Class Proceedings Committee.[31] The Fund was established by the Ontario legislature as part of, and contemporaneously with, the class proceedings regime introduced by the Class Proceedings Act, 1992. It was initially endowed with $500,000, in two tranches, provided by that Law Foundation.[32] The Law Foundation (the third of its type established in Canada[33]) was set up in 1974 to receive the interest on lawyers' mixed trust accounts and to use those monies to support legal education, legal aid, legal research, and law libraries.[34] When the Class Proceedings Fund was established in 1992, the Law Foundation used that interest, as statutorily designated, to seed the Fund.

Hence, whilst the monies used to establish the Class Proceedings Fund were not donated by the Ontario government via consolidated revenue, so was **not** 'public money' as such,[35] the *permission* for such a fund – and for its seed funding from the Foundation – were facilitated by the Ontario

---

[26] Noted in: *Martin v Barrett* [2008] CanLII 25062 (Ont SCJ, Cullity J) [6].

[27] *Fehr v Sun Life Ass Co of Canada* [2012] ONSC 2715, [76].

[28] In Québec (which is not one of the Comparator Jurisdictions for the purpose of this book), the Fonds d'aide aux recours collectifs (the Class Actions Assistance Fund) was established by An Act Respecting the Class Action 1978, RSQ, c R-2.1, c 8, ss 5–37; and Regulation respecting the percentage withheld by the Fonds d'aide aux recours collectifs, RRQ 1981, c R-2.1. The Fonds is an independent agency which was financed by the Québec government. It may assist a Québec claimant with legal fees and disbursements, in exchange for a percentage of the recovery, as discussed in: *Stanway v Wyeth Canada Inc* [2013] BCSC 1585, 56 BCLR (5th) 192, [11].

[29] *Houle v St Jude Medical Inc* [2018] ONSC 6352, [33].

[30] Law Society Act 1990, s 59.1(1)(a), (d).

[31] This is a statutory committee created by the Law Society Act, RSO 1990, s 59.2.

[32] First $300,000, and then a further $200,000, was paid from the funds of the Foundation: per ibid, s 59.1(1)(b), (c).

[33] Following those of British Columbia (1969) and Saskatchewan (1971).

[34] Following its establishment, the Foundation was continued as a corporation by virtue of the Law Society Act, RSO 1990, c L.8, s 53(1). See the discussion at: 'Highlights in the Foundation's history', available at: www.lawfoundation.on.ca/who-we-are/history/.

[35] See, e.g., the discussion in: D Collins, 'Public Funding of Class Actions and the Experience with English Group Proceedings' (2005) 31 *Manitoba Law Journal* 211, 233.

government by means of multiple statutory enactments. It was a legislative decision to assist with the funding of class actions in this way. The Fund has now collated twenty-five years of jurisprudence by which to exemplify the sorts of problems, issues and advantages which this funding avenue attracts. The purpose of this chapter is to capture that experience, by reference (primarily) to relevant statutes, case law, and the Law Foundation's official documentation.

B   How the Ontario Fund Works

1   From a Monetary Perspective

(a)   What the Fund Will Give

Where the Ontario Law Foundation's Class Proceedings Committee agrees to fund a class action from the Class Proceedings Fund, then the following arrangement applies:

- the Fund provides 'financial support' for **disbursements** related to the class action,[36] 'in the amount that the Committee considers appropriate'.[37] Disbursements may include, for example: experts' fees; the costs of preparing and distributing to the class members notices of certification and/or the settlement approval hearing; the costs of administering the claims process; and the costs of establishing a system of electronic document management for the case;[38]
- where the representative claimant receives support from the Fund for its disbursements, and loses the certification hearing, the common issues trial, or an appeal therefrom, then the Fund also indemnifies that representative claimant against any awards for **adverse costs** made against that losing representative claimant (on application by the successful defendant).[39] In that event, the representative claimant cannot be liable for any part of the adverse costs award made against him.[40] Simply put, the Fund 'is statutorily responsible for honouring

---

[36] Law Society Act, RSO 1990, c L.8, ss 59.1(2) and 59.3(1).
[37] ibid, s 59.3(3).
[38] As noted, e.g., in *Parker v Pfizer Canada Inc* [2017] ONSC 2418, [13].
[39] Law Society Act, RSO 1990, ss 59.1(2) and 59.4(1). The information required from the defendant in order to seek that payment of adverse costs is set out in Ontario Regulation 771/92, s 11.
[40] Law Society Act, RSO 1990, s 59.4(3). In *Garland v Consumers' Gas Co* [1998] 3 SCR 112, 165 DLR (4th) 385, a personal costs award against Mr Garland of $500 was set aside by the SCC for that reason.

any award made against the Plaintiffs for costs'.[41] Indeed, once the representative claimant receives funding from the Fund, and loses, there is absolutely 'no legal authority or mechanism to deny payment of an adverse costs award from the Fund'.[42] That payment is a financial burden that the Fund cannot escape from, and the impact that payment of that adverse costs award may have upon the financial health of the Fund is irrelevant.[43] That protection is, probably, the 'main benefit' of the Class Proceedings Fund's involvement in any Ontario class proceeding, and it also definitively ensures recovery of adverse costs by the successful defendant.[44] However, it is not possible for the defendant to request a court to compel the representative claimant to apply to the Class Proceedings Fund for funding, in order to protect the defendant's ability to recover adverse costs, should the representative claimant fail;[45]

- *supplementary funding* is also possible for the representative claimant as the case progresses, should the Class Proceedings Committee consider that appropriate, 'having regard to all the circumstances';[46]
- *but*: the Fund does not fund any legal representatives who are engaged by the representative claimant (whether they be class lawyers or any others who 'provide legal services') for their legal fees.[47] This means that, if class lawyers are realistically not able to carry their fees for the life of the case without billing them to the representative claimant and having them paid, then that effectively eliminates the Class Proceedings Fund from the funding equation. The Fund does not fund legal fees. In such cases, succinctly put, 'that limited support [provided by the Fund] does not meet the Plaintiffs' resource needs'.[48]

---

[41] *Hughes v Liquor Control Bd of Ontario* [2018] ONSC 4862, [13].
[42] Recently affirmed, in the context of a failed certification application, and where United States defendants were involved, in: *Berg v Canadian Hockey League* [2019] ONSC 2106 (Div Ct) [126].
[43] ibid, [125].
[44] *Holmes v London Life Ins Co* (2000), 50 OR (3d) 388 (SCJ) [24]; and *Peter v Medtronic Inc* [2008] CanLII 56712 (Ont SCJ) [20] ('[t]he involvement of the Fund is beneficial to both the representative plaintiffs and defendants').
[45] As made plain in: *Medtronic* (n 44) [17], [41].
[46] Law Society Act, RSO 1990, c L-8, s 59.3(5).
[47] ibid, s 59.3(2).
[48] *JB & M Walker Ltd/1523428 Ontario Inc v TDL Group* [2019] ONSC 999, [11] (third-party funding was sourced to provide financial assistance for the case, an arrangement which was judicially approved).

(b)   What the Fund Will Receive

The support of a representative claimant by the Fund 'has a price'.[49] In essence:

- if the class action is successful (whether by virtue of a judgment award or a judicially approved settlement award), the Class Proceedings Fund takes *a levy of 10 per cent of the proceeds of the action*.[50] That levy operates as a 'charge' on the judgment award or settlement fund.[51] Its purpose is to replenish the Fund, as a top-up mechanism, for the benefit of future litigants who may require recourse to the Fund. In some cases, it has been suggested that the representative claimant has declined to apply for funding from the Fund, precisely because he did not wish to give up 10 per cent of any recovery.[52] Courts have also commented at times (particularly when being asked to approve proposed settlement agreements, including counsel's fees) that other funding options may be 'less expensive' to the class, whereas the Fund 'would have charged a 10% levy on any settlement or recovery';[53]

- if there is a recovery by the class, then the Class Proceedings Fund is also entitled to the *reimbursement of any 'financial support'* (i.e., disbursements) that it funded in the successful action.[54] These must be repaid to the Fund 'as soon as is reasonably practicable, and cannot

---

[49] *Hughes v Liquor Control Bd of Ontario* [2018] ONSC 4862, [85]; and earlier: *Das v George Weston Ltd* [2017] ONSC 5583, [54].

[50] Ontario Regulation 771/92, s 8(4)(c)(ii).

[51] Law Society Act, RSO 1990, s 59.5(5).

[52] e.g., *Henault v Bear Lake Gold Ltd* [2010] ONSC 4474, [24] ('[n]o application was made to the Class Proceedings Fund, saving the Class the statutory 10% tariff that would otherwise have been payable had the Class Proceedings Fund agreed to provide the costs indemnity and fund disbursements'); *Osmun v Cadbury Adams Canada Inc* [2010] ONSC 2752, [26] (the representative claimant 'has not applied to the Class Proceedings Fund for assistance. If the class had received disbursements funding from the Fund, it would now be obligated to repay any financial support provided by the Fund and pay an additional 10% of the settlement funds'); *Trillium Motor World Ltd v General Motors of Canada Ltd* [2016] ONCA 702, [35].

[53] The advantage of class lawyers agreeing to indemnify the representative claimant against an adverse costs award has been oft-cited, e.g.: *Baker (Estate) v Sony BMG Music (Canada) Inc* [2011] ONSC 7105, 98 CPC (4th) 244, [42]; *Marcantonio v TVI Pacific Inc* [2009] CanLII 43191 (Ont SCJ) [34] ('thereby saving the class from having to pay the statutory 10% to the Class Proceedings Fund'); *Bellaire v Daya* [2007] CanLII 53236 (Ont SCJ) [81] ('thereby saving the Class $990,000 which otherwise would have been payable to the Class Proceedings Fund'); *Kranjcec v Ontario* [2006] CanLII 31730 (Ont SCJ) [21] ('a potential savings of $2 million has been achieved').

[54] Ontario Regulation 771/92, s 8(4)(c)(i).

be used for any other purpose without the consent of the [Class Proceedings] Committee';[55]

- ***but***: where the representative claimant receives his party-and-party costs from the unsuccessful defendant, that sum is not paid to the Fund, as the Fund did not provide any cover for those legal fees which the representative claimant incurred;
- (***and***): in the event that there is no judgment award or creation of a settlement fund to which the class members become entitled, then the Fund receives nothing.

In summary, and 'distilled to its essence', where the representative claimant has received funding from the Fund, that has very beneficial consequences for both that party and for the defendant.[56] The Fund is designed to be self-sustaining. From those levies that it receives on successful cases, the Fund then uses those to provide disbursement funding in new and ongoing proposed class actions, as well as adverse costs in current and future funded cases which are unsuccessful.[57]

2   The Criteria for Funding

The Class Proceedings Committee must approve the application for financial support, which written application may be buttressed by oral submissions.[58]

In many cases – from complex competition law class actions[59] to securities actions instituted by pension funds[60] – the amount of funding required for the disbursements in the action, and for the potential exposure to adverse costs, has been judicially noted to have been well beyond the capacity or willingness of the Class Proceedings Fund to finance. In that event (and short of discontinuing the class action in Ontario and re-filing it in a no-costs jurisdiction such as British Columbia if possible[61]), other funding sources – i.e., a third-party

---

[55] See: *Practice Direction #3*, 'Repayment of Funded Disbursements' (dated 7 May 2008), available at: www.lawfoundation.on.ca/class-proceedings-fund/practice-directions/.

[56] *Davies v Corp of the Municipality of Clarington* [2019] ONSC 2292, [63].

[57] Per: *McCracken v Canadian National Rwy Co* [2012] ONSC 6838, [51].

[58] Law Society Act, RSO 1990, s 59.3; and Ontario Regulation 771/92, s 2(3).

[59] *David v Loblaw* [2018] ONSC 6469, [4]. Instead, the judgment concerned approval for a third-party funding agreement, which was given.

[60] *Bayens v Kinross Gold Corp* [2013] ONSC 4974, 117 OR (3d) 150.

[61] As occurred, e.g., in: *Lieberman and Morris v Business Devp Bank of Canada* [2006] BCSC 242, [19]–[20].

funder,[62] the class lawyers,[63] the representative claimant himself,[64] the class members,[65] an insurer,[66] or others[67] – must be found in order to fund the class's own case, and to cover the unpalatable prospect of adverse costs should that occur.[68] Two decades on from when the Ontario class actions regime (and the Class Proceedings Fund) were implemented, it has been judicially observed that 'anecdotal evidence' suggested that representative claimants were more likely to seek an indemnity against adverse costs from their class lawyers than from the Class Proceedings Fund,[69] and that class lawyer indemnities were

---

[62] See, e.g.: *Houle v St. Jude Medical Inc* [2017] ONSC 5129, [44]; *Labourers' Pension Fund of Central and Eastern Canada (Trustees of) v Sino-Forest Corp* [2012] ONSC 2937; *Dugal v Manulife Financial Corp* [2011] ONSC 1785, 105 OR (3d) 364; *Rooney v Arcelor Mittal SA* [2013] ONSC 7768; *Musicians' Pension Fund of Canada (Trustees of) v Kinross Gold Corp* [2013] ONSC 4974, 117 OR (3d) 150.

[63] As in, e.g.: *Gariepy v Shell Oil Co* [2002] CanLII 12911 (Ont SCJ) [63] ('[c]lass Counsel funded all of the disbursements associated with advancing the claims . . . in excess of $1,279,507 to date'); *Mancinelli v Royal Bank of Canada* [2018] ONSC 4206, [11] ('[c]lass Counsel have agreed to provide indemnities to the Plaintiffs for any adverse costs awards, [and] did not seek the support of the Class Proceedings Fund or from a third-party funder'); *Fanshawe College v Hitachi Ltd* [2016] ONSC 8212, [22]; *Vell v Mattel Canada Inc* [2016] ONSC 5789, [7]; *Goodridge v Pfizer Canada Inc* [2013] ONSC 2686, [42].

[64] See, e.g.: *Sondhi v Deloitte Management Services LP* [2018] ONSC 271, [23] ('[t]here is no third-party funding or funding from the Class Proceedings Fund, and Mr Phillip refused to disclose whether he has an indemnity agreement from Class Counsel. He deposed that he has the financial means to be responsible for an adverse costs award but refused to answer any questions about his financial assets or resources').

[65] With the leave of the court, a notice of certification may include a solicitation of contributions from class members to assist in paying class lawyers' fees and disbursements: CPA 1992, s 17(7). See, e.g.: *405341 Ontario Ltd v Midas Canada Inc* [2013] ONSC 5714, [15] ('[t]he representative plaintiff was unable to raise money for disbursements from class members. After certification, it instructed class counsel to apply to the Class Proceedings Fund and the Fund agreed to fund the action').

[66] In *Mackinnon v Ontario (Municipal Employees Retirement Board)* (2006), 52 CCPB 158 (Ont SCJ) [4], an indemnity was provided by insurer CUPE Ontario in favour of the representative claimant.

[67] Funds provided by teachers' unions or the 'legal aid test case fund' were cited as possibilities in: *Buffet v Ontario (AG)* (1998), 42 OR (3d) 53. A trust fund was set up with judicial approval to pay adverse costs in a group of class actions in: *Segnitz v Royal & Sun Alliance Ins Co of Canada* [2003] CanLII 36378 (Ont SCJ) [12]. The trust fund was terminated when funding from the Class Proceedings Fund was forthcoming.

[68] Noted, e.g., in: *Lundy v VIA Rail Canada Inc* [2015] ONSC 1879, [57]; *1250264 Ontario Inc v Pet Valu Canada Inc* [2016] ONSC 5496, [5]; *Fehr v Sun Life Ass Co of Canada* [2012] ONSC 2715, [53].

[69] Noted in: *Bayens v Kinross Gold Corp* [2013] ONSC 4974, 117 OR (3d) 150, [31]; *Fehr* (n 68) [65].

'typical'[70] – with this being a development unlikely to have been foreseen by the Ontario Law Reform Commission or by the Ontario Legislature back in 1992.[71] However, it is undeniably the case that, especially in recent cases, the Fund has agreed to fund very significant amounts of disbursements per class action (including over $1.5M in an insurance takeover dispute alone[72]).

The Class Proceedings Committee applies the following criteria to determine funding applications:[73]

(a) the merits of the plaintiff's case;
(b) whether the plaintiff has made reasonable efforts to raise funds from other sources;
(c) whether the plaintiff has a clear and reasonable proposal for the use of any funds awarded;
(d) whether the plaintiff has appropriate financial controls to ensure that any funds awarded are spent for the purposes of the award; and
(e) any other matter that the Committee considers relevant.

In addition, the following criteria are specified to which the Committee may have regard:[74]

1 The extent to which the issues in the proceeding affect the public interest.
2 If the application for financial support is made before the proceeding is certified as a class proceeding, the likelihood that it will be certified.
3 The amount of money in the Fund that has been allocated to provide financial support in respect of other applications or that may be required to make [adverse costs awards] payments to defendants.

In an early reported decision, the Class Proceedings Committee noted that, of these criteria, the merits of the case 'will typically be the most important and determinative factor to be considered';[75] and that claims

---

[70] *Williams v Canon Canada Inc* [2012] ONSC 1856, [4], citing: *McCracken v Canadian National Rwy* [2010] ONSC 6066, 100 CPC (6th) 334 (SCJ). Also: *Martin v Astrazeneca Pharmaceuticals plc* [2012] ONSC 4666, [24] ('[c]lass counsel routinely assume the risk of costs whether the plaintiffs are disadvantaged members of society or not').
[71] *Bayens v Kinross Gold Corp* [2013] ONSC 4974, [32].
[72] *Jeffery v London Life Ins Co* [2018] ONCA 716, [18].
[73] Law Society Act, RSO 1990, s 59.3(4).
[74] Ontario Regulation 771/92, s 5.
[75] See: *Edwards v Law Society of Upper Canada* (1995), 36 CPC (3d) 116 (Ontario Class Proceedings Committee) 124, 130 (in a very helpful and proactive step, the Committee wrote that it considered that 'it would be useful to the public and to the profession if

with a prospect of success of less than 50 per cent were unlikely to receive funding.[76] On this basis, the Class Proceedings Committee acted, and continues to do so, as a 'partial gate-keeper'[77] of the types of cases that are brought into the regime (as with any external funder, such as third-party funders or class lawyers, who are acting on a contingent basis).

It has been frequently judicially noted that the purpose of the Class Proceedings Fund was to assist access to justice.[78] Specifically, it has also been suggested over the years (including in the very first Ontario court judgment to consider the impact of the Class Proceedings Fund[79]) that some financial impecuniosity on the representative claimant's part was relevant to a successful funding application from the Class Proceedings Fund.[80] However, it is plain from the abovementioned list of criteria that impecuniosity is **not** an explicit factor. Further, whilst the likelihood of certification does matter, it is certainly not a prerequisite that the action has already been certified before funding can be applied for.[81] The Fund is entitled to be used by any representative claimant who meets the criteria, and it is plainly a nuanced and complex analysis which the Class Proceedings Committee must undertake.[82]

---

reasons for its decision could be issued in appropriate cases, particularly in these early days under the legislation': at 124). The decision is available on the Law Foundation of Ontario's website at: www.lawfoundation.on.ca/wp-content/uploads/edwards_v_lsuc .pdf.

[76] ibid, 135.

[77] A Pritchard and J Sarra, 'Securities Class Actions Move North: A Doctrinal and Empirical Analysis of Securities Class Actions in Canada' (2010) 47 *Alberta Law Review* 881, fn 39.

[78] *Broutzas v Rouge Valley Health System* [2019] ONSC 559, [15]; *Hughes v Liquor Control Bd of Ontario* [2018] ONSC 4862, [82]; *Martin v Barrett* [2008] CanLII 25062 (Ont SCJ) [6]–[8]; *Garland v Consumers' Gas Co* (1995), 22 OR (3d) 767 (Gen Div) [15]–[16] ('[t]he purpose of the ... Fund is to improve access to justice in the Province of Ontario': Winkler J), *aff'd*: (1996), 30 OR (3d) 414 (CA).

[79] *Garland* (n 78) (the Fund 'enable[s] potential plaintiffs ... in class action lawsuits to bring ... actions which they would not otherwise have the financial resources to support').

[80] *Dominguez v Northland Properties Corp* [2012] BCSC 539, [82], referring to Ontario's regime. Also: *Nantais v Telectronics Proprietary (Canada) Ltd* (1996), 28 OR (3d) 523, 134 DLR (4th) 470 ('to provide assistance to litigants in need, the Class Proceedings Fund of the Law Foundation was created').

[81] *Holmes v London Life Ins Co* [2000] CanLII 22412 (Ont SCJ) [22]–[23]; and cited in: *Perron v Canada (AG)* (2003), 105 CRR (2d) 92, 121 ACWS (3d) 588, [115]–[116].

[82] See, too, the comments by the Chair of the Class Proceedings Committee in the *Class Proceedings Fund Annual Report* (2016) (available at: www.lawfoundation.on.ca/wp-content/uploads/Report-on-Class-Proceedings-2016-EN.pdf).

3   The Operation of the Levy

(a)   The Order of Distribution

To reiterate, where the class has achieved a recovery, whether by judgment award or by the creation of a settlement fund, the amount to be repaid to the Class Proceedings Fund is the sum of the financial support provided by the Fund in respect of disbursements, plus the 10 per cent levy.

As the case law has developed, in cases of *settlement*, the Class Proceedings Fund is entitled to 10 per cent of the *net* settlement amount (i.e., 10 per cent of whatever is left, following payment of legal fees to the class lawyers and administrative costs[83]). Furthermore, the 10 per cent levy operates as 'a charge' on the recovered pot of the money,[84] *before* the class members have an opportunity to come forth to claim their individual sums. This order of distribution is for the parties to negotiate, and is then for the court to assess as part of the 'fairness hearing' to which all class action settlements must be subjected.

It is always open to Parliament to stipulate legislatively the order in which the distribution should occur – as occurred in the UK's Competition Law Class Action. Under that regime, and in the event of an award of damages being made in a judgment, the representative claimant may be reimbursed from a damages award for the 'costs and expenses' associated with the class proceeding – but only after the class members have been provided with an opportunity to claim their individual damages awards *in full*.[85] Hence, sums such as the funder's success fee, or lawyers' fees, may only be claimed against the *unclaimed* damages fund.[86] In a deliberate departure from the longstanding US 'common fund' doctrine,[87] the UK legislators ensured that, in the case of judgments, claiming class members would not lose a portion of their damages because of payment of those costs and expenses. The UK Government's

---

[83] See, e.g.: *Zwaniga v Johnvince Foods Distribution LP* [2017] ONSC 888, [14]; *Houle v St Jude Medical Inc* [2017] ONSC 5129, [41]; *Markson v MBNA Canada Bank* [2012] ONSC 5891, [9]; and the discussion in: J Brown *et al.*, *Defending Class Actions in Canada* (3rd edn, CCH Canadian Ltd, 2011) 350.

[84] Law Society Act, RSO 1990, s 59.5(5).

[85] CA 1998, s 47C(6), and discussed earlier in Chapter 3, Section C(6).

[86] As examined by the author in: 'Third Party Funding and Class Actions Reform' (n 7) 307–10.

[87] e.g., *Alyeska Pipeline Service Co v Wilderness Socy*, 421 US 240, 257 (1975) (re 'the creation, preservation or increase of a fund in which others have an interest'); and discussed, by reference to US case law, in Mulheron, ibid, 296–98.

focus upon the 'compensation principle' as the 'fundamental premise' of the UK Competition Law Class Action[88] meant that compensating those class members who came forth was the first and foremost priority of the class action, and if insufficient funds remained from a damages award to pay the funder's success fee[89] (and any other 'costs and expenses' of the proceedings), then that remained the risk of the representative claimant and any other party who may be left out-of-pocket. The *quid pro quo* of full compensation to the class members is that those who possess a statutory charge over the unclaimed damages could miss out altogether (unless the representative claimant has access to some other resources with which to pay those sums).

This particular dilemma is avoided in Ontario. Although a fee agreement between class lawyers and the representative claimant has been judicially described in Ontario case law as a 'first charge' upon the judgment award or settlement fund created,[90] it is evident that any payment of the levy to the Class Proceedings Fund is also to be paid *before* the class members are entitled to individual damages assessment and receipt.[91] Whilst it has been judicially said that 'third party funding comes at the expense of class members because the third party funder will share in the proceeds of a successful action', the same is true of any levy which is paid to the Class Proceedings Fund.[92] The Ontario view is plainly that this reduced recovery by class members is a price worth paying, to ensure that those who assume the risk of funding these chancy and expensive actions are reimbursed in full.

As the levy payable to the Class Proceedings Fund is a prior charge, it is necessary (per statute[93]) that any class actions notice to the class

---

[88] BIS, *Private Actions in Competition Law: Government Response* (January 2013) [5.28], [6.18], [6.26].

[89] A funder's success fee was held to be encompassed by the phrase, 'costs and expenses', in: *Merricks v Mastercard Inc* [2017] CAT 16, [109]–[117].

[90] *Jeffery v London Life Ins Co* [2018] ONCA 716, [28].

[91] See, e.g.: *Zwaniga v Johnvince Foods Distribution LP* [2017] ONSC 888, [6] (in a settlement agreement, '$62,925.12, less approved legal fees and the Class Proceedings Fund levy, would be distributed *pro rata*, based on the number of peanut vending machines purchased, to each Class Member who identifies himself or herself following court approval'); *Fulawka v Bank of Nova Scotia* [2016] ONSC 1576, [9] (in a settlement agreement, 'payments to claimants will be subject to all tax and source deductions, including the 10% levy owing to the Class Proceedings Fund'). The same occurred in, e.g.: *Roveredo v Bard Canada* [2013] ONSC 6979, [5]; and *Garland v Enbridge Gas Distribution Inc* [2006] CanLII 36243 (SCJ) [30].

[92] *Kowalyshyn v Valeant Pharmaceuticals Intl Inc* [2016] ONSC 3819, [178].

[93] Ontario Regulation 771/92, s 8(4)(a), (b).

members inform them that the representative claimant has received financial support from the Class Proceedings Fund in respect of the proceeding, and that, consequently, there will be a levy that reduces the amount of any award or settlement funds to which the class members may become entitled, should the class action succeed. That statement must be contained in the first class actions notice that is disseminated after the representative claimant receives financial support in the action from the Fund.[94]

(b)   The Trigger for the Charge

The trigger for the levy being imposed in favour of the Fund is as follows:[95]

A levy is payable in favour of the Fund,

(a)   when a monetary award is made in favour of one or more persons in a class that includes a plaintiff who received financial support under section 59.3 of the Law Society Act; or

(b)   when the proceeding is settled and one or more persons in such a class is entitled to receive settlement funds.

This important provision has given rise to a few interpretative points of interest.

First, the term, 'monetary award', is not defined anywhere in the relevant Ontario statutes. However, in the recent case of *Jeffery v London Life Insurance Co*, the term was defined widely to mean 'a payment of money, imposed by judicial authority, for the benefit of the class members'.[96] The payment may not be damages as such; but both the preceding Ontario Law Reform Commission report,[97] and Ontario case law,[98] have supported a wide notion of what should amount to a 'monetary award' or 'monetary relief'. In *Jeffery*, the Fund had supported the action by payment of the experts' reports and other

---

[94]   ibid, s 8(5).

[95]   ibid, s 10(2)(a), (b).

[96]   *Jeffery v London Life Ins Co* [2018] ONCA 716, [46], [60]. That interpretation was stated to apply, regardless of whether the term 'monetary award' appears in the CPA 1992 or in the Ontario Regulations 771/92, for the sake of consistency in statutory interpretation.

[97]   *Report on Class Actions* (1982) 520–21. Notably, Ontario's CPA 1992 refers extensively to 'monetary relief', in ss 24, 26, and 30. It only refers to 'damages' once, in s 6(1).

[98]   *Hislop v Canada* [2009] ONCA 354, 95 OR (3d) 81, [41]–[44] (Watt JA), cited in: *Jeffery v London Life Ins Co* [2018] ONCA 716, [45].

disbursements. The benefit obtained was the reparation of money to certain accounts in which the class members, as policy-holders of insurance bonds, had an interest – but those class members did not receive monies in their hands, and they had no right to spend the funds as they wished. Nevertheless, it was a 'monetary award', which could properly trigger a levy in favour of the Fund. There is clearly a significant policy dimension to such a decision, in that the Fund must be sought to be protected, and be able to serve its purpose of being self-perpetuating and of assistance to future class actions. In *Jeffery*, Benotto JA emphasised that a wide interpretation of a 'monetary award' was justifiable, because it:

> best serves the purpose … of ensur[ing] that the Foundation gets compensated for the risk it undertakes in funding class actions. The wording of s 10(2)[99] indicates that the monetary award may not necessarily be physically received in the hands of a class member when the levy is determined and payable, such as where a monetary award is ordered payable into a trust or pension plan.[100]

Secondly, it may be that not **all** class members receive the benefit of a monetary award. Does that preclude a levy being ordered to be paid to the Class Proceedings Fund? Clearly it does not, given the wording that is used in the relevant Regulation, that 'one or more persons in the class' receive a benefit. Even if one person in the class receives a monetary award or settlement payout, that is a sufficient trigger for the Fund to be reimbursed for all of its disbursements, and to receive a 10 per cent levy of the monetary award. In *Jeffery*, Benotto JA noted that, 'class action proceedings often result in a settlement fund or monetary award that is payable to a circumscribed group within the class as a whole. The fact that an award benefits some, but not all, members of the class does not remove that award from the ambit of s 10 of the Regulation.'[101]

C   Statistics

The Ontario Class Proceedings Fund has been subject to criticism on the basis that it has not been as used as may have been expected. However, it is fair to view the operation of the Fund in two tranches.

Various suggestions were made by academic scholars and commentators, over the course of the first decade of its operation, as to

---

[99] Reproduced at p 144.
[100] [2018] ONCA 716, [67].
[101] ibid, [65].

why the Fund was under-utilised. These included the following suggestions[102] – that:

- the 10 per cent levy was too high, deterring low-income class members **and** those with strong cases who may not wish to forfeit 10 per cent (the problem of 'adverse selection');
- the initial seed-funding of $500,000 was too low, meaning that, from the outset, the Class Proceedings Committee was too tentative in granting funding applications;
- far fewer representative claimants than were expected applied for funding, and hence, the Fund was not replenished nearly as often as intended;
- as the Fund was only entitled to a levy from those cases which it funded, it missed out on those early cases which settled for multi-million dollar amounts and which did not apply for funding; and
- pursuant to the costs-shifting rule, the risk of an adverse costs award could be just as large a deterrent to those administering the Fund as to the representative claimant, especially if the ameliorating factors in section 31(1) are not liberally interpreted.

Two decades after its implementation, the landscape did not look entirely promising. Take a snapshot of comments made in 2012. The Hong Kong Law Commission referred (in its report of that year) to the Fund being 'under-utilised',[103] and considered its viability to be 'questionable'.[104] Canadian legal practitioners noted, in a publication of that year, that 'funding through public agency has not been used with any great frequency. The dominant financing device has been, and will continue to be, the contingent fee.'[105] In *Fehr v Sun Life Assurance Company of Canada* (2012), Perell J noted that '[t]he conventional wisdom is that a request for funding from the Fund is made only in a minority of cases. In the majority of cases, where funding is not sought or where funding is refused by the [Class Proceedings] Committee, Class Counsel provide indemnities to the representative plaintiffs.'[106] The statistics bear this out. In its review of

---

[102] Summarised by the author in: *Costs and Funding of Collective Actions* (n 15) 98; and earlier: *The Class Action* (n 2) 457–59. See too: Collins, 'Public Funding of Class Actions' (n 35) 235–36; M Capes, 'Book Review: A Guide to the Class Proceedings Act 1992' (1993) 25 *Ottawa Law Review* 655, 656.
[103] *Class Actions* (2012) [8.62].
[104] ibid, [2.34].
[105] Brown *et al.*, *Defending Class Actions* (n 83) 350.
[106] [2012] ONSC 2715, [64].

Table 4.1 *Twenty years of the Ontario Class Proceedings Fund, 1992–2012*

Total of applications received:	131
Number of funding applications approved:	82
Number of funding applications denied:	24
Number of funding applications deferred:	9
Number of funding applications withdrawn:	16
	131
Of the funding applications approved:	
Number of approved applications ongoing:	41
Number of approved applications not certified or dismissed with no further right of appeal:	11
Number of approved applications leading to judgments or settlements:	30
	82

the Fund, two decades on, the Class Proceedings Committee noted that it had approved eighty-two applications over that period. Judicially, it has been said that those eighty-two cases must represent a very small proportion of the total number of class actions commenced over those two decades.[107] Table 4.1 above reproduces a summary of the results of the review undertaken by the Class Proceedings Committee, over the course of the period between the commencement of the Fund in 1992 and the end of 2012:[108]

As at December 2012, **thirty** cases funded by the Class Proceedings Fund have resulted in settlements or awards in favour of class members. Hence: '[t]he 10 per cent levies on these awards and settlements are, in turn, what has enabled the Fund to be financially self-sustaining'.[109] According to that list of thirty applications, the amounts recovered by the class exceeded $10M in eleven of those cases.[110]

Over that twenty-year period:[111]

- the Class Proceedings Fund received $24,240,918 by way of the 10 per cent levies on those thirty cases;

---

[107] *Dugal v Manulife Financial Corp* [2011] ONSC 1785, 105 OR (3d) 364, [31].
[108] See: *Class Proceedings Fund 20 Years in Review* (2013) 14–15, available at: www.lawfoundation.on.ca/wp-content/uploads/CPF-Brochure-2013.pdf.
[109] ibid, 13.
[110] ibid, 16–18.
[111] ibid, 19.

- it paid $7,468,844 in adverse costs awards to successful defendants in class actions; and
- it also paid $11,541,963 by way of disbursements to representative claimants over that period;
- this meant that, as at 31 December 2012, and after other adjustments, the Fund had a credit balance of $7,820,241.

However, since 2012, the picture has changed somewhat, and increasingly for the better. The number of approved funding applications has increased, no doubt signifying the surer financial footing upon which the Fund is based. The figures in Table 4.2 overpage (derived from the Fund's annual reports[112]) are of considerable interest:

Plainly, the financial health of the Fund has considerably and impressively improved over the past few years. The balance of the Fund in 2016 was certainly 'significant',[113] and in 2017, the Chair stated that, 'it is fair to say that the Fund has grown from being relatively unknown and underutilized to a significant part of the class action landscape ... We estimate that the Fund provides funding to 10% of class actions commenced in Ontario.'[114] It is also worth noting that, for the period 1994–2017, the amount of money received by the Fund via the 10 per cent levies was almost $50M; and the amount of adverse costs paid out to winning defendants over the same period has been over $13M.[115] After twenty-five years, the Fund has clearly gained for itself a position in which it can afford to fund more applications, and may be prepared to take a risk upon those in which the merits may not be as strong, but which have a novel, public interest, or test case character.

However, a cautionary note has been sounded about the ongoing utility of the Fund, for three reasons.[116] First, if some adverse costs awards were to deplete the Fund, the consequences would be disastrous

---

[112] These are available in full text at: www.lawfoundation.on.ca/class-proceedings-fund /resources-reports/.

[113] See comment by the Chair of the Class Proceedings Fund, quoted in the *Class Proceedings Fund Annual Report* (2016), available at: www.lawfoundation.on.ca/wp-content/uploads/Report-on-Class-Proceedings-2016-EN.pdf

[114] *Class Proceedings Fund Annual Report* (2017), 'Message from the Chair', 29, available at: www.lawfoundation.on.ca/wp-content/uploads/CPF_Annual_report_2017_EN.pdf.

[115] ibid, p 31, 'Class Proceedings Fund financial highlights' ($47,807,957 and $13,447,253 respectively).

[116] Law Reform Commission of Ontario, *Review of Class Actions in Ontario – Issues to be Considered* (November 2013) 7, as cited in: British Columbia Law Institute, *Study Paper on Financing Litigation* (2017) 233.

Table 4.2 *The Class Proceedings Fund, 2012–17*

	Number of funding applications	Number of funding applications approved	10 per cent levies received by the Fund	Adverse costs awards paid to successful defendants	Balance of the Fund at year's end
2017	27	18	$3,242,185	£3,506,003	$16,650,003
2016	22	17	$5,961,678	$528,767	$19,861,537
2015	17	12	$1,114,211	$676,520	$16,750,105
2014	20	11	$10,350,989	$258,750	$19,313,255
2013	13	7	$2,897,976	$977,397	$9,495,618
2012	12	7	$1,911,337	$2,916,515	$7,820,241

for presently funded (and future) cases, as 'there is no statutory requirement for the government or the Law Foundation to replenish its funds'. Secondly, the 'jurisprudence of costs in class actions lacks consistency, and this makes it difficult for the Class Proceedings Committee to evaluate risk when choosing potential cases'. Thirdly, the Fund 'is not competitive with third party funders who can offer lower rates [of success fees] for lower risk cases', because the Fund cannot vary its statutorily designated levy of 10 per cent. On this latter point, the Law Commission of Ontario has recently consulted upon whether the levy should have some in-built flexibility in order to cater for those lower-risk cases.[117]

Hence, it is plain that the operation of Ontario's Fund is continuing to evolve and to be tweaked, to best suit that jurisdiction's costs-shifting class actions landscape. Its significance is now undeniably very marked, after some rather spartan earlier years.

D   Where the Representative Claimant Loses

The advantage obtained by a winning defendant, who secures an adverse costs award against the representative claimant and who can then apply to have that award enforced against the Class Proceedings Fund, has already been discussed.[118] This section draws out, instead, various

---

[117] *Class Actions: Objectives, Experiences and Reforms* (March 2018), 'Consultation Question 3', 22.
[118] See Section B(1)(b).

protective mechanisms afforded to the claimant 'side' of the litigation: the representative claimant; the Law Foundation; and the class lawyers.

1 Primary Protection: For the Representative Claimant

As already stated,[119] where a Class Proceedings Fund-funded representative claimant either fails to achieve certification, loses on the common issues, or loses on appeal, and recovers nothing in the action, then it is the Fund – and not the representative claimant – that is liable (upon application by the defendant) to pay that adverse costs award.[120] This protection or 'shield'[121] afforded to the representative claimant by the Fund 'is important for the purposes of the Class Proceedings Act',[122] and to the whole ethos of how the regime was set up.[123]

Ontario courts have regularly pointed out the consequences of preserving the costs-shifting rule for class actions litigation – that it was: 'designed to be a significant economic barrier to [such] litigation',[124] to act as a 'litigation chill … built into the system selected by the legislature';[125] especially given 'the extraordinary and indeed financially devastating legal expense of a class action'.[126] In a non-costs-shifting regime such as British Columbia, of course, the motivation to implement a public fund is much reduced (and, in fact, no such fund exists in British Columbia).[127]

The value of this protection cannot be overstated. Two recent Ontario Court of Appeal cases illustrate the potential exposure. In the case of *Das v George Weston Ltd*,[128] a class action was instituted in Ontario in respect of the collapse of the Rana Plaza building in Savar, Bangladesh in 2013, due to significant structural flaws. Thousands were killed or injured,

---

[119] See Section B(1)(a).

[120] Law Society Act, RSO 1990, c L.8, s 59.4.

[121] *Hughes v Liquor Control Bd of Ontario* [2018] ONSC 4862, [83].

[122] *Garland v Consumers' Gas Co* [1998] 3 SCR 112, 40 OR (3d) 479, 165 DLR (4th) 385, [68].

[123] See, e.g., the judicial discussion in: *Hughes v Liquor Control Board of Ontario* [2018] ONSC 4862, [74]–[126]; *Das v George Weston Ltd* [2017] ONSC 5583, [36]–[73], and on appeal, the judgment of Doherty JA dealt with the costs appeal, with further important analysis of Ontario's costs and funding regime: [2018] ONCA 1053; *Fantl v Transamerica Life Canada* [2013] ONSC 5198, [26]–[43]; *McCracken v Canadian National Rwy Co* [2012] ONCA 797, [10]–[11].

[124] *Houle v St Jude Medical Inc* [2017] ONSC 5129, 9 CPC (8th) 321, [43].

[125] *Cavanaugh v Grenville Christian College* [2012] CanLII 47233, [37].

[126] *Houle* [2017] ONSC 5129, [44].

[127] Noted in: *Stanway v Wyeth Canada Inc* [2013] BCSC 1585, 56 BCLR (5th) 192, [12].

[128] [2018] ONCA 1053.

mostly factory workers making garments for international export for Joe Fresh Apparel Canada Inc, a famous brand owned and controlled by George Weston Ltd, Canada's largest food, clothing, and pharmacy retailer. The class action was struck out on the basis that it was plain and obvious that a claim based on vicarious liability against the defendant could not succeed under the law of Bangladesh (that law being the governing law of the dispute). The costs awards against the representative claimant totalled approximately $2.4M – and it was the Fund, and not the representative claimant, that was thereafter embroiled in an (ultimately successful) appeal as to those costs.[129]

Similarly, in *Lavender v Miller Bernstein LLP*,[130] a class action was instituted against the defendant auditors, alleging that they had been negligent in their audit of Buckingham Securities. It was ultimately held that the auditors did not owe any duty of care to Buckingham Securities' investor clients, and that the trial judge had erred, in particular, in his 'proximity' analysis. The auditors sought, and obtained an order for, costs against the Fund in the region of $1,170,000.[131] These are very significant sums of money claimed against the Fund.

2   Secondary Protection: For the Law Foundation

Given that the Law Foundation of Ontario administers the Fund, it is the body that has standing at the costs hearing to argue for an appropriate level of costs[132] (and to argue any appeal therefrom, for which leave is required, but rarely granted[133]).

(a)   Exceptions to Costs-Shifting

A frequent submission by the Foundation pertains to section 31(1) of Ontario's Class Proceedings Act 1992. This provision represents a further

---

[129] The costs were reduced by 30 per cent (see ibid, [225]) – which still left an adverse costs order of about $1.5M.

[130] [2018] ONCA 955.

[131] ibid, [14].

[132] The Law Foundation has a right to be provided with notice, should the court consider that the defendant to the class action may be entitled to an award of costs: Rules of Civil Procedure, RRO 1990, Reg 194, r 12.04(2). Thereafter, the Foundation has the right to make submissions and to be heard on costs: r 12.04(3)(a). For discussion, see, e.g.: *JK v Ontario* [2017] ONCA 902, [36]; *Hodge v Neinstein* [2014] ONSC 6366, [6]; and *Fantl v Transamerica Life Canada* [2013] ONSC 5198, [6].

[133] *Das v George Weston Ltd* [2018] ONCA 1053, [224] (the costs award reduced on appeal, per n 129 above).

avenue by which the Ontario legislature sought to soften the effects of the costs-shifting ('loser-pays') rule which operates in Ontario class actions.[134] As one court put it:

> [s]ince access to justice is at the very heart of class proceedings, one of the major public policy factors to address in establishing any class proceedings regime is, of course, the cost of litigation to the representative plaintiff and to the class members. The nature of the Ontario legislature's response to this factor is to be gathered largely from s 31 of the Class Proceedings Act, 1992 and by its creation of the Class Proceedings Fund.[135]

Section 31(1) facilitates a judicial direction that there be no order as to costs, or alternatively, that any costs awarded to the successful defendant should be reduced significantly from the amounts claimed, in three specific circumstances which are set out in the statute:

> **s 31(1)** In exercising its discretion with respect to costs under subsection 131(1) of the Courts of Justice Act, the court may consider whether the class proceeding was a test case, raised a novel point of law, or involved a matter of public interest.

The 'ameliorating' effect[136] of this provision – and when its three factors have, or have not, been met – has been analysed in detail by the author elsewhere.[137] The Ontario legislature enacted an approach for class actions whereby: fixing costs is to be the same as in ordinary actions, albeit with 'special weight' given to the factors in section 31(1);[138] the provision does not displace the 'normal rule that costs will ordinarily follow the event',[139] nor undermine the general purposes of an adverse costs award;[140] and there is no *presumption* against making adverse cost

---

[134] *Fischer v IG* [2015] ONSC 2491, [14].

[135] *Ruffolo v Sun Life Ass Co of Canada* (2008), 90 OR (3d) 59 (Ont SCJ) [16], with this point not disputed on appeal: [2009] ONCA 274, 95 OR (3d) 709.

[136] As termed in: *Smith v Canadian Tire Acceptance Ltd* (1995), 22 OR (3d) 433, 36 CPC (3d) 175 (Winkler J).

[137] 'Costs Shifting, Security for Costs, and Class Actions: Lessons from Elsewhere', in D Dwyer (ed), *The Tenth Anniversary of the Civil Procedure Rules* (Oxford University Press, 2010), ch 10.

[138] *Cavanaugh v Grenville Christian College* [2012] CanLII 47233, [17] (citations omitted).

[139] *Pearson v Inco* (2006), 79 OR (3d) 427 (CA) [13].

[140] These have been identified in Ontario case law to be as follows: (1) to indemnify successful litigants for the costs of litigation, although not necessarily completely; (2) to facilitate access to justice, including access for impecunious litigants; (3) to discourage frivolous claims and defences; (4) to discourage and sanction inappropriate behaviour by litigants in their conduct of the proceedings; and (5) to encourage settlements: *Berg*

awards against the representative claimant, even should one or more of the section 31(1) factors apply in a given case.[141]

(b) The Status of the Law Foundation

In an appropriate case, the Law Foundation may rely upon one or more of the section 31(1) factors, in order to seek to reduce or remove the adverse costs order for which the Fund is liable. However, the recent cautionary tone of the following judicial comments in Ontario are worth noting –

> in this world, nothing can be said to be certain, except death, taxes, and the submission that a class action is in the public interest [adapted from Benjamin Franklin];[142]
>
> if the Legislature wished every class action to be regarded as in the public interest, it could have introduced a no-costs regime or an asymmetric costs regime, but it did neither;[143]
>
> like a forest fire in this era of climate change, costs in class proceedings have gotten out of control;[144]
>
> in the immediate case, the costs regime is working as it was intended by the Legislature to operate; the defendants have justified their claims for costs; and the plaintiffs and the Class Proceedings Fund have not justified any reduction from the amounts claimed. The Plaintiffs lit the costs fire, and the immediate case is not the occasion for judicial disaster relief.[145]
>
> The defendant 'does not have a bottomless supply of money with which to defend claims. [It] is clearly out-of-pocket for its legal fees and for its legal disbursements. [It] should not be made to suffer the consequences of an inadequate costs order.'[146]

Given its status as a promotor of access to justice, is there any ground for adopting a more lenient attitude towards the Class Proceedings Fund by invoking section 31's grounds more willingly, where the representative claimant is unsuccessful? On this point, the majority judicial opinion

---

v Canadian Hockey League [2017] ONSC 5382, [43] (citations omitted), appeal allowed, but the relevant point was not adversely commented upon: *Berg v Canadian Hockey League* [2019] ONSC 2106 (Div Ct); *McCracken v Canadian National Rwy Co* [2010] ONSC 6066, [10].

[141] *Ruffolo v Sun Life Ass Co of Canada* [2009] ONCA 274, [35], leave to appeal *ref'd*: [2009] SCCA No 226.

[142] *Hughes v Liquor Control Bd of Ontario* [2018] ONSC 4862, opening comment, and fn 1 (Perell J).

[143] ibid, [102].

[144] *Heller v Ubertechnologies Inc* [2018] ONSC 1690, [1] (Perell J again)

[145] *Hughes v Liquor Control Bd of Ontario* [2018] ONSC 4862, [14].

[146] *Smith v Inco Ltd* [2013] ONCA 724, [64], citing the trial judge, Henderson J.

declares 'no'. The potentially disruptive and detrimental effect of a costs award against the Fund is not a matter that a court should consider as being relevant, when deciding whether or not section 31's prerequisites are proven. Where the Law Foundation has made submissions to seek a reduced or nil costs award, the general judicial view has been that 'the issues of entitlement, scale, and quantum of costs must be determined without reference to whether the Fund provided support to the applicant for certification'.[147] Rather, the potential for disruptive impact should be considered by the Class Proceedings Committee in deciding whether to grant funding to a particular claimant in the first place.[148] Of course, it goes without saying that large adverse costs award against the Fund, should a funded action lose, may seriously compromise its ability to fund future class actions (and, in the early days, could have depleted the Fund altogether) – but that is (and always was) the price of the Committee's decision-making as to which cases it should accept for funding and which it should reject. After all, as courts have not been loath to emphasise, the possible rewards of funding a high-value claim are potentially very large to the Fund, where it nets 10 per cent of the recovery by way of levy.[149]

However, on the other hand, there is some sentiment to the effect that the factors in section 31(1) should be given substantial weight if the Fund has supported an unsuccessful class action. In *McCracken*,[150] Winkler CJO noted that '[t]he Fund was created to facilitate access to justice. If the Fund was required to absorb steep costs awards imposed on litigants even though the proposed action displays the factors in section 31(1) of the CPA, this would have an undesirable chilling effect on class proceedings.' Subsequent courts have supported these specific

---

[147] *Hughes v Liquor Control Bd of Ontario* [2018] ONSC 4862, [86]; *Cannon v Funds for Canada Foundation* [2014] ONSC 953, [11]; *Fischer v IG Investment Management Ltd* [2010] ONSC 2839, [28].

[148] See, e.g.: *Edwards v Law Society of Upper Canada (No 2)* (2000), 48 OR (3d) 329 (CA) [52] ('this was a consideration for the Committee recommending funding, not one for the court in deciding to award costs to an otherwise deserving defendant'), citing: *Garland v Consumers' Gas Co* (1995), 22 OR (3d) 767 (Gen Div). Also: *Cavanaugh v Grenville Christian College* [2012] CanLII 47233 (Ont SCJ) [9]; *Sutherland v Hudson's Bay Co* [2008] CanLII 5967 (Ont SCJ) [14].

[149] e.g., *McCracken v Canadian National Rwy Co* [2012] ONCA 797, [11]; *Singer v Schering-Plough Canada Inc* [2010] ONSC 1737, [20]; *David Polowin Real Estate Ltd v Dominion of Canada General Ins Co* (2008), 93 OR (3d) 257 (CA) [29].

[150] *McCracken* (n 149) [10].

comments,[151] including the following recent remark by the Ontario Court of Appeal:

> I agree with Winkler CJO's observation. I would think that the CPC would inevitably take a more restrictive view of the cases it would fund if, in cases that were found to involve matters of public interest, the courts routinely give little or no weight to that factor when assessing costs payable by the Fund to the successful defendant.[152]

Hence, it is possible that the status of the Law Foundation may come to matter in assessments of the section 31(1) factors to a greater extent than may previously have occurred. It is clearly an important and relevant point for the financial welfare of the Fund.

(c) An Uneven Landscape

That tactic of trying to invoke section 31's ameliorating effect has been successful for the Foundation in various cases. For example, in *Das*,[153] the costs award was reduced by 30 per cent on appeal to reflect the public interest component in the claims ('[t]he claim ... lays bare important public policy questions going to the role Canada and, more specifically, its business community, play and should aspire to play in the global marketplace'[154]), albeit that it was important that the costs award should 'remain substantial and reflective of [Ds'] success in the proceedings'.[155]

Even more recently, in *Broutzas v Rouge Valley Health System*,[156] the Fund escaped any adverse costs awards, where the proposed action for breach of privacy (arising from former employees accessing patient contact information) was not certified. Perell J noted that, '[w]hile there is a juridical "I know it when I see it" quality in characterizing a case as justifying no order as to costs because of the novelty of the issues and the public interest in them ... the case at bar has many objective indicia that support the conclusion that there should be no order as to costs.'[157] In earlier cases too, the Foundation has benefited from a reduction in the

---

[151] *Das v George Weston Ltd* [2018] ONCA 1053, [251]; *Green v Canadian Imperial Bank of Commerce* [2014] ONCA 344, [9]; *Smith v Inco Ltd* [2013] ONCA 724, [66]; *Good v Toronto Police Services Bd* [2013] ONSC 5826, [12].
[152] *Das* (n 151) [251] (Doherty JA).
[153] ibid.
[154] ibid, [262].
[155] ibid, [273].
[156] [2019] ONSC 559.
[157] ibid, [23].

adverse costs award to reflect the 'novelty' of the claim,[158] the 'rarity' of the circumstances of the claim,[159] or for the 'public interest' factor.[160]

However, the Law Foundation has been unsuccessful in seeking to engage the effect of section 31(1) in some cases, thus exposing it to significant adverse costs orders. For example, the following costs awards have been ordered against the Fund, where submissions relating to section 31(1) were rejected: in *Lavender v Miller Bernstein LLP*, over $1.16M (the class's claim fell 'within a relatively common category of claims asserting auditors' negligence and involved the application of settled law');[161] in *Hughes v Liquor Control Board of Ontario*, over $2.3M ('and it should not be forgotten that in supporting the plaintiffs' case, the *quid pro quo* was a 10% mandatory share of a pleaded $3 billion damages claim');[162] in *Hodge v Neinstein*, $300,000 ('the issues were no more novel than those that arise in any other class action');[163] and in *Healey v Lakeridge Health Corporation*, over $260,000 ('the bulk of the time was spent on the threshold for compensable damages, which is not a novel issue').[164]

(d)   Other Potential Protection

Quite apart from what is provided in the class actions regime itself, there are more generalist reasons, in accordance with the rules of civil procedure operative in Ontario, as to why the Law Foundation may seek to have the adverse costs award against it reduced because of the defendant's conduct.[165]

---

[158] *Sankar v Bell Mobility* [2015] ONSC 1976, [13] (reduced 'to reflect some measure of novelty in the interpretation of the Gift Card Regulation').

[159] *David Polowin Real Estate Ltd v Dominion of Canada General Ins Co* [2008] ONCA 703, 93 OR (3d) 257, 300 DLR (4th) 491, [40]–[41]. The case was novel; 'it is a rare circumstance that this court reverses one of its own decisions, ... [especially] when the reversal takes place within such a short time-frame. The plaintiffs, armed with this court's decision in *McNaughton*, proceeded with these actions in the reasonable expectation that they were on firm ground in doing so', referring to: *McNaughton Automotive Ltd v Co-operators General Ins Co* [2008] ONCA 597.

[160] *Good v Toronto Police Services Bd* [2013] ONSC 5826, [47] ('the costs award must reflect the presence of the "public interest" factor').

[161] [2018] ONCA 955, [9].

[162] [2018] ONSC 4862, [119].

[163] [2014] ONSC 6366, [87].

[164] [2011] ONCA 55, 103 OR (3d) 401, 328 DLR (4th) 248, [79].

[165] See: Rules of Civil Procedure, r 57.01(1)(g), and evidenced in, e.g.: *Boucher v Public Accountants Council for the Province of Ontario* (2004), 71 OR (3d) 291 (CA) [24]; *Das v George Weston Ltd* [2018] ONCA 1053, [226]; *Lavender v Miller Bernstein LLP* [2018] ONCA 955, [6]; *Hodge v Neinstein* [2014] ONSC 6366; *McCracken v Canadian National Rwy Co* [2012] ONSC 6838, [37]. This conduct may include where: the defendant refused

3 Tertiary Protection: For the Class Lawyers

As already noted,[166] the Class Proceedings Fund does not fund the legal fees incurred by the class lawyers during the life of the class action.

However, the point has been usefully made, by the British Columbia Law Institute,[167] that the existence of a public fund such as the Class Proceedings Fund can help with the legal representation of the class in a variety of other ways. For example, a successful application to the Fund can secure the specialist legal services that class actions law firms typically provide – these are not the sorts of cases which advocacy organisations or publicly funded legal services programmes typically conduct.[168] Furthermore, appeal cases often involve important issues of public interest or importance, but are expensive:

> [a] public fund may also fill the very large gap in services available for appellate proceedings ... Faced with a loss at first instance, litigants are often too discouraged by costs penalties and their lack of resources to consider pursuing an appeal. A publicly funded litigation fund could help litigants pursue appeals in important cases by subsidizing the cost of litigation.[169]

Additionally, for those smaller law firms which do not have the 'war chests' to fund the disbursements of the class action themselves, the Law Foundation can provide both financial support for disbursements, essential administrative support, and not to mention the peace of mind of knowing that any adverse costs award will be covered by the Fund, should the claim lose.[170] The fact that funding can pre-date certification means that it can be a 'useful model' for funding the representative claimant's disbursements whilst the claim is being investigated – often a very expensive stage of the proceedings.[171]

---

to admit uncontroversial or already-admitted facts; the costs claimed by the defendant were disproportionate to the (lack of) complexity of the issues; the amounts claimed by the defendant were excessive and unreasonable; or the defendant unnecessarily increased the costs of the certification motion by a meritless challenge to the representative claimant's qualifications to act in that capacity.

[166] See Section B(1)(a).

[167] *Study Paper on Financing Litigation* (Study Paper 9, October 2017).

[168] ibid, 237.

[169] ibid, 238.

[170] ibid, 238–39.

[171] As noted by: Collins, 'Public Funding of Class Actions' (n 35) 236, 238. See too, for a judicial notation about this advantage: *Bozsik v Livingston Intl Inc* [2016] ONSC 7168, [168].

E   Miscellaneous Issues

This section of the chapter canvasses a number of issues that have arisen in relation to the Class Proceedings Fund, which could assist those law-makers and policymakers in other jurisdictions who are contemplating the implementation of such a fund to support the funding of class actions:

1   Interplay with Other Sources of Funding

A litigation funding agreement (LFA) entered into between a third-party funder and the representative claimant requires the approval of the court, in order to take effect in Ontario.[172] Whilst third-party funding is not 'categorically illegal on the grounds of champerty or maintenance' in Ontario law, courts have reiterated that a particular LFA might be illegal as being champertous, for which judicial vetting is essential.[173]

There has been a rather interesting interplay between third-party funding and the Class Proceedings Fund, with three points arising in the case law.

First, the legislative implementation of the Class Proceedings Fund has **not** been judicially taken to indicate any legislative policy to preclude third-party funding.[174] They remain alternative avenues of funding, depending upon the representative claimant's circumstances.

Secondly, whether or not an LFA is reasonable and non-champertous has regularly been adjudged by reference to the fact that the LFA provides a better return to the class members than the Class Proceedings Fund does, which mandates an uncapped levy of 10 per cent.[175] For example, in *Marriott v General Motors of Canada Company*, it was held that the LFA

---

[172] See, e.g.: *McIntyre Estate v Ontario (A-G)* (2002), 61 OR (3d) 257 (CA); *Metzler Investment GMBH v Gildan Activewear Inc* [2009] OJ No 3315 (SCJ); *Dugal v Manulife Financial Corp* [2011] ONSC 1785; *Labourers' Pension Fund of Central and Eastern Canada (Trustees of) v Sino-Forest Corp* [2012] ONSC 2937; *Bayens v Kinross Gold Corp* [2013] ONSC 4974.

[173] *Fehr v Sun Life Ass Co of Canada* [2012] ONSC 2715, [69]–[95], quote at [71].

[174] *Fehr*, ibid, [57].

[175] See, e.g: *Berg v Canadian Hockey League* [2016] ONSC 4466, [7], not adversely commented on appeal: *Berg v Canadian Hockey League* [2019] ONSC 2106 (Div Ct); and *Bayens v Kinross Gold Corp* [2013] ONSC 4974, 117 OR (3d) 150, [41] ('[t]he court must be satisfied that the access to justice facilitated by the [LFA] remains substantively meaningful and that the representative plaintiff has not agreed to over-compensate the third party funder for assuming the risks of an adverse costs award. . . . the comparable benchmark of the Class Proceedings Fund's percentage uncapped levy may assist the court in determining whether the [LFA] is fair and reasonable'); *JB & M Walker Ltd/ 1523428 Ontario Inc v TDL Group* [2019] ONSC 999, [23]–[27].

'is fair and reasonable. The 7% commission in the Funding Agreement is less than the 10% premium applied by the Class Proceedings Fund, and is capped at a fixed amount, unlike the Fund.'[176] In *Rooney v ArcelorMittal SA* too, Rady J noted that LFAs 'are becoming increasingly common, and represent an alternative to seeking funding from the Class Proceedings Fund. Its terms represent a savings of a minimum of 3% over the Fund'.[177] On the other hand, where a comparison between the LFA and the Fund suggests to the court that the third-party funder is being over-compensated, then Ontario judges have been prepared to intervene by insisting that the LFA's success fee be reduced to 10 per cent to match that of the Fund's, and that any fee exceeding that amount must be judicially approved.[178] It is not only the rate of return that can be adversely-considered in an LFA – the right of termination may be judicially perceived to be 'over-broad' too.[179]

Thirdly, when the representative claimant seeks judicial approval for an LFA, it is (presently) not necessary to have first applied to the Class Proceedings Fund for funding – and when considering the reasonableness of the LFA, 'if approval from the Fund is sought and refused, nothing can be taken from the fact that the Class Proceedings Fund was not prepared to provide litigation funding'.[180] After all, as another court noted, the Class Proceedings Fund 'has limited resources, and it is not obliged to accept all applications. ... the Fund should not be regarded as a filtering mechanism to determine what class actions are worthy or unworthy to be financially supported by third-party funders.'[181] There have certainly been cases in which the Class

---

[176] [2018] ONSC 2535, [9(xii)].

[177] [2013] ONSC 7768, [3]. See too: *Labourers' Pension Fund v Sino-Forest Corp* [2012] ONSC 2937, [16] (the LFA 'is preferable to the alternative of funding from the Class Proceedings Fund. The commission is less than the 10% uncapped levy that would be extracted by the Fund').

[178] *Houle v St Jude Medical Inc* [2017] ONSC 5129, 9 CPC (8th) 321, [42] (Perell J), for comparisons between the LFA and funding by the Class Proceedings Fund, with appeal dismissed: *Houle v St Jude Medical Inc* [2018] ONSC 6352 (Div Ct), and with further comparisons of the LFA with the Fund at [20], [37]–[42].

[179] ibid (Perell J) [91]–[93], and (Div Ct) [25]. As one commentator has noted, the *Houle* decision, whilst demonstrating 'a renewed focus on access to justice and protecting class members ... may also have a chilling effect on third-party funders who are averse to the courts rewriting their agreements': M McKinnon (ed), *2018 Class Action Case Law Year in Review* (Siskinds LLP, 2018), available via the CanLII database at: https://commentary.canlii.org/.

[180] *David v Loblaw* [2018] ONSC 6469, [12].

[181] *Bayens v Kinross Gold Corp* [2013] ONSC 4974, 117 OR (3d) 150, [28].

Proceedings Committee rejected funding from the Fund, and the representative claimant then successfully obtained financial support from a third-party funder.[182] In these circumstances, scholarly commentary has questioned whether the option of obtaining third-party funding will come to form part of the assessment matrix by the Class Proceedings Committee, when deciding whether or not to grant an application for funding from the Fund.[183]

As an aside, applications for funding to the Class Proceedings Fund have become relevant in carriage motions, i.e., where two or more class actions arise out of the same event; where two or more representative claimants have filed viable statements of claim, with plausible causes of action; where the representative claimants have refused to co-operate with each other; and where, for the purposes of judicial efficiency and consistency of outcomes, the court must select one claim to proceed and the other/s to be stayed. In Ontario case law, an extensive and non-exhaustive list of factors are considered to be relevant in deciding carriage motions; one of which is 'funding'.[184] In a recent case,[185] one of the representative claimants had applied for, and obtained, funding from the Class Proceedings Fund; whilst the other representative claimant decided to self-fund their costs and disbursements. Mr Justice Belobaba selected that representative claimant who was self-funding, and noted that, 'there is nothing laudatory' in one claimant's applying for Class Proceedings Fund indemnification, as compared to the other claimant's decision to self-fund, 'where the likelihood of an early settlement is high and the risk and financial impact of any non-recoverable costs is very low'.[186]

2 At the End of the Action

(a) Discontinuance

In the event that the class action is discontinued or abandoned, the representative claimant must repay the amount of any payments which have been received from the Fund.[187]

---

[182] See, e.g.: *Bayens v Kinross Gold Corp* [2015] ONSC 3944, [10].
[183] M Malone, 'Judicial Scrutiny of Third Party Litigation Funding Agreements in Canadian Class Actions' (2017–18) 13 *Canadian Class Action Rev* 193, 203.
[184] *Mancinelli v Barrick Gold* [2016] ONCA 571, 131 OR (3d) 497, [14]–[16].
[185] *Chu v Parwell Investments Inc* [2019] ONSC 700.
[186] ibid, fn 12.
[187] Ontario Regulation 771/92, s 9.

Where discontinuance of a class action is sought, then under Ontario law, court approval is required.[188] Before so ordering, the court must be satisfied that the interests of the class members, and the defendant, will not be prejudiced.[189] The 'policy rationale' for requiring court approval for a discontinuance is two-fold: '(1) deterring plaintiffs and class counsel from abusing the class action procedure by bringing a meritless class proceeding (a so-called strike suit) to extract a payment as the price of discontinuing the class proceeding; and (2) providing an opportunity to ameliorate any adverse effect of the discontinuance on class members who might be prejudiced by the discontinuance'.[190] However, where the Class Proceedings Fund is funding the action, then its interests must be taken account of in respect of the discontinuance too. As one court put it (in circumstances where the medical research surrounding a particular treatment for nicotine addiction, obtained subsequent to certification, did not support generic causation, and where the representative claimant wished to withdraw the class action): '[g]iven the remote prospects of success, it is opportune to allow the Fund to end its exposure to costs in what is now an extraordinarily risky litigation to pursue'.[191]

As with all external funders, the Fund will be affected greatly if the merits of the case change during its progress. Presently, counsel acting for the class must give an undertaking to 'submit a comprehensive annual report on the progress of the action', and to 'promptly advise the [Class Proceedings] Committee of any significant event during the course of the action which may have an impact on, or implications with respect to the Class Proceedings Fund'.[192] Undoubtedly, the grounds for terminating the provision of funding is one of the most vexed issues for all external funders, and raises the tricky question as to whether exclusive grounds for termination should be inserted in the relevant legislation,[193] or whether that should be

---

[188] CPA 1992, s 29(1).

[189] *Parker v Pfizer Canada Inc* [2017] ONSC 2418, [17]–[18].

[190] *Parker*, ibid, [19], citing, e.g.: *Hudson v Austin* [2010] OJ No 2015 (SCJ).

[191] *Parker*, ibid, [20].

[192] By virtue of the 'Class Counsel Undertaking', available for perusal at the Law Foundation of Ontario website at: www.lawfoundation.on.ca/class-proceedings-fund/practice-directions/.

[193] This was the option (in cl 11.2) chosen by the drafters of the *Code of Conduct for Litigation Funding in England and Wales*, which (since 2011) has governed the conduct of those third-party funders who are members of the Association of Litigation Funders. The Code (amended 2014 and 2017) is available at: http://associationoflitigationfunders.com/wp-content/uploads/2018/03/Code-Of-Conduct-for-Litigation-Funders-at-Jan-2018-FINAL.pdf. The author was a member of the original drafting committee, and served as peer reviewer of the Code in 2014 and 2017.

left entirely to consensual contractual agreement.[194] However, given the public nature of a class actions fund, it seems preferable that the former option be employed, to remove uncertainty and debate.

(b) Settlement

When a funded representative claimant seeks judicial approval of any proposed settlement agreement arrived at with the defendant/s (as the class action regime requires[195]), then the welfare of the Fund is one of the factors to which courts have specifically had regard. Albeit that the Law Foundation is not a party to the class action, it is a stakeholder in a settlement, precisely for the reason that it is entitled to both the 10 per cent levy and the reimbursement of disbursements if any recovery is forthcoming to one or more members of the class. In order to approve a settlement of a class proceeding, the court must find that the terms of the settlement are fair, reasonable, and in the best interests *of those affected by it*.[196] That is clearly a wider class than merely the litigants and the absent class members. Hence, courts have properly taken judicial note of whether or not the Fund has objected to the terms of the proposed settlement, when deciding whether the settlement is fair, just and reasonable.[197]

In particular, the court will consider whether the proceeds of settlement are sufficient to permit the Fund to be paid for its disbursements, and to permit the Fund to be paid the 10 per cent levy – whilst also allowing for sufficient monies to pay legal fees and any additional disbursements of the class lawyers and others who provided legal services, whilst still leaving a reasonable sum to be either distributed to the class members or via some other means.[198] The 10 per cent levy is compulsorily set by statute, and hence, if the court is uncomfortable that the combined payout to the Fund and to class lawyers is too high, then it is the latter's fees which may be reduced, or modified, by the court.[199] However, it is impermissible for the

---

[194] This was the option chosen for damages-based agreements for civil contentious matters, which were introduced by the Courts and Legal Services Act 1990, s 58AA, and the Damages-based Agreements Regulations 2013, which are silent on the grounds of termination for any non-employment-related matter.

[195] CPA 1992, s 29(2).

[196] *Dabbs v Sun Life Ass* [1998] OJ No 1598 (Gen Div) [9]; *Parsons v Canadian Red Cross Socy* [1999] OJ No 3572 (SCJ) [68]–[73].

[197] See, e.g.: *Krajewski v TNow Entertainment Group Inc* [2012] ONSC 3908, [18].

[198] See, e.g., the discussion in *Cass v Western One Inc* [2018] ONSC 4794, [107].

[199] As occurred in: *Welsh v Ontario* [2018] ONSC 3217, [17] ('the quality of the success achieved did not merit a combined contingency fee of approximately $5.3 million for

court to insist unilaterally upon counsel donating part of its fees to a designated charity under a *cy-près* order, rather than reverting to the defendant, without the consent of the parties.[200]

Finally, where a *cy-près* distribution to the Law Foundation of Ontario is approved as part of the judicially approved settlement, this has been judicially held to be subject to the limitation that the monies passing *cy-près* would not be mixed with the funds of the Class Proceedings Fund.[201]

3   The Adequacy Criterion

It has long been a contentious point in Canadian certification jurisprudence as to whether the financial wherewithal of the representative claimant to fund his own side of the litigation and to pay any adverse costs award should be a relevant criterion by which to judge the adequacy of the representative claimant.[202] Some cases have held that the financial capability of the representative claimant does matter;[203] others have held that such a requirement would constitute a 'halfway house towards requiring security for costs', and which would 'limit recourse to class proceedings to cases where the proposed representative plaintiffs were either wealthy or could demonstrate that a commitment for funding assistance was in place';[204] whereas other cases have dismissed the representative claimant's financial capacity from the certification analysis altogether.[205] The UK Competition Law Class Action, by contrast, removes any such

---

a $15 million settlement of a $325 million class action in which 90% of the Student Class Members and 100% of the Family Class Members would receive nothing in exchange for their forced releases'; class lawyers' fees adjusted). See too: *Smith v National Money Mart* [2010] ONSC 1334, with that aspect not affected on appeal: [2011] ONCA 233, 106 OR (3d) 37, 331 DLR (4th) 208; and suggested, on other facts, in: *Martin v Barrett* [2008] CanLII 25062 (Ont SCJ) [56].

[200] *Welsh v Ontario* [2019] ONCA 41, [10]–[12]. On this narrow point, the decision in 2018 (n 199) was reversed.

[201] *Cassano v Toronto-Dominion Bank* (2009), 98 OR (3d) 543, [37].

[202] Discussed by the author in: 'Costs Shifting, Security for Costs, and Class Actions' (n 2) ch 10, 202–05.

[203] e.g., *Pearson v Inco Ltd* (2005), 78 OR (3d) 641, 261 DLR (4th) 629 (CA) [94]–[96].

[204] e.g., *Mortson v Ontario (Municipal Employees Retirement Bd)* (2004), 4 CPC (6th) 115 (Ont SCJ) [91], [94].

[205] e.g., *2038724 Ontario Ltd v Quizno's Canada Restaurant Corp* (2008), 89 OR (3d) 252 (SCJ) [139].

uncertainty by stipulating that the financial capabilities of the representative claimant **do** matter.[206]

In any event, the fact that the representative claimant has applied successfully to the Class Proceedings Fund has been cited, in some Ontario case law, as relevant to a finding that the representative claimant was indeed an adequate representative for the class, because adverse costs would be covered;[207] and conversely, where no such application had been made, and there were no other feasible methods put forward for funding the class action disbursements, adequate representation has been judicially refuted.[208]

F Potential Tweaks to the Model

1 Identifying a 'Gap'

The primary justification for implementing a special class actions fund is that there is a 'gap' in the funding market, which may cause meritorious claims not to be brought. That 'gap' could feasibly arise because of limited options for funding the representative claimant's own disbursements; or it could also arise because of the limited options for covering adverse costs, should the representative claimant lose.

The latter scenario has arisen in England and Wales. As one organisation noted, a class actions fund similar to that of Ontario's would be of advantage to English litigation, in that it could potentially assist representative claimants, 'and not just those with incomes low enough to qualify for legal aid'.[209] Furthermore, and contrary to the position which has been widely evident in Ontario, the extent to which lawyers acting for the representative claimant under the UK Competition Law Class Action would be prepared to cover adverse costs should their client lose, in return for a contingent form of funding, is doubtful at best. It seems that they *could* theoretically do so, where the funding of their client's case is being undertaken by means of a legislatively sanctioned and compliant conditional fee

---

[206] The representative claimant must be 'able to pay the defendant's recoverable costs if ordered': CAT Rules, r 78(2)(d); or satisfy any undertaking as to damages re injunctive relief: r 78(2)(e).

[207] *Cavanaugh v Grenville Christian College* [2012] ONSC 2995, [177]; *Segnitz v Royal & Sun Alliance Ins Co of Canada* (2003), 40 CPC (5th) 391 (Ont SCJ) [12]–[13].

[208] *Defazio v Ontario (Labour)* [2007] CanLII 7403 (Ont SCJ) [128].

[209] R Cranston, *Class Actions* (Society of Labour Lawyers, 2007) 22.

agreement[210] (to reiterate, percentage contingency fees are prohibited under the UK Competition Law Class Action[211]). Whilst there is no legislation permitting a solicitor or barrister to underwrite a client's liability to pay the costs of the defendant in the proceedings, earlier case law (in the context of unitary litigation) has held that an agreement between the lawyer and the client to indemnify the client for adverse costs does not constitute champerty or maintenance.[212]

However, in risky cases (of which class actions would be a prime example), the practice has been that lawyers in England and Wales will seek to ensure that their client's adverse costs liability is covered by either after-the-event insurers or by third-party funders.[213] Moreover, the 'green light' for indemnifying a client's adverse costs has not necessarily been clearly spelt out in the relevant case law (e.g., whether it should be limited to cases in which ATE insurance, third-party funding, or some other source of funding is unavailable or prohibitively expensive). As one commentator has noted, '[t]he case for a [valid] indemnity is less convincing in circumstances where the client has ample resources available to fund the litigation'.[214] Another has noted that the consequences of any solicitor not meeting the indemnity for adverse costs could be profound for the Solicitors' Regulation Authority, and that giving indemnities against adverse costs in a large and risky case could cause the solicitor to breach the outcome-focussed requirement in the Solicitors' Code of Conduct, that a solicitor should run his or her 'business or carry out your role in the business effectively and in accordance with proper governance and sound financial and risk management principles'.[215] There has also been a lingering doubt amongst

---

[210] Sanctioned by the Courts and Legal Services Act 1990, s 58, which entitles a litigant to employ 'a person providing advocacy or litigation services' to provide such services under a conditional fee agreement, i.e. what is sometimes called a 'no win no fee' arrangement. In 1999, s 58(1) was amended, to provide that any such agreement which did not comply with the requirements of section 58 'shall be unenforceable'.

[211] Per: CA 1998, s 47C(8).

[212] *Sibthorpe v Southwark LBC* [2011] EWCA Civ 25, [2011] 1 WLR 2111, commenting that the trend of recent UK authorities 'ha[d] been to foreshorten [champerty's] shadow' (at [44]), and also 'given that the legislative trend [was] clearly in favour of restricting the scope [of champerty]' (at [47]).

[213] See, e.g.: M Harvey, 'Case Comment: *Sibthorpe v Southwark LBC*' [2011] *J Personal Injury Law* C98.

[214] A Sedgwick, 'Case Comment: *Sibthorpe v Southwark LBC*' (2011) 30 *Civil Justice Quarterly* 261, 265.

[215] D Marshall, 'Solicitor Indemnity against Adverse Costs' [2012] *Journal of Personal Injury Law* 62, 66, citing: *SRA Handbook*, 'SRA Principles', principle 8.

commentators[216] (but not, to date, the English Court of Appeal[217]) as to whether a solicitor's indemnity for a client's exposure to adverse costs amounts to a 'contract of insurance'.

It is in these types of circumstances that a special class actions fund could be very useful, to fill a 'gap' in funding that is available in other class actions jurisdictions. Whether that becomes a reality under the UK Competition Law Class Action remains to be seen (and, whilst third-party funders are willing to fund the representative claimant's costs and fees and cover adverse costs, any perceived gap is probably filled for the present time).

2   Potential Modifications to Ontario's Model

For the sake of completeness, it is important to note that there are various modifications to Ontario's Class Proceedings Fund which have been implemented or recommended elsewhere, and which may be of interest to any policymakers and lawmakers who are contemplating the introduction of such a fund. Table 4.3 overpage sets out the key tweaks across the models (where the defendant = D, and the representative claimant = C):

This table contains numerous 'variations on the theme', for the consideration of drafters of present and future class actions regimes. Other issues, such as whether the representative claimant should be means- or merits-tested, and possible destination of fund monies to Consolidated Revenue should the fund accumulate excessive sums, have also arisen. There are, as the Civil Justice Council understatedly remarked, 'a very large number of variables' for the creation of a fund by which to support class actions.[218]

G   Conclusion

The establishment, by the government of the day, of a self-generating fund for class actions raises broad policy (and political) issues. The

---

[216] e.g., D Chalk, 'Solicitor Client Costs Indemnities: Unregulated Insurance or Benign Assistance?' [2013] *Journal of Business Law* 59.

[217] Leave to appeal was refused in: *Sibthorpe v Southwark LBC* [2011] EWCA Civ 25, [2011] 1 WLR 2111, [58]–[59]. The CA approved the court below, that: 'this, on any view, was a contract for the provision of legal services. ... To characterise it as a contract of insurance, albeit that the indemnity created some principles similar to an insurance contract, is to go too far': *Morris v Southwark LBC* [2010] EWHC B1 (QB) [46] (Macduff J).

[218] *The Future Funding of Litigation* (n 16) [98].

Table 4.3 *Tweaking Ontario's class fund: some options*

Jurisdiction	Are C's costs and legal fees covered?	Is the winning D's costs covered?	Where may the funding come from?
Québec[219]	the Fonds pays for both class lawyers' disbursements and legal fees	the Fonds does not automatically cover the adverse costs of an unsuccessful C, but this can be agreed specifically between the Fonds and C	where an action is successful, C must reimburse to the Fonds any party-and-party costs received from the losing defendant
South Australia[220]	the proposed fund would provide 'legal assistance for plaintiffs in class actions' (the type of assistance was not specified)	Yes	the fund could be replenished via any unclaimed (residual) monies arising from any class action (and not just from those actions which were funded via the fund); plus from a levy on successfully funded cases
Hong Kong[221]	the expanded fund was to pay for *all* the costs and expenses incurred by C, including legal fees	Yes	if the case won, then C must reimburse the fund with what was paid, plus 10 per cent of the amount recovered by the class, but with the amount

---

[219] See n 28; and see too, s 29; and *Lieberman and Morris v Business Devp Bank of Canada* [2006] BCSC 242, [77].

[220] Law Reform Committee of South Australia, *Relating to Class Actions* (Rep 36, 1977) 10.

[221] The Consumer Legal Action Fund was recommended to be extended to class actions, were those introduced to Hong Kong law: Hong Kong LRC, *Class Actions* (2012), ch 8, [8.146], and Recommendation 8(2) and (3). The Fund was established in 1994 to give assistance to consumers to bring or defend a representative action against a manufacturer: at [3.50]. For other points in the table, see: ibid, [8.62], [8.116], [8.123], [8.152], and Recommendation 8(1).

Table 4.3 (*cont.*)

Jurisdiction	Are C's costs and legal fees covered?	Is the winning D's costs covered?	Where may the funding come from?
Australia[222]	the fund should 'provide support for the applicants' proceedings' and 'to provide for the costs of parties involved in grouped proceedings' (hence, not entirely clear whether the fund would only cover costs, or legal fees as well)	yes, and 'if sufficient funds are available, this indemnification should be without limit'	capped at 25 per cent of the amount recovered for small claims, and at 50 per cent for all other matters; and the levy could be imposed on *all* class action judgments or settlements, regardless of whether or not they were funded by the fund, which could facilitate a lower levy as well as 'parliamentary appropriations', other sources of funding could include unclaimed residual damages or settlement funds, as well as interest which has accrued on those unclaimed monies
England[223]	the funding assistance could be	yes, but where the fund was liable	a levy could be paid by C to the fund 'in

---

[222] ALRC, *Grouped Proceedings in the Federal Court* (1988) [310]–[313].

[223] CJC, *The Future Funding of Litigation* (n 16) ch B, recommending the introduction of a 'supplementary legal aid scheme' to accompany the implementation of any new group action regime: [93]–[98].

Table 4.3 (*cont.*)

Jurisdiction	Are C's costs and legal fees covered?	Is the winning D's costs covered?	Where may the funding come from?
	any one of: full legal fees incurred; funding at prescribed legal aid rates; or funding of disbursements only (the latter being the Ontario model)	for adverse costs, then the level of adverse costs could be capped at the level of the fund's investment in the proceedings (similar to the '*Arkin* cap'[224])	addition to normal costs and damages liability', rather as a deduction from any damages that could relate to future costs of care in a personal injury case; and the levy could be calculated as an uplift (multiplier) on costs, rather than as a percentage of recovery
Victoria[225]	the fund would provide financial assistance for disbursements and for legal fees	yes, the fund would indemnify C for any adverse costs order; plus the fund would be liable for any security for costs order made against C; but the '*Arkin* cap' would apply (at least 'initially' – five years was suggested)	any costs order obtained by C against a losing D would be payable to the fund; plus explicit *cy-près* orders in favour of the fund would be possible as a possible destination of unclaimed damages or settlement funds

---

[224] This cap, which applies in the case of third-party funding in England and Wales, is sourced to: *Arkin v Borchard Lines Ltd* [2005] EWCA Civ 655, [2005] 1 WLR 3055. The author has critically examined that cap in the context of unitary litigation: 'England's Unique Approach' (n 7) Section C(2); and in the context of class actions: 'Third Party Funding and Class Actions Reform' (n 7) Section V(2).

[225] *Civil Justice Review* (Rep 14, 2008), ch 10, Section 3.1, 615–19, and see Recommendation 133, p 42, re the proposal to create a 'Justice Fund', which would operate for Victorian opt-out class actions as well as for unitary litigation. Those class actions would include: opt-out class actions pursuant to the Supreme Court Act 1986, Pt 4A; representative actions under Supreme Court (General Civil Procedure) Rules 2005; and federal class actions where that court was sitting in Victoria (at 618–19, and fn 83).

analysis in this chapter gives rise to the following suggestions for reform, should a public fund be contemplated:

RECOMMENDATIONS: GOVERNMENT AS FUNDER

§ 4.1 A Class Proceedings Fund should only be implemented where there is a proven 'gap' in the funding landscape, that warrants the implementation of a public source of funding via seed funding provided by either:

(1) the government, or
(2) charitable sources.

In the absence of any gap, the utility of any such Fund must be seriously in doubt.

§ 4.2 The legislature must clearly identify:

(1) the type of assistance which the Fund will provide to the representative claimant by way of financial support;
(2) the sources of income to which the Fund will become immediately or potentially entitled, in the event of success or failure of the representative claimant's action;
(3) the precise trigger/s by which the Fund would be entitled to that receipt;
(4) whether the charge received by the Fund upon the recovery:
(a) should take effect prior to, or following, the compensation of those class members who come forward to claim their individual compensation; and
(b) should be a variable, rather than a fixed, percentage, depending upon the risks of the case;

(5) the circumstances, if any, in which the costs-shifting rule should be softened, or ameliorated, so as to reduce or negate an adverse costs order against a losing representative claimant.

§ 4.3 The criteria for funding:

(1) should be stipulated (whether or not with priority accorded to some or none); and
(2) should confirm whether the impecuniosity of the representative claimant/the class is either determinative, relevant, or irrelevant, amongst the criteria which are legislatively prescribed for funding.

§ 4.4 The amount of seed funding for the Fund, and the sources of replenishment, must be sufficient to ensure that the administering body is not hamstrung, or overly cautious, in approving funding, particularly in the early days of the Fund's operation.

§ 4.5 The legislation governing the operation of the Fund should stipulate, for the sake of clarity and certainty, matters such as:

(1) the grounds upon which the provision of funding of the class action can be terminated;

(2) the extent (if any) of input into decisions upon settlement, withdrawal and discontinuance of the class action to which the Fund is entitled;

(3) the specific liabilities, and rights of refund, of the Fund, should the class action be terminated for any of the reasons referred to in (1) or (2).

5

Government as 'Gate-Keeper': Cross-Border Class Actions

A Introduction

The modern reality is that a domestic court which is tasked with adjudicating a class action is, at some stage, likely to have to deal with class members who reside in other jurisdictions altogether. As the International Bar Association has explained, there are two reasons for this:

> In an age in which businesses offer products and services on a global basis, it is inevitable that when an allegation is made that a defendant business acted culpably in providing a product or service, the group of possible claimants who have similar claims may cross borders. Similarly, with mass disasters such as aircraft accidents or human rights violations, claimants may come from several different countries. That is, the group of individuals who are ostensibly damaged by the culpable behaviour may be drawn, potentially, from multiple jurisdictions.[1]

To cope with these complexities, two types of 'cross-border' class actions have emerged. The first is 'parallel class actions', which arise when competing class actions are commenced in different jurisdictions and are then conducted in parallel, ostensibly seeking to cover the same class members in respect of the same cause of action.[2] The second is

---

[1] IBA Legal Practice Division, *Guidelines for Recognising and Enforcing Foreign Judgments for Collective Redress* (adopted October 2008) [4]. The IBA Working Party was chaired by John Brown, Partner, McCarthy Tetrault, Toronto. The purpose of those guidelines is further described by the Chair in: J Brown and B Kain, 'Cross-border Actions for Collective Redress: Some Lessons from Canada', in E Lein *et al.* (eds), *Collective Redress in Europe: Why and How?* (BIICL, 2015) 203, 213–17. The author assisted in drafting and reviewing those *Guidelines*, as a member of the Working Party.

[2] i.e., 'proceedings where different proposed representative plaintiffs, acting in separate jurisdictions, have commenced similar claims': *Englund v Pfizer Canada Inc* [2007] SKCA 62, 284 DLR (4th) 94, [31]. For an example, see: *Asquith v George Weston Ltd*

'transnational (or multijurisdictional) class actions', which arise where a class action in one jurisdiction purports to cover those entities and individuals who reside outside of that jurisdiction (hereafter, 'non-resident class members').[3] It is the second of these which particularly forms the focus of this chapter. A 'jurisdiction', for the purposes of the conundrum studied herein, may be a country, or a state/province within a country, because both national legislatures, and state/provincial legislatures, are potentially confronted with the problem of non-resident class members who are situated outside of the territorial competence of the domestic court.

The Ontario class action of *McSherry v Zimmer*,[4] which arose out of an allegedly defective component part of a hip transplant, offers a good example of the cross-border class action conundrum. Perell J eloquently described the litigation arising: 'concurrent class actions in several provinces, some of them cohort class actions, some of them rival class actions, some of them regional class actions, some of them national class actions, some of them opt-in class actions, some of them opt-out class actions, some of them active class actions, and some of them dormant claim-staking class actions'. All up, there were 'four class actions in Ontario, 2 Québec, 1 Alberta, 1 British Columbia, 1 New Brunswick, and 1 Nova Scotia class action that are in play, 10 in all'.[5]

From amidst the 'chaos and confusion'[6] which can accompany such complex litigation, the spotlight of this chapter is narrowly focused upon one issue. How have those legislatures from the Comparator Jurisdictions which have enacted opt-out class action regimes handled non-resident

[2018] BCSC 1557, [79] ('running a parallel class action in BC [parallel to proceedings in Ontario] in relation to the Bread Claims is not an abuse of process').

[3] This distinction is common in class actions literature, e.g.: J Brown *et al.*, *Defending Class Actions in Canada* (3rd edn, CCH Canadian Ltd, 2011) 126; D Hamer and S D'Souza, 'Multijurisdictional and Transnational Class Litigation: Lawsuits Heard "Round the World"', in P Karlsgodt (ed), *World Class Actions: A Guide to Group and Representative Actions around the Globe* (Oxford University Press, 2012), ch 27, 617–19.

[4] [2012] ONSC 4113, 226 ACWS (3d) 351, [2].

[5] ibid, [1]. There was also a Québec action, later discontinued.

[6] To quote: *Wilson v Dupay Intl Ltd* [2018] BCSC 1192, [92] and [100], citing: Uniform Law Conference of Canada, Civil Law Section, *Report of the Uniform Law Conference of Canada's Committee on the National Class and Related Interjurisdictional Issues: Background, Analysis, and Recommendations* (Vancouver, 9 March 2005); and *Merck Frosst Canada Ltd v Wuttunee* [2009] SKCA 43, [16]. See, too, the several concerns about overlapping and multi-jurisdictional class actions in: *Kowalyshyn v Valeant Pharmaceuticals Intl Inc* [2016] ONSC 3819, [231]–[257], including 'several hidden agenda items, including court parochialism and insularity, lawyer avarice, and lawyer conflicts of interest' (Perell J).

... expressly requires that non-resident
class members opt in (**Section C**)

OR

... is silent about whether non-resident
class members can be included (**Section D**)

OR

the class actions   ... expressly permits an 'all-comers' or
legislation ...   global class of both resident and non-
                             resident class members (**Section E**)

OR

... expressly excludes non-resident class
members in specific
circumstances (**Section F**)

OR

... expressly leaves it for the court decide
how a non-resident
class may be formed (**Section G**)

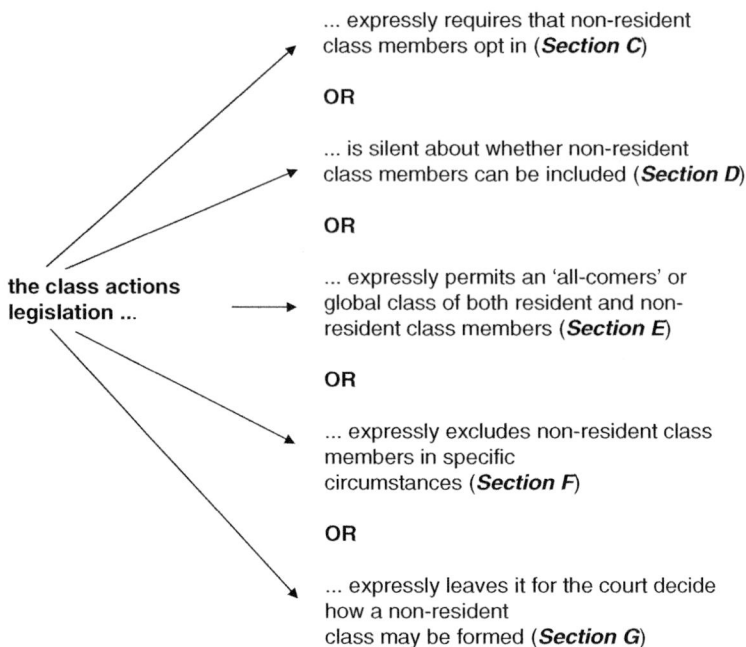

Figure 5.1   The legislative options for dealing with non-resident class members

class members? How 'open' or 'closed' have they been to the participation of the non-resident? Have they been pro-active – or silent? In fact, to date, no fewer than **five** options have been legislatively implemented in the Comparator Jurisdictions. These are shown in Figure 5.1:

Each of the five models will be considered strictly in the order in which they appear in Figure 5.1 above.

The extraordinary diversity of legislative approach towards the treatment of non-resident class members is one of the great surprises emerging from the comparative analysis undertaken for this book. It truly has been, as one Canadian court said, a 'dynamic phase' in class actions jurisprudence.[7] Even if some legislatures in the earlier stages did not provide for non-resident class members because, perhaps, they did not contemplate their existence in class proceedings, that can hardly be a factor in modern class actions drafting. The issue of what to do about non-resident class members can no longer be ignored by legislatures.

---

[7] *R v Brooks* [2009] SKQB 54, 7 WWR 137, [25].

In the first instance, however, it may be helpful to set the context, by noting some well-known examples of cross-border class actions, and the problems which have manifested under them.

B   Setting the Context

1   Some Notable Cross-Border Consumer Grievances

Consumer class actions, in particular, provide a rich seam of cross-border class actions from which to draw examples of the convolutions of litigation to which the widespread provision of goods and services can give rise.

(a)   The 'Defeat Devices' Relating to Vehicle Emissions

On 18 September 2015, a Notice of Violation of the Federal Clean Air Act was issued by the US Environmental Protection Agency against the Volkswagen Group,[8] concerning the manufacture and installation of 'defeat devices' in diesel vehicles, by which to conceal the true level of nitrogen oxide emissions. It was alleged that certain Volkswagen vehicles manufactured in the period 2009–15 had been fitted with a device which (a) detected when the vehicle was being tested for compliance with emissions standards, and (b) manipulated the results. The resulting litigation has straddled country borders.[9] It has also given rise to very different forms of collective redress.

As well as a $25 billion settlement achieved in the United States to compensate owners of Volkswagen Group vehicles (which only covered US-domiciled class members),[10] there have been collective redress

---

[8] Including Volkswagen, Audi, Skoda, and Seat.

[9] As noted at one website, '[a]ccording to a plea agreement between VW and US authorities, the development of cheating software began in 2006, when VW engineers struggled to develop a diesel engine to meet strict US guidelines without sidelining performance': 'Dieselgate scandal roots revealed as industry in spotlight for German election' (*Autovista Group*, 29 August 2017), available at: www.autovistagroup.com/news-and-insights/diesel gate-scandal-roots-revealed-industry-spotlight-german-election.

[10] *In re Volkswagen 'Clean Diesel' Marketing, Sales Practices, and Prods Liab Litig*, WL 3341912 (9th Cir, 9 July 2018), confirming the settlement approved by the US District Court for the Northern District of California (Breyer J). The settlement class 'consists of a nationwide class of all persons (including individuals and entities)' who owned, leased, or held a bill of title over an 'eligible vehicle': at *3. Some opted out of the settlement, which has led to further litigation, e.g.: *In re Volkswagen 'Clean Diesel' Marketing, Sales Practices, and Prods Liab Litig* (ND Cal, 5 April 2019, Breyer J).

proceedings in four different EU Member States.[11] This includes an *opt-in* class action (group litigation order) which has been commenced in England and Wales,[12] and in which about 117,000 class members have opted in at the time of writing.[13] Additionally, there have been opt-out class actions instituted in Australia[14] and Canada,[15] and multiparty litigation commenced in Ireland.[16] The European Commission has commented that the pending cases in the Member States could 'lead to different results depending on the Member State where judgments will be rendered. This situation could incentivise forum shopping, where, in a case of a clear cross-border nature, potential claimants will address their claim where the possibility for success seems higher. … [including] other risks … such as the risk of double compensation or, indeed, of conflicting decisions.'[17]

The contrast in legal outcome for US vehicle owners versus European vehicle owners has frequently made headlines. According to reports,[18]

---

[11] i.e., in the Netherlands, Italy, and Germany, with relevant links to the individual countries' actions, discussed in: www.autovistagroup.com/news-and-insights/vw-dieselgate-compensation-cases-europe-and-us-dropped.

[12] *The VW NOx Emissions Group Litigation* (GLO #105, dated 11 May 2018), details available at: www.gov.uk/guidance/group-litigation-orders#VW-NOx-emissions-group-litigation.

[13] Noted in the first case management conference: *Crossley v Volkswagen Aktiengesellschaft* [2019] EWHC 698 (QB) [1] (Waksman J). Approximately 1.2M affected vehicles are situated in England: at [4].

[14] e.g., *Dalton v Volkswagen AG (No 1)* [2018] FCA 123, [7], in which Foster J refers to seven sets of proceedings 'involving the so-called diesel scandal'.

[15] *Quenneville v Robert Bosch GmbH* [2018] ONSC 4378; and earlier: *Quenneville v Volkswagen* [2017] ONSC 3594. As explained in *Leon v Volkswagen AG* [2018] ONSC 4265, '[t]he first wave of class actions in the US and Canada focussed on the vehicles themselves and the misrepresentations relating to the affected automobiles. The class actions were settled, with VW providing a relatively generous vehicle buy-back program and compensation payments. … The more recent wave of class actions are the securities actions that seek damages for the "fraudulent misrepresentations" made by VW in the sale of its shares … during the affected time period': at [4]–[5]. As one such example, see: *Chandler v Volkswagen Aktiengestllchaft* [2019] QCCS 467.

[16] An Irish Seat owner has claimed compensable damage for breach of contract, arising from the purchase of her affected vehicle: *Volkswagen Group Ireland Ltd v Higgins* [2017] IEHC 809. A number of 'identical proceedings' commenced by other car owners are referred to in that judgment.

[17] 'Report from the Commission to the European Parliament, etc, on the implementation of the Commission Recommendation of 11 June 2013 on common principles for injunctive and compensatory collective redress mechanisms in the Member States concerning violations of rights granted under Union law' (2013/396/EU) (COM (2018) 40, final, 25 January 2018), at 11.

[18] K Oloschakoff and N Hirst, 'VW is winning, at least in Europe' *Politico* (Brussels, 27 July 2016); A de Carbonnel, 'EU says VW yet to guarantee emissions fix does not impair cars',

approximately 8.4M diesel cars in Europe were fitted with the 'defeat device' software, compared to fewer than half a million in the USA[19] – but for the latter, up to $10,000 compensation per vehicle owner is available (in addition to a buy-back programme), whereas no offers of monetary compensation have been made to European vehicle owners at the time of writing. There is a dispute between the defendant and the car owners. The former have claimed that due to the differing emission limits in Europe, this permitted the affected vehicles to be corrected with a software update, thus obviating any proof of damage on the part of the car owners beyond 'minor inconvenience'. On the other hand, the car owners (and their representatives) have claimed that they have suffered compensable damage, and that the installation of the 'defeat device' software infringed European environmental law.[20]

Closer to home, the UK Government has lamented[21] that, 'Volkswagen's treatment of customers in Europe compared to its treatment of customers in the US is deeply unfair', and that it 'strongly agrees with the [UK Transport Select] Committee that the treatment of UK consumers has not been acceptable and that vehicle owners should be compensated for the inconvenience, uncertainty and worry caused by Volkswagen's cheating, as well as for any loss in the value of affected vehicles which may become apparent'. But undoubtedly, the paucity of opt-out class actions in most European Member States does not assist those European owners who are caught up in the worldwide scandal.[22]

Reuters (London, 17 July 2018); European Consumers' Assn (BEUC), *Volkswagen Emission Affair* (website at: www.beuc.eu/volkswagen-emission-affairs).

[19] Also confirmed in the preliminary approval of settlement by Breyer J, per *In re Volkswagen 'Clean Diesel' Marketing, Sales Practices, and Prods Liab Litig,* 2016 WL 4010049 (ND Cal, 29 July 2016), at *1.

[20] See, e.g., the litigation commenced on behalf of 15,000 German consumers on 6 November 2017 in the Braunschweig District Court, as discussed in, e.g.: 'German Consumer Group Files Suit in VW Diesel Scandal' *Associated Press* (1 November 2018); and J Posaner, 'German consumer group files class suit against VW' *Politico* (Brussels, 1 November 2018); and see too, the Hausfeld LLP website at: www.hausfeld.com/case-studies/volkswagen-clean-diesel-litigation?lang_id=3.

[21] *Volkswagen emissions scandal and vehicle type approval: Government Response to the Committee's Third Report of Session 2016–17 (Hansard,* HC699, Appendix: Government Response), Recommendation 3, available at: https://publications.parliament.uk/pa/cm201617/cmselect/cmtrans/699/69902.htm.

[22] See, e.g.: E Thomasson, 'In Germany, test cases aim to resolve generic or common issues for other related cases, but unlike in a US class action, they do not have the legal effect of resolving all individual claims', in: 'German consumer group plans more compensation cases against Volkswagen' *Reuters* (London, 30 August 2017); J Panichi, 'European

Moreover, the opt-out class action embodied in the UK Competition Law Class Action[23] is inapplicable to these facts, as no anti-competitive conduct was in issue. All in all, as one industry body accurately put it, 'enforcement in the United States is far more effective and stringent than in Europe'.[24]

(b)   The Illinois and Ontario McDonald's Actions

There have been some notable class actions in which a domestic court has certified an opt-out class action which included a non-resident class (also formed on an opt-out basis), but where there was inadequate due process for those non-resident class members. This can have tangible consequences for that non-resident class (and for the defendant who had hoped to achieve 'global peace' by virtue of that class action).

This scenario manifested, for example, in the well-known Canadian case of *Currie v McDonald's Restaurants of Canada Ltd.*[25] A class action was earlier instituted in Illinois, on behalf of 'all customers of McDonald's who paid money for McDonald's food products in order to receive a contest game piece'. Those pieces would have entitled the customers to participate in promotional games, whereas the prizes allocated for those games were actually embezzled by a firm engaged by McDonald's.[26] The Illinois class action was settled on behalf of an American and international class of McDonald's customers, including the customers of McDonald's Canada (the '*Boland* judgment'[27]). The Illinois court directed that notice of the proposed settlement which was

---

drivers hoping to get even with Volkswagen are stuck in a legal slow-lane. Unlike Americans, European VW owners lack the legal tools to set up a pan-EU class-action lawsuit', in: 'American lawyers bank on European VW woes' *Politico* (Brussels, 14 March 2016); M Hausfeld, 'The resolve of European consumers not to back down in the face of Volkswagen's defiant refusal to offer similar compensation in Europe for similar harm underscores the need for European-wide collective redress mechanisms', quoted in: *Hausfeld Press Release* (6 November 2017), available at: www.hausfeld.com/news-press /hausfeld-files-for-15000-volkswagen-customers-in-single-largest-consumer-co.

[23]   As described in Chapter 1, Section B(4).

[24]   Intl Council on Clean Transportation (authored by J German), *VW Defeat Devices: A Comparison of US and EU Required Fixes* (December 2017) 1.

[25]   (2005), 74 OR (3d) 321, 250 DLR (4th) 224 (CA).

[26]   McDonald's retained the marketing firm, Simon Marketing Inc, to provide and operate promotional games or contests at its restaurants. A senior employee of Simon Marketing, and others, were indicted for embezzling prizes allocated to McDonald's games and for directing prizes to specific individuals.

[27]   *Boland v Simon Marketing Inc and McDonald's Corp* (as described in *Currie* (n 25) [3]).

judicially approved at the class action fairness hearing[28] be given to Canadian class members (these were, of course, non-resident class members for the purposes of the Illinois class action) by means of various magazines circulated in Canada.[29]

Both Preston Parsons and Greg Currie, who were Ontario residents, were members of the non-resident Canadian class which was included in the Illinois class action. Contemporaneously with the timing of the settlement of the Illinois class action, Mr Parsons commenced a class action in Ontario,[30] on substantially the same grounds that had been settled in the *Boland* judgment. This class action was instituted 'on behalf of all customers of McDonald's restaurants in Canada who purchased food and participated in games or contests conducted by McDonald's for promotional purposes in such restaurants between January 1995 and December 2001'.[31] McDonald's sought to have the *Parsons* class action stayed on the basis that the claims asserted therein had been finally disposed of by the Illinois Circuit Court in *Boland*. Ultimately, the *Parsons* class action was stayed by the Ontario Superior Court of Justice, because Mr Parsons had *participated* in the Illinois action, in order to object to the terms of the proposed settlement (those objections were dismissed by the Illinois court). This meant that he (and five other Canadian objectors) had submitted (or attorned) to the jurisdiction of that Illinois court, necessarily giving rise to the result that the *Boland* judgment should be recognised and enforced against him and the other Canadian objectors who appeared in the Illinois court to contest the *Boland* settlement.[32] Mr Parsons was (ironically) in the position 'as if [he] had voluntarily agreed to the settlement. In consequence, . . . [his] claims are *res judicata* as against the Canadian objectors, and the defendants are entitled to an order staying any attempt by the objectors to relitigate them.'[33] The *Parsons* action was stayed permanently.[34]

---

[28] A final fairness hearing (i.e., to judicially assess whether the proposed settlement was 'fair, just and reasonable') was held on 17 September 2002; with objections by some Canadian class members dismissed on 3 January 2003: noted (2005), 74 OR (3d) 321, [3].

[29] These are itemised in ibid, [3], point 7, and [34].

[30] *Parsons v McDonald's Restaurants of Canada Ltd* [2004] CanLII 28275 (Cullity J).

[31] ibid, [3].

[32] ibid, [60].

[33] ibid, [73]. Objecting to a settlement is only one way in which a non-resident class member may be taken to have submitted to the jurisdiction of a court in another jurisdiction, as discussed in detail by the author in: 'The Recognition, and *Res Judicata* Effect, of a United States Class Actions Judgment in England: A Rebuttal of *Vivendi*' (2012) 75 *Modern Law Review* 180, 200–202.

[34] ibid, [78].

Mr Currie, however, was in quite a different position. He was **not** one of the Canadian objectors who had sought to intervene in the Illinois class action. It was held that Mr Parsons' attornment to the jurisdiction of the Illinois court did not bind other members of that Canadian non-resident class, other than those who had actually objected.[35] Hence, the *Boland* judgment was not recognised, nor enforceable against, Mr Currie, and Mr Currie duly filed his class action. That was met with an application by the defendant to have Mr Currie's proposed class action dismissed on the basis that it was frivolous, vexatious, and an abuse of process, because it was seeking to re-litigate that which had already been determined in the Illinois *Boland* judgment. However, Cullity J refused to stay or to dismiss the *Currie* action.[36] Specifically, this was because of problems with the class action notice directed to the non-resident Canadian class members. For one thing, only about 30 per cent of potential Canadian class members had received notice of the Illinois action, as opposed to 72 per cent of domestic US class members, which Cullity J called 'woefully inadequate'.[37] For another, the notice was extremely technical ('reference to "wall to wall legalese" conveys no more than a hint of its eye-glazing opaqueness').[38] Cullity J did not believe that those Canadian class members who did read it would have understood the implications of the proposed settlement on their legal rights in Canada or that they had the right to opt out.

The Ontario Court of Appeal affirmed Cullity J's view that the dissemination and the content of the notice to Canadian non-resident class members in the *Boland* action was inadequate, with the result that, 'Ontario courts should not recognise and enforce the *Boland* judgment against Currie and the non-attorning Canadian class members he seeks to represent'.[39] Had Mr Currie and the non-attorning Canadian class members been provided with adequate due process, then the Ontario Court of Appeal was prepared to accept that the Illinois court did have jurisdiction to determine the legal rights of those Canadian non-resident class members, on the basis that there was a 'real and substantial connection' between the alleged wrong and Illinois.[40] But that was not this

---

[35] ibid, [32]–[34]. The fact the claims pleaded in *Parsons* and *Currie* were identical, and the same law firm acted for both representative claimants, did not mean that Mr Currie was bound by Mr Parson's attornment or submission.

[36] (2004), 45 CPC (5th) 304 (SCJ).

[37] ibid, [58].

[38] ibid.

[39] (2005), 74 OR (3d) 321, 250 DLR (4th) 224 (CA) [31].

[40] ibid, [21]–[27]. This raises the vexed issue as to how a domestic court should validly assert personal jurisdiction over non-resident class members, absent any opt-in requirement,

scenario, as due process had not been met. Sharpe JA pointed out in
Currie that 'respect for procedural rights' for absent class members would
need to include 'the adequacy of representation, the adequacy of notice,
and the right to opt out'.[41] Given the inadequacies of the various requirements which should have afforded the non-resident Canadian class
members with due process but which did not, the *Currie* class action
could not be dismissed as being an abuse of process. The *Boland* judgment was not binding upon Mr Currie, and the Ontario courts would not
recognise it nor give it preclusive effect.

The Québec Court of Appeal subsequently endorsed the reasoning
in *Currie*, and noted, in a memorable turn of phrase, that whilst
multijurisdictional or cross-border class actions are said to achieve
efficiencies for the litigants and the court, it was not appropriate to
then 'pinch pennies' when it came to appropriate dissemination and
content of the notice sent to those residing outside of the domestic
court's jurisdiction.[42]

(c)   The US Breast Implants Settlement

Some cross-border class litigation has also demonstrated the problem of
how to achieve adequate and *equivalent* results for the non-resident class
members. The United States breast implant settlement case of *Lindsey
v Dow Corning Corp*[43] is an oft-cited example.

In fact, the notice for non-resident class members was also at issue in
that case – a 'major complaint' of the non-resident class members being
that the court-sanctioned notice programme allowed for over US$ 2M for
advertising within the United States (via newspapers, magazines, televi-
sion, and radio); but paid advertisements were not provided for in foreign
jurisdictions.[44] Some non-resident claimants pointed to this disparity as

---

discussed below: Section D(3), and in far more detail in: Mulheron, 'Asserting Personal
Jurisdiction over Non-Resident Class Members: Comparative Insights for the United
Kingdom' (2019) 15 *Journal of Private International Law* 445.

[41] ibid, [25].

[42] *Hocking v Haziza* [2008] QCCA 800, [2008] RJQ 1189 ('the significant increase in
dissemination requirements is the other side of the coin ... of the national or multi-
jurisdictional nature of the proceeding. Resources cannot be preserved on all fronts. If
a national or multi-jurisdictional class action is accepted for reasons of convenience and
efficiency, it is not appropriate to pinch pennies at the same time with regard to the
notices informing the members of the group in question': at [244]), and citing *Currie*,
ibid.

[43] Also called: *In re Silicone Gel Breast Implant Prods Liab Litig*, 1994 WL 578353 (ND Ala,
1994).

[44] ibid, at *3.

infringing the 'best practicable notice' requirement of FRCP 23.[45] However, the District Court disagreed: 'the proper focus is not the differences between domestic and foreign notice, but the adequacy of the notice program outside the United States, with emphasis on the consequences of failure to be exposed to notice'.[46] The non-resident class members were also entitled to other protections, such as greater rights of opt-out, prior to the settlement hearing, and so-called 'super opt-out rights' later in the settlement process.

However, another key problem was that the terms of the global settlement provided that the funds allocated to the claims of non-US breast implant claimants were not to exceed 3 per cent of the total amount of the fund.[47] On 1 September 1994, Judge Pointer approved of the global settlement.[48] Class members could choose whether or not they wished to be bound (and within a year, approximately 6,000 class members had chosen not to participate in the settlement, opting instead to pursue their own actions on an individual basis).[49] On 15 May 1995, less than a year later, Dow Corning Corporation filed for Chapter 11 bankruptcy, as a result of which the US Bankruptcy Court, in 1999, approved of the 'Dow Corning Reorganization Plan',[50] which established a settlement fund of $US2.35 billion for class members who agreed to settle their suits.[51] That Plan divided class members into thirty-three classes. According to the US Court of Appeals for the Sixth Circuit, Classes 6.1 and 6.2 'are composed of foreign breast-implant claimants who are given the opportunity to either settle or litigate their claims. Settlement payments to foreign breast implant claimants are between 35% and 60% of the amounts to be paid to domestic breast-implant claimants.'[52] Unsurprisingly, various groups of foreign claimants argued that their claims 'were not worth less than those of the domestic tort claimants and,

---

[45] Currently enacted in FRCP 23(c)(2)(B), effective 1 December 2003, and worded very similarly to the former FRCP 23(c)(2).

[46] ibid.

[47] As outlined in: P Cashman, *Class Action Law and Practice* (Federation Press, 2007) 690.

[48] See n 43 above.

[49] Noted in: *In re Dow Corning Corp, Debtor* (US Bankruptcy Court, ED Mich, 9 August 1995).

[50] *In re Settlement Facility Dow Corning Trust*, 670 Fed Appx 887, 887 (ED Mich, 2016) (Korean claimants objected to the conditions upon which the Plan was implemented; these objections ultimately failed).

[51] That fund was established with monies contributed by Dow Corning's products liability insurers, its shareholders, and its operating cash reserves.

[52] *In re Dow Corning Corp, Debtor*, 280 F 3d 648, 655 (6th Cir, 2002).

therefore, should not be classified separately from domestic claims'.[53] The Court of Appeals for the Sixth Circuit ultimately concluded that the Plan met the US Bankruptcy Code's classification requirements, and did not improperly classify the non-resident claimants detrimentally compared with domestic claimants, nor treat claims in the same class unequally.[54]

All of this prompted comment from the Australian lawyer who acted for the Australian women (most of whom recovered up to 60 per cent of the recovery accorded to US class members[55]) that, 'the reality was that a price had been set for the foreign claims by a number of foreign lawyers, and the US courts were not very sympathetic to the plight of foreign women'.[56]

These three examples of cross-border consumer grievances highlight just how easily a 'simple' product may morph into an item of multi-jurisdictional importance and disputation, affecting hundreds of thousands, if not millions, of consumers. The cases also evidence a variety of issues that may arise, quite apart from what the class action regime itself may say about non-resident class members. Before turning to that particular question, however, it is worth dealing with a point of terminology.

2 Residence versus Domicile

This chapter essentially turns upon whether or not a class member has a sufficient connecting factor to the *domestic* jurisdiction to be treated as being part of the *domestic* class. If not, then either the legislature or the courts must set out some basis for asserting jurisdiction over the non-domestic class, or excluding them altogether from the auspices of the class action.

There are a variety of potential connecting factors which are recognised in various systems of private international law: domicile, residence (whether habitual or simple), and nationality.[57] The last-mentioned has not figured in the field of class actions regimes to date, but the other two

---

[53] ibid, 661.
[54] ibid, 662–63.
[55] Cashman, *Class Actions* (n 47) 691.
[56] 'Implant Victims' Payout Attacked', *The Age* (Melbourne, 23 January 2005), quoting barrister Peter Cashman (available at: www.theage.com.au/national/implant-victims-payout-attacked-20050123-gdzf4t.html).
[57] A Briggs, *The Conflict of Laws* (3rd edn, Oxford University Press, 2016) 22–28.

have done so. It is worth reiterating that the concepts of 'residence' and 'domicile' are not identical.

'Domicile' means, generally speaking, the country that a person treats as his permanent home and to which he has the closest legal attachment.[58] From the variety of principles which govern domicile,[59] only a few are necessary to note for the purposes of this chapter. No person can be without a domicile.[60] Nor can a person have more than one domicile at the same time and for the same purpose.[61] There are three types of domicile recognised at law: domicile of origin;[62] domicile of choice;[63] and domicile of dependency.[64] Residence (simple) means, technically speaking, the mere physical presence within the borders of a country, establishing the most basic link between a person and a country,[65] although it requires that it be somewhere that the person resides, as opposed to where the person merely visits or owns property.[66] Unlike the concept of domicile, a person can be resident in two countries at the same time.[67] A person can acquire a domicile of choice by actual residence (even if it is for only part of a day), but only when there is 'a fixed intention of establishing a permanent residence in some other

---

[58] E Martin and J Law, *Oxford Dictionary of Law* (6th edn, Oxford University Press, 2006) 177.

[59] See the ten principles articulated in *Barlow Clowes Intl Ltd v Henwood* [2008] EWCA Civ 577 (Arden LJ) [8], and cited with approval, as being 'uncontentious' and a 'convenient summary of the relevant principles of the law of domicile', in, e.g.: *Kebbeh v Farmer* [2015] EWHC 3827 (Ch) [19]; *Z v C* [2011] EWHC 3181 (Fam) [13]; and *Ray v Sekhri* [2014] EWCA Civ 119, [10]. These are generally sourced to: *Udny v Udny* (1869) LR 1 Sc & D 441, 448, 453, 457 and *Bell v Kennedy* (1868) LR 1 Sc & D 307, 320.

[60] *Barlow*, ibid, [8(ii)].

[61] ibid, (8[iii]).

[62] i.e., the domicile assigned by law to a child at birth, which will be the child's father's domicile, or that of the child's mother if the child is born out of wedlock or born after the father's death.

[63] i.e., the domicile acquired by making a home in a country with the intention that it should be a permanent base (i.e., it is acquired by a combination of intention and residence).

[64] i.e., the domicile of dependent persons (i.e., persons under the age of majority, and mentally incompetent persons), which changes with the domicile of that person's parent or guardian. All three definitions explained, e.g., in: D McClean and V Abou-Nigm, *The Conflict of Laws* (9th edn, Sweet and Maxwell, 2016) [2–010]–[2–016]; and Briggs, *The Conflict of Laws* (n 57) 22–25.

[65] McClean and Abou-Nigm (n 64) [2–016]–[2–018]; and Briggs (n 57) (noting that, '[w]hat constitutes residence is hard to say; and the definition of "present as a resident" hardly advances matters very much': at 25).

[66] *Pierburg v Pierburg* [2019] EWFC 24, [47].

[67] ibid, [46].

country'.[68] Without the requisite intention, mere residence cannot confer domicile by choice.

The concept of domicile is the most significant connecting factor in English law, and it is, predictably, determinative under the UK Competition Law Class Action too. The relevant legislation refers throughout to the 'domicile' of the class members – e.g., the CAT Rules provide, in the definitions section, that:[69]

'domicile date' means the date specified in a collective proceedings order or collective settlement order for the purpose of determining whether a person is domiciled in the United Kingdom

. . .

'represented person' means a class member who ... was domiciled in the United Kingdom on the domicile date and has not opted out of opt-out collective proceedings.

By contrast with the UK Competition Law Class Action, the Canadian class action statutes typically refer to a person who is a 'resident' of the relevant province. The term, 'resident', is not defined in the Canadian class action statutes. However, the word has been occasionally considered in the context of those particular statutes. For example, in *Ernewein, Bonneau v General Motors of Canada*,[70] the Supreme Court of British Columbia had to resolve whether or not the representative claimant was 'a resident' of that province. The Court quoted Black's Law Dictionary,[71] and its definition of 'residence', and applied it to the facts at hand to hold that the representative was a resident of British Columbia:

1. The act or fact of living in a given place for some time.
2. The place where one actually lives, as distinguished from a domicile. Residence usually just means bodily presence as an inhabitant in a given place; domicile usually requires bodily presence plus an intention to make the place one's home. A person thus may have more than one residence at a time but only one domicile. Sometimes, though, the two terms are used synonymously.[72]

---

[68] *Bell v Kennedy* (1868) LR 1 Sc & D 307, 319.
[69] CAT Rules, r 73(2). See too: CA 1998, s 47B(11).
[70] [2004] BCSC 1462, 135 ACWS (3d) 994.
[71] (8th edn, West Publishing Co, 2004) 1335.
[72] [2004] BCSC 1462, [99].

Consistently with that latter quoted statement, it is notable that, in several Canadian class actions, the relevant class definitions often refer to persons 'wherever they *may reside or be domiciled*, other than Excluded Persons and Opt-Out Parties'.[73]

To clarify, throughout this chapter, the phrase, 'non-resident class member', will be used for the purposes of convenience, albeit that it must be reiterated that it is a person's *domicile* that matters under the UK Competition Law Class Action.

3   Some Key Assumptions

A domestic court must have jurisdiction to hear and to adjudicate the claim brought by the representative claimant, and to adjudicate the claims of all persons on behalf of whom that party brings the action. As a leading scholar notes, '[t]o say that a court has jurisdiction means that the law regards it as having the power to hear and determine a case against a defendant. It must have jurisdiction over the subject matter of the claim, and personal jurisdiction over the defendant to it.'[74]

At common law, according to the classic Dicey Rules of private international law, jurisdiction over the defendant has traditionally depended upon whether that party is present in,[75] or has otherwise submitted to,[76] the jurisdiction of the domestic court. This is in addition to 'special jurisdiction grounds connecting the forum to defendants outside of the

---

[73] e.g., *Zaniewicz v Zungui Haixi Corp* [2013] ONSC 5490, 44 CPC (7th) 178, [21]; *Leslie v Agnico Mines* [2013] ONSC 2290, [8]; *Kowalyshyn v Valeant Pharmaceuticals Intl Inc* [2016] ONSC 3819, [30]; *Yip v HSBC Holdings plc* [2017] ONSC 5332, [77]. Emphasis added in all cases.

[74] A Briggs, *The Conflict of Laws* (3rd edn, Clarendon Law Series, 2013) 50. Also: C Clarkson and J Hill, *The Conflict of Laws* (4th edn, Oxford University Press, 2011) 102 ('[u]nder the traditional rules, the English court has jurisdiction ... (i) if the defendant is present in England when the claim form is served (though the court may stay the proceedings on the ground that another court is the more appropriate forum); (ii) if the defendant submits to the court's jurisdiction').

[75] See Rule 31 of Lord Collins of Mapesbury (gen ed), *Dicey, Morris and Collins on The Conflict of Laws* (15th edn, Sweet & Maxwell, 2012), vol 1, 411–12 ('[t]he court has jurisdiction ... to entertain a claim *in personam* against a defendant ... who is present in England and duly served there with process') (footnotes omitted). According to Briggs, '[t]he common law takes the view that any person present in England is liable to be summoned to court by anyone else': *Conflict of Laws*, ibid, 112.

[76] See Rule 32, ibid, 421 ('the court has jurisdiction to entertain a claim *in personam* against a person who submits to the jurisdiction of the court'). For discussion of what amounts to 'presence' or 'submission' by the defendant, see, e.g.: P Rogerson, *Collier's Conflict of Laws* (4th edn, Cambridge University Press, 2013) 142–47; P Torremans, *Cheshire, North and Fawcett Private International Law* (15th edn, Oxford University Press, 2017) 323–34.

jurisdiction, justifying in certain circumstances, the service of process abroad'.[77] Statutorily, for the purposes of the UK Competition Law Class Action, the Competition Appeal Tribunal's (CAT's) jurisdiction over a defendant to proceedings in that Tribunal draws from, but is not limited to, those rules.[78] Either way, it is assumed herein that the defendant to a class action **is** amenable to the domestic court's jurisdiction – the difficulty lies with those class members who reside outwith that court's territorial competence, and who have neither opted in nor opted out. They have, quite simply, done nothing. How is jurisdiction to be competently asserted over them?

The chapter proceeds upon two further assumptions: that *the representative claimant* who files an application for certification in the domestic court has, by that very act, necessarily submitted to that court's jurisdiction;[79] and that the domestic court has *subject matter jurisdiction* over the dispute upon which the class action is based.[80]

---

[77] See ibid, Rule 29 and associated text, 371ff; and, e.g., D McClean and V Ruiz Abou-Nigm (n 64) 155. This process is governed by CAT Rules, r 31.

[78] The CAT's jurisdiction over the defendant will depend upon whether that party is domiciled within the UK jurisdiction; or whether the defendant is domiciled outside of the CAT's territorial jurisdiction but has been validly served with process (whether with, or without, the CAT's permission, depending upon the circumstances); or the defendant is one of a number of defendants, at least one of whom is UK-domiciled; or because the UK is the place where the harmful event occurred. See CAT, *Guide to Proceedings 2015*, [5.36]–[5.45], [6.22], for a convenient exposition of those scenarios, and of the relevant provisions governing jurisdiction and service cited therein: Regulation (EU) No 1215/2012 (Brussels recast), especially arts 2(1), 5(3); its sister convention, the Lugano Convention (which is in similar terms, and which applies where the defendant is domiciled in Iceland, Norway, or Switzerland); and the Brussels Convention (which applies where the defendant is domiciled in the territory of a Member State which falls within the territorial scope of that Convention, but is excluded from the recast Brussels Regulation under Art 355 TFEU).

[79] An obvious point, as to which see, e.g.: *Glencore v Exter* [2002] EWCA Civ 528, [45] (claimant who commences a claim submits to the court's jurisdiction 'without reservation').

[80] In the UK, the CAT, as a specialist and statutorily created body, has a wide province of subject matter jurisdiction, which is conveniently set out at: www.catribunal.org.uk/about, under 'The Current Functions of the Tribunal'. In Australia, subject matter jurisdiction is also statutorily limited, because any claim instituted under Pt IVA must fall within the specified, and limited, jurisdiction of the Federal Court of Australia. The federal court has no inherent or general jurisdiction. Federal judicial power is limited to dealing with a 'matter' within s 75 and s 76 of the Australian Constitution. Each federal court principally deals with claims under federal legislation under its original jurisdiction, widened somewhat by an accrued jurisdiction, i.e., 'the litigious or justiciable controversy between the parties of which the federal claim or cause of action forms part': *Re Wakim, ex p McNally* (1999) 198 CLR 511, 583–84, citing: *Stack v Coast Securities (No 9) Pty Ltd*

Finally, this chapter is not concerned with those circumstances whereby, by virtue of specific cross-vesting legislation, the domestic court is able to assert original jurisdiction over the defendant, the representative claimant, and the class members under the opt-out class action.[81]

It is now apposite to examine the five types of legislative models which have been enacted in the Comparator Jurisdictions.

C The Compulsory Opt-In Model

The compulsory opt-in model means that class members who reside outside of the domestic jurisdiction must take a positive step to opt in to the class action, whereas the class of domestic residents is compulsorily formed on an opt-out basis.

1 Legislative Precedents

The model has been enacted in several of the Comparator Jurisdictions.

(a) The United Kingdom

The UK Competition Law Class Action provides that non-resident class members (defined as those not domiciled in the UK on the 'domicile date'[82]) must *opt in* to the class action. The CAT, as the

---

(1983) 154 CLR 261 (HCA) 290. See further: ALRC, *Legal Risk in International Transactions* (Rep 80, 1996) [6.24]–[6.28]; The Hon Justice James Allsop, *An Introduction to the Jurisdiction of the Federal Court of Australia* (Federal Judicial Scholarship, 1 October 2007); and D Grave, K Adams and J Betts, *Class Actions in Australia* (2nd edn, Lawbook Co, 2012) [3.180].

[81] As occurred in relation to the Queensland Floods Class Action being adjudicated by the New South Wales Supreme Court, *Rodriguez & Sons Pty Ltd v Queensland Bulk Water Supply Authy* [2015] NSWSC 838. At the time of filing, Queensland lacked any opt-out class action on its statute books. The fact that the NSW Court had jurisdiction to hear a claim for damages that occurred in Brisbane, alleging negligence by Queensland dam operators of Wivenhoe Dam located in Queensland, was permitted by virtue of the Jurisdiction of Courts (Cross-Vesting) Act 1987 (Qld). This legislation is part of a set of reciprocal statutes across the Australian states, which establishes a national legal system. Section 4 states that, '[t]he Supreme Court of another State or of a Territory has and may exercise original and appellate jurisdiction with respect to State matters'. This cross-vesting legislation 'continues to assist courts in operating across the jurisdictional lines that exist between law areas within Australia': M Davies *et al.*, *Nygh's Conflict of Laws in Australia* (8th edn, Lexis Nexis, 2010) [1.26].

[82] To reiterate, the 'domicile date' is defined in the CAT Rules, r 73(2), to mean 'the date specified in the collective proceedings order' issued by the CAT upon certification.

certifying court under the regime,[83] must decide whether a domestic class should proceed as an opt-in or an opt-out class,[84] and also specify the 'domicile date'.[85] However, even where the CAT may adopt an opt-out approach for *domestic* class members, it cannot do so for non-resident class members; the latter must always be an opt-in class. The relevant statutory provisions state (with emphasis added):[86]

---

s 47B(11) 'Opt-out collective proceedings' are collective proceedings which are brought on behalf of each class member except –

    (a) any class member who opts out by notifying the representative, in a manner and by a time specified, that the claim should not be included in the collective proceedings; and

    (b) *any class member who –*

        (i) *is not domiciled in the United Kingdom at a time specified, and*

        (ii) *does not, in a manner and by a time specified, opt in by notifying the representative that the claim should be included in the collective proceedings.*

r 80(1)(h) A collective proceedings order shall ... specify the time and the manner by which:

    (iii) in the case of opt-out collective proceedings, *a class member who is not domiciled in the United Kingdom on the domicile date may opt in.*

A non-resident class member who opts in then becomes a 'represented person' in the class action.[87] A similar compulsory opt-in arrangement applies to collective *settlements* which include non-resident class members.[88] The same approach has been adopted by the Scottish Parliament, with respect to its recent generic 'grouped proceedings' regime.[89]

---

[83] Prescribed by CA 1998, s 47B(1).

[84] CA 1998, s 47B(7)(c); and CAT Rules, r 80(1)(f).

[85] CAT Rules, r 80(1)(g). This is the date for determining whether a person is a non-domiciled class member who must opt in to the class action: CAT, *Guide to Proceedings 2015*, [6.51].

[86] CA 1998, s 47B(11); and CAT Rules, r 80(1)(h)(iii). Also see the differentiation between opt-in and opt-out in r 82(1)(b)(ii).

[87] Noted in CAT, *Guide to Proceedings 2015*, [6.8]; and CAT Rules, r 73(2).

[88] CA 1998, s 49A(10)(b); and CAT Rules, r 94(10)(b) and r (11)(b).

[89] See: Civil Litigation (Expenses and Group Proceedings) (Scotland) Act 2018, s 20(8)(b).

This model was, in fact, proposed much earlier in England and Wales, in relation to a regime for financial services claims[90] that was never enacted, due to the timing of the 2010 general election, and associated 'horse-trading' of sections of bills which occurred prior to Parliament rising.[91] At that time, a set of rules was developed,[92] which permitted a judicial election as to how to form the domestic class (i.e., opt-in or opt-out[93]); but by this, the drafters sought to ensure that a UK court would assert personal jurisdiction over non-resident class members by virtue of an express opt-in requirement for those class members.[94] That was the approach that the rules-drafting committee ultimately followed for the UK Competition Law Class Action. In doing so, they were not adopting a novel legislative approach to the issue, as some Canadian provincial statutes had already provided similarly.

(b)   The Canadian Statutes

In 1996, the British Columbia legislature implemented an opt-out class action,[95] but with an opt-in requirement for non-resident class members:

---

s 8(1) A certification order must:

...

(g) state the manner in which and the time within which a person who is not a resident of British Columbia may opt in to the proceeding;

s 16(2) Subject to subsection (4), a person who is not a resident of British Columbia may, in the manner and within the time specified in the

---

[90] Per the Financial Services Bill 2009, cll 18–25, introduced to Parliament on 19 November 2009 by HM Treasury.

[91] The fascinating history of this failed law reform attempt is described by the author in: 'Recent Milestones in Class Actions Reform in England: A Critique and a Proposal' (2011) 127 *Law Quarterly Review* 288.

[92] These were intended to be inserted as Pt 19.IV of the CPR, and are available for perusal at: http://ec.europa.eu/competition/consultations/2011_collective_redress/herbert_smith_llp_cjc_en.pdf. The working group was comprised of members of the judiciary, the CJC, the MOJ, and the CPR Committee. The author was a member of that working group, and supported the requirement for an opt-in non-resident class. However, to emphasise, this chapter is written in a personal academic capacity only.

[93] Per CPR 19.IV, rr 19(2), 19.22(1)(f).

[94] Per proposed CPR 19.IV, r 19.22(g)(ii).

[95] Class Proceedings Act, RSBC 1996, c 50.

> certification order made in respect of a class proceeding, opt in to that class proceeding if the person would be, but for not being a resident of British Columbia, a member of the class involved in the class proceeding.
>
> (4) A person may not opt in to a class proceeding under subsection (2) unless the subclass of which the person is to become a member has or will have, at the time the person becomes a member, a[n] [adequate] representative plaintiff.

At the time, Ontario's class actions statute[96] was the only common law provincial regime in operation – and it said nothing about non-resident class members (and still does not). Hence, concerns about jurisdiction over non-residents was (according to some academic commentary[97] and judicial opinion[98]) one feature to which the drafters of the British Columbia regime specifically turned their mind when enacting their own regime. There could be no doubt about it – the British Columbia regime 'expressly permits participation of non-residents'.[99]

After the British Columbia statute was enacted, certain other Canadian provincial legislatures, *viz*, those of Alberta,[100] Newfoundland and Labrador,[101] Saskatchewan,[102] and New Brunswick,[103] adopted a similar approach of requiring non-residents to opt in to those provinces' respective class proceedings. For many years in British Columbia, courts duly divided residents and non-residents along opt-out and opt-in lines, with opt-out and opt-in dates set, respectively.[104] Some Canadian commentary has termed this model a 'hybrid' class action.[105]

---

[96] Class Proceedings Act, SO 1992, c 6.

[97] J Walker, 'Cross-border Class Actions: A View from Across the Border' (2004) *Michigan State Law Review* 755, 767.

[98] Noted in: *McSherry v Zimmer GMBH* [2012] ONSC 4113, [119].

[99] *Stanway v Wyeth Canada Inc* [2011] BCSC 1057, [36].

[100] Class Proceedings Act, SA 2003, c C-16.5, s 17(1)(b) (as it then existed; that earlier version of the provision is available for perusal at: www.canlii.org/en/ab/laws/stat/sa-2003-c-c-16.5/84566/sa-2003-c-c-16.5.html#history).

[101] Class Actions Act, SNL 2001, c C-18.1, s 17(2).

[102] Class Actions Act, SS 2001, c C-12.01, s 18(2).

[103] Class Proceedings Act, RSNB 2011, c 125, s 18(3).

[104] *Bartolome v Mr Payday Easy Loans Inc* [2008] BCSC 132, [57]–[58]; *Hoy v Medtronic* [2002] BCSC 96, 97 BCLR (3d) 109 (Annex); *Gerber v Johnston* [2001] BCSC 687, [23], [58]; *Ewert v Canada (A G)* [2018] BCSC 147, [26].

[105] M Brown, 'Our Aging CPA: It's Time for Ontario to "Opt-In" to a Modern Global Class-Actions Framework' (2017–18) 13 *Canadian Class Actions Review* 395, 414–17.

It is interesting to note, however, that each of British Columbia,[106] Saskatchewan,[107] and Alberta[108] has chosen to *reverse* their legislative positions over the past decade, and instead, have restructured their class actions such that non-resident class members (i.e., those who do not reside within British Columbia, Saskatchewan, and Alberta, respectively) are to be formed on an *opt-out* basis. All provinces now permit 'multi-jurisdictional' class proceedings to be certified,[109] and where that occurs, both the class of domestic class members, and any sub-classes of members from other jurisdictions, can only be formed on an opt-out basis. Indeed, all of these regimes are framed as 'all-comers actions' because they explicitly contemplate that non-resident class members[110] can be included in a multijurisdictional class action unless they opt-out. These regimes are discussed later in the chapter.[111]

2   Why the Compulsory Opt-In Requirement Was Adopted

The reasons which underpinned the UK and Canadian legislatures' drafting choice – which compels non-residents to opt in – is deliberately condensed herein, as the author has explored that issue in detail elsewhere.[112]

---

[106] The original legislative provision was repealed by British Columbia's Class Proceedings Amendment Act, 2018, s 8.

[107] The original legislative provision was repealed by the Class Actions Amendment Act, SS 2007, c 21, s 10.

[108] The original legislative provision was repealed by Alberta's Class Proceedings Amendment Act, 2010, c 15, s 9. Section 17 of Alberta's statute now only provides for opting out.

[109] e.g., in British Columbia, multijurisdictional class proceedings can now be certified, by virtue the Class Proceedings Act, 1996, s 4. This provision was inserted by the Class Proceedings Amendment Act, 2018, s 5. In Alberta, multijurisdictional certification is now governed by the Class Proceedings Act, SA 2003, ss 9 and 9.1.

[110] e.g., in British Columbia, a 'multi-jurisdictional class proceeding' is defined to mean 'a proceeding that is brought on behalf of a class of persons that includes persons who do not reside in British Columbia': Class Proceedings Act, RSBC 1996, s 1, 'Definition'. In Alberta, s 1(h2) does not define a 'multi-jurisdictional class proceeding' in terms of residents and non-residents. However, in Saskatchewan, the Class Actions Act, SS 2001, s 2, defines a 'multi-jurisdictional class action' to mean 'an action that is brought on behalf of a class of persons that includes persons who reside in Saskatchewan and persons who do not reside in Saskatchewan.' All previously existing references to opting in have been removed from these statutes.

[111] See Section E.

[112] For analysis of judicial reasoning, law reform, and academic opinion as to the various reasons underlying the compulsory opt-in requirement, see: 'Asserting Personal Jurisdiction' (n 40); and earlier: 'In Defence of the Requirement for Foreign Class

Suffice to say for present purposes that UK lawmakers took the view that, by analogy to the Dicey rules governing defendants, the most obvious and practical way to achieve non-residents' submission to the CAT's jurisdiction was to require those class members to opt in, and hence, take some pro-active step amounting to submission.[113] Section 47B(11) (previously reproduced[114]) implemented that view. Earlier, regarding the (ultimately unenacted[115]) financial services regime in 2010, law reformers had observed that the compulsory opt-in model for non-resident class members was 'intended to avoid any arguments in relation to national sovereignty which might arise if the provisions purported to assert jurisdiction to decide cases for foreign domiciliaries who have taken no active part in the proceedings'.[116] The department which promulgated the UK Competition Law Class Action explicitly acknowledged that too: 'business would rightly have concerns if a claim could be brought against them in the UK courts on behalf of anyone in the world and these concerns would be exacerbated if there was any risk of them paying compensation twice for the same offence'.[117] As a result, '[t]he Government has therefore decided that the "opt-out" aspect of a claim will only apply to UK-domiciled claimants, though non-UK claimants would be able to opt-in to a claim if desired.'[118]

The prospect of 'paying compensation twice' was theoretically possible, if non-resident class members simply remained part of an amorphously described class and did not opt out of the UK Competition Law Class Action. The prospect was that any English judgment rendered over those non-resident class members who had done nothing at all in relation

---

Members to Opt Into an English Class Action', in D Fairgrieve and E Lein (eds), *Extraterritoriality and Collective Redress* (Oxford University Press, 2012), ch 14, 252–65.

[113] Practically speaking, this step may be acquitted by non-residents giving notice in writing either by mail or by email in a form and by a date determined and approved by the court, as directed in: *Haghdust v British Columbia Lottery Corp* [2013] BCSC 16, [158]. Note, however, the possibilities that social media and other technologies may provide for the dissemination of class action opt-out notices, especially to non-resident class members, postulated in: C Piche, 'The Coming Revolution in Class Action Notices: Reaching the Universe of Claimants through Technologies' (2018) 16 *Canadian Journal of Law and Technology* 227.

[114] See p 189.

[115] See nn 90–91.

[116] See CJC, *Draft Court Rules for Collective Proceedings* (2009), 'Explanatory Notes', Section 5, 11.

[117] BIS, *Private Actions in Competition Law: Government Response* (January 2013) [5.56], 'Jurisdiction', citing the CJC's 'Explanatory Notes', ibid.

[118] BIS, ibid, [5.57].

to that class action would not be recognised by the court in the non-resident class members' own jurisdictions, and nor would it have preclusive effect there. A lack of any recognition or preclusive effect would thereby permit those non-resident class members to re-litigate the same grievance against the same defendant, in another jurisdiction. The concern was that, as argued in one Canadian case (albeit unsuccessfully), that could open the way to permitting non-resident class members who were unhappy with the outcome in the domestic class action to take a 'second bite' at the defendant in their own home countries.[119] This would, as one leading Canadian class actions scholar notes, 'result in unfairness and increased uncertainty for all class action litigants'.[120]

Potential detriment to the defendant was not the only consideration, however. Ultimately, a class action judgment or settlement issued by an English court which ran the risk of not being binding and enforceable as against the non-resident class members would severely compromise the objective of judicial economy for which any class action in England was promulgated.[121] Nor would it promote the efficient and economical use of UK judicial resources, or achieve a just and proportionate allocation of those resources across all cases. It would add to the complexity of the domestic class action for no valid reason. All of this is contrary to the 'overriding objective' which governs English procedure, both generally,[122] and specifically in relation to claims litigated in the CAT.[123] The importance of ensuring that the domestic UK courts should have binding and competent jurisdiction over non-resident class members was the key reason behind the 2010 unenacted reforms, and it played

---

[119] *Ramdath v George Brown College* [2010] ONSC 2019, [52]. Also discussed in: *Excalibur Special Opportunities LP v Schwartz Levitsky Feldman LLP* [2014] ONSC 4118, [115]–[117], although that court was more concerned as to whether to include the non-resident class members would be fair to *them*.

[120] J Brown, 'The Perils of Certifying International Class Actions in Canada', in Fairgrieve and Lein (eds), *Extraterritoriality and Collective Redress* (n 112) [16.06]. The argument is also discussed and developed in: M Brown, 'Our Aging CPA' (n 105), by reference predominantly to Canadian case law.

[121] The importance of achieving improved litigation efficiency by means of an opt-out class action was emphasised by the Civil Justice Council in: *Improving Access to Justice Through Collective Actions: Developing a More Efficient and Effective Procedure for Collective Actions: Final Report* (November 2008), especially Pts 4 and 7. It has been an oft-cited goal of class actions reform, as discussed in: Mulheron, *The Class Action in Common Law Legal Systems: A Comparative Perspective* (Hart Publishing, 2004) 57–60, 'Judicial Economy', and the numerous sources cited therein.

[122] According to CPR 1.1(2)(a)–(f).

[123] See CAT Rules, rr 4(1), (2), outlining the 'governing principles' for litigation conducted in the CAT.

an important part in the legislative choice that was implemented in the 2015 UK Class Action regime too.

Notably, some academic opinion,[124] and Canadian law reform analysis,[125] have supported the view that an express requirement to opt in is the most straightforward method of ensuring that personal jurisdiction over non-resident class members is established. Some Canadian judges too have been very supportive of an opt-in requirement for non-resident class members for the same reason, indicating that the approach was 'prudent',[126] that it 'avoids potential difficulties in exercising jurisdiction over class members outside the province who have not taken any initiative to attorn to the [court's] jurisdiction',[127] and that it 'is seen as having [an] advantage' over other bases.[128] The UK rule-making committee took note of the Canadian statutory precedents then-existing, together with the judicial commentary accompanying that model, and both were influential in explaining and supporting the legislative model enacted in section 47B(11).

This is not, by any means, the *only* justification for prescribing a compulsory opt-in model for non-resident class members. The

---

[124] e.g., M Brown, 'Our Aging CPA' (n 105); L Sandstrom Simard and J Tidmarsh, 'Foreign Citizens in Transnational Class Actions' (2011) 97 *Cornell Law Review* 87, 124; M Murtagh, 'The Rule 23(b)(3) Superiority Requirement and Transnational Class Actions: Excluding Foreign Class Members in Favor of European Remedies' (2011) 34 *Hastings International and Comparative Law Review* 1, 27–28; T Main, 'Judicial Discretion to Condition' (2006) 79 *Temple Law Review* 1075, 1103; D Bassett, 'US Class Actions Go Global: Transnational Class Actions and Personal Jurisdiction' (2003) 72 *Fordham Law Review* 41, and by the same author, 'Just Go Away: Representation, Due Process, and Preclusion in Class Actions' (2009) *Brigham Young University Law Review* 1079; T Monestier, 'Transnational Class Actions and the Illusory Search for *Res Judicata*' (2011) 86 *Tulane Law Review* 1, and by the same author, 'Personal Jurisdiction over Non-Resident Class Members: Have We Gone Down the Wrong Road?' (2010) 45 *Texas International Law Journal* 537.

[125] Alberta Law Reform Institute, *Class Actions* (Rep No 85, 2000) [232] (recommending that non-resident class members opt in; it 'indicat[es] that the non-resident accepts the jurisdiction of the court such that they would be precluded by the doctrine of *res judicata* from later suing, or benefiting from a suit brought, in another jurisdiction').

[126] *Nantais v Telectronics Proprietary (Canada) Ltd* (1995), 25 OR (3d) 331, 127 DLR (4th) 552 (Ont Gen Div) [82] ('[p]erhaps prudence would dictate that such questionnaires include an opting in provision for non-residents, to avoid any doubt as to jurisdiction': Brockenshire J).

[127] *Harrington v Dow Corning Corp* (1997), 29 BCLR (3d) 88 (SC) [9], and cited with approval in: *Ewert v Canada (Attorney General)* [2018] BCSC 147, [18], as being directed to the establishment of jurisdiction.

[128] *Harrington v Dow Corning Corp* [2000] BCCA 605, 193 DLR (4th) 67, [74], citing: Alberta Law Reform Institute, *Class Actions* (Consultation Memo No 9, 2000) [31]. See too: *McSherry v Zimmer* [2012] ONSC 4113, [120].

achievement of equivalent and appropriate due process for resident and non-resident class members alike; the endorsement of personal autonomy and personal choice for those who are domiciled outwith the domestic court's jurisdiction; the avoidance of any doubt about an improper and premature closing of the non-resident class which may otherwise subvert the opt-out ethos of the regime; ensuring that the defendant 'knows the numbers' of non-resident class members – all have been cited in support of the compulsory opt-in model. However, the very fact that there are four other legislative models for dealing with non-resident class members; and that three Canadian provincial legislatures have seen fit to switch from this model to one in which non-resident class members who fall within the class description are bound by the outcome of the domestic court's judgment or judicially approved settlement unless they opt out, bear testament to the fact that it is not a one-sided debate.[129]

Of course, this model requires definition of what does, and does not, constitute a valid act of opting in by the non-resident class members, and which is clearly set out in the legislation. Unfortunately, as the author has discussed elsewhere,[130] this clarity has not been achieved under the UK Class Action, and undoubtedly requires remedying to avoid doubt arising in future litigation under the regime on this important point.

D   The No-Provision Model

This model entails that the statute is entirely silent about non-resident class members.

1   Legislative Precedents

Several opt-out class action statutes enacted in the Comparator Jurisdictions do not refer to how non-resident class members are to be involved in the domestic class action whatsoever. These statutes typically provide, in very generalist terms, that a class member means a person on whose behalf the class action has been 'commenced or otherwise

---

[129] The many arguments against the opt-in model are discussed in: 'Asserting Personal Jurisdiction' (n 40).

[130] 'Joining the United Kingdom's Class Action as a Non-Resident: A Legislative Drafting Conundrum' (2020) 39 *Civil Justice Quarterly* 69, analysing the inconsistency between the CA, 1998, s 47B(11) and the CAT Rules, r 80(1)(h)(iii) and r 82(1)(b)(ii), and the potential ramifications of that variation in drafting.

conducted'.[131] Such generalist descriptors, of course, may prima facie encompass non-resident class members.

Examples of class actions regimes from the Comparator Jurisdictions which do not address the issue of non-resident class members include: the US federal regime;[132] the Ontario[133] and Nova Scotia[134] provincial statutes; the Australian federal regime;[135] and the three currently enacted Australian state opt-out regimes in Victoria,[136] Queensland,[137] and New South Wales.[138]

2 The General Judicial Response

The practical effect of the 'no-provision' model is to leave it to the courts to divine whether or not a class of non-resident class members should be formed on an opt-out basis, or on an opt-in basis, or excluded from the ambit of the class action altogether.

In that regard, courts have sometimes noted, without much enthusiasm, that Parliament (or rule-making bodies) simply have not provided for non-resident class members at all because their inclusion was probably not even thought about. For example, in *Hocking c Haziza*, the Québec Court of Appeal noted that, whilst there was much 'ink spilt' by academic commentators as to whether the class of people covered by a class action could include people who do not reside or otherwise fall within the jurisdiction, '[t]he various provincial laws governing class actions ... are not always very explicit on the subject [citing Ontario's and Québec's statutes as examples]'.[139] In *McSherry v Zimmer GMBH*, an Ontario court suggested that that province's legislature simply 'did not contemplate the circumstances that class members might reside outside Ontario'.[140] Interestingly, this is one area which the law reform

---

[131] See, e.g., the UK's CAT Rules, r 73(2); and Alberta's Class Proceedings Act, SA 2003, c C-16.5, s 1(c).

[132] Contained in FRCP 23(b)(3).

[133] Class Proceedings Act, SO 1992, c 6.

[134] Class Proceedings Act, SNS 2007, c 28.

[135] Federal Court of Australia Act 1976, Pt IVA.

[136] Supreme Court Act 1986 (Vic), Pt 4A.

[137] Civil Proceedings Act 2011 (Qld), Pt 13A.

[138] Civil Procedure Act 2005 (NSW), Pt 10.

[139] [2008] QCCA 800, [137]–[138]. Indeed, the Ontario statute's silence on the issue is at variance with most other Canadian provincial regimes, as demonstrated in: *Charbonneau c Apple Canada Inc* [2016] QCCS 5770, Annex A.

[140] [2012] ONSC 4113, 226 ACWS (3d) 351, [119].

commission report which preceded that reform[141] did not advert to
either. Similarly, in the Victorian case of *Cook v Pasminco Ltd*, Hedigan
J remarked that, '[i]t is true that the legislature may not have specifically
envisaged large numbers of persons wholly outside the State constituting a group for the purpose of Part 4A ... That is of limited assistance
when endeavouring to decide the issue here raised [i.e., whether
a Victorian class action could include class members who were resident
in other Australian states and territories]'.[142]

Practically speaking, it is evident that, under several of the 'no-provision'
regimes the subject of analysis in this chapter, non-resident class members
have been included solely *on an opt-out basis*. This amounts, in realistic
terms, to the judicial creation of either global or national classes – binding
all of those who fall within the class definition and who do not, by the time
and manner prescribed, opt out. For example, in the (pre-*Morrison
v National Australia Bank Ltd*[143]) US securities class action of *In re
Vivendi Universal SA Securities Litigation*,[144] class members who resided
in France and the Netherlands were included in the suit pursued under
FRCP 23 on an opt-out basis. Under the Victorian opt-out regime, the case
of *Dagi and Gagarimabu v BHP & Ok Tedi*[145] showed a similar tack. The
class members lived in relatively isolated villages in the western province of
Papua New Guinea, but were included in the class action (and the Supreme
Court of Victoria could validly assert jurisdiction over them) on an opt-out
basis. Residents from other Australia state jurisdictions have been properly
included as class members under that regime too because they did not opt
out, according to both state[146] and appellate[147] authority (although with

---

[141] Ontario LRC, *Report on Class Actions* (1982).

[142] [2000] VSC 534, [16]. See also the comments about the silence of the legislation at [22].

[143] 130 S Ct 2869, 2879 (2010), in which the US Supreme Court held that the relevant federal
securities law, § 10(b) of the Securities Exchange Act of 1934, did not permit non-
resident class members to sue foreign defendants in relation to activities on foreign (i.e.,
non-US) foreign exchanges, because the federal law lacked extra-territorial effect.

[144] 242 FRD 76 (SDNY, 2007), and the inclusion of French members *aff'd*: 2009 US Dist
LEXIS 31198 (SDNY, 31 March 2009).

[145] [2000] VSC 486. This case concerned the discharge into the Ok Tedi and Fly Rivers of
ore-tailings, waste products and allegedly dangerous and poisonous substances emanating from, or used in connection with, the defendant's mining operations at the Ok Tedi
copper mine.

[146] *Cook v Pasminco Ltd* [2000] VSC 534, re toxic emissions from two smelting plants at
Cockle Creek, New South Wales, and Port Pirie, South Australia, with class members
residing in those two states, noted at [1].

[147] *Mobil Oil Aust Pty Ltd v Victoria* [2002] HCA 27, 211 CLR 1. This case arose out of the
manufacture in Victoria, by Mobil, of allegedly contaminated aviation fuel, and the

some strong dissent at that appellate level[148]). National and international class actions involving class members residing in jurisdictions outside of Ontario have been certified,[149] and have been recognised in Nova Scotia too[150] – all of these including those non-resident class members on an opt-out basis.

Of course, where a court certifies a non-resident class on an opt-out basis, the prospect of those non-resident class members being included in some *other* class action which is on foot too may arise. Academic scholars have explained the potential detriments of overlapping classes, caused by the certification of national classes in one or more Canadian provinces, aptly:

> It is increasingly possible for persons to be included in more than one class action. These persons can become subject to conflicting determinations of their rights. Defendants and class counsel may also be confronted with situations in which they are uncertain of the actual size and composition of plaintiff classes in actions in which they are involved. This can make it difficult for them to plan for the litigation or for the settlement negotiations.[151]

subsequent supply of that fuel to consumers in Victoria and in other Australian States and Territories.

[148] Callinan J strongly dissented in *Mobil Oil*, ibid, preferring the view that, in light of the Victorian regime's silence as to its extra-territorial coverage, 'its operation is confined to each of the following: (i) group members resident in Victoria; (ii) group members carrying on business in Victoria; (iii) group members registered or incorporated in Victoria; (iv) group members wherever resident, registered or carrying on business outside Victoria, positively electing (and not merely not opting out) to be group members': ibid, [190]. His Honour noted that, 'the claims of some claimants may arise out of events and transactions occurring wholly outside Victoria, and the claimants may have no connexion at all with that State . . . there is no doubt that the Victorian Supreme Court has jurisdiction [over D]. It is questionable however, whether it should have an unfettered right to exercise that jurisdiction in respect of group members outside Victoria who have either failed to become aware of the proceedings, or have not opted out': at [188].

[149] e.g., *Wilson v Servier Canada Inc* (2000), 50 OR (3d) 219 (SCJ); *Webb v K-Mart Canada Ltd* (1999), 45 OR (3d) 389 (SCJ); *Pollack v Advanced Medical Optics Inc* [2011] ONSC 1966; *Peter v Medtronic Inc* [2007] CanLII 53244 (Ont SCJ); *Nantais v Telectronics Pty (Canada) Ltd* (1995), 25 OR (3d) 331 (Gen Div), leave to appeal denied: (1995), 40 CPC (3d) 263 (Div Ct), (1996), 7 CPC (4th) 206 (Ont CA); *Carom v Bre-X Minerals Ltd* (1999), 43 OR (3d) 441 (Gen Div); *Robertson v Thomson Corp* (1999), 43 OR (3d) 161 (Gen Div); *Mondor v Fisherman* [2002] OTC 317 (SCJ). Some of these involved national, and others covered international, classes.

[150] *BCE Inc v Gillis* [2015] NSCA 32, 384 DLR (4th) 111, 358 NSR (2d) 39 (although not ultimately certified).

[151] J Walker, 'Coordinating Multijurisdictional Class Actions through Existing Certification Processes' (2006) 42 *Canadian Business Law Journal* 112, 112.

The prospect of overlapping classes has troubled several Canadian judges too. Recently, in *Wilson v Dupay Intl Ltd* (re hip implants)[152] Branch J noted that 'the creation of overlapping classes should generally be avoided, barring unique circumstances', and that the Canadian *Vioxx litigation*[153] was 'generally recognized as an example of the inter-jurisdictional chaos that can develop when overlapping cases are allowed'.[154] In *Heyder v Canada (Attorney General)*, it was noted that no fewer than six overlapping class actions were instituted in respect of allegations of sexual harassment, sexual assault and gender-based discrimination made by current and former servicemen and women in the Canadian Armed Forces.[155] It has been judicially remarked that overlapping class actions can give rise to 'constitutional issues, issues of choice of law, applicable limitation periods, substantive defences and the ability of a provincial court to bind class members resident in another jurisdiction',[156] and that they 'are abusive when they are duplicative and no legitimate purpose would be served by allowing more than one class action to proceed on behalf of overlapping class members from one or more provinces'.[157] In *McKay v Air Canada* (part of the Canadian air cargo cartel action),[158] where a British Columbia class was certified for the purposes of settlement, but where those British Columbia class members were also members of an Ontario national class covering the same grievance, from which none of the British Columbia class members had opted out, the British Columbia Supreme Court chided that all of this 'is by no means an efficient use of judicial resources', or of a saving of

---

[152] [2018] BCSC 1192.

[153] *Tiboni v Merck Frosst Canada Ltd* (2008), 295 DLR (4th) 32 (Ont SCJ), *aff'd*: (2009), OR (3d) 269 (Ont Div Ct).

[154] ibid, [91] (citations omitted).

[155] Noted in: [2018] FC 432, [3].

[156] *Gill v Yahoo! Canada Co* [2018] BCSC 290, [42], citing claimant's counsel.

[157] *Hafichuk-Walkin v BCE Inc* [2016] MBCA 32, 395 DLR (4th) 734, [39]. See too: *Englund v Pfizer Canada Inc* [2007] SKCA 62, [40] ('[t]his is all quite unusual. We would not suggest that it is always or necessarily an abuse of process for a plaintiff to launch claims against the same defendant, and arising out of the same subject matter, in more than one jurisdiction. . . . But where, as here, there is no suggestion that multiple claims serve any legitimate interest of the plaintiffs, the complexion of things changes. . . . [then] the courts are being used in a manner which serves no proper purpose or which is vexatious or oppressive.').

[158] [2016] BCSC 1671, [24]. There were three class actions arising in Canada in relation to cargo fees charged by various airline defendants between 2000 and 2006: *McKay* in BC; *Airia Brands Inc v Air Canada* in Ontario; and *Cartise Sports Inc v AC Cargo Ltd Partnership* in Québec.

litigants' expenses, where stays and other decisions needed to be adjudicated upon across the class actions.

The prospect of a class member being included in two or more class actions is only one of the significant issues arising from the 'no provision' model. Another concerns how, where confronted with legislative silence which does not require the non-resident class members to opt in, domestic courts can validly assert personal jurisdiction over the non-resident class members who have not opted out, according to private international law principles. The numerous and wide-ranging grounds utilised to date are outlined in the following section.

3 Options for Asserting Personal Jurisdiction over Non-Resident Class Members

The 'no-provision' regimes bring the issue of how personal jurisdiction is properly asserted very much to the fore, because the non-resident class member will have done nothing to submit to that court's jurisdiction – and, conceivably, may not even be aware of the proceedings into which he has been swept.

Academically speaking, this issue has been vexed. Take a Canadian snapshot. The issue was identified very early under Ontario's new statute, with Watson noting that it would have to be determined as to how, precisely, an Ontario court should assert jurisdiction over out-of-province class members.[159] But there has been a marked disagreement among leading Canadian class actions scholars about the assertion of jurisdiction over non-class members, with some arguing that submission and pro-active opting in is necessary to enable provincial courts to assert jurisdiction over non-residents;[160] with others arguing that an adherence to due process requirements is sufficient, so that '[c]ourts should exercise jurisdiction over the largest possible class that meets [those due process

---

[159] G Watson, 'Initial Interpretations of Ontario's Class Proceedings Act: The Anaheim and the Breast Implant Actions' (1993) 18 *Carswell Practice Cases – Articles* (3rd series) 344.

[160] P Hogg and S McKee, 'Are National Class Actions Constitutional?' (2010) 26 *National J of Constitutional Law* 279, and a 'sequel' article by the same authors: 'Are National Class Actions Constitutional? – A Reply to Walker' (2013) 31 *National Journal of Constitutional Law* 183; J Martin, 'Sui Generis: Common Law Solutions to Constitutional Problems in Multijurisdictional Class Proceedings' (2013) 69 *University of Toronto Faculty Law Review* 55, 71–73; C Irving and M Bouchard, 'National Opt Out Class Actions, A Constitutional Assessment' (2009) 26 *National Journal of Constitutional Law* 111.

requirements]';[161] and with others contending that provincial legislatures cannot assert personal jurisdiction because the inherent jurisdiction of provincial superior courts simply does not allow for the certification of national opt-out class actions.[162] The numerous problems associated with opt-in regimes have long been ventilated by law reform agencies,[163] and these are, of course, revisited in the event of an opt-in class for non-resident class members.

The problem is that, where non-resident class members are not legislatively compelled pro-actively to opt in to the domestic class action, then some other 'tie' or 'anchor' that binds them to the domestic jurisdiction must be established. Across the Comparator Jurisdictions, these ties have been judicially formulated with vast creativity and not much consistency. A detailed analysis of those ties falls outside the purview of this chapter, given this book's focus upon the government as legislature (the author has explored those ties or anchors in detail elsewhere[164]). For present purposes, it is convenient to merely list those various bases in Table 5.1 overpage.

These grounds demonstrate a remarkable breadth and diversity of judicial reasoning which is illustrative of the evolving and emerging nature of cross-border class actions. In many respects, the principles of private international law are struggling to keep up with the evolution of class actions jurisprudence, and there is certainly no uniformity or consistency of judicial approach across the Comparator Jurisdictions as to how a domestic court should aptly assert personal jurisdiction over class members who reside outwith the jurisdictional competence of that domestic court. The problem arises just as acutely under the 'all-comers' model discussed in the following section as it does to the 'no-provision' model. Clearly, those legislatures which expressly prescribe an

---

[161] J Walker, 'Are National Class Actions Constitutional? A Reply to Hogg and McKee' (2010) 48 *Osgoode Hall Law Journal* 95, 141; and by the same author: 'Coordinating Multijurisdictional Class Actions' (n 151) ('opt-in requirements for non-residents are not necessary to ensure that a decision in a class action binds non-resident plaintiffs. Further, opt-in requirements reduce access to justice for non-residents in multijurisdiction classes in the same way that opt-in requirements reduce access to justice for residents of the province in single-jurisdiction classes').

[162] J Krusell, 'Are National Class Actions Constitutional? A Reply to Walker, Hogg and McKee' (2012) 90 *University of Toronto Faculty Law Review* 9.

[163] These arguments are collected in: Mulheron, *The Class Action* (n 121) 37–38; and discussed further in: *Reform of Collective Redress in England and Wales: A Perspective of Need* (November 2008), Section 7.

[164] 'Asserting Personal Jurisdiction' (n 40), Section III.

Table 5.1 *The 'ties' or 'anchors' for asserting personal jurisdiction*

	The test	The domestic court can validly assert personal jurisdiction over non-resident class members who have not opted in, where . . .
1.	a close alignment of grievances	. . . those class members have grievances which are so closely aligned with those of the domestic class members that adequate representation of the non-resident class members in the suit is assured
2.	achieving finality of litigation	. . . that is necessary and appropriate to achieve finality of litigation
3.	the defendant's presence or submission	. . . although the non-resident class members may be absent from the territorial competence of the domestic court, *the defendant* is present in, or has submitted to, that court's jurisdiction. That is sufficient, on the basis of the classic rules which have traditionally applied to establish jurisdiction
4.	the satisfaction of due process thresholds	. . . their interests are adequately represented and they are accorded sufficient procedural fairness (i.e., adequate notice, equivalent outcomes, and the right to opt out of the action)
5.	the 'reasonable expectation' test	. . . the non-residents have done something that would give rise to a reasonable expectation that legal claims arising out of the activity could be litigated in the domestic jurisdiction
6.	the 'jurisdiction follows recognition' test	. . . the domestic court is satisfied that its judgment would, more likely than not, be recognised in those jurisdictions in which the non-resident class members reside
7.	the 'access to justice' test	. . . to assert jurisdiction is the only realistic avenue by which the non-resident class members may achieve a resolution of their grievances, and where it is probable that non-resident class members would not commence a proceeding in their home jurisdiction
8.	a 'real and substantial connection'	. . . there is a real and substantial connection between the subject matter of the action (and, some courts state, the non-resident class members) and the domestic jurisdiction

opt-in requirement for non-resident class members remove the conundrum of how validly to assert personal jurisdiction from the judicial arena altogether.

E   The 'All-Comers' or 'Global' Model

An 'all-comers' class action is one in which the legislature explicitly provides that the class can be comprised of both resident and non-resident class members on an opt-out basis, so that all such members are bound by the outcome of the class action unless they opt out.

1   Legislative Precedents

The model has been enacted at provincial level in Canada. The Manitoba legislature was the earliest to do so, in a fairly simple drafting manner. The Class Proceedings Act 2002[165] provides as follows:

---

s 6(3) A class that comprises persons resident in Manitoba and persons not resident in Manitoba may be divided into resident and non-resident subclasses.

The regime only provides for opt-out classes,[166] and hence, by necessity, the non-resident sub-class has to be formed on that basis too. A separate representative claimant for each sub-class will be appointed, to ensure adequate protection for both sub-classes.[167] As academic commentary has noted, the Manitoba legislature 'took an approach that essentially codified the "national class" decisions of the Ontario courts, allowing the certification of opt-out classes including non-residents'.[168]

The term, 'non-resident', could conceivably cover non-Canadian residents as well as non-Manitoban residents. So far as the author's searches can ascertain, the only occasion on which the Manitoba provision has been judicially considered was in *Meeking v Cash Store Inc.*[169] Hanssen J stated of section 6(3) that it constituted a 'specific

---

[165] CCSM 2002, c C130, and proclaimed in force 1 January 2003.
[166] Per s 16.
[167] Per s 6(1).
[168] C Jones, 'New Solitudes: Recent Decisions Call into Question the National Class Action' (2007) 45 *Canadian Business Law Journal* 111.
[169] [2012] MBQB 58, 276 Man R (2d) 142.

provision ... which contemplate[s] the creation of a national class'[170] and that the 'Manitoba legislature endorsed the recognition of national class actions',[171] and drew upon the preceding law reform commission report[172] to substantiate that interpretation of section 6(3). The authors of that report did not make it entirely plain as to whether their intention (and recommendation[173]) for that provision was to cover national class actions, as well as transnational class actions. However, given that the relevant section of the report is headed, 'Certification of a National or Foreign Class',[174] and the report notes that, 'American courts have assumed the jurisdiction to certify foreign classes',[175] both national and transnational class actions were probably contemplated.

By means of more detailed legislative provisions than Manitoba's, the provincial legislatures of Saskatchewan,[176] Alberta,[177] and British Columbia[178] have amended their regimes since their original enactments. They now all provide for the possibility of their respective courts certifying multijurisdictional class actions, where the non-residents are to be included in the domestic class action *on an opt-out basis*. Under each provincial regime, if any non-resident persons or entities do not opt out, then they are bound by the outcome on the common issues. Saskatchewan's statute provides a useful example – via the definition of a multijurisdictional class action, and then, what can be ordered:[179]

---

[170] ibid, [63].

[171] ibid, [65].

[172] Manitoba LRC, *Class Proceedings* (Rep 100, January 1999).

[173] Recommendation 22 provided that, '[t]he court should be permitted to certify classes that include non-residents of Manitoba' (at ibid, 67). Section 6(3) of the Manitoba Class Proceedings Act faithfully reproduced the wording of s 6(2) of the Draft Bill, which was appended to the report (at 120).

[174] ibid, 67.

[175] ibid.

[176] Class Actions Act, SS 2001, c C-12.01, s 6.1. The relevant provisions governing multijurisdictional class actions were inserted by the Class Actions Amendment Act, SS 2007, c 21, especially ss 6 and 7.

[177] Class Proceedings Act, SA 2003, c C-16.5, s 9.1. The original legislative provision was repealed, and s 9.1, and other consequential amendments dealing with multijurisdictional classes, were inserted by Alberta's Class Proceedings Amendment Act 2010, c 15, s 7.

[178] The original legislative provision was repealed by British Columbia's Class Proceedings Amendment Act, 2018, s 8. Multijurisdictional class proceedings can be certified by virtue of the Class Proceedings Act, RSBC 1996, s 4. This provision was inserted by the Class Proceedings Amendment Act 2018, s 5 (which was Bill 21 of 2018).

[179] The emphasis is added in both provisions.

s 2   Interpretation

   . . .

"multi-jurisdictional class action" means an action that is brought on behalf of a class of persons that includes persons who reside in Saskatchewan *and persons who do not reside in Saskatchewan*

s 6.1(2)   If the court certifies a multi-jurisdictional class action, the court may:

(a)   divide the class into resident and non-resident subclasses;

(b)   appoint a separate representative plaintiff for each subclass; and

(c)   *specify the manner in which, and the time within which, members of each subclass may opt out of the action.*

As already noted,[180] all three provinces formerly had regimes which implemented an opt-in requirement for non-resident class members, but those positions were reversed in 2007, 2010, and 2018, respectively.

As the author has discussed elsewhere,[181] the primary reasons as to why these provinces changed their positions on this crucial issue were to expand the inclusiveness of their regimes, and to aid judicial economy. According to the British Columbia Attorney-General, that legislature decided to change from opt-in-non-resident-classes to multijurisdictional opt-out classes to 'increase access to justice and improve judicial efficiency by reducing the necessity for parallel proceedings to take place in other provinces or territories.'[182] Parliamentary debates confirmed that these twin objectives motivated the legislative change.[183]

2   *The Legislative Criteria for Deferring to a Class Action Elsewhere*

As something of an understatement, it has been judicially said that '[m]ulti-jurisdictional class actions create difficulties'.[184] The Saskatchewan Queen's Bench noted in *R v Brooks* that these all-comers' class actions 'present new

---

[180]   See p 192.

[181]   'Asserting Personal Jurisdiction' (n 40) Section IV.

[182]   See: AG (British Columbia), 'Legislation introduced to modernize class actions' (*Information Bulletin*, 23 April 2018), available at: https://news.gov.bc.ca/releases/2018AG0024-000707.

[183]   See, e.g., *Hansard* (Legislative Assembly, 23 April 2018, Mr D Eby, First Reading, at 1.55pm), commenting on Bill 21, the Class Proceedings Amendment Act 2018; and *Hansard* (Legislative Assembly, 25 April 2018, A Olsen, Second Reading, at 6.15pm).

[184]   *Walter v Western Hockey League* [2018] ABCA 188, [12].

and likely numerous challenges both for parties involved in them and the courts. New approaches and likely court-to-court communications and protocols will need to be developed. Issues of *forum non conveniens*, jurisdiction, the scope of comity and recognition of [judgments from other jurisdictions] issued in multi-jurisdictional class action suits illustrate only some of the challenges to be addressed.'[185] The Canadian Bar Association has sought to assist with the management of multijurisdictional class actions;[186] whilst it has been noted, academically, that an 'inevitable consequence' of national class actions is a flux of carriage motions, and a change of ethos at the bar: the 'lucrative nature of class proceedings in general and national class actions in particular serves as an effective guarantee that class proceedings will continue to propagate beyond the control of the contemporary "gentlemen's agreement" atmosphere in the established plaintiffs' bar'.[187]

Where all-comers' class actions are proposed in more than one jurisdiction in respect of the same grievance and covering the same, or substantially similar, class members, then the same problem arises as under the 'no provision' model. The prospect of overlapping classes increases markedly. Recently, in *Johnson v Equifax Inc*,[188] a case arising out of a cyber-security breach, six class actions were filed, arising out of that one incident![189] These consisted of: a national class action in Saskatchewan; two national class actions filed in Ontario; a Québec class action; and a national class action and a provincial class action both filed in British Columbia. The Saskatchewan Queen's Bench permanently stayed the class action filed in that jurisdiction as amounting to an abuse of process.[190]

Where multijurisdictional class actions are legislatively permitted, the legislature may provide for criteria (a 'Forums Framework') to which

---

[185] [2009] SKQB 54, 7 WWR 137, [25].

[186] See: *Canadian Judicial Protocol for the Management of Multi-Jurisdictional Class Actions* (Canadian Bar Assn, 13 August 2011), available at: www.cba.org/getattachment/Our-Work /Resolutions/Resolutions/2011/Canadian-Judicial-Protocol-for-the-Management-of -M/11–03-A-Annex01.pdf. Its stated purpose was to 'make use of existing class action legislation, the Rules of Court and Rules of Civil Procedure in various provincial jurisdictions to facilitate the management of multijurisdictional class actions' (at 1). The *Judicial Protocol* was revised by the Canadian Bar Assn and published in 2018: *Canadian Judicial Protocol for the Management of Multijurisdictional Class Actions and the Provision of Class Action Notice* (15 February 2018), available at: www.cba.org/getattachment/Our-Work /Resolutions/Resolutions/2018/Class-Action-Judicial-Protocols-(1)/18–03-A.pdf.

[187] Martin, '*Sui Generis*' (n 160) 78.

[188] [2018] SKQB 305.

[189] *Johnson v Equifax Inc* [2018] SKQB 305.

[190] ibid, [22]–[26].

a domestic court should have regard, when deciding whether to certify an all-comers' class action, or whether it would be preferable to stay some or all of the claims in favour of a class action instituted (or proposed) elsewhere. Alberta's class actions regime[191] provides an example of a Forums Framework which Parliament enacted for the court's assistance (with Saskatchewan's[192] and British Columbia's[193] statutes containing very similar provisions):

---

s 5(6) If a multi-jurisdictional class proceeding or a proposed multi-jurisdictional class proceeding has been commenced elsewhere in Canada that involves subject-matter that is the same as or similar to that of a proceeding being considered for certification under this section, the Court must determine whether it would be preferable for some or all of the claims or common issues raised by the prospective class members to be resolved in the proceeding commenced elsewhere.

(7) When making a determination under subsection (6), the Court must be guided by the following objectives:

   (a) ensuring that the interests of all parties in each of the relevant jurisdictions are given due consideration;
   (b) ensuring that the ends of justice are served;
   (c) where possible, avoiding irreconcilable judgments;
   (d) promoting judicial economy.

(8) When making a determination under subsection (6), the Court may consider any matter that the Court considers relevant but must consider at least the following:

   (a) the alleged basis of liability, including the applicable laws;
   (b) the stage each of the proceedings has reached;
   (c) the plan for the proposed multi-jurisdictional class proceeding, including the viability of the plan and the capacity and resources for advancing the proceeding on behalf of the prospective class members;
   (d) the location of the class members and representative plaintiffs in the various proceedings, including the ability of the representative plaintiffs to participate in the proceedings and to represent the interests of the class members;
   (e) the location of evidence and witnesses;
   (f) the advantages and disadvantages of litigation being conducted in more than one jurisdiction.

---

[191] Class Proceedings Act, SA 2003, c C-16.5.
[192] Class Actions Act, SS 2001, c C-12.01, s 6(2), (3).
[193] Class Proceedings Act, RSBC 1996, c 50, s 4(3), (4).

Judicially, it has been noted of this legislation that it is, essentially, a *forum non conveniens* analysis which the legislatures have stipulated to be undertaken,[194] as part of the certification analysis,[195] wherever an all-comers' class action is sought to be certified. In *Kohler v Apotex Inc*,[196] the Alberta court remarked that the Forums Framework was an unusual legislative step, in prescribing mandatory prerequisites for the court to analyse – but that the listed considerations were somewhat similar to (if more extensive than) the types of factors that a court might consider, at common law, in the context of applications for carriage, stays of proceedings, *forum conveniens* decisions, and to avoid multiplicity of actions.[197] A Saskatchewan court has also suggested[198] that, whilst the Forums Framework is 'very broad'[199] and 'extensive'[200] as to the 'core considerations'[201] that must be addressed, there may *still* be circumstances in which a party may seek to stay a multijurisdictional class action as an abuse of the court's process, above and beyond the criteria stipulated in the Forums Framework (but this case 'is not one of them').[202] In other words, an abuse of process application can be instituted by the defendant, and judicially determined, quite separately from any attempt under the Forums Framework to have a domestic class action stayed in favour of one commenced elsewhere. As Perell J recently noted, the way that the case law has developed, insofar as 'global' or multijurisdictional classes are concerned, is actually two-pronged:

> in the context of proposed class actions, . . . *forum non conveniens* problems arise in two ways; i.e., first, as an aspect of a jurisdiction motion, where the defendant moves to have the action stayed; and second, as an aspect of a certification motion, where the defendant resists certification by arguing that it would be preferable for the putative class members to advance their claims in the court of another jurisdiction and, therefore, the proposed class action does not satisfy the criteria for certification, especially the preferable procedure criterion.[203]

---

[194] *Babin v Bayer Inc* [2017] ONSC 3200, [34].
[195] *R v Brooks* [2009] SKQB 54, [22].
[196] [2015] ABQB 610.
[197] ibid, [19]–[20].
[198] *R v Brooks* [2009] SKQB 54.
[199] ibid, [22].
[200] ibid, [18].
[201] ibid, [18].
[202] ibid, [24]. See too: *Ammazzini v Anglo American plc* [2016] SKQB 53, [21]; and [61] ('[t]he principles of abuse of process remain potentially applicable') (Currie J), citing: *R v Brooks* [2009] SKQB 54, 7 WWR 137, [23]–[24] (Zarzeczny J). The point was not commented on appeal in *Ammazzini*: [2016] SKCA 164.
[203] *Paniccia v MDC Partners Inc* [2017] ONSC 7298, [60].

Indeed, the Saskatchewan case of *Johnson v Equifax Inc* provides a neat example. The defendant was not actually seeking to invoke the Forums Framework[204] on the basis that the Saskatchewan action overlapped with litigation in other provinces. Rather, it submitted that the Saskatchewan action was abusive because it was not commenced or continued with a bona fide purpose of adjudicating the class members' claims (and the court agreed).[205] All of this shows a flexible and multifaceted legislative landscape by which to deal with overlapping classes.

The complexities and nuances of the Forums Framework is one reason why, as one author put it, 'there has been a doctrinal effervescence in Canadian scholarship over multi-jurisdictional class actions'.[206] A study of that topic lies beyond the scope of this book, as it falls outside the focus of the *legislature's* activity as 'gate-keeper' (or otherwise).

However, for present purposes, it is important to note that the 'no-provision' model and the 'all-comers model' by which to handle non-resident class members share one common feature. The domestic court must be able to assert personal jurisdiction over the non-resident class members on some basis that complies with the principles of private international law. Because those non-residents are joining the class on an opt-out basis, there is no question of their opting in, and hence, submission to the domestic court's jurisdiction is simply not an option. Some other basis for 'anchoring' those non-resident class members within the jurisdiction of the domestic court must properly be asserted – from one (or more) of those 'ties' listed in Table 5.1 (and examined by the author in detail elsewhere[207]). By implementing the compulsory opt-in model for non-resident class members, the UK lawmakers have deliberately chosen a model that differs significantly from the Canadian adoption of all-comers, multi-jurisdictional, classes formed on an opt-out basis. The former have arguably placed a higher price on the assertion of personal autonomy and class member choice, whilst the latter have emphasised the desirability of seeking to achieve both 'global peace' for the defendant, and judicial economy.

---

[204] Contained in the Class Actions Act, SS 2001, c C-12.01, s 6(2).
[205] [2018] SKQB 305, [6], [22]–[26].
[206] V Scott, 'Access to Justice and Choice of Law Issues in Multi-Jurisdictional Class Actions in Canada' (2013) *Ottawa Law Review* 233, 236.
[207] 'Asserting Personal Jurisdiction' (n 40), Section III.

F   The Exclusion Model

Under this model, non-resident class members may be excluded for legislatively prescribed reasons, although the model does not ban the participation of non-resident class members per se.

1   The Caveat

At the outset, it must be acknowledged that any blanket attempt to restrict the ambit of a class actions regime merely to those who are resident within the domestic court's jurisdiction *may* be regarded as being discriminatory.

That was certainly the view of the European Commission. In its 2013 Recommendation relating to collective redress mechanisms,[208] it stated that, 'Member States should ensure that, where a dispute concerns natural or legal persons from several Member States, a single collective action in a single forum is not prevented by national rules on admissibility or standing of the foreign groups of claimants or the representative entities originating from other national legal systems.'[209] By the time that the Commission reported on the implementation of its Recommendation five years later, there had been some limited 'movement' among EU Member States in improving their collective redress regimes.[210] Of the current nineteen Member States in which some form of compensatory collective redress has now been enacted (including the United Kingdom's), the Commission was able to say that none 'have general obstacles to the participation of any natural or legal person from other Member States in group actions before their courts. Participation in a group of claimants is not restricted to those domiciled or established in the Member State in which collective action is undertaken.'[211] The Commission said that

---

[208] EC, 'Commission Recommendation of 11 June 2003 on common principles for injunctive and compensatory collective redress mechanisms in the Member States concerning violations of rights granted under Union Law' (2013/396/EU) (OJ 2013 No L201/60).

[209] ibid, 'Cross-border cases', [17].

[210] The EC reported that, '[a]fter adoption of the Recommendation new legislation on compensatory collective redress has been adopted in 4 Member States: in 2 of them (BE, LT) for the first time ever, while in 2 others (FR, UK) important legislative changes have taken place': ibid, [2.1.1], p 3.

[211] ibid, [2.1.7], p 10.

this 'reaffirm[ed] the principle of non-discrimination in the context of civil proceedings'.[212]

However, the lesson from the Comparator Jurisdictions is that exclusions of non-resident class members may be desirable in some circumstances, which are legislatively prescribed rather than open-ended.

2   Legislative Precedents

(a)   The Canadian Statutes

For an all-comers' class action, in which the *entire* class of residents and non-residents is formed on an opt-out basis under the regime, a limited exclusion is sensible, where some of the non-resident class members are, or may become, part of a class action elsewhere (e.g., in their 'home' jurisdiction). The prospect of double recovery is unpalatable, unfair, and inefficient.

To that end, Alberta's Class Proceedings Act 2003 provides that:[213]

> s 9.1(3) **Orders in Multi-Jurisdictional Certification** The Court may refuse to certify a portion of a proposed class if that portion contains members who may be included within a class proceeding, or a proceeding that is the subject of a certification application, in another jurisdiction.

The revised class actions regimes in British Columbia[214] and Saskatchewan,[215] which enacted multijurisdictional class actions on an opt-out basis, now include similar provisions. As far as the author's searches can ascertain, these provinces' provisions have not been the subject of judicial consideration as yet.

(b)   Victoria

The state regime enacted in Victoria, Australia, also contains a judicial discretion to exclude non-resident class members, for broadly stated reasons:[216]

---

[212] EC, 'Report from the Commission, etc, on the implementation of the Commission Recommendation of 11 June 2013 on common principles for injunctive and compensatory collective redress mechanisms in the Member States concerning violations of rights granted under Union law' (2013/396/EU) (COM(2018), final, 25 January 2018) [2.1.7], p 10.

[213] Class Proceedings Act, SA 2003, c C-16.5, inserted by: Class Proceedings Amendment Act 2010, c 15, s 8.

[214] Class Proceedings Act, RSBC 1996, c 50, s 4.1(1)(c).

[215] Class Actions Act, SS 2001, c C-12.01, s 6.1(1)(c).

[216] Supreme Court Act 1986, Pt 4A.

s 33KA   Court powers concerning group membership

(1)   On the application of a party to a group proceeding or of its own motion, the Court may at any time, whether before or after judgment, order—
  (a)   that a person cease to be a group member;
  (b)   that a person not become a group member.

(2)   The Court may make an order under subsection (1) if of the opinion that—
  (a)   the person does not have sufficient connection with Australia to justify inclusion as a group member; or
  (b)   for any other reason it is just or expedient that the person should not be or should not become a group member.

(3)   If the Court orders that a person cease to be a group member, then, if the Court so orders, the person must be taken never to have been a group member.

This is a unique provision among the Australian opt-out class actions regimes. Neither the federal regime, nor the other state opt-out regimes in New South Wales and Queensland, contains anything similar.[217] It has been judicially noted that section 33KA specifically refers to a lack of connection with *Australia* and not with Victoria,[218] and that it is drafted 'in very wide terms'.[219]

Before considering the rather sparse case law arising under the Victorian provision, it is worth noting how jurisdiction over non-resident class members is asserted under that opt-out regime. According to the Supreme Court of Victoria in *Cook v Pasminco Ltd* (a toxic emissions case)[220] – which made only passing reference to section 33KA[221] – the Victorian class action regime contained in Part 4A 'is the

---

[217]   As one leading Australian class actions scholar notes, s 33KA is a very rare instance in which the Victorian class action regime differs from the federal regime enacted almost a decade earlier: V Morabito, *Group Litigation in Australia* (National Report for Australia prepared for the Globalisation of Class Actions Conference, Oxford, December 2007), fn 83.

[218]   *Cook v Pasminco Ltd* [2000] VSC 534, [21].

[219]   *Mobil Oil Aust Pty Ltd v Victoria* (2002) 211 CLR 1 (HCA) [41] (Gaudron, Gummow and Hayne JJ), and cited subsequently in: *Clarke v Great Southern Finance Pty Ltd (No 2)* [2012] VSC 338, [4].

[220]   [2000] VSC 534.

[221]   ibid, [21].

creation by this State of a means of enforcing obligations arising from acts arguably done both inside and outside the territorial jurisdiction of the State of Victoria', and that '[w]hilst there might be arguably good policy reasons for limiting the ambit of Part 4A [to those residing within Victoria], Part 4A does not itself create any limitation.'[222] The assertion of personal jurisdiction over the non-resident class members was said to be met sufficiently, if *the defendant was validly served* with proceedings in Victoria.[223] That would mean that non-resident class members, 'without any connection with the State of Victoria, can be included in the class action and be bound by judgment or settlement in that action, without any action by them'.[224] According to Hedigan J, 'I am not prepared to take the view that interstate groups are excluded from the operation of Part 4A. The legislation is intended to be enabling, not restrictive.'[225] As the author has discussed elsewhere,[226] this particular basis for asserting personal jurisdiction over non-resident class members – that the defendant was validly served with the claim within the jurisdiction – has been the subject of vehement disagreement across the class actions common law jurisdictions. Separately, a majority of the High Court of Australia also endorsed the service upon the defendant within the state of Victoria as a valid basis for asserting jurisdiction over non-resident class members under that Victorian regime.[227]

The interpretation of section 33KA recently arose for consideration in 2018 in *Murray v Great Southern Managers Aust Ltd*.[228] Mr Parker was an investor in a financial scheme managed by the defendant. In a class action commenced in August 2011 brought on behalf of all investors, it was claimed that the scheme's product disclosure statements contravened relevant corporations law. Mr Parker was a class member in the action as defined, and he did not opt out of the action. However, in September 2011, Mr Parker moved from Australia to Singapore, following which he almost completely severed ties with Australia, apart from brief visits for either family or business reasons. The class action then settled in December 2014. The first time that Mr Parker became aware of

---

[222] ibid, [21].
[223] ibid, [22].
[224] ibid, [23].
[225] ibid.
[226] 'Asserting Personal Jurisdiction' (n 40), Section III(B).
[227] [2002] HCA 27, 211 CLR 1. [52]–[53], [61], [68] (Gaudron, Gummow and Hayne JJ) (emphasis added), citing: *John Pfeiffer Pty Ltd v Rogerson* [2000] HCA 36, 203 CLR 503 (HCA) 517, [14].
[228] [2018] VSC 416.

the class action was in July 2017. Mr Parker applied under section 33KA to cease to be a class member – so that he would not be bound by the settlement of the action, and would be free to commence his own proceedings against the defendant (subject to any relevant limitation period). On the basis of Mr Parker's insufficient connection with Australia, the Victorian Supreme Court ordered that he cease to be a group member. He was a 'wholly unknowing' class member, who had moved away from the Australian jurisdiction prior to judgment or settlement.[229] As Croft J pointed out, whether the class member has 'connections to Australia' will inevitably turn on evidence given by the class member which the defendant will find difficult to challenge.[230] However, Croft J applied the caveat that section 33KA could only be applied for the benefit of class members such as Mr Parker, where the opt-out notice did not reach that group member.[231] He agreed with earlier authority[232] that a class member could **not** apply to be excluded, on the basis of an insufficient connection with Australia, where he **did** receive notice of the class action, and had a meaningful opportunity to decide whether or not to opt out.[233] By reference to Parliamentary debates accompanying the passage of section 33KA,[234] Croft J concluded that Parliament's intention in enacting this unique provision was that 'damages awarded in a successful class action could be exhausted before all group members become aware of its outcome, in which case section 33KA could be applied to enable them to pursue a damages claim themselves; unburdened by group membership, *res judicata* and the expiry of a limitation period'.[235]

This particular application of section 33KA – to exclude a class member who resided elsewhere and who had not received the opt-out notice, and who did not wish to be bound by a judicially approved settlement – has been judicially endorsed, in dicta, since.[236]

However, the provision is clearly so much wider than that. Plainly, the Victorian Supreme Court can, of its own volition, exclude a non-resident (or a class of non-residents) *prior to* judgment or settlement.

---

[229] ibid, [8].
[230] ibid, [11]–[12].
[231] ibid, [20].
[232] *Clarke v Great Southern Finance Pty Ltd (in liq)* [2014] VSC 569, [25] (Judd J).
[233] [2018] VSC 416, [15]–[16].
[234] *Hansard* (Legislative Assembly of Victoria, 21 November 2000, Mr Robert Dean, at 1768–69).
[235] [2018] VSC 416, [21].
[236] *Bendigo & Adelaide Bank Ltd v Nye* [2018] QDC 256, [116].

Furthermore, if the terms of section 33KA(2)(b) are to be 'coloured', or take their meaning from, the terms of section 33KA(2)(a), then it may be apposite for the Victorian Supreme Court to consider why it should decline the exercise of personal jurisdiction over non-resident class members, for reasons such as: the due process requirement of adequate representation was not afforded to non-resident class members; those class members were actually or potentially included within a class action in another jurisdiction; or their inclusion in the Victorian class action would render the class action unmanageable and 'inappropriate'.

That application of section 33KA is, of course, a world away from the factual circumstances of *Murray*, and there has been no judicial suggestion of the provision being utilised in that fashion as yet. However, those types of factors are, arguably, very relevant, if the grounds for a domestic court's asserting personal jurisdiction over non-resident class members entails more than simply ascertaining whether the defendant resides in the Victorian jurisdiction. In that regard, this author respectfully disagrees with the Victorian Supreme Court's ground of asserting jurisdiction in *Cook v Pasminco*; and with academic commentary that section 33KA 'serves little purpose in respect of foreign group members. It is the defendant's amenability to the jurisdiction that is critical. There seems little need to consider then the sufficiency of the group members' connection with Australia.'[237] To the contrary, this author takes the view that, where an opt-out class includes non-resident class members, there are far preferable ways in which personal jurisdiction may be asserted, quite apart from the defendant's presence in, or submission to, the domestic court's jurisdiction.[238] Section 33KA should be capable of being used to exclude non-resident class members, in circumstances where there is not a sufficient basis for asserting personal jurisdiction over them upon those preferable bases.

G　The Judicial Choice Model

The final legislative option is that the legislature explicitly places the decision entirely with the court, as to whether a sub-class of non-resident class members should be formed on opt-out or opt-in principles in a given case. The court can, at its discretion, insist that non-resident

---

[237] Grave *et al.*, *Class Actions in Australia* (n 80) [3.280] (quote), and [6.155].

[238] As discussed in: 'Asserting Personal Jurisdiction' (n 40).

class members pro-actively opt in to the action, even where the regime is an opt-out one for domestic class members.

1 Legislative Precedent

The recently enacted UK Competition Law Class Action[239] provides that, for *domestic* class members, the class action can proceed either on an opt-in or an opt-out basis, depending upon judicial choice. However, as already discussed,[240] the UK lawmakers certainly did not extend that judicial-choice model to non-resident class members. They *must opt in*, should they wish to participate in and be bound by the outcome of the UK class action.[241]

However, one US state legislature – that of Pennsylvania – has taken that step of explicitly leaving the decision to the court. At least, the regime has been interpreted that way, precisely because it explicitly allows a sub-class to be formed on an opt-in basis. Pennsylvania courts have considered the possibility of using that permission to compose a non-resident sub-class on an opt-in basis, whilst leaving the domestic class to be formed on an opt-out basis. Such a regime has been judicially called a 'modified opt-out class action'.[242] The Pennsylvania Code, in which Chapter 17 deals with 'Class Actions', provides that:[243]

Rule 1711   The Plaintiff Class. Exclusion. Inclusion.

    (a) Except as provided in subdivision (b) or as otherwise provided by the court, in certifying a plaintiff class or subclass the court shall state in its order that every member of the class is included unless by a specified date a member files of record a written election to be excluded from the class.

    (b) *If the court finds that:*

        (1) *the individual claims are substantial, and the potential members of the class have sufficient resources, experience and sophistication in business affairs to conduct their own litigation; or*

---

[239] See CA 1998, s 47B(7)(c); and CAT Rules, r 79(3).

[240] See pp 188–190.

[241] Per the definition of 'opt-out collective proceedings' in CA 1998, s 47B(11)(b); and CAT Rules, r 80(1)(h)(iii).

[242] *De Asencio v Tyson Foods Inc*, 342 F 3d 301, fn 15 (3rd Cir, 2003).

[243] The Rule was adopted on 30 June 1977, and took effect 1 September 1977. The emphasis is added.

> (2) *other special circumstances exist which are described in the order,*
>
> *the court may state in its order that a person shall not be a member of the plaintiff class or subclass unless by a specified date the person files record of a written election to be included in the class or subclass.*

Hence, class actions under rule 1711 are designated to be opt-out, unless the provisions of rule 1711(b) apply.[244] As the *Explanatory Memorandum* confirms,[245] the rule 'do[es] not deal specifically with jurisdiction over non-resident members of the class'; but '[o]ne of its uses [may be] that the court will have no jurisdiction over non-residents unless they voluntarily appear. The opt-in procedure would provide a simple method of doing this. In such case there could be a dual form of order under Rule 1710; an opt-out for residents, an opt-in for nonresidents.' The *Explanatory Memorandum* referred to the case of *Klemow v Time Inc*,[246] in support of the aforementioned propositions.

2   Judicial Interpretations

In *Klemow*, the representative claimant sought authorisation as representative of a class composed of all Pennsylvania residents with unexpired LIFE subscriptions who had not settled their claims.[247] The Supreme Court of Pennsylvania held (in a footnote) that, '[b]ecause the jurisdiction of the courts of the Commonwealth is territorially limited, the class may consist only of Pennsylvania residents. The class may also include non-residents who submit themselves to the jurisdiction of the state courts.'[248] Some other US state courts had contemporaneously declared that, '[s]imply put, a state court cannot exercise binding jurisdiction over persons residing outside its boundaries unless there is some reasonable basis for doing so.'[249] Hence, requiring non-residents

---

[244] *Katlin v Tremoglie*, 1999 WL 1577980 (Pa Com Pl, 1999), at n 23 ('[u]nder Rule 1711, all class actions meeting the prerequisites of [the Code] are opt-out class actions unless the provisions of Rule 1711(b) apply'); as cited in: *Lorah v Suntrust Mortgage Inc*, US Dist LEXIS 12318 (2009), at *5.

[245] Available at: www.pacode.com/secure/data/231/chapter1700/chap1700toc.html (no pinpoints available).

[246] 466 Pa 189, 352 A 2d 12 (SC Pa, 1976) (citations omitted), cert denied: 97 S Ct 86 (1976).

[247] ibid, 197.

[248] ibid, fn 15.

[249] *Feldman v Bates Manufacturing Co*, 143 NJ Super 84, 89, 362 A 2d 1177 (1976).

to opt in and submit to the court's jurisdiction was a clear and unequivocal basis, providing the requisite 'contact' with the state. The *Klemow* decision preceded the enactment of rule 1711(b) by a year; but once that rule was implemented, it provided a practicable means of dealing with non-resident class members. They had to form an opt-in sub-class.

However, whether the *Klemow* footnote survived rule 1711(b), and still required non-resident class members to opt in to be bound by any judgment or settlement in a Pennsylvania class action, has been the subject of some distinct judicial disagreement since.

On the one hand, the accuracy of the *Klemow* footnote was later doubted in *Parsky v First Union Corp.*[250] The Court of Common Pleas of Pennsylvania stated that an opt-in procedure was unnecessary for non-resident class members, because the decision of the Supreme Court several years later in *Phillips Petroleum Co v Shutts*[251] had 'supplanted' it. The *Shutts* court had held that an opt-out procedure for non-resident class members (in that case, a multistate class action commenced in the Kansas state court) was constitutionally permissible, provided that due process requirements in relation to those non-resident class members were met. In addition to being adequately represented,[252] and receiving appropriate 'best practicable' notice of the class action,[253] the minimum due process thresholds required that non-resident class members be provided the right to exclude themselves from the class actions suit.[254] Even further, the *Shutts* court explicitly rejected any requirement that the non-resident class members had to have some minimum contact with the domestic jurisdiction of Kansas,[255] or that the non-resident class members must expressly consent to the Kansas court's jurisdiction via an opt-in requirement.[256] As one leading US class actions text notes, *Shutts* stands for the very important proposition that 'personal jurisdiction for judgment purposes may be exercised over non-resident class members without minimum contacts with the forum, and without affirmative opt-in consent having been made'.[257] Hence, according to *Parsky*, the decision in *Shutt* rendered the earlier reasoning in *Klemow* no longer applicable, 'leading

---

[250] WL 987764 (2001).
[251] 472 US 797, 105 S Ct 2965 (1985), cited ibid, at *3.
[252] ibid, 808.
[253] ibid, 812–13.
[254] ibid, 813–14.
[255] ibid, 808.
[256] ibid, 812.
[257] A Conte and H Newberg, *Newberg on Class Actions* (4th edn, Thomson West Group, 2002) [1.15], p 48.

this Court to question whether present-day non-resident class members are generally required to "opt in".[258] That court concluded that non-residents of Pennsylvania could be included in the class action on an opt-out basis, and that approach has been followed in Pennsylvania since.[259]

But, on the other hand, in *Weitzner v Vaccess America Inc*, a Pennsylvania court stated that it 'remained guided' by the *Klemow* footnote.[260] The problems of establishing jurisdiction over non-Pennsylvania residents, where there was no consent on the part of those non-residents to join a Pennsylvania state class action, was judicially adverted to in *Linkous v Medtronic Inc* too.[261]

The *Explanatory Memorandum* to the Pennsylvania Code makes plain that, '[j]urisdiction over non-residents is clearly substantive and not procedural, and for this reason is not dealt with in the rules.'[262] This harks back to the basic tenet that, generally speaking, the powers of a civil procedure rule-making body or committee are limited to the making or amending of rules of court for governing a court's practice or procedure, and have no power to modify any substantive matter of law.[263] Hence, the better view appears to be that, where *Shutts* provides a substantive basis upon which a domestic court can assert personal jurisdiction over non-resident class members (i.e., where due process thresholds in relation to non-resident class members are met), then that 'trumps' any *requirement* that non-residents must opt in as a sub-class under rule 1711(b). However, that rule still leaves *the possibility* of a sub-class of non-residents being formed on opt-in principles at the discretion of the court.

3   Relevant Criteria

The final issue under the 'judicial choice' model for non-residents is whether, and if so how, relevant criteria for deciding opt-in versus opt-out should be drafted for inclusion in the regime.

Some indicative criteria are already encapsulated in rule 1711(b)(1), reproduced above. The *Explanatory Memorandum* of the Pennsylvania Code notes that, 'this provision is not intended as a blank check to permit

---

[258] WL 987764 (2001), at *3.
[259] *Milkman v American Travellers Life Ins Co*, WL 1807376 (2001), at *9.
[260] 5 Pa D&C 5th 95, 112 (2008). See too: *Janicik v Prudential Ins Co of America*, 305 Pa Super 120, 451 A 2d 451, fn 14 (1982).
[261] US Dist LEXIS 16277 (1985), at *20.
[262] See: www.pacode.com/secure/data/231/chapter1700/chap1700toc.html.
[263] Discussed in: Mulheron, *The Class Action* (n 121) 38–42, and the sources cited therein.

unbridled discretion in the court to require members of the class to opt in. . . . Obviously, the provision may never be applied to conventional consumer class actions involving numerous members of a class claiming only small amounts who could not conduct their own litigation.'[264]

The drafters of the UK Competition Law Class Action thought the same, for the judicial election as to how domestic classes should be formed. Those drafters included the following criteria within the regime itself: 'the strength of the claims',[265] 'whether it is practicable for the proceedings to be brought as opt-in collective proceedings having regard to all the circumstances',[266] and the 'estimated amount of damages that individual class members may recover'.[267] Further, the CAT's *Guide to Proceedings* (which has the status of a Practice Direction[268]) explains that '[g]iven the greater complexity, cost and risks of opt-out proceedings, the Tribunal will usually expect the strength of the claims to be more immediately perceptible in an opt-out than an opt-in case, since in the latter case, the class members have chosen to be part of the proceedings and may be presumed to have conducted their own assessment of the strength of their claim.'[269] Opt-in classes might also be indicated where 'the class is small but the loss suffered by each class member is high, or the fact that it is straightforward to identify and contact the class members'.[270] Although these factors were drafted (and may potentially be applied[271]) with domestic class members in mind, they would be equally as applicable, if a court had to make the decision between opt-in and opt-out for a sub-class of non-resident class members.

H   Conclusion

How lawmakers handle non-resident class members is clearly a matter upon which legislatures around the Comparator Jurisdictions have

---

[264] Noted at: www.pacode.com/secure/data/231/chapter1700/chap1700toc.html

[265] CAT Rules, r 79(3)(a).

[266] CAT Rules, r 79(3)(b).

[267] CAT Rules, r 79(3)(b).

[268] Pursuant to CAT Rules, r 115(3), and noted in CAT, *Guide to Proceedings 2015*, at p 1.

[269] *Guide*, ibid, [6.39].

[270] ibid.

[271] A follow-on action re a trucks cartel is proposed as an opt-in class action, given the 'sufficiently large' amount of damages likely to be recoverable per class member: *Road Haulage Assn Ltd v Man SE* (Case 1289/7/7/18), whilst another action in respect of the same cartel has proposed an opt-out action, or an opt-in class action in the alternative: *UK Trucks Claim Ltd v Fiat Chrysler Automobiles NV* (Case 1282/7/7/18).

differed significantly, and where reasonable opinion will vary. For future legislatures, the issue cannot be ignored, and it is surely inappropriate to leave this important decision to the courts, given the huge variation of judicial opinion which has flourished throughout those jurisdictions. This is one of the most complex and still-unresolved issues afflicting modern class actions jurisprudence – and, as cross-border consumer grievances continue to proliferate, the search for elegant and workable solutions will continue. What is posited below is the author's recommendations, but with fulsome acknowledgement that others may see it differently.

RECOMMENDATIONS: GOVERNMENT AS 'GATE-KEEPER'

§ 5.1 The pro-active submission of non-resident class members to the domestic court's jurisdiction, by a positive act of opting in, pursuant to the compulsory opt-in model, is the surest method by which to ensure that the domestic court has asserted personal jurisdiction over that class member. The various disadvantages of opt-in regimes are more than offset by the achievement of a judgment rendered in favour of, or against, those non-resident class members which will be recognised and enforced in another jurisdiction.

§ 5.2 Alternatively, where the legislature does not insist upon an opt-in requirement for non-resident class members, then some other legislative basis upon which to assert jurisdiction over those class members may be appropriate. For example, the legislature may elect to define the precise due process requirements that must be met in respect of those class members (including, but not limited to, adequate notice of the proposed action, equivalent outcomes, adequate representation, and appropriate opt-out rights).

§ 5.3 Given the array of judicially created 'anchors' or 'ties' which have been developed by domestic courts to assert personal jurisdiction over non-resident class members, and the disagreements at appellate level which the issue has witnessed, it would seem preferable to settle and to clarify this issue via legislation, rather than to leave it to case law precedential development.

PART II

As a Participant in the Match

6

Government as Representative Claimant

A   Introduction

Whilst a government has no choice as to whether or not it is sued in a class action,[1] its decision to sue on behalf of a class, as representative claimant, must be consciously and deliberately taken. Whether that step is open to the government depends upon how the class action regime is designed, and whether that decision is to be made on a case-by-case basis, or was already made by the legislature.

For the purposes of this chapter, the government, as representative claimant for the class, is taken to include the following: (1) any level of government, from federal to state/provincial to local council/authority to indigenous councils/bands; (2) any government entity or instrumentality (e.g., a department, statutory authority, or regulator); and (3) any special purpose/ad hoc government vehicle which is established by statute and which receives some public funding from Consolidated Revenue. Together, these will be generically referred to as a 'government instrumentality' in this chapter.

In any scenario in which a government instrumentality can, and chooses to, act as representative claimant, there are significant advantages for the class. It is the representative claimant's role: to engage and to instruct legal representatives; to obtain funding for own-side disbursements on the common issues and to arrange cover for the risk of adverse costs, should the class lose; to provide disclosure on the common issues; to arrange significant interim steps such as opt-out and/or settlement notices to the class; and to represent the class at certification, fairness hearings, and other interlocutory steps in the case. Any government

---

[1] A topic tackled in Chapter 8, 'Government as Class Actions Defendant'.

instrumentality may also provide a more formidable negotiating position for the class against a well-resourced defendant.

At the outset, it must be noted that, should a class actions regime require that the consent of a government, government minister or government instrumentality is required in order for it to become a group member (which some regimes do[2]), then that sort of require-ment does **not** apply, where that party is the actual class representative. At the very least, one judge put it thus: 'the mere act of instituting the proceeding is abundant evidence that the party [the government] is consenting to be a group member: and in that case it would be unne-cessary for a separate form of consent to be exhibited.'[3] Hence, there is no requirement that some form of written consent by the government should be required as a 'condition precedent' to its commencing a class action in those circumstances.

None of the regimes of the Comparator Jurisdictions bars a government instrumentality from acting in the capacity of representative claimant. However, how that instrumentality does so has been the source of some controversy. This chapter must necessarily consider the standing of a government instrumentality to sue on behalf of a class of aggrieved persons in **three** different circumstances, as Figure 6.1 below shows:

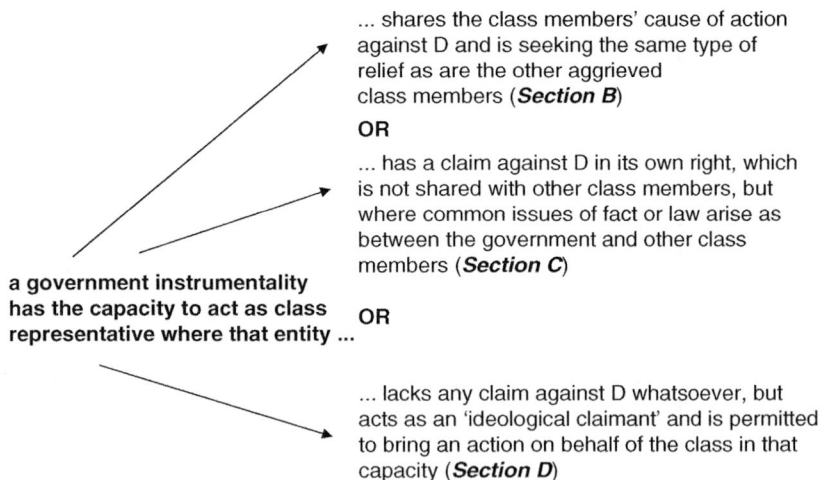

a government instrumentality has the capacity to act as class representative where that entity ...

... shares the class members' cause of action against D and is seeking the same type of relief as are the other aggrieved class members (**Section B**)

OR

... has a claim against D in its own right, which is not shared with other class members, but where common issues of fact or law arise as between the government and other class members (**Section C**)

OR

... lacks any claim against D whatsoever, but acts as an 'ideological claimant' and is permitted to bring an action on behalf of the class in that capacity (**Section D**)

Figure 6.1   Government as 'class representative'

---

[2] A topic considered in detail in Chapter 7, 'Government as Class Member'.

[3] *Australian Competition and Consumer Comm (ACCC) v Golden Sphere Intl Inc* [1998] FCA 598, accessed via austlii.edu.au, no pinpoint available.

These options will be considered strictly in the order in which they are outlined in Figure 6.1.

B   An Identical Cause of Action with Other Class Members

In some circumstances, cases have been commenced by a government instrumentality for the same cause of action, and for the same type of relief, as that which the class members are suing upon too – because all class members have suffered the same type (but not quantum) of harm arising from the same alleged or proven infringement. This is the most straightforward scenario in which the government instrumentality may act as representative claimant.

After all, governmental entities may be affected by the consequences of D's anti-competitive conduct, the same as any other entity or individual who purchased the relevant goods and services. Some examples will suffice. In *Gold Coast City Council v Pioneer Concrete (Qld) Pty Ltd*,[4] the local authority commenced an action under Australia's federal class action regime, on its own behalf and on behalf of class members (individuals and organisations, including government instrumentalities[5]), on the basis that certain companies allegedly engaged in collusive pricing and collusive tendering in respect of some grades of pre-mixed concrete over a five-year period. The action was ultimately discontinued as a class action for a variety of reasons which had nothing to do with the capacity of the local council to sue.[6] In *Gloucester Shire Council v Fitch Ratings Inc (No 2)*,[7] the Council alleged that it, together with the class members which it represented, suffered loss and damage as a result of their investment in sophisticated financial products called synthetic collateralised debt obligations,[8] and that in making that investment, it relied on credit

---

[4] FCA, Drummond J, 9 July 1997.

[5] Given this fact, the case is revisited in Chapter 7, at pp 252–253.

[6] Various 'de facto' certification requirements were not met, according to Drummond J: e.g., difficulties with meeting the minimum numerical threshold; doubt that there was any need for a class action; and that the costs incurred if the case were to proceed as a class action were likely to exceed the costs that would be incurred if each class member litigated individually, given the high costs of disclosure and third party disclosure; and that causation was likely to be a variable issue across class members, as some class members may have purchased that concrete in any event: FCA, 9 July 1997 (no pp available).

[7] [2017] FCA 248.

[8] Wigney J described the financial products in this way: 'SCDOs are particularly complex, some would say bewildering, financial products. One wonders whether anyone at the time ever truly understood or appreciated exactly what they were, or how they worked, other than perhaps the Wall Street masterminds who conjured them up': ibid, [17].

ratings that Fitch Ratings assigned to the products. The Council alleged that those ratings were misleading and deceptive, or were the product of a negligent ratings process. In each of these cases, the government instrumentality, as representative claimant, and each of the class members, were purporting to sue for an identical cause of action and for similar relief (i.e., damages).

In Canada too, 'band governments',[9] i.e., 'a basic unit of government for those peoples subject to the Indian Act (i.e. Status Indians or First Nations)',[10] have sued under provincial class actions statutes.[11] For example, in *Athabasca Chipewyan First Nation v British Columbia*,[12] the suit arose out of the construction, in the late 1960s, of the Bennett Dam on the Peace River in British Columbia. The Peace River eventually flows into northern Alberta's Peace Athabasca Delta, where the Athabasca Chipewyan had exercised various fishing and other treaty rights for a century. The Chief of the band commenced the class action on his own behalf and on behalf of all members of the Athabasca Chipewyan band, claiming that the dam's construction had altered the natural flow of the Peace River and had adversely affected the Delta's ecosystem. The causes of action sued upon included nuisance, interference with riparian rights, and breaches of various licenses and federal and provincial statutes.[13] A similar type of class action was instituted by the chief of the Kwicksutaineuk/Ah-Kwa-Mish First Nation,[14] on behalf of 'all aboriginal collectives who have or assert constitutionally protected aboriginal and/or treaty rights to fish wild salmon for food, social, and ceremonial purposes within the Broughton Archipelago';[15] although the certification of that case was ultimately overruled on the grounds that the 'aboriginal collectives' of the class definition did not have capacity to sue. For present purposes, however, it is relevant to note that the relief sought was common to the representative claimant and all class members, *viz*: a declaration, an injunction, and damages, in both cases.

---

[9] Also called a 'First Nation band'.
[10] See the description noted under 'Band government', at: https://en.wikipedia.org/wiki/Band_government.
[11] See, e.g.: *Chippewas of Sarnia Band v Canada (AG)* (1996), 29 OR (3d) 549, 137 DLR (4th) 239 (the claimant Band sued for a declaration that no surrender of certain lands by the Band had ever taken place).
[12] [2001] ABCA 112, 199 DLR (4th) 452.
[13] ibid, [67].
[14] *Kwicksutaineuk/Ah-Kwa-Mish First Nation v Canada (AG)* [2012] BCCA 193, leave to appeal *ref'd*: [2012] CanLII 70221 (SCC).
[15] ibid, [1].

However, the situation becomes more complicated where the government instrumentality has not been adversely affected in the same way as the class members, and may not even share the same cause of action with the class members. Whether that scenario can be accommodated by a class actions regime depends upon an exercise in statutory interpretation, as discussed in the following section.

C A Dissimilar Cause of Action from Other Class Members

Scenarios can easily arise in which a government instrumentality has a different cause of action from that which the class members are advancing.

For example, the instrumentality may have a statutorily conferred right to sue the defendant for injunctive relief under a consumer protection, environmental protection, or other 'public interest' statute; whereas the class members may have suffered loss and damage arising from a breach of contract which each of them has with the defendant. In other words, the causes of action are quite different, because the government instrumentality is pursuing a claim as 'protector' without having suffered any harm itself; whereas the class members are suing in their private capacities for recompense for the individual harm suffered by each of them. The remedies being sought by the government instrumentality and by the class members are entirely divergent, and so are the causes of action upon which they are suing. Can the government act as representative claimant in that scenario? On this important issue, class actions jurisprudence does not coalesce across the Comparator Jurisdictions, either legislatively or judicially.

The fact that the class action regimes in both Australia and Canada explicitly permit that class members may seek *different remedies* was a direct legislative response to the strictures that had accompanied the traditional representative rule enacted in England and elsewhere.[16] Hence, the regimes would definitely allow injunctive relief to be pursued by the government instrumentality, whilst damages were sought by the

---

[16] See, e.g.: Ontario's Class Proceedings Act, SO 1992, c 6, s 6(3); British Columbia's Class Proceedings Act, RSBC 1996, c 50, s 7(c); Australia's federal regime, FCA 1976, s 33C(2)(a)(iv); New South Wales' Civil Procedure Act 2005, s 157(2)(a)(iv). The reasoning behind these provisions is discussed by the author in: 'From Representative Rule to Class Action: Steps rather than Leaps' (2005) 24 *Civil Justice Quarterly* 424, 429–30.

government, as representative claimant, is suing upon a claim to protect the public or consumer interest, conferred by statute, in which the government instrumentality seeks injunctive relief

AND:

Defendant (D)

private individuals or entities, as class members, are suing for a cause of action in, say, tort, contract, or breach of statutory duty, and are claiming compensatory damages

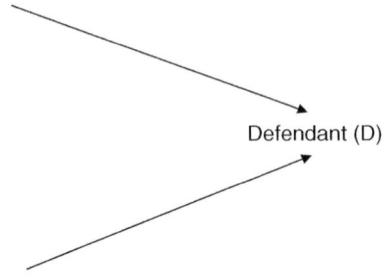

Figure 6.2   Different causes of action, or different types of relief

class. However, what if those different remedies were being pursued under different causes of action? That is where the uncertainty has arisen.

The scenario may be diagrammatically depicted in Figure 6.2 above.

This issue needs to be examined in two parts: first, whether or not a requirement of 'typicality' arises on the face of the class actions regime; and secondly, an exercise of statutory interpretation as to what 'a claim' means, where it appears in class actions statutes.

Dealing with each in turn:

1   The Significance (if Any) of a Typicality Requirement

(a)   Where the Requirement Arises

Of the Comparator Jurisdictions under consideration, only the federal opt-out class action regime of the United States contains a typicality requirement. FRCP 23(a)(3) states that:

Prerequisites. One or more members of a class may sue or be sued as representative parties on behalf of all members only if:

. . .

    (3) the claims or defenses of the representative parties are typical of the claims or defenses of the class

---

Such a requirement is not contained in the text of any of the Canadian federal or provincial statutes (an omission which has been judicially noted across that jurisdiction[17]) or the Australian federal or state statutes (where the omission has been similarly noted[18]). That approach was deliberate. For example, the Ontario Law Reform Commission[19] did not recommend a typicality requirement. It concluded that it added nothing to the other certification requirements such as commonality and adequacy and, hence, was redundant; that it had an uncertain meaning in US class actions case law; and that, strictly interpreted, it would be a further onerous requirement that could halt otherwise meritorious class claims. The law reform reports which preceded the implementation of the Alberta provincial,[20] Manitoba provincial,[21] Victorian state,[22] and Australia federal[23] regimes were obviously fully aware of the typicality requirement arising under FRCP 23(a)(3), but declined to recommend any equivalent. Law reform consideration in Ireland,[24] South Africa,[25] and Hong Kong[26] has not favoured the requirement either.

The question for present purposes is whether, under US jurisprudence, a typicality requirement imposes any need that the causes of action and/or the types of relief sought must be identical as between the representative claimant and the class members. If it did – and if that requirement were to be repeated in another class action regime under consideration either now or in the future – then that would rule out

---

[17] e.g., *Banque de Montréal c Marcotte* [2012] QCCA 1396, [46]–[47]; *Hudspeth v Whatcott* [2017] ONSC 1708, 98 CPC (7th) 40, [259]; *Markson v MBNA Canada Bank* (2004), 71 OR (3d) 741, [88]; *Pardy v Bayer Inc* [2004] NLTD 72, 237 Nfld & PEIR 179, [164]; *Campbell v Flexwatt Corp* (1997), 44 BCLR (3d) 343 (CA) [44], [134], [153], [166]; *Peppiatt v Royal Bank of Canada* (1996), 27 OR (3d) 462; *Abdool v Anaheim Management Ltd* (1995), 21 OR (3d) 453, 121 DLR (4th) 496.

[18] e.g.: the extra-curial comment by The Hon John Basten, writing about the New South Wales state opt-out class action contained in Pt 10 of the Civil Procedure Act 2005 (NSW), *Procedural Reform: The New Part 10* (paper presented to the Judges of the Court, NSW Judicial Scholarship 19, 2011) 3 ('[w]e have not adopted that language and, accordingly, much of the US case-law is irrelevant in construing our rules').

[19] *Report on Class Actions* (1982) 366–71.

[20] *Class Actions* (Rep 85, 2000) [216].

[21] *Class Proceedings* (Rep 100, 1999) 54–56.

[22] See the discussion in: Victorian Attorney-General's Law Reform Advisory Council: *Class Actions in Victoria: Time for a New Approach?* (1997) [6.28]–[6.31].

[23] The discussion of the 'connecting link: common question' did not refer to typicality, notwithstanding the description of the US federal regime contained later in the report: *Grouped Proceedings in the Federal Court* (1988) [136]–[138], and App C.

[24] *Multi-Party Litigation* (Rep 76, 2005) [2.61].

[25] *The Recognition of Class Actions and Public Interest Actions in South African Law* (Rep 88, 1998) [5.6.22].

[26] *Class Actions* (Law Reform Commission of Hong Kong, Rep 85, May 2000) [216].

a government instrumentality acting as representative claimant in the scenario depicted in Figure 6.2.

(b)   The Possible Meanings of 'Typicality'

The meanings given to typicality have been numerous (as the author has explored elsewhere[27]) – and US case law over the course of just 2018 only confirms that impression. It has been judicially said that the requirement is 'not demanding',[28] represents a 'low threshold',[29] is a 'permissive standard',[30] and is to be interpreted 'in common sense terms'.[31]

Some earlier judicial statements indicated that the claims of the representative claimant and of the class members should fairly closely match – e.g., in *General Telephone Co of the Northwest Inc v EEOC*, the US Supreme Court stated that '[t]he typicality requirement is said to limit the class claims to those fairly encompassed by the named plaintiff's claims'.[32] However, the reality remains that many of the judicial definitions of 'typicality' under FRCP 23(a)(3) do **not** prescribe the same claim, cause of action, nor relief as between representative claimant and class members. To take a sample of comments from 2018 case law in Table 6.1 overpage.

The abovementioned quotations continue to illustrate the contention, most aptly, that it is difficult to see what the typicality criterion adds to the commonality or adequacy criteria. On that basis, its inclusion in any certification matrix must be seriously questioned. Those US judges who have stated that typicality's relationship to commonality is 'murky'[33] and 'interchangeable'[34] must surely be as correct now as when those sentiments were put. The author has argued elsewhere[35] that the only aspect of

---

[27] *The Class Action in Common Law Legal Systems: A Comparative Perspective* (Hart Publishing, 2004) 310–13.

[28] *Mallory v Lease Supervisors LLC*, WL 1281555, at *5 (WD Texas, 13 January 2017).

[29] *In re Lamictal Indirect Purchaser and Antitrust Consumer Litig*, WL 6567709, at *4 (DNJ, 12 December 2018), citing: *Newton v Merrill Lynch, Pierce, Fenner & Smith Inc*, 259 F 3d 154, 183 (3d Cir, 2001).

[30] *Caudle v Sprint/United Management Co*, WL 6618280, at *4 (ND Cal, 18 December 2018).

[31] *Arrington v Optimum Healthcare IT LLC*, WL 5631625, at *4 (ED Penn, 31 October 2018), citing: *Beck v Maximus Inc*, 457 F 3d 291, 295–96 (3d Cir, 2006).

[32] 446 US 318, 330, 100 S Ct 1698 (1980).

[33] e.g., *Harriss v Pan Am World Airways Inc*, 74 FRD 24, 41 (ND Cal, 1977) ('[t]he line between the commonality requirement and the typicality requirement is murky undoubtedly, there is much overlap between the two').

[34] e.g., *Droughn v FMC Corp*, 74 FRD 639, 642 (Ed Pa, 1977).

[35] *The Class Action* (n 27) 313–17.

Table 6.1 *The United States' test of typicality*

According to US federal case law, the test of typicality is met where:

- the class members have the same or similar injury, the action is based on conduct which is not unique to the named plaintiff, and other class members have been injured by the same course of conduct;[36]
- the representative claimant's claims are reasonably co-extensive with those of absent class members; [but] they need not be substantially identical;[37]
- the representative claimant's claim has the same essential characteristics of those of the putative class, [and] factual differences will not defeat typicality;[38]
- regardless of the strength of the claims brought by each member, there is similarity between the class representative and class members' claims;[39]
- the representative claimant's claim arises from the same event, practice or course of conduct that gives rise to the claims of other class members, and if his or her claims are based on the same legal theory;[40]
- the claims of the class representative and class members are based on the same legal or remedial theory;[41]
- there is enough congruence between the named representative's claim and that of the unnamed members of the class to justify allowing the former to litigate on behalf of the group;[42]
- the claims of the representative claimant in a class action need not be absolutely identical in every way to the claims of other plaintiffs; it need only be identical in the ways that matter [i.e., provided there is a common element of fact or law].[43]

---

[36] *Caudle v Sprint/United Management Co*, WL 6618280, at *4 (ND Cal, 18 December 2018), citing: *Wolin v Jaguar Land Rover N Am LLC*, 617 F 3d 1168, 1175 (9th Cir, 2010) (citation omitted).

[37] *Caudle*, ibid, citing: *Hanlon v Chrysler Corp*, 150 F 3d 1011, 1020 (9th Cir, 1998).

[38] *Mallory v Lease Supervisors LLC*, WL 1281555, at *6 (WD Tex, 13 January 2017), citing: *Stirman v Exxon Corp*, 280 F 3d 554, 562 (5th Cir, 2002).

[39] *Mallory*, ibid, citing: *Langbecker v Electronic Data Systems Corp*, 476 F 3d 299, 314 (5th Cir, 2007).

[40] *Humphrey v Stored Value Cards*, WL 6011052, at *4 (ND Ohio, 16 November 2018), citing: *In re Am Med Sys Inc*, 75 F 3d 1069, 1082 (6th Cir, 1996) (quoting *Newberg on Class Actions*, vol 1, §3–13). See too: *Doe L v Pierce County*, 2018 WL 4006594, at *20 (CA Wash, 21 August 2018).

[41] *Shahlai v Comcast Cable Communications Management LLC*, WL 3870129, at *4 (D Colo, 15 August 2018), citing: *Menocal v GEO Grp Inc*, 882 F 3d 905, 914 (10th Cir, 2018).

[42] *Laughlin v Jim Fischer Inc*, WL 2538356, at *5 (ED Wis, 4 June 2018), citing: *Spano v Boeing Co*, 633 F 3d 574, 587 (7th Cir, 2011).

[43] *McNamee v Nationstar Mortgage LLC*, WL 1557244, at *7 (SD Ohio, 30 March 2018). Also: *State ex rel U-Haul Co of West Virginia v Tabit*, WL 2304282, at *4 (SC App W Va, 21 May 2018), citing: *In re W Va Rezulin Litig*, 214 W Va 52, 585 S E 2d 52 (2003).

the typicality criterion that has been transposed to later class actions regimes is the need to affirmatively establish the existence of a class – but even if that is correct, that does not relate to the question the subject of this section: does typicality require an identical cause of action as between the representative claimant and the class members?

The answer to that question, under US jurisprudence, appears to be 'no'. To recall,[44] the criterion is not intended to be a difficult threshold to meet. Hence, even should such a requirement be included in any class action regime, the better view is that the scenario in Figure 6.2 is permissible under a criterion of that type. Where that criterion is not contained on the face of the class action regime, however, there is a further potential interpretative obstacle.

2   Statutory Interpretation: The Meaning of 'a Claim'

In the absence of any typicality criterion, the question of whether a government instrumentality could pursue a separate cause of action or claim from that which is pursued on behalf of the class, turns upon the statutory interpretation accorded to the standing requirements – and inevitably, what the word, 'claim', means. This conundrum requires that the government instrumentality has the requisite standing, itself, to sue the defendant. (If it does not, then the realm of the 'ideological claimant', explored later in the chapter,[45] is its only remaining option.)

The relevant provisions of Australia's federal regime (which the state regimes of New South Wales, Victoria and Queensland identically or substantially replicate) state that:[46]

> s 33D(1) A person [one of at least 7 persons who have **claims** against the same person] who has a sufficient interest to commence a proceeding on his or her own behalf against another person has a sufficient interest to commence a representative proceeding against that other person on behalf of other persons referred to [in the bracketed phrase].

Meanwhile, the Ontario regime (which the other Canadian provincial regimes substantially replicate) provides that:[47]

---

[44] See nn 28–31.
[45] Per Section D.
[46] The bracketed section is from FCA 1976, s 33C(1)(a), with added emphasis.
[47] Class Proceedings Act, SO 1992, c 6 (with emphasis added).

> s 5(1) The court shall certify a class proceedings . . . if,
>
> . . .
>
> (b) there is an identifiable class of two or more persons that would be represented by the representative plaintiff . . . ; [and]
> (c) the **claims** . . . of the class members raise common issues; . . .

Under these provisions, what the government instrumentality may sue for as a representative claimant, on behalf of the class, all depends upon what a 'claim' means. There are divergent possibilities – and they have variously received judicial support in both Canada and in Australia, signifying the difficulty of the issue wherever the legislation itself does not make the issue plain.

(a) The Narrow View

At its strictest, the word, 'claim', means the cause of action being sued upon.[48] It means 'the prosecution or pursuit through the legal process of a legal claim founded upon one cause of action'.[49] A cause of action is defined[50] **either** by reference to an act or type of conduct (say, for strict liability torts which do not depend upon proof of harm, such as the trespassory torts); **or** by reference to harm suffered (say, for torts which require proof of some compensable damage, such as the torts of negligence or privacy).

Judicial support for this interpretation is to be found in the judgment of Finkelstein J in *Bray v F Hoffmann-La Roche Ltd.*[51] His Honour held that the word 'claim' in section 33C(1)(a) meant a cause of action, i.e., 'the facts which give rise to the action as well as to the legal basis of the action.'[52] His view was that it was 'loose language' to refer to a remedy as 'a claim'.[53] However, the other members of the Full Federal Court did not agree (discussed below), aptly demonstrating that reasonable judicial opinion will differ upon the meaning of the word 'claim', where it appears in a statute.

---

[48] See: E Martin and J Law (eds), *Oxford Dictionary of Law* (6th edn, Oxford University Press, 2006) 93.

[49] J Penner, *The Law Student's Dictionary* (Oxford University Press, 2008) 7.

[50] *Oxford Dictionary of Law* (n 48) 77.

[51] [2003] FCAFC 153.

[52] ibid, [245].

[53] ibid.

Under this strict interpretation, it may be said that if, say, the representative claimant was only able to sue for injunctive relief against the defendant, because a statute conferred that right upon the representative claimant – but where that representative had not had any wrongful act committed against it personally, nor had it suffered any harm itself – then that would not constitute a 'claim' at all. This line of reasoning emerged under the Australian federal class action regime, although not without controversy.

The Australian Competition and Consumer Commission (ACCC) is a statutorily created government instrumentality which is self-described as 'Australia's competition regulator and national consumer champion'.[54] In a series of class actions brought within the first decade of Australia's federal regime, the ACCC sued on behalf of itself and a defined class, relating principally to pyramid selling by defendants. The ACCC sued solely for injunctive relief under section 80 of the Trade Practices Act 1974 (TPA 1974)[55] (as then enacted), whilst the class members sued for repayment of sums paid and/or damages for losses suffered pursuant to section 82 of that statute.[56] As the High Court of Australia had earlier noted, section 80 was enacted so that the ACCC could protect the public interest: '[t]his is a common feature of the legislation'.[57] Undoubtedly, the ACCC was also a 'person' for the purposes of section 33D(1) – given that it was established by an Act of Parliament as a body corporate,[58] and was entitled to sue and to be sued in its corporate name.[59] However, did the ACCC have 'a claim' that was permissible to bring under section 33D(1)? If not, then it had no 'claim' to share with the class members, and the class action would be invalidly constituted.

---

[54] See, 'About Us', at: www.accc.gov.au/.

[55] It relevantly provided that: 'where, on the application of the Commission or any other person, the Court is satisfied that a person has engaged, or is proposing to engage, in conduct that constitutes or would constitute: (a) a contravention of any of the following [various specified] provisions [including]: (i) a provision of Part IV, . . . ; the Court may grant an injunction in such terms as the Court determines to be appropriate.

[56] Section 82(1) relevantly provided that: '[a] person who suffers loss or damage by conduct of another person that was done in contravention of a provision of Pt IV or V may recover the amount of the loss or damage by action against that other person or against any person involved in the contravention.'

[57] *Truth About Motorways Pty Ltd v Macquarie Infrastructure Investment Management Ltd* [2000] HCA 11, 200 CLR 591, [17], cited in: *Bray v F Hoffmann-La Roche Ltd* [2003] FCAFC 153, [205].

[58] TPA 1974, s 6A(2)(a).

[59] ibid, s 6A(2)(d).

In *ACCC v Giraffe World Australia Pty Ltd*,[60] the class members were members of the Giraffe Club and the Grow Rich System, a pyramid selling scheme, and claimed for repayment/damages. Of course, baldly put, in such cases, the ACCC 'represented a group of which the ACCC was not and could not be a part',[61] because it had not, itself, suffered any loss or damage from any investment in the pyramid selling scheme. However, and using its powers conferred by section 80, it sued instead for various heads of injunctive and declaratory relief, including an order for corrective advertising. Lindgren J preferred the view that the ACCC could **not** act as representative claimant, as it did not share a 'claim' as representative claimant with the class members – primarily because it did not, itself, have a 'claim' at all. It was not that different remedies were being sought by the ACCC and by the class members which was the problem (the opt-out class action itself permitted that, of course[62]). Rather, the class members had a purely *private* interest and were pursuing their remedy in damages to protect that; whereas the ACCC could **only** mount a statutory claim for injunctive relief in the *public* interest, which was not a 'claim' that the opt-out class action envisaged on the part of the representative claimant:

> a statutory *locus standi* of the kind given by s 80 . . . lies outside [s 33D(1)]. This view is consistent with the Second Reading Speech . . . which evinced an intention that Part IVA would be used by persons who brought proceedings to prevent, or obtain relief for, loss or damage to their own interests and the interests of other group members, rather than by persons who sought only to protect public interests and whose private interests had not been specially affected at all.[63]

This *Giraffe World* view has been judicially cited since as being the correct view,[64] or at the very least, 'important to bear in mind'.[65] However, the issue was clouded by the fact that, ultimately, Lindgren J, whilst doubting the correctness of contrary decisions,[66] decided to follow them, and to allow the ACCC to represent the class in *Giraffe World*[67]

---

[60] [1998] FCA 819, (1998) 84 FCR 512.

[61] As noted in: *ACCC v Golden Sphere Intl Inc* [1998] FCA 598.

[62] Per FCA 1976, s 33C(2)(a)(iv).

[63] [1998] FCA 598, 524.

[64] *Bray v F Hoffmann-La Roche Ltd* [2003] FCAFC 153, [210] (Branson J).

[65] *Kirby v Centro Properties Ltd* [2010] FCA 1115, [20] (Ryan J).

[66] Viz, *ACCC v Chats House Investments Pty Ltd* (1996) 71 FCR 250 and *ACCC v Golden Sphere Intl Inc* [1998] FCA 598, considered shortly.

[67] *ACCC v Giraffe World Australia Pty Ltd* [1998] FCA 819, 'Conclusion', point 1, *ibid*; and discussed too in: *Bray v F Hoffmann-La Roche Ltd* [2003] FCAFC 153, [196]; and *Rod Investments (Vic) Pty Ltd v Clark (No 2)* [2006] VSC 342, [18]–[19].

(and in a similar case of misrepresentation in relation to domain name registration services[68]).

(b)   The Wide(r) View

In another of the pyramid selling cases with the ACCC as representative claimant, *viz*, *ACCC v Golden Sphere International Inc*,[69] O'Loughlin J held that the ACCC (pursuing injunctive relief pursuant to section 80) and each investing member in the pyramid selling scheme (pursuing repayment and damages under section 82) all had 'claims'. It has been judicially accepted[70] that *Golden Sphere* is at odds with the views expressed earlier in *Giraffe World* on that point. It did not matter that the former was pursuing a relief in the nature of a *private* interest, whereas the ACCC was pursuing a claim in the nature of protecting a *public* interest for the protection of consumers. This 'difference of interest was not a disqualifying feature'.[71]

The same wider interpretation as to what amounts to a 'claim' was held to apply under the Victorian opt-out class action regime. In *Rod Investments (Vic) Pty Ltd v Clark (No 2)*,[72] Hansen J held that a claim for mere declaratory relief qualified as a 'claim': '[t]he legislature had imposed limitations on the types of claims that can be made using the Part 4A procedure, these limitations going to number, relatedness and commonality, not fine distinctions between a cause of action and an element of a prayer for relief or any public/private ... dichotomy'.[73]

Furthermore, whilst they were not the *same* claims being prosecuted by the ACCC and by the class members, O'Loughlin J held that they could be claimed in the *one* class action. The reasoning underpinning this conclusion demonstrates the complexities that can arise regarding statutory interpretation. The ACCC and the class members were all *capable* of bringing the *same* claim, under section 80, for injunctive relief (given the

---

[68] *ACCC v Internic Technology Pty Ltd* [1998] FCA 818 ('their Honours were not clearly wrong in holding that the terms of Pt IVA are, upon their proper construction, wide enough to encompass the commencement of a representative proceeding under Pt IVA by the ACCC as representative party on behalf of itself and on behalf of other persons whose suffering of loss or damage is an essential element in their causes of action').

[69] [1998] FCA 598.

[70] *Bray v F Hoffmann-La Roche Ltd* [2003] FCAFC 153, [196] (Branson J).

[71] [1998] FCA 598, citing also, for the same view: *ACCC v Chats House Investment Pty Ltd* (1996) 71 FCR 250, 254 (Branson J), although (it was subsequently noted) without the benefit of submissions to the contrary.

[72] [2006] VSC 342.

[73] ibid, [30].

opening words of section 80, that an application for injunctive relief can be 'on the application of the Commission *or any other person*'). According to O'Loughlin J: '[o]nce it is established that Golden Sphere promoted a pyramid selling scheme in contravention of section 61 of the TPA ... then it can be accepted that the ACCC and separately each member of the public who invested in the scheme would be entitled to seek injunctive relief under section 80 of the TPA'.[74] However, ultimately, the class members were **not** seeking injunctive relief – only the ACCC was – but the class members themselves were all *capable* of bringing that claim under section 80, if they were victims of a contravention of the TPA. The fact that they were bringing a separate claim which the ACCC could not prosecute did not matter, as there was *one claim* common to them all.

This view was reiterated in other Australian class actions jurisprudence too. In *Finance Sector Union of Australia v Commonwealth Bank of Australia*,[75] the union, as representative claimant, sued for the imposition of a penalty and the payment of underpayments by the employer bank, which claims were permissible by virtue of statute;[76] whereas the class member employees sued for those claims, and also for breach of their individual employment contracts with the bank.[77] The union had no contract claim of its own, but it was permissible that the union acted as representative claimant for the class members: '[t]here is no reason to read down the plain words of s 33C(1)'.[78] In *King v GIO Australia Holdings Ltd*[79] too, Moore J also approved of the view that at least **one** common claim or cause of action amongst the class members and representative claimant was sufficient,[80] and that the class members may permissibly have other causes of action that the representative claimant cannot personally plead.[81]

---

[74] [1998] FCA 598.

[75] [1999] FCA 1250 (Full FCA), affirming the earlier decision of O'Connor J: [1999] FCA 824.

[76] Pursuant to the Workplace Relations Act 1996, ss 178(1) and 178(6), respectively.

[77] The fact that the class members were suing on their individual contracts with the defendant did not bar the class actions, as expressly provided for in s 33C(2)(b)(i), and reiterated at first instance by O'Connor J in *Finance Sector Union of Australia v Commonwealth Bank of Australia* [1999] FCA 824, [33], [35].

[78] [1999] FCA 1250, [23].

[79] (2000) 100 FCR 209.

[80] *Viz*, for a declaration pursuant to the TPA 1974, s 163A.

[81] (2000) 100 FCR 209, [35], and not ultimately considered on appeal: *King v GIO Aust Holdings Ltd* [2000] FCA 1543 (Full FCA), because interim repleading meant that the representative claimant and class members claimed the same four causes of action against each defendant, thereby removing the problem: at [8].

But would it always be possible to show that a government instrumentality, as representative claimant, and the class members, shared a common cause of action? If not, then an even wider interpretation has occurred under the Australian (and Canadian) regimes.

(c)   The Widest View

At its widest, a 'claim' means '[a] demand for a remedy, or the assertion of a right, especially the right to take a particular case to court (right of action)'.[82] If representative claimant and class members have to share a 'claim' and this meaning applies, then this widens the possibilities considerably. The class members could assert a cause of action which is not identical to that being asserted by the government instrumentality as representative claimant, and yet, they would all be 'claims' capable of being brought in the one class action. There would **not** need to be one claim or cause of action which they all shared.

In Canadian jurisprudence, this widest view of the word, 'claim', has plenty of support. A decade into the life of the Ontario opt-out regime, the case of *Boulanger v Johnson & Johnson Corp*[83] held that the cause of action as between the representative claimant and the class members did not have to be the same. The Divisional Court held that the 'scheme' of the Act was to allow the representative claimant 'to plead causes of action which are not [his own] personal causes of action, but which are the causes of action of members of the class, asserted by the plaintiff in a representative capacity'.[84] In other words, provided that the representative claimant could assert a cause of action (a 'claim') against the defendant, it was not necessary for it to be able to plead, personally, the causes of action that the class members were asserting against the defendant. They all had 'claims' – and provided that there were common issues of fact or law across those claims, the requirements of the legislation were met. That view was affirmed subsequently in *Fournier v Mercedes-Benz Canada*.[85] The representative claimants were car dealers who imported vehicles into Canada, whereas the class members were mainly consumers who had purchased such vehicles. As they were not consumers, the importers could not assert certain claims under the Consumer Protection Act that were available to the class members.[86] In light of

---

[82] See: *Oxford Dictionary of Law* (n 48) 93.
[83] (2003), 226 DLR (4th) 747, 64 OR (3d) 208 (Div Ct).
[84] ibid, [33].
[85] [2012] ONSC 2752.
[86] As discussed in ibid, [108]–[110].

Boulanger, that was nevertheless held to be permissible: '[c]an a claim be asserted on behalf of proposed class members where the representative plaintiff would not be able to assert such a claim? The answer to this question appears to be "yes", provided that the representative plaintiff has a cause of action against the defendants, and the two causes of action share a common issue of law or fact.'[87]

Some Australian judges have also supported this very wide view of what amounts to a 'claim'. In *Bray v F Hoffmann-La Roche Ltd*,[88] Carr J opined that, as it appears in section 33C(1)(a), a 'claim' does not only mean a 'cause of action', but was able to extend to any right to demand of payment, or a type of relief, or a claim to enforce the performance of a statutory duty (by means of a declaration) or to restrain the contravention of a statutory provision (by means of an injunction)[89] – i.e., that it was to be interpreted very widely. Branson J also considered that the word 'claim' bore a wide meaning, certainly wide enough to include a claim by the ACCC for injunctive relief under section 80.[90] The very wide view was also supported by Moore J in *King v GIO Australia Holdings Ltd* as dicta:[91] '[i]t may be that the word 'claim' in section 33C(1)(a) is not be to be treated as a reference to one common cause of action or one common "(any)thing that might lawfully be brought before the court for a remedy". .... Section 33C(1)(a) does not speak of seven or more persons having "the same claim" against the same person, and the language of the section does not warrant some narrow view of what is a claim.'[92] As the author has noted elsewhere,[93] Moore J's view accords precisely with the *Boulanger* view[94] (and, of course, with the numerous other Canadian authorities which have held similarly[95]).

---

[87] ibid, [111], and citing *Boulanger* at [113], together with: *Healey v Lakeridge Health Corp* [2006] OJ No 4277 (SCJ) (at [117]); *Matoni v CBS Interactive Multimedia Inc* [2008] OJ No 197 (SCJ) (at [118]); and *Dobbie v Arctic Glacier Income Fund* [2011] ONSC 25 (at [119]), as illustrating the same point. See too: *Macleod v Viacom Entertainment Canada Inc* (2003), 28 CPC (5th) 160 (SCJ) [23].

[88] [2003] FCAFC 153.

[89] ibid, [110]–[119].

[90] ibid, [195]–[196].

[91] (2000) 100 FCR 209.

[92] ibid, [35]. The issue was not dealt with on appeal: *King v GIO Aust Holdings Ltd* [2000] FCA 1543 (Full FCA), because of interim amendments to the pleadings.

[93] *The Class Action* (n 27) 215.

[94] Per *Boulanger v Johnson & Johnson Corp* (2003), 226 DLR (4th) 747, 64 OR (ed) 208 (Div Ct).

[95] See n 87 above.

Of course, this interpretation of 'claim' is the most helpful, in opening up a class actions regime to government instrumentalities to act as representative claimant. Provided that the instrumentality has a claim itself, then it could still represent class members who had other causes of action to assert which it would not be able to pursue itself.

The predominant lesson to be learnt from this experience is that it would be strongly advisable for any opt-out class action regime to specifically state that: (1) different claims asserted among the class members does not preclude the commencement of a class action and (2) a 'claim' includes, but should **not** be taken to be limited to, a 'cause of action'. That would provide maximum flexibility for the government instrumentality to act as representative claimant.

(d)   Where More than One Regime Applies

Finally, government instrumentalities often have specific statutory entitlements to sue on behalf of members of the public – quite apart from any opt-out class action regime. For example, the ACCC already had the explicit statutory regime[96] under which to apply to the Federal Court for relief, on behalf of persons who had suffered loss and damage, but *only where those persons consented to be represented by the ACCC*.[97] Did that mean that the power of that government instrumentality to pursue an opt-out class action under a more generalist regime should be ruled out, because there was already a specific opt-in regime available to it?

This was emphatically answered 'no' by the Australian Federal Court. In *ACCC v Chats House Investment Pty Ltd*,[98] members of the public gave over moneys to the defendant for investment, specifically, for foreign exchange trading. The defendant had maintained a facade designed to convince its clients that it was engaging in genuine foreign exchange

---

[96] The TPA 1974, s 87(1B), relevantly provided that: 'The Commission may make an application . . . on behalf of one or more persons identified in the application who: (a) have suffered, or are likely to suffer, loss or damage by conduct of another person that was engaged in contravention of [named Parts] or a provision of the Australian Consumer Law; and (b) have, before the application is made, consented in writing to the making of the application.' There are numerous other statutory provisions under which the ACCC can bring actions on behalf of victims, as discussed in: D Grave, K Adams and J Betts, *Class Actions in Australia* (2nd edn, Lawbook Co, 2012) [5.420].

[97] In *Golden Sphere*, the ACCC had not sought that consent, and hence, why it was pursuing the action under the federal opt-out regime: noted in [1998] FCA 598. This type of opt-in representative action has been successfully utilised by the ACCC since: *ACCC v Allphones Retail Pty Ltd* [2011] FCA 538, and was noted to be distinct from the opt-out Pt IVA regime in other respects too: at [22].

[98] (1996) 71 FCR 250.

margin trading when, in fact, no such trading was taking place. The ACCC instituted a class action under the federal opt-out regime (again pursuing injunctive relief under section 80, whilst the class members' claims were for damages suffered). Branson J rejected the argument that any claim of the ACCC's under the generally cast federal class action should be read down (i.e., precluded) because of the opt-in regime which was available to the ACCC to seek relief on behalf of aggrieved persons. Provided that the ACCC had a 'claim' under the opt-out class action regime (which it did, according to her Honour, again diverging from the *Giraffe World* view), then it could bring a federal class action as representative claimant.[99]

However, in any circumstances in which competing regimes are potentially applicable, it will inevitably form part of the superiority analysis, undertaken at certification, as to whether or not some other form of dispute resolution is preferable to the determination of the claim under the opt-out class action.[100]

D   Government as 'Ideological Claimant'

For a representative claimant who does not possess any claim against the defendant at all, the only basis upon which that party could represent the class is as a so-called 'ideological claimant' – and even then, only where the class action regime either expressly or impliedly permits that route of standing.

Trade associations, consumer organisations, unions, lobby groups, individuals who have a longstanding interest in and association with the affected class, and former class members who are no longer so, are the more usual ideological claimants. However, in some circumstances, a government instrumentality, which otherwise lacks any standing to sue because it does not possess any 'claim' against the defendant whatsoever, may be willing to represent the class. Whether or not it may do so depends upon two matters: first, whether the relevant class action regime permits a party lacking any direct cause of action to sue; and secondly (if it does), whether that representative claimant can meet the typical prerequisites of the ideological claimant.[101] Dealing with each in turn:

---

[99]   ibid, 254.
[100] See, e.g., the relevant 'suitability' factor in the UK Competition Law Class Action, CAT Rules, r 79(2)(g).
[101] This section of the chapter draws upon and updates the discussion of this topic undertaken by the author elsewhere: 'The United Kingdom's New Opt-Out Class Action'

1   Drafting for an 'Ideological Claimant': The Options

There are **five** options for drafting for the ideological claimant. Taking them in no particular order:

Option 1: Even though the class actions regime may read, on its face, that only members of the class may sue on behalf of other class members, the regime may nevertheless be taken impliedly to permit the use of an ideological claimant. That drafting model has been evident in the earlier class actions regimes of the United States[102] and Australian[103] federal opt-out regimes. However, such an approach appears to be undesirable and controversial, given that the permissibility of using an ideological claimant has been the subject of legal dispute under both regimes (especially under the US doctrine of 'representational standing'[104]). In modern class actions jurisprudence, the preference is to articulate explicitly the status of an ideological claimant, rather than to leave it to parties' litigation and judicial interpretation.

Option 2: The regime may permit an ideological claimant, in circumstances where a directly affected class member is the default position, but where an ideological claimant is exceptional (i.e., its appointment is only to occur 'if it is necessary to do so in order to avoid a substantial injustice to the class'). This is commonly enacted in the Canadian provincial regimes.[105] It has been judicially stated that 'the burden under the section is high, and involves consideration of both the suitability of the plaintiff and the circumstances of the class members themselves';[106] and that a class action statute drafted in this manner 'presumes … that the representative plaintiff normally will be a member of the class'.[107]

(2017) 37 *Oxford Journal of Legal Studies* 814, 827–33; and: *The Class Action* (n 27) 303–09.

[102] Pursuant to FRCP 23(a), opening words.

[103] FCA 1976, ss 33C(1)(a), 33D(1).

[104] See, e.g.: A Conte and H Newberg, *Newberg on Class Actions* (4th edn, Thomson West Group, 2002), §3.34, 484–86.

[105] British Columbia's Class Proceedings Act, RSBC 1996, s 2(4); Newfoundland and Labrador's Class Actions Act 2001, s 3(4); Saskatchewan's Class Actions Act 2001, s 4(4); Manitoba's Class Proceedings Act 2002, s 2(4); Alberta's Class Proceedings Act 2003, s 2(4); New Brunswick's Class Proceedings Act 2011, s 3(5).

[106] *Cantlie v Canadian Heating Products Inc* [2017] BCSC 286, [364].

[107] *MacKinnon v Instaloans Financial Solution Centres (Kelowna) Ltd* [2004] BCCA 472, 33 BCLR (4th) 21, [47]. Note, e.g., the failure to appoint any such representative in: *Leonard v Manufacturers Life Ins Co* [2016] BCSC 534, [235]–[236].

Option 3: An ideological claimant may be the only party which is permitted by the regime to pursue a class action on the class's behalf. Directly affected class members are not permitted to sue. For example, the opt-in follow-on competition law class action enacted in the United Kingdom in 2013[108] only permitted the English Consumers' Association[109] to constitute the 'specified body'[110] required to commence proceedings on behalf of the class. Amid significant difficulties, limitations, and under-utilisation of the regime,[111] it was repealed and replaced by the present UK Competition Law Class Action in 2015.[112]

Option 4: The regime may permit both directly affected class members and ideological claimants to sue, but may ban certain types or descriptions of ideological claimants from so acting. This model was almost enacted for the UK Competition Law Class Action – one of the amendments proposed before the Public Bills Committee (Lords) was that '[a] person may not be authorised [to act as representative claimant] if they have a direct financial interest in the proceedings, other than as a claimant'[113] – but the provision was not, ultimately, enacted. Had it been so, it would have explicitly ruled out third-party funders as representative claimants, for example (although such an entity is likely to be forestalled from acting in that capacity in any event,[114] as the UK Government itself foreshadowed[115]).

Option 5: The regime may adopt a flexible 'either/or' approach to the use of a directly affected class member or an ideological claimant, permitting

---

[108] Per the CA 1998, s 47B, which was inserted by the Enterprise Act 2002, s 19 (in force 20 June 2003).

[109] Also called Which?.

[110] Pursuant to the Specified Body (Consumer Claims) Order 2005.

[111] Discussed in, e.g.: M Raja and P Lomas, 'A Lawyer's Perspective' in E Lein *et al.* (eds), *Collective Redress in Europe: Why and How?* (BIICL, 2015) 67–72; and Mulheron, 'The Case for an Opt-Out Class Action for European Member States: A Legal and Empirical Analysis' (2009) 15 *Columbia Journal of European Law* 409, 439–41, and the sources cited therein.

[112] Per the Consumer Rights Act 2015, Sch 8, which inserted new provisions in the CA 1998, in Pt 1, ch 4.

[113] 'Bill Documents', *Second Marshalled List of Amendments*, 11 March 2010 (Baroness Noakes).

[114] By virtue of the requirement that the Competition Appeal Tribunal must consider whether the representative claimant is 'a pre-existing body, and the nature and functions of that body': CAT Rules, r 78(3)(b).

[115] BIS, *Private Actions in Competition Law: Government Response* (January 2013) 26, Box 5, Recommendations (claims should not be brought by 'law firms, third party funders or special purpose vehicles').

either to act as representative claimant, 'if the [certifying court] considers that it is just and reasonable for that person to act as a representative in those proceedings'.[116] This was the option ultimately chosen for the UK Competition Law Class Action. Widening the capacity to sue in this way was driven, in that jurisdiction, by the political wish to enable trade and consumer associations – 'those who have a genuine interest in the case' – to act as representative claimants, as an alternative to directly affected class members.[117]

Hence, the drafting approaches are manifold. And if any government instrumentality wishes to act as an ideological claimant, the first enquiry is that it must be permissible under the relevant regime for it to do so.

2   Prerequisites for Representation

The circumstances in which an ideological claimant will be appointed have commonly required that the claimant prove some or all of the following (as shown in Table 6.2 overpage):[118]

Clearly, a government instrumentality will ordinarily be in a position to meet these criteria. However, there may be political reasons as to why the government may not wish to fund the class action; nor be perceived to take one action forward in comparison with other actions that it permits to languish; and may prefer that the action be funded by 'private' representative claimants. These matters, whilst predictable, are quite separate to the legal prerequisites noted above.

E   Conclusion

Any decision to take on the 'mantle' of the representative claimant – whether via legislative choice or by a choice on a case-by-case basis – carries with it political ramifications. As this chapter has demonstrated, the legal standing to do so can be less-than-straightforward, depending upon the statutory drafting used in the class actions regime. The analysis in this chapter gives rise to the following suggestions for reform, in order to cater for the governmental instrumentality as representative claimant:

---

[116] Per CA 1998, s 47B(8)(b); and CAT Rules, r 78(1)(b).

[117] *Private Actions in Competition Law* (n 115) [5.30], [5.32].

[118] This list is reproduced from: Mulheron, 'The United Kingdom's New Opt-Out Class Action' (n 101) 830.

Table 6.2 *The general prerequisites for the ideological claimant*

It is essential that the ideological claimant:

- does not have a direct financial interest in the proceedings;
- is willing to seek instructions from class members where required, and to keep class members informed of key developments in the action;
- is willing to fund, or to arrange funding, for own-side disbursements and fees, to arrange cover for the risk of adverse costs, should that be necessary (i.e., in a costs-shifting regime), and to provide security for costs where that is legitimately sought and awarded;
- has retained competent and experienced lawyers to represent the class;
- has adequately participated in the course of the litigation leading up to the certification hearing and/or fairness hearing at which any settlement agreement is scrutinised;
- has demonstrated a willingness to undertake evidence-gathering responsibilities on the class's behalf, and an ability to offer disclosure (or arrange relevant class members to provide disclosure) on matters having to do with the class;
- has no conflict of interest with the class members on the common issues;
- has demonstrated that, without its intervention, a class of vulnerable people would, or may, go unrepresented, because of a manifest unwillingness of any class member to prosecute the action;
- that it has been in existence for some time prior to the commencement of the class action, and was not formed merely for the purposes of that litigation;
- has demonstrated that it has sufficient knowledge of the history of the litigation to assist the class lawyers with the conduct of the litigation.

RECOMMENDATIONS: GOVERNMENT AS REPRESENTATIVE CLAIMANT

§ 6.1   Even where the class action regime requires that governmental entities must consent in order to be class members, the legislation may preferably specify (for the avoidance of any doubt) that the requisite consent is not required in order for the class action to have been validly commenced (i.e., that consent is assumed to have been given by the very act of commencing the class action on behalf of the class).

§ 6.2   There is no valid basis for incorporating a 'typicality requirement' in a class action; experience dictates that it does not add anything useful to the certification requirements of commonality, adequacy, and suitability.

§ 6.3   In order to avoid uncertainty and contentious litigation, it would be helpful for an opt-out class action statute to explicitly provide that:

    (1) different claims asserted among the class members do not preclude the commencement of a class action;

    (2) it is not necessary that at least one claim should be shared by the class members (including the representative claimant); and

    (3) a 'claim' includes, but should not be taken to be limited to, a 'cause of action'.

§ 6.4 A government instrumentality should not be automatically precluded from commencing a class action under an opt-out class action regime, where another representative action is available to that government instrumentality as the explicitly designated representative claimant. However, the former should only be permitted if it is superior to the latter.

§ 6.5 Whether or not an ideological claimant is permitted under the class actions regime should be explicitly stated, together with whether it should act:

    (1) exclusively and solely;

    (2) exceptionally;

    (3) as an alternative to a directly affected class member; or

    (3) not at all, because that particular type of ideological claimant is barred.

The appropriate drafting model will apply equally to a government instrumentality as to any other representative claimant.

§ 6.6 Whether the legislation should specify the prerequisites for assessing the suitability of an ideological claimant, and if so, a list of the particular prerequisites which should apply, should be explicitly considered by the legislature or rules-makers.

7

Government as Class Member

A   Introduction

The purpose of this chapter is to consider the scenario in which government is not the representative claimant, bringing suit on behalf of those who allege loss or damage arising from D's conduct, but rather, is a member of the class. Another party is filing the suit – but because of the width of the class definition, it is conceivable that government – and more specifically, government ministers, agencies, employees, and officers – are caught up within it.

The legislative approach to the scenario of how to handle government as a class member has differed across the Comparator Jurisdictions. None of the regimes has entirely excluded the government from involvement and membership in a class action. However, two legislative options have been evident, as shown in Figure 7.1 overpage.

Dealing with each option in turn:

B   Membership Only with Consent

1   Legislative Precedents

The relevant Australian federal provision, reproduced in the box overpage,[1] was repeated in the state opt-out regimes of Victoria,[2] New South Wales,[3] and Queensland.[4] It has also been suggested for the proposed opt-out class

---

[1] Federal Court of Australia Act 1976, Pt IVA, s 33E(2).
[2] Supreme Court Act 1986 (Vic), s 33E(2).
[3] Civil Procedure Act 2005 (NSW), s 159(2).
[4] Civil Proceedings Act 2011, s 103D(2). Oddly, the Queensland provision does not mention Ministers, body corporates, and officers, of *Territories*. This was pointed out in the Australian Lawyers' Alliance submission, but was apparently not taken account of:

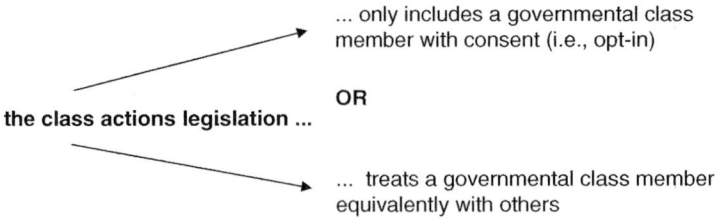

... only includes a governmental class
member with consent (i.e., opt-in)

OR

the class actions legislation ...

... treats a governmental class member
equivalently with others

Figure 7.1   The legislative options for dealing with government as a class member

action for the state of Tasmania.[5] These provisions have been little-cited, judicially speaking, but they are important:

---

s 33E(2) None of the following persons is a group member in a representative proceeding unless the person gives written consent to being so:

(a) the Commonwealth, a State or a Territory;

(b) a Minister or a Minister of a State or Territory;

(c) a body corporate established for a public purpose by a law of the Commonwealth, of a State or of a Territory, other than an incorporated company or association; or

(d) an officer of the Commonwealth, of a State or of a Territory, in his or her capacity as such an officer.

None of the persons specified in the abovementioned subsection ('the Excepted Persons') is a class member in an otherwise opt-out class action, unless that person gives a written mandate to be included. It is the **only** facet of the Australian federal regime which explicitly imposes an opt-in regime, albeit for a very specific group of persons.[6] By enacting section 33E(2) so as to deliberately exclude from the class 'the Commonwealth and State, as well as a number of persons and entities related to those bodies politic',[7] the federal and state legislatures followed the Australian Law Reform Commission's recommendation.[8]

Submission 18 (16 September 2016), 15, 17, available at: www.parliament.qld.gov.au/documents/committees/LACSC/2016/22-LimitationActions/submissions/018.pdf.

[5] See: Supreme Court Civil Procedure Amendment Bill 2018 (Bill 52/2018), cl 68(2), unenacted at the time of writing.

[6] Noted also in: V Morabito, 'Class Actions Instituted only for the Benefit of the Clients of the Class Representative's Solicitors' (2007) 29 *Sydney Law Review* 5, text accompanying fn 100.

[7] *Matthews v SPI Electricity Pty Ltd* [2012] VSC 549, [19].

[8] *Grouped Proceedings in the Federal Court* (Rep 46, 1988) [128] and cl 8(2) of the Draft Bill, App A.

A number of practicalities have been clarified, insofar as this opting-in provision is concerned. First, where one of those Excepted Persons is the representative claimant (rather than merely a class member), then the very act of filing suit is 'abundant evidence that the party is consenting to be a group member'.[9] No separate act of opting in is necessary. Secondly, the Australian federal regime requires that notice be provided to the court by the Excepted Persons via a designated opt-in form.[10] Thirdly, there is 'no temporal limitation' in section 33E(2), as to when consent can be given. Hence, it has been interpreted that 'the section is ambulatory, and intended to have application at any stage in the proceeding', so that an Excepted Person 'can give consent to being a group member at any point in time whilst the proceeding is on foot'.[11] Fourthly, it is impossible to compel or force the Excepted Persons to opt in and to become part of the class, should the defendant want to widen the class to encompass all possible claimants.[12] State entities, where they allege loss or damage, are entitled to 'remain outside the group and litigate independently', rather than opt in under section 33E(2). That is their choice.[13]

Whether or not a class member actually falls within one of the 'limited exceptions'[14] in section 33E(2) is a question of fact. This requires that both the role and status of that class member, and the capacity in which the class member is suing, be scrutinised.[15]

The federal provision has been applied to the Australian Competition and Consumer Commission (ACCC),[16] which is a body corporate within the meaning of section 33E(2)(c). That case clarified that it is not necessary for any entity mentioned in section 33E(2) ('such as a loss-suffering Commonwealth officer') to be claiming the same type of relief as the other class members. Different remedies as between class members, and as between class members and the representative claimant, are perfectly permissible; the legislation says so.[17] The provision also arose for consideration in *Community & Public Sector Union*

---

[9] *ACCC v Golden Sphere Intl Inc* (1998) 82 FCR 424, [24] (O'Loughlin J).

[10] Form 20, pursuant to Federal Court Rules, r 9.33; formerly Form 130, pursuant to Ord 73, r 4.

[11] *Matthews v SPI Electricity Pty Ltd* [2012] VSC 549, [7] (Forrest J).

[12] ibid, [19].

[13] ibid, [21].

[14] *Multiplex Funds Management Ltd v P Dawson Nominees Pty Ltd* [2007] FCAFC 200, 244 ALR 600, [56].

[15] *Community & Public Sector Union v Commonwealth of Australia* [1999] FCA 653, [64].

[16] *ACCC v Giraffe World Australia Pty Ltd* [1998] FCA 819, 156 ALR 273, 282 (Lindgren J).

[17] Pt IVA, s 33C(2)(a)(iv).

v Commonwealth of Australia[18] on a different point – *viz*, whether a group of Deputy Registrars of the Family Court were members of the class, *in their capacity as such officers* (for it is only then that their consent is required[19]). Those Deputy Registrars were officers of the Commonwealth (that had been clarified previously[20]) – but the question was whether they were claiming in their individual, rather than in their official, capacity. It was held that this claim was brought by them in their official capacity (it was not, 'for example, a consumer-related complaint' on their part[21]). Hence, they were required to opt in, in order to be bound by the outcome of the action.

One case in which section 33E(2) was not flagged up, but arguably could (and should) have been, was in the early Australian class action of *Gold Coast CC v Pioneer Concrete (Qld) Pty Ltd*.[22] This case involved an alleged cartel involving pre-mixed concrete during the period 1989–94. The victims were allegedly 'not only private sector contractors but the municipal governments of the Gold Coast [and others]'.[23] Indeed, Drummond J noted that the evidence before him suggested that 'a limited number of public bodies in addition to the applicant might be within the group definition: they are various Queensland government instrumentalities (such as Queensland Rail and the Queensland Department of Transport), the Tweed Shire Council, and the New South Wales Department of Main Roads'.[24] In fact, given that both the state of Queensland and Queensland Rail had already chosen to commence their own individual proceedings against the same four defendants for the same kind of damages that the Gold Coast City Council was claiming,[25] Drummond J considered that there was no evidence that any Queensland governmental instrumentality was willing to seek to recover damages through the vehicle of a class action. For this, and other reasons,[26] the class action was discontinued (albeit that the Council subsequently elected to continue its proceedings against the defendants for

---

[18] [1999] FCA 653.
[19] Per s 33D(2)(d).
[20] *Re Winton; ex p Jolliffe* (1997) 17 FCR 89, 93, 96, cited in *CPSU v Cth* [1999] FCA 653, [60].
[21] [1999] FCA 653, [65].
[22] (FCA, Drummond J, 9 July 1997).
[23] Noted in related proceedings: *Gold Coast CC v Pioneer Concrete (Qld) Pty Ltd* (1998) 99 LGERA 263 (FCA), accessed via LexisNexis, no pinpoint available.
[24] FCA, 9 July 1997, no pinpoint available.
[25] See: *Queensland v Pioneer Concrete (Qld) Pty Ltd* [1999] FCA 499.
[26] Nor was Drummond J convinced, e.g., that the minimum numerical threshold of seven class members was met.

its own benefit[27]). Drummond J also stated that, '[i]t is highly probable that the State of Queensland and Queensland Rail will opt out of the representative action, if it proceeds and an opt-out notice is published'.[28] However, it is suggested that, in light of section 33E(2), those instrumentalities would have to have opted in, had the action proceeded in class action form.

2 Justifications for the Requirement

Why include such a provision? At least three reasons have been suggested.

First, the *Explanatory Memorandum* which accompanied the Federal Court of Australia Amendment Bill 1991 stated that, '[t]he activities of Governments, government agencies, Ministers and officials may be subject to legislative and other restraints which make inappropriate, the inclusion of such persons in a representative proceeding without consent'.[29] In fact, this reproduces the reasoning of the Australian Law Reform Commission as to why these parties should be required to opt in.[30] However, it has been judicially said that the *Explanatory Memorandum* may have provided '*a* reason as to why the Federal Government felt it necessary to introduce the provision, [but] it does not purport to provide the *only* reason for such inclusion'.[31] What other reasons could there be, in support of an opt-in requirement for Government, its employees, and agencies?

Secondly, the Australian Law Reform Commission hinted at a second reason: that the proposed regime was 'intended to enhance access to legal remedies by private individuals who may otherwise be deterred by cost or other barriers from enforcing their legal rights'.[32] The implication is that government and its agencies and employees, when injured in their governmental capacities, may have other means of redress – e.g., a re-allocation of budget to either compensate the injured or to file suit; or legislative redress may be possible to compensate or to prevent future conduct from injuring the government and its agencies in a similar way.

---

[27] *Gold Coast City Council v Pioneer Concrete (Qld) Pty Ltd* [1998] FCA 791 (14 July 1998).

[28] FCA, 9 July 1997, no pinpoint available.

[29] Federal Court of Australia Amendment Bill 1991, *Explanatory Memorandum*, [14], available at: http://classic.austlii.edu.au/au/legis/cth/bill_em/fcoaab1991339/memo_0.html.

[30] *Grouped Proceedings in the Federal Court* (Rep 46, 1988) [128].

[31] *Community & Public Sector Union v Commonwealth of Australia* [1999] FCA 653, [64] (emphasis added).

[32] *Grouped Proceedings in the Federal Court* (Rep 46, 1988) [128].

These avenues are simply not available to private, non-governmental parties.

Thirdly, conflicts of interest on the part of government may manifest, should a government minister, agency, or corporation, be part of a class action without its/his/her express consent. Certainly, governments may be victims of wrongdoing. That much is evident, for example, from the alleged facts giving rise to the ultimately discontinued class action in *Gold Coast City Council v Pioneer Concrete (Qld) Pty Ltd*, discussed above.[33] However, where government is a class member, it is suggested that apparent or actual conflicts could arise in any one of four scenarios:

 (i) the defendant itself may be the government or a governmental agency, such that it could be a suit by government against government;
 (ii) it may be politically sensitive if government were seen to be benefitting, financially, from a suit filed and conducted by a private individual or entity;
(iii) it may be equally as sensitive, should a private entity be subject to a security for costs or other costs award against it, for which third-party funding (or other externally sourced funding) is required, from which the government could benefit; or
(iv) should the representative claimant lose the class action on the common issues, or reach a settlement which the government as class member considered was unsuitable, then it could be politically naive or impossible for the government either to object to the settlement or to legislate to reverse/amend the outcome.

These three reasons are powerful justifications for requiring government entities, officers, and employees, to be required to opt in to an otherwise opt-out class action.

3   What about Judges?

When Denning LJ stated that 'justice is best done by a judge who holds the balance between the contending parties without himself taking part in their disputation',[34] his Lordship was not speaking (in 1957) with class actions in mind (although the Australian Law Reform Commission subsequently quoted him precisely in that context[35]). More recently,

---

[33] (FCA, Drummond J, 9 July 1997).
[34] *Jones v National Coal Board* [1957] 2 QB 55 (CA) 56.
[35] *Access to the Courts II – Class Actions* (DP 11, 1979) [66].

Lord Mance has reiterated, extra-curially, that, 'a judge must also be both honest and incorruptible and independent of the parties and issues before him'.[36]

These sentiments are particularly apposite, when appreciating that a judge can feasibly be caught up in the membership of a class action in which that judge is adjudicating. After all, judges may buy goods and services which are defective, or which are the subject of price-fixing too. One can imagine such membership occurring even without realisation!

For example, in the second case to be filed under the UK Competition Law Class Action – that of *Merricks v Mastercard Inc*[37] – the Competition Appeal Tribunal (CAT) noted that any members who were assigned to hear the certification application must be excluded, given that those members fell within the class definition of potential price-fixed victims of interchange fees.[38] This direction that the tribunal members be excluded was done (said the CAT) 'to avoid the appearance of any conflict of interest'.[39] *Merricks* demonstrates that consumer class actions have the real potential to sweep judges in as part of the class.

It is suggested that the better tack is for the lawmakers to address the role of judges in opt-out class actions, and some experiences garnered from the Australian jurisdiction are of interest in that regard.

(a)   The Australian Federal Regime

Notably, judges are not referred to explicitly within the Australian federal regime, in section 33E(2), as Excepted Persons. Quite how those parties are to be treated under this provision of the federal class actions legislation is not entirely clear, but it **is** plain that judges 'are not public servants, and are not subject to supervision and control by the executive'.[40] Nevertheless, the pertinent question, for current purposes, is whether

---

[36] Lord Mance, 'The Role of Judges in a Representative Democracy' (Lecture given during the Judicial Committee of the Privy Council's Fourth Sitting in The Bahamas, 24 February 2017) [10], available at: www.supremecourt.uk/docs/speech-170224.pdf.

[37] [2019] EWCA Civ 674, overruling the refusal to certify: [2017] CAT 16.

[38] This was ordered at a preliminary directions hearing: *Merricks v Mastercard Inc* (CAT, President Roth J, 21 November 2017), and confirmed at the certification hearing: *Merricks v Mastercard Inc* [2017] CAT 16, [6]. The experts appearing for each of the representative claimant and the defendant were also excluded by the order.

[39] ibid, [6]. There was no similar self-exclusion evident in the subsequent appellate judgments in which permission to appeal was allowed: [2018] EWCA Civ 2527, and in which the appeal was allowed, thereby overturning the CAT's refusal to certify the action as a collective proceeding: [2019] EWCA Civ 674.

[40] P Nygh (ed), *Concise Australian Legal Dictionary* (Butterworths, 1997) 223.

they are 'officers of the Commonwealth, State or Territory'?[41] That phrase is not defined in the Federal Court of Australia Act 1976.[42]

If they are not 'officers', then they are not Excepted Persons. Hence, if they are to be excluded from a class action in which they would otherwise be included, then they must be expressly excluded from the action under the class definition; or otherwise they must opt out, just as with any other class member who does not wish to be bound by the outcome of the action.[43] It has been academically suggested[44] that, as section 33E(2) does **not** cover judges, then consideration should be given to excluding those parties from the class definition, at least wherever the represented group could feasibly cover those judges who could potentially hear the class action.

That tactic has indeed occurred in Australian federal jurisprudence,[45] where the class included 'domestic users' of gas supplies in Victoria who had suffered loss and damage arising from the interruption of gas supplies as a result of an explosion and fire which occurred at Esso's Longford Gas Plant in Victoria in 1998.[46] In that litigation, the class was said to exclude '[a]ny person who is a judge of the Federal Court of Australia or the High Court of Australia'.[47] A further argument in support of the view that judges are not 'officers of the Commonwealth, State or Territory for the purposes of section 33E(2) is that one Australian state regime (that of Victoria) includes judges in the list of Excepted Persons explicitly (as discussed below[48]), suggesting that its legislature did not consider judges to be otherwise covered by that list.

---

[41] i.e., whether they fall within the terms of s 33E(2)(d).

[42] The phrase appears neither in s 33A, the interpretative provision for the class actions regime in Pt IVA, nor in s 4, the interpretative provision for the Act as a whole.

[43] Per FCA 1976, Pt IVA, s 33E(1).

[44] D Grave, K Adams and J Betts, *Class Actions in Australia* (2nd edn, Lawbook Co, 2012) [7.235].

[45] *Johnson Tiles Pty Ltd v Esso Aust Ltd* [2000] FCA 1572. See too, e.g.: *Wright Rubber Pty Ltd v Bayer AG (No 3)* [2011] FCA 1172 (as outlined in the Notice of Settlement reproduced in the judgment, whereby the class definition excluded 'Justices or Registrars of the High Court of Australia or the Federal Court of Australia'); *Darwalla Milling Co Pty Ltd v F Hoffman La Roche Ltd (No 2)* [2006] FCA 1388, [5] (same exclusion).

[46] This action was brought under the federal class action contained in Pt IVA. Hence, the differently worded provision in Victoria's state opt-out regime could not be relied upon in this litigation.

[47] [2000] FCA 1572, [16].

[48] Section (b).

On the other hand, some judicial and academic opinion supports the notion that judges **are** 'officers' of the Commonwealth or State or Territory, depending upon which Government appointed them. If this is also true for the purposes of section 33E(2), then judges are Excepted Persons and could only be bound by an Australian class action (whether federal or state) if they opted into it. The High Court of Australia decreed, in *R v Commonwealth Court of Conciliation & Arbitration; ex parte Brisbane Tramways Co Ltd*,[49] that where the phrase appears in section 75(v) of the Australian Constitution, then it 'naturally and properly include[s] both judicial and non-judicial officers'.[50] Justice Isaacs put it thus: 'a Judge holds an office, and when directly appointed by the Commonwealth, and accepting his office and salary from and removable by the Commonwealth, he is an officer of the Commonwealth'.[51] This provision in the Constitution was interpreted in the context of enabling the High Court, by virtue of its original jurisdiction under section 75(v), to review the decision of any justice of a federal court or a family court,[52] all of which is a world away from the meaning of the phrase in section 33E(2).

Academic scholarly opinion has also considered the phrase to have a wide meaning. Some have noted that '[a]n "officer" connotes an "office" of some conceivable tenure, and connotes an appointment, and usually a salary'.[53] As a result, state judges 'are State officers, namely, Judges of the State'.[54]

Similarly, the Australian Law Reform Commission has opined that the term, 'officer of the Commonwealth' has 'generally [been] regarded as having a wide meaning, such as "a person who is appointed by the Commonwealth to carry out a Commonwealth function or purpose"'.[55] Of course, where a judge is a member of the class by virtue solely of his or her *private capacity* (e.g., as a consumer who suffered loss or damage by reason of the defendant's

---

[49] (1913) 18 CLR 54 (HCA). Earlier: *R v Commonwealth Court of Conciliation and Arbitration; ex parte Whybrow & Co* (1910) 11 CLR 1 (HCA).

[50] Thus, in that case, it included the President of the Commonwealth Court of Conciliation and Arbitration.

[51] (1913) 18 CLR 54 (HCA) 79.

[52] Per: *Edwards v Santos Ltd* (2011) 242 CLR 421 (HCA).

[53] See: J Boughey and G Weeks, '"Officers of the Commonwealth" in the Private Sector: Can the High Court Review Outsourced Exercises of Power?' (2013) 36 *UNSW Law Journal* 316, text accompanying fn 54.

[54] ibid. However, state judges are not 'officers of the Commonwealth' when exercising federal jurisdiction: The Hon James Allsop, *An Introduction to the Jurisdiction of the Federal Court of Australia* (Federal Judicial Scholarship, 1 October 2007), available at: www.fedcourt.gov.au /digital-law-library/judges-speeches/chief-justice-allsop/allsop-cj-200710.

[55] *The Judicial Power of the Commonwealth* (Rep 92, 2001) [7.60] (internal citations omitted).

conduct), then section 33E(2) would not 'bite' regardless, and the judge would be a member of the class unless he/she opted out.

(b)   Other Options

It is decidedly odd that inadvertent class membership on the part of judges could occur under Australia's federal legislation, given the steps that had diligently been taken by the Commonwealth legislature to seek to avoid embarrassing conflicts of interest on the part of other Excepted Persons. Notably, this oddity has been rectified by the Victorian legislature. In addition to the Excepted Persons listed by the federal legislature (and reproduced previously[56]), the following clause was added in Victoria's relevant provision:[57]

---

s 33E(2)   None of the following persons is a group member unless the person gives consent in writing to being so—

    . . .

    (d)   any judge, magistrate or other judicial officer of the Commonwealth, a State or a Territory;

However, the subsequently enacted Australian state opt-out regimes,[58] including the most recently proposed regime in Tasmania,[59] do not replicate that provision. That omission is a mistake, in this author's view. For the avoidance of potential embarrassment, inconvenience and uncertainty, judges should be explicitly excluded from the ambit of any class action, unless they choose to affirmatively opt in to that action.

Indeed, for the removal of all doubt, the list of those who are not class members in the Queensland Floods class action (which is presently being litigated before the New South Wales Supreme Court under that state's class action regime) provides a useful categorisation of suggested 'Excepted Persons' for legislative drafting purposes:

> The following persons are not Group Members for the purposes of this proceeding:

---

[56]   See p 250.

[57]   This provision was inserted in the Supreme Court Act 1986 (Vic) in 2000, by the Courts and Tribunals Legislation (Miscellaneous Amendments) Act 2000, s 13.

[58]   e.g., Queensland's Civil Proceedings Act 2011, s 103D(2), enacted in 2016, and inserted by the Limitation of Actions (Child Sexual Abuse) and Other Legislation Amendment Act 2016, s 10; and New South Wales' Civil Procedure Act 2005, s 159(2).

[59]   Supreme Court Civil Procedure Amendment Bill 2018, s 68(2).

a) the Commonwealth, or any agency or instrumentality thereof;
b) the States or Territories, or any agency or instrumentality thereof;
c) a Minister of the Commonwealth, a State or Territories; or
d) any judicial officer of the Commonwealth, State or Territories.[60]

To reiterate, it should always be open to any individual from this list to opt in to the class action if that individual is suing in a purely private, rather than official, capacity.

C   The No-Differentiation Model

The majority of class actions statutes in the Comparator Jurisdictions do not treat government, agencies, employees or officers any differently from other class members.

Ontario's Class Proceedings Act 1992[61] (and some other Canadian class actions statutes[62]) provides that:

s 36 This Act binds the Crown.

In its preceding report, the Ontario Law Reform Commission considered that the Crown should be subject to the same rules as was the ordinary citizen, hence the enactment of the abovementioned clause.[63] There was no specific discussion in that report[64] (or, indeed, in other notable law reform reports[65]) about government as a class member.

Interestingly, the inclusion of a government as class member has been mooted in Canadian class actions jurisprudence without adverse

---

[60] As contained in the Statement of Claim for *Rodriguez & Sons Pty Ltd v Queensland Bulk Water Supply Authy* filed in the NSW Supreme Court registry on 8 July 2014, at [7], and available for perusal at: www.supremecourt.justice.nsw.gov.au/Documents/Class%20Actions/Queensland%20Floods/qld_floods_statementofclaim_080714.pdf/.

[61] SO 1992, c 6.

[62] New Brunswick's Class Proceedings Act, RSNB 2011, c 125, s 2(1); Manitoba's Class Proceedings Act, CCSM c C130, s 43; Newfoundland and Labrador's Class Actions Act, SNL 2001, c C-18.1, s 42.

[63] *Report on Class Actions* (1982) 845–46, and cl 54 of the Draft Bill.

[64] Nor did that entity feature in the discussion of opt-in versus opt–out: ibid, 478–91.

[65] Government as class member did not feature, e.g., in: Alberta Law Reform Institute, *Class Actions* (Rep 85, 2000); or in Manitoba LRC, *Class Proceedings* (Rep 100, 1999). The case discussed in the following footnote was cited in the recent Consultation Paper published by the Ontario LRC, but without reference to the fact that the Province of British Columbia was a class member: *Class Actions: Objectives, Experiences and Reforms* (CP, March 2018), fn 245.

comment. In *Burnett v St Jude Medical Inc*,[66] the Province of British Columbia was originally within the class definition (in respect of a class action against the defendants in connection with the research, development, design, testing, manufacture and release of allegedly defective Silzone-coated heart valves). The representative claimant then amended the claim to delete the Crown's possible claim in connection with health care costs related to the allegedly defective valve. The Province brought an application that it be reinstated as a class member.[67] That application failed, but not because the government could not be a class member under the British Columbia class actions statute. Rather, 'there is no real prejudice if the Province decides to advance its possible subrogated claims by way of a separate action'.[68]

D   Conclusion

The consequence of judges, government, and its associated entities and agencies being inadvertently included in a class action giving rise to compensation, or where a class action fails on the common issues, could give rise to difficult political and judicial sensitivities. Both the Australian gas supplies case and the *Merricks* litigation in the United Kingdom clearly demonstrate that, in consumer actions, there is the very real possibility of judges being included in the class action by virtue of their falling within the class definition, unless that definition expressly excluded them. To avoid any doubt on the issue, and to preclude any need to frame class definitions in particular actions accordingly, the Victorian regime is by far the preferable provision by which to achieve the opt-in requirement for government, for its associated entities and bodies politic, and judiciary.

RECOMMENDATIONS: GOVERNMENT AS A CLASS MEMBER

§ 7.1   Government, government ministers, government agencies and body corporates, and government employees, should have to opt in to any opt-out class action, in order to be bound by the outcome.

---

[66] [2008] BCSC 148.
[67] Noted ibid, [3].
[68] ibid, [79]. In fact, the Province then commenced its own class action, on 14 March 2008, 'seeking recovery of past and future health care costs in relation to all BC residents that received Silzone-coated implants manufactured by the defendants', as noted in: *Burnett v St Jude Medical Inc* [2009] BCSC 82, [16].

§ 7.2 Judges should also be included in the statutory list of those who must opt in to any opt-out class action, in order to ensure that any judge who may potentially hear a class action is not inadvertently included in the very case over which the judge is presiding.

§ 7.3 A statutory opt-in provision would be preferable to relying on a case-by-case exclusion of the parties referred to in §§ 7.1 and 7.2 from the relevant class definition.

8

Government as Class Actions Defendant

A   Introduction

As one senior judge succinctly put it, '[c]itizens blame governments for many kinds of misfortune'.[1] Two reasons account for this: first, governments at all levels – federal, state/provincial, and local/band – have an intrinsic and intricate involvement in the day-to-day life of citizens and businesses; and secondly, they are typically deep-pocketed defendants who are attractive litigation targets.[2] In fact, a cursory examination of class actions instituted against the Crown, as represented by federal, state, or provincial governments, reveals a remarkable array of subject matters, causes of action, and grievances. The complexity and sensitivity of some of the suits discussed in this chapter are remarkable,[3] and have raised

---

[1]   *Graham Barclay Oysters Pty Ltd v Ryan* [2002] HCA 54, 211 CLR 540, [6] (Gleeson CJ).

[2]   For similar comment, see, e.g.: L Sossin, 'Revisiting Class Actions Against the Crown: Balancing Public and Private Legal Accountability for Government Action', in J Kalajdzic (ed), *Accessing Justice: Appraising Class Actions Ten Years After Dutton, Hollick & Rumley* (LexisNexis, 2011), ch 3, 33, as cited in: LRC of Ontario, *Class Actions: Objectives, Experiences and Reforms* (CP, March 2018) 43.

[3]   e.g., the case of *William v British Columbia* [2012] BCCA 285, [2012] 10 WWR 639, 33 BCLR (5th) 260, [24]–[27], was striking: '[t]he trial commenced in November 2002 and occupied 339 court days over a span of nearly five years. Twenty-four Tsilhqot'in witnesses testified, and five additional Tsilhqot'in witnesses provided evidence by affidavit. The parties adduced expert evidence from a wide range of disciplines including anthropology, archaeology, cartography and biology. A very large number of historical documents were entered as exhibits. ... This was very complex and difficult litigation. A great deal was at stake ... for Aboriginal title and rights claims ... The trial was a massive undertaking for the parties, their counsel, and for the trial judge. Mr Justice Vickers was the presiding judge. He retired after giving the judgment, and, sadly, passed away shortly thereafter. One is struck, in reading the transcript of the proceedings, by the incredible patience and conscientiousness shown by the trial judge.'

several unusual and difficult issues[4] – although it must be stated, at the outset, that many of the suits have not survived the 'cause of action' threshold test at certification, or have otherwise been either struck out or the subject of summary dismissal on the application of the governmental defendant.

Whether litigation is instituted against the Crown via either unitary or class action, it is necessary that such a suit is permissible and is not subject to any immunity conferred on the Crown in respect of the conduct for which it is being sued. A short summary of the law concerning proceedings against the Crown is contained in Section C.

Thereafter, Section D sets out the types of scenarios in which governments have been sued as class action defendant in the Comparator Jurisdictions of Australia and Canada. Those two have been selected because they offer more comparative lessons for common law jurisdictions than does the United States. This is primarily because of the different (statute-specific) causes of action that are typically pleaded in, and which commonly underpin, class actions in the United States. As the Ontario Law Reform Commission noted[5] many years ago, 'the vast majority of class suits [in relation to actions in the federal courts] are based upon statutory causes of action, either express or implied'; and additionally, US courts are far more willing to hold that a contravention of a statutory provision gives rise to a civil cause of action for breach of statutory duty than are courts in English and Commonwealth jurisdictions (where severe restrictions tend to apply to that cause of action[6]).

---

[4] See, e.g., *Richard v British Columbia* [2008] BCCA 53, 290 DLR (4th) 336, [24] ('[t]his proceeding has raised some unusual and difficult legal issues as it has unfolded, and seeking the assistance of the court, including the appeal process, is entirely consistent with the jurisprudence').

[5] *Report on Class Actions* (1982) 214–19 (quote at 215).

[6] Canadian law does not recognise a nominate tort of breach of statutory duty: *Wu v Vancouver (City)* [2019] BCCA 23, [43], citing: *Canada v Saskatchewan Wheat Pool C* [1983] 1 SCR 205 (SCC) 227, which confirmed that there is no separate or independent tort of breach of statutory duty in that jurisdiction; the proper remedy for breach of statutory duty by a public authority, traditionally viewed, is judicial review for invalidity; and that whilst Canadian law does not recognise an action for 'negligent breach of statutory duty', the civil consequences for a breach of statute are subsumed in the law of negligence if the common law principles which establish a private law duty of care can be established (see also: *Canada (AG) v TeleZone Inc* [2010] 3 SCR 585, [2010] SCC 62, [28]–[29]; and *Cimaco Intl Sales Inc v British Columbia (AG)* [2010] BCCA 342, [56]). English law circumscribes the availability of the cause of action for breach of statutory duty by insisting, inter alia, that: Parliament intended to confer a private law right of action for damages if the statutory duty or obligation imposed upon the defendant was breached; the statute was enacted for the benefit of a particular class of persons of whom the claimant

... for vicarious liability

OR

... for direct systemic wrongdoing

OR

**the Crown may be sued as a defendant
under one or more bases of liability ...**

... for breach of a non-delegable duty of care

OR

... as a principal for an agent's misconduct

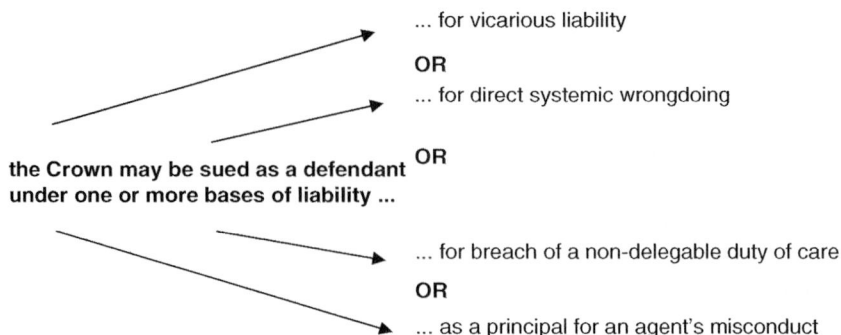

Figure 8.1   Government as a defendant under a class action regime

The chapter then examines, in Section E, the theories of liability for which governments have typically been sued in class action litigation. These are illustrated in Figure 8.1 above.

Some interesting and novel claims have been instituted against governments in both Comparator Jurisdictions, and samples of tort claims are also outlined in that final section by way of illustration.

However, first, it is apposite to consider, in Section B, the ramifications of sectoral-versus-generic reform, from a governmental perspective.

B   Sectoral versus Generic Class Action Reform

1   The Most Common Enactments

It almost goes without saying – but it must be said – that the major difference between a sectoral and a generic opt-out class action regime is that the latter type poses significant risk to a government of its being sued itself under the very legislation which it (or a predecessor government) promulgated. The former practically never does. Politically speaking, it is important that no conflict of interest arises on this basis, so as to prevent the implementation of a generic scheme – and, as this chapter demonstrates, that conflict may be more real than merely suggestive. Dissuading an impression of that conflict of interest, by transparent reasoning and law reform explanation, is an important part of law reform in this area.

---

was one; and the relevant loss was of a kind which the statute protected the claimant against: *X (Minors) v Bedfordshire CC* [1995] 2 AC 633 (HL) 731–32. This 'difficult and controversial area of law' (per *Todd v Adams* [2002] EWCA Civ 509, [32]) is discussed further by the author in: *Principles of Tort Law* (Cambridge University Press, 2016), chapter 5D.

The Australian, Canadian, and US opt-out class actions the focus of this book are, and were always intended to be, generic. They were intended to cater for **any** cause of action which properly arose within the court's subject matter jurisdiction and personal jurisdiction, and which did not otherwise fall foul of legislative exclusions of jurisdiction.[7] Those relevant legislatures promulgated the policy of facilitating access to legal redress and of promoting judicial efficiency – and chose not to differentiate between sectors of the economy, the nature of the activities out of which the grievance arose, the types of claimant, or the category of defendant.

Law reform opinion has been very alive to the 'dangers' that generic regimes pose to government, and to the benefits that such regimes provide to citizens and businesses with a grievance against government. For example, the Australian Law Reform Commission remarked: '[t]he activities which could give rise to a multiple claim may be undertaken by government or private individuals. ... The respondent to grouped proceedings could be the Commonwealth government or its agencies.'[8] The government of the day was under no illusions when it enacted Pt IVA in 1992: and indeed, within five years of the enactment, that anticipation became a reality. Class suits were instituted against the governments of Queensland and New South Wales in respect of the approval and registration of an insecticide used on cotton;[9] and against a local government authority and the New South Wales government in respect of the contamination of oyster farms.[10] The Manitoba Law Reform Commission also noted[11] that many class actions claims litigated against government

---

[7] e.g., under Australia's federal regime in the FCA 1976, s 33G prohibits the commencement of a class action if it would be concerned only with the claims in respect of which the Federal Court has jurisdiction solely by virtue of the Jurisdiction of Courts (Cross-Vesting) Act 1987 (Cth) or state law equivalent. The famous native title case of *Wik Peoples v Queensland* [1994] FCA 967, (1994) 120 ALR 465, was one such case; and hence, any reliance upon Pt IVA was 'expressly disclaimed' by the aboriginal claimants for that reason (at [24]).

[8] *Grouped Proceedings in the Federal Court* (Rep 46, 1988) [325].

[9] *McMullin v ICI* [1996] FCA 1511, [72] (in addition to an action against its manufacturers and distributors), although the claims against the governments were eventually dismissed: [1997] FCA 541.

[10] *Graham Barclay Oysters Pty Ltd v Ryan* [2002] HCA 54, (2002) 211 CLR 540, although the claims against the local authority and the state were ultimately dismissed. Neither owed a duty of care to a consumer in negligence; and no action lay by statute. The action was also commenced against the relevant oyster growers and distributors.

[11] *Class Proceedings* (Rep 100, 1999) 20–21, citing, e.g., cases arising from: contaminated blood; prison riots; and abuses and discriminatory policies arising in Aboriginal residential schools.

in Canada prior to that report 'would not [have] come within the specific narrow categories of the representative order rule'.[12] This (said the Commission) emphasised the need to accommodate the governmental defendant under the proposed class action in Manitoba. Most recently, the Law Reform Commission of Ontario has stated that:

> Class action lawsuits often involve thousands – if not hundreds of thousands – of potential litigants and millions – if not billions – of dollars in compensation. They can result in huge awards and have a significant impact on the general public, corporate, *or government behavior and reputations*, public policy, and the justice system. It is fair to describe class actions as one of the most high-profile and far-reaching legal procedures in the Canadian justice system. ... Class actions have systemic implications for access to justice, court procedures and efficiency, and *government ... liability.*[13]

One of the 'founding fathers' of the Australian federal opt-out regime has also noted that one of the objectives of class actions reform is to hold governments to account for illegal or improper behaviour.[14] Consistently with this, one leading Australian academic scholar has noted that, over the course of the regime, '[t]he favourite "targets" of plaintiff lawyers have included banks; and *governments and their various agencies, instrumentalities and entities*',[15] and that many of the claims against government (whether state or federal) have been instituted by those who are disadvantaged, whether socially, economically, intellectually, or psychologically.[16] It is a powerful motivator for enacting a generic regime – but it is not an approach that has found favour elsewhere.

2   The Experience of the United Kingdom

The UK Competition Law Class Action enacted in 2015 was at the other end of the spectrum from the Australian and Canadian regimes. Whereas the Civil Justice Council (CJC) had recommended, in 2008, that a generic class

---

[12] ibid, 10.

[13] *Class Actions: Objectives, Experiences and Reforms* (CP, March 2018) 2 (emphasis added).

[14] The Hon Justice Ronald Sackville, 'Law and Poverty: A Paradox' (2018) 41 *UNSW Law Journal* 80, 92, and cited in: ALRC, *Integrity, Fairness and Efficiency: An Inquiry into Class Action Proceedings and Third-Party Litigation Funders* (Rep 134, December 2018) [9.89].

[15] V Morabito, 'Lessons from Australia on Class Action Reform in New Zealand' (2018) 24 *NZ Business Law Quarterly* 178, 183 (footnotes omitted) (emphasis added).

[16] The various categories are discussed, by reference to case law, in: V Morabito and J Ekstein, 'Class Actions Filed for the Benefit of Vulnerable Persons: An Australian Study' (2016) 35 *Civil Justice Quarterly* 61.

action, of an opt-in or an opt-out nature (depending upon judicial discretion), be introduced,[17] what eventuated was *sectoral* reform – permitting follow-on or stand-alone *competition law* claims only.

As described in an earlier chapter,[18] this political decision represented a significant divergence as between the preceding reform recommendation and the enactment in the Consumer Rights Act 2015. (In fact, the sectoral regime also contravened the European Commission's recommendation that compensatory collective redress should be 'applied horizontally and equally', i.e., generically.[19]) The CJC had based its preference for generic reform upon four key reasons.[20] These consisted of the following: the evidence showed that there were unredressed grievances across a range of sectors (e.g., competition law, financial and banking services, employment, consumer transactions, and the pharmaceutical and medical sector);[21] the generic regime would not preclude a sectoral regime, where appropriate;[22] the clear view expressed during consultation by participants (including the judiciary) was that generic reform was preferable;[23] and there were already examples of generic multiparty regimes in England and Wales, *viz*, the representative rule[24] and the group litigation order,[25] and hence, it was a wide-standing approach which had already been adopted in English civil procedure.

---

[17] CJC, *Improving Access to Justice through Collective Actions: Final Report* (November 2008), Recommendation 3, at p 5.

[18] See Chapter 3, 'Government as Class Actions Designer', Section C(1).

[19] See: EC, *Recommendation on Common Principles for Injunctive and Compensatory Collective Redress Mechanisms in the Member States Concerning Violations of Rights Granted under Union Law* (EC, 2013/396/EU, OJ 2013 No L201/60), Recital 7, L201/60, and Articles 1–2, 'Purpose and Subject Matter', L201/62. This aspect of the EC's Recommendation was discussed in detail by the author in: 'A Channel Apart: Why the United Kingdom has Departed from the European Commission's Recommendation on Class Actions' (2015) 17 *Cambridge Yearbook of European Legal Studies* 36.

[20] CJC, *Improving Access to Justice: Final Report* (2008) (n 17) Recommendation 1, p 21, and 137–40.

[21] This was primarily based upon the 'evidence of need' study conducted by the author, *Reform of Collective Redress in England and Wales: A Perspective of Need* (2008), citing, e.g. OFT, *Unfair Contract Terms Guidance: Consultation on Revised Guidance for the Unfair Terms in Consumer Contract Regulations 1999* (OFT311, 2007), and the response of the Citizens' Advice Bureau (CAB), *Unfair Contract Terms Guidance: Response* (2007), plus a variety of other sources.

[22] Indeed, the CJC recommended that the competition law sector or the employment sector may provide a suitable exemplar regime: *Improving Access to Justice: Final Report* (2008) (n 17) Recommendation 1, p 5.

[23] ibid, 139.

[24] Contained in: CPR 19.6.

[25] Contained in: CPR 19.10–19.15.

However, in its formal response to the CJC's recommendations,[26] the
Ministry of Justice (MOJ) accepted that there was a place for class actions
brought on an opt-out basis – but it categorically rejected the generic
approach. Instead, 'the Government considers that the only practical way
forward is on a sector by sector basis'.[27] The pathway of sectoral reform
in the UK was firmly set thereafter, culminating in the regime for
competition law grievances implemented in 2015.

It is almost unthinkable that government, in any of its national or local
authority guises, will be sued under the UK Competition Law Class
Action. Governments do not tend to engage in, nor authorise, anti-
competitive conduct! Although (naturally) the MOJ did not allude to
any concerns about the prospect of the UK government being sued as
a reason for rejecting the generic approach, there is no doubt that the
caution exhibited by the UK legislature has effectively precluded any
governmental fault from being prosecuted on an opt-out basis to date.

This is important, given relatively recent *opt-in* group litigation orders
(GLOs) which have been brought against the government, its officers, or
its agencies. For example, GLOs have been authorised (certified) in
relation to: claims against the government-run post office for alleged
accountancy flaws in the post office's computer system;[28] claims against
the South Yorkshire Police and the West Midlands Police, alleging that
the police sought to deliberately conceal the true circumstances of the
Hillsborough tragedy in order to deflect blame from themselves for the
deaths and injuries suffered as a result of that tragedy;[29] and claims
against Her Majesty's Revenue and Customs Service for taxes levied on
pension scheme contributions.[30] All of this litigation must be conducted
on opt-in principles, as the GLO regime countenances nothing else.[31]

Hence, there is no opt-out formation of the class (or aggregate assessment of damages on a class-wide basis) possible against the UK
Government or its agencies, either presently, or in the foreseeable future.

---

[26] MOJ, *The Government's Response to the Civil Justice Council's Report: Improving Access to
Justice through Collective Actions* (July 2009).
[27] ibid, [12].
[28] GLO #97, 'The Post Office Group Litigation' (26 January 2017).
[29] GLO #96, 'The Hillsborough Victims Litigation' (23 January 2017).
[30] GLO #90, 'The Recognised Overseas Self Invested International Pensions Group
Litigation' (22 June 2012).
[31] Per CPR 19.11(2)(a), re the establishment of a 'group register'; and Practice Direction
19B, s 6.1A, whereby a claim must be issued before it can be entered upon the group
register.

The contrast with the generic regimes operative in the other Comparator Jurisdictions is stark.

C   Proceedings against the Crown

1   Retreating from Crown Immunity

Historically, the royal prerogative of perfection (encapsulated in the common law maxim, 'the King can do no wrong') meant that the sovereign personally, and the Crown (where prerogative acts were performed by the government on behalf of the Crown), had complete immunity from all civil and criminal proceedings at common law.[32] For the purposes of the immunity, the 'Crown' included governments, government departments, and all other public bodies that were agencies of the Crown,[33] as well as the agents or employees of the Crown.[34]

The ambit and nature of Crown immunity, and the background to its general revocation, lie outside the scope of this chapter.[35] However, suffice to quote, for present purposes, varying scholarly views of what underpinned the Crown's immunity: that '[b]eing himself the first source and the fountain of justice, the Sovereign could not, indeed, be arraigned before his own courts. Consequently, no court of justice had the power to compel him to appear before it';[36] or that 'the Crown was generally

---

[32] E Martin and J Law (eds), *Oxford Dictionary of Law* (6th edn, Oxford University Press, 2006) 473–74.

[33] See, e.g.: *Feather v The Queen* (1865) 122 All ER 1191 (CA) ('the maxim that the King can do no wrong applies to personal as well as to political wrongs; and not only to wrongs done personally by the Sovereign, if such a thing can be supposed to be possible, but to injuries done by a subject by the authority of the Sovereign'), as cited in: J Allen, 'The Office of the Crown' (2018) 77 *Cambridge Law Journal* 298, fn 75. Also: *Oxford Dictionary of Law*, ibid, 143.

[34] See, e.g., the discussion in: *Kemmy v Ireland* [2009] IEHC 178.

[35] This topic is covered in substantial detail in the following, e.g.: A Bradley, K Ewing and C Knight, *Constitutional and Administrative Law* (17th edn, Pearson, 2018) 735–44; T Arvind, 'Restraining the State Through Tort? The Crown Proceedings Act in Retrospect', in T Arvind and J Steele (eds), *Tort Law and the Legislature* (Hart Publishing, 2013), ch 19; A Tettenborn and R Blackburn, *Halsbury's Law of England: Crown and Crown Proceedings*, vol 29 (5th edn, LexisNexis, 2014); and for short summaries, see: Office of Parliamentary Counsel, *Crown Application* (HMSO, 14 February 2018) [3.10]–[3.11]; and J Alder and K Syrett, *Constitutional and Administrative Law* (11th edn, Palgrave Master Series, 2017) 340–41.

[36] JL Baudouin, P Deslauriers and B Moore, *La Responsabilité Civile* (8th edn, Yvon Blais, 2014), vol 1, [1–127], 108, as cited in: *Canada (AG) v Thouin* [2015] QCCA 2159. See too: *Lord Bamff v The Laird of Rosa-Solis* [1677] 3 Brn 127, 128 ('[b]y the law of England, the

considered to be subject to the law, as consonant with principles of justice. Procedural particularities did however severely thwart opportunities for redress. One of the King's prerogatives was that he could not be sued in the central courts, in the same way that a feudal lord could not be sued in his own court.'[37] As Lord Bingham once said, '[f]ew common law rules were better-established or more unqualified than that which precluded any claim in tort against the Crown'.[38] The maxim that 'the King can do no wrong' may have actually meant that the King was not privileged to commit illegal acts, but 'it came to be understood to be a rule barring actions in tort against the Crown'.[39]

The scenario was not entirely hopeless, for certain actions (for breach of contract or for the recovery of property) came to be possible to commence against the Crown by means of a petition of right. This was a 'special process',[40] which dated from either the thirteenth[41] or the fourteenth century,[42] by which a citizen had to petition the King for permission to sue him, and where an action could proceed only if the King signified his consent by endorsing the petition *fiat justitae*, translated as 'let right be done'. There was no right of appeal against the King's refusal of consent either.[43] That process eventually became

---

King can do no wrong; that is one of their maxims; and therefore he cannot be pursued in any court').

[37] M Andenas and D Fairgrieve, 'Reforming Crown Immunity – The Comparative Law Perspective' [2003] *Public Law* 730, 732–33, citing: W Holdsworth, *A History of English Law* (3rd edn, Methuen, 1923), vol 3, 465.

[38] *Matthews v MOD* [2003] UKHL 4, [4]. This judgment usefully sets out the nature and effect of the Crown immunity, and the various steps that were potentially available to ameliorate its effects.

[39] *Mulcahy v MOD* [1996] EWCA Civ 1323, [1996] QB 732, [15]. Neill LJ cited the case of *Canterbury v AG* (1843) 12 LJ ch 281, in which an ex-Speaker sued the Crown for compensation for damage to his furniture in the fire which destroyed the Houses of Parliament in 1834 which (he alleged) was caused by the negligence of certain Crown servants; the claim failed.

[40] Described, e.g., in: *Roberts v Swangrove Estates Ltd* [2007] EWHC 513 (Ch) [119]. It was not an 'ordinary action': *Macgregor v Lord Advocate* [1921] SLR 558.

[41] R Mohammed-Davidson, 'Show me the Money: Enforcing Original Jurisdiction Judgments of the Caribbean Court of Justice' (2016) 29 *Leiden Journal of International Law* 113, 120, citing: W Baker Clode, *The Law and Practice of Petition of Right Under the Petitions of Right Act 1860* (1887).

[42] *C v Nova Scotia (AG)* [2015] NSSC 199, [41], and fn 18 ('[t]here is some debate as to whether the petition of right had its origin in legislation that dates from the time of Edward I or arose from feudal practise'), citing: P Hogg *et al.*, *Liability of the Crown* (Carswell, 2011) 5 and H Street, *Governmental Liability* (Cambridge University Press, 1953) 3.

[43] Mohammed-Davidson (n 41) 120.

regulated by statute, as an attempt at simplification.[44] However, the concept became outmoded. As one court notes, '[t]he idea that the state should be immune from any form of claim based on the concept that the king can do no wrong or that the king could not be sued in his own courts is difficult to sustain and pay proper regard to practical modern reality'.[45] There was also another option. As Lady Hale remarked of the doctrine of Crown immunity: '[t]he officials who carried out his policies could be sued for their unlawful actions, and the practice developed of nominating an official as a defendant to claims in tort'.[46] If, say, a claim was brought for damages for negligent driving against a Crown employee acting in the course of his employment, the Crown would pay the damages on an *ex gratia* basis in appropriate cases, indemnifying the said employee against any liability for those damages.[47] However, Lady Hale acknowledges that 'the courts had to grapple with the circumstances in which the King's prior authority or subsequent ratification might import the doctrine that the King could do no wrong and thus afford a defence to such a claim'.[48] In essence, 'that system attracted widespread criticism' too.[49]

Much of that changed in the United Kingdom by virtue of the passage of the Crown Proceedings Act 1947.[50] Not only did that statute abolish the old petition of right system,[51] but it also sought to place the Crown on the same legal footing as an ordinary citizen, insofar as some actions were concerned. The Crown became liable for the tort of any servant or agent committed in the course of employment,[52] for breach of its duties as an employer,[53] for breach of its duties as an occupier or owner of property,[54] and for breach of any statutory duty that was binding on the Crown.[55] There are still major differences between Crown proceedings and claims

---

[44] Pursuant to the Petitions of Right Act 1860, 23 and 24 Vict, c 34. This statute reformed the procedure for petitions of right in the UK.

[45] *C v Nova Scotia (AG)* [2015] NSSC 199, fn 23.

[46] *Rahmatullah (No 2) v MOD (Rev 1)* [2017] UKSC 1, [2017] AC 649, [16].

[47] Discussed, but not awarded, in: *Re De Keyser's Royal Hotel Ltd* [1920] AC 508 (HL).

[48] *Rahmatullah (No 2) v MOD (Rev 1)* [2017] UKSC 1, [2017] AC 649, [16].

[49] *Mulcahy v MOD* [1996] QB 732 (CA) 740 (Neill LJ).

[50] c 44, receiving Royal Assent on 31 July 1947, and fully in force on 1 January 1948.

[51] Per s 1 ('the claim may be enforced as of right, and without the fiat of His Majesty, by proceedings taken against the Crown for that purpose in accordance with the provisions of this Act').

[52] Per s 2(1)(a).

[53] Per s 2(1)(b).

[54] Per s 2(1)(c).

[55] Per s 2(2).

between private parties, and some significant limitations still apply,[56] but the landscape was still levelled significantly by the 1947 Act. It had a transformatory effect.[57] The UK House of Lords remarked (in separate cases) that the statute, 'as a whole, had the effect of removing, to a large extent but not to an unlimited extent, a general pre-existing immunity expressed in the ancient maxim that the King can do no wrong';[58] and that it recognises that, '[u]nder the rule of law, the Crown (i.e., the executive government in its various emanations) is in general subject to the same common law obligations as ordinary citizens'.[59]

Similar legislation exists in the Comparator Jurisdictions the subject of consideration in this chapter.[60] As stated in a leading Australian class action in which the Crown was sued, the legislative position 'reflects an aspiration to equality before the law, embracing governments and citizens, and also a recognition that perfect equality is not attainable. ... the first principle is that the tortious liability of governments is, *as completely as possible*, assimilated to that of citizens.'[61] This important passage was quoted by the Australian Law Reform Commission in its subsequent report, *Traditional Rights and Freedoms: Encroachments by Commonwealth Laws*,[62] as illustrating

---

[56] Notably, s 2(5) exempts the Crown from liability for any person exercising 'responsibilities of a judicial nature'. Until 1987, s 10 of the Crown Proceedings Act 1947 created a 'blanket immunity' in respect of the death of, or personal injury to, a member of the armed forces caused by the negligence of another member of the armed forces and attributable to service. However, s 2 of the Crown Proceedings (Armed Forces) Act 1987 removed the blanket protection of s 10 – thereby bringing back into the judicial arena questions such as the existence and ambit of the duty of care owed to one who is injured or killed whilst on active service. Nevertheless, the Government retains a power to re-introduce Crown immunity under the 1987 Act (which is executable via an order of the Secretary of State for Defence, per s 2(1)(a)).

[57] See, e.g., the interesting comment in *Hansard* in 1956 that 'cases involving the Crown in the High Court since the passing of the Crown Proceedings Act have numbered about 200 a year; that is, about 1,800 since the passage of the Act': *Hansard* (HC, 26 October 1956, JES Simon, vol 558, col 1026).

[58] *Matthews v MOD* [2003] UKHL 4, [116].

[59] *Deutsche Morgan Grenfell Group plc v Inland Revenue* [2006] UKHL 49, [2007] 1 AC 558, [133].

[60] See, e.g.: federally in Canada: Crown Liability and Proceedings Act, RSC 1985, c C-50, formerly the Crown Liability Act, SC 1952–53, c 30, which was proclaimed on 14 May 1953; Nova Scotia's Proceedings against the Crown Act, RSNS 1989, c 360; Ontario's Proceedings against the Crown Act, RSO 1990, c P.27; British Columbia's Crown Proceedings Act, RSBC 1996, c 89; New South Wales' Crown Proceedings Act 1988; Queensland's Crown Proceedings Act 1980.

[61] *Graham Barclay Oysters Pty Ltd v Ryan* [2002] HCA 54, 211 CLR 540, [12] (emphasis added).

[62] (Rep 129, 2015).

the proposition that, '[p]erfect equality before the law between government and citizen is not possible'; that '[e]xposure to some types of liability might make a government agency's task very difficult, or prohibitively costly, to perform'; and that government liability in negligence is an area rife with uncertainty and complexity.[63] On that note, the problem of 'regulatory negligence' is described shortly.[64]

Various issues have arisen in the class actions context, arising from the Crown proceedings legislation which fall outside the purview of this chapter.[65] One particular issue which *is* of interest, however, is that of class definition, in cases arising from allegations of historical abuse and mistreatment of children at state-owned and operated care homes and schools. The representative claimant will typically plead a direct negligence claim against the Crown for operational, management, and administrative decisions (which is more likely to attract a duty of care, as opposed to purely policy decisions which typically do not), on behalf of those who resided at an institution and who alleged grievances over several decades leading up to the filing of the class action. In such cases, those claims for negligence have been limited to the period *after* the relevant crown proceedings statute came into effect (and certification orders have, at times, excluded all claims prior to the dates that such statutes become operational[66]). For example, in *Seed v Ontario*,[67] where the representative claimant alleged negligence against the province of Ontario for its operation and management of a school for the blind from 1 September 1963 to the date of the class action suit, Horkins J noted, '[t]he decision to limit claims for negligence to the period after 1963 is based on the Ontario Proceedings Against the Crown Act, which bars claims in negligence against the defendant for conduct occurring before the statute came into force in September 1963'.[68] In such cases, the Crown may plead the statute of limitations; some or all of the class members may plead an extension

---

[63] ibid, [16.39]–[16.41], citing: M Aronson, 'Government Liability in Negligence' (2008) 32 *Melbourne University Law Review* 44, 46.

[64] See pp 295–303.

[65] e.g., *Skibinski v Community Living British Columbia* [2010] BCSC 1500; *Dolmage v Ontario* [2010] ONSC 6131, 6 CPC (7th) 221, and *Dolmage v Ontario* [2010] ONSC 1726.

[66] e.g., *Richard v British Columbia* [2009] BCCA 185, 93 BCLR (4th) 87; *Welsh v Ontario* [2016] ONSC 5319, [8].

[67] [2012] ONSC 2681, 31 CPC (7th) 76.

[68] ibid, [87].

thereto;[69] and that may be such an individual issue for each class member as to preclude certification.[70]

2   A Tactical Difference?

Before turning to specific categories of class actions suits which have frequently been brought against governmental defendants, it is of interest to note that, in the views of some, the government cannot – and should not – always take the same approach to settlement as would private defendants.

In its study of the Australian federal justice system,[71] the Australian Law Reform commission outlined the contrasting views about governmental defendants. Some respondent law firms who often acted for such defendants commented that government lawyers often lacked authority or instructions to settle until litigation was approaching trial; that government employees were sometimes reluctant to take responsibility for any settlement decisions, for fear of criticism from within their agencies; and that federal government agencies could display 'an inability to take properly into account the implications of litigation risk on resources and outcomes, as private litigants must do. The common experience of this firm ... is that the Crown often goes to trial because it is easier for the bureaucracy to accept a judgment from the courts, than it is for someone to take responsibility for, and to justify, an outcome reached by settlement negotiation.'[72]

On the other hand, the Australian Government Solicitor's office (AGS) pointed out that 'such critical comments on government litigants often derive from practitioner or party misunderstanding of government model litigant obligations. The model litigant rules require fair play,

---

[69] As occurred, e.g., in: *PG v AG of Canada* [2003] SKQB 41, [20]. This invokes the common law principle of 'reasonable discoverability', now oft-encapsulated in statute, e.g., the Limitation Act 1980 (UK), s 14(1), *viz*, that a limitation period will not begin to run until the claimant has discovered, or should with reasonable diligence have discovered, the wrongful nature of D's acts, and the nexus between those acts and his injuries. Discussed further by the author in: *Principles of Tort Law* (n 6), online chapter BE, 118–29.

[70] That outcome occurred, e.g., in: *Daniels v Canada (AG)* [2003] SKQB 58, 230 Sask R120 (class of Indians sued the federal Canadian government, alleging that they enlisted in the Canadian Army to serve in WWII and the Korean War; did not receive the same benefits for their services as did non-Aboriginal veterans; and that such benefits were either negligently administered or misappropriated by officials of the relevant Dept).

[71] *Managing Justice: A Review of the Federal Civil Justice System* (Rep 89, 1999).

[72] ibid, [3.136]–[3.138], citing various submissions.

but not acquiescence, and government lawyers must press hard to win points and defend decisions they believe to be correct.'[73] Furthermore, the AGS 'indicated that they give assessments on the risks, and the commercial and policy implications of litigation. Federal government agencies had to consider policy and the need to set precedents. Private parties tended to look at their own cases in isolation.'[74] Although it is not plain that the same reasons motivate, the willingness of governmental defendants to go to trial – and specifically in the context of class actions – has been noted in Canada too.[75] These comments are worth bearing in mind when considering the case law discussed in the following section.

D   Scenarios Involving Government as Defendant

The following scenarios do not purport to be exhaustive – and the case law discussed is a sample only – but they give an indication of how the intricate involvement of government, its employees, instrumentalities, and agencies in every facet of modern-day life can leave these parties exposed to a class actions lawsuit. It is very important to emphasise upfront that not all of them proceeded, much less succeeded. However, they demonstrate the reach of potential class litigation against government defendants. By reference to Australian and Canadian jurisprudence,[76] actions *instituted* against government defendants have included the following:

1   Immigration Matters

Governments have frequently been targets of class action claims for damages on behalf of immigrants and asylum seekers. The suits have frequently focused upon the alleged failure to provide reasonable care for the class members' health and wellbeing, whilst in transit, in detention facilities, or lawfully resident. Alternatively, rejection of applications for,

---

[73] ibid, [3.139].

[74] ibid, [3.140]. In the same report, the ALRC considered federal class actions under Pt IVA, but did not comment specifically upon governmental defendants. It opined that, '[p]rocedures for representative proceedings generally appear to be working well and in accordance with the legislative intentions. The Federal Court does not view such cases as more problematic than other complex cases': at ibid, [7.92].

[75] J Foreman and G Meisenheimer, 'The Evolution of the Class Action Trial in Ontario' (2014) 4 *Western Journal of Legal Studies* 1, 5.

[76] The case law referenced in this section is derived from a perusal of reported and unreported case law on the CanLII and AustLII databases.

say, permanent resident status, temporary visa protection, or asylum status, have also formed the basis of some class actions (more generally for judicial review rather than for compensatory redress).

For example, in Australia, class actions against the Australian Government have been commenced by each of the following:

- a class of 'boat people' whose boat, travelling from Indonesia to Australia, was destroyed on rocks at Christmas Island;[77]
- a class of persons who arrived in Australia by boat seeking asylum, and who were allegedly detained in immigration detention centres;[78] and
- a class who alleged that they sustained personal injury (physical and psychological) as a result of their detention at the Christmas Island detention centre whilst detained as 'unlawful non-citizens'.[79]

In addition, class actions seeking judicial review[80] of rejected applications for refugee status or for the grant of permanent or temporary visas have also been instituted against the Australian Government, on the grounds that:

- the government's delegates allegedly breached natural justice and procedural fairness in failing to adhere to the requisite processes[81] (e.g., that an oral hearing was not afforded to each of the class members[82]); or

---

[77] *Ibrahimi v Cth of Australia* [2018] NSWCA 321 (the action was brought under the New South Wales opt-out class action contained in the Civil Procedure Act 2005, Pt 10).

[78] *DBE17 v Cth of Australia* [2018] FCA 1307, aff'd: *DBE17 v Cth of Australia (No 2)* [2018] FCA 1793.

[79] *AS v Minister for Immigration (Ruling No 7)* [2017] VSC 137 (this action, brought under Pt 4A of the Supreme Court Act 1986, Victoria's state opt-out class action, failed).

[80] Pursuant to the Administrative Decisions (Judicial Review) Act 1977, s 15.

[81] e.g., *Lek Kim Sroun v Minister of Immigration, Local Govt and Ethnic Affairs* [1993] FCA 297, (1993) 43 FCR 100 (applications for refugee status or domestic protection (temporary) visas rejected; claim of representative claimant rejected); *Nguyen Thanh Trong v Minister of Immigration, Local Govt and Ethnic Affairs* [1996] FCA 1481 (applications for refugee status refused; class action permitted to proceed); *Wu Yu Fang v Minister of Immigration and Ethnic Affairs and Cth of Australia* [1996] FCA 1272 (class of refugees failed to apply for protection visas within the statutory time limit; substantive claim failed); *Wu Shan Liang v Minister of Immigration and Ethnic Affairs* [1995] FCA 1327, (1995) 130 ALR 367 (class members denied refugee status, and claimed that the government minister's delegates did not properly consider whether there was a real chance of the class members being persecuted if they were returned to China; class action permitted to proceed).

[82] *Zhang de Yong v Minister of Immigration, Local Govt and Ethnic Affairs* [1993] FCA 489; and on appeal: *Chen Zhen Zi v Minister of Immigration and Ethnic Affairs* [1994] FCA 985 (substantive claims failed; oral interviews by the decision-maker not mandatory in every case); with further litigation by some class members: *Li Chan Tian v Minister of Immigration, Local Govt and Ethnic Affairs* [1994] FCA 1020.

- the time, place, and content of English proficiency tests were not nominated by the Minister nor appropriately delegated[83]).

Such class actions typically did not seek damages or compensatory redress, but sought instead, that the refusals to grant refugee status be set aside, and that injunctive relief be awarded to restrain the government from taking any action to remove any class member from Australia. However, and notably, in 2001, the Australian Parliament decided to carve out an exception to the otherwise generic nature of its federal opt-out class action in this field.[84] By virtue of an amendment to the Migration Act 1958, Parliament provided an 'unqualified prohibition on representative or class actions'.[85] Section 486B relevantly provides that:[86]

---

s 486B(1) This section applies to all proceedings (migration proceedings) in the High Court, the Federal Court or the Federal Circuit Court that raise an issue in connection with visas (including if a visa is not granted or has been cancelled), deportation, taking, or removal of unlawful non-citizens.

  . . .

(4) The following are not permitted in or by a migration proceeding:
 (a) representative or class actions;

(5) This section has effect despite any other law, including in particular:
 (a) Part IVA of the Federal Court of Australia Act 1976; and
 (b) any Rules of Court.

As academic scholars and the judiciary have noted, this amendment has had a profound effect upon the number of class actions against government and government agencies instituted in this category, by effectively prohibiting them.[87] Leading up to that amendment, there were twenty-

---

[83] *Fazal Din v Minister for Immigration and Multicultural Affairs* [1997] FCA 780 (substantive claim succeeded).

[84] Introduced by the Migration Legislation Amendment Act (No 1) 2001 (Cth).

[85] *DZY17 v Minister for Home Affairs* [2018] FCAFC 196, [31].

[86] There was an application filed in 2016 for a declaration that s 486B(4)(a) was invalid, as noted in: *Plaintiff S195/2016 v Minister for Immigration and Border Protection (Cth)* [2016] HCA Trans 251. The outcome of this application is not apparent from any further transcript available via the AustLII database.

[87] e.g.: D Grave, K Adams and J Betts, *Class Actions in Australia* (2nd edn, Lawbook Co, 2012) [1.440]; The Hon Justice Bernard Murphy, 'The Operation of the Australian Class Action Regime' (Bar Assn of Queensland, Gold Coast, 9 March 2013) [5.7]; The Hon Justice Ronald Sackville, 'Judicial Review of Migration Decisions: An Institution in Peril?'

five migration-related federal class actions (constituting 20 per cent of the total number of class actions brought), whereas in the period of 2000–9 (the second eight years), there were none.[88] In the previously mentioned federal class action relating to detention in immigration centres, the Australian Government did not seek to rely on section 486B.[89]

In Canada too, the federal Canadian government has been sued by each of the following:

- a class of persons who applied for permanent resident status as part of a skilled trades programme intended for economic immigrants and whose applications were denied;[90]
- a class of investors who lost the opportunity to obtain permanent resident status when the Canadian Government terminated all applications for permanent residence from foreign investors that had not been approved prior to February 2014, and who claimed that returning their application fees and their investments would not compensate for the loss of the opportunities to obtain permanent resident status through investment;[91] and
- a class of Pakistani refugees who were denied permanent resident status because they had been identified as persons who might be inadmissible to Canada due to membership of a terrorist organisation (which the class members disputed).[92]

2   Agricultural, Food, and Environmental Disputes

Given that much of agricultural and food production depends upon governmental permission and regulation, it is unsurprising that this field of activity has given rise to many class suits against governments.

(2000) 23 *UNSW Law Journal* 190, 196; J MacLean, 'In What Circumstances Can You Apply to Review a Government Decision?', in *Western Australia Law Handbook* (31 July 2018); and ALRC, *Integrity, Fairness and Efficiency: Final Report* (2018) (n 14) [2.6].

[88] As recorded in: V Morabito, *An Empirical Study of Australia's Class Action Regimes: Class Action Facts and Figures (First Report)* (December 2009) 25–27.

[89] *DBE17 v Cth of Australia* [2018] FCA 1307, [74].

[90] *Cabral v Canada (Citizenship and Immigration)* [2018] FCA 4 (class claim failed, as showing no genuine issue for trial; defendant obtained summary judgment).

[91] *Sin v Canada* [2015] FC 276 (claim did not disclose a cause of action).

[92] *Mohiuddin v Canada* [2006] FC 664, 295 FTR 96 (some class claims had to be pursued via judicial review before any claim for compensatory damages, and others struck out as not disclosing a cause of action).

In Australia, class actions have been commenced by the following:

- a class of graziers, who sued two state governments, alleged that their stock was contaminated as a result of ingestion of chlorfluazuron (which was a component of an agricultural pesticide used on cotton crops), and its presence in animal fat meant that Australian beef exports were rejected by numerous overseas markets, causing significant financial losses to those graziers;[93]
- a class of consumers and businesses alleged that a local authority failed to supply dam water which was fit for (agricultural) purpose;[94]
- a class of Victorian abalone fishermen alleged that the Victorian state government (and a company, SOM) negligently allowed the release of a herpes-like virus, abalone viral ganglioneuritis, from an abalone aquaculture farm operated by SOM near Port Fairy, thereby decimating the wild abalone population off the Victorian coast;[95]
- a class of residents and businesses alleged that a Queensland government entity which operated Wivenhoe Dam negligently permitted major flooding downstream in and around the capital city of Brisbane, thereby causing deaths, property damage, and economic loss;[96] and
- a class of consumers alleged that a local authority and the state of New South Wales caused them to contract Hepatitis A as a result of their consuming oysters grown in Wallis Lake, New South Wales, which were contaminated with human faeces.[97]

In Canada, and in the same category, class actions have been instituted against various federal and provincial governments, on the bases that:

- a class alleged that their persons and homes were contaminated by their living near a steel plant, coke ovens, tar ponds and related by-products operations, located in Sydney, Nova Scotia, and that the

[93] *McMullin v ICI Aust Operations Pty Ltd* [1997] FCA 541 (the state governments of Queensland and New South Wales were sued vicariously for the acts and omissions of government employees involved in the oversight of pesticide use, plus for direct negligence and for breach of statutory duty; all failed at trial).
[94] *Tongue v Tamworth CC* [2004] FCA 209, and associated litigation.
[95] *Regent Holdings Pty Ltd v State of Victoria* [2012] VSCA 221, (2012) 36 VR 424.
[96] *Rodriguez & Sons Pty Ltd v Queensland Bulk Water Supply Authy t/as Seqwater* (No 19) [2019] NSWSC 262.
[97] The contentious nature of this claim is illustrated by the fact that, on earlier appeal, the Full Federal Court had held (2:1, Lee and Lindgren JJ in the majority) that the Council was not liable in negligence; but that (2:1, Lee and Kiefel JJ in the majority) the State was liable: *Graham Barclay Oysters Pty Ltd v Ryan* [2000] FCA 1099.

federal Canadian government had allegedly operated the ovens without emissions controls;[98]
- a class of First Nation band members alleged that the Crown's regulation of salmon aquaculture was responsible for serious decline in wild
  salmon stocks within an archipelago where Aboriginal collectives had
  rights to fish;[99]
- a class of tobacco producers in Ontario alleged that the Canadian
  federal and Ontario provincial governments allowed the sale of contraband tobacco products illegally across Canada at smoke shops, bingo
  parlours, flea markets and in the work place, which diminished the
  market for the sale of legal tobacco;[100] and
- a class of commercial cattle farmers in Canada (except in Québec)
  alleged that they suffered economic losses arising from the discovery of
  the fatal neurological disease of cattle, bovine spongiform encephalo-
  pathy (BSE) in a cow in Alberta in 2003, that the federal government
  was negligent as the regulator of the cattle industry in Canada in
  allowing BSE to enter the feed chain that infected the Alberta cow,
  and was responsible for the ensuing international bans on the importation of Canadian beef and cattle.[101]

3   Pharmaceutical and Medical Matters

In Australia, it will be recalled[102] that one of the reasons that prompted
the implementation of class actions reform was precisely because a blood
contamination case[103] was not capable of being decided under any opt-
out regime, for no such regime then existed anywhere in Australian civil
procedure. However, there have been other class actions in the pharmaceutical and medical sector that have been commenced in that jurisdiction. For example, a group of companies alleged that the Commonwealth
agency, the Therapeutic Goods Administration, improperly suspended
the licence of Pan Pharmaceuticals and cancelled the registration of all

---

[98] *MacQueen v Sidbec Inc* [2006] NSSC 208, 246 NSR (2d) 213, [52]–[54] (that part of the
class action survived strike-out; but allegations of regulatory negligence were struck out).
[99] *Kwicksutaineuk/Ah-Kwa-Mish First Nation v Canada (AG)* [2012] BCCA 19 (but the
class was de-certified because of an unworkable and ill-defined class definition).
[100] *Weninger Farms Ltd v Canada (Minister of National Revenue)* [2012] ONSC 4544 (class
action struck out as disclosing no cause of action).
[101] *Sauer v Canada (Agriculture)* (2009), 246 OAC 256.
[102] See Chapter 2, Section D.
[103] *E v Australian Red Cross Socy* [1991] FCA 20, 27 FCR 310.

therapeutic goods (i.e., vitamins, health supplements, and complementary medicines) manufactured by Pan Pharmaceuticals.[104]

In Canadian class actions jurisprudence, this category of claim has featured quite prominently.[105] For example, the government of Ontario and other provinces were sued, in addition to the Canadian Red Cross Society, in the national blood contamination class action of *Parsons v Canadian Red Cross Society*[106] and related litigation. The class actions were litigated in three provinces on behalf of those who received blood transfusions or who suffered from haemophilia and who received blood or blood products, and all of whom were infected with the Hepatitis C virus.[107] In 1999, all the actions settled, with judicial approval, pursuant to the 1986–90 Hepatitis C Settlement Agreement. One of the reasons that the settlement proposal was considered to be fair, just and reasonable, and in the best interests of the class members, was that there was (in the view of the Ontario settlement judge, Winkler J) a 'substantial litigation risk of continuing to trial'.[108] This was primarily because the Canadian Red Cross Society, the 'primary defendant', was 'involved in protracted insolvency proceedings', and so even if the court-ordered stay of litigation proceedings against it were to be lifted, it was unlikely that there would be any meaningful assets available to satisfy any judgment in favour of the class members. The Crown was 'secondary defendant' in these proceedings – and against that party, there was (said Winkler J) 'a real question as to [its] liability'.[109] The Canadian federal, provincial and territorial governments paid up to $1.118 billion to compensate the class members under the settlement agreement.

In Canada, other notable cases in this category have included the following:

- a class of recipients of breast implants alleged that the implants were inherently dangerous, and that the government and its agencies were

---

[104] *Pharm-a-Care Laboratories Pty Ltd v Cth of Australia (No 3)* [2010] FCA 361, and associated litigation.
[105] As noted in: Manitoba LRC, *Class Proceedings* (Rep 100, 1999) 20.
[106] [2016] ONSC 4809.
[107] See, in British Columbia: *Endean v Canadian Red Cross Socy* [1999] CanLII 6357 (BCSC). In Ontario: *Parsons v Canadian Red Cross Socy* [1999] OJ No 3572 (SCJ). In Québec: *Honhon c Canada (Procureur général)* [1999] CanLII 11813 (QCCS); *Page c Canada (Procureur général)* [1999] JQ No 4415 (CS); *Page c Canada (Procureur général)* [1999] JQ No 5325 (CS).
[108] *Parsons* [2016] ONSC 4809, [92].
[109] ibid.

negligent in their statutory obligation to regulate the import, manufacture, distribution, and use of breast implants in Canada;[110]

- a class of patients, who were incarcerated and medically treated at
  a psychiatric hospital which was administered by the province of
  Ontario, alleged that the medical treatment they received ('social
  therapy') was unethical and illegal, and amounted to experimentation
  and torture;[111]

- a class of dental patients alleged that the use of mercury in dental
  practice was harmful to their health, and that the British Columbia
  provincial and federal Canadian governments owed them a private law
  duty of care to prohibit or regulate the use of mercury in dental
  practice;[112]

- a class of recipients of a medical device designed to alleviate or cure
  female incontinence sued the federal Canadian government on the
  basis that it regulated the sale and marketing of medical devices, that it
  had a duty to examine and test products to be sold in Canada, and that
  it negligently allowed the device to be licensed for sale and use in
  Canada;[113]

- a class of children (and their parents) alleged that children diagnosed
  with autism had their requests for funding for intensive behavioural
  treatment rejected by the provincial government of British Columbia
  and that this constituted a violation of their right to equality[114] under
  the Canadian Charter of Rights and Freedoms;[115] and

- a class of persons who contracted SARS alleged that employees of the
  province of Ontario prematurely announced that a SARS outbreak in

[110]   *Chapman v Canada (Health and Welfare Canada)* [2007] SKQB 151. The representative
        claimants did not sue the manufacturers and/or distributors of the implants, and
        a dispute arose when the Crown sought to claim contribution and indemnity from
        those third parties.

[111]   *Barker v Ontario* [2013] ONSC 7381.

[112]   *Holland v The Queen* [2008] BCSC 965 (negligence claim against province of
        Saskatchewan struck out).

[113]   *Klein v American Medical Systems Inc* (2006), 84 OR (3d) 217, 278 DLR (4th) 722 (claim
        struck out; the federal government did not owe a private law duty of care to class
        members).

[114]   Per s 15(1).

[115]   *Auton (Guardian of) v British Columbia (Minister of Health)* (1999), 12 Admin LR (3d)
        261, 32 CPC (4th) 305, [57] (class action not certified, because it was not the preferable
        procedure, a judicial review application was). For a similar claim, see: *Sagharian
        v Ontario (Minister of Education)* [2012] ONSC 3478 (autistic children and their parents
        alleged that defendant failed to provide or to fund Applied Behavioural Analysis inter-
        vention, speech therapy, occupational therapy, and other programmes and services for
        persons with autism, as part of Ontario's education system; class claim discontinued).

Toronto in 2003 was under control and contained and that a state of emergency was over – when, in fact, the outbreak was not contained at all.[116]

4 Police, Prison, and Civil Liberty Matters

The government's management and operation of prisons and detention centres has proven to be a fertile sector in which class actions have been commenced.

In Australia, a class action has been commenced in relation to each of the following:

- a class of Aboriginal and Torres Strait Islander people, who were residents on Palm Island, sued the state of Queensland and the Queensland Police Commissioner in relation to a riot on the Island in 2004, alleging racial discrimination by members of the Queensland Police Service[117] (this case being singled out by the recent Australian Law Reform Commission report, as constituting an example of 'the Part IVA regime promoting access to justice'[118]); and
- a class of Aboriginal persons detained in a youth detention centre in the Northern Territory alleged that they had suffered false imprisonment, assault and battery, and racial discrimination, on the basis that such systemic or routine conduct would not have been engaged in, had the detainees not been Aboriginal;[119] and
- a class of children and young adults alleged that they had been wrongly arrested and jailed because of out-of-date or incorrect bail information in the New South Wales police computer system;[120]

In Canadian jurisprudence, class actions have been brought against various governments on the following bases:

---

[116] *Williams v Canada (AG)* (2005), 76 OR (3d) 763, 257 DLR (4th) 704 (class action struck out as disclosing no cause of action in negligence).

[117] *Wotton v State of Queensland (No 7)* [2017] FCA 406, and associated litigation. The class action settled; with a rare *cy-près* distribution; $233,540 was set aside from the settlement sum so that financial counselling, advice, and assistance could be provided by the Indigenous Consumer Assistance Network Ltd to registered group members: *Wotton v State of Queensland (No 11)* [2018] FCA 1841.

[118] *Integrity, Fairness and Efficiency: Final Report* (2018) (n 14) [2.6]. See too, the discussion in: [7.173].

[119] *Jenkings v Northern Territory* [2017] FCA 1263 (claim in relation to racial discrimination struck out as being inadequately particularised).

[120] *Konneh v State of New South Wales* [2011] NSWSC 1170.

- a class of members alleged that the Ontario provincial government operated or oversaw the operation of several youth detention centres where child detainees were regularly subjected to lengthy and inappropriate periods of solitary confinement;[121]
- a class of male prisoners alleged that they were systemically sexually abused by a prison officer who was employed within the British Columbia prison system for over twenty years;[122]
- a class of detained individuals who were not remanded into pre-trial custody alleged that the province of British Columbia was in breach of the Canadian Charter of Rights and Freedom by carrying out routine strip searches at the Vancouver city jail;[123]
- a class of prisoners at a federally operated correctional centre alleged that they were prevented from wearing commemorative t-shirts of an inverted maple leaf for those inmates who died of unnatural causes whilst in custody, the confiscation breaching their rights to freedom of expression;[124]
- a class of prisoners at the Kingston Penitentiary in Ontario alleged that, during a fire set by some prisoners during a riot, the government failed to maintain proper fire safety equipment and procedures;[125] and
- a class of prisoners alleged that, during a lockdown at a jail operated by the province of British Columbia, their activities were restricted and searches were conducted of inmates and their cells, which exceeded the authority of correctional staff, prison administrators, and the emergency response and tactical units of the Correctional Service of Canada and were unlawful.[126]

5 Indigenous and Aboriginal Matters

Apart from cases instituted by Aboriginal class members canvassed in the previous category of claim arising from prison and detention claims, disputes arising from Aboriginal ownership and property rights have been commenced fairly frequently.

---

[121] *JK v Ontario* [2017] ONCA 902, and associated litigation.

[122] *Lakes v MacDougall* [2011] BCSC 1273.

[123] *Thorburn v British Columbia (Public Safety and Solicitor General)* [2013] BCCA 480 (class action did not meet four out of five certification threshold requirements).

[124] *Lauzon v Canada (AG)* [2015] ONSC 2620 (certification refused; a grievance process established by the Corrections and Conditional Release Act, SC 1992, c 20, had potential to effectively redress the substance of the prisoners' claims, despite the unavailability of damages).

[125] *Nixon v Canada (AG)* (2002), 21 CPC (5th) 269 (Ont SCJ).

[126] *Ewert v Canada (AG)* [2016] BCSC 962.

Australian class actions in this area have included the following:

- a class of Australian 'traditional aboriginal owners' objected to the nomination of certain lands as a potential site for a repository for radioactive waste, and to the settlement of that proposal on their behalf by an Aboriginal Land Council;[127] and
- a class of Aboriginal persons objected to the Australian Government's manifesto to improve the living conditions in Alice Springs town camps in the Northern Territory, and to the joint announcement by the Commonwealth Minister for Aboriginal Affairs and the Northern Territory Chief Minister of a multi-million commitment to improve living conditions in those town camps, on the basis that the federal government lacked the power to compulsorily acquire prescribed areas of the Northern Territory where aboriginal residents occupied parts of the land under tenancy agreements, and had not afforded procedural fairness.[128] However, given that there was another procedural vehicle[129] (which was, itself, a 'representative proceeding') by which to enable a person authorised by all members of a native title claim group to bring an application for determination of native title, a class action was held to be unnecessary.[130]

In Canadian class actions jurisprudence, Indian bands and their elected chiefs have commenced class actions too, on the following bases:

- the class members sought declarations relating to aboriginal title to lands and relating to aboriginal fishing rights;[131]
- the class members alleged that the federal Canadian government devised and implemented a systemic assimilation policy (the Sixties Scoop[132]) which was purposely designed to destroy First Nations families and communities, and that 16,000 Aboriginals were the

---

[127] *Bill v Northern Land Council* [2018] FCA 1823 (claim failed; substantive causes of action impermissibly pleaded; and inappropriately constituted as a class action because of procedural deficiencies).

[128] *Shaw v Minister for Families, Housing, Community Services and Indigenous Affairs* [2009] FCA 1397, [2]. The Northern Territory government was also sued; the substantive claims in the class action failed.

[129] Pursuant to the Native Title Act 1993 (Cth), s 61.

[130] *Roe v Kimberley Land Council Aboriginal Corp* [2010] FCA 809.

[131] *Cowichan Tribes v Canada (AG)* [2018] BCSC 2254, and associated litigation.

[132] Described as 'a dark and painful chapter in Canada's history': The Hon Carolyn Bennett, Minister of Indigenous and Northern Affairs, *Press Release* (1 February 2017), as cited in: *Brown v Canada (AG)* [2018] ONSC 3429 (SCJ) fn 1. The episode generated 23 actions in superior and federal courts across Canada, as noted *ibid*, [1].

victims of a deliberate programme of 'identity genocide of children' operative in Ontario over a twenty-year period;[133] and

- the class members alleged that an area of 438,000 hectares in the central interior of British Columbia was an area of traditional territory over which they could preclude certain activities such as commercial logging, mining, and commercial road building.[134]

6   Employment Disputes

As with any employer, disputes may arise between government on the one hand, and their employees or former employees on the other.

In Australian class actions jurisprudence, class actions have been commenced by employees in relation to the following:

- employees' entitlement to retirement benefits;[135]
- whether duress was applied to employees in relation to their entry into workplace agreements;[136] and
- whether the government replaced employees (*viz*, deputy registrars of the Family Court) without regard to the scheme provided by federal statute for removing an office-holder from office.[137]

In Canada, employment disputes with government have given rise to class action suits in a variety of circumstances, including the following:

- class members alleged that the Ontario government appropriated their employees' pension benefits without compensation, as a result of restructuring activities;[138]

---

[133]   *Brown v Canada (AG)* [2010] ONSC 3095, (2010), 102 OR (3d) 493 (SCJ). The action was certified: *Brown v Canada (AG)* [2013] ONSC 5637 (SCJ); leave to appeal to the Divisional Court was permitted: *Brown v Canada (AG)* [2014] ONSC 1583 (Div Ct), but that appeal was dismissed: *Brown v Canada (AG)* [2014] ONSC 6967 (Div Ct), and summary judgment establishing Canada's legal liability in tort was granted: *Brown v Canada (AG)* [2017] ONSC 251 (SCJ). A national settlement was recently approved: *Brown* [2018], ibid.

[134]   *William v British Columbia* [2012] BCCA 285.

[135]   *Mulcahy v Hydro-Electric Comm* [1998] FCA 1780 (the Commission was established as a body corporate by the Hydro-Electric Commission Act 1929 (Tasmania) to manage and control that state's hydro-electric works).

[136]   *Schanka v Employment National (Administration) Pty Ltd* [1998] FCA 1123 (the defendant was incorporated as a publicly owned provider, with all shares owned by the Commonwealth), and associated litigation.

[137]   *Community and Public Sector Union (CPSU) v Cth of Australia* [1999] FCA 653.

[138]   *Ontario Public Service Employees Union v Ontario* [2005] OJ No 1841 (Ont SCJ) (class action was certified and settled).

- employees of a timber mill alleged that, in permanently shutting down the mill, the province of British Columbia had inadvertently removed from a tree farm licence a provision which would have prevented the mill from being closed without the Minister of Forests' approval;[139]
- a class of employees alleged that a branch of the government of British Columbia installed machines for crushing empty liquor bottles at retail outlets, and that the use of glass-crushing technology was harmful to their health and safety, exposing them to glass dust and infectious spores and fungus;[140] and
- a class of current and former employees of the Canadian Forces, who were injured, physically or psychologically, in the course of duty, alleged that their compensation/benefits were arbitrary, substandard, and inadequate for supporting themselves and their families, and less favourable than those available to injured persons claiming under tort law or workers compensation laws.[141]

7 Financial Products and Gambling Services

Governments may develop, promote, underwrite, and/or manage various financial schemes, which then prove to be defective or problematical for the relevant investors. Additionally, governmental oversight and regulation of gaming operations have given rise to class actions. As one Canadian judge put it:

> lotteries have become big business for governments. Realizing that they could be a useful way of raising money without overt taxation, governments decided that lotteries were not such a bad thing after all, if they could be controlled by the state and if the profits flowed to the treasury. The 'numbers game', formerly orchestrated by shady gangsters collecting slips and distributing cash in seedy neighbourhoods, is now played in thousands of convenience stores across the nation.[142]

Gaming operations have given rise to several class actions in Canadian jurisprudence:

---

[139] *James v British Columbia* [2005] BCCA 136, 38 BCLR (4th) 263 (class action permitted to proceed as disclosing a reasonable cause of action).

[140] *R v Price* [2001] BCSC 1494, 109 ACWS (3d) 400 (class action struck out as disclosing no cause of action for misfeasance in public office).

[141] *Scott v Canada (AG)* [2013] BCSC 1651.

[142] *Loveless v Ontario Lottery and Gaming Corp* [2011] ONSC 4744, [2].

- in one novel case,[143] class members sought recovery of jackpot prizes which they had won when they gambled at various casinos operated on behalf of the British Columbia Lottery Corporation (which was a Crown corporation, a government corporation,[144] and an agent of the government[145]). Those jackpot prizes were withheld because class members – categorised as those with a pathological gambling habit – had been participants in the Corporation's voluntary self-exclusion programme. The class members alleged that over 400 jackpot prizes were forfeited due to the winner being a participant in the programme; that the rules which underpinned that programme were *ultra vires* the Corporation's rule-making powers;[146] and that the Corporation was in breach of their gaming contracts by withholding jackpot prizes from them.[147] On the substantive claim, the class members succeeded. The representative claimant proved that, until the situation was rectified, the rules were not validly enacted and could not be enforced against the class members;[148]

- however, in *Dennis v Ontario Lottery & Gaming Corp*,[149] the Ontario Superior Court of Justice declined to certify a class action against a provincial gaming corporation, by persons who had signed self-exclusion forms, on the basis that the claims were preferably brought as individual actions rather than as a class action. For one thing, the class definition was over-inclusive, because not all class members were pathological gamblers; and within the category of problem gamblers, there were degrees of severity and moments of clarity (which was an individual issue).[150] For another, the personal circumstances and gambling history of the class members pointed to the individualistic nature of the proposed common issues, which could not be resolved by the use of statistical evidence.[151] None of this was amenable to class determination;

---

[143] *Haghdust v British Columbia Lottery Corp* [2014] BCSC 1327.

[144] Pursuant to the Financial Administration Act, RSBC 1996, c 138, s 1.

[145] [2014] BCSC 1327, [43]. The corporation had over 900 employees, and performed a variety of functions.

[146] ibid, [40], citing: *Barbour v Uni of British Columbia* [2009] BCSC 425, [38] ('[h]istorically, the presumption of common law was that corporations created by or under a statute have only those powers which are expressly or impliedly granted to them. To the extent that a corporation acted beyond its powers, its actions were *ultra vires* and invalid').

[147] ibid, [213]

[148] ibid, [214], 'Answers to the Common Issues'.

[149] [2010] ONSC 1332.

[150] ibid, [198]–[200].

[151] ibid, [209].

- another class action concerned whether the province of British Columbia was entitled to retain licence fees paid by a class of charitable and religious organisations over the period of a decade with respect to bingo and casino gaming operations which they had conducted over that period, or whether those fees were unconstitutional and contrary to the Criminal Code (ultimately, they were not[152]); and

- finally, a class suit concerned whether the Ontario Lottery and Gaming Corporation failed to protect Ontario class members from fraud committed by the retailers who were largely responsible for the sale and redemption of tickets.[153]

Turning to government-operated and funded financial products, the Australian class actions landscape has witnessed some significant suits. For example, the New South Wales government was sued in relation to a 'HomeFund' scheme, which had, as its purpose, 'to ensure that every person in Australia has access to adequate and appropriate housing at a price within his or her capacity to pay'.[154] However, a combination of falling interest rates, relatively stable incomes, and static or falling property values, caused the amount owing by many borrowers who entered into a mortgage under the scheme to increase to such a degree as to decrease, or even eliminate, their equity in their properties. This meant that those borrowers were not able to refinance at the lower interest rates available from other financial institutions. Those class members sued the financial institutions and co-operative institutions involved in the scheme, and also sued the government for breaches of consumer protection legislation[155] and for breach of fiduciary duty. However, as a result of Crown immunity, ultimately the government could not be sued in relation to its activities relating to the HomeFund scheme.[156]

---

[152] *Nanaimo Immigrant Settlement Socy v British Columbia* [2004] BCCA 410, 242 DLR (4th) 394. Ultimately, the licence fees paid with respect to their charitable casino and bingo gaming operations were direct taxes which were constitutional and did not offend the Criminal Code.

[153] *Loveless v Ontario Lottery and Gaming Corp* [2011] ONSC 4744.

[154] *Woodlands and Ballard v Permanent Trustee Co Ltd* [1996] FCA 1643.

[155] Pursuant to ss 51AB, 52, 52A, and 74 of the Trade Practices Act 1974, and of ss 42 and 43 of the Fair Trading Act 1987 (NSW).

[156] [1996] FCA 1643, [56] ('the State of New South Wales is not estopped from relying on Crown immunity. . . . [it] is not bound by the Trade Practices Act, and no claim under that Act is maintainable against it in these proceedings').

8   Educational Services

Government-funded and -operated educational institutions have been the subject of several class actions, for systemic abuse (both physical and sexual), and for inadequate educational systems and policies.

In Canada, there has been 'a line of cases relating to the treatment of children in the care of the provincial government',[157] in which claims have alleged, inter alia, negligence and breach of fiduciary duty in the operation and management of various institutions funded and operated by provincial governments:

- in relation to schools for the deaf, it was alleged that the defendant government knew (or ought to have known) of physical, emotional, and sexual abuse being perpetrated against the students and yet took no reasonable steps to prevent, halt, eliminate, or report these abuses (alleged deficiencies in the care and education of the students included: failing to implement appropriate practices and policies; failing to follow proper staff hiring, training, and supervisory practices; disciplining students in a way that was unprofessional, inept, inconsistent, harsh, and excessive; failing to report child abuse; and implementing education facilities which were antiquated, unsuitable, and unsafe[158]);
- in relation to residential schools operated by the Crown which were established for various purposes (e.g., for students with developmental disabilities;[159] for students who were blind[160] or deaf;[161] for students engaged in a residential programme associated with a psychiatric

---

[157] *Templin v HMQ Ontario* [2016] ONSC 7853, [3], citing many of the relevant cases. In this case, unusually, the defendant consented to certification, which was positively commented upon by the certification judge.

[158] *Welsh v Ontario* [2018] ONSC 3217, and associated litigation.

[159] e.g., *Slark v Ontario* [2017] ONSC 4178; *Dolmage, McKillop and Bechard v The Queen* [2014] ONSC 1283, and *Dolmage v Ontario* [2010] ONSC 1726 (Cullity J, who certified the action), leave to appeal to the Div Ct against aspects of that certification denied: [2010] ONSC 6131 (Herman J). These actions related to three provincially operated residential facilities for individuals with developmental disabilities. For an earlier class action seeking judicial review in relation to the same dispute, which was partially successful, see: *Gray v Ontario* (2006), 264 DLR (4th) 717 (Ont Div Ct). See too: *Richard v British Columbia* [2008] BCCA 53, 290 DLR (4th) 336 (class claim brought on behalf of those who were sexually, physically, emotionally, and psychologically abused while resident at the Woodlands School, a facility operated by the province of British Columbia for the care and control of mentally handicapped persons and persons needing psychiatric care; claim certified and settled with judicial approval).

[160] *Seed v Ontario* [2017] ONSC 3534, and associated litigation.

[161] *Rumley v British Columbia* [2001] 3 SCR 184, 205 DLR (4th) 39.

research institute;[162] for First Nations children who were former students of a residential school;[163] and for more than 150,000 First Nations, Inuit, and Métis children who, from the 1860s to the 1990s, were required to attend Indian Residential Schools operated by religious organisations and funded by the Government of Canada[164]), it was alleged that cruel and systemic abuse, brutality and mistreatment occurred at those government-operated and/or -funded institutions; and

- the *non-monetary* benefits conferred by a settlement agreement with the Crown has been judicially considered to be important in approving the settlement. In *McKillop and Bechard v The Queen*,[165] the class members were participants (mostly children) who were mildly, moderately, severely or profoundly disabled, who were entered into a residential programme of hospital care, activity, educational programmes and adult training operated by the province of Ontario, and who suffered abuse, mistreatment and harm during their residencies. In addition to the monetary compensation offered by the settlement fund, proposed non-monetary benefits for the class included a formal apology; the preservation of voluminous documents for scholarly research; and commemorative plaques at each institution, stating that, in 2014, the government of Ontario issued an apology to former residents of the centres who were harmed. Conway J approved the settlement as being fair, just, reasonable, and in the best interests of the class members[166] – partly because the Crown's apology was a vital and extraordinary component of this settlement, the commemorative plaques would constitute an enduring public record of that apology; and the other non-monetary benefits recognised the dignity of class

---

[162] *Templin v HMQ Ontario* [2016] ONSC 7853.

[163] *Cloud v Canada (AG)* (2004), 73 OR (3d) 401, 247 DLR (4th) 667 (CA) (class action certified), leave to appeal dismissed: *MCC v Canada (AG)* [2005] SCCA No 50.

[164] *Canada (AG) v Fontaine* [2017] 2 SCR 205, [2017] SCC 47, and associated litigation. As noted in *Fontaine v Canada (AG)* [2018] ONSC 6381, across Canada, approximately 18,000 individual actions by former students of the residential schools, and numerous class actions, were commenced against Canada and the churches that operated the schools: at [19].

[165] [2014] ONSC 1282. This was companion litigation to that brought on behalf of residents of the Huronia Regional Centre, which settlement was judicially approved on 3 December 2013: *Dolmage v The Queen* [2013] ONSC 6686 (Conway J). Both actions related to provincially operated residential facilities for adults with developmental delays.

[166] ibid, [37].

members and enabled the history of the centres to be recorded and preserved.[167]

The case aptly illustrates the sensitive and unique litigation in which governments may become involved as class actions defendants.

In Australia too, a class of former residents of residential schools for immigrant British children alleged that they were subjected to systemic physical and sexual abuse perpetrated by a significant number of staff and others during their time at the schools over the period of 1938–74 and sued the Commonwealth Government on the basis that its Ministers were 'legal guardians' of the residents, and sued the state government of New South Wales on broadly the same basis.[168]

9   Social Services, Support, and Cohesion

Governments are involved inextricably in social services and support-oriented activities. Where either the financial support and assistance is less-than-required, or the services themselves are alleged to fall below the standard of reasonable care, governments have frequently been on the end of class action suits.

In Canadian jurisprudence, suits in negligence (amongst other causes of action[169]) against the government have been attempted in a variety of circumstances – where:

- the government provided social support services for developmentally disabled persons who had been approved to receive support and services under established programmes, but those persons were allegedly negligently placed on indeterminate waiting lists, with inconsistent prioritisation processes for the wait-listed services, and poor matching programmes;[170]

---

[167] ibid, [26].

[168] *Giles v Cth of Australia* [2014] NSWSC 83 (pursued under the Civil Procedure Act 2005, Pt 10, the New South Wales opt-out class action regime). An application to discontinue the class action failed; 'at this stage of the proceedings, I am satisfied that the most efficient and cost effective method of disposition of these claims is by a representative proceeding as it is presently constituted' (at [140]–[144]). The poignant background to this action, and the potential limitation problems arising therefrom, were discussed in: A Cheshire, 'Fairbridge Farm School child migrant class action' (2010) 100 *Precedent* 49.

[169] Breach of fiduciary duty, and breach of the Canadian Charter of Rights and Freedoms, Pt I of the Constitution Act, 1982, being Schedule B to the Canada Act 1982 (UK) 1982, c 11, both frequently feature in such class actions.

[170] *Leroux v Ontario* [2018] ONSC 6452.

- class members were removed from their families and made Crown wards when they were children (because they had suffered criminal assaults, neglect, or abuse at the hands of their family members), but suffered further abuse whilst in the care of the province of Ontario, and where the Crown failed to advance the children's claims for compensation from the Criminal Injuries Compensation Board or in the civil courts for harms suffered by those children;[171]
- a class of elderly residents of Alberta's long-term care facilities alleged that the Alberta government artificially inflated the accommodation charges at those nursing homes in order to subsidise the cost of medical expenses, rather than ensuring that the accommodation charges were used exclusively for the actual costs of accommodation and of meals;[172]
- current and former wards of the province of Nova Scotia were placed in the Nova Scotia Home for Coloured Children and claimed that, during their residence there, they suffered physical, mental, and sexual abuse;[173] and
- welfare recipients under the Ontario Disability Support Program disputed the adjudications of benefit claims, alleging that their treatment amounted to breaches of the Canadian Charter of Rights and Freedoms because the procedures used to process, evaluate, and adjudicate claims for benefits were irrational, inefficient, inaccessible, and demeaning.[174]

In Australia, a class action was brought against the Victorian government, arising from strife caused when that government sought to improve, or restore, 'peace and harmony' among sectors of the

---

[171] *Papassay v The Queen (Ontario)* [2017] ONSC 2023, and associated litigation. For a similar claim by those in the custody of British Columbia's child welfare system, family and foster care services, see: *Strohmaier v British Columbia (AG)* [2015] BCSC 1189. See too, for similar claims in other provinces: *TL v Alberta (Director of Child Welfare)* [2006] ABQB 104, 58 Alta LR (4th) 23; and *CP v Saskatchewan (Minister of Social Services)* [2014] SKQB 416.

[172] *Alberta v Elder Advocates of Alberta Socy* [2011] 2 SCR 261, [2011] SCC 24. Ultimately, no duty of care was triggered on these facts. The fact that the province of Alberta may have audited, supervised, monitored, and generally administered the accommodation fees did not create sufficient proximity; and 'floodgates concerns' was a strong policy reason negating a duty of care, per that well-known dictum of 'the spectre of unlimited liability in an indeterminate amount for an indeterminate time to an indeterminate class': *Ultramares Corp v Touche*, 255 NY 170, 179 (1941): at [67]–[74].

[173] *Elwin v Nova Scotia Home for Coloured Children* [2013] NSSC 411, 339 NSR (2d) 35.

[174] *Wareham v Ontario (Minister of Community and Social Services)* [2008] ONCA 771 (claim struck out as disclosing no cause of action).

community.[175] In 1994, the Victorian Premier directed state ministers, government departments, and governmental agencies, to refer to those people living in, or originating from, the Former Yugoslav Republic of Macedonia as 'Slav Macedonians'. It was the first occasion upon which any Australian government had sought to change the name of the language of an immigrant community. The reason for the directive was that the Victorian government considered it imperative to take action to restore peace and harmony to the Greek, Macedonians, and Slavic communities. In a judicial review application brought by the class of Macedonian Greek residents, it was claimed that the directive suggested that the Macedonian language was to be singled out for different treatment, and that it was not regarded by the government as being on an equal footing with every other officially recognised language. The class action was permitted to proceed. Whilst it was found that there was no 'bad faith' or 'any ulterior agenda' on the part of the Victorian government, there was an error in the decision that it was not non-discriminatory.

10   Tax-Related Matters

It is convenient to round out the discussion of the types of class actions commenced against governments by mentioning some tax-related matters of note:

- a class of Chinese immigrants argued that the so-called 'head tax' payable by each Chinese person upon entry to Canada between 1885 and 1923 was a breach of the Canadian Charter of Rights and Freedoms, and should be repaid to the class members' estates;[176]
- a class of taxpayers claimed against the Australian Commissioner of Taxation, for its assessment of certain arrangements as tax avoidance schemes;[177] and
- a class of persons who owned land in an area in New South Wales near Jervis Bay, zoned as rural since 1964, alleged that the Commonwealth and state governments, and Shoalhaven Council, had collaborated and conspired to acquire their property without just compensation.[178]

---

[175] *Macedonian Teachers Assn of Victoria Inc v Human Rights & Equal Opportunity Comm* [1998] FCA 1650.

[176] *Mack v Canada (AG)* (2001), 55 OR (3d) 113 (action struck out; the Charter had no retrospective application).

[177] *Meredith v Commr of Taxation* [2002] FCAFC 271, and associated litigation.

[178] *Esposito v Commonwealth* [2013] FCA 546.

This case law study demonstrates the extraordinary diversity of class actions instituted against governments of all types – federal, state and provincial, local authorities, and indigenous councils and bands.

E Claims in Tort: Some Examples

1 Principal Theories of Liability against Governments

Typically, claims against a governmental defendant – whether brought in unitary or class litigation – are brought on one (or more) of four bases of liability.[179] These are described in Table 8.1 overpage (where defendant = D), and with some examples drawn from the two Comparator Jurisdictions the focus of this chapter:

2 The Problematical Concept of 'Regulatory Negligence'

Governments have an intimate involvement in the daily life of citizens and of entities, precisely because of the extensive legislative framework that governs and regulates society. However, just because a government instrumentality or employee or statutory (public) authority does not carry out a statutory duty or a statutory power, either competently or at all, does **not** give rise to an automatic suit in negligence. In the context of English common law, there are **four** difficulties which any claimant – representative or otherwise – will confront, when seeking to sue the Crown or any government instrumentality or employee in negligence:[180]

(i) The Crown does not owe a duty of care to any claimant, merely by undertaking (via its employees or statutory authorities) a statutory duty or statutory power without reasonable care, or by its failing to perform a statutory duty or a statutory power at all. In other words, a duty of care towards the claimant cannot arise *automatically* out of a statutory duty or power that the Crown exercised, or failed to exercise, properly for the claimant's benefit;[181]

(ii) Where a Crown employee or public authority has exercised its discretion under a statutory duty or power which is purely policy

---

[179] These differentiations are well-articulated, e.g., in: *Razumas v MOJ* [2018] EWHC 215 (QB) [125]–[126].

[180] These difficulties are examined by the author in more detail in: *Principles of Tort Law* (n 6), ch 13.

[181] Pursuant to the so-called 'East Suffolk principle': *East Suffolk Rivers Catchment Board v Kent* [1941] AC 74 (HL) 102, discussed in ibid, principle §13.2 and accompanying text.

Table 8.1 *How governments have been sued in class actions*

The basis	Description	Examples of plea
direct wrongdoing	this is where the claim consists of allegations of direct wrongdoing on the part of the government itself – *viz*, that it committed a breach of contract; a tort; an equitable wrong (such as breach of fiduciary duty); a restitutionary cause of action; or contravened a statutory duty or a statutory power that gives rise to a civil remedy on the part of those affected	Discussed in text below
vicarious liability	the government, D, is vicariously liable for the wrongdoing of another where (citing UK jurisprudence[182]): i. the wrongdoer committed a tort or other legal wrong; ii. the wrongdoer was D's employee, or his or her relationship with D was sufficiently 'akin to employment' to render D vicariously liable; but the wrongdoer was not an independent contractor;	*Daniels v Canada (AG)*[183] *M v Nova Scotia (AG)*[184] *Lakes v MacDougall*[185] *McMullin v ICI Aust Operations Pty Ltd*[186]

[182] *Catholic Child Welfare Socy v Institute of the Brothers of the Christian Schools* [2012] UKSC 56, [2013] 2 AC 1, [47].

[183] [2003] SKQB 58, 230 Sask R120 (Crown sued for vicarious liability; but certification denied).

[184] [2006] NSSC 293, 248 NSR (2d) 230 (representative claimant, one of sixty-two former residents of the Nova Scotia Home for Coloured Children, claimed for physical, mental, and sexual abuse allegedly perpetrated by employees; issue permitted to proceed to trial).

[185] [2011] BCSC 1273, [9] (Crown admitted vicarious liability for acts of sexual abuse by an employee during course of his employment with the government as a prison officer).

[186] [1997] FCA 541, no pinpoint available (vicarious liability failed; '[i]n relation to the claim that the two state governments are vicariously liable for the negligence of officers involved in recommending feeding cotton gin trash to cattle, I hold there is no liability. It is not shown that any officer knew, or ought to have known, that the feeding of cotton trash might lead to a significant contamination problem').

Table 8.1 (*cont.*)

The basis	Description	Examples of plea
	iii. the wrongdoer committed the wrong within the course, or the scope, of his or her employment; or, where the relationship was 'akin to employment', there was a close relationship between that relationship and the wrongdoer's wrong.	
a non-delegable duty of care	this claim operates where the government, D, owes a duty of care to the class members; but there is no actual breach by the government, because it entrusted or delegated the actual task or work to another individual or entity (third party), who did the task or work carelessly. What is alleged against D is not merely a duty to take care, but a duty to provide that care was taken. Non-delegable duties of care are inconsistent with the fault-based principles on which the law of negligence is based, and are hence exceptional. Certain features of a relationship point towards the imposition of a non-	*Griffiths v Winter*[187] *Das v George Weston Ltd*[188] *AS v Minister for Immigration and Border Protection*[189] *Giles v The Commonwealth*[190]

[187] [2002] BCSC 1219, [19] (issue certified to proceed to trial).
[188] [2018] ONCA 1053, affirming: [2017] ONSC 4129 (no non-delegable duty of care applied).
[189] [2014] VSC 593 (Crown conceded that the Commonwealth owed a non-delegable duty of care to those kept in detention on Christmas Island), and see too: *AS v Minister for Immigration (Ruling No 7)* [2017] VSC 137, [99].
[190] [2011] NSWSC 582 (representative claimant pleaded a non-delegable duty in favour of group of school residents).

Table 8.1 (*cont.*)

The basis	Description	Examples of plea
	delegable duty upon D in favour of class members:[191] i. the class members were vulnerable or dependent on the protection of D against the risk of injury (e.g., medical patients, prisoners, children, residents in care homes); ii. there was an antecedent relationship between the class members and D which put the class members in the custody, charge, control or care of D and from which it can be inferred that D assumed a positive duty to protect the class members from harm; iii. the class members had no control over how D chose to perform those obligations, i.e., whether personally, or through employees, or through third parties; iv. D delegated to a third party an integral function of D's positive duty towards the class members, which means that the third party was exercising D's custody, charge, control, or care over the class members; v. the third party was negligent, not in some collateral respect,	

---

[191] *Woodland v Essex CC* [2013] UKSC 66, [2014] 1 AC 537, [23] (Lord Sumption), but 'subject to usual proviso that such judicial statements are not to be treated as if they were statutes and can never be set in stone': [38] (Baroness Hale). Also see: *KLB v British Columbia* [2003] SCC 51, [2003] 2 SCR 403, [30]–[37], where the bases for non-delegable duties on the part of the government were analysed.

Table 8.1 (*cont.*)

The basis	Description	Examples of plea
	but in the performance of the very function assumed by D and which was delegated by D to that third party.	
principal–agent liability	the government may have appointed a general agent (one who has authority to act for the government, as principal, in all of its business of a particular kind, or who acted for the government in the course of the agent's usual business or profession); or it may have appointed a special agent (one who is authorised to act only for a special purpose that is not in the ordinary course of the agent's business or profession). The government, as principal, is bound by, and liable for, the acts of the agent that are within the authority conferred.	*Ibrahimi v Commonwealth of Australia*[192] *Endean v Canadian Red Cross Socy*[193] *Kequahtooway v Saskatchewan*[194]

---

[192] [2018] NSWCA 321 (representative claimant alleged that Border Protection Command was agent of the Australian Government, and had stationed vessels on Christmas Island to conduct surveillance on northern approaches by illegal immigrants to Christmas Island by boat; but the agent did not breach the principal's duty by failing to cause their ships to proceed with all practicable speed to passengers of the shipwrecked boat).

[193] (1997), 148 DLR (4th) 158, 36 BCLR (3d) 350, [12] (blood contamination case; representative claimant alleged that the provincial and federal governments were liable for acts of their agent, the Canadian Blood Committee, in intentionally destroying relevant documentary evidence, thereby prejudicing the ability to prosecute the action).

[194] [2018] SKCA 68, [9]–[10]; and *Safioles v Saskatchewan* [2015] SKQB 183, 472 Sask R 38, [11]; and *WP v Alberta (No 2)* [2013] ABQB 296, 563 AR 47, [34], [77], all of which arose from alleged institutional abuse, re physical, sexual or psychological abuse alleged to have been carried out by, inter alia, agents at the schools.

in nature, courts cannot assess such decisions in a negligence action, because Parliament intended for those decisions to be made by those parties alone. Hence, any purely policy decision of the Crown is 'non-justiciable', and is not capable of founding a duty of care to a claimant;[195]

(iii) The reluctance of the common law to impose a duty of care in respect of pure omissions applies as equally to the Crown (via its employees and public authorities) as to a private entity or individual;[196] and

(iv) 'Something more' than merely failing to perform a statutory duty or power competently is required to trigger a duty of care on the Crown's part. The most common way of seeking to establish that is by proving that the Crown, in undertaking its statutory powers or duties, assumed responsibility for the safety or welfare of the claimant *as an individual*, rather than merely acting for the common good or in the public interest.[197] Alternatively, the Crown may owe a duty of care to a claimant where, in undertaking its statutory powers or duties, the Crown was in a closely proximate relationship with the claimant, and where public policy supported the imposition of a duty upon the Crown.[198]

Class actions jurisprudence instituted against governments, emanating from the Comparator Jurisdictions of Canada and Australia, illustrate broadly the same principles. Numerous class actions have fallen foul of them. Indeed, what precisely was required to satisfy the relationship of proximity in a claim of regulatory negligence was said, in one Canadian case, to be 'in conflict', and with '30 other cases waiting in the wings for the issue to be resolved' in that jurisdiction.[199] It is a landscape of real complexity. Some Canadian scholars have declared that, in the field of regulatory negligence, 'many cases are "contradictory" and "in a state of lamentable confusion"',[200] whilst in Australia, it has been said that 'the

---

[195] Noted, e.g., in *Carty v Croydon LBC* [2005] EWCA Civ 19, [36] (Dyson LJ), and discussed in *Principles of Tort Law* (n 6) §13.4, and accompanying text.

[196] Per, e.g., *Stovin v Wise* [1996] AC 923 (HL), and discussed ibid, §§3.9 and 13.5, and accompanying text.

[197] Per, e.g., *Gorringe v Calderdale MBC* [2004] UKHL 15, [38] (Lord Hoffmann), [100] (Lord Brown), and discussed ibid, §13.7, and accompanying text.

[198] As exemplified, e.g., in *Dorset Yacht Co Ltd v Home Office* [1970] AC 1004 (HL), and discussed ibid, §13.8ff, and accompanying text.

[199] *Taylor v Canada (AG)* [2011] ONCA 181, 104 OR (3d) 481, [28].

[200] F Kristjansen and S Moreau, 'Regulatory Negligence and Administrative Law' (2012) 25 *Canadian Journal of Administrative Law and Practice* 103, 127, as cited in: *Paradis Honey*

common law on the liability of government authorities in negligence is remarkably confused'.[201] A detailed study of the issue lies outside the scope of this chapter. However, a few illustrative class action cases will suffice.

Canadian courts have frequently concluded that legislative schemes created for the purpose of regulating commerce, industry, society, medicine, food production, and so on, were **not** legislatively intended to protect *individual* users, consumers, businesses or entities. In *Cooper v Hobart*,[202] the proposed representative action instituted in British Columbia failed on the basis that the pleadings did not disclose a cause of action in negligence against the government defendant. The Canadian Supreme Court held that the Crown entity, the Registrar of Mortgage Brokers, did not owe a duty of care to investors who had lost money after investing it with a broker that was subject to the oversight of the Registrar. It was alleged by the class members that the Registrar was aware that the broker was violating the governing statute, but failed either to suspend the broker or to warn investors that the broker was under investigation.[203] However, no duty of care was triggered, because the Registrar's duty was not to investors or to individual members of the proposed class, but 'to the public as a whole. Indeed, a duty to individual investors would potentially conflict with the Registrar's overarching duty to the public.'[204] The principle has been applied frequently in Canadian class actions law to preclude a class action against governments or government instrumentalities, on the basis that there is no cause of action for 'regulatory negligence'.[205]

---

[201] *Ltd v Canada* [2016] 1 FCR 446, [2015] FCA 89, [123]. For a review of mixed case law outcomes, outside the class actions context, see too: W Braul *et al.*, 'Water Use Challenges to Oil and Gas Developments' (2015) 53 *Alberta Law Review* 323, 336–41.
M Aronson, 'Government Liability in Negligence' (2008) 32 *Melbourne University Law Review* 44, 46, and cited in: ALRC, *Traditional Rights and Freedoms: Encroachments by Commonwealth Laws* (Rep 129, 2015) [16.41].

[202] [2001] SCC 79, [2001] 3 SCR 537, 206 DLR (4th) 193.

[203] ibid, [40].

[204] ibid, [44] (quote), and see too, [49].

[205] e.g., *Cimaco Intl Sales Inc v British Columbia (AG)* [2010] BCCA 342, [54] ('*Cooper* precludes a claim because a regulator does not owe a duty of care to the consumers of a regulated industry'); *Pearson v Inco Ltd* (2001) 0J No 4990; *MacQueen v Sidbec Inc* [2006] NSSC 208, 246 NSR (2d) 213; *Kimpton v Canada (AG) and British Columbia* [2004] BCCA 72, 236 DLR (4th) 324; *Holtslag v Alberta* [2004] ABQB 268, 28 Alta LR (4th) 284, [59]–[60] ('it is necessary to inquire whether these Acts or regulations impose a duty of care on the Defendant to individual members of the public. In making this inquiry, it is necessary to examine the entire legislative scheme created by the Acts and regulations, including the Alberta Building Code. The duty of care, if it exists, must arise

Moreover, an insufficient proximity between the government and the class members has precluded any common law duty of care, especially where the government did not have any direct involvement in the day-to-day conduct of the activity in question, and was 'simply too far removed from the daily activities of the boards to be under a private law obligation to ensure compliance with the law and policy governing the collection of school fees', as one British Columbia court put it.[206] More recently, a claim of regulatory negligence has been prosecuted upon the basis of a new tort of 'misconduct by a civil authority' (distinct and different from the tort of misfeasance in public office). This new tort was developed in the context of a federal class action instituted by bee keepers against the Crown;[207] although a class action by beer consumers against the Liquor Control Board of Ontario was considered 'not to be the case to give birth to the Misconduct by a Civil Authority cause of action.'[208]

Australian courts have also recognised the distinct problems of assessing negligence on the Crown's part where decisions made by governmental employees and entities were solely policy decisions which did not, and could not, give rise to a duty of care actionable in negligence.[209] Some have remarked, for example, that 'there may also be a large step from the existence of power to take action to the recognition of a duty to exercise the power. Issues as to the proper role of government in society, personal autonomy, and policies as to taxation and expenditure may intrude';[210] and that whether or not a government or government minister owes a private law duty of care in tort involves complex questions of control, vulnerability, reliance, indeterminacy, and the role of government in society.[211] In *Graham Barclay Oysters Pty Ltd v Ryan*,[212] which involved the contamination of oysters in Wallis Lake, an action in negligence against the State of New South Wales failed. The class of persons who had contracted the Hepatitis A virus as a consequence of that

---

from the legislative scheme'); *Williams v Canada (AG)* (2005), 76 OR (3d) 763, 257 DLR (4th) 704, [60] ('[t]he legislative scheme is not concerned with durability or service life of products approved for use. There is no authority for the proposition that this legislative scheme is concerned with economic interests of [individual] consumers').

[206] *Wiggins v British Columbia* [2009] BCSC 121, [42].

[207] *Paradis Honey Ltd v Canada* [2016] 1 FCR 446, [2015] FCA 89, 382 DLR (4th) 720.

[208] *Hughes v Liquor Control Board of Ontario* [2018] ONSC 1723, [273]–[285], quote at [285], having conducted a detailed and scholarly review of the proposed new tort.

[209] *McMullin v ICI Aust Operations Pty Ltd* [1997] FCA 541.

[210] *Graham Barclay Oysters Pty Ltd v Ryan* [2002] HCA 54, (2002) 211 CLR 540, [9].

[211] *Gunns Ltd v State of Tasmania* [2016] TASFC 7, [4].

[212] [2002] HCA 54, (2002) 211 CLR 540.

contamination alleged that the government did not act to take reasonable steps to ensure that the food consumed by the class members was fit for human consumption, but did not succeed. In rejecting the claim, the High Court of Australia stated that:

> At the centre of the law of negligence is the concept of reasonableness. When courts are invited to pass judgment on the reasonableness of governmental action or inaction, they may be confronted by issues that are inappropriate for judicial resolution, and that, in a representative democracy, are ordinarily decided through the political process. Especially is this so when criticism is addressed to legislative action or inaction. Many citizens may believe that, in various matters, there should be more extensive government regulation. Others may be of a different view, for any one of a number of reasons, perhaps including cost. Courts have long recognised the inappropriateness of judicial resolution of complaints about the reasonableness of governmental conduct where such complaints are political in nature.[213]

The High Court refused to accept that the state owed any duty of care to the oyster consumers which would have obliged it to exercise greater control (and, presumably, to permit less industry self-regulation) of that industry. After all, that 'takes the debate into the area of political judgment. By what criterion can a court determine the reasonableness of a government's decision to allow an industry a substantial measure of self-regulation?'[214] Furthermore, the requisite proximity was lacking, for the state 'was not in the position of a highway authority having actual physical control of the land from which the effluent was released'.[215]

As a result, a common law duty of care was not owed by the state to the class of oyster consumers.

3   Novel Claims against the Government in Tort

Class action regimes can attract claims of direct wrongdoing against a government that are of an entirely novel type, and in which the boundaries of substantive law are contentious or evolving, as cases of 'first impression'. However, it is essential to always bear in mind –

---

[213] ibid, [6] (Gleeson CJ).
[214] ibid, [27] (Gleeson CJ). See too: [162]–[186] (Gummow and Hayne JJ), [90]–[95] (McHugh J), [246]–[249] (Kirby J). These principles have been subsequently applied, to negate any duty of care on the part of a governmental defendant, outside of the class actions context, in, e.g.: *Electro Optic Systems Pty Ltd v State of New South Wales* [2014] ACTCA 45, [283]–[357].
[215] ibid, [323] (Callinan J).

especially where novel claims are pleaded against a deep-pocketed defendant such as the government – that a class actions statute does not create any new substantive rights or amend the substantive law (except to the extent that the statute legislates for that[216]). That has been reiterated in both Comparator Jurisdictions of Australia[217] and Canada.[218] It is not the class action that renders defendants liable; the regime merely facilitates the enforcement of substantive laws.

From the wide array of class suits instituted against government, it is useful to take some illustrative scenarios in tort law of cases which fell on either side of the 'permissible' line.

(a)   Negligence

In *Ibrahimi v Commonwealth of Australia*,[219] the ambit of the tort of negligence was considered, for the first time, in the context of a claim arising from a shipwreck of a boat of illegal immigrants who had been bound for Australia from Indonesia. The boat was destroyed on the rocks at Christmas Island during a severe storm. Approximately fifty people died, and forty-one were rescued. The illegal immigrants, and government employees who witnessed the shipwreck, were amongst those who sued the Commonwealth of Australia for damages arising from alleged negligence. In 2010, Border Protection Command, an agent of the Commonwealth, had stationed vessels on Christmas Island in order to conduct surveillance on northern approaches to Christmas Island and,

---

[216] Re, e.g., the tolling of limitation periods for those who never file suit; and the aggregation of damages which do not relate to the individual quantum of class members, as discussed in: Mulheron, *The Class Action in Common Law Legal Systems: A Comparative Perspective* (Hart Publishing, 2004) 38–42; and 'The Mere Mirage of a Class Action? A Challenge to *Merricks v Mastercard Inc*' (2018) 37 *Civil Justice Quarterly* 216, 230–33 (co-authored with D Edlin).

[217] See, e.g.: Australian LRC, *Grouped Proceedings in the Federal Court* (Rep 46, 1988) [348], [355], [357].

[218] See, e.g.: *Kenora Police Services Board v Savino* [1997] OJ No 2768 (Div Ct) [3] ('[t]he Class Proceedings Act does not create any new substantive rights'); *Davidson v Canada (AG)* [2015] ONSC 8008, 262 ACWS (3d) 648, [56] ('the Class Proceedings Act 1992 cannot be used as a source of substantive law to circumvent the substantive law of the Crown Liability and Proceedings Act'); *Briones v National Money* [2013] MBQB 168, 295 Man R (2d) 101, [24] ('[n]otwithstanding the important policy objectives that underlie class action legislation, as procedural legislation, it does not nullify the parties' choice of a different forum, which is a matter of substantive law'); *Reid v Ford Motor Co* [2006] BCSC 712, [26] ('the Class Proceedings Act does not change the substantive law. It is a procedural statute, and therefore neither its objects nor provisions should be given effect to in a manner which affects the substantive rights of the parties').

[219] [2018] NSWCA 321.

amongst other things, to intercept boats and transfer their crew and passengers to Christmas Island for processing under the Migration Act 1958 (Cth). The class submitted that the Australia Government's ongoing and continuous engagement in an operation to intercept the regular and foreseeable arrival of illegal immigrants gave rise to a duty of care owed by the Government to the class members; and that it was reasonably foreseeable that a shipwreck risk to these boats arose when approaching Christmas Island in dangerous conditions.

The duty of care contended for was rejected by the New South Wales Court of Appeal as being an entirely novel duty of care which Australian tort law[220] did not support. Quite apart from a real issue of causation of damage (i.e., there was no evidence that any rescuer or onlooker had suffered mental harm as a result of the pleaded events[221]), no duty could arise. For one thing, it was an example of a 'pure omission', in which no duty could be imposed which required Commonwealth officers or agents to rescue persons at sea at the risk of several dangers to themselves.[222] For another, the risk posed by the class members' activities was both inherent and obvious, against which a defendant did not need to take reasonable precautionary steps.[223]

In Canada too, class action suits in negligence against governments can, even after more than two decades of jurisprudence, represent novel claims, the precise type of which has not been litigated previously. *Brown v Canada (Attorney General)*, a case of 'protracted procedural litigation' against the Canadian federal government, was one such example.[224] At first instance, the Ontario Superior Court of Justice noted that any alleged duty of care owed by the federal Crown to Aboriginal First Nation children, to preserve and protect their Aboriginal culture and identity following the extension of a provincial welfare programme to 'Indians with Reserve Status in the Province', did not fall within an established category of negligence, and hence, required resort to first principles of analysis. Such a common law duty was held to be arguable,[225] and the

---

[220] The relevant law that applied to the territory of Christmas Island was that of the common law of Australia, as amended by Western Australian legislation: at ibid, [165].

[221] ibid, [191].

[222] ibid, [200], [207].

[223] ibid, Annexure A.

[224] Commencing with: *Brown v Canada (AG)* [2010] ONSC 3095, (2010), 102 OR (3d) 493 (SCJ).

[225] *Brown v Canada (AG)* [2013] ONSC 5637, [53]–[66] (Belobaba J), with leave to appeal to the Divisional Court being permitted: *Brown v Canada (AG)* [2014] ONSC 1583 (Div Ct).

class action was certified. Ultimately, that was upheld on appeal, on the basis that the certification judge had taken an entirely proper analysis of the novel negligence claim.[226] Eventually, summary judgment was granted in favour of the class members on the basis that, over the years of the class period, the Canadian Government had a common law duty of care to take reasonable steps to prevent on-reserve Indian children in Ontario, who had been placed in the care of non-Aboriginal foster or adoptive parents, from losing their Aboriginal identity, and that the Government had breached this common law duty of care.[227]

Leroux v Ontario[228] is another noteworthy negligence case. The claim was brought by developmentally disabled class members who had turned eighteen, and who had been approved by the provincial government to receive support and services, but who (it was alleged) had not received those adequately, or at all. One of the claims advanced against the government was negligence, in respect of the Ontario government's operation and administration of its social assistance programme.[229] Given the novelty of that claim, recourse to first principles was again necessary in order to establish a duty of care.[230] In relation to the requisite proximity analysis, every disabled class member directly inter-acted with the Ontario governmental entities, through their receipt of developmental services whilst minors; they had further direct contact after turning eighteen by receiving formal approval for continuing sup-port and services; and representations were directly made to them as to the type of social support and assistance that would be provided. Hence, there was 'at least a chance that the requisite level of proximity can be

---

[226] *Brown v Canada (AG)* [2014] ONSC 6967 (Div Ct) [31]–[38].

[227] *Brown v Canada (AG)* [2017] ONSC 251 (SCJ). A national settlement was recently approved: *Brown v Canada (AG)* [2018] ONSC 3429 (SCJ).

[228] [2018] ONSC 6452.

[229] Specifically, the 'negligent utilization and administration of existing resources. ... [including] indeterminate delays in the waitlisted services, flawed computer programs and bad databases, and the poor prioritization and matching of available resources': ibid, [13], quoting Belobaba J's summary.

[230] Canadian law prescribes that the existence of a duty of care owed by the Crown must be assessed by an application of the two-part test established by the House of Lords in *Anns v Merton LBC* [1978] AC 728 (HL) 751–52, which has now been overtaken and discredited in UK tort jurisprudence. However, the *Anns* test has been modified in Canada in *Cooper v Hobart* [2001] SCC 79, [2001] 3 SCR 537, in terms which closely resemble the tripartite test applicable in the United Kingdom per *Caparo Industries plc v Dickman* [1990] 2 AC 605 (HL), *viz*: (1) reasonable foreseeability of harm; (2) legal proximity between the claimant and defendant; and (3) no policy reasons negating a duty of care, as Belobaba J's analysis in *Leroux* demonstrates (at [30]–[37]).

established as this matter proceeds'.[231] Further, whilst this was a novel claim, at its essence, it was about 'the allegedly deficient and negligent operation of a social assistance system within existing resources. The viability of a negligence claim that focuses on operational deficiencies, as opposed to inadequate funding issues, in the context of a challenge to a social assistance program [has been] acknowledged ... the focus of the complaint is the operational failures in the implementation of a government program.'[232] The class action was certified in relation to that negligence claim.[233]

These suits against government were cases of first impression in Australia and Canada, and a couple of which were instituted at least twenty-five years after the implementation of their respective opt-out regimes.

(b) Misfeasance in Public Office

The tort of misfeasance in public office is not infrequently pleaded in class actions instituted against government. The tort requires (according to the famous *Three Rivers* line of authority) that: a public officer purported to exercise some public power or authority; some act or omission was done or made in the exercise of that power; the defendant either knew that his disregard of the duty would injure the claimant or was recklessly indifferent to the consequences for the claimant; the defendant's exercise of power or authority was done with malice, or dishonestly, or 'in bad faith'; the claimant had sufficient interest to sue the defendant; and the claimant suffered loss as a result.[234] The tort particularly suits the class actions context, for a public officer's alleged misconduct can potentially affect large numbers of people. As one scholar has remarked, 'the applicability of the representative (or class) action to the misfeasance claim in *Three Rivers* seems to have passed without comment',[235] but the case was an example of one claim avoiding a multiplicity of actions for the same event.[236]

---

[231] [2018] ONSC 6452, [32].

[232] ibid, [36].

[233] ibid, [37]. The claim for breach of fiduciary duty, however, was struck out.

[234] *Three Rivers DC v Governor of the Bank of England (No 3)* [2000] UKHL 33, [2000] 2 WLR 1220, 1230; and later: *Three Rivers DC v Governor and Company of The Bank of England* [2001] UKHL 16, [2003] 2 AC 1, [42]; *N v Sec of State for the Home Dept* [2014] EWHC 3304 (QB).

[235] M Aronson, 'Misfeasance in Public Office: A Very Peculiar Tort' (2011) 35 *Melbourne University Law Review* 1, fn 91.

[236] The case was brought by a class of liquidators and creditors of the Bank of Credit and Commerce International SA (BCCI), but was not instituted under the representative rule.

Of its elements as construed in Australian tort law,[237] at least two were at issue in a recent suit brought by a class of traditional Aboriginal owners against the Northern Land Council.[238] The latter is an independent statutory authority of the Commonwealth of Australia,[239] which is responsible for assisting Aboriginal peoples in the Top End of the Northern Territory to acquire and manage their traditional lands and seas.[240] Some novel issues arose in this case, which did not ultimately need resolving (given other defects with the class action,[241] which meant that it could not proceed). One was whether the tort could only be committed by a natural person (as opposed to a statutory authority);[242] and another was whether, in order to show that a corporate entity acted with 'malice', it was necessary to specify some person so closely and relevantly connected with the entity that the state of mind of that person could be treated as being the state of mind of the entity.[243]

The tort has been problematical in some Canadian class actions against the government and government instrumentalities too. The tort's elements, as set out in UK jurisprudence,[244] have been cited with approval in Canadian law,[245] and with similar elements articulated by the Supreme Court of Canada.[246] In *Strohmaier v British Columbia (Attorney General)*,[247] the Crown was sued in a proposed class action by a class of

---

[237] They are broadly similar: (i) an invalid or unauthorised act; (ii) done maliciously; (iii) by a public officer; (iv) in the purported discharge of his public duties; and (v) which causes loss or harm to the claimant: *Northern Territory of Australia v Mengel* [1995] HCA 65, (1996) 185 CLR 307.

[238] *Bill v Northern Land Council* [2018] FCA 1823.

[239] Established under the Aboriginal Land Rights (Northern Territory) Act 1976 (Aus), s 21.

[240] The Council's functions are described at: www.nlc.org.au/about-us.

[241] e.g., the class was ill-defined; it 'does not enable the NLC to determine who is and who is not within the group. Nor are potential group members able to determine whether they are members of the represented group'; and given its reference to 'other Aboriginals interested in' the claim: [2018] FCA 1823, [144]–[145].

[242] ibid, [107].

[243] ibid, [108]–[110].

[244] See text accompanying n 234.

[245] e.g., *R v Price* [2001] BCSC 1494, 109 ACWS (3d) 400, [9].

[246] Per *Odhavji Estate v Woodhouse* [2003] SCC 69, [2003] 3 SCR 263, [32] ('the tort of misfeasance in a public office is an intentional tort whose distinguishing elements are twofold: (i) deliberate unlawful conduct in the exercise of public functions; and (ii) awareness that the conduct is unlawful and likely to injure the plaintiff. Alongside deliberate unlawful conduct and the requisite knowledge, a plaintiff must also prove the other requirements common to all torts. More specifically, the plaintiff must prove that the tortious conduct was the legal cause of his or her injuries, and that the injuries suffered are compensable in tort law').

[247] [2015] BCSC 1189.

children who had been in the custody of British Columbia's child welfare system and family services. The allegation was that the Crown did not make a claim under the relevant Criminal Injuries Compensation Acts, nor commence a civil action against those who had committed abuse and mistreatment against those children, nor did it hire a lawyer to represent the children's interests. The tort of misfeasance in public office was 'bound to fail', said the British Columbia Supreme Court. The Crown's conduct was not deliberate nor intentional, as the tort required;[248] any negligence in not pursuing compensation on the children's behalf did not render a decision not to pursue compensation unlawful in the requisite sense;[249] and given that the class members were suing the Crown in negligence too, it was an inherently inconsistent plea to allege that the Crown was also carrying out a public function for the purposes of the tort of misfeasance in public office.[250] In the class action in *Weninger Farms Ltd v Canada (Minister of National Revenue)*,[251] the tort also failed. The Minister of National Revenue was sued as a Crown agency, on the basis that it administered and enforced the tobacco excise legislation which regulated the manufacture, importation and sale of tobacco. The class members, who were tobacco producers, alleged that the agency had a positive duty to prevent the importation and sale of contraband tobacco; and that the agency 'knowingly and deliberately failed' to fulfil that statutory duty. However, there was no allegation of conduct which was 'unlawful', 'dishonest', or made in 'bad faith', as the tort required.[252] The class also alleged that the Minister had a policy of non-intervention to appease and to placate the Aboriginal community at the expense of the tobacco producers. However (said the court), that did not amount to 'misfeasance'. Rather, it was a policy that took into account economic, social, and political factors, and which happened to have unfortunate financial consequences for one constituency (i.e., the tobacco producers).[253]

Each of these cases raised novel scenarios and submissions relating to the tort of misfeasance in public office, but as the results of these selected

---

[248] ibid, [112].
[249] ibid, [113].
[250] ibid, [114].
[251] [2012] ONSC 4544.
[252] ibid, [30].
[253] ibid, [30].

cases demonstrate, the tort can be difficult to prove in the class actions context.

(c) Conversion

The tort of conversion requires that: the claimant owned, possessed or was entitled to immediate possession of goods, and that the defendant dealt with the goods in a manner that was inconsistent with those rights; the defendant's conduct was intentional, not accidental; and the defendant's conduct was sufficient to exclude the claimant from being able to use and/or possess the goods.[254]

A novel instance of this was recently instituted in a class action against the province of British Columbia in *Trapp v British Columbia*.[255] The representative claimant (who had 'paid taxes throughout his working life and retirement'[256]) proposed a class action on behalf of all British Columbia taxpayers, alleging that the British Columbia Liberal Party engaged in taxpayer-funded, non-essential, partisan advertising leading up to the 2017 provincial general election. It was alleged that, inter alia, the Party committed conversion by using provincial tax dollars to fund that advertising; and that the government of British Columbia committed the same tort, or alternatively, was liable for conspiracy to commit conversion.[257] However, the class members' claims failed, on the basis that it was 'not viable' to characterise tax dollars as the goods of those class members.[258] The British Columbia Supreme Court held that, '[o]nce tax dollars enter the Government's coffers, it would not be proper to characterize those as "goods of the plaintiff". Rather, they become the property of the Government.'[259] As a result, the class action was struck out against both defendants as disclosing no reasonable cause of action.

(d) Defamation

The Australian competition regulator's class suit against those who were allegedly engaging in pyramid selling schemes has been discussed in a previous chapter.[260] What has not been quite so often discussed in

---

[254] *Kuwait Airways Corp v Iraqi Airways Co (Nos 4 and 5)* [2002] UKHL 19, [2002] 2 AC 883, [37]–[44]; and defined in much the same terms in Canadian case law: *Boma Manufacturing Ltd v Canadian Imperial Bank of Commerce* [1996] 3 SCR 727, [31].

[255] [2018] BCSC 580.

[256] ibid, [6].

[257] ibid, [10].

[258] ibid, [57].

[259] ibid, [47], citing: *Troops in Cape Breton* [1930] SCR 554, [56].

[260] See Chapter 6, 'Government as Representative Claimant', Section C(2)(a).

Australian class actions case law and secondary literature, however, is that there was a related class action for defamation *against that government regulator*.

The Australian Competition and Consumer Commission (ACCC) commenced its class action against Giraffe World Australia Pty Ltd (Giraffe World) on 6 May 1998, alleging that Giraffe World engaged in conduct that amounted to misleading or deceptive conduct, pyramid selling, and referral selling, in contravention of the Trade Practices Act 1974. On 14 July 1998, Giraffe World instituted its own class action against the ACCC,[261] alleging that the ACCC's act in commencing its class action, in effect shutting down Giraffe World's business, was precipitous, when the parties were then in communication about the question whether any aspect of that business contravened the aforementioned statute. It also alleged that a media release and a memo published by the ACCC contained several defamatory imputations. Giraffe World brought the class action on its own behalf, and on behalf of seven class members (the requisite minimum class under the Australian regime), who were identified as being a director/chairman of Giraffe World, the president of the company, and five individuals who were involved in the direct selling operations.

The difficulty was that the seventeen pleaded defamatory imputations did not relate specifically to those class members other than Giraffe World. Lindgren J observed that the statement of claim contained 'no pleading of defamation of the individuals. A pleading of defamation of the individuals would involve different allegations (a pleading of different imputations) from those in the existing statement of claim, although there would be some overlap.'[262] It was a reminder that defamation requires an injury to the reputation of *each* class member, and that the defamatory imputation must identify each such claimant as an individual.[263] The court concluded that '[t]he existing statement of claim does not even attempt to satisfy' the threshold requirements of a class action under the Australian opt-out regime, and the action was discontinued.[264]

---

[261] *Giraffe World Australia Pty Ltd v ACCC* [1998] FCA 1560.

[262] ibid, no pinpoint available.

[263] As cited in the early cases of: *Youssoupoff v MGM Pictures Ltd* (1934) 50 TLR 581 (CA) 587; *Monson v Tussauds Ltd* [1894] 1 QB 671 (CA) 692; and with a wide array of jurisprudence since, as discussed by the author elsewhere: *Principles of Tort Law* (n 6), ch 15.

[264] Pursuant to FCA 1976, s 33N.

An unusual claim for defamation was also brought as a class action in Canada by a class of refugees against the federal Canadian government.[265] The allegation was that each of the class members was identified as a member of the Altaf branch of the Mohajir Quami Movement (MQM) in Pakistan, and that an information package gathered and prepared by various officials within Citizenship and Immigration Canada, the Canada Border Services Agency, and the Canadian Security Intelligence Service, were sent by the Minister of Citizenship and Immigration to immigration officers who assessed, *and rejected*, those class members' applications for permanent residency. It was alleged that branding the MQM as a terrorist organisation[266] was capable of adversely affecting the reputation of the representative claimant and of other members of the MQM.

However, the claim in defamation was struck out. The ostensible reason given was that the precise words or statements that were alleged to be defamatory were not set out in the pleadings.[267] However, the Canadian court also appeared to impute a 'serious harm' requirement (explicitly part of the English common law,[268] and since 2013,[269] statutorily enshrined), whereby the number of publishees was so small and narrowly construed that the imputations (if they could be pleaded) did not sufficiently injure the class members' reputation 'in the public'. Although the representative claimant described the internal documents as being 'widely circulated', the reality was that they were provided to local immigration officers who processed the applications for permanent residence. In those circumstances, '[t]here is no explanation for how information which was kept internal to the immigration system would affect the Plaintiff's reputation in the public'.[270]

Neither the Australian nor Canadian case law referenced above engaged with the conundrum of group defamation (although several earlier Canadian class actions against media defendants have had to grapple with the issue[271]). The law of defamation provides that it is necessary for claimant

---

[265] *Mohiuddin v Canada* [2006] FC 664, 295 FTR 96.

[266] Pursuant to the Immigration and Refugee Protection Act, SC 2001, c 27, s 34(1)(f).

[267] [2006] FC 664, 295 FTR 96, [39].

[268] The so-called '*Jameel* principle', named after: *Jameel v Dow Jones & Co Inc* [2005] EWCA Civ 75, [55].

[269] Defamation Act 2013, s 1(1), discussed in: *Principles of Tort Law* (n 6) 763–67.

[270] [2006] FC 664, 295 FTR 96, [38].

[271] See, e.g.: *Elliott v Canadian Broadcasting Corp* (Ont SCJ, 22 December 1993) [16]–[30] ('[n]o individual member of the class of 25,000 has a cause of action in defamation, as none has been singled out by the words complained of as an individual'), aff'd: (1993), 16 OR (3d) 677 (Gen Div), aff'd: (1995), 25 OR (3d) 302 (CA); *McCann v The Ottawa Sun* (1993),

group members to prove that the defamatory statement was reasonably understood as referring to them individually,[272] but these principles can be difficult to apply, especially to 'cases at the borderline',[273] and where policy inevitably plays some significant part[274] ('the group aspect of the defamatory statements should not distract the court from the real issue, namely whether the published words refer to the plaintiff'[275]). However, a class member does not, simply because he is a member of a group, sustain an injury to his reputation because of some defamatory statement directed towards the group *as a group*, and that essential principle of law is not dispensed with in the context of a class action.[276]

Hence, as these cases demonstrate, class action claims which are underpinned by tortious causes of action against the government, and against government instrumentalities, continue to push the boundaries of substantive tort doctrine, even where unsuccessful.

F   Conclusion

The vast array of types of subject matter and grievances which have been the subject of class actions commenced against government and

16 OR (3d) 672 (SCJ) ('there is nothing in the words complained of that specifically identify McCann as distinct from the larger group'); *Bou Malhab v Diffusion Métromédia CMR Inc* [2011] 1 SCR 214, [2011] SCC 9 (a class of Montreal taxi drivers whose mother tongue was Arabic or Creole sued for injury to reputation allegedly suffered as a result of racist comments made by a radio host; by majority, the SCC held that class members had not been personally affected and had not suffered injury individually).

[272] *Knupffer v London Express Newspaper Ltd* [1944] AC 116 (HL) 122, cited in several of the cases noted ibid.

[273] *Braddock v Bevins* [1948] 1 KB 580 (CA) 587, quote at 589. See too: *Brady v Ottaway Newspapers Inc*, 84 AD 2d 226 (NY App Div, 1981); *Algarin v Town of Wallkill*, 421 F 3d 137 (2d Cir, 2005); and *AIDA v Time Warner Entertainment Co LP*, 332 Ill App 3d 154 (2002), all cited in: *Hudspeth v Whatcott* [2017] ONSC 1708, 98 CPC (7th) 40, [263] ('[g]enerally speaking, in the United States, defamation claims are possible for groups of 25 and fewer people, because it is easier to identify each individual in such small groups'). Unions can have particular difficulties: e.g., *Seafarers Intl Union of Canada v Lawrence* (1979), 24 OR (2d) 257 (CA) 263, 97 DLR (3d) 324; *EETPU v Times Newspapers Ltd* [1980] QB 585. Discussed further in: Mulheron, *Principles of Tort Law* (n 6) 787–88.

[274] *Bou Malhab v Diffusion Métromédia CMR Inc* [2011] 1 SCR 214, [2011] SCC 9, [111], and citing: J Tanenhaus, 'Group Libel' (1950) 35 *Cornell Law Quarterly* 261, 263; and J Broome, 'Group Defamation: Five Guiding Factors' (1985) 64 *Texas Law Review* 591, 595.

[275] *Butler v Southam Inc* [2001] NSCA 121, 197 NSR (2d) 97, [53], cited in: *Bou Malhab*, ibid, [111].

[276] *Hudspeth v Whatcott* [2017] ONSC 1708, 98 CPC (7th) 40, [210], citing: *Bou Malhab*, ibid (an appeal from the Québec Court of Appeal, but on the principle of group defamation, civil and common law 'take the same approach': *Hudspeth*, ibid, [209]).

governmental agencies invokes the concern that was expressed at the outset of this chapter – that a government that is charged with the responsibility for law reform consideration and implementation may be conflicted, when it is the government, itself, that is likely to be a frequent target of such litigation. The suitable response to this concern is **not** to eschew a generic class action regime. It is unacceptable to restrict access to justice in such a manner, in order to protect governmental defendants from class action suits. Rather, the concern is best addressed by avenues which are contained in the Recommendations below.

RECOMMENDATIONS: GOVERNMENT AS CLASS ACTIONS DEFENDANT

§ 8.1 The implementation of suitable preliminary merits criteria within the generic regime, and a close regard to the relevant commonality, suitability, and representative threshold criteria, will provide a government defendant with adequate protection in those cases which are not appropriate to commence or to continue against that defendant in class action form.

§ 8.2 When framing a class claim against a government defendant, four principal theories of liability should be investigated, given how such claims have typically been pleaded: a claim for direct wrongdoing by the governmental defendant; a claim for vicarious liability; a claim for breach of a non-delegable duty of care; and a claim for principal liability for the wrongs committed by an agent.

§ 8.3 Except to the extent that a class actions statute permits modification of the substantive law, the statute is procedural only. Hence, the elements of any cause of action pleaded against a government defendant should not be modified or abrogated in any way, merely because the claim is being prosecuted on behalf of a class. To date, this cautionary note has been evident in three contexts, for example:

(a) claims for group defamation are only permissible where injury to the reputation of the class members as individuals, and where adequate identification of those class members, is proven;

(b) novel duties of care, giving rise to a possible claim in negligence, are possible by reference to 'first principles' (i.e., reasonable foreseeability of harm; legal proximity between the class members and the defendant; and public and legal policy favours, or does not negate, a duty of care from arising), but should be assessed no differently, merely because the defendant is a government or government entity;

(c) any claim for 'regulatory negligence' should be treated with the aversion that it usually deserves, given the fact that any failure to execute a statutory duty properly, or at all, does not automatically generate a duty of care owed to those who suffered loss or injury as a result of that omission on the government's part.

9

Government as Class Actions Beneficiary

A   Introduction

Government may become a class actions beneficiary in multifarious ways. As a (rare) class member, government may be a *direct* beneficiary of any successful outcome that is obtained by the representative claimant (as discussed in a previous chapter[1]). However, this chapter focuses upon other, less obvious, ways in which, monetarily, a government may derive benefits from class actions litigation. Figure 9.1 overpage summarises these potential avenues:

These monetary benefits to government – which are analysed in the order in which they appear in Figure 9.1 – arise when there are unclaimed damages remaining, where either aggregate damages have been awarded, or settlement funds have been judicially approved, in favour of the class, and after direct distributions have been made to class members.

An undistributed residue in the context of a class action settlement is, of course, a very common scenario. What has been true in US jurisprudence ('as most class action settlements result in unclaimed funds, a plan is required for distributing those funds'[2]) has applied in the other Comparator Jurisdictions too. Whatever happens to that residue is likely to be less 'personal' as a form of compensatory redress – and some potential recipients of those unclaimed damages may not be class members at all. There is no doubt that the manner of dealing with undistributed residues has been considered, from a class actions drafting point of

---

[1]   Per Chapter 7, 'Government as Class Member'.
[2]   *Six Mexican Workers v Arizona Citrus Growers*, 904 F 2d 1301, 1305 (9th Cir, 1990). See too: *Powell v Georgia-Pacific Corp*, 843 F Supp 491, 499 (WD Ark, 1994) ('[i]t is not uncommon in a class action settlement to have undisbursed funds in the registry of the court').

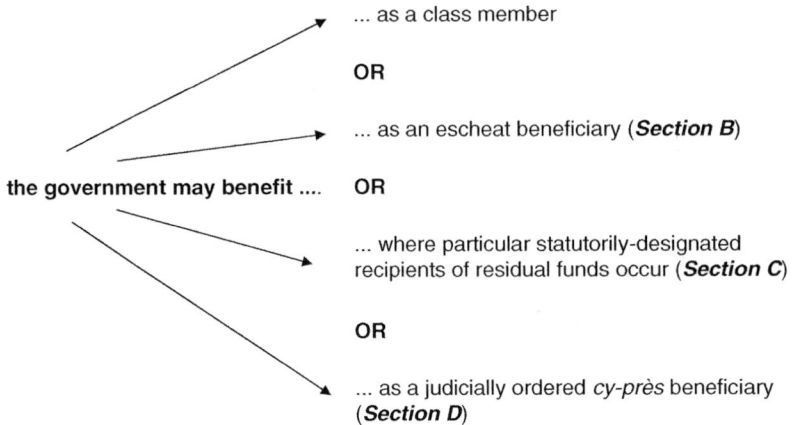

Figure 9.1   How the government may be a beneficiary of class actions

view, to be 'controversial'[3] and 'one of the more contentious design details'.[4] The options potentially available for distributing any unclaimed damages sum are six-fold:[5]

(1) a *pro rata* distribution amongst those class members who came forth to claim;[6]

(2) a reversion to the defendant;[7]

---

[3] Alberta Law Reform Institute, *Class Actions* (Rep 85, 2000) [348].

[4] BIS, *Private Actions in Competition Law: Government Response* (2013) [5.64].

[5] The first five of these were cited in *In re Lease Oil Antitrust Litig (No II)*, WL 4377835 at *18 (SD Tex, 2007). Many US federal courts have articulated some, but not all, of these options: see ibid, citing: *Wilson v Southwest Airlines Inc*, 880 F 2d 807, 813–16 (5th Cir, 1989) (approving options (1), (2), (3), and (5)); *Powell v Georgia-Pacific Corp*, 119 F 3d 703, 706 (8th Cir, 1997) (approving options (1), (2), (4), and (5)); *Six Mexican Workers v Arizona Citrus Growers*, 904 F 2d 1301, 1307 (9th Cir, 1990) (same); *Zaber v City of Dubuque*, 902 NW 2d 282, 291 (CA Iowa, 2017) (same). Also see, e.g.: *Diamond Chemical Co Inc v Akzo Nobel Chems BV*, 517 F Supp 2d 212, 216 (DDC, 2007); *In re Motorsports Merch Antitrust Litig*, 160 F Supp 2d 1392, 1393–94 (ND Ga, 2001).

[6] For discussion of US case law and academic opinion about this option, see: Mulheron, *The Modern Cy-près Doctrine: Applications and Implications* (Routledge Cavendish, 2006) 245–47.

[7] As well as being implemented by some US courts, the option is statutorily permitted in some Canadian provincial regimes. To mention a few, e.g.: Ontario's Class Proceedings Act, SO 1992, c 6, s 26(10); Manitoba's Class Proceedings Act, CCSM 2002, c C130, s 34(5) (c); New Brunswick's Class Proceedings Act, RSNB 2011, c 125, s 36(1)(d). Notably, under the UK Competition Law Class Action, any reversion to the defendant is on the basis that, 'a [settlement] provision that any unclaimed balance of the settlement amount reverts to the defendants shall not of itself be considered unreasonable': CAT Rules, r 94(9)(g); and r 97(7)(g). The reversion option is discussed further in: *The Modern Cy-près Doctrine*, ibid, 250–52.

(3) payment of legal practitioners' fees and disbursements (to the extent that those are not recoverable from the defendant);[8]
(4) an escheat distribution;
(5) a distribution to some pre-determined statutorily prescribed recipient; or
(6) a *cy-près* distribution to a designated entity.

Where implemented or permitted by the lawmakers, then it is the last three of these options which may render indirect benefits to a government.

Debates as to which of the six abovementioned options should prevail, should an undistributed residue arise,[9] are relatively common. This is a debate into which the court is inevitably drawn in the context of settlement agreements, given that, in each of the Comparator Jurisdictions, these must be judicially sanctioned before they can take effect.[10] Perell J of the Ontario Superior Court of Justice spoke for all class actions jurisdictions when he remarked that:

> Settlement approval is the most important and difficult task for a judge under all class action regimes … Since most class actions settle, the integrity and the legitimacy of class actions as a means to secure access to justice largely depends upon the court properly exercising its role in the settlement approval process. In scrutinizing a settlement, the court is called on to protect the interests of the class members who are to be bound by the outcome and who will be compelled to release their claims against the defendant in exchange for their participation in the class action settlement.[11]

---

[8] This has been statutorily enacted in some class actions regimes across the Comparator Jurisdictions, e.g.; Nova Scotia's Class Proceedings Act, SNS 2007, c 28, s 37(1)(b); Manitoba's Class Proceedings Act, CCSM 2002, c C130, s 34(5)(a); New Brunswick's Class Proceedings Act, RSNB 2011, c 125, s 36(1)(b); and the UK Class Action in CA 1998, s 47C(6). British Columbia's Class Proceedings Act, RSBC 1996, c 50, s 34(5)(a), was in identical terms to the aforementioned Canadian regimes, until its repeal on 27 November 2018.

[9] See recently, e.g., *Zaber v City of Dubuque*, 902 NW 2d 282, 291–92 (CA Iowa, 2017) (a *cy-près* distribution to four entities preferred over escheat or reversion); *Rosser v A&S Contracting Inc*, WL 666121 (SD Ohio, 17 February 2017) (*cy-près* also preferred); *Gerken v Sherman*, 484 SW 3d 95, 105 (Mo App WD, 2015), citing: *Kansas Assn of Private Investigators v Mulvihill*, 159 SW 3d 857, 860 (Mo App WD, 2005). See earlier: *Six Mexican Workers v Arizona Citrus Growers*, 904 F 2d 1301, 1307 (9th Cir, 1990).

[10] e.g., in Australia's federal regime: FCA 1976, s 33V, with the state regimes of New South Wales, Queensland and Victoria containing similar provisions. In Canada, see, e.g.: Ontario's Class Proceedings Act, SO 1992, c 6, s 29, with the other provincial common law regimes containing similar provisions. In the US, see, e.g.: FRCP 23(e).

[11] *Waldman v Thomson Reuters Canada Ltd* [2014] ONSC 1288, [80].

Although some law reform opinion has put forward the view that judicial scrutiny of class actions settlements is neither required nor prudent,[12] this is very much the exceptional view. Class actions **are** different from unitary litigation, and the process of compulsory judicial scrutiny is (coupled with certification) the most tangible recognition of that. In addition to preserving fairness for those class members who are not before the court, there are many others whose interests will be vitally affected by the settlement obtained: a defendant who should not be subjected to extortionate or 'blackmail' settlements; the class representative's lawyers and funders, who are seeking reasonable remuneration for assistance rendered to the representative claimant and whose fee agreements will likely be the subject of scrutiny too; the representative claimant, in those jurisdictions which permit a fee to be paid to that representative; and the potential beneficiaries of any undistributed residue of damages.[13] It is a complex landscape, which has not always demonstrated the best of integrity of litigation, according to law reform[14] and academic[15] opinion. It is against this backdrop that distributions to government and to governmental entities must be considered.

US class actions judges have broad discretion to shape orders by which unclaimed class settlement funds should be distributed,[16] whereby the

[12] Scottish Law Comm, *Multi-Party Actions* (1996) [4.92], and Recommendation 19; and earlier: the provisional views in: *Multi-Party Actions: Court Proceedings and Funding* (DP 98, 1994) [7.49]–[7.54].

[13] Many aspects of procedural and substantive law to do with class action settlements are discussed by the author in: 'A Spotlight on the Settlement Criteria under the United Kingdom's New Competition Class Action' (2016) 35 *Civil Justice Quarterly* 14; *The Class Action in Common Law Legal Systems: A Comparative Perspective* (Hart Publishing, 2004), ch 11; and 'Cy-Près Damages Distributions in England: A New Era for Consumer Redress' (2009) 20 *European Business Law Review* 307.

[14] Law reform opinion has frequently emphasised the importance of preserving the integrity of the settlement process and of avoiding collusive settlements (e.g., Ontario LRC, *Report on Class Actions* (1982), vol III, ch 20), and the comment (at 806) that 'there is a real possibility that, without the benefit of appropriate safeguards, parties and their counsel might be tempted to abuse the class action procedure in reaching a settlement'). For reference to similar opinions, see *The Class Action* (n 13) 390–96.

[15] Perhaps the most vociferously criticised class action settlement under FRCP 23 occurred in the asbestos-related personal injury class action in: *Georgine v Amchem Products Inc*, 83 F 3d 610 (3rd Cir, 1996), where a number of problems with the settlement were highlighted in: S Koniak, 'Feasting While the Widow Weeps' (1995) 80 *Cornell Law Review* 1045, 1048. The settlement was ultimately set aside.

[16] A district court has 'broad discretionary powers' with regard to 'equitable decrees involving the distribution of any unclaimed class action fund': *Van Gemert v Boeing Co*, 739 F 2d 730, 737 (2d Cir, 1984). Also: *Everett v Verizon Wireless Inc*, 460 F 3d 818, 827 (6th

court's choice among distribution options 'should be guided by the objectives of the underlying statute [if any], and the interests of the silent class members'.[17] Canadian judges share that wide discretionary decision-making role. However, Australian judges are seemingly more circumscribed as to how undistributed residues should be handled. These differences are largely attributable to the drafting and design decisions which were taken by their respective legislatures to begin with.

There are also *non-monetary* benefits that may be derived by a government from class actions implementation. The class action device can serve to shine a light upon substantive legislative law that is not fit for purpose, and is either too stringent or too lax to serve the ends of justice by which society is governed. As the Australian Law Reform Commission highlighted many years ago, class actions can 'result in inadequacies in substantive law being revealed, [as being] . . . too harsh [or] . . . ineffective. If such problems exist, effective enforcement should lead to the operation of the substantive law being examined more closely and, if necessary, amended to reflect accurately the public interest.'[18] More recently, the Law Commission of Ontario noted, of Ontario's class action, that several interviewees 'stated that class actions cannot be viable vehicles for certain types of claims, such as environmental damage, mass torts and human rights, without reform of the substantive law surrounding these claims'.[19] Even more recently, the Australian Law Reform Commission[20] reviewed class actions which have been brought on behalf of shareholders against companies that are alleged to have breached their continuous disclosure obligations under the Corporations Act 2001 (Cth).[21] In light of the facts that (1) this category of class action is, at the time of writing, the most commonly prosecuted class action in Australian federal class actions law;[22] and (2)

Cir, 2006), citing: *Six Mexican Workers v Arizona Citrus Growers*, 904 F 2d 1301, 1307 (9th Cir, 1990).

[17] *Lessard v City of Allen Park*, 470 F Supp 2d 781, 782–83 (ED Mich, 2007), citing *Six Mexican Workers*, 904 F 2d 1301, 1307 (9th Cir, 1990).

[18] *Grouped Proceedings in the Federal Court* (1988) [67].

[19] *Class Actions: Objectives, Experiences and Reforms* (CP, March 2018) 11.

[20] *Inquiry into Class Action Proceedings and Third Party Litigation Funders* (DP 85, 2018). The author was a member of the Academic Expert Panel which assisted that Inquiry.

[21] The statutory requirements for continuous disclosure, which were enacted as a response to the 1987 stock market crash, are contained in ch 6CA of the Corporations Act.

[22] Since the continuous disclosure obligations were introduced, eighty-two shareholder class actions had been filed in the Australian Federal Court: ALRC, *Integrity, Fairness and Efficiency – An Inquiry into Class Action Proceedings and Third-Party Litigation*

the 'industry' of litigation funding has limited its attention to these 'most commercially rewarding' claims, as opposed to those that could be instituted by impecunious and disadvantaged groups,[23] the ALRC recommended that the Australian Government commission a further review of the legal and economic impact of the operation, enforcement and effects of the continuous disclosure obligations operative in that jurisdiction.[24] Highlighting deficiencies in the substantive laws which a government has enacted is an indirect benefit of class actions reform.

This chapter, however, focuses upon when, and in what circumstances, a government may potentially benefit *monetarily* from distributions of unclaimed residues – by means of an escheat distribution (Section B), by means of a statutorily designated beneficiary whose expenditure of the class funds will assist the government with providing social and legal support services (Section C), and by means of an earmarked *cy-près* distribution (Section D).

B An Escheat Beneficiary

An escheat distribution, in the class actions context, means a sum of money which is allocated (whether by judgment or by judicially approved settlement) for payment to class members, but which is, either statutorily or by judicial order, forfeited to the Crown (also referred to variously as 'the state', 'Treasury', or 'consolidated revenue') instead. It is also called a 'forfeit distribution' in some sources.[25] An escheat to the Crown is derived from feudal principles,[26] i.e., '[t]he King is the owner of everything which has no other owner.'[27] It is a common law doctrine designed

---

Funders (Rep 134, December 2018), ch 9, [1.1], citing the observations of Prof Vince Morabito via correspondence with that Commission.

[23] ibid, [9.89].

[24] ibid, [9.89]–[9.90].

[25] See, e.g., OLRC, *Report on Class Action* (1982) 582 (i.e., discussing whether 'the remnants of the fund should … be forfeited to the Province as a form of unclaimed property').

[26] The concept originated in thirteenth century feudal land law, whereby 'a fief reverted to the lord when the tenant died without leaving a successor qualified to inherit under the original grant. Hence, the lapsing of land to the Crown or to the lord of the manor, on the death of the owner intestate without heirs': *Oxford English Dictionary* (online, 2018). Real or personal property could also revert to the lord of the fee or the Crown where there was a gross breach of the feudal bond: *Butterworths Concise Australian Legal Dictionary* (Butterworths, 1997) 140.

[27] *In re Wells* [1933] Ch 29 (CA) 43.

to ensure 'that property is not left in limbo and ownerless'.[28] Since all property, real or personal, must have an owner, then in the absence of any other owner, the Crown is 'the owner of last resort'.[29]

This type of distribution is called a 'general escheat', which means that those unclaimed monies 'are unconditionally deposited into the treasury of a governmental body for the benefit of *the public at large*'.[30] Where ordered, the unclaimed sum unconditionally becomes the government's monies, to spend 'as it sees fit'[31] – subject, of course, to the law governing appropriations and payments from that Fund.[32] A general escheat is distinguishable from a distribution to a governmental entity which is destined for special purposes that 'map' or are linked to the objectives of the class action litigation. The latter, called a 'specific' or 'earmarked escheat',[33] is a true *cy-près* distribution, and represents another avenue of potential benefit to a government (discussed later in Section D).

1 Legislative Precedents for a General Escheat

(a) Those that Permit

Legislative provisions pertaining to escheat distributions may be divided into two categories: those that amount to general escheat provisions of

---

[28] Quoted from: Parliament of Australia, Treasury Legislation Amendment (Unclaimed Money and Other Measures) Bill 2012 (*Bills Digest*, No 50 2012–13), 'Origins of unclaimed money laws'.

[29] *Confederation Financial Services (Canada) Ltd v Confederation Treasury Services Ltd* [2003] OJ No 1259, [51], citing: *Re Wells* [1933] Ch D 29; and *British Columbia (AG) v Royal Bank of Canada* [1937] SCR 459 (SCC).

[30] *Democratic Cent Committee of District of Columbia v Washington Metro Area Transit Comm*, 84 F 3d 451, 456 (Ct App DC, 1996) (emphasis added), citing: *State of California v Levi Strauss & Co*, 224 Cal Rptr 605, 613, 715 P 2d 564, 572 (1986).

[31] *Nanaimo Immigrant Settlement Socy v The Queen* [2003] BCSC 1852, (2003), 22 BCLR (4th) 308, [28], citing the trial judgment with approval.

[32] Typically, in the United Kingdom, any money received by the government which is not taxation or fines is classed as a 'Consolidated Fund Extra Receipt' (CFER). These are to be paid into the Consolidated Fund as soon as they are received, but arise only rarely, i.e., where unexpected types of income 'outside the ambit' arise: Scrutiny Unit, House of Commons, *Finance Glossary*, 4 (available at: www.parliament.uk/documents/commons/Scrutiny/120515-finance-glossary.pdf). The monies in the Consolidated Fund are generally appropriated via 'Supply and Appropriation Acts': ibid, 13.

[33] *Democratic Cent Committee of District of Columbia v Washington Metro Area Transit Comm*, 84 F 3d 451, 456 (Ct App DC, 1996). See too, outlining these 'two forms of governmental escheat': N DeJarlais, 'The Consumer Trust Fund: A *Cy Près* Solution to Undistributed Funds in Consumer Class Actions' (1987) 38 *Hastings Law Journal* 729, 751–52.

general application, and those that were specifically enacted in class actions statutes. Where enacted, each may potentially apply to the class actions context.

The United States federal class action is absolutely silent as to what should happen with unclaimed residues of damages. However, escheat provisions of general application (reproduced below[34]) have been applied in the context of unclaimed monies which have been paid into court as a result of either a class actions aggregate damages award or a settlement agreement:

> § **2041** Deposit of moneys in pending or adjudicated cases
> All moneys paid into any court of the United States, or received by the officers thereof, in any case pending or adjudicated in such court, shall be forthwith deposited with the Treasurer of the United States or a designated depositary, in the name and to the credit of such court. This section shall not prevent the delivery of any such money to the rightful owners upon security, according to agreement of parties, under the direction of the court.
>
> § **2042** Withdrawal
> No money deposited under section 2041 of this title shall be withdrawn except by order of court.
> In every case in which the right to withdraw money deposited in court under section 2041 has been adjudicated or is not in dispute and such money has remained so deposited for at least five years unclaimed by the person entitled thereto, such court shall cause such money to be deposited in the Treasury in the name and to the credit of the United States. Any claimant entitled to any such money may, on petition to the court and upon notice to the United States attorney and full proof of the right thereto, obtain an order directing payment to him.

Whilst these provisions may not have been enacted with unclaimed damages sums arising from class actions in mind, it has been judicially held that a federal court may escheat unclaimed funds derived from class action litigation to the federal government pursuant to 'the spirit of those provisions.[35] As *Jones v National Distillers* explained: '[t]he option [of

---

[34] 28 USC §§ 2041, 2042.
[35] See, e.g.: *In re Folding Carton Antitrust Litig*, 744 F 2d 1252, 1255 (7th Cir, 1984). It was conceded that the precise technical triggers for an escheat distribution may not be met, in

escheat] ... remains a context-specific, discretionary determination' in the class actions context.[36]

When it undertook its 1982 reform project, the Ontario Law Reform Commission was not enamoured with the unclear and varied approach towards escheat which had been adopted in US class actions:

> Although the American case law suggests that the unclaimed residue of funds resulting from class ... litigation might well escheat, even in the absence of express legislation on this point, there is much to be said for expressly resolving this question. An express statutory provision has a potential for flexibility that is not present if this matter is left to the common law and escheat statutes of general application. .... As a matter of policy, considerations of equity and behaviour modification may interact in a manner that suggests that the fund should be forfeited [to the Crown] in some cases [e.g., where the defendant had perpetrated a consumer fraud[37]] and should be returned to the defendant in others [e.g., where the cause of action proven against the defendant was one of strict liability and in which the damage was unforeseeable[38]]'.[39]

Instead, the OLRC recommended that any class actions statute enacted in Ontario should contain the following provision:[40]

> **cl 28** The court may order that any money that has not been distributed under sections 23–27 be forfeited to the Crown or returned unconditionally to the defendant as the court considers proper.

That is, the OLRC recommended that any new class actions statute should contain an in-built escheat distribution, to be available for unclaimed damages or settlement sums, should the court wish to so order. However, in a scenario which was not by any means limited to

respect of unclaimed damages arising from a class action, but it could nevertheless be permitted ('the technical Congressional requirements present no real obstacles'). The ruling in *Folding Carton* was subsequently criticised as causing some 'confusion': *In Re Folding Carton Antitrust Litig*, 687 F Supp 1223, 1225–26 (ND Ill,1988), and the 7th Circuit later conceded that its original order in the aforementioned 1984 judgment 'appears not to have been acceptable to anyone': *Houck on behalf of US v Folding Carton Admin Comm*, 881 F 2d 494, 500 (7th Cir, 1989). However, successful examples of escheat distributions in US class actions jurisprudence are discussed in Section 3 below.

[36] 56 F Supp 2d 355, 358 (SDNY, 1999), citing: *Van Gemert v Boeing Co*, 739 F 2d 730, 735 (2d Cir, 1984).

[37] Suggested by the OLRC in: *Report on Class Actions* (1982) 595.

[38] ibid, 595–96.

[39] ibid, 595.

[40] As discussed at ibid, 596. The provision of the Draft Bill appears at 871.

this point,[41] several Canadian provincial legislatures subsequently chose to adopt something quite similar to clause 28 – whilst the Ontario legislature itself disregarded the OLRC's recommendation and did not include anything resembling clause 28. Manitoba's Class Proceedings Act, CCSM 2002, provides one such example of an escheat provision:[42]

> **s 34(5)** If any part of an award that, under section 32(1), is to be divided among individual class or subclass members remains unclaimed or otherwise undistributed after a time set by the court, the court may order that the unclaimed or undistributed part of the award:
>
> (a) be applied against the cost of the class proceeding,
> (b) be forfeited to the government, or
> (c) be returned to the party against whom the award was made.

Other Canadian provincial legislatures, whilst very similar, have nominated recipients by another name which is synonymous with the 'government'.[43] By contrast, other Canadian regimes probably permit an escheat distribution, just by virtue of the extremely wide discretion vested in the court which is adjudicating the class action. Alberta's Class Proceedings Act, SA 2003,[44] provides one such example:

> **s 34(5)** If any portion of an award that, under sections 31 and 32, is to be divided among individual class members or subclass members remains unclaimed or otherwise undistributed after the time provided for by the Court, *the Court may make any order that the Court considers appropriate* with respect to the distribution or other use or application of the unclaimed or undistributed portion of the award.

British Columbia's legislature did originally enact an escheat provision almost identical in terms with that of Manitoba (reproduced

---

[41] e.g., British Columbia's legislature included an express requirement that the common issues 'predominate' over individual issues, just as the OLRC had recommended, whilst the Ontario legislature chose to ignore that recommendation, as discussed in: Mulheron, *The Class Action* (n 13) 191–95.

[42] c C130 (emphasis added).

[43] Newfoundland and Labrador's Class Actions Act, SNL 2001, c C-18.1, s 34(5)(b) (payment permitted to the 'consolidated revenue fund'); Saskatchewan's Class Actions Act, SS 2001, c C-12.01, s 37(5)(b) (payment permitted to 'the Crown in right of Saskatchewan'); New Brunswick's Class Proceedings Act, RSNB 2011, c 125, s 36(1)(c) ('be forfeited to the Crown in right of New Brunswick'); Nova Scotia's Class Proceedings Act, SNS 2007, c 28, s 37(1)(c) ('be forfeited to Her Majesty in right of the Province').

[44] Class Proceedings Act, SA 2003, c C-16.5 (emphasis added). Broadly similar wording is used in the federal Canadian class action too: Federal Courts Rules, r 334.28(2).

previously),[45] but on 27 November 2018, that provision was repealed and replaced by a provision which favours a statutorily designated beneficiary (an important amendment which is discussed later in this chapter[46]).

To date, the relevant Canadian provisions have not been judicially applied in order to confer escheat distributions upon the government or governmental entities, so far as the author's searches can ascertain.[47] Some scholars have noted the lack of uniformity amongst the provinces about this option[48] (which may have possibly hindered its application), whilst others have suggested that the lack of usage has been the result of a deliberate strategy at settlement fairness hearings in Canadian class actions jurisdictions, on the basis that it is 'common practice to make express provision for *cy-près* distribution in a way that ensures there is no undistributed surplus'[49] – a practice which appears to have continued quite effectively. However, the US escheat provisions certainly **have** been applied. Hence, it is that jurisdiction's case law which will form the focus of the judicial examples of escheat discussed shortly,[50] for the interesting and insightful comparative lessons that such jurisprudence reveals.

(b) Those that Prohibit

Some class actions regimes take quite the opposite tack. They expressly prohibit an escheat distribution, by providing for the distribution or reversion of any unclaimed damages sum or settlement fund to a stated recipient, and to no other.

For example, Ontario's regime provides for unclaimed damages to be compulsorily paid to the defendant,[51] should any part of an award remain undistributed, following direct distributions to class members[52]

---

[45] Per Class Proceedings Act, RSBC 1996, c 50, s 34(5)(b).

[46] See Section C(1)(b), 'British Columbia'.

[47] An escheat distribution was rejected by the court in its scrutiny of the settlement agreement proposed in Re Canadian Red Cross Socy [2012] ONSC 7124, without discussion as to why that option was inappropriate.

[48] J Kalajdzic, 'The "Illusion of Compensation": Cy-Près Distributions in Canadian Class Actions' (2013) 92 *Canadian Bar Review* 173, 176, fn 9, and fn 21.

[49] Victorian LRC, *Civil Justice Review* (Rep 14, 2008) 554, citing: J Berryman, 'Class Actions' (paper presented to the Second Intl Symposium on the Law of Remedies, Auckland, 16 November 2007) 15.

[50] See Section 3 below.

[51] Ontario's Class Proceedings Act, 1992, SO 1992, c 6, s 26(10).

[52] Per CPA 1992, s 26(2)–(3).

or *cy-près* distributions.[53] That is expressed in mandatory terms.[54] As already mentioned,[55] the Ontario legislature did not implement the OLRC's recommendation for escheat distributions.

The UK Class Action provides that unclaimed damages arising from a judgment **must** be paid to a stated charitable entity[56] (as discussed later in the chapter[57]). There is absolutely no other destination possible in the event of a judgment. However, the same restriction does not apply in the event that a residue is left over from a settlement fund, when the full array of distribution options (including escheat) are theoretically permissible. The legislation itself is silent about those potential destinations, leaving it to the general discretion of the court to approve settlement agreements 'only if satisfied that its terms are just and reasonable'.[58]

Australia's federal class action does not expressly permit escheat distributions either. However, it does permit reversions to the defendant. The regime provides that, should any residue following direct distributions to class members arise, then on the defendant's application, the court may make an order that that residue be refunded to that party.[59] This is the only express provision contained in the regime which deals with unclaimed damages remaining in the aggregate damages fund.[60] Unlike the two previously-mentioned regimes, the Australian federal provision (and the equivalent provision in the country's three state opt-out regimes[61]) is expressed permissively (i.e., that 'the court *may* make such orders as are just' for the return of the money to the defendant). Perhaps this wording may be seen to have left the door open to escheat orders; this remains to be seen. However, given that the law reform commission report preceding the enactment of the federal regime strongly recommended against an escheat distribution of unclaimed residues,[62] and given that no other recipient of the unclaimed funds is referred to in the regime at all, it is unsurprising that there has never been

---

[53] Per CPA 1992, s 26(4)–(6).
[54] i.e., any unclaimed or undistributed sum 'shall be returned [to the defendant], without further order of the court'.
[55] See p 324.
[56] *viz*, the Access to Justice Foundation, per CA 1998, s 47C(5).
[57] See Section C(1).
[58] Per CA 1998, s 49A(5), and discussed further in: Mulheron, 'A Spotlight' (n 13) 21–23.
[59] FCA 1976, s 33ZA(5).
[60] P Cashman, *Class Action Law and Practice* (Federation Press, 2007) 413.
[61] Queensland's Civil Proceedings Act 2011, s 103W(5); Victoria's Supreme Court Act 1986, s 33ZA(5); New South Wales' Civil Procedure Act 2005, s 178(5).
[62] See Section 2(b) below.

an escheat distribution judicially awarded or approved under that regime, so far as the author's searches can ascertain.

There are, of course, *general* escheat statutes operative in these jurisdictions. For example, Ontario's Escheats Act 2015[63] provides that 'possession in the name of the Crown of any property' can be taken under that statute, where 'the property has become the property of the Crown by escheat'[64] or 'the property has become the property of the Crown because it forfeited to the Crown for any cause.'[65] Similarly, New South Wales has legislation[66] which provides that unclaimed funds will revert to state governments, and must be paid into the Consolidated Fund. The legislation applies to 'enterprises' that hold unclaimed money, which is a widely defined term[67] that could feasibly include a court that holds an undistributed aggregate award of damages.[68] However, given that these situation-specific class actions statutes do not refer to escheat distributions, it is unlikely that these general statutes would be successfully invoked in an opt-out class action brought under any of the Australian state opt-out regimes.

It is plain from the foregoing analysis that legislatures across the Comparator Jurisdictions were divided over escheat distributions. And so, too, were law reform bodies. The views of the latter are of interest, should any legislature be considering the introduction, or amendment, of class actions legislation relating to escheat payments to government.

2   Divided Law Reform Opinion

There is no doubt that the prospect of escheat distributions to the Crown arising from unclaimed class actions funds gives rise to 'strong opinions'.[69] Even where esteemed law reform opinion has recommended in favour of the possibility of escheat, it has been viewed as rather down the pecking order of favouritism as a destination of undistributed residues, vying neck-and-neck with reversionary distributions to the defendant.[70]

---

[63] SO 2015, c 38, Sch 4. Other provinces have broadly similar legislation.
[64] Per s 2(1), para 3.
[65] Per s 2(1), para 4.
[66] The Unclaimed Money Act 1995 (NSW). Other states have broadly similar legislation.
[67] Per s 3, 'Definitions'.
[68] The Act 'binds the Crown . . . in all its other capacities': per s 6.
[69] BIS, *Private Actions in Competition Law: Government Response* (2013) [5.66].
[70] The judicial and academic criticisms of reversionary distributions are examined in: Mulheron, *The Modern Cy-près Doctrine* (n 6) 250–52, and by: Kalajdzic, 'The "Illusion of Compensation"' (n 48) 176–77.

(a)   Those in Favour (and Why)

As already mentioned,[71] the Ontario Law Reform Commission favoured a class action statute which granted explicit permission for a court to order an escheat distribution to the Crown. This was to be an alternative option to a *cy-près* distribution, reversion to the defendant, or an order that class members could share in a judgment on an average or proportional basis.[72] A majority of the Commission could see no problem with an escheat distribution, given that the deterrent potential of class actions was a factor in its decision to recommend 'the adoption of an expanded class action procedure for Ontario'[73] in the first place – provided that the court should have a broad and overarching discretion to award an appropriate recipient the unclaimed damages, as one case would differ from another.[74] However, this was, as stated, a *majority* opinion. Within the Commission, there was some strong dissent on the part of one member (and concurred with by the Chairman[75]), who opposed escheat distributions, and preferred the view that any unclaimed damages should be returned to the defendant[76] (and, ultimately, that is what the legislature enacted[77]).

The Manitoba Law Reform Commission also favoured a wide range of possible destinations for unclaimed damages sums, including escheat distributions ('the Commission believes that it best serves the ends of class proceedings legislation').[78]

The Alberta Law Reform Institute also recommended that a court should be permitted to order that all or part of an aggregate award that remained unclaimed or undistributed could be forfeited to the government.[79] Somewhat in line with the OLRC Report, the Institute recommended that the reversion of any undistributed residue to the defendant should be preferred to an escheat to the Crown, 'unless the court considers that in all the circumstances it would be inappropriate to

---

[71] See n 40.
[72] See cll 23–26 of the Draft Bill, in *Report on Class Actions* (1982) 870, and the associated commentary for those provisions earlier in the report.
[73] ibid, 595.
[74] ibid, 596, and Recommendation 8, p 602.
[75] See ibid, 'Chairman's Reservations', 852, para (e) ('I share the view of my colleague . . . that the undistributed residue of an aggregate award should be returned to the defendant, and I join in his dissent').
[76] Noted ibid, 596, fn 364.
[77] Per CPA 1992, s 26(10).
[78] *Class Proceedings* (Rep 100, 1999) 102, and Recommendation 13.
[79] *Class Actions* (Rep 85, 2000) [356] and Recommendation 20(2) at p 140.

do so'.[80] However, ironically, the Alberta legislature did not, as indicated previously,[81] follow that recommendation, instead leaving it very open as to which recipients may receive those undistributed residues.

(b)   Those Against (and Why)

The dissenting opinion within the OLRC (including the Chairman's) has already been mentioned.[82] In the views of these dissenters, reversion to the defendant was the **only** course that should be adopted in the event of an undistributed residue – because its entitlement to the rest of the aggregate award was superior to that of either a *cy-près* beneficiary or the Crown.

The Australian Law Reform Commission opposed escheat distributions too.[83] Part of the reason for this was that the ALRC did not favour the behaviour modification or deterrent objectives of a class actions statute, preferring the view that such a regime should be implemented solely to achieve improved compensatory redress.[84] It remarked that, whilst 'the expansion of access to legal remedies might lead to greater enforcement of legal liabilities [and compliance with the law], and as a result, increase the amount of monetary relief paid' by defendants, that was only 'incidental' to the primary goal of providing access to the remedy the law prescribes.[85] By corollary, that Commission noted that, '[a]ny money ordered to be paid by the defendant should be matched, so far as possible, to an individual who has a right to receive it. If this cannot be done, there is no basis for . . . letting it fall into Consolidated Revenue, simply because the procedure used was the grouping procedure.'[86] More recently, the Victorian Law Reform Commission did not favour the forfeiture-to-Consolidated-Revenue option either.[87]

The policy consultation conducted by BIS, prior to the enactment of the UK Competition Law Class Action,[88] stipulated that one entity (and *only* that entity) could be paid unclaimed damages arising from

---

[80]   ibid, Recommendation 20(3), p 141.

[81]   See the provision reproduced at text accompanying n 44 above.

[82]   See n 75 above.

[83]   *Grouped Proceedings in the Federal Court* (Rep 46, 1988).

[84]   ibid, [354], 'Policy goals achieved'.

[85]   ibid, [67], [323]. The divided opinion amongst law reform commissions upon whether behaviour modification and deterrence should ever underpin a class actions statute is explored by the author in: *The Class Action* (n 13) 63–66.

[86]   ibid, [239].

[87]   *Civil Justice Review* (Rep 14, 2008) 554.

[88]   *Private Actions in Competition Law: Government Response* (January 2013).

a judgment.[89] It considered,[90] but rejected, the option that Treasury's Consolidated Fund could be a suitable destination for undistributed residues. It noted that 'many respondents expressed strong opinions against escheat to the Treasury and that this option was supported by only one respondent.'[91] However, BIS was far more relaxed when it came to an unclaimed residue arising from *settlements*, suggesting that the court may be asked to consider and approve a variety of possible destinations of unclaimed funds.[92]

3 Judicial Observations about Escheat Distributions

(a) Arguments in Favour

Although escheat distributions have not been frequently ordered in US class actions jurisprudence, various judges have expressed support for this option, by which to deal with unclaimed damages, for the right case.

Escheat to the state has been judicially stated[93] to be advantageous over other avenues for distribution, because: (1) it 'preserves the deterrent effect' of class actions (whereas reversion to the defendant 'risks undermining the deterrent effect of class actions by rewarding defendants for the failure of class members to collect their share of the settlement'); whilst (2) it also 'benefits the community-at-large rather than those harmed by D's conduct'. There may be limited circumstances in which reversion to the defendant would be appropriate – say, because it was likely that the claims of each of the class members was smaller than what was originally contemplated; or where the defendant acted in good faith (albeit unlawfully).[94] However, wherever deterrence and behaviour modification are legitimate objectives of the suit, then reversion is considered to be inappropriate in US jurisprudence.

The interests of the non-claiming class members can also be equated with general citizens, and as the US Court of Appeals for the Seventh Circuit has stated, at least those class members will receive some benefit as a result of an escheat, whereas some other options would give them no 'compensation' at all:

---

[89] See n 56 above.
[90] *Private Actions in Competition Law: Government Response* (2013) [5.64].
[91] ibid, [5.66].
[92] ibid, [5.65], [5.72].
[93] *In re Baby Prods Antitrust Litig*, 708 F 3d 163, 172 (3d Cir, 2013).
[94] *Lessard v City of Allen Park*, 470 F Supp 2d 781, 783 (ED Mich, 2007); *Wilson v Southwest Airlines Inc*, 880 F 2d 807, 815 (5th Cir, 1989).

non-claiming class members will benefit indirectly to the extent that the state uses the fund to benefit all of its citizens. Obviously, this results in an imperfect fit between the class harmed – the non-claiming class members – and the class benefitted – all citizens. However, awarding the fund to either the defendants or the claiming class members results in an even less perfect fit because it ensures that non-claiming members will receive no benefit.[95]

Some US judges have further defended an escheat distribution (ahead of other options) on the basis that it provides some compensation to the state for the judicial and physical resources which it provides for the parties' benefit.[96] The Court of Appeals for the Third Circuit explained thus:

> [t]raditionally, unclaimed monetary awards have escheated to the state. The application of that rule seems reasonable and in accordance with general legal and equitable principles. Here, the parties benefitted by the action of the state in providing a forum to resolve their differences and, in that light, repayment to the government to defray some of the costs of the court system would be in the nature of a user fee.[97]

Of course, escheat distributions are simple and inexpensive too. They involve minimal administrative costs, which gives them a tangible advantage (indeed, one court said it was their 'only advantage'[98]) over other distribution options. As one District Court put it, '[r]elying on Jeremy Bentham's principle of utility, the obvious answer is transfer the remaining money to the United States Department of Treasury to be used by the Government for its operations. Pragmatism, simplicity and the need for finality also counsel this denouement.'[99] Such transfers to the US Treasury 'would involve virtually no administrative expense, and would benefit the public at large by increasing federal revenues'.[100]

Finally, where an escheat distribution applies, as opposed to a reversion to the defendant, then the defendant has no standing or input into the discretionary decision which the court must make about the distribution. In that event, the US Supreme Court has confirmed that the defendant 'has no more standing to press its appeal than would

---

[95] *In re Folding Carton Antitrust Litig*, 744 F 2d 1252, 1258 (7th Cir, 1984) (deciding that, instead of invoking the *cy-près* doctrine, the money should escheat to the US Treasury).

[96] *SEC v Drexel Burnham Lambert Inc*, 956 F Supp 503, 508 (SDNY, 1997).

[97] *In re Pet Food Prods Liab Litig*, 629 F 3d 333, 363–64 (3rd Cir, 2010, Weis J, concurring and dissenting).

[98] *State of California v Levi Strauss & Co*, 224 Cal Rptr 605, 613–14, 715 P 2d 564, 572 (1986).

[99] *SEC v Bear, Stearns & Co Inc*, 626 F Supp 2d 402, 419 (SDNY, 2009).

[100] *In re Dept of Energy Stripper Well Exemption Litig*, 578 F Supp 586, 595 (D Kans, 1983).

a losing defendant have standing to contest the division of an award between plaintiff and his attorney pursuant to a contingent-fee arrangement'.[101] The same court noted that class members (whether or not they claim), and not the defendant, are 'the equitable owners of their respective shares in the recovery'.[102] At the very least, given that the equitable ownership of the residue does not lie with the defendant, 'it would appear that there is no underlying impropriety for a court to direct that unclaimed common funds will ultimately escheat to the state'.[103]

It is also worth noting that escheat has its academic supporters.[104] This is partly because it may spread the benefit across all citizens rather than confer benefits upon the class members (whether claiming or non-claiming) who were harmed by the defendant's unlawful conduct – but '[i]n theory, this criticism applies as much or more to other solutions' to damages distribution.[105] And it is partly because it 'wastes virtually no money on administrative costs', and it also 'disincentivize[s] certain parties' from seeking *cy-près* distributions in their favour.[106]

(b)   Arguments Against

The key disadvantage of escheat distributions, vis-à-vis *cy-près* distributions (which are considered in further detail shortly[107]), is that *cy-près* awards 'also preserve the deterrent effect, but (at least theoretically) more closely tailor the distribution to the interests of class members, including those absent members who have not received individual distributions.'[108] As various US District Courts have noted, '[c]y près is often preferred over escheat to the government,' principally because the recipient will be an entity whose interests more closely match those of the class and/or

---

[101]   *Boeing Co v Van Gemert*, 444 US 472, 100 S Ct 745, fn 4 (1980).

[102]   ibid, 481–82.

[103]   A Conte and H Newberg, *Newberg on Class Actions* (4th edn, Thomson West Group, 2002), vol 3, §10.19, 526, fn 9, citing: *Friar v Vanguard Holding Corp*, 509 NYS 2d 374, 376 (1986).

[104]   e.g., G Jois, 'The *Cy Près* Problem and the Role of Damages in Tort Law' (2008) 16 *Virginia Journal of Social Policy and Law* 258, 267.

[105]   J Johnston, '*Cy Près* Comme Possible to Anything is Possible: How *Cy Près* Creates Improper Incentives in Class Action Settlements' (2013) 9 *Journal of Law, Economics and Policy* 277, 298–99.

[106]   ibid, 299. See too: K Barnett, 'Equitable Trusts: An Effective Remedy in Consumer Class Actions' (1987) 96 *Yale Law Journal* 1591, 1599.

[107]   See Section D(1).

[108]   *SEC v Bear, Stearns & Co Inc*, 626 F Supp 2d 402, 419 (SDNY, 2009).

who offer services that are relatable to the class members,[109] and where an escheat distribution 'would serve no public purpose'.[110]

There have also been reservations in US courts as to just how willing the federal Treasury is to spend escheat monies. One class action judge in the US District Court of Texas put it thus: '[an] escheat to the federal government would be inappropriate, as the majority of the remaining funds would likely languish unspent, providing no benefit to anyone'.[111] This concern probably stems from the fact that (unlike with *cy-près* distributions or reversions to the defendant), unclaimed sums deposited with the US Treasury pursuant to § 2041 are not deposits in the final, permanent and irreversible sense. The concluding words of § 2042 provides that, '[a]ny claimant entitled' can apply to recover the sum from the United States Treasury, *after* the escheat. As a result, it has been judicially suggested that the US Government is not the true owner of undistributed class action residues: '[a]lthough the term escheat is used, the United States obtains no beneficial interest in the funds but merely holds the money as trustee for the rightful owners,'[112] meaning that the US Government 'cannot obtain title to the money',[113] and '[a] claimant with title does not lose it thereby.'[114] The concern may be overstated. The US Court of Appeals for the Seventh Circuit noted, in *Folding Carton*, that, '[i]n view of the generous time period afforded by the district court and us, it is doubtful that any claimants will come along thereafter.'[115] Still, the fact that class members can even *apply* for a refund from the Treasury means that, whilst 'the interests of the silent class members are fully protected',[116] some judges have worried about the money languishing unspent.

---

[109] *Rosser v A&S Contracting Inc*, WL 666121, at *2 (SD Ohio, 2017), citing: American Law Institute, *Principles of the Law: Aggregate Litigation* (2010), 218–19, §3.07 cmt b. See too: *In re Polyurethane Foam Antitrust Litig*, 178 F Supp 3d 621, 623 (ND Ohio, 2016) ('[r]ather than see money escheat to the state or revert to the defendant, *cy près* distributes unclaimed funds to a third-party charity').

[110] *Schwartz v Dallas Cowboys Football Club Ltd*, 362 F Supp 2d 574, 577 (ED Pa, 2005).

[111] *In re Lease Oil Antitrust Litigation (No II)*, WL 4377835 at *19 (SD Tex, 12 December 2007).

[112] *Powell v Georgia-Pacific Corp*, 843 F Supp 491, 497 (WD Ark,1994), citing: *In re Folding Carton Antitrust Litig*, 744 F 2d 1252, 1257 (7th Cir, 1984) (Flaum J, concurring in part and dissenting in part); and *US v Klein*, 303 US 276, 279–80 (1938).

[113] Per Flaum J, ibid.

[114] *United States v Seventeen Thousand, Four Hundred Dollars in Currency*, 524 F 2d 1105, 1109 (DDC, 2016) (Doyle J, dissenting) (deposit under §2042 does not act as an escheat).

[115] *In re Folding Carton Antitrust Litig*, 744 F 2d 1252, 1255 (7th Cir, 1984).

[116] *Six Mexican Workers v Arizona Citrus Growers*, 904 F 2d 1301,1308 (9th Cir, 1990).

An escheat distribution will not be able to ensure that the substantive law that was infringed in the class action will be supported or enforced in the future either. The California Supreme Court was undoubtedly correct when it described a general escheat as 'the least focused compensation';[117] whereas *cy-près* distributions better achieve 'indirect benefit to the class members'.[118] In other words, escheat distributions are a very blunt tool of achieving redress, although a sharp tool by which to achieve deterrence.

Finally, in any jurisdiction such as the United States in which various state laws governing escheat distributions are not necessarily uniform, another factor against an escheat distribution is the prospect of the significant additional expense which would be required for class lawyers (or a settlement administrator) to review those laws and then allocate the undistributed funds according to those varying laws.[119]

Some academic commentators vehemently discount the utility of escheat distributions, on the basis that the 'benefits are thinly spread throughout the general public and there is no focus on future deterrence of the offense';[120] that 'the government's entitlement to the funds is weak at best';[121] that escheat is highly inappropriate where the money is rightfully the property of consumers;[122] and that it 'is overly cumbersome and risks only benefiting local governments rather than advancing the goals of the underlying claims'.[123]

The divisive views surrounding escheat distributions, both at judicial and law reform levels, are indicative of the controversy that undistributed residues attract. However, in the author's view, escheat distributions do have their place, alongside the panoply of options to which a court may have regard. The advantages that such a distribution may offer, as outlined in this chapter, cannot be discounted out-of-hand. Whilst the option may rarely be invoked, it is a legitimate destination,

---

[117] *State of California v Levi Strauss & Co*, 41 Cal 3d 460, 475, 224 Cal Rptr 613 (1986).

[118] *Mace v VanRu Credit Corp*, 109 F 3d 338, 345 (7th Cir, 1997), and approved/applied in: *Rosser v A&S Contracting Inc*, WL 666121, at *2 (SD Ohio, 2017).

[119] *In re Lease Oil Antitrust Litig (No II)*, WL 4377835 at *20 (SD Tex, 12 December 2007). In that event, the court moved to consider, and approve, a *cy-près* distribution to the 'Neighborhood Air Toxics Modeling Project for Houston and Corpus Christi'.

[120] J McCall et al., 'Greater Representation for California Consumers: Fluid Recovery, Consumer Trust Funds, and Representative Actions' (1995) 46 *Hastings Law Journal* 797, 809.

[121] J Tidmarsh, 'Cy Près and the Optimal Class Action' (2014) 82 *George Washington Law Review* 767, 769.

[122] D Nelthorpe, 'Consumer Trusts Funds' (1988) 13 *Legal Services Bulletin* 26, 26.

[123] C Bartholomew, 'Saving Charitable Settlements' (2015) 83 *Fordham Law Review* 3241, 3249.

and the government of the day (and general public) may benefit from
the windfall.

4   The Criteria That Point towards, or away from, an Escheat Distribution

An analysis of US class actions case law demonstrates that one or more of
the following factors will need to be present, before any escheat distribution will be ordered by which to deal with an undistributed residue:

(i) the state is more likely to be an appropriate recipient where the
underlying statute infringed was a statute which was enacted by the
US Government precisely to serve deterrence and enforcement
objectives. In such circumstances, an escheat distribution would
enforce the substantive law, and it would be appropriate that any
unclaimed monies revert to the state.[124] The types of federal statutes
which have typically been considered to serve those deterrent goals
are antitrust, securities, and civil rights statutes.[125] As one court put
it, where 'the original sources of the Distribution Funds were disgorgement and penalties' arising from infringements of securities
statutes, then 'those origins ... answer the question of how the
money can be used to do "the greatest good for the greatest number
of people"';[126]

(ii) an escheat distribution is appropriate where neither a *cy-près* award
nor reversion of the funds to the defendant is considered to be appropriate on the facts. This scenario has arisen where using unclaimed
funds to establish a proposed charitable foundation would be an
unneeded use of the money and 'would be carrying coals to
Newcastle'; and where a reversion was also inappropriate because the
goals of the underlying statute meant that disgorgement from the
defendant was necessary.[127] In some cases, appellate courts have

---

[124] *Hodgson v YB Quezada*, 498 F 2d 5, 6 (9th Cir, 1974) (reversion of unclaimed settlement
funds to Treasury authorised by enforcement goals of the Fair Labor Standards Act,
where the employer was successfully sued for violating that Act's overtime and book-
keeping requirements, and restrained from withholding overtime compensation), and
cited, on this point, in: *Six Mexican Workers v Arizona Citrus Growers*, 904 F 2d 1301,
1307–8 (9th Cir, 1990).

[125] *Newberg on Class Actions* (n 103) §10.19, 525 (case law references per statute omitted).

[126] *SEC v Bear, Stearns & Co Inc*, 626 F Supp 2d 402, 419 (SDNY, 2009).

[127] *In re Folding Carton Litig*, 744 F 2d 1252, 1254–55 (7th Cir, 1984) (rejecting *cy-près* under
circumstances and requiring escheat of settlement funds to federal government). Also
evident in: *Six Mexican Workers v Arizona Citrus Growers*, 904 F 2d 1301, 1309 (9th Cir,

emphasised the order of preference, *viz*, that it is only where a suitable *cy-près* beneficiary cannot be located that a district court should consider escheating the funds to the United States Treasury;[128]

(iii) escheat distributions benefit *all* citizens, and in some cases, that may match the purpose of why the litigation was instituted better than any *cy-près* order would do.[129] For example, where there is a clear crossover between the general public and the injured class members (say, where those aggrieved class members were users of public transport), so that it could be said with reasonable confidence that a distribution to the US Treasury would probably compensate the injured class members too, then an escheat distribution is particularly apposite;[130]

(iv) an escheat distribution may be 'particularly fitting' if the government has (via its regulator) sought to compel the particular defendant's compliance with the law on many occasions: '[p]aying the money to the Treasury will help defray the cost of those efforts';[131] and

(v) an escheat distribution may also be appropriate where it would be 'impracticable' or 'infeasible' to pay the unclaimed damages to those class members who were injured by the defendant's conduct, because say, 'numerous victims suffered relatively small amounts', or 'the victims cannot be identified', or 'there are no victims entitled to damages'.[132]

On the other hand, some factors have pointed away from an escheat distribution in US jurisprudence, *viz*:

1990) ('If the district court is unable to develop an appropriate *cy-près* distribution, or finds *cy-près* no longer appropriate, it should consider escheating the funds pursuant to 28 USC § 2042. In light of the deterrence objective of FLCRA and the nature of the violations, we find that reversion of the funds to the defendants is not an available option').

[128] *Nachshin v AOL LLC*, 663 F 3d 1034, 1041 (9th Cir, 2011), citing: *Six Mexican Workers*, 904 F 2d 1301, 1307, 1309 (9th Cir, 1990). Also: *In re Lupron Marketing and Sales Practice Litig*, 677 F 3d 21, 33 (1st Cir, 2012).

[129] *Folding Cartons* 744 F 2d 1252, 1254–55 (7th Cir, 1984).

[130] An example provided in: *In re Dept of Energy Stripper Well Exemption Litig*, 578 F Supp 586, 595 (D Kans, 1983).

[131] *SEC v Drexel Burnham Lambert Inc*, 956 F Supp 503, 508 (SDNY, 1997) (and noting, 'in light of the Posners' long and inglorious history of preying on public companies').

[132] *SEC v Lorin*, 869 F Supp 1117, 1129 (SDNY, 1994), *aff'd* 76 F 3d 458 (2d Cir, 1996) ('[w]here distribution to identifiable injured parties is not feasible or appropriate, the money disgorged by the defendant is paid to the Treasury', citing: *SEC v Dimensional Entertainment Corp*, 1996 WL 107290 (SDNY, 1996) and *SEC v Marcus Schloss & Co Inc*, 714 F Supp 100 (SDNY, 1989). Also see *United States v Exxon Corp*, 561 F Supp 816 (DDC, 1983), where those who were victims of overcharging by the defendant for oil were impossible to trace; escheat distribution ordered).

(i) an escheat to a governmental body has been held to not be appropriate if 'this option is not urged by any party';[133]

(ii) nor is an escheat distribution appropriate where 'a more precise distribution approach is available', *viz*, where a *cy-près* distribution that achieves a better overlap between the injured class and the benefitted class is possible. To reiterate, '[u]nder the general escheat, the funds are unconditionally deposited into the treasury of a governmental body for the benefit of the public at large. Because this approach provides the least focused compensation to the injured class, it is used only when a more precise method cannot be found';[134] and

(iii) also, it has been judicially suggested that an escheat distribution is inappropriate, if the governmental regulator 'has already had an opportunity to pursue the defendants, has in fact done so, and has collected an amount that satisfied it.'[135]

C A Statutorily Designated Beneficiary

The second manner in which a class action may monetarily benefit a government is by more indirect means, where the services of a statutorily designated beneficiary serve as a substitute for, or assistance with, legal and social support services that the government is unable or unwilling to provide.

1 Legislative Precedents

In earlier class actions law, it was unusual (although not unheard of) that legislatures would design their regimes so as to provide that undistributed

---

[133] *Diamond Chemical Co Inc v Akzo Nobel Chems BV*, 517 F Supp 2d 212, 217–18 (DDC, 2007) ('[t]he Court shall therefore consider those options that are advanced by Class Plaintiff and Defendants – reversion and *cy près* distribution'). Also: *Kansas Assn of Private Investigators v Mulvihill*, 159 SW 3d 857, fn 2 (Ct App WD Mo, 2005); and *Powell v Georgia-Pacific Corp*, 119 F 3d 703, 706 (8th Cir, 1997) ('[b]ecause neither party challenges the court's decision not to allow a reversion of the funds to GP or to escheat them, we need determine only whether the court correctly settled on a *cy près* distribution or, alternatively, whether the money should have been distributed *pro rata*').

[134] *State of California v Levi Strauss & Co*, 224 Cal Rptr 605, 613–14, 715 P 2d 564, 572–73 (1986). This was the reason that no general escheat was ordered in *Democratic Centre Committee of District of Columbia v Washington Metropolitan Area Transit Comm*, 84 F 3d 451, 457 (DC Ct App, 1996).

[135] *Six Mexican Workers v Arizona Citrus Growers*, 904 F 2d 1301, 1313 (9th Cir, 1990, Fernandez J, concurring).

residues arising from either judgments or settlements in class actions suits should be paid to a particular entity which was statutorily designated. However, that option, by which to benefit government 'in kind', has been adopted relatively recently by two different legislatures, discussed next. This suggests that modern legislatures wish to exert more control over the destination of unclaimed residual funds arising in class actions, and to remove the decision, partially or completely, from the judicial arena.

(a) The United Kingdom

Under the UK Competition Law Class Action, where the Competition Appeal Tribunal (CAT) makes an aggregate award of damages, a time period in which class members may come forward to claim their individual quantum of damages must be prescribed (the 'specified period'[136]). If undistributed funds remain thereafter, then the regime provides, in the Competition Act 1998, as follows:

> **s 47C(5)** Subject to subsection (6),[137] where the Tribunal makes an award of damages in opt-out collective proceedings, any damages not claimed by the represented persons within a specified period must be paid to the charity for the time being prescribed by order by the Lord Chancellor under s 194(8) of the Legal Services Act 2007.

According to delegated legislation,[138] the prescribed charity, for the purposes of section 194(8), is the Access to Justice Foundation (the AtJF).[139] That Foundation is a registered charity[140] which uses its acquired monies 'to promote access to justice.'[141] It thus fulfils the statutory requirement, set out in the Legal Services Act, of any prescribed charity 'provid[ing] financial support to persons who provide, or

---

[136] See: CAT Rules, r 93(3)(a). It means that time 'specified in a direction made by the Tribunal', as clarified in: CA 1998, s 47B(14).

[137] That sub-section permits all or part of the costs or expenses incurred by the representative in connection with the proceedings to be paid from the residual damages. The history and purpose of that provision, which represents a statutory 'first charge' upon the residuary damages, is discussed by the author in: 'Third Party Funding and Class Actions Reform' (2015) 131 *Law Quarterly Review* 291.

[138] Per the Legal Services Act 2007 (Prescribed Charity) Order 2008, in force 3 November 2008.

[139] For further information, see the entity's website at: www.atjf.org.uk/#. The Foundation was launched as a charity on 8 October 2008.

[140] Charity registration number 1126147.

[141] See AtJF, and the description under 'About us', at: www.atjf.org.uk/about-us.html.

organise or facilitate the provision of, legal advice or assistance (by way of representation or otherwise) which is free of charge'.[142]

Hence, this means that: where an award of aggregate damages is made;[143] an undistributed residue remains following direct distributions to claiming class members; any payment in respect of the 'costs and expenses incurred in connection with the proceedings' has been made to the representative claimant (if ordered);[144] and some funds remain, then the AtJF is the **only** recipient specified. The monies can go absolutely nowhere else. However, in this regard, the UK Competition Law Class Action followed the recommendation of the Government.[145] Earlier, Sir Rupert Jackson had also identified an 'opportunity' for the AtJF to act as a suitable destination of unclaimed damages which may arise from any opt-out class action that may be introduced to UK law.[146]

On the other hand, the situation is more fluid where the parties have reached a judicially approved *settlement* under the UK Competition Law Class Action.[147] In that case, the representative claimant must specify how settlement sums are to be paid and distributed;[148] and any residual unclaimed sum can be distributed howsoever the parties agree and the CAT approves. Conceivably, that distribution could be in favour of any of the six options outlined earlier in this chapter.[149] None of these is 'off the table', insofar as settlements are concerned. That, too, was a deliberate recommendation of the Government – that defendants should be 'free to settle on other bases', other than a distribution to the AtJF.[150]

It is worth noting that a distribution of unclaimed damages to the AtJF was a point upon which the views of consultation respondees were quite divided. Only half of the respondees favoured this recipient as the sole beneficiary.[151] However, for those favouring this option, the charity was considered to be a trustworthy entity, 'experience[d] with receiving funds

---

[142] Per the Legal Services Act 2007, s 194(9)(b).

[143] Per CA 1998, s 47C(2).

[144] Per CA 1998, s 47C(6).

[145] BIS, *Private Actions in Competition Law: Government Response* (January 2013) 6, 26, and [5.70].

[146] See: *Review of Civil Litigation Costs: Final Report* (December 2009), ch 33, 336, [4.10].

[147] Per CA 1998, s 49A, but only where it is 'satisfied that its terms are just and reasonable': s 49A(5).

[148] Per CAT Rules, r 94(4)(d).

[149] See pp 316–317.

[150] BIS, *Private Actions in Competition Law: Government Response* (January 2013), per the box on p 26, and [5.70]. See earlier: BIS, *Consultation Paper* (April 2012) [5.64]–[5.45], and [5.70].

[151] *Private Actions: Government Response*, ibid, [5.46], and Figure 5, green shading.

from litigation and has the necessary expertise when legal issues arise as well as dealing with inherently unpredictable sources of income'.[152] Nonetheless, opponents of the idea of a statutory *cy-près* provision and/or that the AtJF should serve as sole destination, considered that: other more appropriate recipients could consist of: the defendant; the Crown (HM Treasury); *cy-près* destinations; other specifically named recipients; or a range of these to be selected by the court on a case-by-case basis.[153] One respondent considered that any distribution of unclaimed damages to the AtJF would 'cross the line from compensation to punishment'[154] (a view with which some English academic commentary has concurred[155]), whilst another noted that it would create 'an unjustified windfall' to the AtJF.[156] Hence, there was a significant proportion of respondees who considered that other recipients had a preferable claim to unclaimed damages than did the AtJF.

Perhaps for this reason, the Government left open the possibility of another recipient or destination being statutorily prescribed 'at a future date, in response to evidence as to how the system is working'.[157] That evidence will undoubtedly take some years to manifest, given that the regime is sectoral only, and hence the rate of litigation is considerably less than would have been evident under a generic opt-out class action regime.[158]

Nevertheless, the explicit distinction adopted by the UK legislature, between limiting the recipient of unclaimed *judgment-awarded* damages to one statutorily prescribed charity, whilst permitting various entities (including the defendant) to share in unclaimed *settlement* monies, is unique amongst those regimes enacted across the Comparator Jurisdictions. It is a distinguishing feature from its Australian, Canadian and United States earlier counterparts.

---

[152] ibid, [5.47].
[153] ibid, [5.46].
[154] Per Herbert Smith Freehill *Submission* (reproduced ibid, [5.49]).
[155] e.g.: J Sorabji, 'Coping with Complexity and Securing Justice through Multi-Party Litigation: Lessons from the CAT and JJB Sports' [2014] *European Business Law Review* 527, 536 ('[t]he problem at the heart of the statutory *cy-près* mechanism in the 2013 Bill is that it rests on an implicit acceptance that the opt-out action goes beyond the primary purpose of civil proceedings: to secure compensation as a means of rights-vindication').
[156] City of London Law Society *Submission* (reproduced ibid).
[157] ibid, [5.71].
[158] At the time of writing, some three years after the regime took effect on 1 October 2015, only six actions have been filed in total.

(b) British Columbia

In November 2018, the Parliament of British Columbia introduced a Bill,[159] the purpose of which was to considerably change the way in which undistributed residues of aggregate damages sums are treated in that province.[160] That Bill duly received Royal Assent,[161] and its amending provisions now form part of the class actions statute in that jurisdiction.[162] In a provision that is reminiscent of the UK's legislative solution discussed above, the amendment did away with the former regime[163] which vested a broad discretion in the court as to how to distribute that residue. Instead, it legislatively provides that *half* of any such residue (whether arising from judgments or settlements, and not just from judgments as the UK provision provides) must now be paid to the Law Foundation of British Columbia in most (but not all) cases:

> **36.2** (1) Subject to subsection (2), the court must order that, if all or any part of an award under Division 2 or settlement funds under section 35 have not been distributed within a time set by the court,
>
> > (a) 50% of the undistributed amount be distributed to the Law Foundation of British Columbia, and
> >
> > (b) 50% of the undistributed amount be applied in any manner that may reasonably be expected to benefit class or subclass members, including, if appropriate, distribution to the Law Foundation of British Columbia.
>
> (2) If the award or settlement referred to in subsection (1) is in respect of a class proceeding that relates to damage or loss suffered primarily by Indigenous people of Canada or it would be impractical or impossible for the court to make an order under that subsection, the court must order that all or any part of the undistributed amount be applied in any manner that may reasonably be expected to benefit class or subclass members.

---

[159] Attorney General Statutes Amendment Act, 2018 (Bill 57, 2018). The Bill received its First Reading on 19 November 2018.

[160] This significant change is in addition to other 2018 amendments which had the effect of transforming the British Columbia from an opt-in to an opt-out regime for non-resident class members, and of establishing a formal framework for the certification of multi-jurisdictional class proceedings, as discussed in Chapter 5, 'Government as "Gate-Keeper": Cross-Border Class Actions'.

[161] This occurred on 27 November 2018: see *Progress of Bills*, 3rd Session, 41st Parliament (British Columbia), available at: www.leg.bc.ca/parliamentary-business/legislation-debates-proceedings/41st-parliament/3rd-session/bills/progress-of-bills.

[162] Class Proceedings Act, RSBC 1996, c 50, Part 4, and with a new Div 4 inserted.

[163] i.e., the previous s 34, 'Undistributed Award', was repealed.

This means that suits which concern grievances suffered primarily by Indigenous peoples are exempt from these amending rules, thus vesting a broad discretion in the courts to select appropriate *cy-près* recipients of undistributed funds in those cases, just as occurs for all cases under the existing regime.[164]

As of 2001, all Canadian provinces and territories have law foundations in place. These foundations now have two main revenue sources: the interest earned on lawyers and paralegals' mixed trust accounts; and as recipients of *cy-près* awards in class actions litigation.[165] The largest of these Foundations, that of Ontario, describes how it distributes its funds in this way: 'by law, the Foundation gives 75% of the revenue [earned from mixed trust accounts] after operating expenses to Legal Aid Ontario; [it] uses the remaining 25% to make innovative grants to improve access to justice across Ontario; [and] the Foundation uses [*cy-près*] funds to make grants across the country through its Access to Justice Fund'.[166] The Law Foundation of British Columbia, established by statute in 1969,[167] was actually the *first* such foundation established in Canada. It is mandated by statute to distribute its funds in five areas: legal education, legal aid, legal research, law reform, and law libraries.[168] The Government of British Columbia hence considered that it would be appropriate to introduce the recent changes to the class actions statute, given that the funds distributed to the Law Foundation will be required to

---

[164] See *Explanatory Note* accompanying cl 19 of the Bill, available at: www.leg.bc.ca/parlia mentary-business/legislation-debates-proceedings/41st-parliament/3rd-session/bills/ first-reading/gov57-1.

[165] These foundations (and similar foundations existing in Australia and in the United States) were established as a result of the decision of the House of Lords in *Brown v Inland Revenue Commrs* [1965] AC 244 (HL), which held that solicitors who held clients' monies in designated trust accounts were not entitled to retain the interest earned from those sums and use the interest for their own benefit, because the interest in question did not belong to the solicitors (the interest could not be retained 'either by custom or by implied agreement, although a similar practice had long been followed by a number of solicitors': at 245). Hence, an alternative use of those monies had to be found. The legislature in New South Wales decided to deal with the issue by creating, in 1967, a Law Foundation to receive the interest and use it for legal aid, legal education and legal research purposes, and other jurisdictions have followed suit.

[166] See: 'Who we are', available at: www.lawfoundation.on.ca/who-we-are/.

[167] *viz*, by the Legal Profession Act, and established in April 1969, as described at: 'History of the Law Foundation' at: www.lawfoundationbc.org/about-us/history/.

[168] Per: Legal Profession Act, SBC 1998, c 9, s 61(1), and described in further detail at: 'Mandate, Mission and Strategic Priorities', available at: www.lawfoundationbc.org /about-us/mandate-mission-and-strategic-priorities/.

be used to facilitate access to justice, which in turn 'is a core principle of class proceedings'.[169]

At the time of writing, the new British Columbia provisions have not been judicially applied. However, there are certainly cases in which the Law Foundation of British Columbia has already been judicially approved as a *cy-près* recipient of undistributed residues, on the basis of its impressive 'role in promoting consumer rights and access to justice'.[170]

(c) US State Statutes

The aforementioned United Kingdom and British Columbia provisions, which statutorily designate a specific beneficiary of unclaimed class action funds, is not a new idea. Some US states enacted statutes, much earlier, and these stipulated that a certain percentage of undistributed funds should be sent to certain recipients.[171]

For example, the Illinois Civil Procedure Code[172] provides that undistributed residues (whether arising under judgments or settlements) must be distributed to 'eligible organizations':

---

735 Residual funds in a common fund created in a class action

Definitions. 'Eligible organization' means a not-for-profit organization that:
  (i)   has been in existence for no less than 3 years;
  (ii) has been tax exempt for no less than 3 years from the payment of federal taxes . . . ;
  (iii) . . .
  (iv) has a principal purpose of promoting or providing services that would be eligible for funding under the Illinois Equal Justice Act;
  (v)   . . .

Settlement. An order approving a proposed settlement of a class action that results in the creation of a common fund for the benefit of the class shall . . . provide for the distribution of any residual funds to one or more eligible organizations, except that up to 50% of the residual funds may be distributed to one or more other nonprofit charitable organizations or other organizations that serve the public good if the court finds there is good cause to approve such a distribution as part of a settlement.

---

[169] As cited in: 'Introduction of Miscellaneous Bill' (*British Government News*, 19 November 2018), available at: https://news.gov.bc.ca/releases/2018AG0097-002221.

[170] *Park v Nongshim Co Ltd* [2019] ONSC 1997, [96]. Also a *cy-près* recipient in: *Steele v Toyota Canada Inc* [2015] BCSC 1014; *Marshall v Yellow Cash Centre Inc* [2015] BCSC 365.

[171] As discussed in: Jois, 'The *Cy Près* Problem' (n 104) 259.

[172] ch 735, Code of Civil Procedure, Art II, Civil Practice Pt 8, 'Class Action'.

Judgment. A judgment in favor of the plaintiff in a class action that results in the creation of a common fund for the benefit of the class shall provide for the distribution of any residual funds to one or more eligible organizations.

Notably, the court has more discretion under settlements than it does under judgments – reminiscent of the position under the UK Competition Law Class Action. By way of further, and differential, example, North Carolina's relevant statute[173] provides that any undistributed monies arising from a class action settlement be directed to a fund to subsidise legal services for the indigent population of that state.

§ 1–267.10. Distribution of unpaid residuals in class action litigation

(a) It is the intent of the General Assembly to ensure that the unpaid residuals in class action litigation are distributed, to the extent possible, in a manner designed either to further the purposes of the underlying causes of action or to promote justice for all citizens of this State. . . .

(b) . . . the court, unless it orders otherwise consistent with its obligations under FRCP 23, shall direct the defendant to pay the sum of the unpaid residue, to be divided and credited equally, to the Indigent Person's Attorney Fund and to the North Carolina State Bar for the provision of civil legal services for indigents.

Some academic commentary has preferred the less discretionary approach of the North Carolina statute as 'a step in the right direction, as it requires the entirety of the remaining fund to be distributed to a single organization and therefore takes the guesswork out of determining where the funds will go. On the contrary, the . . . Illinois statute still leaves the distribution of a substantial amount of the remaining funds to the judge's discretion.'[174]

2   How Is the Government a 'Beneficiary'?

(a)   Enhancing the Third Sector

How does a distribution of unclaimed damages or settlement funds to these statutorily designated entities in the United Kingdom and British

---

[173] ch 1, Civil Procedure, Sub-chapter 08, Judgment Article 26B, 'Distribution of Unpaid Residuals in Class action Litigation'.

[174] Johnston, '*Cy Près* Comme Possible' (n 105) 298, discussing the state statutes discussed in the text above.

Columbia benefit their governments? It is, of course, via an indirect means. They are statutory examples of a government's relying upon the third sector[175] – that of charity and non-profit foundations – in order to provide funding and resources which the government is not willing or able to fund itself. At a higher level, it is an example of 'a general policy trend towards the inclusion and use of the third sector to provide some public services, services which have traditionally been regarded as the responsibility of the state. Over this time, the government has viewed the third sector as a "key partner in a mixed economy of public service provision, alongside the public and private sectors".'[176] At a specific level, these entities offer a 'flexible source of funding for legal help that is not reliant on taxation or government spending decisions.'[177]

Given that any legally advanced society requires the observance, monitoring and enforcement of the rule of law, the range of projects which has been funded by both the AtJF (United Kingdom)[178] and the Law Foundation (British Columbia)[179] is impressively wide – and socially important (as Table 9.1 overpage illustrates). The Law Foundation of

[175] 'Third sector' covers 'the range of organisations that are neither public sector nor private sector. It includes voluntary and community organisations (both registered charities and other organisations such as associations, self-help groups and community groups), social enterprises, mutuals and co-operatives. [They] generally: are independent of government . . . are "value-driven" . . . and reinvest any surpluses generated in the pursuit of their goals': National Audit Office, *What are third sector organisations and their benefits for commissioners?* (October 2010), available at: www.nao.org.uk/successful-commissioning/introduction/what-are-civil-society-organisations-and-their-benefits-for-commissioners/.

[176] N Glover-Thomas and W Barr, 'Enabling or Disabling? Increasing Involvement of Charities in Social Housing' [2009] *Conveyancing and Property Lawyer* 209, 209, citing, as the internal quote: DTI, *Social Enterprise: A Strategy for Success* (2002) 7. For a summary of several policy documents which had put that governmental position since 1997, see the discussion at 214. Further, '[i]n 2006, the sector's importance to government policy was further strengthened through the establishment of a new Office for the Third Sector within the Cabinet Office, and the appointment of a Minister for the Third Sector. These initiatives, along with continued support for embracing the third sector, have ensured that the role of the voluntary sector in public service provision is regarded as integral to modern provision': at 214–15.

[177] T Brown, 'Rumplestiltskin's New Money' (2010) 154 *Solicitors' Journal* 53, 54.

[178] See, for further information, the several projects described by the Access to Justice Foundation at the following URLs: www.atjf.org.uk/our-impact; www.atjf.org.uk/supporting-litigants-in-person.html; and www.atjf.org.uk/local-trusts.html.

[179] See, for information about the projects funded by the Law Foundation of British Columbia: 'Mandate, Mission and Strategic Priorities', available at: www.lawfoundationbc.org/about-us/mandate-mission-and-strategic-priorities/; and the list of year's priorities provided in: *Law Foundation of British Columbia Annual Report* (2018), 'Report from the Chair', pp 2–3.

Table 9.1 *The indirect benefits provided by statutorily designated beneficiaries*

The Access to Justice Foundation projects (no defined period) included:	The Law Foundation of British Columbia projects (for 2018) included:
• funding the Centre for Criminal Appeals, which challenges unsafe convictions and unjust sentences; • providing funding for Release, an organisation that provides legal advice, assistance and representation to people who engage with drug and/or alcohol treatment, to help resolve issues around debt, benefit payments and housing to create more stable living conditions for those affected by those issues; • providing legal and other support for the homeless, those who are trafficking victims, and those who are subject to domestic violence; • providing support to litigants in person, via the 'Advicenow' website, which provides free legal advice through *pro bono* advice sessions, and also practical and emotional support in person at court; • providing financial and other support to various Legal Support Trusts and committees operating across the UK, to support the provision of free legal help through law centres, advice agencies and local Citizens Advice bureaux.	• approving ten new poverty law advocacy programmes for communities across the province where no other poverty law programmes exist; • funding fifteen family law advocacy programs, to address 'a pressing and widespread need for legal assistance to people who otherwise do not qualify for legal aid'; • using $358,000 received from the provincial government to assist with funding advocacy programs and legal clinics; • approving a $5M contribution towards an Indigenous Legal Lodge planned for the University of Victoria; • organising a Systemic Advocacy Workshop to give public interest lawyers working in funded programmes the chance to meet and discuss common issues; • approving a 10 per cent increase in the overall grants budget available for legal education, etc.; • implementing the Law Foundation's response to the Truth and Reconciliation Commission's Report and Calls to Action, which will likely include financial support for both cultural competency training and First Nations Courts.

British Columbia approved of grants across the five areas of activity in 2018 alone in the sum of over $33M (with 62 per cent of that sum allocated to legal aid; 26 per cent allocated to legal education; 8 per cent allocated to law libraries; 3 per cent to law reform; and 1 per cent to legal research).[180]

This is also in an era whereby some of these projects and services are serving as a substitute for the diminishing legal aid funding. In the United Kingdom, for example, there is no doubt that legal aid funding has significantly decreased over the past decade in that jurisdiction,[181] a fact which the UK Government readily admits.[182] Notably, neither entity under discussion in this section of the chapter actually funds individual litigation and adverse costs. It is specifically provided that the AtJF 'will not fund individual litigation (including disbursements).'[183] Rather, the AtJF 'will only consider requests for funding from organisations which provide, organise or facilitate the provision of legal advice or assistance which is provided free of charge to people who are in charitable need.'[184] Its Memorandum of Association spells out this charitable purpose in more detail, *viz*, that the AtJF 'is primarily established to provide "financial and other support ... to persons who provide, or organise or facilitate the provision of, legal advice or assistance (by way of representation or otherwise) which is free of charge (that is, otherwise than for or in expectation of fee, gain or reward) and which is provided directly or indirectly to people who are in need of such advice or assistance by reason of youth, age, ill-health, disability, financial hardship or other disadvantage'.[185] Similarly, the type of 'legal aid' envisaged as one of the mandated areas of assistance for the Law Foundation of British Columbia, whilst providing some representation of low-income people by volunteer lawyers, does not operate as would a government legal aid service, but rather, funds community-based advocacy schemes, public interest law centres, students' legal advice clinics, and other *pro bono* clinical programmes.[186]

---

[180] *Annual Report*, ibid, 7.

[181] The areas of law which are eligible for legal aid has substantially reduced, especially with the implementation of the Legal Aid, Sentencing and Punishment of Offenders Act 2012. For a recent convenient summary, see: CJC, *The Law and Practicalities of Before-the-Event (BTE) Insurance: An Information Study* (November 2017), Section A2, 'The interplay with legal aid'.

[182] The amount of cuts has exceeded £1 billion over a decade, from £2.6 billion in 2005–6 to £1.5 billion in 2016: noted in O Bowcott, 'Impact of cuts to legal aid to come under review', *The Guardian* (London, 31 October 2017).

[183] See: AtJF, 'Distribution Principles', at: www.atjf.org.uk/distribution-principles.html.

[184] Ibid.

[185] Para 3.1, cited at: www.atjf.org.uk/distribution-principles.html.

[186] The vast range of these funded legal aid projects are outlined in: *Annual Report* (2018), 8–11.

Hence, the legal support provided by these two entities, to those types of charitable, non-profit or volunteer organisations and clinics that seek to assist disadvantaged persons within the general public, provides an indirect benefit to government, in easing the pressure upon diminishing legal aid funding.

(b)   The Amounts of Money Potentially at Stake

As the Law Foundation of British Columbia has recently acknowledged, the amendments to that province's class actions statute in 2018, whereby (with limited exception) 50 per cent of undistributed proceeds from class actions in the province are to be given to the Foundation, will have a significant impact upon its operation. That legislative development (stated the Chair) 'will diversify the sources of revenue available to the foundation, and help provide sustainable funding into the future for our programs'.[187] Prior to that, the Law Foundation had established an 'Access to Justice Fund' as a restricted and administered fund, into which *cy-près* distributions arising from class actions were paid[188] – and some reasonably large amounts were received (e.g., $550,000 from a class action which was paid out to the Access Pro Bono Society of BC;[189] and the Foundation Child Welfare Fund received $158,000 to support initiatives on children's legal issues, which was 'a very welcome contribution to work in a key area at a time when other Law Foundation income is limited'[190]). However, now that the statutory changes have taken effect in British Columbia, the Law Foundation may be expected to receive very significant monies arising from undistributed residues.

It is also undeniably the case that receiving unclaimed residues from class action judgments has the potential to change the AtJF's role in UK society dramatically. Presently, in addition to donations,[191] monies from dormant client accounts,[192] and fundraising amounts,[193] the AtJF receives funds via *pro bono* costs orders. Since 2008, section 194 of the Legal Services Act 2007 has permitted a *pro bono*-assisted litigant to recover costs from a losing party in respect of legal representation that was provided to that litigant free of charge, with those *pro bono* costs to be

---

[187]   ibid, 'Report from the Chair', 2.
[188]   See, e.g.: *Annual Report* (2015), 11.
[189]   Noted in: *Annual Report* (2017), 22, note 9.
[190]   *Annual Report* (2015), 11.
[191]   See: AtJF plea for donations, at: www.atjf.org.uk/donations.html.
[192]   Noted at: www.atjf.org.uk/unclaimed-client-accounts.html.
[193]   Described at: www.atjf.org.uk/local-trusts.html, including legal walks.

paid to the AtJF.[194] These *pro bono* costs awards typically are in the vicinity of a few thousand pounds.[195] All in all, that funding was described by commentators as variously amounting to 'new money to promote access to justice'[196] and 'recycle[d] costs ... disbursed to legal aid providers'.[197] However, the amounts of damages arising under the UK Competition Law Class Action may be eye-wateringly large, depending upon the length of the infringement period and the number of class members affected by the anti-competitive conduct. For example, in the second class action for which certification was sought, *viz*, that of *Merricks v Mastercard Inc*,[198] the infringement period was sixteen years; the class members were those who were resident in the UK for a continuous period of three months or more, and were over sixteen years of age; and the estimated damages was £14 billion.[199] Any unclaimed damages fund would, by any measure, be very significant in such a case.

None of this is unexpected. Unclaimed funds in some notable US cases have been very large too – $125M in one case,[200] $600M in another.[201] Still, the sums of money which are potentially available to statutorily designated beneficiaries of undistributed residues means that those entities' ability to finance access to justice projects – and to redistribute monies to those in legal need – offers a very viable alternative, and considerable support, to the governmental provision of such services.

A final point relates to lobbying. There is no doubt that the potential for 'distasteful' lobbying of judges was a key reason as to why the UK Government elected not to legislatively stipulate *cy-près* beneficiaries as a potential destination of undistributed residues, but to specify the AtJF

---

[194] See, in particular, s 194(3).

[195] Such an order was granted in, e.g.: *Daejan Investments Ltd v Benson (includes Costs Judgment)* [2013] UKSC 14 (£3,000), and *Grand v Gill* [2011] EWCA Civ 554 (£2,500); but refused in, e.g.: *V v Associated Newspapers Ltd* [2016] EWCOP 29; and *Hurst v Denton-Cox* [2014] EWHC 3948 (Ch). See, for procedural guidance on seeking such orders: C Carter, 'Unlocking funds, restoring balance' (November 2017) *Counsel* 18; E Alabaster, 'Clawing back *pro bono* costs' (May 2016) *Counsel* 16; T Jones, 'Pro bono costs orders' (2012) 17 *Judicial Review* 120; J Morgan, 'Laying the foundation' (2008) 105 *Law Society Gazette* 14.

[196] Sir Rupert Jackson, *Review of Civil Litigation Costs: Final Report* (December 2009), ch 33, 336, [4.10].

[197] R Smith, 'Blinded by Statistics?' (2008) 158 *New Law Journal* (9 October 2008) 1391.

[198] [2019] EWCA Civ 674; overturning the refusal of certification in: [2017] CAT 16, and remitting the case to the CAT for a re-hearing. At the time of writing, an appeal to the UK Supreme Court has been filed.

[199] *Merricks v Mastercard Inc* [2017] CAT 16, [2].

[200] *Allapattah Services v Exxon Corp*, 157 F Supp 2d 1291 (SD Fla, 2001).

[201] *In re Holocaust Victim Assets Litig*, 2000 US Dist LEXIS 20817 (EDNY, 22 November 2000).

as the appropriate recipient for judgment awards that remain undistributed. Without citing any empirical evidence on the point, it stated:

> [t]he Government remains of the view . . . that allowing *cy-près* would be undesirable, due to the fact that there would be frequently substantial difficulties in determining a suitable candidate for organisational distribution and that this in turn would likely lead to the lobbying of judges and potentially also satellite litigation disputing the party chosen.[202]

The corollary of that legislative class actions design decision to statutorily designate a third sector entity, however, is that the court's discretion and flexibility, when choosing an appropriate destination for what can constitute very significant sums of money, is much-reduced. To reiterate, however, the UK Competition Law Class Action embodies the legislative drafting oddity that *cy-près* distributions are expressly ruled out for distributing the remainder of judgment awards, but remain distinctly possible in a *settlement* context.

D   Government as a *Cy-Près* Beneficiary

The third avenue by which government may constitute a financial beneficiary of a class action is where a court orders an earmarked escheat distribution to government or to a governmental instrumentality for a specific purpose which is allied to the underlying purpose of the class litigation.

1   Cy-près *Distributions Generally*

This is not the forum in which to discuss the law and the practicalities of *cy-près* distributions, and how the doctrine moved from the context of testamentary charitable trusts to that of class actions jurisprudence (the author has undertaken that detailed analysis elsewhere[203]). Suffice to say, for present purposes, that the equitable doctrine of *cy-près*, in the class actions context, applies where undistributed damages or settlement funds exist because it was impossible or impracticable to locate the class members individually; and where those funds are distributed to the 'next best' class – so as to match the intended use of the funds as

---

[202] BIS, *Private Actions in Competition Law: Government Response* (2013) [5.64].
[203] *The Modern Cy-près Doctrine* (n 6). The book considers the doctrine across many subject areas of law, including charitable trusts; non-charitable trusts; contractual specific performance; and class actions. The last-mentioned is dealt with at chs 7 and 8.

nearly as possible to the original objectives of the class litigation and the victim class who sued successfully in that litigation.[204] A *cy-près* distribution 'provides indirect compensation to silent class members'.[205] That, however, is something of a misnomer, for even non-class members – those who suffered no loss or damage whatsoever – may benefit under an earmarked escheat distribution.

As a remedy, *cy-près* distributions have **not** been universally adopted in the Comparator Jurisdictions as a means of dealing with undistributed residues. In fact, the acceptance of this doctrine as a means of dealing with undistributed residues is one of the most variable points of comparative class actions jurisprudence. It essentially entails a philosophical question as to whether class actions should be deterrent (which such distributions support), or whether class actions serve a solely compensatory objective (for which *cy-près* distributions are an anathema).[206]

Cy-près distributions are permitted under Canadian provincial class actions because they are expressly authorised by statute. They are 'envisioned under the Act as an aspect of distributing a judgment for aggregated damages . . . as part of the court's broad discretion', as one Canadian court put it.[207] For example, Ontario's Class Proceedings Act, SO 1992[208] enacted a *cy-près* provision (on the basis of a recommendation on the part of the preceding law reform commission report,[209] but only by majority[210]) as follows:

---

[204] See, e.g.: *In re Holocaust Victim Assets Litig*, 311 F Supp 2d 407, 415–16 (EDNY, 2004); *In re Folding Carton Antitrust Litig*, 557 F Supp 1091, 1108 (ND Ill, 1983); and for law reform definition, see, e.g.: South African Law Comm, *The Recognition of a Class Action in South African Law* (Working Paper 57, 1995) [5.38]; and Ontario LRC, *Report on Class Actions* (1982) 572–74.

[205] *Powell v Georgia-Pacific Corp*, 119 F 3d 703, 706 (8th Cir, 1997), citing: *Newberg on Class Actions* (3rd edn, Shepard McGraw-Hill, 1992) §10.17; and *State of California v Levi Strauss & Co*, 715 P 2d 564, 573 (Cal 1986).

[206] These divergent positions are described in detail by the author in: *The Modern Cy-près Doctrine* (n 6) ch 7, Section C.

[207] *Slark v Ontario* [2017] ONSC 4178, [35].

[208] SO 1992, c 6.

[209] See Ontario LRC, *Report on Class Actions* (1982) 602, and Recommendation 7.1 ('[w]here it proves impossible to distribute all or an aggregate award to individual class members . . . the court should be able to order a *cy-près* distribution of the residue in a manner that may reasonably be expected to benefit some or all of the members of the class').

[210] See: 'Chairman's Reservations', ibid, 852, para (e), concurring with a dissenting commissioner on this point.

> s 26(4) The court may order that all or a part of an award [of damages] that has not been distributed within a time set by the court be applied in any manner that may reasonably be expected to benefit class members, even though the order does not provide for monetary relief to individual class members, if the court is satisfied that a reasonable number of class members who would not otherwise receive monetary relief would benefit from the order.
>
> ...
>
> s 26(6) The court may make an order under subsection (4) even if the order would benefit,
>
> (a) persons who are not class members; or
> (b) persons who may otherwise receive monetary relief as a result of the class proceeding.

These provisions may have been judicially described as 'novel'[211] – but they have been followed by subsequently enacted provincial legislatures,[212] and have been judicially applied frequently throughout the provinces.[213] It has been judicially acknowledged in Canadian case law that *cy-près* provisions in class action regimes serve the important policy objectives of general and specific deterrence of wrongful conduct, and of improving access to justice,[214] and that 'the private class action

---

[211] *Smith v Canadian Tire Acceptance Ltd* (1995), 22 OR (3d) 433 (Gen Div) [41].

[212] Alberta's Class Proceedings Act, SA 2003, c C-16.5, s 34(2), (4); Saskatchewan's Class Actions Act, SS 2001, c C-12.01, s 37(2), (4); Nova Scotia's Class Proceedings Act, SNS 2007, c 28, s 37(2), (4); Newfoundland and Labrador's Class Actions Act, SNL 2001, c C-18.1, s 32(2), (4); New Brunswick's Class Proceedings Act, RSNB 2011, c 125, s 36(2), (4); Manitoba's Class Proceedings Act, CCSM, c C130, s 34(2), (4). British Columbia's Class Proceedings Act, RSBC 1996, c 50, did replicate those provisions, in s 34(2), (4), until the repeal of that section on 27 November 2018.

[213] A significant amount of Canadian case law is discussed variously, e.g., in: Kalajdzic, 'The "Illusion of Compensation"' (n 48); and by the same author, 'Access to a Just Result: Revisiting Settlement Standards and *Cy-près* Distributions' (2010) 6 *Canadian Class Action Review* 217; J Berryman, 'Nudge, Nudge, Wink, Wink: Behavioural Modification, *Cy-Près* Distributions and Class Actions' (2011) 53 *Supreme Court Law Review* 2d 133; P Williams, '*Cy-près* Distributions: Uses and Controversies', *McCarthy Tetrault News* (18 January 2019, available at: www.mccarthy.ca/en/insights/blogs/canadian-class-actions-monitor/cy-pres-distributions-uses-and-controversies); J Brown *et al.*, *Defending Class Actions in Canada* (3rd edn, CCH Canada Ltd, 2011) 267–68; Mulheron, *The Modern Cy-près Doctrine* (n 6) ch 7, Section C(2). The topic of *cy-près* settlement distributions will also form a focus of the forthcoming project of the Law Reform Commission of Ontario, *Class Actions: Objectives, Experiences and Reforms* (CP, March 2018), 'specific question 13', and 13.

[214] *Carom v Bre-X Minerals Ltd* [2014] ONSC 2507, [123] ('*[c]y-près* distributions are generally intended to meet at least two of the principal objectives of class actions. They

litigation Bar functions as a regulator in the public interest for public policy objectives'.[215] Although the Canadian Supreme Court has remarked the *cy-près* provisions 'authorize . . . awards made to charities in situations where some class members cannot be identified',[216] there is actually nothing on the face of the statutes to limit the *cy-près* recipients to charities.

By contrast with the Canadian position, the US federal class action is silent on the matter of *cy-près* distributions. Remarkably, though, creative and innovative judicial decision-making has meant that the US jurisdiction possesses the most developed *cy-près* jurisprudence in the class actions context. As one prominent US scholar has recently put it, from the 'acorn' of the famous and controversial case of *Daar v Yellow Cab Co*[217] arising from alleged overcharges by Yellow Cab in Los Angeles, 'a mighty oak of *cy-près* doctrine and creativity has grown.'[218] Despite considerable opposition from some quarters,[219] such distributions have received judicial endorsement on the part of many US federal appellate[220] and district[221] courts. It is perceived as a superior alternative to reversion to the defendant: '[w]ithout fluid recovery, defendants may be permitted to retain ill gotten gains simply because their conduct harmed large numbers of people in small amounts instead of small numbers of people

are meant to enhance access to justice by directly or indirectly benefitting class members, and they may provide behaviour modification by ensuring that the unclaimed portion of an award or settlement is not reverted to the defendant'), and cited in: *Slark v Ontario* [2017] ONSC 4178, [38].

[215] *Alfresh Beverages Canada Corp v Hoechst AG* (2002), 16 CPC (5th) 301 (SCJ) [15]–[16]; *Tesluk v Boots Pharmaceutical plc* (2002), 21 CPC (5th) 196 (SCJ) [16], cited in: *Ford v F Hoffmann-La Roche Ltd* (SCJ, 23 March 2005) [133].

[216] *Sun-Rype Products Ltd v Archer Daniels Midland Co* [2013] 3 SCR 545, [2013] SCC 58, [101].

[217] 67 Cal 2d 695, 63 Cal Rptr 724 (1967).

[218] R Marcus, 'Revolution v Evolution in Class Action Reform' (2018) 96 *North Carolina Law Review* 903, 925.

[219] Described in: Mulheron, *The Modern Cy-près Doctrine* (n 6) 236–44. Also, as cited in Marcus, ibid, 925 and fn 112, A Liptak, 'Doling Out Other People's Money', *NY Times* (New York, 26 November 2007) A14: '[j]udges all over the country have gotten into the business of doling out leftover class action settlement money, sometimes to organizations only tangentially related to the subject of the lawsuit'; and also noting the lobbying of some judges by charities.

[220] e.g., *Simer v Rios*, 661 F 2d 655 (7th Cir, 1981); *Powell v Georgia-Pacific Corp*, 119 F 3d 703 (8th Cir, 1997); *Six Mexican Workers v Arizona Citrus Growers*, 904 F 2d 1301 (9th Cir, 1990).

[221] e.g., *In re Wells Fargo Securities Litig*, 991 F Supp 1193 (ND Cal, 1998); *In re Holocaust Victim Assets Litig*, 302 F Supp 2d 89 (EDNY, 2004); *Jones v National Distillers*, 56 F Supp 2d 355 (SDNY, 1999).

in large amounts'[222] ('fluid recovery' being a term used synonymously with *cy-près* distributions in relevant US case law[223]). Various state courts have also permitted *cy-près* distributions.[224] In addition to that, some state legislatures have expressly legislated for *cy-près* remedies in class actions. The Californian Code of Civil Procedure[225] is one such example:

> s 384(a)   It is the policy of the State of California to ensure that the unpaid cash residue and unclaimed or abandoned funds in class action litigation are distributed, to the fullest extent possible, in a manner designed either to further the purposes of the underlying class action or causes of action, or to promote justice for all Californians. The Legislature finds that the use of funds for these purposes is in the public interest, is a proper use of the funds, and is consistent with essential public and governmental purposes.
>
> (b)   ... the court shall amend the judgment to direct the defendant to pay the sum of the unpaid residue or unclaimed or abandoned class member funds ... to nonprofit organizations or foundations to support projects that will benefit the class or similarly situated persons, or that promote the law consistent with the objectives and purposes of the underlying cause of action, to child advocacy programs, or to nonprofit organizations providing civil legal services to the indigent. The court shall ensure that the distribution of any unpaid residue or unclaimed or abandoned class member funds derived from multistate or national cases brought under California law shall provide substantial or commensurate benefit to California consumers. ...

To note, *cy-près* distributions are far more common in US jurisprudence for unclaimed sums arising from class action *settlements* than they are for *judgment awards*. Indeed, whilst some courts have considered that the latter are not precluded from the operation of the *cy-près* doctrine,[226] other courts have held that settlement sums are the doctrine's **only** province of

---

[222] *State of California v Levi Strauss & Co*, 224 Cal Rptr 605, 715 P 2d 564 (1986).

[223] Noted in, e.g.: *Democratic Centre Committee of District of Columbia v Washington Metropolitan Area Transit Comm*, 84 F 3d 451, 455 (DC Ct App, 1996).

[224] See, e.g.: in Missouri: *Buchholz Mortuaries Inc v Director of Revenue*, 113 SW 3d 192 (S Ct Mo, 2003); in New Jersey: *Mui v GPU Inc*, 851 A 2d 799 (SC, 2004); in District of Columbia: *Boyle v Giral*, 820 A 2d 561 (DC Ct App, 2003); and in California: *In re Vitamin Cases*, 107 Cal App 4th 820 (Ct App, 2003).

[225] Code of Civil Procedure, Pt 2, Title 3, ch 5, 'Permissive Joinder', amended by Stats 2018, ch 45, s 2 (SB 847), effective 27 June 2018.

[226] e.g.: *Powell v Georgia-Pacific Corp*, 843 F Supp 491, 497 (WD Ark, 1994); *In re Toys 'R' Us Antitrust Litig*, 191 FRD 347 (EDNY, 2000); *Matzo Food Prods Litig*, 156 FRD 600, 605 (DNJ, 1994).

operation.[227] The legal picture in the United States is quite mixed and uncertain on that point.[228]

The scenario is far from straightforward in Australia too. *Cy-près* distributions are not countenanced under its federal regime. This seemingly puts Australia as the 'odd one out' amongst the Comparator Jurisdictions, insofar as *cy-près* distributions are concerned.[229] Instead, where an aggregate damages award is not fully distributed, then the legislature expressly provided for the funds to revert to the defendant.[230] The preceding law reform commission report was very critical of the *cy-près* remedy for several reasons;[231] subsequent ALRC consideration of civil litigation generally has not seen fit to revisit the issue;[232] and it has not been embraced by any of the state opt-out regimes enacted since either.[233] As the author has posited elsewhere:

> the Australian legislature would do well to consider amending the class action regime in Pt IVA to expressly permit, but not mandate, *cy-près* distributions for that jurisdiction. In doing so, and in learning from the experiences of jurisdictions elsewhere, statutory restrictions … could be usefully imposed upon the use of the doctrine, and the worst excesses of coupon recovery could be either statutorily or judicially disallowed.[234]

---

[227] e.g., *Weber v Goodman*, 1998 US Dist LEXIS 22832, at *17 (EDNY, 1998); *Beecher v Able*, 575 F 2d 1010, 1015 (2d Cir, 1978).

[228] See, for analysis: Mulheron, *The Modern Cy-près Doctrine* (n 6) 236–44. The area continues to attract academic debate in US literature, e.g.: A Dyk, 'A Better Way to *Cy-près*: A Proposal to Reform Class Action *Cy-près* Distribution' (2019) 21 *NYU Journal of Legislation and Public Policy* 635; L Mullenix, 'Ending Class Actions As We Know Them: Rethinking the American Class Action' (2014) 64 *Emory Law Journal* 399; Tidmarsh, '*Cy près* and the Optimal Class Action' (n 121); R Bone, 'Justifying Class Action Limits: Parsing the Debates over Ascertainability and *Cy près*' (2017) 65 *University of Kansas Law Review* 913; B Hills, 'Never Settle for Second Best? *Cy près* Distributions in Securities Class Action Settlements' (2017) *Missouri Law Review* 507.

[229] Discussed in: *The Modern Cy-près Doctrine*, ibid, 230–32.

[230] FCA 1976, s 33ZA(5).

[231] ALRC, *Grouped Proceedings in the Federal Court* (Rep 46, 1988) [237]–[239].

[232] ALRC, *Managing Justice* (Rep 89, 1999).

[233] New South Wales' Civil Procedure Act 2005, s 178; Victoria's Supreme Court Act 1986, s 33ZA, and Queensland's Civil Proceedings Act 2011, s 103W, make no allowance whatsoever for *cy-près* distributions, closely adopting the wording of the federal regime. Interestingly, the NSW government did propose a *cy-près* distribution for the Bill, but it met with such opposition that the clause was deleted, as noted in, e.g.: Clayton Utz, 'NSW rolls back contentious *cy-près* rule in class actions bill' (*Lexology*, 3 December 2010); V Morabito, *An Empirical Study of Australia's Class Action Regime: The First 25 Years of Class Actions in Australia (Fifth Report)* (July 2017) 16.

[234] Mulheron, *The Modern Cy-près Doctrine* (n 6) 232.

In the absence of any express authorisation for *cy-près* remedies, very sporadic instances of *cy-près* distributions have arisen in Australian class actions settlements, by virtue of this generalist provision contained in the Australian federal class actions regime:

---

s 33ZF General power of Court to make orders

(1)   In any proceeding (including an appeal) conducted under this Part, the Court may, of its own motion or on application by a party or a group member, make any order the Court thinks appropriate or necessary to ensure that justice is done in the proceeding.

In *King v AG Holdings Ltd (formerly GIO Holdings Ltd)*,[235] the first shareholder class action commenced under the Australian federal class actions regime, Moore J approved a settlement distribution scheme which provided that residue settlement funds would be paid to the Australian Institute of Management for the benevolent purpose of training corporate officers and directors, or to the Australian Shareholders Association. Although Moore J himself did not refer to section 33ZF, subsequently it has been suggested, in dicta, that such a distribution of unclaimed settlement funds to a third party was an appropriate exercise of this generalist judicial power.[236] The law reform picture across Australia is mixed too. On the one hand, the Western Australian Law Reform Commission recently studied the issue and decided against *cy-près* remedies.[237] On the other hand, earlier Victorian law reform opinion[238] stated that, to remove doubt and to expand the scope of remedies available in the event that unclaimed residues of judgment awards or settlement funds arise, the Australian federal and state legislatures should

---

[235]   [2003] FCA 980, noted in para 4.11 of the 'Settlement Scheme' contained in Ann A. For academic and law reform discussion, see, respectively: V Morabito, 'The Victorian Law Reform Commission's Class Action Reform Strategy' (2009) 32 *UNSW Law Journal* 1055, 1069; and Victoria LRC, *Civil Justice Review* (2008), 545, fn 243, noting the Submission by law firm Maurice Blackburn.

[236]   *Wotton v State of Queensland (No 11)* [2018] FCA 1841, [22] (Murphy J).

[237]   *Representative Proceedings* (Rep 103, 2015) [5.108].

[238]   See: Victorian LRC, *Civil Justice Review* (Rep 14, 2008), ch 8, 'Improving Remedies in Class Actions', 550–55, and Recommendations 101–7. That Commission recommended the express authorisation of *cy-près* distributions where: (a) there was a proven contravention of the law, (b) a financial or other pecuniary advantage has accrued to the contravener, (c) the loss suffered by others, or the pecuniary gain obtained by the contravener, was capable of reasonably accurate assessment, and (d) it was not possible, reasonably practicable or cost effective to identify some or all of those who had suffered loss. However, that recommendation was not implemented by the state legislature.

make *specific* provision for *cy-près* distributions where statutorily prescribed circumstances are met. The author strongly concurs with this latter view.[239] Reliance upon some generalist power is neither desirable nor sufficiently transparent.

Finally, it is worth noting that the UK legislature also turned its face against the prospect of general *cy-près* distributions, insofar as the distribution of residual amounts arising from *judgment awards* was concerned (as discussed previously,[240] the Access to Justice Foundation is the statutorily-designated recipient of such monies). The preceding Government consultation document foreshadowed three difficulties: the difficulty of identifying 'a suitable candidate' for the *cy-près* distribution; the 'likely' lobbying of judges; and potential satellite litigation disputing the *cy-près* beneficiaries who were selected.[241] However, the Government did not disagree with *cy-près* distributions for the disposition of residual settlement sums[242] (presuming that the terms of the settlement met the 'just and reasonable' threshold specified by statute[243]).

Having set the scene, it is now appropriate to turn attention to whether, and if so, in what circumstances, the government or a government entity may be judicially designated as a *cy-près* beneficiary.

2   Earmarked Escheat Distributions

(a)   Divided Viewpoints

A distribution to a governmental entity which permits the unclaimed funds to be applied or used for a particular purpose that matches the objectives underlying the class actions suit itself – an 'earmarked escheat'[244] – is a form of *cy-près* distribution. As one court put it, 'escheat to the state . . . [is] one form of fluid recovery'.[245]

---

[239]   But *only* where the requisite elements for a *cy-près* distribution can be met, as outlined by the author elsewhere: '*Cy-près* Damages Distributions in England' (n 13) Section IV.

[240]   See pp 338–340.

[241]   BIS, *Private Actions in Competition Law: Government Response* (2013) [5.64].

[242]   ibid, [5.65].

[243]   CA 1998, s 49A(5).

[244]   Also referred to as 'escheat to the government for . . . specified purposes': *Democratic Centre Committee of District of Columbia v Washington Metropolitan Area Transit Comm*, 84 F 3d 451, 455 (DC Ct App, 1996), citing: *State of California v Levi Strauss & Co*, 715 P 2d 564, 571 (1986).

[245]   *Kraus v Trinity Management Services Inc*, 23 Cal 4th 116, 134, 999 P 2d 718 (SC, 2000).

'Earmarked escheat' distributions (which have been judicially[246] and academically[247] distinguished from 'general escheat' orders) have been judicially defined in US case law to apply 'where the funds are distributed to a governmental body which uses them to ameliorate the effects of past harm and to reduce the risk of future harm'.[248] It is important that the governmental entity be selected so that it can use the funds 'on projects that benefit non-collecting class members and promote the purposes of the underlying cause of action'.[249]

It is said that one of the benefits of an earmarked escheat is that the administration costs of distributing the unclaimed monies tend to be reduced significantly. One court put it this way: where 'funds are disbursed to a particular governmental agency for the purpose of benefiting a group of persons who approximate the injured class; the details of the distribution are left to the agency. The advantage of the earmarked escheat is that it utilizes already extant governmental bodies to administer the fund.'[250] Moreover, by reason of the reach of its programmes and its publicly funded entities, the government may be uniquely positioned to utilise the unclaimed funds for the indirect benefit of class members. As academic commentary has pointed out, distribution to a government-authorised and funded consumer trust fund 'directs awarded funds to specific organizations that are in a position to use the funds for lawsuits, lobbying, or other projects aimed at benefiting class members and those similarly situated'.[251]

It follows from the discussion in the preceding section that the Australian class actions regimes, whether federal or state, **may** permit earmarked *cy-près* distributions to the government by virtue of a general judicial discretion.[252] Similarly, given its express differential treatment

---

[246] e.g., *Kraus v Trinity Management Services Inc*, 23 Cal 4th 116, 135, 999 P 2d 718 (2000); *Democratic Centre Committee of District of Columbia v Washington Metropolitan Area Transit Comm*, 84 F 3d 451, 457 (DC Ct App, 1996).

[247] e.g., McCall *et al.*, 'Greater Representation for California Consumers' (n 120) 808–10; G Hillebrand and D Torrence, 'Claims Procedures in Large Consumer Class Actions and Equitable Distribution of Benefits' (1988) 28 *Santa Clara Law Review* 747, 764–65; DeJarlais, 'The Consumer Trust Fund' (n 33) 751–53; Barnett, 'Equitable Trusts' (n 106) 1591, fn 75.

[248] *People v Thomas Shelton Powers Inc*, 2 Cal App 4th 330, 342 (CA Cal, 1992).

[249] *State of California v Levi Strauss & Co*, 224 Cal Rptr 605, 613, 715 P 2d 564, 572 (1986).

[250] *Democratic Centre*, ibid, 456, citing: *Levi Strauss*, ibid, 613.

[251] S Karas, 'The Role of Fluid Recovery in Consumer Protection Litigation: *Kraus v Trinity Management Services*' (2002) 90 *California Law Review* 959, 971.

[252] Per FCA 1976, s 33ZF. For an excellent analysis of the wide array of orders that have been made under this catch-all provision, and with a critique of the inconsistencies of

between the unclaimed sums arising from judgment awards (where *cy-près* is rejected) and settlement funds (where it is permitted), earmarked escheat distributions cannot be ruled out under the UK Competition Law Class Action in future litigation, where settlement agreements are being devised for judicial approval.

When deciding whether or not to exercise its discretion in favour of any *cy-près* distribution, including an earmarked escheat distribution, it is to US and Canadian jurisprudence that the focus inevitably turns, given the vast judicial experience garnered in those jurisdictions. Those courts have typically considered one or more of the following factors in favour of such a distribution:[253]

(i) it is not practical to distribute the benefits in any other manner; and a direct distribution to the class members would be uneconomic, considering the modest damages, and the fact that there is no cost-effective way of locating those class members, determining if they suffered damage and, if so, establishing their loss;

(ii) the *cy-près* distribution is directly related to the issues in the lawsuit, and the degree to which the spillover benefits will effectuate the purposes of the underlying substantive law;

(iii) the amount of compensation distributed to class members prior to the *cy-près* distribution is manifestly inadequate;

(iv) the proportion of class members sharing in the direct recovery is also inadequate, compared with those claiming class members who would benefit from the *cy-près* recovery;

(v) the extent to which benefits of any *cy-près* distribution would 'spill over' to non-class members is appropriate (i.e., '[a] reasonable number of class members who would not otherwise receive monetary relief must benefit from the order'[254]); and

(vi) the costs of administering the *cy-près* distribution are appropriate.

There are caveats and disadvantages, however, which may countenance against earmarked escheat distributions. For example:

approach, see: M Legg and J Metzger, 'Section 33ZF: Class Actions Problem Solver?', in D Grave and H Mould (eds), *25 Years of Class Actions in Australia* (Ross Parsons, 2017), ch 16.

[253] See, e.g., in the United States: *Jones v National Distillers*, 56 F Supp 2d 355, 357 (SDNY, 1999); *Six (6) Mexican Workers v Arizona Citrus Growers*, 904 F 2d 1301, 1305 (9th Cir, 1990). In Canada, e.g.: *Serhan (Trustee of) v Johnson & Johnson* [2011] ONSC 128, [58]–[59]; *Cass v WesternOne Inc* [2018] ONSC 4794, [91].

[254] *Slark v Ontario* [2017] ONSC 4178, [36].

(i) since earmarked escheat 'depends for its success upon the active cooperation of the government, it should not be employed where . . . the relevant governmental body opposes its use';[255] and

(ii) it was argued recently in an Ontario class action[256] that it would be inappropriate to direct unclaimed funds to 'large well-funded organizations [which] are *already* directly funded by the Crown, [so that] the settlement funds should not be used to augment already established government programs already in receipt of funding' – the court rejected the proposed earmarked *cy-près* distribution, without expressly resolving that issue;

(iii) there is (as the California Supreme Court acknowledged[257]) a 'danger that the recovery will be submerged in the state's general fund' rather than be earmarked at all. Where this happens, then the governmental entity may use the funds for purposes that do not benefit class members,[258] and may simply be 'absorbed into Government allocations';[259]

(iv) there is also a risk that monies that were already allocated by the government to that earmarked agency or body will be reduced with the expectation of the forthcoming escheat distribution, thus 'diluting' the benefits of the earmarked escheat. The Californian Supreme Court noted[260] that earmarked escheats 'can be conditioned on the state's promise not to divert previously budgeted funds' – and presumably, can also seek an undertaking that the escheat will not disappear into general consolidated revenue. The Court acknowledged that its ability to enforce those types of undertakings 'may be limited, [but] there is no reason to assume that the state would act in bad faith'.[261] Academically, however, this risk has been viewed seriously, with scholars suggesting that '[t]he lack of control over governmental use of damages or settlement funds threatens its effectiveness',[262] and that earmarked

---

[255] *State of California v Levi Strauss & Co*, 224 Cal Rptr 605, 613, 715 P 2d 564, 573 (1986). That scenario applied here, and hence, earmarked escheat could not be implemented.

[256] *Slark v Ontario* [2017] ONSC 4356, [6]–[7].

[257] *State of California v Levi Strauss & Co*, 224 Cal Rptr 605, 614, 715 P 2d 564, 573 (1986).

[258] McCall *et al.*, 'Greater Representation for California Consumers' (n 120) 809.

[259] R Higgins, 'The Equitable Doctrine of *Cy-près* and Consumer Protection' (Annex 1, ACA Submission, *Trade Practices Rev*, 15 July 2002) 9. See too: W Rubenstein, 'On What a "Private Attorney General" Is – and Why it Matters' (2004) 57 *Vanderbilt Law Review* 2129, fn 112; and Barnett, 'Equitable Trusts' (n 106) 1599.

[260] *State of California v Levi Strauss & Co*, 224 Cal Rptr 605, 715 P 2d 564, fn 10 (1986).

[261] ibid, fn 10.

[262] DeJarlais, 'The Consumer Trust Fund' (n 33) 753.

distributions can 'be viewed as a windfall by the legislature or executive, resulting in reduced appropriations to the [governmental] agency, thereby minimizing the benefit of the escheated funds';[263] and

(v) on the odd occasion, an earmarked escheat distribution would not achieve anything, because the charges which were unlawfully rendered were, in fact, taxes that had already been paid into the Treasury coffers. It has been held in some US jurisprudence[264] that the expense and burden of progressing with the class action outweighed the benefits of doing so – the court preferred to leave the money where it was, i.e., with the government. The class action would have permitted individual recoveries, but the amount of individual damages was small, and the overcharges had been paid to the state Treasury, thereby benefiting state residents in general.[265]

(b)   Examples of 'Governmental Benefit'

Examples of earmarked escheat distributions to governmental entities and instrumentalities are difficult to find in Canadian jurisprudence. For example, in the *Canadian Vitamins Class Actions National Settlement Agreement*, which resulted from the settlement of several class actions arising from a complex global, multiparty, price-fixing and market-sharing conspiracy relating to the sale of vitamins in Canada,[266] the settlement fund created for *the intermediate purchasers* was judicially approved to be distributed *cy-près* to a number of industry organisations, trade associations, non-profit foundations, and charitable entities.[267] The *cy-près* recipients of the settlement fund which was created to benefit *the consumers* affected by the vitamin cartel were also considered against a number of criteria, including 'whether the organization was non-denominational; and whether the organization had a charitable or non-profit designation'.[268] This approach to selecting *cy-près* destinations has typified Canadian *cy-près* distributions, and seems to have gained a marked ascendancy over escheat distributions to governmental bodies.

However, a few examples of earmarked escheat distributions which have been evident in US class actions include the following:

---

[263] McCall *et al.*, 'Greater Representation for California Consumers' (n 120) 809.

[264] *Blue Chip Stamps v Superior Court*, 18 Cal 3d 381, 556 P 2d 755 (1976).

[265] ibid, 386–87. The class members had alleged that excessive sales taxes had been collected by a trading stamp company.

[266] *Ford v F Hoffmann-La Roche Ltd* (2005), 74 OR (3d) 758 (SCJ).

[267] ibid, [83]–[91].

[268] *See* ibid, [96]. None of the numerous recipients listed at [99] was a governmental body.

- an antitrust class action was successfully brought on behalf of consumers against drug companies accused of price-fixing antibiotics, and the unclaimed balance of the settlement fund was distributed to state governments for use in public health programmes, including drug addiction treatment, pollution control, and public education about environmental pollution laws;[269]
- the Department of Housing was successfully sued for violating oil price regulations by overcharging, and unclaimed funds were ordered to be given to the US Treasury to be divided among the states to be applied toward federal energy conservation programmes;[270] and
- bus fares were unlawfully overcharged to those who used bus services in the Washington metropolitan area. Congress gave consent to the establishment of the Washington Metropolitan Area Transit Authority, which was exclusively responsible for the provision of transportation services by bus in the metropolitan area; and unclaimed settlement monies were paid to this transit authority to enable it to purchase new buses for use in those affected service areas (this was considered to benefit the 'next best' class of beneficiaries, i.e., current bus riders, given the transit authority's experience in providing bus transportation).[271]

E Conclusion

It is very much a drafting design choice as to whether government chooses to provide itself with the option of deriving monetary benefits from class actions litigation, by virtue of how it chooses to demarcate appropriate recipients of undistributed residues. As the chapter has discussed, some legislatures have distinguished between judgment awards and settlement funds, providing a court with greater flexibility in the settlement context. The three key avenues by which a government

---

[269] *State of West Virginia v Pfizer & Co*, 314 F Supp 710 (SDNY, 1970), *aff'd*, 440 F 2d 1079 (2d Cir, 1971), cert denied, 404 US 871 (1971).

[270] *United States v Exxon Corp*, 561 F Supp 816 (DDC, 1983).

[271] *Democratic Centre Committee of District of Columbia v Washington Metropolitan Area Transit Comm*, 84 F 3d 451, 457 (DC Ct App, 1996). The court drew support for this avenue of distribution from the much earlier non-class action case of: *Market St Rwy Co v Railroad Comm*, 28 Cal 2d 363, 171 P 2d 875 (1946) (fund established, representing overcharges made by defendant railway company; few patrons filed claims for refunds; unclaimed sum paid to the City of San Francisco, which had owned the railway and would use funds to improve its services).

may financially benefit from a class action – by means of an escheat distribution, by means of a statutorily designated beneficiary whose expenditure of the class funds will assist the government with providing social and legal support services, and by means of an earmarked *cy-près* distribution – have not been implemented within the Comparator Jurisdictions uniformly, or (in some cases) at all. However, each of them does have a degree of judicial and/or law reform support, and add depth and utility to the panoply of options for undistributed residues. From the experiences derived from the Comparator Jurisdictions, the following recommendations are suggested, where class actions design (or amended design) is under consideration or review.

RECOMMENDATIONS: GOVERNMENT AS BENEFICIARY

§ 9.1 Although a general escheat distribution (whether to the Crown/Treasury/ Consolidated Revenue/the state) lacks both precision and a focus upon the aggrieved class members, there are at least five circumstances in which (singularly or in combination) such a distribution may be appropriate, and preferable to other avenues, by which to deal with the distribution of undistributed residues of damages or a settlement fund arising from a class action suit. Hence, it is recommended that a discretion vested in the court to award a general escheat distribution in the event of an undistributed residue arising should be included in any provision which deals with undistributed residues. However, it would be appropriate to designate an escheat distribution as an avenue of 'last resort', to be awarded if, and only if, the other specified avenues were not appropriate nor feasible on the facts of a particular case.

§ 9.2 The legislative prescription of a charitable entity to which undistributed residues of damages or a settlement fund arising from a class action suit is to be paid, has the advantages of: (1) removing the potential for a 'lobbying effect'; (2) providing certainty for courts and litigants alike; and (3) providing an indirect method by which governments may benefit from the outcome of a successful class action. However, it is recommended that such an option should be one of a range of options to which undistributed residues could be distributed (whether in the context of judgment awards or settlement funds), instead of constituting a legislatively designated sole destination of undistributed residues. This would maximise the opportunities by which the outcome of a successful class action could benefit the aggrieved class members for whom the suit was litigated, and whose interests are paramount.

§ 9.3 An earmarked escheat distribution to a governmental entity may achieve a better rate of 'cross-over' as between the original class and the *cy-près* class than any other avenue of recipient or method of distribution of undistributed residues of damages or a settlement fund. It is recommended that the option be encompassed, whether legislatively or judicially, when considering an appropriate distribution of such residues. However, the concerns about government resources being diverted away from the governmental recipient should be explicitly addressed by the court when making such an order (albeit that enforcement of any governmental undertaking may be infeasible).

10

Conclusion: Levelling the Playing Field

A   Some Closing Thoughts

Many claims stand out from amongst the plethora of cases which have been considered in this book. Two are particularly worthy of mention.

In 1909, Kingsley Fairbridge founded a society at the University of Oxford, in order to promote the emigration of children from Great Britain to its colonies. He envisioned that schools would be established in rural communities in some of these colonies, so that children who were living in poor and unhealthy conditions in Great Britain could be sent to these schools, and thereby have an opportunity to be raised, to be educated, and to learn a variety of skills, in a much better and healthier environment. For that purpose, a farm and a school were established at Molong in New South Wales, Australia, called the Fairbridge Farm which continued to operate until 1974. Just over a century after the Fairbridge Society was created in Oxford, a class action was instituted against the Commonwealth of Australia and the State of New South Wales,[1] in which Geraldine Giles and Vivian Drady alleged that, during much of the time at the Fairbridge Farm, children were subjected to systemic physical and sexual abuse perpetrated by a significant number of staff and others. It was claimed, on behalf of former child residents, that those government defendants should be legally liable in damages to the children who had suffered from such abuse, and for the harm sustained, both physical and psychological. The class action ultimately settled for $24M.[2]

---

[1]   *Giles v Cth of Australia* [2014] NSWSC 83.

[2]   See the statement by the class lawyers, Slater and Gordon: '[t]he settlement established a $24 million fund to compensate those victims of child abuse at the Fairbridge Farm School in Molong who registered in accordance with the Court's orders. That registration period has since closed and the distribution of the compensation fund has been

Half a world away, Marc Leroux, who resided in Timmins, Ontario, was father to Briana, who was diagnosed with a rare brain disorder when she was two. Throughout her life, Briana remained non-verbal, functioned at the level of a three-year-old; and required constant care in relation to activities such as eating, mobility, and personal hygiene. Her father relied upon financial support and social services provided by the Ontario provincial government. He brought an action[3] against the province of Ontario on behalf of all acutely disabled persons who had turned eighteen, and who had thereafter been approved by government to receive support and services. It was alleged that these disabled persons had then been relegated by the relevant provincial Ministry to indeterminate waiting lists, inconsistent prioritisation processes for the waitlisted services, and poor matching programmes. All of this, said Mr Leroux, had pushed his family life, and those of other class members, to 'the brink of disaster' and to 'breaking point', in seeking to provide disabled loved ones with care, often whilst also holding down employment. Mr Leroux believed that his experiences with the provincial Ministry were common to thousands of Ontario families, and sought damages (including punitive damages) against the province of Ontario. At the time of writing, the class action has been certified.

Both scenarios are poignant. Indeed, the vulnerability and other characteristics of the class members may have particularly suited these cases to the opt-out class action, to preclude the need for all class members to come forward at the outset. However, perhaps the most remarkable aspect of these two cases is that they could be brought at all. In both New South Wales and Ontario, at some point distantly earlier, a vote was taken by their respective Parliaments to permit opt-out class actions, without restricting the ambit of possible defendants, and without taking any measures to protect government from such suits. Those decisions were taken with a full and complete awareness that government could become a litigation 'target'. Where activities by a government could be alleged to have been deleterious to a sector of society, to a group of people, or to a cluster of businesses, and across a generic range of grievances and causes of action, then the respective Parliaments accepted that the procedural vehicle of the class action could be taken for a lengthy and expensive ride, in order to seek compensatory redress against that particular defendant.

---

completed': available at: www.slatergordon.com.au/class-actions/past-class-actions/fair bridge-farm-school.

[3] *Leroux v Ontario* [2018] ONSC 6452 (judgment dated 14 December 2018, Belobaba J).

For any jurisdiction – such as that of the United Kingdom – where that possibility is not a reality, the courageous and far-sighted decisions made by those lawmakers from the Comparator Jurisdictions cannot be over-stated. Opt-out class actions have levelled the playing field, and have served as a vehicle by which claimants such as Mr Leroux and Ms Giles may at least have the opportunity to test the legitimacy and strength of their claims against a well-resourced and powerful defendant.

Of course, there are constant concerns as to how the opt-out class action vehicle is operating, as very recent reports by law reform bodies in Australia (federally, and in Victoria), and in Ontario, demonstrate. Rule changes to FRCP 23 in 2018 also highlight the continuous 'review-in-motion' to which class action procedure is rightly subject. However, in these jurisdictions, the question has moved from 'whether to implement' to 'how to improve'. It a question of an entirely different order in other jurisdictions, where the absence of an opt-out generic class action makes the commencement of the type of suits brought by Ms Giles and Ms Drady, and Mr Leroux a much more difficult proposition, procedurally speaking.

The landscape is also in a constant state of flux. At the time of writing, opt-out reform may possibly come to pass, for example, in Tasmania, Prince Edward Island, New Zealand, and Scotland, given developments which have occurred in each of those jurisdictions. If and when that occurs, then at least a hundred design issues associated with class actions commencement, conduct, costs, and funding, will eventually require consideration by lawmakers and jurists.

As this book has sought to demonstrate, government, in all of its guises, is central to class actions reform and implementation – from enabling and designing the regime, to choosing whether to fund the regime with seed funding and to establish a self-replenishing funder, to legislating for the extent to which the courts should 'gate-keep' against 'all-comers' class actions. Then, quite apart from its role as potential defendant, the mantles which government may occupy as class member, as representative claimant, or as financial beneficiary of class actions litigation, require careful and measured class action design.

By any measure, the interplay between government and the opt-out class action has been an extraordinary evolution of political will, leaps of faith, jurisprudential 'nous', and social responsibility. The ancient maxim, 'the King can do no wrong' in the feudal society that he ruled, has truly been transformed to that of, 'the government can bring great benefit' to modern society, via the class action vehicle.

B　The Recommendations Collected

The recommendations contained throughout this book are collected for convenience below. It is hoped that they may be of assistance and utility, to those policy-makers and/or law-makers who are considering class actions reform and/or implementation.

§ 2.1　Upon a review of a civil procedural landscape, class actions reform may tend to be indicated where a number of the following circumstances are present –

    (1)　the existing procedural regimes are struggling, or unable, to cope with group actions, because the requirements contained within those regimes cannot be met, whether because of legislative drafting or judicial interpretation;

    (2)　a number of 'missing cases' are recognised, i.e., where mass disasters, regulatory fines, equivalent litigation elsewhere, yield no compensatory redress in the domestic landscape, or where anecdotal evidence from claimant lawyers points to 'deserving' cases not instituted;

    (3)　multiple claims arising out of the same dispute or event create burdensome or duplicative litigation;

    (4)　a senior and respected judicial figure adverts to the need for class actions reform, either curially or extra-curially;

    (5)　legislative regimes which were enacted in order to diversify and expand the collective redress regimes available have been under-utilised or otherwise unsuccessful;

    (6)　attempts have been made to create 'add-on' classes of domestic class members to class actions instituted in other jurisdictions, and another 'backyard';

    (7)　public regulators either state on the record, or exhibit from their litigious (non)activity, that they are unable or unwilling to devote the resources necessary to institute civil actions for compensatory redress, over and above their public enforcement function; and

    (8)　empirical and/or anecdotal evidence suggests that groups of people or businesses have been unwilling to litigate grievances or disputes, for economic, social, psychological, or personal reasons.

§ 2.2　The potential for class actions regimes to modify defendant behaviour and to create a deterrent effect upon potential defendants or across an industry or sector of enterprise/society may be a by-product of litigation, but should not be regarded as a motivator or objective of class actions reform. Compensatory redress (e.g., damages, restitutionary relief, and other permissible damages awards) is the objective.

§ 3.1 Across the ambit of class actions commencement, conduct, costs, and funding, there are at least a hundred design issues which arise. Not all of these will be dealt with via either legislative enactment or court rules; judicial precedent, practice directions, and practices developed in the legal marketplace may govern some of these design issues.

§ 3.2 No legal regime is entirely transplantable to another jurisdiction. Cultural, historical and legal factors will dictate the extent to which the design of a class action in one jurisdiction may be successfully transposed to another, by reference to the lessons learnt from the former's experiences.

§ 4.1 A Class Proceedings Fund should only be implemented where there is a proven 'gap' in the funding landscape that warrants the implementation of a public source of funding via seed funding provided by either:
(1) the Government, or
(2) charitable sources.

In the absence of any gap, the utility of any such Fund must be seriously in doubt.

§ 4.2 The legislature must clearly identify:
(1) the type of assistance which the Fund will provide to the representative claimant by way of financial support;
(2) the sources of income to which the Fund will become immediately or potentially entitled, in the event of success or failure of the representative claimant's action;
(3) the precise trigger/s by which the Fund would be entitled to that receipt;
(4) whether the charge received by the Fund upon the recovery:
(a) should take effect prior to, or following, the compensation of those class members who come forward to claim their individual compensation; and
(b) should be a variable, rather than a fixed, percentage, depending upon the risks of the case;

(5) the circumstances, if any, in which the costs-shifting rule should be softened, or ameliorated, so as to reduce or negate an adverse costs order against a losing representative claimant.

§ 4.3 The criteria for funding:
(1) should be stipulated (whether or not with priority accorded to some or none); and
(2) should confirm whether the impecuniosity of the representative claimant/the class is either determinative, relevant, or irrelevant, amongst the criteria which are legislatively prescribed for funding.

§ 4.4 The amount of seed funding for the Fund, and the sources of replenishment, must be sufficient to ensure that the administering body is not hamstrung, or overly cautious, in approving funding, particularly in the early days of the Fund's operation.

§ 4.5 The legislation governing the operation of the Fund should stipulate, for the sake of clarity and certainty, matters such as:
(1) the grounds upon which the provision of funding of the class action can be terminated;
(2) the extent (if any) of input into decisions upon settlement, withdrawal and discontinuance of the class action to which the Fund is entitled;
(3) the specific liabilities, and rights of refund, of the Fund, should the class action be terminated for any of the reasons referred to in (1) or (2) above.

§ 5.1 The proactive submission of non-resident class members to the domestic court's jurisdiction, by a positive act of opting in, pursuant to the compulsory opt-in model, is the surest method by which to ensure that the domestic court has asserted personal jurisdiction over that class member. The various disadvantages of opt-in regimes are more than offset by the achievement of a judgment rendered in favour of, or against, those non-resident class members which will be recognised and enforced in another jurisdiction.

§ 5.2 Alternatively, where the legislature does not insist upon an opt-in requirement for non-resident class members, then some other legislative basis upon which to assert jurisdiction over those class members may be appropriate. For example, the legislature may elect to define the precise due process requirements that must be met in respect of those class members (including, but not limited to, adequate notice of the proposed action, equivalent outcomes, adequate representation, and appropriate opt-out rights).

§ 5.3 Given the array of judicially created 'anchors' or 'ties' which have been developed by domestic courts to assert personal jurisdiction over non-resident class members, and the disagreements at appellate level which the issue has witnessed, it would seem preferable to settle and to clarify this issue via legislation, rather than to leave it to case law precedential development.

§ 6.1 Even where the class action regime requires that governmental entities must consent in order to be class members, the legislation may preferably specify (for the avoidance of any doubt) that the requisite consent is not required in order for the class action to have been validly commenced (i.e., that consent is assumed to have been given by the very act of commencing the class action on behalf of the class).

§ 6.2 There is no valid basis for incorporating a 'typicality requirement' in a class action; experience dictates that it does not add anything useful to the certification requirements of commonality, adequacy, and suitability.

§ 6.3 In order to avoid uncertainty and contentious litigation, it would be helpful for an opt-out class action statute to explicitly provide that:
(1) different claims asserted among the class members do not preclude the commencement of a class action;
(2) it is not necessary that at least one claim should be shared by the class members (including the representative claimant); and
(3) a 'claim' includes, but should not be taken to be limited to, a 'cause of action'.

§ 6.4 A government instrumentality should not be automatically precluded from commencing a class action under an opt-out class action regime, where another representative action is available to that government instrumentality as the explicitly designated representative claimant. However, the former should only be permitted if it is superior to the latter.

§ 6.5 Whether or not an ideological claimant is permitted under the class actions regime should be explicitly stated, together with whether it should act:
(1) exclusively and solely;

(2) exceptionally;

(3) as an alternative to a directly affected class member; or

(3) not at all, because that particular type of ideological claimant is barred.

The appropriate drafting model will apply equally to a government instrumentality as to any other representative claimant.

§ 6.6 Whether the legislation should specify the prerequisites for assessing the suitability of an ideological claimant, and if so, a list of the particular prerequisites which should apply, should be explicitly considered by the legislature or rule-makers.

§ 7.1 Government, government ministers, government agencies and body corporates, and government employees, should have to opt in to any opt-out class action, in order to be bound by the outcome.

§ 7.2 Judges should also be included in the statutory list of those who must opt in to any opt-out class action, in order to ensure that any judge who may potentially hear a class action is not inadvertently included in the very case over which the judge is presiding.

§ 7.3 A statutory opt-in provision would be preferable to relying on a case-by-case exclusion of the parties referred to in §§ 7.1 and 7.2 from the relevant class definition.

§ 8.1 The implementation of suitable preliminary merits criteria within the generic regime, and a close regard to the relevant commonality, suitability, and representative threshold criteria, will provide a government defendant with adequate protection in those cases which are not appropriate to commence or to continue against that defendant in class action form.

§ 8.2 When framing a class claim against a government defendant, four principal theories of liability should be investigated, given how such claims have typically been pleaded: a claim for direct wrongdoing by the governmental defendant; a claim for vicarious liability; a claim for breach of a non-delegable duty of care; and a claim for principal liability for the wrongs committed by an agent.

§ 8.3 Except to the extent that a class actions statute permits modification of the substantive law, the statute is procedural only. Hence, the elements of any cause of action pleaded against a government defendant should not be modified or abrogated in any way, merely because the claim is being prosecuted on behalf of a class. To date, this cautionary note has been notable in three contexts, for example:

(a) claims for group defamation are only permissible where injury to the reputation of the class members as individuals, and where adequate identification of those class members, is proven;

(b) novel duties of care, giving rise to a possible claim in negligence, are possible by reference to 'first principles' (i.e., reasonable foreseeability of harm; legal proximity between the class members and the defendant; and public and legal policy favours, or does not negate, a duty of care arising), but should be assessed no differently, merely because the defendant is a government or government entity;

(c) any claim for 'regulatory negligence' should be treated with the aversion that it usually deserves, given the fact that any failure to execute a statutory duty properly, or at all, does not automatically generate a duty of care owed to those who suffered loss or injury as a result of that omission on the government's part.

§ 9.1 Although a general escheat distribution (whether to the Crown/ Treasury/Consolidated Revenue/the state) lacks both precision and a focus upon the aggrieved class members, there are at least five circumstances in which (singularly or in combination) such a distribution may be appropriate, and preferable to other avenues, by which to deal with the distribution of undistributed residues of damages or a settlement fund arising from a class action suit. Hence, it is recommended that a discretion vested in the court to award a general escheat distribution in the event of an undistributed residue arising should be included in any provision which deals with undistributed residues. However, it would be appropriate to designate an escheat distribution as an avenue of 'last resort', to be awarded if, and only if, the other specified avenues are not appropriate or feasible on the facts of a particular case.

§ 9.2 The legislative prescription of a charitable entity to which undistributed residues of damages or a settlement fund arising from a class action suit is to be paid, has the advantages of: (1) removing the potential for a 'lobbying effect'; (2) providing certainty for courts and litigants alike; and (3) providing an indirect method by which governments may benefit from the outcome of a successful class action. However, it is recommended that such an option should be one of a range of options to which undistributed residues could be distributed (whether in the context of judgment awards or settlement funds), instead of constituting a legislatively designated sole destination of undistributed residues. This would maximise the opportunities by which the outcome of a successful class action could benefit the aggrieved class members for whom the suit was litigated, and whose interests are paramount.

§ 9.3 An earmarked escheat distribution to a governmental entity may achieve a better rate of 'cross-over' as between the original class and the *cy-près* class than any other avenue of recipient or method of distribution of undistributed residues of damages or a settlement fund. It is recommended that the option be encompassed, whether legislatively or judicially, when considering an appropriate distribution of such residues. However, the concerns about government resources being diverted away from the governmental recipient should be explicitly addressed by the court when making such an order (albeit that enforcement of any governmental undertaking may be infeasible).

BIBLIOGRAPHY

[This bibliography contains a record of those materials which are cited in the book. Whilst every effort has been made to attribute and to trace authorships correctly, where it has not been possible to identify individual authorship, the author has indicated this with —. The author apologises in the event of any errors contained in the bibliography of materials cited.]

Texts, Monographs, and Published Research Papers

Alder J and K Syrett, *Constitutional and Administrative Law* (11th edn, Palgrave Master Series, 2017)

Allsop (The Hon Justice James), *An Introduction to the Jurisdiction of the Federal Court of Australia* (Federal Judicial Scholarship, 1 October 2007)

American Law Institute, *Principles of the Law: Aggregate Litigation* (2010)

Berryman J, *Class Actions* (published paper presented to the Second Intl Symposium on the Law of Remedies, Auckland, 16 November 2007)

Bradley A, K Ewing and C Knight, *Constitutional and Administrative Law* (17th edn, Pearson, 2018)

Briggs A, *The Conflict of Laws* (3rd edn, Clarendon Law Series, 2013)

Briggs A, *The Conflict of Laws* (3rd edn, Oxford University Press, 2016)

Brown J, *et al.*, *Defending Class Actions in Canada* (3rd edn, CCH Canadian Ltd, 2011)

Canadian Bar Assn, *Canadian Judicial Protocol for the Management of Multi-Jurisdictional Class Actions* (13 August 2011)

Canadian Bar Assn, *Canadian Judicial Protocol for the Management of Multijurisdictional Class Actions and the Provision of Class Action Notice* (15 February 2018)

Cashman P, *Class Action Law and Practice* (Federation Press, 2007)

Chiodo S, 'The Class Actions Controversy: The Origins and Development of the Ontario Class Proceedings Act' (2018–19) 14 *Canadian Class Action Review* (whole issue, with chapters noted separately under 'Periodicals')

Clarkson C, and J Hill, *The Conflict of Laws* (4th edn, Oxford University Press, 2011)

Collins (Lord) of Mapesbury (gen ed), *Dicey, Morris and Collins on The Conflict of Laws* (15th edn, Sweet & Maxwell, 2012)

Competition Appeal Tribunal, *Guide to Proceedings* (2015)

Conte A, and H Newberg, *Newberg on Class Actions* (4th edn, Thomson West Group, 2002)

Cranston R, *Class Actions* (Society of Labour Lawyers, 2007)

Davies M, *et al.*, *Nygh's Conflict of Laws in Australia* (8th edn, Lexis Nexis, 2010)

Frankel M, *Law Without Order* (Hill & Wang, 1973)

German J, *VW Defeat Devices: A Comparison of US and EU Required Fixes* (Intl Council on Clean Transportation, December 2017)

Grave D, and K Adams, *Class Actions in Australia* (Lawbook Co, 2005)

Grave D, K Adams and J Betts, *Class Actions in Australia* (2nd edn, Lawbook Co, 2012)

Grave D, *et al.* (eds), *Class Actions in England and Wales* (Sweet & Maxwell, 2018)

Hodges C, *Multi-Party Actions* (Oxford University Press, 2001)

Hodges C, and S Voet, *Delivering Collective Redress: New Technologies* (Hart Publishing, 2018)

Hogg P, *et al.*, *Liability of the Crown* (Carswell, 2011)

Holdsworth W, *A History of English Law* (3rd edn, Methuen, 1923)

Huschelrath K, and S Peyer, *Public and Private Enforcement of Competition Law: A Differentiated Approach* (CCP Working Paper 13–5, April 2013)

Huschelrath K, and H Schweitzer (eds), *Public and Private Enforcement of Competition Law in Europe: Legal and Economic Perspectives* (Springer-Verlag, ZEW Economic Studies Series Title, 2014)

International Bar Assn Legal Practice Division, *Guidelines for Recognising and Enforcing Foreign Judgments for Collective Redress* (October 2008)

Karlsgodt P, (ed), *World Class Action: A Guide to Group and Representative Actions around the Globe* (Oxford University Press, 2012)

Kirby M, *Reform the Law: Essays on the Renewal of the Australian Legal System* (Oxford University Press, 1983)

Kliebard K, *et al.*, *Class/collective Actions in the United States: Overview* (Class Actions Global Guide, Practical Law, updated as at 1 September 2018)

Knigge A, and I Wijnberg, *Class/collective Actions in The Netherlands: Overview* (Class Actions Global Guide, Practical Law, updated as at 1 July 2018)

Legg M, and R McInnes, *Annotated Class Actions Legislation* (LexisNexis, 2014)

Lein E, *et al.* (eds), *Collective Redress in Europe: Why and How?* (British Institute of International and Comparative Law, 2015)

McClean D, and V Abou-Nigm, *The Conflict of Laws* (9th edn, Sweet and Maxwell, 2016)

Markesinis B, *Foreign Law and Comparative Methodology* (Hart Publishing, 1997)

Morabito V, *Group Litigation in Australia* (National Report for Australia prepared for the Globalisation of Class Actions Conference, Oxford, December 2007)

Morabito V, *An Empirical Study of Australia's Class Action Regimes: Class Action Facts and Figures (First Report)* (December 2009)

Morabito V, *An Empirical Study of Australia's Class Action Regimes: Litigation Funders, Competing Class Actions, Opt Out Rates, Victorian Class Actions and Class Representatives (Second Report)* (September 2010)

Morabito V, *Class Action Facts and Figures – Five Years On (Third Report)* (November 2014)

Morabito V, *An Empirical Study of Australia's Class Action Regimes: Facts and Figures on Twenty-four Years of Class Actions in Australia (Fourth Report)* (August 2016)

Morabito V, *An Empirical Study of Australia's* Class Action Regimes: The First 25 Years of Class Actions in Australia (*Fifth Report*) (July 2017)

Mulheron R, *The Class Action in Common Law Legal Systems: A Comparative Perspective* (Hart Publishing, 2004)

Mulheron R, *The Modern Cy-près Doctrine: Applications and Implications* (Routledge Cavendish, 2006)

Mulheron R, *Competition Law Cases under the Opt-out Regimes of Australia, Canada and Portugal* (Research Paper for the BERR Dept, October 2008)

Mulheron R, *Reform of Collective Redress in England and Wales: A Perspective of Need* (A Research Paper for submission to the Civil Justice Council of England and Wales, 2008)

Mulheron R, *Costs and Funding of Collective Actions: Realities and Possibilities* (A Research Paper for the European Consumers' Organisation (BEUC), February 2011)

Mulheron R, *Principles of Tort Law* (Cambridge University Press, 2016)

Newbold B, *et al.*, *Class/collective actions in Australia: Overview* (Class Actions Global Guide, Practical Law, updated as at 1 August 2018)

Polinsky M, and S Shavell, *Public Enforcement of Law* (Stanford Institute for Economic Policy Research, May 2006)

Public Interest Advocacy Centre, *Representative Proceedings in New South* Wales – *A Review of the Law and a Proposal for Reform* (1995)

Rogerson P, *Collier's Conflict of Laws* (4th edn, Cambridge University Press, 2013)

Street H, *Governmental Liability* (Cambridge University Press, 1953)

Tettenborn A, and R Blackburn, *Halsbury's Law of England: Crown and Crown Proceedings*, vol 29 (5th edn, LexisNexis, 2014)

Torremans P, *Cheshire, North and Fawcett Private International Law* (15th edn, Oxford University Press, 2017)

Yeazell, *From Medieval Group Litigation to the Modern Class Action* (Yale University Press, 1987)

Zuckerman A, *Zuckerman on Civil Procedure: Principles of Practice* (3rd edn, Thomson Sweet and Maxwell, 2013)

—*Class and Group Actions 2019* (11th edn, Global Legal Group, 2018)

—*The Class Actions Law Review: Ireland* (2nd edn, *The Law Reviews*, May 2018)
—*The Law of Class Action: Fifty-state Survey 2015–16* (American Bar Assn, 2016)
—*A Practitioner's Guide to the December 2018 Federal Rule Amendments* (Practical Law, 1 December 2018)
—*Ripe for Reform: Improving the Australian Class Action Regime* (US Chamber Institute for Legal Reform, March 2014)

Official Reports and Discussion Papers

(in chronological order per jurisdiction)

Australia

Law Reform of Committee of South Australia, *Report Relating to Class Actions* (Rep 36, 1977)
ALRC, *Access to the Courts–II (Class Actions)* (DP 11, 1979)
ALRC, *Grouped Proceedings in the Federal Court* (Rep 46, 1988)
ALRC, *Legal Risk in International Transactions* (Rep 80, 1996)
Victorian Attorney-General's Law Reform Advisory Council (authored by V Morabito and J Epstein), *Class Actions in Victoria – Time for a New Approach* (1997)
ALRC, *Managing Justice: A Review of the Federal Civil Justice System* (Rep 89, 1999)
ALRC, *Annual Report* (Rep 90, 2000)
ALRC, *The Judicial Power of the Commonwealth* (Rep 92, 2001)
Victorian LRC, *Civil Justice Review Report* (Rep 14, 2008)
Law Reform Commission of WA, *Representative Proceedings* (DP 103, 2013)
ALRC, *Traditional Rights and Freedoms: Encroachments by Commonwealth Laws* (Rep 129, 2015)
Western Australia LRC, *Representative Proceedings: Final Report* (Project 103, 2015)
ALRC, *Traditional Rights and Freedoms: Encroachments by Commonwealth Laws* (Rep 129, 2015)
Victorian LRC, Access to Justice – Litigation Funding and Group Proceedings (CP, 2017)
Federal Court of Australia Law and Practice, *Class Actions Statistics* (2018)
Victorian LRC, *Access to Justice: Litigation Funding and Group Proceedings* (March 2018)
ALRC, *Inquiry into Class Action Proceedings and Third-Party Litigation Funders* (DP 85, May 2018)
ALRC, *Integrity, Fairness and Efficiency – An Inquiry into Class Action Proceedings and Third-Party Litigation Funders* (Rep 134, December 2018)

Canada

Ontario LRC, *Report on Class Action* (1982)

Ontario Attorney-General's Dept, *Report of the Attorney-General's Advisory Committee on Class Action Reform* (1990)

British Columbia Ministry of the Attorney General, Class Action Legislation for British Columbia (Consultation Document, 1994)

Manitoba Civil Justice Litigation Committee, *Civil Justice Review Taskforce Report* (1996)

Manitoba LRC, *Class Proceedings* (Rep 100, 1999)

Rules Committee of the Federal Court of Canada, Class Proceedings in the Federal Court of Canada (DP, 2000)

Alberta Law Reform Institute, *Class Actions* (Memo No 9, 2000)

Alberta Law Reform Institute, *Class Actions* (Rep 85, 2000)

Uniform Law Conference of Canada, Civil Law Section, *Report of the Uniform Law Conference Of Canada's Committee on the National Class and Related Interjurisdictional Issues: Background, Analysis, and Recommendations* (Vancouver, 9 March 2005)

Class Proceedings Fund 20 Years in Review (2013)

Law Reform Commission of Ontario, *Review of Class Actions in Ontario – Issues to be Considered* (November 2013)

Law Foundation of British Columbia, *Annual Report* (2015)

Class Proceedings Fund Annual Report (2016)

Class Proceedings Fund Annual Report (2017)

British Columbia Law Institute, *Study Paper on Financing Litigation* (2017)

Law Foundation of British Columbia, *Annual Report* (2017)

Law Commission of Ontario, Class Actions: Objectives, Experiences and Reforms (CP, March 2018)

Law Foundation of British Columbia, *Annual Report* (2018)

England and Wales

See too, the numerous additional reports, 1988–2003, noted in: Mulheron: *The Class Action in Common Law Legal Systems: A Comparative Perspective* (Hart Publishing, 2004) 509–10

Lord Woolf MR, *Access to Justice: Final Report to the Lord Chancellor on the Civil Justice System in England and Wales* (1996)

Lord Chancellor's Dept, *Representative Claims: Proposed New Procedures* (2001)

Dept of Trade and Industry, *Social Enterprise: A Strategy for Success* (2002)

Office of Fair Trading, *Unfair Contract Terms Guidance: Consultation on Revised Guidance for the Unfair Terms in Consumer Contract Regulations 1999* (OFT311, 2007)

Civil Justice Council, *The Future Funding of Litigation: Funding Options and Proportionate Costs: Alternative Funding Structures* (June 2007)

Ministry of Justice, *Claims Management Services Regulation: Claims in Respect of Bank Charges: Guidance Note* (27 July 2007)

Civil Justice Council (J Sorabji, M Napier and R Musgrove (eds)), *Improving Access to Justice through Collective Actions: Final Report (A Series of Recommendations to the Lord Chancellor)* (November 2008)

HM Treasury, *Reforming Financial Markets* (Cm 7667, 2009)

Civil Justice Council, *Draft Court Rules for Collective Proceedings* (November 2009)

Sir Rupert Jackson, *Review of Civil Litigation Costs: Final Report* (December 2009)

Ministry of Justice, *The Government's Response to the Civil Justice Council's Report: 'Improving Access to Justice through Collective Actions'* (July 2009)

Ombudsman Schemes: Guidance for Departments (Cabinet Office, April 2010)

Assn of Litigation Funders, *Code of Conduct for Litigation Funding in England and Wales* (2011), and with amended versions published in (2014) and (2017)

Dept of Business, Innovation and Skills, *Private Actions in Competition Law: A Consultation on Options for Reform* (April 2012)

Dept of Business, Innovation and Skills, *Private Actions in Competition Law: A Consultation on Options for Reform: Government Response* (2013)

Competition Appeal Tribunal Rules of Procedure: Review by the Rt Hon Sir John Mummery (3 April 2015)

Dept of Business, Innovation and Skills, *Competition Appeal Tribunal (CAT) Rules of Procedure: Government Response* (September 2015)

Competition and Markets Authority, *Competition Law Redress: A Guide to Taking Action for Breaches of Competition Law* (CMA 55, May 2016)

Civil Justice Council, *The Law and Practicalities of Before-the-Event (BTE) Insurance: An Information Study* (November 2017)

Office of Parliamentary Counsel, *Crown Application* (HMSO, 14 February 2018)

European Union

Competition Directorate-General, Green Paper on Damages Actions for Breach of the EC Antitrust Rules, COM (2005) 672 (19 December 2005)

Comp, *EC Staff Working Paper accompanying the Green Paper*, SEC (2005) 1732

White Paper on Damages Actions for Breach of the EC Antitrust Rules, COM (2008) 165 (2 April 2008)

EC Staff Working Paper accompanying the White Paper, SEC (2008) 404 (2 April 2008)

European Parliament, *Resolution on the White Paper on Damages Actions for Breach of the EC Antitrust Rules*, 2008/2154 (INI) (26 March 2009)

European Parliament, *Directive 2009/22/EC of the European Parliament and of the Council of 23 April 2009 on injunctions for the protection of consumers' interests* (OJEUL110/30, 1 May 2009) (codifying Directive 98/27/EC on injunctions for the protection of consumers' interests)

SANCO Directorate-General, Green Paper on Consumer Collective Redress, COM (2008) 794 (27 November 2009)

SANCO, Staff Working Document, Practical Guide on Quantifying Harm in Actions for Damages Based on Breaches of Art 101 or 102 of the Treaty on the Functioning of the European Union, SWD (2013) 205 (11 June 2013)

Proposal for a Directive of the European Parliament and of the Council on Certain Rules Governing Actions for Damages under National Law for Infringements of the Competition Law Provisions of the Member States and of the European Union, COM (2013) 404 (11 June 2013)

European Commission, *Commission Recommendation of 11 June 2003 on common principles for injunctive and compensatory collective redress mechanisms in the Member States concerning violations of rights granted under Union Law* (2013/396/EU) (OJ L201/60, 26 July 2013)

European Commission, *Report from the Commission to the European Parliament, the Council and the European Economic and Social Committee on the Implementation of the Commission Recommendation of 11 June 2013 on Common Principles for Injunctive and Compensatory Collective Redress Mechanisms in the Member States Concerning Violations of Rights granted under Union law* (2013/396/EU), COM (2018) 40 final (25 January 2018)

Hong Kong

Law Reform Comm of Hong Kong, *Class Actions* (CP, 2009)
Law Reform Comm of Hong Kong, *Class Actions* (2012)

Ireland

Irish LRC, Multi-Party Litigation (Class Actions) (CP, 25, 2003)
Irish LRC, *Report on Multi-Party Litigation* (Rep 76, 2005)

New Zealand

New Zealand Law Comm, *Review of Class Actions and Litigation Funding* (May 2018)

Scotland

Scottish Law Comm, Multi-Party Actions: Court Proceedings and Funding (DP 98, 1994)
Scottish Law Comm, *Multi-Party Actions* (Rep 154, 1996)
Report of the Scottish Civil Courts Review (2009)

Sheriff Principal (J Taylor), *Review of Expenses and Funding of Civil Litigation in Scotland* (October 2013)
Scottish Civil Justice Council, *Annual Report 2017/18 and Annual Programme 2018/19* (2018)

South Africa

South African Law Comm, *The Recognition of a Class Action in South African Law* (Working Paper 57, 1995)
South African Law Comm, *The Recognition and Class Actions and Public Interest Actions in South African Law* (Project 88, 1998)

United States

Report of the Committee on Rules of Practice and Procedure of the Judicial Conference of the United States, Standing Committee on Rules of Practice and Procedure, 'Preliminary Draft of Proposed Amendments to Rules of Civil Procedure for the United States District Courts' (1964) 34 *Federal Rules Decisions* 325
US Advisory Committee on Rules of Civil Procedure (1996)
Advisory Committee on Civil Rules and Working Group on Mass Torts, *Report on Mass Tort Litigation* (1999)Hensler D, *et al.*, *Class Action Dilemmas: Pursuing Public Goals for Private Gain* (RAND Institute for Civil Justice, 1999)
Administrative Office of the US Courts, *Report of the Civil Rules Advisory Committee to the Standing Committee on Rules of Practice and Procedure* (May 2002)
Report of the Judicial Conference Committee on Rules of Practice and Procedure to the Chief Justice of the United States and Members of the Judicial Conference of the United States (September 2002)
Notes Accompanying Federal Rules of Civil Procedure, Title IV, Parties, Rule 23, Class Actions, 'Notes of Advisory Committee on Rules – 1966 Amendment' (Legal Information Institute, Cornell Law School)
United States Courts, *How the Rulemaking Process Works* (US Courts Newsletter, 2018)
US Advisory Committee Note to Rule 23 (2018)

Contributions to Edited Texts/Chapters

Arvind T, 'Restraining the State Through Tort? The Crown Proceedings Act in Retrospect', in T Arvind and J Steele (eds), *Tort Law and the Legislature* (Hart Publishing, 2013), ch 19
Betts J *et al.*, 'Litigation Funding for Class Actions', in D Grave and H Mould (eds), *25 Years of Class Actions in Australia* (Ross Parsons, 2017), ch 10
Brown, J, 'The Perils of Certifying International Class Actions in Canada', in D Fairgrieve and E Lein (eds), *Extraterritoriality and Collective Redress* (Oxford University Press, 2012), ch 16

Brown J, and B Kain, 'Cross-border Actions for Collective Redress: Some Lessons from Canada', in E Lein *et al.* (eds), *Collective Redress in Europe: Why and How?* (British Institute of International and Comparative Law, 2015) 203

Fleming J, and J Kuster, 'The Netherlands', in P Karlsgodt (ed), *World Class Actions: A Guide to Group and Representative Actions around the Globe* (Oxford University Press, 2012), ch 14

Geisker J, and J Tallis, 'Australia', in *Third Party Litigation Funding Law Rev* (2nd edn, 16 November 2018)

Grave D, and J Betts, 'The Commission Recommendation on Common Principles for Collective Redress: Some Reflections from Australia', in E Lein *et al.* (eds), *Collective Redress in Europe: Why and How?* (British Institute of International and Comparative Law, 2015) 219

Hamer D, and S D'Souza, 'Multijurisdictional and Transnational Class Litigation: Lawsuits Heard "Round the World"', in P Karlsgodt (ed), *World Class Actions: A Guide to Group and Representative Actions around the Globe* (Oxford University Press, 2012), ch 27

Jackson H, and J Zhang, 'Private and Public Enforcement of Securities Regulations', in J Gordon and W Ringe (eds), *The Oxford Handbook of Corporate Law and Governance* (Oxford University Press, 2018)

Khouri S, *et al.*, 'Litigation Funding and Class Actions: Idealism, Pragmatism and a New Paradigm', in D Grave and H Mould (eds), *25 Years of Class Actions in Australia* (Ross Parsons, 2017), ch 11

Kim I, 'Public Enforcement', in A Marciano and G Ramello (eds), *Encyclopaedia of Law and Economics* (Springer, 2016)

Legg M, and J Metzger, 'Section 33ZF: Class Actions Problem Solver?', in D Grave and H Mould (eds), *25 Years of Class Actions in Australia* (Ross Parsons, 2017), ch 16

MacLean J, 'In What Circumstances Can You Apply to Review a Government Decision?', in *Western Australia Law Handbook* (31 July 2018)

Martineau Y, and A Lang, 'Canada', in P Karlsgodt (ed), *World Class Actions: A Guide to Group and Representative Actions around the Globe* (Oxford University Press, 2012), ch 2

Morabito V, 'Empirical Perspectives on 25 Years of Class Actions', in D Grave and H Mould (eds), *25 Years of Class Actions in Australia* (Ross Parsons, 2017), ch 4

Mulheron R, 'Costs-Shifting, Security for Costs, and Class Actions: Lessons from Elsewhere', in D Dwyer (ed), *The Tenth Anniversary of the Civil Procedure Rules* (Oxford University Press, 2010), ch 10

Mulheron R, 'Disgruntled Customers and Bank Charges: Class Action (Reform) Activity', in S Grundmann *et al.* (eds), *Financial Services, Financial Crisis and General European Contract Law: Failure and the Challenges of Contracting* (Wolters Kluwer, 2011), ch 11

Mulheron R, 'The Impetus for Class Actions Reform in England arising from the Competition Law Sector', in S Wrbka *et al.* (eds), *Collective Actions: Enhancing Access to Justice and Reconciling Multilayer Interests?* (Cambridge University Press, 2012), ch 15

Mulheron R, 'In Defence of the Requirement for Foreign Class Members to Opt Into an English Class Action', in D Fairgrieve and E Lein (eds), *Extraterritoriality and Collective Redress* (Oxford University Press, 2012), ch 14

Mulheron R, 'Class Actions and Law Reform: Insights from Australia and England, a Quarter of a Century Apart', in D Grave and H Mould (eds), *25 Years of Class Actions in Australia* (Ross Parsons, 2017), ch 14

Murphy (The Hon Justice Bernard) and V Morabito, 'The First 25 years: Has the Class Action Regime Hit the Mark on Access to Justice?', in D Grave and H Mould (eds), *25 Years of Class Actions in Australia* (Ross Parsons, 2017), ch 3

Overington R, 'Resolving Multiple Claims: How Efficient is the Class Action Regime?', in D Grave and H Mould (eds), *25 Years of Class Actions in Australia* (Ross Parsons, 2017), ch 7

Raja M, and P Lomas, 'A Lawyer's Perspective', in E Lein *et al.* (eds), *Collective Redress in Europe: Why and How?* (British Institute of International and Comparative Law, 2015) 67

Sorabji J, 'Collective Actions Reform in England and Wales', in D Fairgrieve and E Lein (eds), *Extraterritoriality and Collective Redress* (Oxford University Press, 2012), ch 3

Sossin L, 'Revisiting Class Actions Against the Crown: Balancing Public and Private Legal Accountability for Government Action', in J Kalajdzic (ed), *Accessing Justice: Appraising Class Actions Ten Years After Dutton, Hollick & Rumley* (LexisNexis, 2011), ch 3

Stuart-Clark S, *et al*, 'Australia', in Paul Karlsgodt (ed), *World Class Actions: A Guide to Group and Representative Actions around the Globe* (Oxford University Press, 2012), ch 22

Wilcox (The Hon Murray), 'Class Actions in Australia: Recollections of the Early Days', in D Grave and H Mould (eds), *25 Years of Class Actions in Australia* (Ross Parsons, 2017), ch 2

Periodical Articles

Allen J, 'The Office of the Crown' (2018) 77 *Cambridge Law Journal* 298

Andenas M, and D Fairgrieve, 'Reforming Crown Immunity – The Comparative Law Perspective' [2003] *Public Law* 730

Aronson M, 'Government Liability in Negligence' (2008) 32 *Melbourne University Law Review* 44

Aronson M, 'Misfeasance in Public Office: A Very Peculiar Tort' (2011) 35 *Melbourne University Law Review* 1

Barkett J, *The 2018 Amendments to the Federal Class Actions Rule* (American Bar Assn, 2018)

Barling (The Hon Mr Justice Gerald), 'Collective Redress for Breach of Competition Law: A Case for Reform?' (2011) 10 *Competition Law Journal* 5

Barnett K, 'Equitable Trusts: An Effective Remedy in Consumer Class Actions' (1987) 96 *Yale Law Journal* 1591

Bartholomew C, 'Saving Charitable Settlements' (2015) 83 *Fordham Law Review* 3241

Bassett D, 'US Class Actions Go Global: Transnational Class Actions and Personal Jurisdiction' (2003) 72 *Fordham Law Review* 41

Bassett D, 'Just Go Away: Representation, Due Process, and Preclusion in Class Actions' (2009) *Brigham Young University Law Review* 1079

Beaton-Wells C, 'Private Enforcement of Competition Law in Australia – Inching Forwards?' (2016) 39 *Melbourne University Law Review* 681

Berryman J, 'Nudge, Nudge, Wink, Wink: Behavioural Modification, *Cy-Près* Distributions and Class Actions' (2011) 53 *Supreme Court Law Review* 2d 133

Black M, 'Class Actions Pursuant to Tennessee Rule of Civil Procedure 23' (1979) 46 *Tennessee Law Review* 556

Bone R, 'Justifying Class Action Limits: Parsing the Debates over Ascertainability and *Cy près*' (2017) 65 *University of Kansas Law Review* 913

Boughey J, and G Weeks, '"Officers of the Commonwealth" in the Private Sector: Can the High Court Review Outsourced Exercises of Power?' (2013) 36 *UNSW Law Journal* 316

Braul W, *et al.*, 'Water Use Challenges to Oil and Gas Developments' (2015) 53 *Alberta Law Review* 323

Broome J, 'Group Defamation: Five Guiding Factors' (1985) 64 *Texas Law Review* 591

Brown T, 'Rumplestiltskin's New Money' (2010) 154 *Solicitors' Journal* 53

Brown M, 'Our Aging CPA: It's Time for Ontario to "Opt-In" to a Modern Global Class-Actions Framework' (2017–18) 13 *Canadian Class Actions Review* 395

Burbank S, and S Farhang, 'Class Actions and the Counter-revolution against Federal Litigation' (2017) 165 *University of Pennsylvania Law Review* 1495

Capes M, 'Book Review: A Guide to the Class Proceedings Act 1992' (1993) 25 *Ottawa Law Review* 655

Carroll M, 'Class Action Myopia' (2016) 65 *Duke Law Journal* 843

Chalk D, 'Solicitor client costs indemnities: unregulated insurance or benign assistance?' [2013] *Journal of Business Law* 59

Chamberlain N, 'Contracting-Out of Class Action Litigation: Lessons from the United States' [2018] *New Zealand Law Review* 371

Chamberlain N, 'Class Actions in New Zealand: An Empirical Study' [2018] *New Zealand Business Law Quarterly* 132

Cheshire A, 'Fairbridge Farm School child migrant class action' (2010) 100 *Precedent* 49

Chiodo S, 'Class Actions in England, North America and Australia' (2018–19) 14 *Canadian Class Action Review* 15

Chiodo S, 'The Early Campaign for Reform and the OLRC Report' (2018–19) 14 *Canadian Class Action Review* 47

Chiodo S, 'The Report of the Attorney General's Advisory Committee on Class Action Reform (1985–1993)' (2018–19) 14 *Canadian Class Action Review* 89

Chiodo S, 'Class Actions Twenty-five Years On' (2018–19) 14 *Canadian Class Actions Review* 189

Cohn S, 'The New Federal Rules of Civil Procedure' (1966) 54 *Georgia Law Journal* 1204

Collins D, 'Public Funding of Class Actions and the Experience with English Group Proceedings' (2005) 31 *Manitoba Law Journal* 211

Crandley M, 'Federal Rule Changes Coming in December' (*National Law Review*, 26 September 2018)

DeJarlais N, 'The Consumer Trust Fund: A *Cy Près* Solution to Undistributed Funds in Consumer Class Actions' (1987) 38 *Hastings Law Journal* 729

Dyk A, 'A Better Way to *Cy-près*: A Proposal to Reform Class Action *Cy-près* Distribution' (2019) 21 *NYU Journal of Legislation and Public Policy* 635

Erichson H, 'Searching for Salvageable Ideas in Ficala' (2018) 87 *Fordham Law Review* 19

Foreman J, and G Meisenheimer, 'The Evolution of the Class Action Trial in Ontario' (2014) 4 *Western Journal of Legal Studies* 1

Frankel M, 'Amended Rule 23 From a Judge's Point of View' (1966) 32 *ABA Antitrust Law Journal* 251

Frankel M, 'Some Preliminary Observations Concerning Civil Rule 23' (1967) 43 *Federal Rules Decisions* 39

Gamble R, 'Jostling for a Piece of the (Class) Action: Third Party Funders and Entrepreneurial Lawyers Stake their Claims' (2017) 46 *Common Law World Review* 3

Glover-Thomas N, and W Barr, 'Enabling or Disabling? Increasing Involvement of Charities in Social Housing' [2009] *Conveyancing and Property Lawyer* 209

Harvey M, 'Case Comment: *Sibthorpe v Southwark LBC*' [2011] *Journal of Personal Injury Law* C98

Higgins A, 'Driving with the Handbrake On: Competition Class Actions under the Consumer Rights Act 2015' (2016) 79 *Modern Law Review* 442

Higgins A, and A Zuckerman, 'Class Actions Come to England (Editorial)' (2016) 35 *Civil Justice Quarterly* 1

Higgins R, 'The Equitable Doctrine of *Cy-près* and Consumer Protection' (Annex 1, ACA Submission, *Trade Practices Rev*, 15 July 2002)

Hillebrand G, and D Torrence, 'Claims Procedures in Large Consumer Class Actions and Equitable Distribution of Benefits' (1988) 28 *Santa Clara Law Review* 747

Hills B, 'Never Settle for Second Best? Cy près Distributions in Securities Class Action Settlements' (2017) *Missouri Law Review* 507

Hogg P, and S McKee, 'Are National Class Actions Constitutional?' (2010) 26 *National Journal of Constitutional Law* 279

Hogg P, and S McKee, 'Are National Class Actions Constitutional? – A Reply to Walker' (2013) 31 *National Journal of Constitutional Law* 183

Irving C, and M Bouchard, 'National Opt Out Class Actions, A Constitutional Assessment' (2009) 26 *National Journal of Constitutional Law* 111

Johnston J, '*Cy Près* Comme Possible to Anything is Possible: How *Cy Près* Creates Improper Incentives in Class Action Settlements' (2013) 9 *Journal of Law, Economics and Policy* 277

Jois G, 'The *Cy Près* Problem and the Role of Damages in Tort Law' (2008) 16 *Virginia Journal of Social Policy and Law* 258

Jones C, 'New Solitudes: Recent Decisions Call into Question the National Class Action' (2007) 45 *Canadian Business Law Journal* 111

Jones T, '*Pro bono* costs orders' (2012) 17 *Judicial Review* 120

Kalajdzic J, 'Access to a Just Result: Revisiting Settlement Standards and *Cy-près* Distributions' (2010) 6 *Canadian Class Action Review* 217

Kalajdizic J, 'Consumer (In)Justice: Reflections on Canadian Consumer Class Actions' (2011) 50 *Canadian Business Law Journal* 356

Kalajdzic J, 'The "Illusion of Compensation": *Cy-Près* Distributions in Canadian Class Actions' (2013) 92 *Canadian Bar Review* 173

Kaplan B, 'Continuing Work of the Civil Committee: 1966 Amendments of the Federal Rules of Civil Procedure' (1967) 81 *Harvard Law Review* 356

Karas S, 'The Role of Fluid Recovery in Consumer Protection Litigation: *Kraus v Trinity Management Services*' (2002) 90 *California Law Review* 959

Koniak S, 'Feasting While the Widow Weeps' (1995) 80 *Cornell Law Review* 1045

Krusell J, 'Are National Class Actions Constitutional? A Reply to Walker, Hogg and McKee' (2012) 90 *University of Toronto Faculty Law Review* 9

Lambert K, 'Class Actions Settlements in Louisiana' (2000) 61 *Louisiana Law Review* 89

Lynch G, 'Marvin Frankel: A Reformer Reassessed' (2009) 21 *Fed Sentencing Rep* 235

McCall J, *et al.*, 'Greater Representation for California Consumers: Fluid Recovery, Consumer Trust Funds, and Representative Actions' (1995) 46 *Hastings Law Journal* 797

Main T, 'Judicial Discretion to Condition' (2006) 79 *Temple Law Review* 1075

Malone M, 'Judicial Scrutiny of Third Party Litigation Funding Agreements in Canadian Class Actions' (2017–18) 13 *Canadian Class Action Review* 193

Marcus R, 'Revolution v Evolution in Class Action Reform' (2018) 96 *North Carolina Law Review* 903

Marcus D, 'The History of the Modern Class Action, Part I' (2013) 90 *Washington University Law Review* 587

Marcin R, 'Searching for the Origin of the Class Action' (1974) 23 *Catholic University Law Review* 515

Marshall D, 'Solicitor Indemnity against Adverse Costs' [2012] *Journal of Personal Injury Law* 62

Martin J, '*Sui Generis*: Common Law Solutions to Constitutional Problems in Multijurisdictional Class Proceedings' (2013) 69 *University of Toronto Faculty Law Review* 55

Miller A, 'Of Frankenstein Monsters and Shining Knights: Myth, Reality, and the "Class Action Problem"' (1979) 92 *Harvard Law Review* 664

Miller A, '*McIntyre* in Context: A Very Personal Perspective' (2012) 63 *South Carolina Law Review* 465

Mohammed-Davidson R, 'Show me the Money: Enforcing Original Jurisdiction Judgments of the Caribbean Court of Justice' (2016) 29 *Leiden Journal of International Law* 113

Monestier T, 'Personal Jurisdiction over Non-Resident Class Members: Have We Gone Down the Wrong Road?' (2010) 45 *Texas International Law Journal* 537

Monestier T, 'Transnational Class Actions and the Illusory Search for *Res Judicata*' (2011) 86 *Tulane Law Review* 1

Morabito V, 'Ideological Plaintiffs and Class Actions: An Australian Perspective' (2001) 34 *University of British Columbia Law Review* 459

Morabito V, 'Class Actions Against Multiple Respondents' (2002) 30 *Federal Law Review* 295

Morabito V, 'Standing to Sue and Multiple Defendant Class Actions in Australia, Canada and the United States' (2003) 41 *Alberta Law Review* 295

Morabito V, 'The Federal Court of Australia's Power to Terminate Properly Instituted Class Actions' (2004) 42 *Osgoode Hall Law Journal* 473

Morabito V, 'Class Actions Instituted only for the Benefit of the Clients of the Class Representative's Solicitors' (2007) 29 *Sydney Law Review* 5

Morabito V, 'The Victorian Law Reform Commission's Class Action Reform Strategy' (2009) 32 *UNSW Law Journal* 1055

Morabito V, and J Caruana, 'Australian Unions: The Unknown Class Action Protagonists' (2011) 30 *Civil Justice Quarterly* 382

Morabito V, and J Caruana, 'Can Class Action Regimes Operate Satisfactorily Without a Certification Device? Empirical Insights from the Federal Court of Australia' (2013) 61 *American Journal of Comparative Law* 579

Morabito V, and J Ekstein, 'Class Actions Filed for the Benefit of Vulnerable Persons: An Australian Study' (2016) 35 *Civil Justice Quarterly* 61

Morabito V, 'Lessons from Australia on Class Action Reform in New Zealand' (2018) 24 *New Zealand Business Law Quarterly* 178

Mulheron R, 'From Representative Rule to Class Action: Steps Rather than Leaps' (2005) 24 *Civil Justice Quarterly* 424

Mulheron R, 'Some Difficulties with Group Litigation Orders – and Why a Class Action is Superior' (2005) 24 *Civil Justice Quarterly* 40

Mulheron R, 'Justice Enhanced: Framing an Opt-Out Class Action for England' (2007) 70 *Modern Law Review* 550

Mulheron R, and P Cashman, 'Third Party Funding of Litigation: A Changing Landscape' (2008) 27 *Civil Justice Quarterly* 312

Mulheron R, 'Building Blocks and Design Points for an Opt-out Class action' [2008] *Journal of Personal Injury Law* 308

Mulheron R, '*Emerald Supplies Ltd v British Airways plc*: A Century Later, the Ghost of *Markt* Lives On' (2009) 8 *Competition Law Journal* 159

Mulheron R, 'The Case for an Opt-out Class Action for European Member States: A Legal and Empirical Analysis' (2009) 15 *Columbia Journal of European Law* 409

Mulheron R, '*Cy-près* Damages Distributions in England: A New Era for Consumer Redress' (2009) 20 *European Business Law Review* 307

Mulheron R, 'Opting In, Opting Out, and Closing the Class: Some Dilemmas for England's Class Action Lawmakers' (2010) 50 *Canadian Business Law Journal* 376

Mulheron R, 'Recent Milestones in Class Actions: A Critique and a Proposal' (2011) 127 *Law Quarterly Review* 288

Mulheron R, 'Recent Milestones in Class Actions Reform in England: A Critique and a Proposal' (2011) 127 *Law Quarterly Review* 288

Mulheron R, 'A Missed Gem of an Opportunity for the Representative Rule' [2012] *Euro Business Law Review* 49

Mulheron R, 'The Recognition and *Res Judicata* Effect of a United States Class Actions Judgment in England: A Rebuttal of *Vivendi*' (2012) 75 *Modern Law Review* 180

Mulheron R, 'A Channel Apart: Why the United Kingdom has Departed from the European Commission's Recommendations on Class Actions' (2015) 17 *Cambridge Yearbook of European Legal Studies* 36

Mulheron R, 'Third Party Funding and Class Actions Reform' (2015) 131 *Law Quarterly Review* 291

Mulheron R, 'A Spotlight on the Settlement Criteria under the United Kingdom's New Competition Class Action' (2016) 35 *Civil Justice Quarterly* 1

Mulheron R, 'The United Kingdom's New Opt-Out Class Action' (2017) 37 *Oxford Journal of Legal Studies* 814

Mulheron R, and D Edlin, 'The Mere Mirage of a Class Action? A Challenge to *Merricks v Mastercard Inc*' (2018) 37 *Civil Justice Quarterly* 216

Mulheron R, 'Joining the United Kingdom's Class Action as a Non-resident: A Legislative Drafting Conundrum' (2020) 39 *Civil Justice Quarterly* 69

Mulheron R, 'Revisiting the Class Action Certification Matrix in *Merricks v Mastercard Inc*' (2019) 30 *King's Law Journal* 396

Mulheron R, 'Asserting Personal Jurisdiction over Non-Resident Class Members: Comparative Insights for the United Kingdom' (2019) 15 *Journal of Private International Law* 445

Mulheron R, 'England's Unique Approach to the Self-Regulation of Third Party Funding: A Critical Analysis of Recent Developments' (2014) 73 *Cambridge Law Journal* 570

Mullenix L, 'Ending Class Actions As We Know Them: Rethinking the American Class Action' (2014) 64 *Emory Law Journal* 399

Munro D, 'Class Actions in Virginia state courts? Or is it just *Bull?*' (2012) 23 *Journal of the Virginia Trial Lawyers Association* 26

Murphy R, 'Competing Ideologies at the Formation of the Federal Class Action Rule: Legal Process versus Legal Liberalism' (2018) 10 *Drexel Law Review* 389

Murtagh M, 'The Rule 23(b)(3) Superiority Requirement and Transnational Class Actions: Excluding Foreign Class Members in Favor of European Remedies' (2011) 34 *Hastings International and Competition Law Review* 1

National Audit Office, *What are third sector organisations and their benefits for commissioners?* (October 2010)

Nelthorpe D, 'Consumer Trusts Funds' (1988) 13 *Legal Services Bulletin* 26

Partridge S, and K Miller, 'Some Practical Considerations for Defending and Settling Products Liability and Consumer Class Actions' (2000) 74 *Tulane Law Review* 2125

Phi B, 'Arming the Courts in Collective Redress: A Move to "Australian-Style" Class Actions in the UK?' (2017) 36 *Civil Justice Quarterly* 197

Piche C, 'The Coming Revolution in Class Action Notices: Reaching the Universe of Claimants through Technologies' (2018) 16 *Canadian Journal of Law and Technology* 227

Pritchard A, and J Sarra, 'Securities Class Actions Move North: A Doctrinal and Empirical Analysis of Securities Class Actions in Canada' (2010) 47 *Alberta Law Review* 881

Rabiej, K, 'The Making of Class Action Rule 23: What Were We Thinking?' (2005) 24 *Mississippi College Law Review* 323

Resnik J, '"Vital" State Interests: From Representative Actions for Fair Labor Standards to Pooled Trusts, Class Actions, and MDLs in the Federal Courts' (2017) 165 *University of Pennsylvania Law Review* 1765

Rubenstein W, 'On What a "Private Attorney General" Is – and Why it Matters' (2004) 57 *Vanderbilt Law Review* 2129

Sackville (The Hon Justice Ronald), 'Law and Poverty: A Paradox' (2018) 41 *UNSW Law Journal* 80

Sackville (The Hon Justice Ronald), 'Judicial Review of Migration Decisions: An Institution in Peril?' (2000) 23 *UNSW Law Journal* 190

Sandstrom Simard L, and J Tidmarsh, 'Foreign Citizens in Transnational Class Actions' (2011) 97 *Cornell Law Review* 87

Schenkkan P, 'State Class Action Reform: Lessons from Texas' (2005) 12 *Andrews Class Action Litigation Reports* 15

Scott V, 'Access to Justice and Choice of Law Issues in Multi-Jurisdictional Class Actions in Canada' (2013) *Ottawa Law Review* 233

Sedgwick A, 'Case Comment: *Sibthorpe v Southwark LBC*' (2011) 30 *Civil Justice Quarterly* 261

Seymour J, 'Representative Proceedings and the Future of Multi-Party Actions' (1999) 62 *Modern Law Review* 565

Seymour J, '*Independiente Ltd v Music Trading On-Line (HK) Ltd*: A little knowledge is a dangerous thing?' (2005) 24 *Civil Justice Quarterly* 16

Sherman E, 'American Civil Justice in a Global Context' (2002) 52 *De Paul Law Review* 401

Smith R, 'Blinded by Statistics?' (2008) 158 *New Law Journal* (9 October 2008) 1391

Sorabji J, 'The Hidden Class Action in English Civil Procedure' (2009) 28 *Civil Justice Quarterly* 498

Sorabji J, 'Coping with Complexity and Securing Justice through Multi-Party Litigation: Lessons from the CAT and JJB Sports' [2014] *European Business Law Review* 527

Spender J, 'Securities Class Actions: A View from the Land of the Great White Shareholder' (2002) 31 *Common Law World Review* 123

Stempel J, 'Erie under Advisement' (2011) 44 *Akron Law Review* 907

Stuart-Clark S, and C Harris, 'Multi-Plaintiff Litigation in Australia: A Comparative Perspective' (2001) 11 *Duke Journal of Comparative and International Law* 289

Stuart-Clark S, and C Harris, ''Class Actions in Australia: (Still) a Work in Progress' (2008) 31 *Australian Bar Review* 63

Tanenhaus J, 'Group Libel' (1950) 35 *Cornell Law Quarterly* 261

Tidmarsh J, '*Cy Près* and the Optimal Class Action' (2014) 82 *George Washington Law Review* 767

Underwood J, 'Rationality, Multiplicity & Legitimacy: Federalization of the Interstate Class Action' (2004) 46 *South Texas Law Review* 391

Walker J, 'Cross-border Class Actions: A View from Across the Border' (2004) *Michigan State Law Review* 755

Walker J, 'Coordinating Multijurisdictional Class Actions Through Existing Certification Processes' (2006) 42 *Canadian Business Law Journal* 112

Walker J, 'Are National Class Actions Constitutional? A Reply to Hogg and McKee' (2010) 48 *Osgoode Hall Law Journal* 95

Watson G, 'Initial Interpretations of Ontario's Class Proceedings Act: The Anaheim and the Breast Implant Actions' (1993) 18 *Carswell Practice Cases – Articles* (3ʳᵈ series) 344

Watson G, 'Is the Price Still Right?' (Administration of Justice Conference, Toronto, 15 October 1997)

Wilcox (The Hon Justice Murray), 'Representative Proceedings in the Federal Court: A Progress Report' (1997) 15 *Australian Bar Review* 91

Wright C, 'Class Actions' (1970) 47 *Federal Rules Decisions* 169

Wright G, 'The Cost-Internalization Case for Class Actions' (1969) 21 *Stanford Law Review* 383

Yeazell S, 'Group Litigation and Social Context: Toward a History of the Class Action' (1977) 77 *Columbia Law Review* 866

Yeazell S, 'From Group Litigation to Class Action Part I: The Industrialization of Group Litigation' (1980) 27 *UCLA Law Review* 514

Yeazell S, 'From Group Litigation to Class Action Part II: Interest, Class, and Representation' (1980) 27 *UCLA Law Review* 1067

—'Class Actions and Interpleader: California Procedure and the Federal Rules' (1953) 6 *Stanford Law Review* 120

—'Aggregation of Claims in Class Actions' (1968) 68 *Columbia Law Review* 1554

—'Federal Class Actions: A Suggested Revision of Rule 23' (1946) 46 *Columbia Law Review* 818

Judicial Speeches

Allsop (The Hon Justice James), 'Federal Jurisdiction and the Jurisdiction of the Federal Court of Australia' (lecture given to the New South Wales Bar Assn, 21 October 2003)

Allsop (The Hon Chief Justice James), 'Class Actions' (keynote address to the Law Council of Australia Forum, 13 October 2016)

Basten (The Hon Justice John), 'Procedural Reform: The New Part 10' (published paper presented to the Judges of the Court, NSW Judicial Scholarship 19, 2011)

Beech-Jones (The Hon Justice Robert), 'Representative Actions in NSW Courts' (23 March 2017)

Jackson (Sir Rupert), 'Sixth Lecture in the Civil Litigation Costs Review Implementation Programme' (Royal Courts of Justice, 23 November 2011)

Mance (Lord), 'The Role of Judges in a Representative Democracy' (lecture given during the Judicial Committee of the Privy Council's Fourth Sitting in The Bahamas, 24 February 2017)

Murphy (The Hon Justice Bernard), 'The Operation of the Australian class action regime' (Bar Assn of Queensland, Gold Coast, 9 March 2013)

Law Newsletters, Legal Bulletins and Press Articles

Alabaster E, 'Clawing back *pro bono* costs' (May 2016) *Counsel* 16

Bowcott O, 'Impact of cuts to legal aid to come under review' (*The Guardian*, 31 October 2017)

British Columbia Attorney-General, 'Legislation introduced to modernize class actions' (*Information Bulletin*, 23 April 2018)

Carter C, 'Unlocking funds, restoring balance' (November 2017) *Counsel* 18

Clayton Utz, 'NSW rolls back contentious *cy-près* rule in class actions bill'; (*Lexology*, 3 December 2010)

Cooper P, 'Mississippi Won't Add Class Action Rule' (*Bloomberg News*, 18 May 2018)

de Carbonnel A, 'EU says VW yet to guarantee emissions fix does not impair cars' (*Reuters*, 17 July 2018)

Emmerig J, *et al.*, 'Supreme Court of New South Wales Relaxes Requirements for Class Actions' (Jones Day Publications, April 2019)

Hausfeld M, *Hausfeld Press Release* (6 November 2017)

Hurst B, 'The "Tidal Wave" of Data Protection-related Class Actions: Why We're not Drowning Just Yet ...' (*Bird & Bird Information Bulletin*, November 2018)

Liptak A, 'Doling Out Other People's Money' (*NY Times*, 26 November 2007) A14

McKinnon M (ed), 2018 *Class Action Case Law Year in Review* (Siskinds LLP, 2018)

Morgan J, 'Laying the foundation' (2008) 105 *Law Society Gazette* 14

Morrison J, 'Proposed Rule 23 Amendment for Class Action Settlement: Sea Change or Codification of the Status Quo?' (*Class Action Lawsuit Defense*, 11 May 2018)

Oloschakoff K, and N Hirst, 'VW is winning, at least in Europe' (*Politico*, 27 July 2016)

Panichi J, 'American lawyers bank on European VW woes' (*Politico*, 14 March 2016)

Piper Alderman, 'Class Actions in Australia: A Plaintiff's Paradise?' (*Lexology*, 19 February 2010)

Posaner J, 'German consumer group files class suit against VW' (*Politico*, 1 November 2018)

Power M, 'Roundtable: Litigation Funding' (*Law Society Gazette*, 13 March 2017)

Ruckin C, 'Cohen Milstein Lands $200 M BA–Virgin Settlement' (*Legal Week*, 15 February 2008)

Schrama H, and M Sinnighe Damste, 'Class Action for Damages in the Netherlands'; (*Loyens Loeff Newsletter*, 20 March 2019)

Thomasson E, 'German consumer group plans more compensation cases against Volkswagen' (*Reuters*, 30 August 2017)

Van Rest C, and B Keizers, 'A Collective Action for Damages in the Netherlands in a Fact!'; (*Hogan Lovells Publications*, 2 April 2019)

Walters M, 'Appeal Court Revives Mammoth £14bn Mastercard Group Action' (*Law Society Gazette*, 16 April 2019)

Williams P, '*Cy-près* Distributions: Uses and Controversies' (*McCarthy Tetrault News*, 18 January 2019)

—'Justice Black Dies at 85; Served on Court 34 Years' (*NY Times*, 25 September 1971)

—'Implant Victims' Payout Attacked' (*The Age*, 23 January 2005)

—'Queensland floods class action to begin in NSW Supreme Court' (*The Weekend Australian*, 8 July 2014)

—'An Introduction to Collective Redress Schemes' (Pinsent Masons, April 2016)

—'2011 Queensland Floods: Class action begins in NSW Supreme Court' (*Courier-Mail*, 3 December 2017)

—'New flood class action seeks compensation for what might have been' (*Brisbane Times*, 23 March 2017)

—'Dieselgate scandal roots revealed as industry in spotlight for German election' (*Autovista Group*, 29 August 2017)

—'Watch Out for GDPR-related Claims: It's Not all about Fines . . . ' (*Walker Morris Update*, 25 July 2018)

—'German Consumer Group Files Suit in VW Diesel Scandal' (*Associated Press*, 1 November 2018)

—'Introduction of Miscellaneous Bill' (*British Government News*, 19 November 2018)

Dictionaries and Similar Reference Works

—*Butterworths Concise Australian Legal Dictionary* (Butterworths, 1997)

—*Oxford Dictionary of English* (2nd edn, revised, Oxford University Press, 2005)

—*Oxford English Dictionary* (online, 2018)

Burchfield R, *New Fowler's Modern English Usage* (3rd edn, revised, Clarendon Press, 1998)

Garner BA (ed), *Blacks Law Dictionary* (8th edn, West Publishing Co, 2004)

Martin E, and J Law (eds), *Oxford Dictionary of Law* (6th edn, Oxford University Press, 2006)

Nygh P (ed), *Concise Australian Legal Dictionary* (Butterworths, 1997)

Penner P, *The Law Student's Dictionary* (13th edn, Oxford University Press, 2008)

Parliamentary Debates and Ministerial Statements

(in chronological order)

Hansard (House of Commons, 26 October 1956, JES Simon, vol 558, col 1026)

Hansard (Legislative Council, 5 December 1986, Mr J Kennan AG, col 1659)

Hansard (Legislative Assembly of Ontario, House Documents, 34th Parliament, 2nd Session, 12 June 1990, Attorney General, Mr Ian Scott, member of the Liberal Party representing St George-St David, at 1530)

Hansard (Legislative Assembly, 35th Parliament, 1st Session, 17 December 1990, moved by Mr Howard Hampton, at 1510)

Hansard (Senate, 13 November 1991, Senator Durack, at 3018 and 3019)

Hansard (Senate, 13 November 1991, Senator Durack, at 3021)

Hansard (Senate, 13 November 1991, Senator Spindler, at 3022–23)

Hansard (Senate, 13 November 1991, Senator Tate, at 3025)

Hansard (Senate, 13 November 1991, at 3028)

Hansard (House of Representatives, 14 November 1991, Mr Duffy MP and A-G, at 3174)

Hansard (House of Representatives, 14 November 1991, Mr Duffy MP and A-G, at 3175)

Hansard (Legislative Assembly, 35th Parliament, 1st Session, 18 November 1991, moved by Mr Winninger, on behalf of Mr Hampton, at 1630)

Hansard (House of Representatives, Peter Costello, 26 November 1991, vote, at 3284)

Hansard (House of Representatives, 26 November 1991, Mr Costello, at 3289)

Hansard (House of Representatives, 26 November 1991, the Rt Hon Peter Staples, Lab, Jagajaga, Minister for Aged, Family and Health Services, at 3297)

Hansard (House of Representatives, 26 November 1991, vote, at 3297)

Hansard (Legislative Assembly of Ontario, 35th Parliament, Second Session, 27 April 1992, moved by Attorney General, Mr Hampton, Member of New Democratic Party (Rainy River), and by Mr Scott, former Attorney General, at 1520–30)

Hansard (Legislative Assembly of Ontario, 35th Parliament, Second Session, 27 April 1992, moved by Mr Chiarelli, Member of the Liberal Party (Ottawa West), at 1530)

Hansard (Legislative Assembly of Ontario, 35th Parliament, Second Session, 27 April 1992, moved by Mr Chiarelli, Member of the New Democratic Party (Cochrane South), at 1640–50)

Hansard (Legislative Assembly, 35th Parliament, Second Session, 25 June 1992, moved by the Speaker, the Hon David Warner, at 2320)

Hansard (Legislative Assembly of Victoria, 21 November 2000), Mr Robert Dean, at 1768–69)

Hansard (House of Lords, 20 July 2009, the Hon Bridget Prentice, Parliamentary Under-Secretary of State for Justice, col 103WS)

The Rt Hon Bridget Prentice, *Justice: Collective Actions* (Written Ministerial Statement, 20 July 2009)

Hansard (New South Wales Legislative Assembly, 24 January 2010, Mr John Hatzistergos AG)

Rt Hon Dr Vince Cable MP, Secretary of State for Business, Innovation and Skills, *Private Actions for Competition Law: Government Response* (January 2013), 'Preface'

Hansard (House of Lords, 3 November 2014, col GC584)

Hansard (House of Lords, 3 November 2014, vol 756, GC585–GC588)

Hansard (HC Deb, 21 January 2015, vol 590, col 677)

Hansard (Legislative Assembly, 55th Parliament, 1st Session, 8 November 2016, Mr Ryan, col 4285, at 4.12pm)

Hansard (Legislative Assembly, 55th Parliament, 1st[st] Session, 8 November 2016, Ms Howard, col 4287, at 4.27pm)

Hansard (Legislative Assembly, 55th Parliament, 1st Session, 8 November 2016, Mr Dick, col 4311, at 5.09pm)

Hansard (Legislative Assembly of British Columbia, 23 April 2018, Mr D Eby, First Reading, at 1.55pm)

Hansard (Legislative Assembly of British Columbia, 25 April 2018, A Olsen, Second Reading, at 6.15pm)

The Rt Hon Meg Hillier MP (*Commons Select Committee Parliament News*, 12 March 2019)

E-Sources and Websites

Access to Justice Foundation: www.atjf.org.uk/about-us.html, and various other sites (e.g., Our Impact; Supporting Litigants in Person; Local Trusts; Distribution Principles)

Assn of Litigation Funders: http://associationoflitigationfunders.com/wp-content/uploads/2018/03/Code-Of-Conduct-for-Litigation-Funders-at-Jan-2018-FINAL.pdf

Australian Competition and Consumer Commission: www.accc.gov.au/

England and Wales Law Commission: www.gov.uk/government/organisations/law-commission

European Consumers' Assn (BEUC), Volkswagen Emission Affair: www.beuc.eu/volkswagen-emission-affairs

Her Majesty's Courts and Tribunals Service: www.gov.uk/guidance/group-litigation-orders,

Law Foundation of British Columbia: www.lawfoundationbc.org/about-us/mandate-mission-and-strategic-priorities/

Law Foundation of Ontario: www.lawfoundation.on.ca/who-we-are/history/, and various other sites (e.g., About Us; Mandate Mission and Strategic Priorities; Class Counsel Undertaking)

Scrutiny Unit, House of Commons, Finance Glossary: www.parliament.uk/documents/commons/Scrutiny/120515-finance-glossary.pdf

Slater and Gordon Solicitors: www.slatergordon.com.au/class-actions/past-class-actions/fairbridge-farm-school

United Kingdom Parliament: www.parliament.uk/site-information/glossary/purdah/

US Courts: www.uscourts.gov/rules-policies/about-rulemaking-process/how-rulemaking-process-works

Wikipedia (various sites)

INDEX